*For my mum, Joan, and my favourite little men, Samuel
and Oliver. And to all the boys I've ever known, but
especially for Nigel, the best one . . . yet.*

First published in Great Britain in 2000
by Piccadilly Press Ltd.,
5 Castle Road, London NW1 8PR

Phototypeset from author's disc
in 10.5 pt Futura Book

A catalogue record for this book is available from the
British Library

ISBN: 1 85340 686 4 (paperback)

1 3 5 7 9 10 8 6 4 2

Printed and bound by Creative Print and Design (Wales),
Ebbw Vale

Design & cover design by Judith Robertson

*Maria Coole is a young journalist who lives in
Greenwich, London. She is Deputy Editor of
Bliss magazine. This is her first book.*

NELSON DEMILLE

THE CHARM SCHOOL

A *Time Warner* Paperback

First published in Great Britain in 1988 by Grafton Books
Published in 1989 by HarperCollins
This edition published in 2000 by Time Warner Paperbacks
Reprinted in 2001, 2002, 2003

A CIP catalogue record for this book
is available from the British Library.

ISBN 0 7515 3118 9

Printed and bound in Great Britain by
Clays Ltd, St Ives plc

Time Warner Paperbacks
An imprint of
Time Warner Books UK
Brettenham House
Lancaster Place
London WC2E 7EN

www.TimeWarnerBooks.co.uk

To the memory of
Joanna Sindel

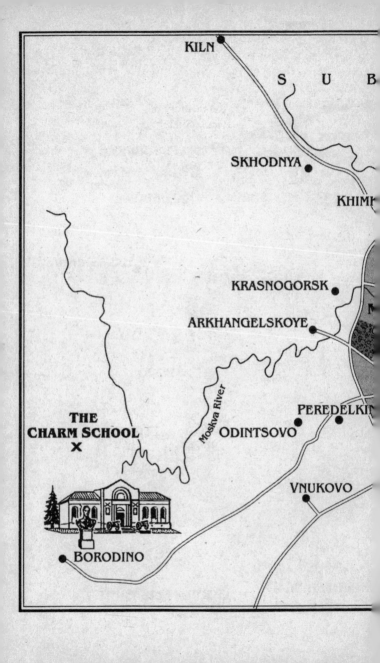

ACKNOWLEDGEMENTS

I wish to thank my half-blooded and full-blooded Russian friends, Nicholas Ellison, Nanscy Neiman-Legette, Nicholai Popoff, and Svetlana, my spiritual guides through the labyrinth of the Russian soul. And thanks, too, to Bob Whiting, who taught me to swear in Russian. And special gratitude to Ginny Witte for her devotion to this work and this writer.

AUTHOR'S FOREWORD

On occasion, I find myself agreeing with the *Washington Post*. About *The Charm School*, they wrote, 'Contemporary Cold War fiction doesn't get much better than this.'

But the Cold War is over, so is *The Charm School* still relevant? That would be like asking if any war novel or historical fiction is relevant. One of the first war novels ever written, *The Iliad*, is still read almost three thousand years after it first appeared, yet some recent novels about the Vietnam War and the Cold War have passed into oblivion, while others are still read and enjoyed. Obviously the question of relevance is not the right question. The question is, What makes for a good, timeless read? The answer, as we all know, is good writing, believable plot, interesting characters, realistic dialogue, suspense, mystery, romance, the battle between good and evil, and sometimes even a happy ending.

We all know that war spawns hundreds of novels, most of them written after the last shot is fired. But the Cold War, for some reason, has not inspired any major retrospective novels since the Berlin Wall fell in 1989. It's as though whatever was written contemporaneously, such as *The Charm School*, or Le Carré's novels and Tom Clancy's earlier books, or the thousands of other East versus West spy novels and nuclear Armageddon thrillers published between 1945 and 1989 are, and will be, the sum total of Cold War literature. The same can be said of motion pictures; with very few exceptions, Hollywood has not touched the subject in any significant way.

To be sure, tomes of non-fiction books, school texts, and film documentaries have been written and produced about the

Cold War since it ended, but as an art form, the subject seems dead.

In any case, even if novelists don't want to write about the Cold War, and movie producers don't want to deal with the subject, what was written and filmed still has the ability to entertain and to educate.

The Charm School is set in the old Soviet Union. The time period is about 1988, and the premise, in a nutshell, is this: American Embassy personnel in Moscow learn of the existence of a Soviet spy school (the Charm School) that trains KGB agents to talk, act, look, and think like Americans. The reluctant instructors at the school are Americans – military pilots shot down and captured over North Vietnam during the Vietnam War. These pilots have all been listed as missing in action and their fate has been unknown for over a decade when the story opens.

I won't give any more of the plot away, but I will say how I came upon this premise. I was an infantry officer in Vietnam in 1968. In April of that year, I was passing through Hue-Phu Bai Air Base and stopped in the Officer's Club for a cold beer. The jet jockeys in the bar had rarely seen an infantry officer and I had rarely seen fighter-bomber pilots up close. They were interested in the life of a ground soldier, and I was interested in the life of jet pilots who dodged surface-to-air missiles and anti-aircraft fire between beers. Ironically, they thought my job was more dangerous than theirs, and I thought they must be suicidal to fly through Missile Alley on the way to Hanoi and Haiphong. In any event, during the conversation, one of the pilots remarked offhandedly about 'the guys who were winding up in Moscow.' When I asked him what he meant, he explained, saying something like, 'You know, the pilots who were seen bailing out safely and not showing up on POW lists or in Hanoi's propaganda films.'

I replied, 'The North Vietnamese aren't necessarily giving out all the names of the guys they capture.'

This pilot replied, 'No, because they're sending some of

them to Moscow. That's the payoff for the Soviets giving them the SAM missiles.'

I recall being somewhat amazed by this statement.

The pilot continued, 'The Red Air Force is using these guys to train their pilots in American tactics and in equipment capabilities.'

It made sense and I nodded.

Another pilot added, 'Those guys will never come home.' He made a cutting motion across his throat.

This exchange stayed with me and when the controversy concerning Americans missing in action grew throughout the 1970s and '80s, I made a point of watching for anything that resembled what I'd heard at Hue-Phu Bai in 1968. But I never saw anything written and never heard anything said about this possibility. Still, it haunted me, and this idea became the central premise of *The Charm School*.

The book was well received when it was published in 1988, and became a bestseller. The publication of the book also added some fuel to the fire of the MIA controversy, raising this new possibility of the Soviets being part of a conspiracy.

I received hundreds of letters asking me where I'd gotten this idea, what further information I had, and if I had any solid proof of what I'd written. Some of these letters were from families of MIAs and they were heartbreaking to read.

I worked for a while with some POW/MIA groups, and without going into agonizing detail, we made little headway in discovering anything concerning the fate of the MIAs. But I, like others, was convinced that there were at least some MIAs being held in the Soviet Union.

Then came the collapse of the Soviet Union, and in the aftermath, there were some hints that Americans – not only from Vietnam but from Korea as well – had been kept prisoner in the Soviet Union. But these sketchy reports from the former Soviet Union did not seem to pan out.

I would have to say that after all this time since the collapse of Russian communism, and the relatively open society that now exists, that if a significant number of US servicemen had been imprisoned or are still imprisoned in the former Soviet Republic, we would have known about it by now. Or would we?

So, once again, is *The Charm School* relevant? I think, yes, if only because it accurately reflects those dark times when we all thought we were on the brink of nuclear annihilation. It is an insight into how we thought about the Evil Empire and how paranoid both sides were about the intentions of the other.

In 1986, I went to the Soviet Union to do research for *The Charm School*. After spending all my life living under this real or imagined threat – air raid drills in grade school, Civil Defense shelters, Dr Strangelove-type movies, and so forth – I had no idea what to expect.

The reception at Moscow airport was every bit as bad as I'd expected – too many questions, bag searches, bureaucracy, and general unpleasantness. I felt like I was in a Grade B Cold War movie.

But after about a week in Moscow, I realized that the people and the system were more to be pitied than hated. I remembered an expression I'd heard or read that went something like, 'Russia is a Third World country with first-class weapons.' The theoretical danger of a world war was real, but the actual possibility that the Russians were willing to roll the dice seemed somehow remote.

By week two, in Leningrad, I became an instant expert on the Soviet Union and decided – either presciently as my reviewers would later say, or optimistically – that the Soviet Union had about ten years left before it imploded. I even made references to this in my novel, and without giving any page numbers where I said so, you can read for yourself where some of my characters made this prediction. As it turned out, the Soviet Union in 1986 had less than three years left to live. The collapse of communism in the Soviet Republics and eastern Europe sort of surprised me, but I wasn't shocked.

In retrospect, we can all be experts now and say we saw a

wave of freedom sweeping the globe in the late 1980s – a new era of global information and communication and economic co-dependence, an unacceptable spiraling of weapons costs and an unwillingness of the people on both sides of the Iron Curtain to die in a needless war.

We can spend the next decade analyzing the reasons for the sudden collapse of the Soviet empire, but that may not be as important as trying to figure out where we're all going from here.

Prior to the collapse of the Soviet Union, I'd written only two Cold War novels – *The Charm School* and *The Talbot Odyssey* – and my career and reputation weren't tied closely to the continuance of the Cold War. Yet among some writers and some Cold Warriors, there is a certain nostalgia for the good old days when their services were needed and appreciated.

And maybe, on a certain level, the old Us versus Them thrillers can be enjoyed and appreciated as nostalgia. On another more important level, a book like *The Charm School* can be read and appreciated as a warning that the past is often prologue to the future – because if we forget what we all went through between 1945 and 1989, we are likely to repeat it some time in the not-too-distant future.

In any case, there must be something about this book that appeals to the reader because it's been in continuous print since its publication and its sales have remained strong long past the demise of the system it portrays.

I've taken the opportunity to replace some material that was deleted in the original hardcover edition and also deleted in earlier paperback editions. Most of this material can be found in Chapters 3 and 23.

In Chapter 3, the deleted and replaced material is at the beginning of the chapter and was originally removed because it was felt that the scene gave away too much, too soon. I don't think it does, and the reader can be the judge.

The material in Chapter 23 is an exchange between Colonel Sam Hollis and Lisa Rhodes, both of the American Embassy, and two American tourists, a man and his wife, both Brown University professors favorably disposed towards the Soviet system. Hollis and Rhodes, on the other hand, are on the run from the KGB. The dialogue among these four is amusing in that the American tourists are totally clueless about the predicament that their compatriots are in, and while the tourists are praising life in Russia, Hollis and Rhodes are expecting the KGB to show up and whisk them away. The original editor of *The Charm School* found something about this scene that she didn't like – too political, I think she said. We argued; she won. But I've replaced the scene and again, the reader can be the judge.

When speaking of the old Soviet Union, it seems always appropriate to quote George Orwell's *1984*, and as he said so brilliantly in that book, 'Who controls the past, controls the future: who controls the present controls the past.' What I did not do, however, is to *change* anything I'd written in the past in order to make me look more clever about predicting what was to come in 1989. Other than replacing what had been deleted, and making a few grammatical and technical corrections, and the addition of this Author's Foreword, the book in your hands is what I wrote in 1987–8.

I have heard from college instructors that they offer *The Charm School* as optional or required reading in English or Contemporary History classes, and in fact, an English teacher in my local high school assigns it every spring semester. This has caused my son and daughter, who've both taken the class, the extreme embarrassment of having one of their father's books discussed aloud by their peers. They survived the experience and are both now in college where they can avoid a repeat of this trauma by carefully reading the course catalogue for any references to *The Charm School*.

In 1994, I published *Spencerville*, which I describe as a post-Cold War novel. My purpose was to examine the life of a former Cold Warrior, Keith Landry, the book's hero. Landry was a fairly typical product of his age – drafted into the army in the 1960s, fought in Vietnam, stayed in the service, and eventually wound up in the Pentagon doing intelligence work. As the book opens, Landry has been pushed into early retirement because of the collapse of the Soviet Union. His unique occupation is no longer relevant and he finds himself in his Saab on the road to his hometown, Spencerville, in rural Ohio. He's going home, but home has changed and so has he and so has his country. This is a sort of nostalgic, bittersweet story of love lost and love found, of trying to rediscover roots, and trying to make sense of the past three decades, especially the turbulence of the 1960s.

The book worked the way most good post-war stories work, and I suppose I meant it to be a companion to *The Charm School* the way *The Odyssey* is a companion to *The Iliad*. The story of a returning soldier is obviously not new, but most novelists will tell you honestly that the war story is more interesting than the coming home story. *The Charm School*, then, written in the waning days of the Cold War, may have predicted the end of that era, but for all that any of us knew at the time, history could easily have gone the other way.

But enough about the present and the future – put yourself back in about 1988, pretend that the nuclear missiles are still targeting Moscow and Washington, New York and Leningrad, Peoria and Smolensk, and think about what James Kirkwood, author of *Good Times/Bad Times* and *Some Kind of Hero*, said: '*The Charm School* grabs hold of you, drags you off to the scariest Russia imaginable . . . and doesn't let you out until the last page.'

Welcome to *The Charm School*.

Nelson DeMille, 1999
Long Island, New York

Part 1

Whenever you are unhappy, go to Russia. Anyone who has come to understand that country will find himself content to live anywhere else.

– **Marquis de Custine**
Russia in 1839.

'You are already staying in Smolensk two days, Mr Fisher?' she asked.

Gregory Fisher was no longer confused or amused by the peculiar syntax and verb tenses of English as it was spoken in this part of the world. 'Yes,' he replied, 'I've been in Smolensk two days.'

'Why don't I see you when you arrive?'

'You were out. So I saw the police – the militia.'

'Yes?' She leafed through his papers on her desk, a worried look on her face, then brightened. 'Ah, yes. Good. You are staying here at Tsentralnaya Hotel.'

Fisher regarded the Intourist representative. She was about twenty-five years old, a few years older than he. Not too bad looking. But maybe he'd been on the road too long. 'Yes, I stayed at the Tsentralnaya last night.'

She looked at his visa. 'Tourism?'

'Right. *Tourizm*.'

She asked. 'Occupation?'

Fisher had become impatient with these internal control measures. He felt as if he were making a major border crossing at each town in which he was obliged to stop. He said, 'Ex-college student, currently unemployed.'

She nodded. 'Yes? There is much unemployment in America. And homeless people.'

The Russians, Fisher had learned, were obsessed with America's problems of unemployment, homeless people, crime, drugs, and race. 'I'm voluntarily unemployed.'

'The Soviet constitution itself guarantees each citizen a job, a place to live, and a forty-hour working week. Your constitution does not guarantee this.'

Fisher thought of several responses but said only, 'I'll ask my congressman about that.'

'Yes?'

'Yes.' Fisher stood in the middle of the office with pale yellow walls.

The woman folded her hands and leaned forward. 'You are enjoying your visit in Smolensk?'

'Super. Wish I could stay.'

She spread his travel itinerary over her desk, then energetically slapped a big red rubber stamp across the paperwork. 'You visit our cultural park?'

'Shot a roll of film there.'

'Yes? Do you visit the Local History Museum on Lenin Street?'

Fisher didn't want to push his credibility. 'No. Missed that. Catch it on the way back.'

'Good.' She eyed him curiously for a few moments. Fisher thought she enjoyed the company. In fact, the whole Smolensk Intourist office had a somewhat forlorn look about it, like a chamber of commerce storefront in a small Midwestern town.

'We see not many Americans here.'

'Hard to believe.'

'Not many from the West. Buses from our socialist brother countries.'

'I'll spread the word around.'

'Yes?' She tapped her fingers on the desk, then said thoughtfully, 'You may travel anywhere.'

'Excuse me?'

'An American is telling me this. Everyone is getting passport. Thirty bucks. Two, three, four weeks.'

'Could take longer. Can't go to Vietnam, North Korea, Cuba, few other places.'

She nodded absently. After a few moments she inquired, 'You are interested in socialism?'

Fisher replied. 'I am interested in Russia.'

'I am interested in your country.'

4

'Come on over.'

'Yes. Someday.' She looked down at a printed form and read, 'You have the required first aid kit and tool kit in your automobile?'

'Sure do. Same ones I had in Minsk.'

'Good.' She continued, 'You must stay on the designated highways. There are no authorized overnight stops between here and Moscow. Night driving in the countryside is forbidden for foreign tourists. You must be within the city of Moscow by nightfall.'

'I know.'

'When you reach Moscow, you must report directly to the Intourist representative at the Hotel Rossiya where you are staying. Before you do this, you may stop only for petrol and to ask directions of the militia.'

'And to use the *tualet*.'

'Well, yes of course.' She glanced at his itinerary. 'You are authorized one small detour to Borodino.'

'Yes, I know.'

'But I would advise against that.'

'Why?'

'It is late in the day, Mr Fisher. You will be hurrying to Moscow before dark. I would advise you already to stay in Smolensk tonight.'

'I am already checking out of my hotel. Yes?'

She didn't seem to notice his parody of her English and said, 'I can arrange for another room here. My job.' She smiled for the first time.

'Thank you. But I'm sure I can make Moscow before dark.'

She shrugged and pushed the paperwork toward him.

'*Spasibo*.' Fisher stuffed it in his shoulder satchel. '*De svedahnya*,' Greg Fisher said with a wave.

'Drive safely,' she replied, adding. 'Be cautious, Mr Fisher.'

Fisher walked out into the cool air of Smolensk, considering

5

that last cryptic remark. He took a deep breath and approached a crowd of people surrounding his car. He sidled through the throng. 'Excuse me, folks . . .' He unlocked the door of his metallic-blue Pontiac Trans Am, smiled, gave a V-sign, slipped inside the car, and closed the door. He started the engine and drove slowly through the parting crowd. '*Da svedahnya*, Smolenskers.'

He proceeded slowly through the center of Smolensk, referring to the map on the seat beside him. Within ten minutes he was back on the Minsk-Moscow highway, heading east toward the Soviet capitol. He saw farm vehicles, trucks, and buses but not a single automobile. It was a windy day, with grey clouds scudding past a weak sun.

Fisher saw that the farther east he drove, the more advanced the autumn became. In contrast to the bustling agricultural activity he'd seen in East Germany and Poland at the same latitudes, the wheat here had been harvested on both sides of the highway, and the occasional fruit orchards were bare.

Greg Fisher thought about things as the landscape rolled by. The restrictions and procedures were not only annoying, he concluded, but a little scary. Yet, he'd been treated well by the Soviet citizens he'd met. He'd written home on a postcard to his parents, 'Ironically this is one of the last places where they still like Americans.' And he rather liked them and liked how his car literally stopped traffic and turned heads wherever he went.

The Trans Am had Connecticut plates, had cast aluminum wheels, a rear deck spoiler, and custom pin-striping; the quintessential American muscle car, and he thought that nothing like it had ever been seen on the road to Moscow.

From the backseat of the car came the aroma of fruits and vegetables given him by villagers and peasants wherever he'd stopped. He in turn had given out felt-tip pens, American calendars, disposable razors, and other small luxuries he'd been advised to bring. Greg Fisher felt like an ambassador of goodwill, and he was having a marvelous time.

A stone kilometer post informed him that he was 290 K from Moscow. He looked at the digital dashboard clock: 2:16 P.M.

In his rearview mirror he saw a Red Army convoy gaining on him. The lead vehicle, a dull green staff car, pulled up to his bumper. 'Hey,' Fisher mumbled, 'that's called tailgating.'

The car flashed its headlights, but Fisher could see no place to pull off the two-lane road bordered by a drainage ditch. Fisher speeded up. The 5-liter, V-8 engine had tuned-port fuel injection, but the local fuel didn't seem to agree with it, and the engine knocked and backfired. 'Damn it.'

The staff car was still on his tail. Fisher looked at his speedometer, which showed 110kph, twenty over the limit.

Suddenly the staff car swung out and pulled alongside him. The driver sounded his horn. The rear window lowered, and an officer in gold braid stared at him. Fisher managed a grin as he eased off the gas pedal. The long convoy of trucks, troop carriers, and cars passed him, soldiers waving and giving him the traditional Red Army 'Ooo-rah!'

The convoy disappeared ahead, and Greg Fisher drew a breath. 'What the hell am I doing here?' That was what his parents wanted to know. They'd given him the car and the vacation as a graduation gift after completing his MBA at Yale. He'd had the car shipped to Le Havre and spent the summer touring Western Europe. Heading into the East Bloc had been his own idea. Unfortunately the visa and auto permits had taken longer than expected, and like Napoleon and Hitler before him, he reflected, his Russian incursion was running about a month too late into the bad season.

The landscape, Fisher noticed, had a well-deserved reputation for being monotonous and infinite. And the sky seemed to be a reflection of the terrain: grey and rolling, an unbroken expanse of monotony for the last eight days. He could swear the weather changed from sunshine to gloom at the Polish border.

The excitement of being a tourist in the Soviet Union, he decided, had little to do with the land (dull), the people (drab), or the climate (awful). The excitement derived from

7

being where relatively few Westerners went, from being in a country that didn't encourage tourism, where xenophobia was a deep-rooted condition of the national psyche; a nation that was a police state. The ultimate vacation: a dangerous place.

Gregory Fisher turned on his car radio but couldn't find the Voice of America or the BBC, both of which seemed to come in only at night. He listened for a while to a man talking in a stentorian voice to the accompaniment of martial music, and he could pick out the words 'Amerikanets' and 'agressiya' being repeated. He snapped off the radio.

The highway had become wider and smoother as he left Tumanovo, but there were no other indications that he was approaching the great metropolis of Moscow. In fact, he thought, there was a singular lack of any visible commercial activity that one would associate with the twentieth century. 'I'm having a Big Mac attack.'

He put a Russian language tape in the deck, listened, and repeated, '*Ya-plo-kho-syebya-choo*. I feel ill. *Na-shto-zhaloo-yetyes?* What's the matter with you?'

Fisher listened to the tape as the Trans Am rolled along the blacktop highway. In the fields women gleaned grain left by the reapers.

In contrast, throughout Western Europe, every village had been a delight, each turn in the road revealed a new vista of pastoral loveliness. Or so it seemed now. In some superficial ways, he realized, rural Russia was not unlike rural America; there was little that was quaint or historical in either heartland, no castles or chateaux, few messages from the past. What he saw here was a functional if inefficient agribusiness, whose headquarters was in Moscow. 'I don't like this,' he said.

Fisher was in the village now. It consisted mostly of log cabins, *izbas*, whose doors, window frames, and flower boxes were all of the same blue. 'People's Paint Factory Number Three is overfilling quota on blue paint number two. Yes?' The entire village stretched along both sides of the highway for half a kilometer or so, like some elongated Kozy Kabin motel in the Adirondacks. He saw a few elderly people and children digging root vegetables from their kitchen gardens in the small fenced-in front yards. An old man was forcing mortar into the chinks between two logs of an *izba* while a group of children were gleefully terrorizing a flock of chickens.

Everyone stopped, turned, and watched as the metallic-blue Trans Am rolled by. Fisher gave a cursory wave and began accelerating as soon as he passed the last cabin. He glanced over his right shoulder and saw a glimpse of the sun hanging lower on the southwest horizon.

Some half hour later he turned off the highway on to a smaller parallel route that had once been the principal western road out of Moscow. In a few minutes he found himself on the outskirts of Mozhaisk, 128 kilometers from Moscow, and he slowed to the urban speed limit. His Intourist guidebook informed him that this was a thirteenth-century town of old Muscovy, but there weren't any signs of antiquity evident in the plain concrete and wooden buildings. His map showed a monastery somewhere in the area, and he saw the spire of the Cathedral of St Nicholas, but he didn't have the time or the inclination to sightsee. There was a flip side to being an American in a Pontiac Trans Am in deepest, darkest Russia. There were limits to the amount of attention one could comfortably take.

He continued through Mozhaisk, affecting a nonchalance behind the wheel, avoiding the stare of the State motor policeman directing traffic through the only major intersection.

Finally, with the town behind him, he saw what he was looking for, a petrol station, *the* petrol station, on the eastern end of Mozhaisk, marked by a picture of a pump. He pulled on to the immaculate, white concrete and stopped beside a yellow pump. A man in clean overalls sat in a chair outside a white concrete-block building reading a book. The man peered over the book. Fisher got out of the car and approached him. 'How's business?' Fisher handed him Intourist coupons for thirty-five liters of 93-octane. 'Okay?'

The man nodded. 'Oo-kay?'

Fisher went back to his car and began pumping gas. The man followed and looked over his shoulder at the meter. Fisher did not wonder why all petrol stations were self-service if the attendant stood there watching you. Fisher had stopped wondering about such things. He hit thirty-five liters, but the tank wasn't full, so he squeezed in another four liters before he put the hose back. The attendant was peering inside the Pontiac now and didn't seem to notice.

Fisher got into his car, started the big engine, and raced the motor. He lowered the electric windows and handed the attendant a packet of postcards from New York City. 'Everyone is being homeless there. Yes?'

The attendant flipped slowly through the cards. Fisher put a Bruce Springsteen tape in the deck, popped the clutch, and left six feet of rubber on the white concrete. He made a tight, hard U-turn and accelerated up the road. 'Surreal. Really.'

He rolled up the windows and lost himself in the music.

Fisher pressed on the gas pedal until he was well past the speed limit. 'Haven't seen a traffic cop in the last thousand miles. They never *heard* of radar here.'

He thought about the Rossiya Hotel in Moscow. That would be his first decent accommodation since Warsaw. 'I need a steak and scotch whiskey.' He wondered what he was going to do with the fruits and vegetables in the rear seat.

Another thought popped into his mind. 'Avoid sexual entanglements.' That was what the embassy man in Bonn had told him when he'd gone there to pick up his Soviet visa, and so far he'd avoided it, though not by much in Warsaw. Still, he had fifteen pairs of panty hose and a dozen tubes of lip gloss. 'We'll see what shakes out at the Rossiya.'

Fisher kept looking for a sign directing him back to the main highway. 'The sun has riz, and the sun has set, and here we is in Roosha yet.'

Greg Fisher pulled off to the side of the deserted road. A stone kilometer post read 108 K, and an arrow pointed back to the main highway via a one-lane road with crumbling blacktop. An arrow to the left pointed toward a rising road in better condition. The sign was in Cyrillic, but he could make out, the word 'Borodino'. He looked at his dashboard clock: 4:38. Impulsively he accelerated, swinging on to the Borodino road, heading west into the setting sun.

He didn't know what he expected to see at Borodino, but something told him it was a not-to-be-missed opportunity. In June he had stood on the beach at Normandy and had been moved by what had happened there. Similarly, he thought, he would like to see the place where Napoleon and Kutuzov had faced off, where fifty years later Leo Tolstoy had stood and pondered his epic, *War and Peace*. Fisher thought perhaps he owed the Russian at least that before he entered Moscow.

The road curved gently and rose gradually. Poplars flanked either side, and Fisher found it pleasant. He drove slowly through a set of stone pillars with open iron gates. The road crested a small hill, and he saw spread before him Borodino Field, where Napoleon's *Grands Armée* met the Russian army led by Field Marshal Kutuzov. The road led down to a small parking area beyond which was a white limestone building with a red-tiled roof and a neoclassical portico. On either side of the portico were wings in which were set arched French windows. Two old, muzzle-loading cannon flanked the entranceway. This building, Fisher knew from his Intourist booklet, was the Borodino Museum. He rummaged through his tapes and found Tchaikovsky's '1812 Overture.' He slid in the tape, turned up the volume and got out of the car, leaving the door open. The overture reverberated over the quiet battlefield, and a flock of wild geese took to the air.

Fisher mounted the steps of the museum and tried the doors, but they were locked. 'Typical.' He turned and looked out at the grass-covered fields and hillocks where a quarter-million French and Russian soldiers met on a September day in 1812, the French intent on taking Moscow, the Russians on defending it. For fifteen hours, according to his guidebook, the two sides fired at each other, and in the evening the Russians withdrew toward Moscow, and the French were in possession of Borodino Field and the little village of the same name. A hundred thousand men lay dead and wounded.

In the distance Fisher saw the memorial to the French soldiers and officers who fought there in 1812, and further away was a newer monument dedicated to the Russian defenders who tried to stop the Germans in this same place in 1941. Fisher noted there was no monument to the Germans.

Greg Fisher was suddenly overcome by a sense of history and tragedy as he gazed out over the now peaceful fields, deathly still in the autumn dusk. The cold east wind blew tiny birch leaves over the granite steps where he stood, and the cannon of Tchaikovsky's overture boomed over the quiet countryside. 'Russia,' he said softly to himself. '*Rodina* – the motherland. Bleeding Russia. But you made them all bleed too. You gave them death in seven-digit numbers.'

Fisher walked slowly back to his car. It was much colder now, and a chill passed through his body. He shut the door and turned the tape lower as he drove slowly on the lanes, past the black granite obelisk honoring Kutuzov, past the common grave of the Soviet Guardsmen who fell in action in 1941, past the monument dedicated to the *Grande Armée* of 1812, and past the dozens of smaller markers dedicated to the Russian regiments of both 1812 and 1941. In the deepening dusk Fisher fancied he could hear the muted sounds of battle and the cries of men. *I'm too hard on them*, he decided. *They got shafted bad. Screwed by the West once too often.*

He had lost track of time, and it had become noticeably darker. He tried to retrace his route through the low hills and clusters of birch trees, but he realized he was lost.

Fisher found himself going upgrade in a towering pine forest and reluctantly continued on the narrow, paved lane, looking for a wide place to turn around. He put on his headlights, but they revealed only walls of dark green pine on either side. 'Oh, Christ Almighty . . .'

Suddenly the head beams illuminated a large wooden sign attached to a tree, and Fisher stopped the car. He stared out the windshield at the Cyrillic lettering and was able to make out the familiar word STOP. The rest of the sign was incomprehensible except for the also familiar CCCP. Government property. But what wasn't these days? 'Do I need this?' He thought he detected a quaver in his voice, so he said more forcibly, 'I don't need this crap. Right?'

As he sat considering what to do next, he noticed what appeared to be a small opening in the trees off the right shoulder. The opening lay beyond the sign, and he didn't want to pass the sign with the car, so he took a flashlight from under his seat and got out. He walked the ten meters to the opening. It was a graveled patch, not five meters square, but obviously meant as a turnaround, a means of allowing the unwary motorist to obey the sign. 'Russian efficiency.' He kicked at the crushed stone and decided it would be alright. He turned back toward his car, them froze.

Over the hum of the engine he heard branches rustling. He remained motionless and breathed through his nose, noticing the resinous scent of the trees. The air was cold and damp, and he shivered in his windbreaker. He heard it again, the brushing of pine boughs, closer this time. *The headlights attracted a deer*, he thought. *Right*. He took a step toward his car. Somewhere in the distance a dog barked – an unfriendly bark, he decided.

The glare of his headlights blinded him, and he shielded his eyes as he walked in long strides the ten meters back toward his car; *one, two, three, four, five –*

'Russian efficiency,' said a voice a few feet to his right.

Fisher felt his knees go weak.

Lisa Rhodes noted it was five o'clock, and she poured a shot of bourbon into her paper Coke cup. She walked to the window of her office in the Press Attaché's section of the American embassy. The seventh-floor windows faced west and looked over the Moskva River. Across the river rose the Ukraina Hotel, a twenty-nine-story structure of bombastic Stalinist architecture that fronted on the Taras Shevchenko Embankment.

The district that was contained within the loop across the Moskva had been one of the poorer quarters of nineteenth-century Moscow. Extensive razing and building under the Soviets had transformed it into a cleaner if less interesting place. In the two years since she'd been in Moscow, she'd seen not only wooden structures demolished, but magnificent stone mansions and churches destroyed. The government seemed to consult no one regarding these matters. Somewhere, she assumed, was a master plan for changing the face of Moscow, but the citizens who lived in the city had never been asked their opinion. 'What a screwed-up social contract they've got here,' she said aloud.

Spanning the river below was the Kalinin Bridge, connecting into Kutuzov Prospect, which ran west alongside the Ukraina Hotel and continued on, becoming the Minsk-Moscow highway. She followed the road with her eyes until it disappeared into the pale sinking sun over the flat horizon. 'Russia . . .' an immense and inhospitable expanse, more suitable for wild horsemen and ruminants, an unlikely place to find a powerful empire of Europeans and their cities. Certainly, she thought, the most frozen empire that ever existed; a civilization whose roots seemed tenuously sunk into the thin soil like the fragile white birch.

The internal phone rang. She turned from the window and answered it. 'Rhodes.'

'Hello,' the male voice said. 'Today is the first day of Sukkot.'

'Is that so?'

'I've been invited to a party in Sadovniki. Religious dissidents. You might enjoy it.'

'I'm D.O. tonight.'

'I'll get you switched.'

'No . . . no, thanks, Seth.'

'Is it completely and finally over?'

'I think so.'

'Will you take a polygraph on that?'

'I have to finish a press release now.'

'Well, at least you won't be able to get in trouble tonight. Think about it, Lisa.'

She didn't know if Seth Alevy meant about them or the party. She replied, 'Sure will.'

'Good night.'

She hung up, slipped off her shoes, and put her feet on the desk. Holding the bourbon in her lap, she lit a cigarette and contemplated the acoustical-tile ceiling. The new American embassy, she reflected, sitting on ten acres of bad bog land about equidistant between the Moskva river and the old embassy on Tchaikovsky Street, had been more than a decade in the building. The work had been done mostly by a West German firm under subcontract to an American concern in New York. If the Soviet government was insulted by this snub to socialist labor and building expertise, they never expressed it verbally. Instead they'd indulged themselves in petty harassments and bureaucratic delays of monumental proportions, which was one of the reasons the project had taken about five times as long as it should have.

The other reason was that each slab of precast concrete that the Soviets had supplied to the building site had been implanted with listening devices. After the bugging scandal broke, there followed the Marine guards' sexual scandals at the old embassy, and the subsequent charges and counter-charges between Moscow and Washington. The American diplomatic mission to the Soviet Union had been in a shambles for over a year, and the whole mess had been making front-page news back in the States. The image of the Secretary of State conducting business in a trailer out on Tchaikovsky Street was rather embarrassing, she thought.

According to Seth Alevy's sources, the Russians had a big laugh over the whole thing. And according to her own personal observations, the American diplomats in Moscow felt like fools and had for some time avoided social contact with other embassies.

Eventually, a little belated Yankee ingenuity and a lot of Yankee dollars had put things right in the new embassy. But Lisa Rhodes knew there was a good deal of residual bitterness left among the American staff, and it influenced their decision-making. In fact, she thought, whatever good-will there had been between the embassy people and their Soviet hosts was gone, replaced by almost open warfare. The State Department was now seriously considering making a clean sweep of the entire staff, replacing the two hundred or so able and experienced men and women with less angry diplomats. She hoped not. She wanted to continue her tour of duty here.

Lisa Rhodes shook the ice in her drink. She closed her eyes and exhaled a stream of cigarette smoke at the ceiling.

She thought of Seth Alevy. Being involved with the CIA station chief in Moscow was not the worst thing for her career. He could pull strings to keep her in Moscow even if State ordered her home. And she did love him. Or once loved him. She wasn't sure. But somehow, being involved with him meant being involved with his world, and she didn't like that. It wasn't what she wanted to do with her career or her life. It was also dangerous. Being in Moscow was dangerous enough by itself.

3

'Russian efficiency.' said the voice again.

Greg Fisher did not turn, did not breathe.

'American?'

Fisher found himself nodding in the dark.

'I'm over here.'

Fisher turned slowly toward the voice. He could make out the figure of a man standing among the pine boughs on the far side of the road. The man was tall, heavily built, and wore matching dark clothing that looked like a uniform.

The man stepped onto the road, and Fisher saw in his right hand the glint of steel. A gun. Fisher took a step back.

The man spoke as he walked. 'Name's Dodson. Yours?'

'Fisher.' He cleared his throat. 'Gregory. American.' Fisher thought that if he had a serial number he'd give him that too. 'Who are *you*?'

'Keep it down.' The man stopped a few feet from Fisher.

Fisher swallowed and inquired, 'Tourist?'

The man smiled without humor. 'Resident.'

'Oh.'

'Are you lost, Fisher?'

'Very.'

'Alone?'

Fisher hesitated, then replied. 'Yes. . . .' He saw now that the steel was not a gun but a knife. The man was about fifty years old with short, dark hair and eyes that glinted like the steel in his hand. There was something – blood, maybe – smeared on his chin.

Dodson said, 'You might just be a graduate student.'

'I am. *Was*. Yale. Business school.'

Dodson smiled again. 'No. I mean . . .' He regarded the

Pontiac Trans Am, its engine running and its headlights on. 'No . . . I think you're the real thing.'

Fisher was confused, but he nodded. He took a deep breath and looked cautiously at the man. It was not a uniform but a blue warm-up suit with red piping. The man wore running shoes. *Unreal*, he thought.

Dodson slipped the knife into a scabbard beneath his waistband, then pointed at the Trans Am. 'You drive that from Yale?'

'Yeah. Sort of. From Le Havre.'

'Amazing.'

'Yeah. Well, I have to get going. Not supposed to be driving after dark. Hey, nice meeting you.' Fisher glanced at his car but didn't move toward it.

A dog barked again, and Dodson motioned Fisher toward the car. Dodson got in the passenger side and closed the door quietly. Fisher got behind the wheel. Dodson said, 'I have to put some distance between me and this place.'

'What place?'

'I'll tell you later. Turn it around. Kill the lights.'

'Right.' Fisher pulled the Trans Am up into the turnaround, backed out, and headed down the narrow road.

'Cut the engine and coast.'

Fisher glanced at his passenger, then put the transmission in neutral and shut off the engine. The car rolled down the slope he'd come up. 'Hard to see the road.'

'Where are you heading, Greg?'

'Moscow.'

'Me, too.'

'Oh . . . well, I guess I can drop you off . . .' Fisher felt his head beginning to swim. 'I mean –'

'Where are we?'

'Russia.'

'Yes, I know. How far are we from Moscow?'

'Oh, about a hundred kilometers.'

Dodson nodded to himself. 'Closer than we thought.'

Fisher considered the big man sitting beside him. *Resident. How far are we from Moscow? You might just be a graduate student.* Clearly the man was nuts. Fisher said tentatively, 'Someone after you?'

'Depends if they know I'm gone yet.'

'Oh.' Fisher stared out the windshield. 'Getting harder to see.'

'Peripheral vision is better at night. Try it.'

'Yeah?' Fisher moved his eyes slightly and found that indeed he could see better. 'Learn something every day.'

'Yes. Escape and evasion,' Dodson said. 'They teach you that course at Yale?'

'No.' The road began to wind, and Fisher found himself gripping the wheel, tugging it left and right to try to make it respond without the power steering.

Dodson picked up a handful of maps and brochures from the console between them. 'Can I borrow some of these?'

'Sure. Help yourself. Take them all.'

Dodson opened the glove compartment and sorted though the maps by the dim light. 'Where are we in relation to Moscow?'

'West. A little north. We're near Borodino. That's where I got a little lost.'

'Borodino. The battlefield.'

'Right. I have to try to find the Minsk-Moscow highway. This road isn't even on the map.'

Dodson nodded. 'No, it wouldn't be.'

Occasionally branches brushed either side of the Pontiac, and Fisher jerked the wheel the opposite way. The car went off the road to the right, and he felt the two tires sink into the sandy shoulder. The car slowed and he tugged at the wheel until he got the tires back on the blacktop and continued down the gradual slope.

Fisher turned his head slightly toward Dodson. As he tried to sort out the dark images in his peripheral vision, he focused now and then on his passenger. He saw the man running his fingers over the dashboard, then touching the rich leather on the side panels – like he'd never sat in an American car before, Fisher thought. Like a Russian.

They sat in silence as the car continued down the ridge line. The pine trees thinned toward the base of the slope, and Fisher was able to see better.

The night had become very still, he noticed, and bright twinkling stars shone down between scattered clouds. He hadn't been in the Russian countryside at night, and the deep, dark quiet surprised him. *Spooky*.

Through an opening in the trees, he saw the rolling fields below. The moon broke through a cloud and revealed a dozen polished obelisks standing like shimmering sentries over the dead. 'Borodino.'

Dodson nodded.

Fisher thought he saw something in his rearview mirror. Dodson noticed and looked back through the rear window.

Fisher ventured, 'Someone following us?'

'I don't see anything.' He added. 'They're searching on foot, because they think I'm on foot.'

'Right.'

'I wish you hadn't left that tire mark in the sand, however.'

'Sorry.' Fisher thought a moment, then added. 'This mother can outrun anything in the USSR.' He smiled in spite of himself.

Dodson smiled in return.

Fisher found the car slowing as the slope flattened. He said, 'Who's after you? What did you do?'

'Long story.'

Fisher nodded. 'Fucked-up country.'

'Amen.' Dodson studied an Intourist highway map, then slipped it into his side pocket. 'You have a city map of Moscow?'

'Under your seat.'

Dodson found the folded map and opened it.

Fisher said, 'It's all in Russian. You know Russian?'

'Hardly a word. Everything was in English. That was rule number one.'

Fisher began to ask something, then thought better of it.

Dodson studied the map. 'I did read in American newspapers that there was a new American Embassy somewhere near the Moskva River, but the articles weren't too specific. I don't see it here.'

'It's near the Kalinin Bridge. You want to go there?'

'Ultimately.'

'Okay . . . we have to cross that bridge on my way to the Rossiya.'

'That's where you're staying?'

'Right. I can drop you off at the embassy.'

'I wouldn't get past the Soviet militia at the gates.'

'Why not?'

'No passport,' said Dodson. He looked at Fisher a moment, then said, 'Let me see your passport.'

Fisher hesitated, then drew his passport from the inside pocket of his windbreaker.

Dodson took it, studied it and the visa stapled to it by the light of the glove compartment, then handed it back.

They were nearly out of the pine forest now. Ahead lay copses of bare birch, a few lonely poplars, and the fields of Borodino. A hundred meters beyond the base of the ridge, the Pontiac came to a gradual halt. Fisher looked at Dodson, waiting for instructions.

Dodson said, 'If they catch us together, they'll shoot you.'

Fisher felt his mouth go dry.

'Or worse, they'll send you to where I just escaped from. So we're going to part company here. I'm going cross-country to Moscow. You're going to find the highway and drive there. You're going to the embassy. I'm going to figure out what to do when I get to Moscow. I may try to contact you at the Rossiya. Understand?'

'Yes.'

'I may try to contact the embassy by phone. I need all the rubles and kopeks you've got on you.'

Fisher took out his wallet and removed the one-, five-, and ten-ruble notes. 'About a hundred and fifty.'

Dodson took the notes.

Fisher found seventy-five kopeks in his pocket and handed them over.

'Can't promise I'll pay you back.'

Fisher shrugged. Fisher didn't care if he never saw the money or Dodson again. Especially if it meant getting shot. He thought he should have listened to the Intourist lady and stayed in Smolensk.

Dodson glanced back in the rear of the car. 'You going to open a farm stand?'

'Huh . . . ? Oh, no. Gifts. You can take what you need.'

'You have candy? Packaged food?'

'Candy in the plastic bag back there. Some peanuts. Snacks.'

Dodson leaned back and retrieved the bag with the name and address of a West Berlin *Konditorei* stamped on it. 'Last outpost of junk food, right, kid?'

Fisher forced a smile. 'Right.'

'Okay, listen to me, Greg Fisher. I am going to tell you something, and you are going to listen like you never listened to a prof at Yale. Okay?'

'Okay.'

'My name is Major Jack Dodson. I am an American Air Force officer.'

Fisher nodded. 'Air Force.'

'I am – I was – a POW. I was shot down over North Vietnam in 1973.'

Fisher looked at Dodson. 'Jesus . . . you're an MIA!'

'Not anymore, kid. Listen. I have been held here in Mrs Ivanova's Charm School since 1974 –'

'Where?'

'That's what we call it. Don't interrupt. I am going to give you some important details. You will get to the embassy before

22

I reach Moscow. I may never reach Moscow. But you will. You will ask to speak to a defence attaché, preferably the Air Force attaché. Got that? Attaché.'

'Yes. Attaché.'

Dodson studied Fisher for a long moment, then said softly. 'I don't know what fate brought us together on this lonely road; Greg Fisher, but I think it was God's will.'

Fisher simply nodded.

'I am going to tell you a very strange story now. About the Charm School.' Dodson spoke and Fisher listened without interruption. Fifteen minutes later Dodson said, 'You make sure they understand you and believe you. There are a lot of men whose lives depend on you as of this moment, Mr Fisher.'

Fisher stared through the windshield with unfocused eyes.

'Are you a patriot, Mr Fisher?'

'I guess . . . I mean in the last few weeks . . .'

'I understand. You'll do what you have to do.'

'Yes.'

Dodson reached out and took Fisher's hand, which was limp and wet. 'Good luck, and as we used to say on the flight line, God speed.' Dodson opened the door and left quickly.

Fisher sat motionless for a few seconds, then looked out the passenger side window. Major Dodson was gone.

Gregory Fisher felt very alone. In a moment of crystal clarity. he completely grasped the meaning and the consequences of the secret that had just been revealed to him, and an awful fear suddenly gripped him, a fear unlike any he had ever known in his short, sheltered life. 'This one's for real.'

Gregory Fisher got his bearings from the Kutuzov obelisk shining in the moonlight. He found the lane flanked by the monuments to the Russian regiments, then spotted the white limestone museum, and within a minute he was on the poplar-lined road heading toward the iron gates.

Approaching the gates, he saw they were now closed. 'Oh, for Christ's sake –' He hit the accelerator, and the Trans Am

23

smacked the gates, flinging them open with a metallic ring that brought him out of his trancelike state. 'Let's get the hell out of here!'

Fisher pressed harder on the accelerator as he negotiated a series of shallow S-turns. Coming out of a long turn, he saw the old Moscow road dead ahead. He cut sharply left onto it with squealing tires.

Fisher snapped on his headlights and saw the signpost he'd passed earlier. He made a hard right into the farm lane that led back to the main Minsk-Moscow highway. 'Should have taken this road the first time. Right? Did I need to see Borodino? No. Saw *War and Peace* once. . . . Read *War and Peace* too . . . that's all I needed to know about Borodino . . .'

His chest pounded as the Pontiac bumped over the potholed pavement. He could see lights from distant farm buildings across the flat, harvested fields. He had an acute sense of being where he wasn't supposed to be, when he wasn't supposed to be there. And he knew it would be some time before he was where he *was* supposed to be: in his room at the Rossiya – and longer still before he was where he wanted to be: in Connecticut. 'I knew it.' He slapped his hand hard on the steering wheel. 'I *knew* this fucking country would be trouble!' In fact, despite his nonchalance of the last eight hundred miles, he had felt tense since he'd crossed the border. Now a neon sign flashed in his head: NIGHTMARE. NIGHTMARE.

The straight farm road seemed to go on forever before his headlights picked out a string of utility poles, and within minutes he was at the intersection of the main highway. 'Okay . . . back where we started.' He turned quickly onto the highway and headed east toward Moscow.

He saw no headlights coming at him and none in his rear mirror, but he still had to resist the urge to floor it. As he drove he realized there were towns and villages ahead, and if there were police in any of them, he would be stopped and questioned.

Greg Fisher concocted several stories to tell the police, but as plausible as they might sound to him, it didn't after the fact that the police – either here or in Connecticut – believed nothing you told them.

The clouds had returned, he noticed, and the night was deep and black with no sign of human habitation on this vast and fabled Russian plain. He had the feeling he was moving through a void, and as the time passed, the sensory deprivation began to work on his mind. He tried to convince himself that what had just happened to him had not happened. But by the time he reached Akulovo, he was left with nothing but the truth. 'Jesus Christ . . . what am I supposed to do?'

Unwilling to think about it any longer, he popped a tape in the deck and tried to immerse himself in the sound of an old Janis Joplin album. She sang 'Bobby McGee' in that deep, husky voice that turned him on. He wondered what she had looked like.

When Fisher's mind returned to the road again, he saw a strange, haunting shimmer of light sitting on the black horizon. For some seconds he stared at it, confused and anxious. Suddenly he looked at his clock and odometer, then back at the glow. 'Moscow!'

The Trans Am rolled eastward, and Greg Fisher kept his eyes on the distant lights. Ahead the road dipped beneath a highway bridge, and he knew this was the Outer Ring Road, the unofficial city limits. The road widened to four lanes as it passed beneath the Ring Road. He saw a farm truck coming toward him, its poultry cages empty. Then a bus heading out of the city went by, and he could see by its bright interior lights that it was filled with darkly clad peasants, mostly old women with head scarves.

Still he saw no signs of urban life along the highway, no suburbs, no streetlights, no signs, only fields of cut grain as though each square meter of earth had to produce something until the moment it was excavated for construction.

Roads began branching off to the left and right, and in the far distance he could see rows of stark prefab apartment houses, some lighted, some under construction. The previous night in his hotel room in Smolensk, he had spent an hour studying his Moscow map for this approach into the city.

To his right in the far distance the land rose, and he knew these were the Lenin Hills. Atop the rise was a massive skyscraper with an ornate spire – Moscow State University, where he had intended to check out the coeds. But his plans had turned indefinite.

Straight ahead up the highway he could see the Triumphal Arch commemorating the Battle of Borodino, and beyond the arch were solid blocks of buildings, like a medieval city, Fisher thought, rural to urban just like that. No Glenwoods subdivisions here.

The highway passed to the right of the Triumphal Arch, and the Minsk-Moscow highway became Kutuzov Prospect, named after the general of Borodino. Suddenly there were streetlights and vehicles.

He did not see a sign that said, 'Welcome to Moscow,' but that was where he was. With the luck of the damned he had made it, had driven through the countryside after dark in a flashy American car without being stopped. He felt somewhat calmer now that he was mingling into the traffic of Moscow. 'So much for the vaunted efficiency of the police state.' He noticed that other drivers were pulling close to him to look at his car. 'Go away,' he muttered.

He drove slowly through Victory Square. To his left was a huge statue of Kutuzov on horseback, and behind that a circular building housing another Borodino museum. 'Moscow branch,' he muttered. Fisher felt an unpleasant association with his side trip to Borodino Field. 'Goddamned museums . . . statues . . . victories . . . wars . . .' The Prospect was flanked by solid walls of grey masonry buildings. Fisher pulled up to his first stoplight. People in the crosswalk were looking at his car and licence plate, then at him. 'Jesus, you people never see a car with Connecticut plates before?'

Fisher savored the sights and sounds. 'Moscow! I'm in

Moscow!' He grinned. All the towns and villages from Brest on had been mere hors d'oeuvres. This was the pièce de résistance. The Capital, the Center, as the Russians called it. He stared at the buildings and the people, trying to absorb every detail, making himself understand that he was actually *in* the streets of Moscow. *'Moskva.'*

The light changed, and Fisher moved forward. The road forked, but he knew to take the left fork. Ahead he saw the spire of the Ukraina Hotel, another Stalinist wedding cake that looked much like the Moscow university building. He passed beside the massive hotel and found himself on the Kalinin Bridge that spanned the Moskva River. On the far bank, off to the left, he could see a modern high-rise building of dark red brick, and he was fairly certain that was the American embassy compound. 'Thank you, God.'

Fisher came off the bridge into a confusing interchange. He was looking for a turnoff that would double him back toward the embassy near the river when a green and white police car pulled up beside him. The policeman in the passenger seat motioned him to pull over. Fisher decided he didn't see him. The policeman shouted, *'Stoi!'*

Fisher considered making a run for the embassy. *Fastest car in the Soviet Union*. But a chase through central Moscow was probably not a good idea. He was past the interchange now and was on the busy Kalinin Prospect.

'Stoi!'

'Up your *stoi*, bozo.' Fisher took a deep breath, cut the wheel, and pulled over to the curb. His knees were so weak and shaky he had trouble applying the brakes.

The police car pulled up behind him, and both men, dressed in green overcoats and fur hats, approached. They carried white billy clubs. One came to his window, and Fisher lowered it.

'Amerikanets?'

'Right. *Da.*'

'Viza. Pasport.'

Gregory Fisher controlled his shaking hands as he produced his visa and passport.

The policeman studied the documents, looking alternately between Fisher and the papers again and again until Fisher thought the man was a half-wit. The other man was walking around the car, touching it. He seemed intrigued by the rear spoiler.

No one said anything for a long time. Suddenly a man in civilian clothing appeared. He stared at Fisher through the windshield, then came to the driver's side. He spoke in heavily accented but correct English. 'The car documents, please. Your international driver's license, your insurance papers, your motoring itinerary.'

'Right. *Da.*' Fisher handed the man a large envelope.

The civilian studied the paperwork for some time, then snapped his fingers, and one of the policemen quickly handed him Fisher's passport and visa. The civilian said to Fisher, 'Turn off your ignition, give me your keys, and step out of the car.'

Fisher did as he was told. As he stood in front of the man he noticed that he was tall and very slender for a Russian. In fact, he was fair and Nordic-looking.

The man studied Fisher's face, then his passport and visa pictures just as the uniformed man had done. Finally he said, 'You come from Smolensk?'

'Connecticut.'

'You just arrived in Moscow from Smolensk?'

'Oh, yes.'

'You were driving in the country at night.'

'No.'

'But you said you just arrived in Moscow. It has been dark for two hours.'

'I didn't say I just –'

'You were seen coming past the Arch.'

'Oh . . . is that the city limit?'

'What is your business in this quarter of the city?'

'Tourism.'

'Yes? Have you gone to your hotel yet?'

'No. I thought. I'd just drive around –'

'Please don't lie. That makes it worse. You were driving in the country at night.'

'Yes.' Fisher looked closely at the man. He was about forty, wore a leather coat and a black fur hat, probably sable. He seemed neither friendly nor hostile, just inquisitive. Fisher knew the type. 'Well, I got a late start from Smolensk.'

'Did you?' The man looked at Fisher's travel itinerary. 'Yet it says here you left the Intourist office at thirteen-fifty – one-fifty P.M.'

'I got lost.'

'Where?'

'At Bor – at Mozhaisk.'

The man stared at Fisher, and Fisher stared back. *Fuck you, Boris.*

'I don't understand.'

'Lost. You know.'

'What did you see in Mozhaisk?'

'The cathedral.'

'Where did you get lost?' The man added in a sarcastic tone, 'Inside the cathedral?'

Fisher's fear gave way to annoyance. 'Lost means you don't *know* where.'

The man suddenly smiled. 'Yes. Lost means that.' The man seemed to be thinking. 'So. That is what you say?'

Fisher stayed silent. He might not have the right to remain so, he thought, but he had enough brains not to incriminate himself any further.

The man regarded Greg Fisher for an uncomfortably long time, then motioned Fisher to follow him. They went to the rear of the car, and the man unlocked Fisher's trunk and opened it. The trunk light revealed Fisher's cache of spare parts, lubricants, and cleaning supplies. The man picked up a can of Rain Dance car wax, examined it, then put it back.

Fisher noticed that the citizens of Moscow slowed imperceptibly but did not stop and did not stare – the only time in the last thousand miles that the Pontiac did not stop traffic. Greg Fisher suddenly comprehended the full meaning of the words 'police state'.

He noticed that the two uniformed men were bent over into the rear seat of his car, examining his luggage and burlap bags of fruit and vegetables.

'What does this mean?'

Fisher turned back to the civilian. 'What?' Fisher saw he was pointing to the nameplate on the car. 'Pontiac,' Fisher said.

'Yes?' Name of the company' – *shithead* – 'General Motors. I think as an Indian word or something. Right. Chief Pontiac.'

The man didn't seem enlightened. He stared at Fisher's nationality plate, a red, white, and blue shield with stars and stripes that Fisher had been required to purchase at Brest. The man snapped his finger against the American shield, almost, Fisher thought, as though he intended to be insulting. He then pointed to the front fender. 'Trans Am?'

'Trans – across. Am – America.'

'Across America.'

'Right.'

'Across Russia.' The man smiled again, and Fisher noticed it wasn't a pleasant smile. The man came around to the driver's side and put his hand on the seat. 'Leather?'

'Yes.'

'How much?'

'Oh . . . about eighteen thousand dollars.'

'Seventy – eighty thousand rubles.'

Fisher noticed the man had given the black market rate of exchange instead of the official rate. Fisher replied, 'No. *Fifteen* thousand.'

The man smirked, then asked, 'Are you a capitalist?'

'Oh, no. I'm an ex-student. I took a course in Soviet

30

economics once. Read Marx and a book called *The Red Executive*. Very enlightening.'

'Marx?'

'Karl. And Lenin. I'm very interested in the Soviet Union.'

'For what reason?'

'Oh, just to know about the Soviet people. World's first socialist state. Fascinating. Did you ever see *Reds?* Warren Beatty –'

The man turned away and joined the two policemen who were now standing on the sidewalk. They spoke for about five minutes, then the tall civilian returned. 'You have broken a law: driving in the country at night. It is very serious, for a foreigner.'

Fisher said nothing.

The man continued, 'You should have stopped in a town along the highway if you were lost.'

'You're absolutely right.'

'I suggest you go now directly to the Rossiya and stay there for the evening. You may be asked to give a full accounting of yourself tomorrow, or perhaps tonight.'

'Okay.' And here, in an ironic twist, Fisher realized, they didn't cuff or frisk you after charging you with a serious offense; they simply had no previous experience with armed or dangerous citizens. Nor did they arrest you on the spot, because the whole country was a sort of detention camp anyway; they simply sent you to your room. The arrest was at their convenience. 'Right. The Rossiya.'

The man handed Fisher his papers and his keys. 'Welcome to Moscow, Mr Fisher.'

'Real glad to be here.'

The man walked away, and Fisher watched him descend into a Metro station. The two policemen got into their car without a word. They remained parked, watching Fisher.

Greg Fisher shut his trunk and his right side door, then climbed behind the wheel and started the engine. He noticed a crowd forming now. 'Sheep.' He replayed the incident in

31

his mind and decided he'd done all right. 'Schmucks.' He threw the car in gear and pulled out into traffic. The police car followed.

'Assholes.' He was trembling so badly now he wanted to pull over but continued up Kalinin Prospect. The police car stayed with him, so the embassy was out of the question for the time being.

Fisher barely noticed his surroundings as he drove. When he did, he realized he had crossed the Inner Ring Road and was heading straight for the Kremlin. He recalled from the map what he was supposed to do and turned hard right onto Marx Prospect, went down to the embankment road, and cut left. On his right was the Moskva, to his left the high crenellated south wall of the Kremlin, punctuated by tall watchtowers. The Moskva reflected the glow of the red stars of the Kremlin's towers and churches, and Fisher stared, mesmerized by a sight of unexpected beauty. He felt that he had come to the end of his uneasy journey.

The embankment road curved to the right, and the Kremlin wall ended at a massive watchtower. Behind him he could still see the headlights of the police car in his rearview mirror. Ahead, he saw an arched underpass beneath the ramp of a Moskva River bridge. Rising up beyond the ramp was the Rossiya Hotel. It was a massive, modern building with a glass and aluminum facade, and its width made its ten stories look squat. Fisher noticed that most of the windows were dark. He drove under the ramp and pulled around to the east side as his Intourist instructions said. In front of the east entrance was a small parking area bordered on three sides by a low stone wall. He came to a stop fifty feet from the front doors and looked around. There were no cars in the lot. The front of the Rossiya was stark. To the left of the entrance doors was another door that led to a Beriozka shop, found in nearly all Soviet hotels where Westerners with Western currency could buy Russian goods and occasionally Western toiletries and sundries. The Beriozka was closed.

Fisher noticed that the parking lot hung out over a steep incline that ran down to the Moskva River. The hotel was a monstrosity, surrounded by small, old buildings and a half dozen tiny churches in bad repair.

Fisher looked in his rearview mirror. On the entrance drive behind him he saw the police car parked. Fisher pulled up to the front doors of the hotel and shut off the engine.

He saw a green-uniformed doorman standing inside the glassed-in outer foyer of the hotel. The man studied the Trans Am but made no move to open the door. Fisher got out of the car with his shoulder satchel. He had discovered that in a Soviet hotel a doorman's job was not to help people in, but to keep Soviet citizens out, especially, but not limited to, black marketeers, prostitutes, dissidents, and the curious who might want to see how people on the West side of the tracks lived. Fisher opened the door himself and approached the doorman. 'Allo.'

'Allo.'

Fisher motioned toward his car. '*Bagazh*. Okay?'

'Okay.'

He handed the doorman his car keys. '*Garazb*. Okay?'

The doorman looked at him quizzically.

It occurred to Fisher that there was probably not a parking garage in the whole of Moscow. Fisher was tired, scared, and annoyed. 'Sweet Jesus . . .' He realized he didn't have a ruble on him. He reached into his satchel and grabbed an item he'd been saving. 'Here.' He held up an eight-inch copper reproduction of the Statue of Liberty, complete with pedestal.

The doorman's eyes darted around, then he took it and examined it suspiciously. '*Religiozni?*'

'No, no. It's the Statue of Liberty. *Svoboda*. For you. *Podarok*. Take care of the auto. Okay?'

The doorman shoved the statue into the pocket of his tunic. 'Okay.'

Fisher pushed through the swinging glass door and entered the lobby, which seemed deserted and, like most public places,

33

over-heated. The Russians equated heat with luxury. Fisher suspected. He looked around. The lobby was mostly grey stone and aluminium. A mezzanine ran from end to end above the pillared lobby. There was no bar, no newsstand, no shops, no services in evidence. There was nothing in fact to suggest he was in a hotel except for a sort of ticket window in the left-hand wall that he assumed was the front desk. He walked to it, and a disinterested young woman looked up. He gave her his Intourist reservation, his passport and visa. She examined the passport a moment, then without a word disappeared through a door behind the desk.

Fisher said aloud to himself, 'Welcome to the Rossiya, Mr Fisher. How long will you be staying with us? . . . Oh, until the KGB comes for me . . . Very good, sir.'

Fisher turned and looked down the long, narrow lobby. There were no bellhops or hotel staff in view except the doorman sitting in the glass-enclosed foyer. He could see his car, and parked right behind it was the police car.

The place not only looked deserted, but spooky. 'This is not a hotel.'

Fisher now noticed a couple near a far pillar arguing in French, which echoed through the lobby. They were well dressed and both were good-looking. The woman seemed on the verge of tears. The man gave a very Gallic wave of dismissal and turned his back on her.

'Oh,' Fisher said, 'give the woman a break. You should have my problems, buddy.' Fisher recalled Paris as he'd last seen it in June and wondered why he'd ever left. Napoleon probably wondered the same thing as Moscow burned around him and the snow was falling. He might have stood right here, Fisher thought, a hundred yards from the Kremlin wall, Red Square to his back and the Moskva to his front. *And he would have felt that sense of doom that the Westerner feels when he enters this foreboding land, like I feel now.*

He noticed that someone had moved his car, but he didn't see his bags being brought in, and that bothered him. He thought

34

about where his car might be. *Probably at KGB headquarters, being stripped to its frame.* The police car was also gone.

Fisher needed a drink. He looked at his watch: 8:30 P.M. Someone behind him said, 'Gree-gory Feesher.'

He turned back to the desk. A middle-aged woman with short red hair, black roots, and a polyester pantsuit of aquamarine said. 'I am from Intourist. I may see your papers?'

Fisher handed her the large envelope. She went through each paper carefully, then looked at him. 'Why are you late?'

Fisher had rarely been asked that question in that tone by anyone, and he felt his anger rising in him again. He snapped, 'Late for *what*?'

'We were worried about you.'

'Well, nothing to worry about now, is there? May I go to my room?'

'Of course. You must be tired.' She added, 'It has been some time since I met an American who traveled by auto from the West. The young are so adventurous.'

'And stupid.'

'Perhaps.' She handed him his papers minus his passport and visa, then gave him a green hotel card. 'This is your *propusk*. Carry this always with you. Your passport and visa will be returned when you check out. You must produce the *propusk* when anyone in authority asks for it.'

'Maybe I should just tape it to my forehead.'

She seemed to appreciate the joke and smiled. She leaned across the counter and said softly, 'You have been here long enough to know that it is not easy for a Westerner traveling without a tour group, Mr Fisher. Don't call attention to yourself.'

Fisher didn't respond.

'Avoid barter, currency deals, prostitutes, political talk, and itinerary violations. I give you good advice because you seem a pleasant young man.'

Fisher thought he'd been anything but pleasant. 'Thank you. I'll be good.'

She stared at him awhile, and Fisher had the disturbing thought that she knew he was already in trouble and was worried about him. He suddenly liked her. He asked, 'Where is my luggage?'

'It will be along.'

'Shortly?'

'Presently.'

He thought it was being searched by now. He asked, 'Will they park my car safely?'

'Of course. Who could steal an American car?'

Fisher smiled. 'Couldn't get too far.'

A bellhop suddenly appeared who Fisher thought looked like Genghis Khan's nephew. He motioned Fisher to follow him to the elevator bank. They waited nearly five minutes before an elevator came. Fisher rode up with the Tartar to the seventh floor. The elevator doors opened to reveal a small vestibule where a pretty young woman sat at a desk. In Paris or Rome, Fisher would have been pleasantly surprised to find a floor concierge in attendance. But in Moscow, Fisher knew this woman was the floor's *dezhurnaya*, a guardian of public morals, and according to a Pole he'd met in Warsaw, also a KGB snoop.

The blond woman looked up from a copy of *Cosmopolitan*. 'Allo. Your *propusk*, please.'

Fisher gave it to her. She handed him his room key. 'Give me key when you leave. I give you *propusk*.'

'Sounds fair.'

The bellman pointed down the hall, and Fisher found himself leading the way. At a turn in the corridor Fisher saw his room, 745, and opened the door with his key. He went in, followed by the bellman. Fisher said, 'Your room, sir.'

'Please?'

'Forget it.' Fisher looked around. It was a medium-sized room decorated in stark Scandinavian blondewood. The two single beds were undersized, and the mattress would be thin foam rubber, and the sheets, coarse cotton. The rug was brick-red, but that didn't hide the fact that it needed a shampoo. He doubted, however, that such a thing existed east of Berlin. *Oh, the things we take for granted.* The rest of the room looked clean enough except for the window. He had not seen a single clean window in the whole of the Soviet Union. 'Windex. I'll sell them Windex.' A smell of pine disinfectant reminded him of his side trip to Borodino.

The bellman said, 'Good room.' He tried a lamp switch and seemed surprised that it worked. 'Good light.'

'Excellent fucking light. Volts, watts, lumens, the works.'

The bellman ducked into the bathroom for a second, opened the closet, pulled out a few bureau drawers, then held out his arms as if to say, 'It's all yours.'

Fisher sighed and rummaged through his satchel, finding a small sampler of Aramis cologne. 'This drives the women wild.'

The Tartar took it and sniffed. 'Ah.' The man beamed, his slanted eyes narrowing. 'Thank you.' He turned and left.

Fisher examined the door. As in all other rooms he'd stayed in east of the curtain, this door had no peephole, no bolt, or security chain. He walked to the bed, fell back onto it, and kicked off his Reeboks. He stared at the ceiling awhile, then sat up and looked at the telephone. The hotel service directory was a single sheet of typed paper. He dialed a three-digit number, got room service, and ordered a bottle of vodka. 'First thing that went right all day.'

He considered the events of the last few hours. He had managed to suppress his fear in front of the police and to act natural and a bit cocky as he checked in. But his resolve was draining away fast in the quiet, empty room. He began to shake, then bounded out of bed and paced the room. *What if they come for me now? Maybe I should try to get to the embassy now. But that bastard said to stay in the hotel. They're watching me. Can they know what happened at Borodino?*

He stopped pacing. 'This is not a business problem. This is life or death.' He realized he had to calm down before he could think. Don't think about getting arrested or shot. *Then* you can go through the bullshit of problem solving.

He walked to the window and looked out through the grime. From his corner room he could see toward Red Square. The Kremlin was to the left, and he could look down into it. St Basil's ten phantasmal onion domes seemed to hang suspended like giant helium balloons above the dark cobbled pavement, and beyond them lay the huge GUM department store. The streets looked deserted, the buildings were dark, but the monuments were bathed in floodlight. A night fog, like a vapor, rolled off the Moskva and swirled around the streetlights, rolled over the Kremlin walls, and seemed to turn covers, as if it were looking for something. There was a sinister essence about this city, Fisher decided. Something unnatural about its cold, dead streets.

There was a loud rap on the door, and Fisher turned with a start. Another knock. Fisher took a breath, went to the door, and threw it open. A matronly woman stood there with an ice bucket from which protruded a liter of Moskovskaya. Fisher showed her in, gave her a tube of toothpaste, and showed her out.

His hand shook as he poured a half tumbler of the chilled vodka. He drank it down, and it made his eyes water. He refilled his glass and continued pacing. *The next knock will be my luggage or the KGB.* 'The fucking K –' He stopped. He'd heard and believed that every room was bugged. He'd read somewhere that some rooms had a fiber optic embedded in the wall or ceiling and everything in the room could be seen. He put his glass on the nightstand, turned off the light, put on his shoes, and took his shoulder satchel. He went into the bathroom, flushed the toilet, and shut the light. As the toilet was still flushing, he left the bathroom and slipped quietly out of his room into the hallway. He looked both ways, then retraced his path and found the elevator lobby. The *dezhurnaya*'s face was hidden by the copy of *Cosmopolitan*. She didn't seem to know he was there or didn't care. Fisher read the string of subheads on the cover: *Beating the Man Shortage! Cosmo Finds the Best*

Place to Meet Them; The Shy Girl – How She Can Compete; Why Friends Make the Best Lovers; The Joy of Resuming an Old Romance.

Fisher put his keys on her desk. She looked up. 'Allo, Mr Fisher.' She gave him his *propusk.*

He pushed the elevator button and prepared for a long wait. The vodka finally reached his brain. He said to the woman, 'Good magazine?'

'Yes. Very sexy.'

'Right.'

'American women have too much.'

'I hadn't noticed.'

She tapped the magazine. 'They have so many problems with men.'

'Cosmo women have more problems than most.'

'Ah.'

Fisher hesitated, then took a tube of lip gloss from his satchel. It was a frosted pink and seemed to match her coloring.

She smiled as she examined it. 'Thank you.' She took a compact mirror from her bag and went to work immediately.

Fisher noticed it wasn't really her color, but she didn't seem to care. He liked the way she puckered her lips. The elevator came, and he stepped in. Two Russian men who smelled of salami stood quietly behind him. Fisher felt perspiration under his arms.

Fisher stepped out into the lobby and felt somewhat better in a public place. He found the foreign exchange window, but it was closed. He went to the front desk and asked the clerk if she would cash an Intourist voucher for five rubles. She said she wouldn't. Fisher asked for the Intourist woman and was told she was gone.

He looked around. All he needed was a lousy two-kopek piece. *For want of a nail* . . . 'Damn it.' He saw that the French couple was still there, and he approached them. *'Pardon, monsieur, madame. J'ai besoin de . . . deux kopeks. Pour le téléphone.'*

The man gave him an unfriendly look. The woman smiled nicely and searched through her bag. *'Voilà.'*

'Merci, madame. Merci.' Fisher moved off and found a single telephone booth in a short corridor that led to the Beriozka. He went inside, pulled the door closed, and took his Fodor guide from his satchel. Fisher found the number of the American embassy, inserted the two-kopek piece, and dialed.

Gregory Fisher listened to the short, distant ringing signals, very unlike the ones he was used to at home. He cleared his throat several times and said 'hello' twice to try his voice. The blood was pounding in his ears. He kept his eyes on the corridor. The phone continued to ring.

Lisa Rhodes sat at the night duty officer's desk on the first floor of the chancery building. The wall clock showed 8:45. The phone had been quiet all evening. This was not an embassy that was likely to be surrounded by angry mobs or blown up by a terrorist. Nor was Moscow a city where the police called to inform you they had a dozen of your compatriots in the drunk tank. She lit a cigarette as she crossed out a line of the press release she was working on.

The door opened, and Kay Hoffman, Lisa's boss, stuck her head into the small office. 'Hello. Anything exciting happening?'

'Yes, but it's happening in Rome. Hello, Kay. Come on in.'

Kay Hoffman entered the office and sat on the windowsill air register. 'Ah, that feels good on my buns. Cold out there.'

Lisa smiled and regarded Kay Hoffman a moment. She was a woman near fifty with thick chestnut hair and large brown eyes. She could be described as pleasantly plump, or perhaps full-figured. In any case, men seemed to like her lustiness and easy manner.

Lisa said, 'I can't offer you a drink.'

'That's alright. I thought I'd drop in on the Friday night follies.'

Lisa nodded. The Friday night cocktail reception, given by the ambassador, was a sort of TGIF affair, except that the weekends were worse than the weekdays. Traditionally all visiting Americans in Moscow were invited to the reception, and in the days when you could count the Americans on two hands, they were contacted individually. Now, with increased trade and tourism, it was sort of an open invitation that you had to know about. The embassy staff seemed to enjoy seeing new faces, and the visiting Americans were usually thrilled to be there. Sort of like sitting at the captain's table, Lisa thought.

Kay said, 'Come with me. Call the guard post and tell them where you'll be.'

'No, thanks, Kay.'

'Sometimes there are interesting men there. That's why I go. You're young and good-looking. Lisa. You attract them, and I'll pounce on them.'

Lisa smiled.

'Last week,' Kay continued, 'I met a single man who was in Moscow to see about exporting Armenian cognac to the States. He comes in about once a month. Stays at the Trade Center Hotel, so he must have money and connections.'

'Was he nice?'

'Yes. Very.' Kay grinned.

Lisa forced a smile in return. 'I'm not up to it tonight.'

Kay shrugged. She said, 'What are you working on?'

'Oh, that rock group, Van Halen, who played at the Kolonnyi Zal.'

'How were they?'

'I got a headache from them. But you'd have thought by the crowd that John Lennon had returned from the dead with free Levis for everyone.'

'Write something nice.'

'I'm trying.' Lisa went back to her work.

'What happened with that political affairs officer? Seth Alevy.'

'I'd rather not talk about it.'

'Alright.' Kay looked at her watch. 'I can make the last half hour. Then I'll be downstairs in the bowling alley bay. Unless I get lucky.'

Lisa smiled. 'Maybe I'll see you later.'

'You need a man, sweetie.' Kay Hoffman left.

A few minute later, the phone rang, and Lisa saw the red

42

light flashing, indicating that the Marine post was calling her. She picked up the receiver. 'Rhodes here.'

'This is Corporal Hines, ma'am. I have a call from a man who says he is a US national. Says he wants to speak to a defense attaché.'

Her eyebrows rose. 'A *defense attaché*. Why?'

'Won't say. Sounds like a young guy. Won't say where he's calling from either.'

'Put him through.'

'Yes, ma'am.'

The phone clicked, and she heard Corporal Hines say, 'Go ahead, sir.'

A male voice said, 'Hello . . . ?'

'This is Ms Rhodes speaking. Can I help you?'

There was no response for several seconds, then the voice said, 'I have to speak to a defense attaché. Air Force, if possible.'

'For what reason, sir?'

'It's important. National security.'

She checked the recording device to make sure it was activated. 'Then perhaps it's not a good idea to speak on the phone.'

'I know that. But I don't have any choice. I have to tell you now – before they come for me.'

'Who is going to come for you?'

'You know who.'

'Alright . . .' She thought a moment. There was a possibility this was a setup or a prank, but her instincts said it was neither. 'What is your name, sir?'

'Why can't I speak to a defense attaché?'

'Do you know what a defense attaché is?'

'No . . . but I was told to speak to one.'

'Who told you that?'

'Is your phone tapped?'

'You must assume it is.'

'Oh, Christ. Can you send someone to get me? I need help.'

43

'Where are you?'

'Maybe I can get there. Can I get through the gate?'

Lisa Rhodes thought he was sounding more distraught and perhaps a bit drunk. 'Listen to me,' she said with a tone of authority. 'Talk to me, and if I think it advisable, I will locate a defense attaché. Alright?'

'Yes . . . yes, okay.'

She found the duty officer's procedure manual in a drawer and flipped through it as she spoke. 'Are you an American citizen?'

'Yes, I –'

'What is your name?'

There was a pause, then the voice answered, 'Fisher. Gregory Fisher.'

'Where are you now?'

'The Rossiya Hotel.'

'Are you checked in there?'

'Yes.'

'Did they take your passport when you checked in?'

'Yes.'

'Well, you can't get past the mili-men – the Soviet militia outside the embassy – without it.'

'Oh.'

'Room number?'

'Seven forty-five. But I'm not in my room.'

'Where are you?'

'In a phone booth in the lobby.'

'What is your business in the S.U.?

'S.U.? . . .'

'Soviet Union.'

'Oh . . . no business –'

'Tourist?'

'Yes.'

'When did you arrive in the country, Mr Fisher?'

'Last week.'

'What tour group are you with?'

'Group? No group. I drove –'

'You *drove* to Moscow?'

'Yes, my own car. That was part of the damned problem.

'What was?'

'The car. A Trans Am sticks out –'

'Yes. Alright, tell me briefly why you need help and why you would like to speak to a defense attaché.'

She heard what sounded like a sigh, then he said softly, 'In case you can't get here in time . . . I'm going to tell you all I can . . . before they get me.'

Lisa Rhodes thought that Gregory Fisher had a good grasp of the situation. She said, 'Then you'd better speak quickly.'

'Okay. I was in Borodino, about five P.M. tonight – visiting the battle-field. I got lost in the woods –'

'Were you stopped by the police?'

'No. Yes, but in Moscow.'

'Why?'

'For driving in the country at night.'

She thought that this wasn't computing. A travel itinerary violation was one thing. Asking to speak to a defense attaché – a person who was more or less an intelligence officer, a spy – was quite another. 'Go on, Mr Fisher.'

'On the road, north of Borodino, I think, I met a man, an American –'

'An American?'

'Yes. He said he was an American Air Force pilot –'

'And he was on the road, north of Borodino, at night? Alone? In a car?'

'Alone. On foot. He was hurt. Listen, I don't know how much time I have –'

'Go on.'

'His name was Major Jack Dodson.'

'Dodson.' Lisa had thought that it might have been a defense attaché at the embassy, but the name was unfamiliar.

'Dodson said he was an MIA – a POW – shot down in Vietnam –'

'What?' She sat up in her chair. 'He told you that?'

'Yes. And he said he had been a prisoner here in Russia for almost twenty years. A place he called Mrs Ivonova's Charm School. Near Borodino. He escaped. I gave him maps and money. He didn't want us to travel together in my car. He's heading cross-country to Moscow. To the embassy. There are other Americans held prisoner who –'

'Stop. Hold the line.' She hit the hold button. In the duty book she quickly found the apartment number of the air attaché, Colonel Sam Hollis, whom she knew casually. She rang him, but there was no answer. 'Damn it, and Seth is at his damned Sukkot party . . .' She considered putting out an all-points page for Hollis but instead tried Hollis' office two floors above. The phone was picked up on the first ring, and a voice answered, 'Hollis.'

She said in a controlled voice, 'Colonel Hollis, this is Lisa Rhodes on the duty desk.'

'Yes?'

'I have a US national on the line, calling from the Rossiya. He sounds very distraught. He also says he wants to speak to a defense attaché, preferably an Air Force attaché.'

'Why?'

'I'll play the tape for you.'

'Go ahead.'

Lisa Rhodes transferred the playback to Hollis' line. When it was finished, Hollis said, 'Put him through.'

She put the phone on conference call and released the hold button. 'Mr Fisher? Are you there?'

There was no answer.

'Mr Fisher?'

'Yes . . . there's someone standing –'

'Here is the gentleman with whom you asked to speak.'

Hollis' voice came on the line. 'Mr Fisher, you say you are calling from the lobby of the Rossiya?'

'Yes. I'm –'

'Is the lobby crowded?'

'No. Why?'

'Who is standing by the phone booth?'

'A man. Listen, should I try to get to the embassy –'

'No, sir. You stay there. Do not leave that hotel. Do not go back to your room. There is a restaurant on the top floor. Go to the lounge there and introduce yourself to some Westerners – English-speaking, if possible – and stay with them until I arrive. Is that clear?'

'Yes . . . yes.'

'What are you wearing?'

'Blue jeans . . . black windbreaker –'

'Okay, son. Get to the lounge quickly. If anyone tries to stop you, kick, scream, yell, and fight. Understand?'

'Yes . . . yes, I . . .' Fisher's voice sounded strained. 'Oh . . . God . . . hurry.'

Hollis' tone was soothing. 'Ten minutes, Greg. Get to the lounge.'

Lisa heard the phone click as Fisher hung up. Hollis' voice came on. 'Ms Rhodes, I need a car –'

'I've already called for one, Colonel. With a driver.'

'I'll be bringing Mr Fisher here. Have a visitor's room ready in the residency and alert the appropriate security people.'

'Yes, sir.'

'Stay in the duty office.'

'Of course.'

There was a silence, then Hollis said, 'Nicely handled, Ms Rhodes.'

She heard him hang up before she could respond. Lisa Rhodes put the phone back in the cradle. 'You, too, Colonel Hollis.'

47

5

Colonel Sam Hollis, American air attaché to the Soviet Union, left his office and took the elevator to the ground floor of the chancery building. He went directly to the duty office adjacent the empty lobby and opened the door.

Lisa Rhodes turned toward him. 'Yes?'

'Hollis.'

'Oh . . .' She stood. 'I didn't recognize you in civvies.'

'Have we met?'

'A few times.' She regarded him a moment. He was wearing a leather bomber jacket, jeans, and leather boots. He was in his late forties, tall, and lanky. She thought he was rather good-looking in a tough sort of way. She remembered his pale blue eyes and unmilitary-length sandy hair. She also remembered that he and Seth had business dealings.

Hollis said, 'I don't want you to breathe a word of this to anyone.'

'I know that.'

'Good. There is someone however . . . do you know Seth Alevy? Political affairs officer.'

'Yes.'

'Mr Alevy is attending a party in town –'

'I know that.'

'How do you know that?'

'He invited me.'

'I see. So you know how to reach him?'

'Yes, through his people there.'

'That's right. Please do that.'

She hesitated, then said, 'I've already asked his people to get him here.'

Hollis gave her a close look.

She returned his stare. 'I guess I know he's involved with things like this.'

Hollis went to the door, then turned back to her. 'Are *you* involved with things like this?'

'Oh, no. I'm just a PIO. Seth and I are social friends.'

They looked at each other a moment. Hollis guessed she was in her late twenties. She was lightly freckled, with reddish auburn hair. She was not the type of woman you forgot meeting, and in fact, he had not forgotten the times they'd met in the embassy. He also knew that she and Alevy had been recent lovers. But by instinct and training he never offered information, only solicited it. 'Hold the fort. See you later.' He left.

Lisa moved to the door and watched him walk quickly through the lobby to the front doors. 'Strong, silent type. Silent Sam.'

Sam Hollis pushed through the glass doors into the damp, misty night. He zipped his leather jacket and headed toward a blue Ford Fairlane that sat in the forecourt with its engine running. Hollis jumped in the passenger side. 'Hello, Bill.'

The driver, a security staff man named Bill Brennan, drove quickly through the court, around the traffic circle that held the illuminated flagpole, and moved toward the gates. 'Where we going, Colonel?'

'Rossiya.' Hollis looked at Brennan. He was a man in his mid-fifties, heavyset and balding, and his nose had once been broken. Hollis always had the impression that Brennan wanted to break someone else's nose. Hollis said, 'You carrying?'

'Yup. You?'

'No. Didn't have time to get it.'

'Loan mine if you promise to kill a commie.'

'That's alright.'

The gates swung open, and the car moved past the Marine guard post, then past the Soviet militia booth on the sidewalk. Brennan kept the speed down so as not to attract the attention of the KGB embassy watchers in the surrounding buildings, but Hollis said, 'Step on it. They know where I'm going.'

'Okay.' Brennan accelerated up the dark, quiet side street and cut right on to the wide, well-lit Tchaikovsky Street. Traffic was sparse and Brennan made good time. He asked, 'Do I stop for police?'

'No, you run them.' Hollis added, 'Don't take the direct route up Kalinin.'

'Gotcha.' The Ford picked up speed in the outside lane, passing buses and trams, and sailed past the Kalinin Prospect intersection. Brennan stuffed his mouth with bubble gum, chewed, and blew bubbles until they popped. 'Want some?'

'No, thanks. Do you know the Rossiya?'

'Know the traffic patterns, parking, and all. Not the inside.'

'Fine.' Brennan knew the streets of Moscow better than a Moscow cabbie, but Hollis thought that Brennan cared not a whit about Moscow. He was into streets, and he claimed he'd never seen Red Square, because he couldn't drive through it.

Brennan asked between chews, 'Is this going to be messy?'

'Maybe. American national up the creek at the Rossiya.'

'How'd the *Komitet* know you were going there?'

'Well, the kid – the US national – called the embassy and said he was in trouble.'

'Oh.'

Hollis thought about Fisher's call. He assumed the traffic police had indeed stopped Fisher for nothing more than an itinerary violation. But Fisher had gotten paranoid because of the Borodino thing. If he'd kept his cool, he would have been able to come to the embassy and tell his story. Instead, Gregory Fisher's two-kopek phone call might have already cost him his freedom – or his life.

Yet, Hollis thought, it was a brave thing to do. Stupid, but brave. Hollis would tell him that without making him feel bad. How to get Fisher out of the country was tomorrow's problem.

Brennan asked, 'What kind of trouble is he in?'

'Itinerary violation.'

'Am I asking too many questions?'

'Not yet.'

'Okay, why am I tear-assing across Moscow with a military attaché in my car to rescue a kid who went to the fucking zoo instead of the fucking park or whatever?'

'You're asking too many questions.'

'Right.'

Neither man spoke for a while. The popping gum was getting on Hollis nerves. Hollis thought about the phone call. Who was Major Jack Dodson? What, in the name of God, was a POW doing in the woods at Borodino? Only Gregory Fisher could answer that.

Brennan said, 'I just passed a parked cop car.'

Hollis glanced back. 'He's on a break.'

'Right.'

Hollis looked at the speedometer and saw they were doing seventy miles per hour. Tchaikovsky Street changed names several times as it curved south and cast in what was generally known as the Second Ring Road. They crossed the Moskva at the Crimea Bridge, skirted Gorky Park to the right, and continued east up the wide, six-lane road. Hollis glanced at his watch. It had been twelve minutes since they'd left the embassy.

'Do you see him?' Brennan asked.

Hollis looked out of the rear window. 'Not yet.'

'Good.' Brennan suddenly cut hard left with squealing tires through Dobrynin Square and headed up Ordynka Street, straight north on a run that would take them to the center of Moscow and the Rossiya Hotel. Hollis knew that Brennan's route may have taken them a few extra minutes, but it had avoided any KGB who were out to intercept them and avoided the militia posts around the Kremlin.

Brennan said, 'If I get nabbed speeding, they kick me out of the country.'

'That bother you?'

51

'No . . . but I have the Colt .45. That can get sticky. My diplomatic immunity status is a little shaky.'

'I'll take the gun and the rap if they nail us.'

'Nah . . . that's okay. I'm tired of this fucking country anyway.'

'Drive on.'

Brennan accelerated up Ordynka Street. He added more bubble gum to the already large mass, and the bubbles got bigger.

Hollis hiked up the left leg of his blue jeans, reached into his boot, and pulled out a grey Air Force survival knife. He slipped the knife under his jacket and into his belt. Brennan watched him out of the corner of his eye but said nothing.

Hollis could see the Moskvoretsky Bridge about a half a kilometer ahead, and beyond the bridge he saw the Rossiya getting bigger with every second. The few cars on the road seemed to be standing still. Hollis heard a continuously honking horn behind them. He looked out the rearview window. 'The fuzz.'

'I hear it. What kind of car?'

'A Lada.'

'A fucking joke. About as much power as an electric shaver.'

'Nevertheless, he's on our tail.'

'Not for long.'

The Ford shot forward, and Hollis watched as the Lada lost ground. The police car had no siren or revolving lights, and the horn grew more distant, though Hollis knew it was still sounding because the Lada's headlights dimmed every time the driver hit the horn.

Brennan took the narrow bridge at eighty miles per hour, and Hollis saw a blur of pedestrians staring at them from the bridge walkway. The Ford sailed off the bridge, bounced hard, then tore across the embankment road, cutting diagonally past the Kremlin's corner tower. As they barreled up the approach lane to the Rossiya, Brennan asked, 'East side?'

'Yes. You keep going. Back to the embassy.'

Brennan pulled the Colt .45 from his shoulder holster. 'You need this?'

'No. You keep it or ditch it. Your choice.'

Brennan swung around toward the east entrance of the hotel. 'Ready.'

Hollis saw that the small parking area did not have a Trans Am in it, and he took this as a bad sign. 'Ready. Nice job.'

Brennan slowed the car in front of the hotel. 'Good luck.' He popped a big bubble.

'You too.' Hollis jumped out of the moving car and slammed the door as Brennan accelerated out the exit ramp.

Hollis pushed through the front doors of the Rossiya, and the doorman said, '*Propusk.*'

'*Komitet,*' Hollis replied as he brushed past him.

The man literally jumped back and tried to open the second door, but Hollis was already through it. Hollis went directly to the elevator and hit the top floor button. *Komitet.* Committee. The Committee for State Security – the KGB. Magic words. Open sesame. The fact that he'd arrived in an American car, wearing American clothing, made no difference to the doorman. No one else would dare utter that word.

The elevator arrived. Hollis rode up to the tenth floor and began the long trek to the west-facing side.

The Rossiya, for the uninitiated, was a confusing amalgam of four separate wings containing over three thousand rooms, attached to form a square around a central court. The east wing was the Intourist hotel, the west wing was a hotel for Soviet and East Bloc citizens only, while the north and south wings were residences for favored communists. The wings were connected at a few floors though not at the ground floor. To pass from one wing to another, Hollis knew, you had to have a good reason. East was east, and west was west, and most Western tourists were not even aware of the presence of the others. Here on the top floor however, east and west nearly met in this Byzantine and schizoid building. Hollis approached the entrance to the restaurant and bar, where one of the ubiquitous angry ladies

53

who seemed to guard every door in Moscow sat at a desk. She looked him over.

'Bar,' Hollis said.

She nodded curtly and pointed to the doors. Hollis went through into a large foyer. To the left was a black, closed door marked with the English word BAR. Straight ahead, two open doors revealed a huge restaurant filled to capacity. Hollis could tell by the din, the toasts, the laughter, and the attire that they were mostly Russians. He looked inside. A band played American jazz, and the dance floor was crowded with people who seemed to have trouble just standing. A wedding party occupied a large round table, and the bride, a pretty young girl in white, was the only person still sitting upright. Hollis had the fleeting impression she was having second thoughts. Hollis surveyed the room and satisfied himself that Fisher would not have gone in there. A man came toward him shaking his head. The man pointed over Hollis' shoulder. 'Bar.'

'*Spasibo*.' Hollis went through the black door and entered the bar, where, for Western hard currency, you could buy Western hard liquor and brand name mixers; a night spot of capitalist decadence, high above Red Square. Hollis scanned the dark lounge.

The bar was full, but in contrast to the Russian restaurant, the drunken chatter was more subdued and less lusty. The clientele, Hollis knew, were mostly Western Europeans, and nearly all were guests at the hotel. The Rossiya attracted few Americans, and he wondered how Fisher wound up here. Mixed with the Europeans were always a few Soviet high rollers with access to Westerners and their money. Every hard currency bar in Moscow also had a resident KGB snoop who could eavesdrop in ten languages.

Hollis walked around the lounge but didn't see anyone who could be Gregory Fisher. This, he decided, was not good.

There was a service bar where patrons were obliged to get their own drinks. Hollis elbowed through the crowd and spoke to the bartender in fluent Russian. 'I'm looking for my friend. An American. He is young and has on blue jeans and a short, black jacket.'

The bartender glanced at him quickly but continued to make drinks as he replied, 'American, you say? No, I didn't see anyone like that.'

Hollis left the bar and walked quickly to the east-wing elevators. He rode down to the seventh floor and got off. The *dezhurnaya* looked at him curiously. '*Gost?*'

'No. Visitor.' He leaned over her desk, looked the blond woman directly in the eye, and said, 'Fisher.'

She looked away.

'Gregory Fisher. American.'

She rolled a tube of lip gloss in her fingers, then shook her head.

Hollis looked at the keyboard behind her desk and saw that the key for 745 was missing. He walked past her and she called after him, 'You may not go there.'

Hollis ignored her. He found room 745 and knocked. There was no answer. He knocked again, harder.

A voice from behind the door said, 'Who is it?'

'I'm from the embassy.'

'Embassy?'

Hollis heard the lock turn, and the door opened. A paunchy, middle-aged man with sleep in his eyes, wearing a robe, peered out. 'Is everything alright?'

Hollis looked at him, then past him into the room. 'I'm looking for Mr Fisher.'

The man seemed relieved. 'Oh, I thought something happened at home. My wife. My name is Schiller. Everything's alright, isn't it?'

'Yes.' Hollis stared at him.

Schiller said, 'I heard "embassy", and you know –'

'Mr Fisher just called me and said he was in seven forty-five.'

Schiller's manner went from worried to slightly annoyed.

55

'So? He's not here, pal. I don't know the guy. Try four fifty-seven. Anything's possible in this fucked-up country.'

Which, Hollis thought, was not only true, but offered another possible explanation. 'They may have assigned you a room-mate. They do that sometimes.'

'Do they? Christ, what a place.'

'Could there be anyone's luggage in your closet?'

'Hell, no. I paid extra for a fucking single, and there's no one here. Hey, is he with that American Express group. Did you see that little Intourist guide they have? Christ, she looked edible. Maybe your friend is talking politics with her.' He laughed. 'Well, see ya at the Bolshoi.' The man closed the door.

Hollis stood there a moment, then walked back to the elevators. The *dezhurnaya* was gone. Hollis went behind her desk and found the drawer full of *propusks*. He flipped through them but could not find one with 745 on it. *How did Schiller get the key to 745 without turning in his propusk?*

Hollis took the elevator down to the lobby, which was deserted. He went to the front desk and rang the bell. The clerk appeared at the door behind the counter. Hollis said in Russian, 'What room is Gregory Fisher in?'

The clerk shook her head. 'Not here.'

'Who is in room seven forty-five?'

'I cannot tell you.'

'Is there an Intourist representative here?'

'No. Tomorrow morning at eight. Good evening.' She turned and disappeared into the inner office. He looked toward the foyer and saw there was a different doorman on duty. 'People are disappearing left and right, before my very eyes. Amazing country.'

Hollis thought a moment. Several possibilities came to mind, including the possibility that this was all a KGB *provokatsiya*, a ruse to draw him into some sort of compromising situation. But if they wanted to entrap him, there were less elaborate schemes. If they wanted to kill him, they'd just pick a morning he was jogging along the Shevchenko Embankment and run him over.

56

Hollis thought about Fisher's voice, the words, the very real fright in his tone. 'Fisher is real.' But Hollis had to prove that Fisher had reached this hotel alive and had fallen into the hands of the KGB. For if he could prove that, then what Fisher had said about Major Jack Dodson was probably true.

Hollis reached over the clerk's counter and took her telephone. He dialed 745 and let the phone ring a dozen times, then hung up. 'Not good.'

Hollis looked round. He realized he was alone and exposed. They could take him anytime they wanted now.

He walked quickly across the lobby, his footsteps echoing on the stone floor. He entered the dark passage that led to the Beriozka shop, drew his knife, and slid into the phone booth that Fisher must have used. Hollis thought that if the Rossiya was causing people to disappear, it might be a good idea if he proved that *he* had reached the Rossiya alive. He inserted a two-kopek piece and dialed the embassy. The Marine duty man answered, and Hollis asked to be put through to the duty office. Lisa Rhodes answered quickly.

Hollis asked, 'Have you heard from our friend?'

'No. Isn't he there?'

'Apparently not.'

There was a silence, then she said, 'Are you returning here?'

'That is my plan.'

'Do you need assistance?'

Hollis did, but he did not want this thing to escalate. He, Seth Alevy, and the other men and women in their profession had been made to understand by the ambassador that their shenanigans were their own business and should never embarrass the diplomatic mission. Hollis continued in that cryptic and stilted way they all spoke over the telephone. 'Have my car and driver returned yet?'

'No. Isn't he with you?'

'No, I let him go on. I thought he should be back there by now.'

'I'm sure he's not. Could he have had an accident or a breakdown?'

'He could very well have. You may be hearing from the authorities on that.'

'I see.' She drew a deep breath. 'Can I send transportation for you?'

'No. I'll find transportation. Is your friend back from his party yet?'

'He should be here within minutes. Do you want him to join you?'

'No need for that,' Hollis replied.

'Can he call you there?'

'No. But I may call you again.'

'What shall we do here if I don't hear from you?'

'Let him make that decision when he arrives.'

'Alright.' She added, 'I've replayed that tape we both like. It sounds realistic.'

'Yes. I've thought about that. I'll do what I can to find the original.'

'Good luck.'

Hollis hung up and went back down the dark corridor, knife in hand. He reached the lobby and slipped the knife under his jacket. 'Well, if I don't make it back, the ambassador can raise a little stink about it.' His estranged wife, Katherine, would get his pension and life insurance. He kept meaning to write to his lawyer in Washington to change his will. The complications inherent in international matrimonial problems were endless. 'Endless.' There were times when he wished he were in his old F-4 Phantom with nothing more to worry about than MiGs and missiles converging on his radar screen.

Hollis considered the evidence. Fisher's phone call to the embassy had tipped the KGB, but they would have needed time to react. 'Therefore Fisher made it to the lounge.'

Hollis took the elevator back up to the top floor and went to the lounge. He ordered a Dewar's and soda at the service

58

bar and said to the bartender in Russian, 'Have you seen my friend yet?'

'No. I'm sorry. Three dollars.'

Hollis paid him.

A well-dressed man next to Hollis thrust his glass toward the bartender and said with a British accent, 'Gin and tonic – Gordon's and Schweppes. Slice of lemon this time, *spasibo*.'

Hollis said to the man, 'They've been out of lemons since, the Revolution.'

The Englishman laughed. 'What a place this is, eh, Yank?'

'Different.'

'Bloody right. Here on holiday, then?'

'Business.'

'Me too.' The man's drink came without the lemon, and the bartender asked for three pounds. Hollis moved away from the service bar, and the Englishman followed. The man said, 'They haven't had cocktail waitresses since the Revolution either. You fetch your own drinks here, and they make their own exchange rates as they go along. Three dollars, three pounds, all the same to them. But I think my gin cost me more than your whiskey.'

'Try giving him three lire next time.'

The man laughed. 'They're not that bloody stupid. Name's Wilson.'

'Richardson,' Hollis replied.

They tipped their glasses toward each other. 'Cheers.'

Wilson said, 'Did I hear you speaking Russian there? *Spasibo* and *pozhalusta*. Which is which?'

'*Spasibo* is "thank you", *pozhalusta* is "please".'

'Oh, I've been getting it backwards. How do you get the bartender's attention?'

'Call out *Komitet*.'

'*Komitet?*'

'Right. That should get his attention. Have you been in here awhile?'

'About an hour, I suppose. Why?'

59

'I'm looking for a friend of mine. American, in his twenties, blue jeans and windbreaker.'

'"Windcheater", you mean?'

'Yes, windcheater.'

'I think I did see him. No one dresses in this benighted country. Damned Reds ruined everything. No manners either, and no style here, if you know what I mean. Of course I don't fault you for wearing a leather jacket if no one else dresses.'

'Did you notice if he was speaking to anyone?'

Wilson looked around the lounge. 'Saw him sitting over there somewhere. Yes, speaking to someone.'

'Who?'

'Ah, now I remember. See those two? Nicely dressed. Frogs, I think. They dress well if nothing else. Had a young chap with them. Could be your fellow. The lad had a few too many, and two people from the hotel helped him out. The boy became a bit . . . belligerent, I suppose you'd say. They hurried him off. I don't think they would make anything of it – half the damned country's drunk at any given moment. Probably took him to his room.'

'When was this?'

'About fifteen – twenty minutes ago.'

'Thanks.' Hollis moved through the cocktail tables and sat in an armchair across from the man and woman. 'May I?'

The man grunted in reply.

Hollis asked, 'Do you speak English?'

The man shook his head.

'And you, *madame*?'

She looked at him. 'A little.'

Hollis leaned across the table and spoke softly and distinctly. 'I am looking for a friend, an American, a young man. I understand he had a drink with you earlier.'

The woman glanced at the man beside her before replying. 'Yes.' She added in good English, 'He was ill. He was aided to his room.'

'This young man told you his name?'

60

'Yes.'

'Fisher?'

'Yes.'

'Did he seem . . . agitated? Worried?'

The woman did not reply but nodded almost imperceptibly.

'Did he tell you what was worrying him?'

The man stood and said to the woman, '*Allons.*'

She remained seated and said to Hollis, 'He did not say. But he said they may come for him. He knew. I think the drink was . . . what . . . ?'

'Drugged.'

'Yes.' She stood. 'My husband wishes to go. There is no more I know. I am sorry.'

Hollis stood also and said to the woman, 'You understand, *madame*, this is a matter of some concern to the authorities here. They know he spoke to you and are curious about what he told you. You may be in danger. Do you understand?'

'Yes.'

The Frenchman walked away impatiently. The woman lingered a moment, and Hollis looked her in the eye. 'What else?'

Her eyes met his. 'Are you the attaché?'

'Yes.'

'He said you would come. He said to tell you some things that he did not say to you on the telephone.' The woman thought a moment, then recited quickly, 'Dodson told him it was once a Red Air Force school. Now it is a KGB school. There are almost three hundred Americans.'

'Three hundred? He said three *hundred*?'

She nodded.

Hollis found himself holding the woman's arm in a tight grip. 'What else did Mr Fisher say?'

'Nothing. He became ill . . . They came for him. A Russian spoke to us in English, asking what the young man was saying. My husband replied in French, saying we spoke no English and could not understand the Russian or the young man.'

61

'Did the Russian believe your husband?'

'I think so.'

Hollis released her arm. 'Then perhaps you will be alright. But take the precaution of contacting your embassy. Tonight. In person. Not on the telephone. Then leave the country immediately.'

'I understand.'

'Good. Thank you, *madame*.'

She smiled weakly. 'The boy borrowed from me two kopeks . . . he seemed a nice sort . . . and now . . . now he is . . . what? Dead?'

Hollis didn't reply.

She shook her head. 'What times we live in.' She walked away.

Hollis finished his drink, then made his way out of the lounge and into the corridor. He went to the south wing of the hotel and took the elevator down to the Zaryadye Cinema, which had just let out. Hollis mixed with the crowd in the lobby and exited the door that faced the Moskva River embankment. He followed a group down a flight of stairs that led to a passageway under the road.

Hollis walked through the long, tiled tunnel, watching his breath mist in the cool air, listening to the echoing footsteps around him. A few of the Russians glanced curiously at him. He recalled a time two years before when he'd first come to Russia. He'd had occasion to walk this underpass at night and had been impressed by the discovery that there was not a scrap of litter on the floor, nor a line of graffiti on the walls. Moreover, the citizens of Moscow walked without fear. He was still impressed, but two years had given him a broader perspective. The streets and subways were immaculate, but little else was. There was no fear of street crime, not because there was none, but because it wasn't reported in the news. This was a society that thrived on good news, most of it manufactured.

Yet the average citizen's own observations told him one thing, and the government told him another. Predictably, Soviet men and women developed frayed circuitry, jerking along through life believing neither their senses nor the newspapers, neither in themselves nor their leaders, neither in God nor their fellow man. It was a nation of illusion, delusion, and collusion, a Potemkin village on a national scale, a place where men and women could disappear without a trace, and all evidence of their ever having existed would disappear with them. 'I tried, Fisher. I tried.'

Hollis came to the end of the tunnel. He ascended the stairs and went out on to the pedestrian walk of the Moskvoretsky Bridge, over which he and Brennan had driven nearly an hour before. He walked about twenty yards on to the bridge and stopped. A fog rose off the Moskva below, and the ruby red stars of the Kremlin towers glowed spectrally through the mist. There may have been a fine rain falling, but Hollis had never been able to distinguish Moscow's mist from its drizzle, and it didn't matter.

Hollis turned up the fleece collar of his leather jacket. Moscow by night, Hollis had discovered, was unlike any other great city he'd lived in. You could walk the streets and squares of Moscow until dawn, as he'd done few times, and never meet with an adventure or a misadventure. There were no public bars, no discos, no prostitutes, no street people, no nightlife. No all-night markets, no midnight movies, no midnight mass, no midnight anything. Most of the city was quiet by ten P.M., shut down by eleven, and the last taxis disappeared by twelve. All public transport ceased at one A.M., and after that you were on your own, which was to say you were stranded.

There was one class of citizen, however, who stayed out until the last possible moment; and one of them, a young man of about eighteen, now approached Hollis. He carried a nylon Adidas bag and wore a cheap synthetic-leather coat, of three-quarter length. He had on American jeans, but his shoes were definitely Soviet. He spoke good English with exceeding politeness. 'Excuse me, sir, do you have a cigarette?'

'No, do you?'

'Yes.' The young man gave Hollis a Marlboro, lit it for him, and lit one for himself. The boy looked up and down the bridge. Hollis noticed a few other black marketeers observing the action. The youth said, 'My name is Misha. I am pleased to meet you.' They smoked awhile. Hollis threw his unfinished cigarette off the bridge. Misha's eyes followed it, then he turned to Hollis. 'Do you see this end of the square?' Misha's gesture took in the south end of Red Square, bordered by the Kremlin wall, the back of St Basil's, the Rossiya, and the Moskva River. 'That is where the German, Matthias Rust, landed his aircraft. I was here that day. What a sight it was.'

Hollis nodded. Rust's landing spot had become part of the unofficial tour of Red Square. The average Muscovite, usually cynical by nature, had been captivated by the young man's flight. The Soviet court gave him four years. Hollis, as an air attaché, had been inconvenienced by the fallout from that flight when some of his better contacts in the Red Air Force and Air Defence Ministry had been sacked. Nevertheless, as a pilot, Hollis could appreciate the young flier's daring. Hollis thought that he would like to try something insane like that one day.

Misha said, 'He flew for peace.'

'So did Rudolph Hess.'

Misha shrugged. 'No politics. Economics. Do you have anything to trade?'

'Perhaps. What do you have, Misha?'

'I have unpressed black caviar. Three hundred grams. Very excellent. It is sixty dollars in the Beriozka. But I would trade it for a carton of American cigarettes.'

'I have no cigarettes on me.'

Misha looked around again, then said, 'Well, forty dollars then.'

'It is against the law for us to deal in currency.'

Misha backed away. 'Excuse me.'

Hollis grabbed his arm. 'Have you been on the bridge all night?'

'A few hours . . .'

'Did you see an American car on the embankment road about two hours ago?'

Misha drew on his cigarette. 'Perhaps. Why?'

'It's none of your business why.' Hollis pressed Misha against the bridge rail. 'Do you want to make forty dollars, or do you want to swim in the river?'

Misha said, 'I didn't see the car myself. A friend told me he saw it. On the embankment road about two hours ago.'

'What sort of car?'

'He thought it was a Pontiac Trans Am. It had a rear spoiler. Dark color.'

'How did your friend know it was a Trans Am?'

'Magazines. You know. I give three dollars American or fifteen rubles for *Car and Driver*. Same for *Track and* –'

'Did your friend see where the car went?'

'The Rossiya.' Misha added, 'Then a strange thing happened. They hurried over to the Rossiya to see the car and to talk to the driver who they saw in the car – a young man – maybe American. But as they got to the Intourist wing, they saw the car going up Razin Street, away from the Rossiya, with two older men.'

'Two Russians?'

'Two Russians.' Misha hesitated, then said, 'The type with closed faces. You know what I mean?'

'Yes. Did you or your friends notice anything else unusual tonight?'

'Yes. About an hour ago. I myself and everyone here saw a blue Ford Fairlane going very fast over the bridge. A cop was chasing it, but the bastard never had a chance. Those Fords can move on the straightaway. The American embassy uses them. Are you from the embassy? Was that your car?'

Hollis turned and walked back 'toward the underpass. Misha followed. They went down the steps, and Hollis handed Misha two twenty-dollar bills. Hollis said, 'I'll take the caviar.'

Misha reluctantly took the tin of caviar from his gym bag

and handed it to Hollis. Misha said, 'I'll give you three more tins and an ancient Russian cross for your jacket.'

Hollis put the caviar in his pocket and said in Russian, 'Go home, Misha, and never come back to this bridge. The men with closed faces will be asking about you.'

Misha's eyes widened, and his mouth dropped open.

Hollis climbed to the top of the stairs and walked back to the bridge. He crossed it on foot, aware of the stares of the other entrepreneurs. Capitalism, Hollis thought, like sex, was hormonal; it existed on the Moskvoretsky Bridge and behind St Basil's, a stone's throw from the Kremlin. It existed around every hotel and every farmer's market throughout Moscow, in small isolated cells that might one day spread and weaken the whole state. Like communism in czarist Russia, capitalism was the new subversive ideology.

Hollis walked out on to Ordynka Street, working out in his mind a Metro route that would get him back alive.

6

Sam Hollis got off the Metro at Smolenskaya station. He walked along the Moskva River embankment and followed the big loop of the river beneath the Kalinin Bridge. The massive Ukraina Hotel rose up across the Moskva, and a dark riverboat slid toward its dock on the Shevchenko Embankment. The autumn was not pretty in Moscow, Hollis decided; it was wet and grey. But when the first snow fell, Moscow was transformed into a sparkling white city of muted sounds and soft curves. The sun shone more often, and the night was starlit, casting iridescent blue shadows over the snowy landscape. The good fur coats appeared, and the women looked better. Children pulled sleds, and ice skaters could be seen in the parks. The snow was like white ermine, Hollis thought, cloaking the hard-featured city.

Hollis turned up a gradually rising street that came off the embankment. At the turn of the century this district, where the new American embassy was located, had been called Presnya. It was then a squalid industrial suburb and fertile ground for Marxist-Leninist ideology. During the revolution of 1905, the workers here had fought the Czar's army, and the whole area had been subject to intense artillery bombardment and – when the revolt was put down – to savage reprisals. The district was now called Krasno Presnya – Red Presnya. It seemed to Hollis that half the streets, squares, and districts of Moscow were prefixed with 'red', to the extent that the word had become meaningless, and the Muscovites in private conversation usually dropped the 'red'. Presnya was largely rebuilt, but Hollis still sensed its tragedy. Russia was a very sad country.

Hollis looked up and saw the towering red brick chancery

building, its windows all alight as per the ambassador's orders. A few minutes later he saw the red brick walls and the embassy residences that rose above them. The streets were deserted, and the low ground was covered with a blanket of river fog.

Hollis could now see the lights of the main embassy gate in the wall. The compound was a sort of mini-Kremlin, Hollis thought, and the use of red brick, rare in Moscow, was supposed to make the Russians think of the red brick Kremlin walls and towers. That, in turn, was supposed to make them associate the American embassy with power, strength, and perhaps even God and sanctuary. Hollis thought the Madison Avenue subtlety might be lost on the average Soviet citizen.

The gate was a hundred meters away, and Hollis could see the Soviet militia booth, though he could not yet see the US Marine guard post just inside the gates. Rising above the wall, the illuminated flagpole flew the Stars and Stripes, which now fluttered in the light breeze.

Sam Hollis heard a car drawing up behind him, and its engine had the slow rpm sound of a Chaika. The car kept pace with him just to his rear. The driver raced the engine and flashed his lights. Hollis did not turn around.

The car drew abreast of him and stopped. Hollis saw it was indeed a Chaika, a black four-door sedan, the type favored by the Committee for State Security. There were three men inside. The driver stayed behind the wheel, and two men got out. They both wore leather coats, black pants, leather gloves, and narrow-brim hats – what Hollis called KGB evening attire. Hollis recognized them as the same two embassy watchers who had followed him one afternoon. The short, squat one Hollis had named Boris. The other one, taller and better built, Hollis called Igor.

Hollis turned and walked toward them, his hands in his pockets, his right hand through a slit in his jacket and around the handle of his knife.

Boris and Igor looked Hollis over. Boris said in English, 'Hand over your wallet and watch, or we'll beat you to a pulp.'

Hollis replied, 'Is the *Komitet* so badly paid?'

Boris snapped, 'You bastard, who do you think you are? Give me your wallet.'

Hollis said, *'Yeb vas.'* *Fuck you.* Hollis turned and walked toward the embassy. He heard the footsteps of the two men behind him. They came up very close, and Igor said, 'What's your hurry? We want to talk to you.'

Hollis kept walking. It occurred to him that the KGB had no difficulty in impersonating muggers. Hollis was abreast of the embassy wall now, and the gate was fifty yards further. Suddenly he felt a powerful blow in the small of his back, and he lurched forward, sprawling across the sidewalk, breaking his fall with his hands. He rolled to the side and barely avoided a kick, then splashed into the wet gutter. Igor and Boris smiled down at him. Igor imparted to Hollis a pithy aphorism in crude Russian. 'You keep drinking like that, and one of these days some queers will fuck you while you're drunk and you'll have a hangover in your asshole instead of your head.'

Both men laughed.

Hollis wanted to bring out the knife, but he knew that's what they wanted too. Hollis remained where he was. Boris glaneed toward the embassy gate, then stared at Hollis. 'The next time, I'm going to crack your skull open.' He spat at Hollis, then slapped Igor on the back and said, 'We taught this shit his lesson. Let's go.' They turned and walked back toward the Chaika.

Hollis stood and brushed the water and filth from his jacket and trousers, noticing that the palms of his hands were bleeding. He felt a raw abrasion on his cheekbone and a dull pain in his back. The two men got into the car, and Hollis could hear them laughing with the driver. The car made a U-turn and sped off.

Hollis continued toward the embassy. As he approached the gate, a young militiaman, who had obviously seen the whole incident, stepped out of the booth and extended his hand palm up. *'Pasport.'*

Hollis snapped back, 'You know who I am!'

'*Pasport!*'

Get out of my way, you *dristui*.'

The militiaman stiffened at the expletive. '*Stoi!*'

The other militiaman came out of the booth. 'What is this?'

A Marine guard appeared at the gate and called out, 'What's going on there?' Hollis saw he was armed and so could not cross the threshold of the property. Hollis called to him, 'Open the gate.'

The Marine opened the gate, and Hollis brushed past the militiamen, walking the ten yards between the militia booth and the entrance to the embassy compound. He took the salute of the guard, who recognized him, and the sergeant on duty asked, 'Are you alright, Colonel?'

'Fine.'

Hollis strode across the courtyard, and in the distance he could hear the bells of Ivan's tower chiming midnight and the raised voices of the two Marines and the two Soviet militiamen shouting at one another. He entered the chancery and went directly to the duty office.

Lisa Rhodes stood as he walked in. 'Oh, Colonel Hollis. We were getting worried. We –'

'Any word on Bill Brennan?'

'He's here. In the infirmary. I don't have the details. What happened to your face?'

'Tripped. Is Seth Alevy here yet?'

'Yes. He's in the sixth-floor safe room, waiting for you.'

Hollis went to the door.

'May I come?'

He looked at her.

'Seth Alevy said I could, if it was alright with you.'

'Is that so? Come along then.'

They walked to the elevator in silence and rode up together. She said, 'Your hands are bleeding.'

'I know that.'

She shrugged, then asked, 'Is Bill Brennan a friend of yours?'

'No. Why?'

'It was the first thing you asked.'

'He was my responsibility.'

'I like that.'

He glanced at her.

The elevator stopped at the sixth floor, and they stepped across the corridor to an interior room. Hollis pressed a buzzer.

The door opened, and Seth Alevy said, 'Come in, please.' He motioned them to a round oak table at which were a dozen leather and chrome chairs.

Lisa Rhodes looked around the dimly lit room. The chancery, she knew, had several safe rooms, but this was the first time she had been in the sixth-floor one. It was an interior room like all the safe rooms, and this one was lit by soft indirect cove lighting around the walls. On the table were individual reading lamps. The floor was covered in a thick royal blue carpet, and the walls and door were carpeted in a camel color. Lisa noticed that the ceiling was the same as in the other safe rooms: black acoustical foam rubber. The room was impervious to underground listening devices, cavity resonators, or directional microphones, and it was swept for bugs two or three times a day. This particular room, she'd heard, was used mostly by the intelligence types, and Lisa saw they treated themselves rather well with a bar in one corner, a sideboard, and a recessed galley counter complete with running water and a refrigerator.

Alevy said to Lisa. 'Drink?'

'No, thanks. I'm still on D.O.'

'Right. Coffee then.'

Hollis said, 'Vodka, neat.'

Alevy poured black coffee for Lisa and a chilled vodka in a crystal flute for Hollis.

Hollis regarded Seth Alevy a moment. He was about forty, some years younger than Hollis. He wore a nicely tailored three-piece tweed suit with a green knit tie. He was too tall and too lean and reminded Hollis of an unbearded Lincoln, though somehow better looking. He'd been married once, but no one here knew anything about that.

Hollis said, 'How was your party?'

'Fine. Lots of dissidents. Good food. Sukkot is a happy holiday. You should have come.'

'Then who would have gone chasing across Moscow?'

'I'm certain,' Alevy said coolly, 'that my people could have handled that.'

Hollis did not hear Alevy add the word 'better', but it was there. Hollis said, 'The kid asked for a defense attaché.'

'I'm sure he didn't know a defense attaché from a middle linebacker. I'm not sure I do either. The next time, Sam, something like this comes up, please call me or someone in my section.'

Hollis didn't respond but recalled what he knew of Alevy. Seth Alevy was a Philadelphian, a Jew, and a Princeton graduate, not necessarily in that order. He had once told Hollis in a rare, candid moment that he hated the Soviets and had joined the CIA 'to do maximum damage to the regime'. Getting into the CIA had not been difficult. Alevy had majored in Russian studies and Russian language and had thereby come to the attention of the CIA, as he knew he would.

Alevy poured himself a vodka.

Hollis threw the tin of caviar on the table. 'Some *tost, maslo*, and *smetana* would be fine.'

Alevy examined the tin. 'Very nice stuff.' Alevy and Lisa got crackers, butter, and sour cream. Hollis opened the tin with his knife.

Alevy regarded Hollis for some time, then asked, 'They rough you up, Colonel?'

Lisa heaped a spoonful of black caviar on a buttered cracker. Hollis said to her, 'I would have asked for red, but I can't stand the word *krasnya* anymore.'

Lisa laughed. 'I thought I was the only one.'

Alevy's eyes went from one to the other. He asked again, 'They rough you up?'

Hollis stared at Alevy across the table. 'You know damned well what happened.'

'Well,' Alevy replied, 'if they had gotten out of hand, my people would have stepped in. You were covered.' Alevy added, 'They tell me you kept your cool.'

'How is Brennan?'

'He didn't fare as well as you. The cops finally caught up with him. They kept him standing around in the rain for half an hour, then just gave him a ticket and left. But before Brennan could get back to his car, a bunch of *khuligans* appeared and beat him with iron pipes, robbed him, then smashed up the car. And there's never a cop around when you need one.' Alevy added, 'He made it back here instead of going to a hospital. He got his nose broken again, but he says he got a few licks in. Doc Logan says he'll be okay, but he has to go West for proper care.'

Hollis nodded. Score another point for the KGB tonight, he thought.

Lisa was spreading sour cream on a plate of crackers. Alevy helped himself to the caviar. 'Where did you get this? How much?'

'Moskvoretsky Bridge. Forty bucks.'

'I could have done better. You ever hear a Jew argue with a Russian about price? Anyway, I assume this black marketeering is part of your tale. If you're feeling up to it now, we're listening.'

Hollis glanced at Lisa.

Alevy said, 'It's alright. I had a top secret clearance done on Ms Rhodes some months ago.'

'Why?'

'Regulations. We were dating.'

Hollis poured another vodka for himself. 'What is her need to know?'

'Let me worry about that.'

73

Hollis thought for a moment, then nodded. 'Okay. From the beginning. I was in my office doing the report you asked for earlier. The phone rang. It was Ms Rhodes.' Hollis related the events of the evening, leaving out what the French woman had told him. A half hour later he poured himself a glass of mineral water and said, 'So, as I approached the embassy, I expected to be met. By friends. But apparently you thought it would be good for me to get up close and personal with the *Komitet*.'

Alevy replied dryly, 'You have diplomatic immunity.'

'Yeah, Seth, but the KGB has a different take on diplomatic immunity.'

'Well, you're here, and a little peroxide will clean up those cuts nicely. I'll even pay for your dry cleaning.'

Hollis began to say something, but Lisa interjected, 'Colonel, what do you think happened to Gregory Fisher?'

'We should assume he is right now in a room with KGB interrogators.'

No one spoke for a while, then Alevy said, 'By the way, Sam, no one is faulting you for anything. You acted as quickly as possible.' He added, 'It's their town.'

Hollis didn't respond.

Alevy changed the subject. 'I'm interested in the man in room seven forty-five.'

'So am I,' Hollis replied.

Alevy asked, 'Was he definitely an American?'

Hollis considered a moment before answering. 'Yes. Right down to the Mennen after-shave lotion.'

'But,' Alevy speculated, 'he could have been an American in the employ of the KGB.'

'Could have been. But maybe Fisher just got his room number wrong.'

Alevy stood and hit a button on the electronic console in the corner. Gregory Fisher's voice filled the room, and they listened again to the entire conversation.

Lisa remarked, 'I think he knew his room number.'

Seth Alevy lit a cigarette and paced around the room in

thought. He said finally, 'Well, I'll handle it from here.' He turned to Lisa. 'Of course you'll discuss this with no one.' He said to Hollis, 'I'll take a report from you and forward it to Langley. You'll want a copy sent to your section in the Pentagon.'

Hollis stood. 'That's right.'

Alevy added, 'We'll have to tell the ambassador something since we've got a car wrecked and a man in the infirmary. I'll handle that of course.' Alevy turned to Hollis. 'I don't see any military intelligence angle here, Sam.'

'No.'

Alevy regarded Hollis keenly and said, 'You might think this Major Dodson thing concerns you because Major Dodson, if he exists, was or is a POW and so on. But I'll let you know if I need you.'

Hollis walked to the door. 'Thank you, Mr Alevy.'

Lisa said, 'What I want to know is, what is Mrs Ivanova's Charm School? And where is Major Dodson? Is he still out there somewhere? Can we help him? Can we help Greg Fisher?'

Alevy looked at his watch. 'It's very late, and I have some sending to do. So good night and thank you, Sam. Lisa, will you stay a moment?'

Hollis opened the door.

Alevy called after him, 'Do you want your caviar?'

'Put it some place warm, Seth, where the sun doesn't shine.' Hollis left.

As Hollis stood waiting for the elevator, Lisa joined him. The elevator came, and they both rode to the ground level in silence. They walked out the rear of the chancery into the cold October night. Sam Hollis and Lisa Rhodes stood a moment on the covered stone terrace. Lisa said, 'My unit is to the left.'

'Mine's to the right.'

'Will you walk me?'

They took the path to the left, which was bordered by newly planted trees, Russian birches, all bare now. To the right was the quadrangle formed on three sides by the row house residences and the Marine barracks, and on the fourth side by the chancery buildings. The grass of the quadrangle held the faint outlines of impromptu softball games and fainter evidence of a short touch-football season. The embassy's few children sometimes played in the quadrangle, and in fact, Hollis saw a few toys lying on the wet grass. The first snow would bring snowmen and snowball fights, and the spring would bring kite-flying, followed by sun-bathing. This little patch of ground – about three acres – was the village commons, a little piece of the America they all missed and had learned at last to love.

Lisa followed his gaze. She said, 'We're building a scarecrow out there as soon as we get the stuff together. Someone in the consular section has located pumpkins in the free market on Mira Prospect. Well, sort of pumpkins. Can you carve a jack-o'-lantern with that knife of yours?'

Hollis replied, 'That's why I carry it.'

'In case you see a pumpkin in the market? I doubt it.'

They kept walking. Lisa said, 'I'm not sure I like living and working in the same place – in a compound. It's like a fort . . . or a jail.'

'It's better for everyone.'

'Is it? The old place at least had charm, and it was right on Tchaikovaky Street, not far from the American Express office.' She smiled. 'And we all lived in that delightfully grim apartment house off Gorky Street. My bathroom – they were prefab, remember? – was pulling away from the rest of the building. There was a six-inch gap, and I could actually see into the bathroom below.'

'Was that you?'

She laughed. They walked on in silence awhile, then Lisa said, 'But I suppose this is better. We have the quadrangle. I guess you're used to this institutional living. I mean, you lived on Air Force bases.'

'Sometimes. Depended on the assignment.'

76

Lisa stopped. 'This is my cell. Actually, they're quite nice. Just a bit sterile.'

'Eight million Muscovites would trade places with you.'

'Oh, I know. I'm just getting cabin fever.'

'Take a leave.'

'In January. There's a place called Jumby Bay, a small island off the coast of Antigua. Very private and very lovely. I may defect there.'

They stood in the cold mist, and he noticed in the dim lamplight that her face and hair were wet. He noticed, too, she was about twenty years younger than he was.

Lisa said, 'I've never seen you at the Friday night follies.'

'I usually wind up at some embassy reception on Fridays.'

'Right. The follies are for the rank and file. But I get to go to a lot of cultural events. Do you like the ballet?'

'Only at the end when the fat lady sings.'

'That's opera.'

'Right. I get them mixed up.' He took his hands out of his jacket pockets. 'Well, I suppose we'd better get out of the rain.' He held out his hand.

She seemed not to notice and said, 'Seth is very intense.'

'Is he?'

'Yes. Some people would mistake it for abrasiveness.'

'Would they?'

'Do you know him well?'

'Well enough.'

'You both seemed short with each other. Are you enemies or just rivals?'

'Neither. We enjoy each other. It's just our way of speaking.'

'Like when you suggested he shove the caviar up his ass?'

'Yes, like that.'

She considered a moment. 'He never mentioned that he knew you.'

'Why should he?'

'I suppose there were a lot of things he didn't discuss with me.' She added, 'He is very professional. There was no loose pillow talk.'

'But you know he's not a political affairs officer.'

'Yes, I know that. And I know that most attachés are military intelligence.'

'How do you know that?'

'One knows these things. Didn't you know I was seeing Seth Alevy?'

'He never mentioned it.'

'I thought it was hot gossip in the lunchroom. Oh, well, as a French philosopher once said, "People who worry about what others think of them would be surprised at how little they did."'

'Precisely.'

She asked, 'Do you have antiseptic for those cuts? You have to be careful in foreign countries.'

'I had three glasses of Russian antiseptic.'

'Be serious. I have some witch hazel . . .'

'I'm going to the infirmary to see Brennan. I'll get something there.'

'Good. Be sure you do.'

'I will. Good night.'

'I have tomorrow off. I usually sleep late after night duty.'

'Good idea.'

'I wanted to go to the Marx and Engels museum tomorrow. I haven't seen it yet. Have you?'

'It's not on my list.'

'Anyway, I'm a little . . . concerned now. About going out alone, I mean. I guess they know who I am now. From the tape. Right?'

'Yes. But I don't think you have anything to worry about.'

She reached out and picked a wet twig from his fleece collar and handed it to him.

He examined the twig thoughtfully, then spoke in a soft voice. 'You see, Ms Rhodes, you can't let them dictate how you are going to live. They are not omnipotent, nor omnipresent. They want you to think that. It makes their job easier.'

'Yes, I know that, but –'

'But you may be right. Perhaps you ought to stay in the compound until we get a better fix on this.'

She replied in an impatient tone, 'That is not what I had in mind, Colonel. I'm asking you if you would like to come with me tomorrow.'

Hollis cleared his throat. 'Well . . . why don't we have lunch and save the Marx-Engels museum for a special occasion?'

She smiled. 'Call for me here at noon.' She turned and walked to her door.

'Good night, Colonel Hollis.'

'Good night, Ms Rhodes.'

'Yes . . . yes, I . . . Oh, God . . . hurry.'

'Ten minutes, Greg. Get to the lounge.'

Seth Alevy hit the stop button on the tape player.

Charles Banks, special aide to the American ambassador to the Union of Soviet Socialist Republics, sat at the head of the long mahogany table in the ambassador's safe room, a worried look on his face.

Sam Hollis sat to his right, across from Alevy. Hollis had been in the room a number of times and was always struck by its patina of age, though the room was barely a year old. Apparently everything in the room, including the wainscoting and moldings, had been taken from somewhere else and reconstructed here. The ambassador, a wealthy man, was supposed to have paid for it himself. Hollis would have wondered why, except that everyone in this loony place had an idiosyncrasy that defied explanation.

Alevy said to Charles Banks, 'A voice-stress analysis was done on the tape early this morning. Our expert says that Gregory Fisher was most probably telling the truth and was under actual stress.'

Banks looked curiously at Alevy. 'Really. They can tell that?'

'Yes, sir.'

'Amazing.'

Hollis regarded Charles Banks, a man near sixty, with snow-white hair, a ruddy, avuncular face, and sparkling blue eyes. Hollis remembered last Christmas when Banks dressed as Santa Claus for the embassy children. When not wearing his Santa suit, Banks favored dark, three-piece pinstripes. He was a career diplomat, with the standard Eastern credentials, easy social graces, and the voice of a 1940s radio announcer. Yet beyond the Santa façade and the diplomat's polish, Hollis recognised a kindred spirit; Hollis thought that Charles Banks was the third spy in this room. But Hollis did not know for whom Banks was spying.

Alevy continued his briefing for Banks. 'And as I've indicated, Colonel Hollis believes he can establish that Mr Fisher was at the Rossiya last night.'

Banks turned to Hollis. 'You have this Englishman, the French couple, and the black-market fellow.'

Hollis replied, 'I don't actually *have* them. I spoke to them.'

'Yes, of course. But they could identify Mr Fisher?'

'I hope so. We're getting facsimiles of passport photos transmitted here from the State Department's files of all passport applicants with the name Gregory Fisher. There are about a dozen.'

'And you will show the photos to these people?'

'I called my counterpart in the French embassy this morning,' Hollis explained, 'and he found out for me that a Monsieur and Madame Besnier have contacted their embassy, stating they were involved in a difficulty at the Rossiya. They are leaving the country on today's Finnair flight out of Sheremetyevo at twelve forty-five. If we miss them there with the photos, we can locate them in Helsinki or in France. Keep in mind, sir, the woman did know the name "Gregory Fisher".'

'Yes, but I would like her to identify a photograph.'

'Of course. And the Englishman, Wilson, is still at the Rossiya, according to John Crane at the British embassy. Mr Wilson is here on the gas pipeline business. The black marketeer, Misha, said that his friends only saw the car, but I believe that was Mr Fisher's car. There are few Pontiac Trans Ams in Moscow. Probably none. So that is my hard evidence, if we should need it, sir.'

Banks nodded. 'Thank you.' He turned to Alevy. 'So, despite the fact that the Rossiya and Intourist say Mr Fisher was never at the hotel, you two are convinced he was and that he called the embassy from there. Let me ask you this: Are you sure there is an American Gregory Fisher in the Soviet Union?'

Alevy answered, 'The Soviet Foreign Ministry has been suspiciously quick to confirm that it issued a visa to a Mr Gregory Fisher of New Canaan, Connecticut, age twenty-four, and Intourist has been helpful for a change, informing us that this Mr Fisher crossed the frontier at Brest seven days ago. He spent a night in Brest, three nights in Minsk, a night in Smolensk, and was on the road in between.'

'And,' Banks asked, 'you believe this is the same Gregory Fisher who called our embassy?'

Alevy seemed somewhat impatient. 'He's the only Gregory Fisher we have in this country at the moment, sir. Intourist also confirms that Gregory Fisher was to have checked in at the Rossiya. The evidence seems conclusive, sir.'

'Has anyone contacted this man's family?'

'That would be premature,' Alevy answered. 'There is no use upsetting them at this stage.'

Banks added, 'And until we are sure he has vanished, as you are suggesting.'

'Actually,' Alevy replied, 'he has not vanished. I think we can tidy up all these questions shortly. We know where Gregory Fisher is now.'

'Where is he, Mr Alevy?'

'He is in Mozhaisk, sir. In the morgue.'

Banks leaned forward across the table. 'Dead?'

Alevy replied dryly, 'Yes, sir. I believe that's why he's in the morgue. Peterson, in the consular section, got the call about twenty minutes ago. The call came from a gentleman who identified himself only as an official of the Soviet government. Mr Fisher had a car accident.'

Banks said, 'How terrible!'

'Yes, sir.' Alevy shuffled some papers in front of him and glanced at a blue sheet. 'According to the militia report, Mr Fisher's car, which they call a *Transamerikanets sportivnyi avtomobil*, was found at daybreak this morning by peasants, eighteen kilometers west, of Mozhaisk in a ravine off the Minsk-Moscow highway. The car apparently had been heading toward Moscow and went off the highway during the night, crashing into a tree. The damage indicates the car was traveling at excessive speed and could not navigate a sudden turn in the road. Mr Fisher was not wearing a seat belt and suffered chest and head injuries. He died of his injuries before the peasants discovered the accident. We are requested to take charge of the body for shipment out of the Soviet Union.'

Banks seemed to be pondering all this, then said, 'That would indicate that Mr Fisher never got to Moscow.'

Hollis added, 'Nor to Borodino, since according to my map, the accident occurred some kilometers before the Borodino turnoff.'

Banks looked at Alevy. 'There is certainly some inconsistency here. Is it at all possible that Mr Fisher never reached Moscow? That he made this call from the road and that he was perpetrating some sort of hoax or prank?'

Alevy replied, 'Fisher's call came through without operator asistance, meaning it was made from metropolitan Moscow. In addition we have the voice-stress test and the witnesses. What else do you need, Charles? Videotape?'

'One has to be absolutely certain.' Banks glanced at his watch and stood. 'You've both done an admirable job of detective work considering the difficulties here. I'm quite proud of you. I think the ambassador should alert the Soviet authorities to these facts and tell them that we suspect foul play and that we want a full investigation.'

Alevy and Hollis glanced at each other. Alevy said, 'Mr Banks, what we are suggesting is that it was the Soviet authorities who *murdered* Gregory Fisher.'

'Oh.' Banks nodded slowly. 'Yes, I see. Because of what Mr Fisher said regarding this Major Dodson.'

Alevy studied Banks' face, then said, 'Charles, are you jerking us around, or are you that dense?'

Banks winked in reply, then said, 'Well, I'll speak directly to the ambassador about this. I trust you'll both keep in mind the political considerations that may arise as a result of this incident.'

Alevy stood. 'As a political affairs officer, that will be foremost in my mind, sir. Foremost.'

'Splendid. Colonel Hollis?'

Hollis remained seated and didn't reply.

'Colonel?'

Hollis said to Banks, 'Once I bombed only politically approved targets. We lost the war.'

Banks responded in a soothing voice. 'As you know, in the Soviet armed forces there is a political commissar attached to every command. The military officers resent this, but they recognize that today war is too important to be left to the generals and colonels. Especially cold war. Good day, gentlemen.' Banks went out the door.

Alevy said to Hollis, 'Why didn't you just say okay? That's all he wanted to hear.'

Hollis stood. 'An American citizen has been murdered, and I'm a little pissed off.'

'They get murdered in America all the time,' Alevy observed. 'Do you feel partly responsible for Fisher's death?'

'I suppose. Wouldn't you?'

'Maybe. Look, Sam, I'm not a politician or a diplomat, but you have to see their point of view as this thing heats up. Some dorks are trying to crank up détente again, and that's the numero uno consideration right now. If I found two KGB men in the basement planting a bomb, the ambassador would tell me to forget it.'

'What if you found a KGB man in bed with the ambassador's wife?'

Alevy smiled. 'Same thing. One can't become personally involved. Détente. Think peace.' He held up two fingers. 'Peace.'

'Okay, forget that Fisher was murdered. *Why* was he murdered?'

'You know. He saw something. Heard something.'

'Something big.'

'Apparently,' Alevy replied.

'We're supposed to find out what it is. That's why they put us here.'

'Yes. That's true. Let's see what comes down from Washington.' Alevy walked to the door. 'If you have nothing further of a sensitive nature, let's go. The snack bar has croissants from Paris this morning. If you stick one in your ear, you can hear the sound of a sidewalk café.'

'I'm going to go for the body.'

'Wrong. Someone in the consular section is going for the body. That's *their* job.'

'I don't think you heard me. *I* am going.'

Alevy looked annoyed but said nothing.

'I'll need two passes from the Foreign Ministry.'

'Two?'

'I'm taking company.'

'Who?'

'Lisa Rhodes.'

'Is that so? How do you know she wants to go?'

'Everyone here would like to get out of Moscow. Even picking up a corpse is a treat.'

'You understand that the Foreign Ministry will inform the KGB that they have issued a pass in your name.'

'I think I understand that,' Hollis replied.

'The *Komitet* does not like you any more than they like me. They may not be able to resist the temptation to get you to the Mozhaisk morgue on *their* terms.'

'Let me worry about that.'

'I'm not worried about you. You're a pain in the ass. I'm worried about Lisa Rhodes.' Alevy added, 'Keep in mind, I can't cover you out in Mozhaisk.'

'You can't cover me fifty yards from the embassy. Two passes in my office before noon.'

Alevy opened the door to leave, but Hollis closed it. Hollis asked, 'Did you find out if a Major Jack Dodson is listed as an MIA in Vietnam?'

'Checking on it.'

'And how about our friend in seven forty-five? Schiller. Any such American in country?'

'I'm checking it, Sam. I'll keep you fully informed.'

'I know you will, Seth. It's a joy working with the CIA.'

Alevy patted Hollis' shoulder. 'Try not to get killed on the Minsk-Moscow highway.' Alevy left.

Hollis looked at his watch: ten A.M. He'd been up all night with this thing. Brennan was in the infirmary, the Besniers were packing to leave Russia, Fisher was in the morgue, Charles Banks and the ambassador were burning the wire to Washington, and Alevy was having croissants in the snack bar. 'I'll try not to get killed on the Minsk-Moscow highway. I want to see how this thing ends.'

8

Sam Hollis pulled on his blue jeans, then his leather boots. He slipped his knife in the left boot and strapped an ankle holster above his right boot. Hollis checked his Soviet Tokarev 7.62mm automatic. It was basically a Colt-Browning design, slightly modified by a Russian armorer named Tokarev who put his name on it and probably forgot to pay Colt or Browning a licensing fee. The Tokarev's advantages were that Hollis found it to be reliable, he was familiar with the American original, and lastly, if he had to shoot someone, it was better to leave a Soviet-made slug in the body.

Hollis screwed a short silencer into the muzzle and stuck the automatic into his ankle holster, pulling the jeans down over it. He put on a black turtleneck sweater and over that his leather jacket, which held four extra magazines of eight rounds each.

Sam Hollis left his apartment and walked across the wide quadrangle. The grass was soggy beneath his boots, but the sky was clearing, and a weak sun was visible between the rolling clouds.

Three boys in their mid-teens were tossing around a football. Hollis recognised the passer as Larry Eschman, son of Commander Paul Eschman, the Naval attaché. Another boy, Tom Caruso, son of the consul general, was running short patterns. The third boy was named Kevin, son of Jane Lowry, a commercial officer. Kevin Lowry was defensive back. Saturday morning normality. Sort of. The Eschman boy called out, 'Colonel Hollis! Ready?'

'Sure.' Hollis ran toward the opposite sideline until Caruso and Lowry moved into defensive positions, then Hollis cut downfield in a deep fly pattern. The two boys were close, and Hollis could hear their cleats slapping on the sodden turf.

Without a prearranged play Hollis thought he should hold the same pattern for Eschman. He held out his arms, glanced back over his right shoulder, and saw the ball as a brown blur hanging in the air, wide and long. He put on a burst of speed and felt the ball hit his fingertips, then got control of it and pulled it to his chest. His boots lost traction, and he shoulder-rolled forward, the ball tucked securely between his right hand and the crook of his elbow. He heard Eschman holler, 'Complete! Way to go, Colonel!'

Hollis sat up as Caruso extended his hand toward him. 'Nice going. Colonel.' Hollis pulled himself up by Caruso's hand.

Lowry walked over and also put out his hand. As Hollis reached toward Lowry, he saw that Lowry was holding an automatic pistol. Hollis took the gun and slipped it back into his ankle holster, pressing hard on the Velcro strap.

Lowry said, 'You move pretty fast, Colonel. Even with an iron ankle weight.'

Caruso stifled a grin.

Hollis said, 'When I played end at the Academy, I shot three defensive backs.'

Both boys laughed.

Hollis looked at the boys. It must be lonely for them, he thought. No high school dances, no Saturday nights, no beaches, skiing, friends, girls. No America. He said, 'Get something out of this tour of duty, guys. Get out into Moscow and meet the Russians.'

They nodded.

'Don't let Vanya see you with those cleats,' Hollis warned, referring to the Russian groundkeeper who was obsessed with the lawn and actually called Scotts in Columbus, Ohio, for advice.

Hollis continued his walk across the quad. He approached the housing units, found Lisa Rhodes' door, and pressed her buzzer. The brick row houses for singles were narrow, but they were three stories high. The first floor, that in the States might have had a garage, was a laundry and storage room. A foyer with a staircase led up to the living room, dining area, and kitchen. The third floor held one or two bedrooms, sometimes a study or home office, depending on the rank of the officer. Lisa was in a one-bedroom unit along the east wall. Hollis heard her footsteps on the stairs, then the door opened. She smiled. 'Hello. I thought you were running to me, then I saw the football.'

'Were you looking for me?'

'Just checking the weather. What did you drop?'

'My wallet.'

'Oh.' She stepped outside and did a complete turn. 'Is this casual enough?'

Hollis glanced her over. She was wearing ankle-high boots, black corduroy slacks, and a dark blue quilt jacket that the Russians called a *vatnik*. From the collar of the jacket rose a black turtleneck like his own. He said, 'Very nice.'

'Are you going to tell me why you requested I dressed in casual clothes of dark colors?'

'I have a fetish. Let's go.'

They walked on the path that ran parallel to the residences toward the pedestrian gate in the rear of the compound. She said, 'Seriously, Sam . . . can I call you Sam?'

'Of course.'

'Why *dark*?'

'I'll tell you later.'

They passed through the rear gate where the Marine barracks were located, and the single Marine watchstander saluted. Hollis walked up to the Soviet militia booth on the sidewalk and greeted the two young men in Russian. They returned the greeting stiffly. Hollis said, 'When you get back to your barracks, you tell the two men who were at the main gate last night that Colonel Hollis apologizes for not acting correctly.'

Neither man spoke, then one of them said, 'We will be sure to tell them, Colonel.'

'Good day.'

Hollis and Lisa walked up Devatinski Street. Lisa asked, 'What was that about?'

Hollis replied, 'I got a little nasty when they asked me for my passport. I guess I was on edge after the Rossiya.'

She said, 'That was good of you to apologize.'

'It was militarily correct.' He added, 'Also I don't want the bastards to think they can get to me.'

They came into Tchaikovsky Street where the old embassy stood. Lisa said, 'Where are we going for lunch?'

'The Prague.'

'Then we can walk up Arbat Street. I have to make a stop.'

They turned right and walked along the wide boulevard. Lisa said, 'The sun is shining, for a change.'

'I see.'

'Do you go to the Prague often?'

'No.'

'Read any good books lately?'

'Can't think of any.'

'Someone told me you were shot down over North Vietnam.'

'That's right.'

'But you weren't a POW.'

'No, I was rescued at sea.'

'This Major Dodson business has special meaning for you.'

'Perhaps.'

'You're not into complex sentence structures, are you?'

'Depends on the subject.'

'Sorry.'

They walked on in silence awhile, then crossed Tchaikovsky Street and turned up Arbat Street where it began at the massive Foreign Ministry building, another Stalinist skyscraper of pinnacles and spires. Lisa asked, 'Have you ever been in there?'

'A few times.'

'What's it like?'

'Have you ever been to the State Department building?'

'Yes.'

'Well, that's what the Soviet Foreign Ministry is like, except the twaddle and bunkum is in Russian.'

They walked up Arbat, an old Moscow street that had recently been made into the Soviet Union's first and only pedestrian shopping street. There were hundreds of people out on this promising Saturday, every one of them carrying a big bag. The street had been repaved with brick, and young trees struggled to take hold in concrete planters. There were benches, decorative streetlamps, and flower boxes running the length of the kilometer-long street that wound through the old Arbat district.

The Arbat was sometimes compared to the Left Bank or Georgetown, Greenwich Village, or Soho. But Hollis thought the Arbat was the Arbat, a unique glimpse of a vanished world that had not been well-known or chronicled even when it existed. For some reason the present regime was trying to preserve the Arbat's heritage, rehabilitating the handsome buildings and restoring the façades of once chic shops. Though, in a society that placed no value on chicness, gentility, tourism, or consumerism, Hollis could not comprehend what the government's purpose was. It might be nothing more than creeping bourgeois sentimentality, though Hollis found that hard to believe. He said to Lisa, 'Do you like this?'

'Sort of. But it's a bit sanitized, if you know what I mean.'

'Have you seen the unsanitized parts of the Arbat?'

'Oh, yes. I know every block of what's left of old Moscow.'

'Do you?'

'I'm doing a photographic essay.'

'Interesting. Hobby?'

'Sort of. I'm going to get it published.'

'Good luck.' He asked, 'Are you a Russophile?'

She smiled with a touch of embarrassment. 'Sort of. Yes, I like . . . the people . . . the language . . . old Russia.'

'No need to be defensive. I won't have you arrested.'

'You make a joke of it, but on this job you have to be careful what you say publicly or privately.'

'I know.'

Lisa and Hollis strolled from one side of the street to the other, looking in shop windows. The shops were mostly of the basic variety, a *svet* – lighting fixture store, an *apteka* – apothecary, and so on. There were a number of snack bars and ice cream kiosks and what the Russians called health food stores that sold mostly processed dairy products. Hollis noticed a long line outside one of them, women, young children, and babies in strollers, which meant, he knew, that fresh milk was available. Lisa stopped at an outdoor stand and bought a bunch of mums from one of the traditionally white-aproned old ladies. Lisa said, 'For a utilitarian people, the Russians spend a lot of money on hothouse flowers.'

'Maybe they eat them.'

'No, they put them in their drab apartments and dingy offices. Flowers are Russian soul food.'

'The Russians are a paradox – are they not? I can't figure them out,' Hollis said. 'They talk a lot about their Russian souls, but they never much mention their hearts.'

'Perhaps –'

'Instead of saying "a heart-to-heart talk", for instance, they say "*dusha-dushe*" – soul-to-soul. I get weary of all the soul talk.'

'It may be a matter of semantics –'

'Sometimes I think their problem is purely genetic.'

'Actually I have Russian blood.'

'Oh, do you? I've put my foot in my mouth.'

She took his arm as they walked. 'I'll forgive you.' She said, 'My paternal grandparents were named Putyatov. They owned a large estate and a big brick house outside of Kazan on the Volga. I have an old picture of the house.'

'Is it still there?'

'I don't know. When my grandmother, Evelina Vasileva, last saw it on the day she fled, it was still intact. My grandfather had five hundred peasants on the estate. I'd try to find it, but I can't get permission from the Foreign Ministry.' She stayed silent awhile, then added bitterly, 'What's it to them if I spend a weekend out in the country looking for my roots?'

'Did you tell them you were an aristocrat and heir to five hundred peasants?'

'Of course not.' She laughed, then said thoughtfully, 'I'll bet the Putyatov name is still remembered there.'

'Fondly?'

'Who knows? This is not like Western Europe where you can go back and trace your ancestry. There's been a complete break here, whole families wiped out, two world wars, revolution, civil war, purges, plagues, forced collectivization . . . what would I do if I found the house or found a Putyatov?'

'I don't know. But *you'd* know what to do. You have a Russian soul.'

She smiled but said nothing and led him toward a shop whose gilded wooden letters spelled *antikvar*. She said, 'This is the best of Moscow's three antique shops. The other two are mostly secondhand-junk shops.'

They went inside, and the chicly dressed proprietress, an attractive young woman, greeted Lisa cordially, and Lisa gave the woman the mums. Lisa said in Russian, 'Anna, this is my friend Sam.'

Hollis said in Russian, 'Good afternoon.'

She appraised him a moment, then asked in Russian, 'Are you with the embassy?'

'Sometimes.'

'Then you must know my good friend Seth Alevy.'

'I've heard of him.'

'Give him my regards, if you see him.'

'I will, if I see him.'

'Please' – she waved her arm – 'look around.'

Hollis watched as Lisa browsed through the shop, crowded mostly with furniture, rugs, and lamps, none of which looked antique. There were, however, tables covered with interesting smaller items: silver pieces, ivory, troika bells, ceramics, gilded picture frames, jasper, porphyry, and other objects of semi-precious Ural stone – bits and pieces of a vanished world. Hollis wondered if Lisa was looking for the Putyatovs here.

Hollis noted there were no crosses or icons and in fact nothing of a religious nature, though religious art had been the predominant art form in pre-Revolution Russia. However there were things here that one would never find in a Moscow store, though nothing of true artistic value. Most of the good pieces had long since been appropriated by the government for museums or for the houses of the Soviet elite. The rest had made its way out of Russia long ago or had been destroyed in the initial frenzy of the Revolution. Now and then something significant surfaced in the West – a previously unknown Fabergé egg, a Rublyev icon, and recently a Levitan landscape had been auctioned at Sotheby's for an anonymous client who was thought to be a Soviet defector. But for the most part, the evidence that Imperial Russia and Holy Russia had once existed could be seen only in Soviet museums between the hours of ten and six, closed Mondays.

Hollis picked up an inkwell made of Lithuanian amber. Embedded in the amber was an insect that he could not identify. He studied the inkwell as he thought about Seth Alevy, Lisa Rhodes, and the antique-shop woman who knew too much.

Lisa called out, 'Do you like this?' She held up a round lacquer box.

Hollis walked over to her and took the small black box. On the lid was an uncommonly lithe Russian milkmaid, carrying a yoke with two milk buckets hanging from it. The black lacquer was deep and lustrous, and the girl's clothing, bright and vibrant. On the bottom of the box was a four-hundred-ruble price sticker.

She said, 'I think it's a real Palekh box. Maybe pre-Revolution. Can you tell?'

Hollis' limited knowledge of Palekh boxes told him that it was difficult to tell the old ones from the ones still made in the village of Palekh. The quality was consistently high, and the style unchanged, despite the Revolution or the fact that the craftsmen were now all state employees. Therefore, age had no meaning with Palekh boxes. Size counted. This one could be bought in a Beriozka for about a hundred rubles. He said, 'I don't think it's worth four hundred.'

'That's what I'd expect a man to say.'

Hollis shrugged.

She added, 'Besides, I like Anna.'

'Anna doesn't own the place. The great Soviet people own it. Anna works for the government.'

'Actually, this is a unique sort of operation. It's called a commission shop. Do you know what that is?'

'No.'

'People bring things here on consignment. Whatever Anna sells, she takes a commission. The rest goes to the person who brought it in. Anna splits her commission with the government. It's almost free enterprise.'

'I've never heard of that.'

'It's only allowed with used goods.'

'Interesting.'

'Anna has what we call incentive. She's nice, and she holds things for me.'

'And Seth.'

'Yes. She likes Camels.'

'Excuse me?'

'Cigarettes. Camel cigarettes.'

'Oh.'

'I'm going to buy this.' She went to the counter and chatted with Anna, then counted out four hundred rubles. Lisa wrapped the Palekh box in a piece of tissue and slipped it into her bag. She pushed a pack of Camels across the counter. 'Let me know if you ever get anything porcelain with inlaid silver or gold.'

'I'll call you if I do.'

They bade farewell, and Hollis walked out into the pedestrian street. Lisa followed and they continued walking in the afternoon sun. Hollis ventured, 'That was a lot of money for that box.'

'I know.'

'Do you usually carry four hundred rubles with you?'

'I'm a real Russian. No credit cards, no checks. Just hundreds of rubles in case I see something to buy.'

'They usually look for food and clothing. That box was – well, it's not my business.'

They walked for a few minutes before she said, 'Does that place remind you of anything?'

'Not offhand.'

'Think. A novel. The one we all think about here.'

'Oh, yes. The secondhand store in *1984*. The one run by the Thought Police, where poor Winston Smith was entrapped. That did cross my mind, now you mention it. Is that place run by the Thought Police?'

'I hope not.'

'How does that woman know you and Alevy and that you are both with the embassy? Why does Seth Alevy frequent that place?'

'That's a good question. I thought you could tell me.'

'I'm sure I can't.'

'Seth gives me money to buy things there. In fact, he tells me what to buy. It's always an overpriced item. This time it was the box. I shouldn't tell you this, but he hasn't been up front with me.'

Hollis did not respond.

'Was that disloyal of me?'

'Do you owe him loyalty?'

She shrugged. 'In some areas. Anyway, I told you, so you wouldn't think I was a complete bubble brain. I was under orders to buy the box.'

Hollis nodded, then said, 'That did seem out of character.'

'Out of character and out of my price range.' She asked, 'So you don't know *anything* about the antique shop?'

'No.' But Hollis thought he might look into it.

They walked on, and Hollis watched the people sitting on the benches and planters, eating ice cream and small meat pies. Most people gave them a passing glance, and some stared. Westerners were still rare enough in Moscow to attract attention, and a Muscovite could pick out a Westerner as easily as a Westerner could pick out a Cossack on horseback. The sun, Hollis thought, had the unfortunate effect of putting Moscow and its citizens in the most unfavorable light; somehow the drabness was not so drab under an overcast sky.

Lisa had taken his arm again, and Hollis gave her a sidelong glance. Now that she'd mentioned it, there was something vaguely Russian about her. But perhaps it was only the power of suggestion, as when he'd seen Julie Christie as Pasternak's Lara against the background of Hollywood's Moscow.

Hollis thought Lisa was quite pretty, and he noticed she had the high cheekbones and sharp features of some Slavic women. But her complexion was light, and her eyes were big and blue. Her auburn hair was cut in a shag-pixie style that Hollis noticed was popular with many younger Moscow women. Her lips, he saw, had the capability of being pouty, though he hadn't seen that so far. Mostly she smiled or bit her bottom lip in thought.

She said without looking at him, 'Do I have a fly on my nose?'

'No . . . I . . . I was just looking for Russian features.'

'Not in the face. Feet and legs. Short, stubby legs and big feet. Fat thighs.'

'I doubt that.'

'Want to bet?'

'Well . . . sure.'

She smiled and led him down a side street called Kalachny, or pastrycook. The streets in the Arbat recalled the names of the sixteenth-century court purveyors who once lived and worked there: Plotnikov – carpenter, Serebryany – silversmith, and so on. The names had been changed after the Revolution but had recently been changed back again. It was, Hollis thought, as if the country was on a nostalgia trip, like in America, a sure sign that the twentieth century had gotten out of hand. Hollis said, 'Where are you taking me now? To see your Russian features?'

'No. To lunch. Didn't you invite me to lunch?'

'Yes, but I called in a favor to get a reservation at the Prague.'

'Oh, I thought I could pick.'

'Alright, but there aren't any restaurants this way.'

'There's one.'

'What's it called?'

'I don't think it has a name.' She crossed Pastrycook Street, and he followed her up the steps of an old stucco building that looked like the former residence of a wealthy merchant. They entered the large foyer, and Hollis smelled cabbage and old fish. She said, 'That's not the restaurant you smell. That's the tenants.' She motioned him to a door under a sweeping staircase, and they descended into the basement.

Lisa opened another door at the end of the stairs, and Hollis could see a large dimly lit room with a low wooden ceiling. The floors and walls were covered with Oriental carpets, and a layer of aromatic tobacco smoke hung in the air. An old woman approached and smiled widely, giving Hollis the impression she was wearing someone else's dentures. The woman said, 'Salaam aleihum.'

Lisa returned the greeting and followed the woman to a low table laid with a dirty red cloth and mismatched flatware. Lisa and Hollis sat, and Lisa exchanged pleasantries with the woman, who spoke flawed Russian. The woman asked Lisa, 'Does your friend like our food?'

'He loves it. Could you bring us a bottle of that plum wine?'

The woman moved off.

Hollis looked at his surroundings. 'Is this place in the Blue Guide?'

'No, sir. But it ought to be. The food is great.'

'Is it Jewish?'

'No. Azerbaijanian. I said *salaam aleihum*, not *sholom aleichem*. Close, but it's sort of Arabic.'

'I see.' Hollis noticed the room was full, and the other diners, mostly men, were obviously not ethnic Russians, and in fact he heard no Russian being spoken. Moscow, Hollis had observed, was becoming ethnically diverse as more of the Soviet minorities found their way to the center of the empire. The regime discouraged this immigration, and the Russian Muscovites were appalled by it. Though the Soviet government claimed they had no figures on ethnic breakdown, Seth Alevy had done a report in which he estimated nearly twenty percent of Moscow's population was now non-Russian. The city had become home to Uzbeks, Armenians, Georgians, Tartars, Turks, and a dozen other Soviet minority groups. Alevy had concluded that Moscow was becoming more cosmopolitan and sophisticated because of this ethnic diversity. He also concluded that it was becoming the sewer of the empire, like former imperial capitals, filled with wheeler-dealers, men on the make, profiteers, and parasites. Such as Misha. Where the Russians saw a problem, Seth Alevy and Sam Hollis saw an opportunity.

Hollis noticed that most of the patrons were glancing at them. Hollis asked, 'Is this place safe?'

'I guess.'

'This doesn't appear to be a government-owned restaurant.'

'It's a catering establishment. Almost a private club. It's owned and operated by an Azerbaijanian produce cooperative. It's legal.'

'Okay.'

'Have you ever eaten in a catering co-op?'

'No.'

'The food is better than in the best restaurants. Especially the co-ops with access to fresh produce such as this one.'

'Okay.'

A young boy came to the table and set down a bowl of small white grapes and another bowl containing tangerines.

Lisa said, 'See? When was the last time you saw a tangerine?'

'In a dream last week.' Hollis took a sharp knife and peeled a tangerine. He pulled the sections apart, and he and Lisa ate in silence, picking at the sweet white grapes between bites of tangerine. Lisa said, 'Do you believe this?'

'You saved me from scurvy.'

Lisa wiped her mouth with her handkerchief as there were no napkins. 'All the Azerbaijanians who live in Moscow come here. The food is genuinely ethnic.'

Hollis nodded. In Moscow's other so-called ethnic restaurants, the Prague, the Berlin, the Bucharest, and the Budapest, the food was distinctly Russian. And in the Havana the only thing Cuban was the sugar on the table. The Peking served borscht. He asked, 'How did you find this place?'

'Long story.'

Hollis thought it could be told in one word: *Seth*.

She said, 'We're allowed to patronize these places. Most Westerners don't know about them, or if they do, won't eat in them.'

'Can't guess why.'

'Do you smell those spices?'

'Sort of. But the tobacco smoke is filled with air.'

Lisa sat back and lit her own cigarette. 'Restaurants,' she said, 'are a sort of barometer of what is wrong with this country.'

'How is that?'

'I mean there are eight million Muscovites, and half of them are trying to get reservations in the twenty passable restaurants.'

'Seating is tight,' Hollis agreed. 'But they may be holding our table at the Prague.'

'You see, if private individuals were allowed to open restaurants, five hundred would spring up overnight. Same with shops and everything else.'

'That would be a threat to the system.'

'What sort of threat?'

'A very formidable threat. It would be like lighting a candle in the dark. Everyone would converge on it and light their own candles from it. Then the dimly perceived flaws in the system would be seen. Then who knows what would happen.'

Lisa studied him for a moment before observing. 'You're rather profound for a military man.'

'I thank you, I think. Read any good Gogol lately?'

She smiled. 'Actually, I'm a great fan of his. Have you read *Dead Souls*?'

'Who hasn't?'

'He's not that widely read in the West, and I think that's because his characters are hard to appreciate outside a Russian context. Don't you think so?'

'Absolutely.'

'Gogol's statue is actually at the end of this street, you know. In the Arbat Square. Have you seen it?'

'Hard to miss it.'

The plum wine came, and Lisa poured. Hollis touched glasses with her and toasted. 'As the peasants say, "To a short winter, ample meat, and dry wood for the fire."'

'You forgot the last line.'

'Yes. "And a warm woman for my bed."'

They drank.

Lisa looked at him over the rim of her glass. She asked, 'Sam, where are you from originally?'

'All over. I'm an Air Force brat.'

'Is this going to be like pulling teeth?'

He smiled. 'Alright, let me tell you about myself. I was born at Travis Air Force Base during the Second World War. I moved all over the globe until I was eighteen. Then I spent four years at the Air Force Academy. I graduated and went on to fighter school. I did a tour in 'Nam in 1988, then another in 1972. That's when I was shot down over Haiphong. I got the craft out to sea, bailed out, and was picked up by air-sea rescue. I was banged up a bit, and the flight surgeons said no more flying. My father was a brigadier general by this time and got me a temporary posting in the Pentagon until I was able to be more active. Somehow I wound up taking a language course in Bulgarian. As you might know, Bulgarian is the root Slavic language, sort of like Latin is to the romance languages. So anyway, I did three years in Sofia as an air attaché, then did stints in a couple of other Warsaw Pact countries, then before I knew it, I was too involved with this business for them to let me go back to the line.' Hollis took a drink of his wine. 'I always suspected my father was behind this embassy attaché business.'

'So you're a reluctant spy.'

'No, not reluctant. But not enthusiastic either. Just sort of . . . I don't know. And I'm not a spy.'

'Okay. And then about two years ago, they sent you here. The big leagues.'

'The only league in this business.'

'And how about your family?'

'My father retired some years ago. He and my mother live in Japan. I'm not sure why. They're rather odd. I think they're into Zen. Too much traveling around. They don't even know America, and what they know they don't like. Reminds me of the Roman centurions or British colonial officers. You know? Since World War Two, America has developed a whole class of people like that.'

'Like us.'

'Yes, like us. The emissaries of empire.'

'Do you have brothers or sisters?'

'A younger sister who married a jet jockey and is currently living in the Philippines. No children. One older brother who works on Wall Street, wears a yellow tie, and makes too much money. He's married, two children. He's the only real American in the family.' Hollis smiled. 'He developed travel burnout as a kid after the fifteenth transfer. His philosophy is that a man should never leave his time zone.'

'Time zone?'

'Yes. You know. He lives in the Eastern time zone. He won't leave it and in fact confines himself to twenty degrees of latitude within the zone. He'll cross zip codes freely but tries to stay within his telephone area code. He's in two one two.'

Lisa stifled a laugh. 'Are you serious?'

'Yes.'

'What an interesting family. Are you all close?'

'There is a bond. How about you? Tell me about Lisa.'

She gave no indication of having heard him and said, 'I seem to remember a wife.'

'Wife? Oh, yes, Katherine. She went to London to shop.'

'I think she's been gone about half a year.'

'Has it been that long?'

'Are you legally separated?'

'Illegally.'

Lisa seemed about to pursue this but poured more wine instead.

The proprietress came to the table, and she and Lisa discussed the day's fare. Lisa ordered for both herself and Hollis. Lisa said to Hollis, 'It's a fixed price. Only three rubles. The menu changes by the hour. Better that than the big restaurants where they keep telling you they're out of everything you order.' She tore a piece of pitta bread and put half of it on his plate. She remarked, 'Bulgarian? I thought your Russian was odd. I don't mean American-accented or anything, but not Russian-accented either.'

'I speak a little Polish too.'

'You've been around the Bloc.' She laughed at her own pun.

Hollis smiled. 'It's an article of faith with the Russians that only a Russian can speak *Russian* Russian. Yet Seth Alevy is nearly perfect. If he were trying to pass, a Muscovite would think he was probably a Leningrader and vice versa.'

'Perhaps on the telephone. But there's more to being a Russian than the language. It's like that with any nationality, but the Russians *are* different in unique ways. Did you ever notice that Russian men walk from the shoulders down? American men use their legs.'

'I've noticed.'

She continued, 'And their facial expressions are different, their mannerisms. To be a Russian is the sum total of the national and cultural experience. Neither you nor I nor Seth could pass for a Russian any more than we could pass for an Oriental.'

'I detect some Russian mysticism there, Ms Putyatova.'

Lisa smiled.

Hollis said, 'Yet I wonder if it could be done? I mean, given the right training, cultural immersion, and so forth, could an American pass for a Russian in a group of Russians? Could a Russian pass for an American at a backyard barbecue?'

Lisa thought a moment before replying. 'Perhaps for a while, if no one was looking for a counterfeit. But not under close examination. Something would betray the person.'

'Would it? What if a Russian who already knew English went to a special school? A school with an American instructor? A sort of . . . finishing school? A total immersion in Americana for, let's say, a year or more. Would you get a perfect copy of the American instructor?'

Lisa considered a moment, then replied, 'The instructor and the student would have to be very dedicated . . . There would have to be a very good reason for an American to go along with that –' She added, 'We're talking about spies, aren't we?'

'You are. I'm not. You're very bright.' Hollis changed the subject. 'Your Russian is grammatically perfect. Your colloquialisms are good. But I noticed your accent, rhythm, and speech patterns are not Muscovite, nor do you sound as if you learned Russian at Monterrey or Weisbaden.'

'No, I didn't go to our language schools. My grandmother taught me Russian.'

'Evelina Vasileva Putyatova?'

'So, you were paying attention. Odd for a man.'

'I'm a spy. I listen.'

'And look and file things away. Anyway, my grandmother was a wonderful woman.' Lisa stubbed out her cigarette and continued, 'I was born and raised in Sea Cliff, a neat sort of village of Victorian houses on Long Island's north shore. Sea Cliff has a large Russian community that goes back to czarist times. Then the Revolution and civil war brought a second wave of immigrants, among whom were my grandmother and grandfather. They were in their early twenties and recently married. My grandfather's father was a czarist officer, and he was killed fighting the Germans, so my grandfather, Mikhail Aleksandrovich Putyatov, inherited the estate and title, which by this time had become a distinct liability. My grandmother's parents had already been arrested by the local Bolsheviks and shot, and Mikhail's mother, my great-grandmother, shot herself. Relatives on both sides of the family were scattered all over Russia or were at the front or already in exile. So sensing the party was over, Mikhail and Evelina grabbed the jewels and the gold and got out. They didn't arrive in America broke. Anyway, Mikhail and Evelina wound up in Sea Cliff, a long way from the Volga.'

'And your grandmother told you all this?'

'Yes. Russians are perhaps the last of the Europeans to put so much emphasis on oral history. In a country where there has always been censorship, who can you go to for the facts if not the old people?'

'They're not always the most reliable witnesses to the past.'

'Perhaps not in the sense of the larger issues. But they can tell you who was hanged for hoarding food and who was shot for owning land.'

'Yes, that's true. Go on.'

'Well, in the parlor of our nice old Victorian house in Sea Cliff, we had a silver samovar, and when I was a child, Evelina would sit me by the samovar and tell me Russian folktales, then when I got older, about her life on her parents' estate and about my grandfather. When I was about sixteen, she told me about the Revolution, the civil war, the epidemics, and the famine. It affected me very deeply, but I suppose her stories were colored by her hate of the communists, and I suppose, too, that I was influenced by her hate, though I don't know if that was her purpose.'

Hollis made no comment.

Lisa continued, 'But she taught me love, too, love of old Russia, the people, the language, the Orthodox church . . .' Lisa stared off into space for a few seconds, then continued, 'In my grandmother's room there were three beautiful icons on the wall and a curio cabinet that held folk art and miniature portraits on porcelain of her family and of Nicholas and Alexandra. The atmosphere in our community, even as late as when I grew up, was vaguely anticommunist – anti-Bolshevik, I suppose you'd say. There is a Russian Orthodox church close by, and ironically the Soviet mission to the United Nations has an old estate that they use as a weekend retreat a few miles from the church. Sundays my grandmother and I would go to church, and sometimes we'd walk with the priests and the congregation to the gates of the Soviet estate and pray. Our Holy Saturday candlelight procession would always march past the Soviet place. Today we'd call that a demonstration. Then, we called it bringing light to the anti-Christs. So you see, Sam, Evelina Putyatova had a deep and lasting influence on me. She died when I was away at college.'

Neither spoke for some time, then Lisa said, 'I went to the University of Virginia and got my degree in Soviet studies. I took the Foreign Service Entrance Exam, went through the oral assessment, the background investigation, and was vetted for a top secret clearance. I placed high on the USIS list but had to wait a year for an appointment. I did my year of consular service in Medan, Indonesia. There were six of us in a run-down two-story house, and I couldn't figure out what we were supposed to do to further American interests there. Mostly we drank beer and played cards. I almost went nuts. Then I got my first real USIS job at the American library in

Madras, India, and spent two years there. Then I came back to Washington for a year of extra training and staff work with the USIS in DC. Then off to East Berlin for two years, where I finally used my Russian. That was a good embassy – exciting, mysterious, spies all over the place, and a ten-minute car ride to the West. After Berlin, I finally got what I wanted. Moscow. And here I am. With another spy.'

'You like spies.'

'I'm a spy groupie.'

Hollis smiled.

She added, 'I've never married and never been engaged.' I'm turning twenty-nine next month.'

'Invite me to your office birthday party.'

'Sure will.'

He asked, 'And your parents?'

'They both still live in that house in Sea Cliff. My father is a banker; my mother a teacher. They can see the harbor from their porch, and in the summer they sit out there and watch the boats. It's very lovely, and they're very happy together. Maybe someday you can stop by.'

Hollis didn't know what to say to that, so he asked, 'Brothers or sisters?'

'An older sister, divorced and living back home. I have a niece and nephew. My parents seem happy for the company. They want me to marry and move close by. They're proud of my career in the diplomatic corps but aren't too keen on my present assignment. Especially my mother. She has a phobia about Russia.'

'You look like you can take care of yourself. You know, my father was stationed on Long Island in the mid-fifties. Mitchel Air Force Base. I vaguely remember it.'

'Yes. It's closed now.'

'I know,' Hollis replied. 'What's become of the place?'

'It's been parceled out to Hofstra University and a community college. Part of the land was used to build the coliseum where the Islanders play. Do you follow hockey?'

107

'No. Like my parents, I'm not much of an American. It's ironic, considering I've devoted my life to the service of my country. I'm a patriot, but I'm not plugged into the pop culture. For years I thought Yogi Bear and Yogi Berra were the same person.'

Lisa smiled. 'So you wouldn't pass the friend-or-foe test if someone asked you who plays center field for the Mets? You couldn't pass for the American that you are.'

'No, I'm afraid I'd be shot on the spot.'

Lisa poured the last of the wine into their glasses. She looked at Hollis. 'Well, now we know something about each other.'

'Yes. I'm glad we had a chance to talk.'

The food arrived, and Hollis inquired, 'What the hell is this?'

'That's *dovta*, a soup made of sour milk and rice. This cuisine is similar to Turkish. It's somewhat complex, with more depth than Slavic cuisine. And the shit on the chipped blue plate is called *gulubtsy*.' She laughed.

Hollis smiled and helped himself. They ate in silence. More plates of spiced food arrived. They washed the meal down with weak Moscow beer. Hollis glanced at his watch.

She noticed and asked, 'Do you have time to see the Train of Mourning?'

'The what?'

'The actual engine and coach that brought Lenin's body back to Moscow. It's on display at Paveletsky Station.'

'Oh, *that* train. I'll pass.'

'Just kidding anyway. I don't really go to places like the Marx-Engels museum either,' Lisa said. 'I think it's a joke how they try to create a secular religion in place of the one they destroyed. But if you *are* free this afternoon, perhaps we can do something.'

'Sure. How would you like to take a ride in the country?'

'Don't joke.'

'No joke,' Hollis replied.

'Where? How?'

'I have to go to Mozhaisk on official business. I have a pass with your name on it.'

'Do you? I'd love to go. What sort of business?'

'Bad business, Lisa. Gregory Fisher is in the Mozhaisk morgue.'

Lisa stopped eating and stared down at the table for some time. She cleared her throat and said, 'Oh, God, Sam. That poor boy . . .'

'Do you still want to go?'

She nodded.

The proprietress brought strong Turkish coffee and honey balls. Hollis had the coffee. Lisa sat silently. She lit a cigarette and said to Hollis, 'Was he . . . trying to escape or what . . . ?'

'No. They say he was heading *toward* Moscow. They say he had a car accident before the Borodino turnoff. They say he never got to the Rossiya.'

'They're lying.'

'Be that as it may, it's their country. I'll brief you in the car. But I want you to understand now that if you come with me, I can't guarantee your safety.'

'Safety?'

'I *think* the KGB is satisfied that they've contained the problem. They probably don't think they have to engineer another accident. On the other hand, they're not logical in the way we understand logic, therefore they're not predictable.'

She nodded.

Hollis added, 'They know you took Fisher's call, and they know your name is on the pass. That shouldn't make you a target, but you never know what they've talked themselves into. Still want to go?'

'Yes.'

'Why?'

'Why are you going, Sam? Anybody from the consular section could go.'

'I'm going to snoop around. You know that.'

109

'And that's why I'm wearing dark, casual clothes and why you have a gun in an ankle holster.'

'That's right.'

'Well . . . I'll help you snoop. I enjoy your company.'

'Thank you.'

'You're welcome. Also, I guess I feel I was in at the beginning of this . . . you know?'

'Yes.' He stood and put six rubles on the table. 'Well, the food wasn't so bad. The place has ambience and no electronic plumbing like at the Prague or the other top twenty. Two and a half stars. Send a letter to Michelin.'

She stood. 'Thanks for being such a good sport. My treat next time.'

'Next time I pick.'

'Can you top this for ambience?'

'You bet,' Hollis said. 'I know a KGB hangout.'

'Are you kidding?'

'No.'

'Neat. Take me.'

They left the restaurant, and Hollis found himself in an agreeable frame of mind for the first time in a long while.

Part 2

Scratch a Russian, and you will wound a Tartar.

– Napoleon Bonaparte

9

Sam Hollis and Lisa Rhodes came out of Arbat Street into the square of the same name. They walked past the statue of Gogol toward the star-shaped pavilion of the Arbatskaya metro station on the far side of the square. The Prague Restaurant was to their left, where a long line of people still waited for their lunch. On the north side of the square was Dorn Svyazi, a glass and concrete post office and telephone exchange. Lisa said, 'That's where the church of Saint Boris used to stand, and over there was the seventeenth-century church of Saint Tikhon. The communists demolished both of them. I have old pictures though.'

'Are you trying to publish a book or draw up an indictment?'

'Both.'

They entered the metro pavilion and jostled their way through the crowd toward the escalators. At the last moment Hollis took Lisa's arm and led her toward the opposite doors of the pavilion. They came back out on to the square behind a fountain. She said, 'What are you doing?'

'We're not taking the metro to the embassy.'

'Oh . . . don't we have to pick up a car?'

'Follow me. Walk quickly.'

Hollis moved rapidly toward the east side of the square. Lisa followed. They passed a number of kiosks and cleaved through lines of people queued up for *kvass*, soft drinks, and ice cream. Lisa said, 'Where are we going?'

He took her wrist and pulled her up to a black Zhiguli parked with its engine running at the curb in front of the Khudozhestvennyi Art cinema. 'Get in.'

Hollis went to the driver's side, and a man whom Lisa recognized from the embassy got out immediately. Hollis slid behind the wheel, and the man closed the door. The man said; 'Full tank, linkage is a bit sticky, your briefcase is in the backseat. Luck.'

'Thanks.' Hollis threw the Zhiguli into gear and pulled out into Kalinin Prospect, then made a sudden U-turn and headed west. He looked in his rearview mirror.

Lisa said nothing.

Hollis accelerated up the broad avenue and within two minutes crossed Tchaikovsky Street, then crossed the Moskva River over the Kalinin Bridge and passed the Ukraina Hotel, continuing west on Kutuzov Prospect. A few minutes later they drove by the Borodino Panorama and left the inner city at the Triumphal Arch. Hollis accelerated to fifty kilometers per hour. He commented. 'How many cities of eight million people can you get clear of in ten minutes? Moscow is a driver's paradise.'

Lisa didn't respond.

Hollis reached under his seat and pulled out a black wool cap and a dark blue scarf. He put the cap on and handed Lisa the scarf. 'A babushka for madam. Please try it on.'

She shrugged and draped the scarf over her head, tying it at her throat. She finally said, 'I saw this in a movie once.'

'A musical comedy?'

'Yes.'

Some minutes later they passed scattered highrise projects, looking like grey concrete ships adrift in a sea of undulating grassland. Lisa said, 'It's against the law for us to drive cars without diplomatic plates.'

'Is it?'

'Where is this car from?'

'The Intourist Hotel. Rented and paid for with an American Express card.'

She said in a sarcastic tone. 'Then you've provided them with hard currency to use against us in Washington. Some spy.'

'It was only forty dollars. A K-man could barely buy a defense worker lunch.'

114

Again she shrugged.

Hollis observed, 'Moscow is getting too big for the KGB. Too much Western influence. Rental cars, AMEX, a couple of Western banks. It's easier for us to operate now.'

'You sound like him.'

'Who?'

'Seth. Very narrow perspective.'

'I know.' Hollis could sense that her good mood had become subdued. Probably, he thought, she was nervous as well as upset over Fisher's death.

Hollis thought too that bringing an amateur along, an innocent, might not be the brightest thing he'd done all week. But in some vague way he felt it would be good for her. Alevy had understood that. And from the standpoint of pure tradecraft, a woman who had no known intelligence connections was good cover. If Alevy and Hollis had applied for the passes together, the KGB would have called out an armored division to follow them.

Hollis realized that he *was* thinking like Alevy. How else could he explain the logic of asking Lisa Rhodes to take a drive with him from which she might not return alive? He said aloud, 'Sorry.'

'For what?'

'For sounding like Seth.'

She smiled. 'Boy, that's a loaded one.'

He didn't respond.

Lisa looked out the window and said thoughtfully, 'If Greg Fisher came in from Smolensk and Borodino, this is the road he took.'

'Yes, it was.'

'He drove right by the embassy.'

'I know.'

They crossed the Outer Ring highway, and Lisa informed him, 'There used to be signs on this road reading "Forward to Communism". But I suppose the authorities realized the unfortunate imagery of that slogan on a road that goes in circles.'

Hollis smiled. 'You're a good guide. I'll speak to Intourist about a weekend job for you.' Hollis pulled a piece of flimsy greyish paper from his pocket and handed it to her. 'Your pass.'

She glanced at the red Cyrillic letters and the Foreign Ministry stamp, then stuffed it in her bag. 'It's only good until midnight.'

'We'll be there and back before then.'

'I thought we could stay in the country overnight.'

Hollis did not reply immediately, then said, 'I don't have a toothbrush.'

Lisa smiled at him, then turned her attention to the countryside. A small village of about two dozen houses sat starkly in an open field. Rough fences sectioned off garden plots from poultry and swine, and mudpaths connected dilapidated dwellings to outhouses. The cottages were roofed with corrugated sheet metal, and she imagined that a hard rain must drive the inhabitants crazy. She wondered, too, how they kept the heat in when the windchill factor got to fifty or sixty below. 'Unbelievable.'

He followed her gaze. 'Yes. It's striking, isn't it? And fifteen kilometers back is the capital of a mighty nuclear power.'

'This is my first trip into the country.'

'I've been around a bit, and it gets worse when you head east toward the Urals or north toward Leningrad. Over half the rural population is ill-housed, ill-clothed, and ill-fed, though they grow the food.'

Lisa nodded. 'You hear and read about this, but you have to see it to believe it.'

Hollis pointed. 'Do you see that rise over there? Beyond that is a pine forest in which is hidden a very sophisticated phased-array radar site that is the command center for all the Soviet antiballistic missile silos around Moscow. For the price of that installation, half the peasants in this region could be put in decent farmhouses with indoor plumbing and central heat. Guns or butter. Some societies can't afford both.'

She nodded. 'Half our national budget and sixty percent of theirs . . . incredible wealth sunk into missile silos.'

'The current optimistic theory in Washington is that we're spending them to death.' He added, 'Forget what I said about the location of that ABM site.'

She nodded distractedly.

They drove on in silence for some time before she spoke again. 'In my work I meet Russians who understand the contradictions in their system. They like us, and they would like to build grain silos instead of missile silos. But the government has made them believe the missiles are necessary because we want to conquer them.'

'Well, they're right. You make a distinction between the people and the government here. But I think people get the kind of government they deserve. In this case, probably better.'

'That's not true, Sam. The Russians may not understand democracy, but in some curious way they are passionately devoted to *svoboda* – freedom.'

Hollis shrugged.

'I always thought that communism is an historical fluke here. It won't make it to its hundredth birthday.'

Hollis replied dryly, 'I'd hate to think what these people will come up with next.'

'Are you really so hard-line, or are you just giving me a hard time?'

'Neither. I'm just processing information. That's what I was told to do here.'

'Sometimes I think I'm the only person in the embassy who is trying to find some good here, some hope. It's so damned depressing being around cynics, hawks, oily diplomats, and paranoiacs.'

'Oh, I know. Look, if we're going to be friends, let's cool the politics.'

'Okay.'

Again they lapsed into silence. The sky had become gloomy again, and drops of rain streaked across the windshield. There

117

was a sense of quiet oppressiveness in the air, a greyishness that entered through the eyes and burrowed its way into the brain, heart, and soul. Lisa said, 'Out here, on the plains, I think I understand that legendary Slavic melancholy.'

'Yes, but you ought to see the endless fields of giant sun-flowers in the summer. They take your breath away.'

She looked at him. 'Do they?' Lisa thought that the statement told her more about Sam Hollis than Hollis had intended. 'You'll have to show me in the summer.'

'Okay.'

'I wish I had a camera.'

'I'll stop at the next camera store.'

'Okay.' She looked at her watch. 'Are we going to get to the morgue on time?'

'If it's closed, someone will open it.' Hollis suddenly cut the wheel, and the Zhiguli angled off on to a dirt track, fishtailing and throwing up a cloud of dust.

'What's the matter?'

'Nothing.' Hollis took the car around the far side of a *kochka*, one of the small knobby knolls that added small terrain relief to the plains that swept west from Moscow. He brought the Zhiguli to a halt out of sight of the road. Hollis reached back, opened the briefcase on the rear seat, and took out a pair of binoculars, then got out of the car. Lisa followed, and they climbed the grassy knoll to the top. Hollis knelt and pulled Lisa down beside him. He focused the binoculars down the long straight road and said, 'I think we're alone.'

Lisa replied, 'In the States men say, "Do you want to go someplace where we can be alone?" Here they say, "I think we're alone" or "I think we have company".'

Hollis scanned the skies, then the surrounding fields. He stood and Lisa stood also. Hollis handed her the binoculars. 'Take a look over there.'

She focused on the eastern horizon. 'Moscow . . . I can see the spires of the Kremlin.'

Hollis stared out over the harvested farmland. 'It was just about here.'

'What was?'

'This is about how far the German army got. It was this time of year. The German recon patrols reported what you just said. They could see the spires of the Kremlin through their field glasses.'

Lisa looked at him curiously.

Hollis seemed lost in thought for a time, then continued, 'The Germans figured the war was over. They were this close. Then God, who probably didn't care much for either army, tipped the scales toward the Reds. It snowed early, and it snowed heavy. The Germans were freezing, the panzers got stuck. The Red army got a breather, then attacked in the snow. Three and a half years later the Russians were in Berlin, and the world has not been the same since.'

Hollis turned and watched the sun sinking in the western sky. His back to Lisa, he said as if to himself. 'Sometimes I try to understand this place and these people. Sometimes I admire what they've done, sometimes I'm contemptuous of what they can't do. I think, though, that they're more like us than we care to admit. The Russians think big, like we do, they have a frontier spirit, and they take pride in their accomplishments.They have a directness and openness of character unlike anything I've encountered in Europe or Asia, but much like I remember in America. They want to be first in everything, they want to be number one. However, there can only be one number one, and the next number is two.'

Hollis walked down the knoll and got into the car. Lisa followed and slid in beside him. Hollis pulled back on to the road and continued along the Minsk-Moscow highway. An occasional produce truck passed, going in the opposite direction toward Moscow. Hollis noted idly that the potatoes looked small and the cabbages were black. He saw no other vegetables, no poultry, livestock, or dairy products. He supposed that was worth a short report, though his discovery was already common knowledge to the housewives of Moscow.

Lisa glanced at Hollis from time to time. She would have liked to draw him out on what he'd said on the knoll, but she knew better. A man such as Hollis, she understood, was capable of occasional bursts of speech from the heart but did not want it to become dialogue. Instead she rolled down the window. 'Smell that.'

'What?'

'The earth. You don't smell that in Moscow.'

'No,' he replied, 'you don't.'

She looked out the window at the Russian countryside, listened to the stillness of the late autumn, smelled the dank, rich earth. 'This is it, Sam. Russia. Not Moscow or Leningrad. *Russia*. Look at those white birches there. See the small leaves, all red, yellow, and gold. Watch what happens when a breeze comes along. See that? What could be more Russian than that – tiny colored birch leaves blowing across a grey sky, across a lonely landscape? It's so desolate, it's beautiful, Sam. The Kremlin can't change this. It's immutable, timeless. My God, this is it. This is *Russia*!'

Hollis glanced at her as she turned to him, and their eyes met. He looked back out the windshield and for the first time *felt* the presence of the land.

She said with growing excitement, 'Look at the smoke curling out the chimneys in that village. The clouds are gathering in the late afternoon. The fires are lit against the dampness. Tea is brewing, potatoes and cabbage are boiling. Father is mending a fence or a plow in the drizzle. The black mud clings to his felt boots. He wants his tea and the warmth of his cabin. I can see horsemen, I can hear balalaikas, I see lonely birch log churches against the purple horizon . . . I can hear their clear bells pealing over the quiet plains . . .' She turned to him. 'Sam, can't we stop in a village?'

He replied softly, 'I think you might be disappointed.'

'Please. We won't have this opportunity again.'

'Maybe later . . . if there's time. I promise.'

She smiled at him. 'We'll find time.'

They continued on in companionable silence, two people in a car, traveling west into the setting sun, cut off from the embassy, the city, the world, alone.

Hollis glanced at her from time to time, and they exchanged smiles. He decided he liked her because she knew what she liked. At length he said, 'I give that kid credit. I hope he had the thrill of a lifetime.'

'What do you know about him? His family, home, how he died.'

Hollis told her what little he knew.

She said simply, 'They murdered him.'

They drove past small villages, collective farms, and state farms. About halfway to Mozhaisk she asked, 'Is this going to be dangerous?'

'Very.'

'Why me?'

'I had the impression you think this stinks. I thought you might want to follow through on your convictions.'

'I'm . . . not trained.'

'But you're a spy groupie.' He smiled. 'You thought East Berlin was exciting. This is a chance to mix it up a bit.'

'You're baiting me, Colonel.' She poked him in the side good-naturedly. 'You didn't even know I was a spy groupie before you decided to ask me.'

'Good point. You see, you're thinking like an intelligence officer already.' Hollis checked his watch, the odometer, and his rearview mirror.

She asked, 'Hollis, are you one of those men who bait liberated women? I'm not one of those women who think that women can do everything a man can do.'

'This is neither a sociological experiment nor a personal matter, Ms Rhodes. I think you can be helpful and you are good cover.'

'Okay.'

Hollis added, 'And good company.'

'Thank you.'

The small Zhiguli was one of the few private cars on the highway, but Hollis knew it would attract far less attention than an American Ford with diplomatic plates. He knew too that he and Lisa could pass for Ivan and Irina out for a weekend drive. The embassy watchers, Boris, Igor, and company, sitting in their cars outside the embassy gates, had by now realized that Hollis had given them the slip again. They were probably very upset with him, and their bosses were very upset with them. Everyone was upset. Except Fisher. Fisher was dead.

She said, 'I guess you can tell I'm not as sprightly and scintillating as I was at lunch.'

'Well, hearing of a death, even of someone you didn't know, is upsetting.'

'Yes, that, and –'

'You're a bit nervous.'

'That too –'

'And you've discovered I'm not as interesting as you first thought.'

'On the contrary. May I speak? I was going to say that I'm worried about this whole mess. I mean, I was sitting in my office last night, before Greg Fisher's call, thinking that we're getting it together with them again. *Glasnost* and all that. You understand?'

'Yes.'

'I said to myself, "Please, God, no more Afghanistans, no KAL airliners, no Nick Daniloffs this time."'

'That's like praying for an end to death and taxes.'

'But why does it always have to be *something*? This thing is going to ruin it all again, isn't it? We'll be kicking out each other's diplomats and staff again, canceling cultural and scientific exchanges, and heading further down that fucking road to the missile silos. Won't we?'

Hollis replied, 'That's not my area of concern.'

122

'It's *everybody*'s area of concern, Sam. You live on this planet.'

'Sometimes. Once I was high above it, sixty thousand feet, and I'd look around and say, "Those people down there are *nuts*." Then I'd come in and release my bombs. Then I'd dodge missiles and MiGs and go home and have a beer. I didn't get cynical or remorseful. I just got narrowed into my little problem of dropping my bombs and getting my beer. That's the way it is today.'

'But you talked to God. You asked Him about the big plan.'

'He never answered.' Hollis added, 'For your information, however, the word still seems to be détente. Think peace. Subject to change without notice.'

She pulled a pack of Kents from her bag. 'Mind?'

'No.'

'Want one?'

'No. Crack the window.'

She lowered the window and lit up.

Hollis cut off the highway on to a farm road and continued at high speed, churning up gravel as the Zhiguli bounced along a narrow lane.

She asked, 'Why did you leave the highway?'

Hollis referred to a sheet of paper in his hand and made a hard left on to another road, then a right. He said, 'A Brit some years ago fortunately charted back routes to bypass a lot of major towns around Moscow. This route bypasses Mozhaisk. No road names, just landmarks. Look for a dead cow.'

She smiled despite her growing anxiety. She said, 'You're committing an itinerary violation.'

'You ain't seen nothin' yet.'

'We're going to Borodino, I suppose.'

'That's correct.' Hollis continued to navigate the intersecting farm lanes. He passed an occasional truck or tractor and waved each time. He said to Lisa, 'The damned linkage does stick, but the car handles alright. They're Fiats, you know, and this one handles like its Italian cousin. Good trail cars.'

'Men. Cars. Football. Sex.'

'Excuse me?'

'Nothing.'

They crossed the Byelorussian railroad tracks, and a short time later Hollis saw the utility poles of the old Minsk-Moscow road and the town of Mozhaisk in the distance. 'Well, we got around Mozhaisk. I wonder if Boris and Igor are pacing up and down Main Street waiting for us.'

'Who are Boris and Igor?'

'Embassy watchers.'

'Oh.'

Hollis crossed the main road and continued on the farm roads. Within fifteen minutes he intersected the poplar-lined road to Borodino Field and turned on to it. Ahead he saw the stone columns and towering gates that led to the battlefield. The gates were closed, and as they drew near they could see the gates were chained.

Lisa said, 'I think these outdoor exhibits and such close early this time of year.'

'That's what I counted on.' Hollis swung the Zhiguli between two bare poplars and into the drainage ditch. He followed the ditch that skirted the gates, then cut back on to the road and proceeded toward the museum. 'You've never been here?'

'As I said, I've never been able to get a pass out of Moscow . . . except to stay at the Finnish *dacha*.'

Hollis nodded. The Finnish dacha – so named because of its architecture and saunas – was a newly built country house for American embassy staffers on the Klyazma River, about an hour's drive north of Moscow. The ambassador's dacha for senior staff such as himself was nearby. An invitation to spend a weekend at the ambassador's house was very nearly a punishment. But the Finnish dacha had quickly earned a reputation, and families did not go there. One night, from his bedroom window in the ambassador's place, Hollis had listened to the happy noises of men and women and splashing hot tubs coming from the Finnish dacha in the woods until dawn.

Katherine, who had been with him then, had commented, 'Why are they allowed to have so much fun and we have to drink sherry with stuffed shirts?' Within the month she had departed on her shopping trip. Hollis asked Lisa, 'Go there much?'

She glanced at him. 'No . . . it was sort of like the office Christmas party and on Monday morning everyone avoided everyone else. You know?'

'I think so.' Hollis saw the gravel parking field ahead with the museum to the right. He said, 'I was here once. A reception of military attachés last October on the anniversary of the German-Russian battle here in 1941. Interesting place.'

'It looks it.' They kept silent as the car continued through the lot on to a narrow lane. The sun was gone, and the night had become very still. She noticed bright twinkling stars between scattered clouds. The deep, dark quiet of the countryside at night surprised her. 'Spooky.'

'Romantic.'

She smiled despite herself. The moon broke through the clouds and revealed a dozen polished obelisks standing like shimmering sentries over the dead.

'Borodino,' Hollis said softly. 'Fisher would have come this way, past the museum. The trick is to retrace how he got lost. Reach back in my briefcase and find the serial survey map.'

She did as Hollis said. 'This it?'

'Yes. Unfold it and put it in your lap. If we're stopped, hit it with your cigarette lighter. It's flash paper and will go up in a second without too much heat, smoke, or ash.'

'Okay.'

'Under your seat should be a red-filtered flashlight.'

She reached beneath her seat and brought out the light.

Hollis said, 'We know he drove through the battlefield, then he said he found himself on a road in the woods north of Borodino Field, about this time at night. Further north is the Moskva River and the power station and reservoir. So he must have been between here and the river. The only woods on that aerial map is the *bor* – the pine forest. See it?'

'Yes.' She looked up from the map. 'I see pine trees there in the hills. See?'

'Yes. Those are the hills just south of the Moskva. Now I'm coming to a fork in the road.'

She shone the red light on the map. 'Yes, I see it here. If you take the left fork it will loop back and begin to climb that hill.'

Hollis nodded. The left fork appeared to head back toward the museum, but did not. This was where Fisher must have made his fatal error. Hollis took the left fork.

With the headlights off they drove on, and the land began to rise. A few pines stood on the grassy fields, then the road entered the thick tree line, and it became very dark. Lisa cleared her throat. 'Can you see?'

'Just shine the red light out the window once in a while.'

She rolled down the window, letting in a cold blast of air. The red light picked out the narrow road, and Hollis followed the beam. He said, 'How you doing?'

'Okay. How're *you* doing?'

'Fine,' Hollis replied. 'Nice woods. I like that word – *bor*. Very evocative, very Russian. I think of a deep, dark pine forest of old Muscovy, woodcarvers and woodcutters, log cabins, pine pitch boiling over fires of crackling logs. Sort of fairytalish. *Bor*.'

She looked at him but said nothing.

They continued up the ridge line, the Zhiguli moving very slowly, its high rpm engine whining in first gear. Lisa said, 'Can I smoke?'

'No.'

'I'm getting shaky.'

'Want to go back?'

She hesitated before replying, 'Later.'

Ten minutes later they approached a sign, and Hollis stopped the car. Lisa shone the light on the sign, and they both read the words: STOP! YOU ARE ENTERING A RESTRICTED AREA. TURN BACK!

'This,' Hollis said, 'must be the place. I was getting worried that we might have taken the wrong road.'

'We did take the wrong road.'

Hollis got out and looked around, discovering the small turnaround off the right side of the road. He opened the trunk and ripped out the wires for the back-up lights and the brake lights, then got in the car. He drove into the turnaround, but instead of backing out, continued between the pine trees until the Zhiguli was some twenty yards into the forest. He turned the car so it pointed back toward the road, then killed the engine.

Lisa said nothing.

Hollis whispered, 'Keep a sharp ear and eye out. Be ready to make a quick getaway. If I'm not back within the hour, you go on to Mozhaisk and take care of the morgue business. Tell whoever asks that I didn't come along. Get behind the wheel and lower the window. See you later.'

Hollis got out, softly closed the door, and began walking through the woods on a course parallel to the road.

Lisa came up beside him. 'You're crazy.'

'Go back.'

'No.'

They walked side by side. The forest floor was springy, covered with a carpet of pine needles and cones. The spaces between the trunks were clear except for clumps of ferns and pine saplings. There was no wind, and the resinous pine scent was overpowering. There was little sound except for the soft tread of their shoes on the needles and the occasional crunch of a pine cone. The forest was very dark. Lisa whispered, 'Sam, we have no business here . . . no . . . cover . . . even with diplomatic immunity.'

'Our cover is that we're gathering mushrooms. The Russians are great mushroom gatherers. They'll relate to that.'

'There are no mushrooms in pine forests.'

'Really? Then we're on a sexual escapade.'

'Then we should be in the backseat of the Zhiguli.'

'Well, think of a cover yourself then. In the meantime, let's not get caught. I assume you're coming with me.'

'Yes.'

Within a few minutes they saw signs nailed to the trees at intervals. Hollis and Lisa approached one, and she turned the red-filtered flashlight on it and read: STOP! GO BACK. YOU ARE IN A RESTRICTED AREA. YOU ARE SUBJECT TO ARREST.

Hollis put his mouth to Lisa's ear and whispered, 'There may be sound sensors. Step lightly, like a deer.'

She nodded.

Hollis put his hand on her shoulder and felt her shaking. 'Do you want to go back to the car?'

She shook her head.

Hollis drew his Tokarev pistol from his ankle holster and slipped it into his pocket. They continued through the forest. A half moon was rising and cast a weak blue light into the patches of clearing, which they avoided. Occasionally they saw signs with the same message, then Lisa pointed to a new sign in a clearing. They approached it cautiously and read: STOP! ARMED GUARDS HAVE ORDERS TO SHOOT.

Hollis whispered, 'We're almost there.'

They heard a noise behind them and spun around. Hollis dropped to one knee and brought out his automatic. Lisa crouched beside him. The pine boughs on the far side of the small clearing moved, then parted. A small doe entered the clearing and came toward them, then abruptly stopped not ten feet away, sniffed the still, heavy air, turned, and ran.

Hollis holstered his pistol and stood. They moved on. Within five minutes they found themselves facing an eight-foot-tall fence of barbed wire, topped with coiled razor wire. A metal sign on the fence warned: HIGH VOLTAGE.

On the other side of the wire, the pine trees had been cut to a depth of about fifty meters. Hollis could see an inner ring of more barbed wire at the far edge of the treeless zone. A watchtower rose up from the inner wire. He whispered, 'Mrs Ivanova's Charm School.'

She nodded. 'Not charming.'

Hollis peered at the watchtower, then scanned the inner fence, beyond which he could make out the glow of lights. He took Lisa's arm, and they walked carefully along the barbed wire, coming across the decomposed carcass of a deer that had been electrocuted. Lisa said, 'Sam, let's go now.'

He pulled her down. 'Listen.'

The stillness of the forest was broken by the sound of a diesel engine, then they saw headlights coming toward them. Hollis whispered, 'Get down.' They both dropped on to the pine carpet, facing the wire. The headlights grew brighter, and they could see the vehicle moving slowly through the raked sand of the clear zone between the barbed wire fences. The vehicle got closer and louder. Hollis could see it was a half-track with an open troop compartment in the rear. There were two men in the cab, and in the rear he saw six helmeted soldiers. Two were manning a swivel-mounted machine gun, two manned a searchlight, and two stood at port arms as though ready to spring from the vehicle. Hollis hoped it was a random patrol, but the soldiers looked too tense and alert. As the vehicle drew within ten yards of them, Hollis could make out the special green uniforms of the KGB Border Guards. He whispered to Lisa, 'Pull the scarf over your face and cover your hands.'

Hollis pulled his knit cap down, and it became a ski mask. He put on black nylon gloves and waited. The half-track drew abreast of them on the other side of the wire, not fifteen feet away. Hollis assumed that the sound or motion sensors had picked up something and the patrol was sent to determine if it was a four-or two-legged animal. He could hear the men talking to one another, then heard a radio crackle in the truck's cab. A transmitted voice said, 'Well, are you all awake out there? What are you doing, Grechko?'

The man sitting beside the driver responded into his handset, '*Khula grushi okolachivahu.*' *Whacking pears with my prick.*

The voice on the radio laughed, then said, 'Shoot a bear for the colonel, and he will get you all laid in Moscow. Shoot a spy, and he will take the credit.'

Grechko replied, 'Then it's bear we're after.'

The driver laughed as he hit the brakes and the half-track came to a halt opposite Hollis and Lisa. The search-light snapped on, and a beam shot down the cleared area, then began sweeping the woods beyond the wire. The beam moved closer to Hollis and Lisa, illuminating the ferns and tree trunks along the ground in a bright bluish light. The beam came toward them, passed over, continued on, then came back quickly and stopped on the carcass of the deer ten yards down the fence. The beam swept away from the deer and continued on.

Hollis felt Lisa shaking beside him. He found her hand under her body and squeezed it. They waited. After a minute the half-track moved on. They remained motionless, barely breathing.

After five full minutes Hollis rose cautiously to one knee, keeping a hand on Lisa's back. He peered intently into the darkness and listened closely, then helped her up. They turned away from the barbed wire, and Hollis saw, not ten feet into the trees, two KGB Border Guards moving toward them, carrying AK-47 rifles at the ready.

In an instant Hollis realized Lisa had not seen them, and they had not seen him or her. Lisa moved toward him to say something. The KGB men saw the motion. Hollis in a single movement pushed Lisa to the ground, dropped into a crouch, and drew his Tokarev automatic from his pocket. Hollis fired the silenced pistol and saw the first man slap his hand to his chest. The second man looked dumbstruck as he stared at his falling companion, then turned to Hollis and brought his rifle into the firing position. Hollis put two rounds into the man's chest, then stepped the ten feet towards them. He saw they were both still alive, lying on their backs, blood bubbling at their lips. They were both very young, perhaps still in their teens. Hollis took both AK-47s by their straps and slung them over his shoulder. As he threw pine branches over the two men, Lisa came up beside him. 'Oh . . . oh, God . . . Sam!'

'Quiet.' He slung a rifle over her shoulder, took her by the arm, and they moved in long rapid strides through the pine forest. Hollis was no longer concerned about the sensors since there were patrols out now, making their own noise.

Within ten minutes they intersected the road some distance from the car. Hollis got his bearings and found the Zhiguli among the trees. They threw the AK-47s into the back and jumped inside. Hollis started the engine and threw the car into gear, but instead of heading on to the road, turned and went deeper into the woods, maneuvering through the widely spaced tree trunks.

'Sam, where are you going?'

'Not back on the road, to be sure. You shine that red light ahead and find room.'

She leaned out the window with the light.

Hollis wove through the pine forest. Behind them they could hear a vehicle and see headlights on the road they'd come up. Lisa said, 'These trees are getting closer. Watch out.'

Hollis crushed both fenders between two tree trunks, and the Zhiguli got stuck. He tried to throw it into reverse but the linkage stuck. 'Damned piece of junk.'

Hollis got it into reverse, pulled out, and found another way through the trees. Low-lying boughs fanned the windshield, leaving sticky needles on the glass. Hollis knew that it was possible to get a vehicle through an evergreen forest, and in fact whole columns of trucks and armor passed through these Russian pine forests during the war without having to knock down a single tree. It was just a matter of finding the spaces. 'Keep that light out there, Lisa.'

'Okay. Look over there.' She pointed the light, and Hollis saw a wide opening toward which he headed. It was a game trail, like a tunnel through the boughs, the width and height of a good-sized buck. The Zhiguli fitted into it nicely, and Hollis accelerated to five kph.

Lisa glanced back. 'I think I see lights in the woods.' She looked at him. 'Are we going to make it?'

'No problem.' Hollis guessed that the Russians didn't know for sure if they were dealing with spies or bears. But if they found the two bodies, the whole countryside would be crawling with militia, Red Army, and KGB.

The ground began to slope down at a steeper angle, and the Zhiguli started to slide, though Hollis was applying the brake. Suddenly the car broke out of the trees and began plunging headlong into a ravine. 'Hold on!' The Zhiguli hit the trough of the ravine and splashed into a shallow stream, nearly overturning. Hollis cut the wheels hard right and accelerated through the streambed. He gave it more gas, pushing the battered car on downstream. The banks flattened, and the stream became wider and deeper. The Zhiguli's engine began coughing. 'Getting wet.' Hollis angled the car toward a low spot in the bank and pushed the gas pedal to the floor. The car went up the bank, faltered, then the engine roared, and the Zhiguli came out of the streambed. A blue half moon shone through the broken cloud cover, and they both looked through the windshield at Borodino Field spread out in front of them. Hollis said, 'Good trail car.'

Lisa lit a cigarette with shaking hands and drew in deeply. She exhaled a long stream of smoke. 'Want one?'

'No, you enjoy yourself.'

She said, 'This is not what I thought you meant by a drive in the country.'

'Well,' Hollis replied, 'this is the country, and we're driving in it.' Hollis pulled the car into a copse of birches. He retrieved the two AK-47s and threw them out the window into the high grass, then flung his pistol, ankle holster, and spare ammunition clips after them. 'Burn the map.'

Lisa hung the map out the window and touched it with her lighter. The map flashed and disappeared in a small puff of smoke. She said, 'We're out of the woods, but we're not out of the woods.'

'Getting there.' Hollis put the car in gear and moved out over the rolling fields of high yellow grass. From the crest of a hill they saw the road they'd taken into the forest. Hollis steered a course parallel to the road, cutting cross-country. They heard a helicopter overhead, and Hollis drove into the moonshadow on the dark side of a granite obelisk. The helicopter passed over, casting a moonshadow of its own. Hollis waited until the helicopter descended into the forest in the vicinity of the Charm School, then moved the car again.

Lisa spoke as though she had just concluded a silent conversation with herself. 'It wasn't in cold blood.'

Hollis glanced at her.

She said, 'I feel sick.'

'It's a sickening thing. Shooting people. I used to bomb people. Never saw them. Take a deep breath.'

She put her head out of the window, inhaled a long breath, and slumped back in her seat.

Hollis drove the car hard over the grassy fields. He knew that time and place were critical. If they could get where they were supposed to be, at the morgue in Mozhaisk, they could bluff it. But if they were caught in the open country, the evidence would be strongly against them.

They came upon a small dirt road that marked the boundary of the historic battlefield. On the other side of the road was furrowed farmland. Hollis didn't think the Zhiguli had any more tolerance for abuse, so he cut on to the dirt tractor road and turned north toward the Moskva River. He accelerated up the straight road and hit ninety kph when the car started to shimmy. He eased off, and the Zhiguli settled down. The tractor road ended at the Moscow river road, and Hollis turned right, approaching Mozhaisk from the west, rather than from the Moscow road where they might be waiting for him. He turned on the headlights and threw his wool cap out the window. Lisa threw her scarf out and brushed herself off, then brushed pine needles off Hollis' clothing as he drove. Hollis made a fast run into Mozhaisk without encountering another vehicle.

The town seemed eerily deserted for an early Saturday evening. Hollis handed Lisa a piece of paper. 'Directions to the morgue.'

She read them, and at length they arrived in front of a squat white stucco building near the railroad tracks. A wooden sign over the door said MORG. Hollis looked at his watch. It was just after eight P.M. They got out of the car and walked to the door. He said to her, 'Are you up to this, or do you want to sit in the car?'

'I'm up to *this*. I've done consular work. I wasn't up to the other thing.'

'You were fine.'

'Thank you. And you have brass balls.'

'I show off around women. That's why I brought you along.' He pushed a button marked NIGHT BELL, and they waited. Hollis put his hand on her shoulder and noted she wasn't shaking. This was a very cool woman, he thought.

The heavy wooden door to the morgue opened, revealing a man wearing the uniform of a KGB colonel. The man said in English, 'Come in.'

10

The KGB colonel cocked his finger under Hollis' nose, turned, and walked away.

Hollis and Lisa followed him through a dark, musty room furnished as a sitting room, and Hollis recalled that a municipal morgue often doubled as a funeral parlor. They entered a cold room of white ceramic tile, and Hollis was hit by that smell of chemicals whose purpose one would instantly recognize. The Russian pulled a hanging string, and a bright fluorescent light flickered on, illuminating a white enameled freezer chest of a type found in America in the 1950s. Without formalities the colonel opened the freezer lid, exposing the body of a naked man lying in the white frost.

The corpse's arms and legs were askew, and his head lolled to one side. Gregory Fisher's eyelids had not been closed, and the staring blue eyes revealed frozen tears. Cracked teeth showed through parted blue lips.

Hollis noticed that Fisher's chest and face were deeply lacerated and that the blood had not been properly cleaned off. The young man's cuts and bruises were deep purple against his white flesh. Hollis studied Fisher's face and was able to discern the features of a once good-looking man in his early twenties. Hollis felt sorry for Gregory Fisher, whose voice had become familiar to him with each replay of the tape. Hollis wondered if they'd had to torture him to make him tell them about Dodson.

The KGB colonel handed Hollis a passport, which Hollis opened to the photo page. He glanced at the color photograph of a tanned, smiling face, then handed the passport to Lisa. She looked at the photo, then at the corpse, and nodded. She slipped the passport into her bag.

The colonel slammed the freezer shut and motioned them

into a small cubicle in which sat a battered birch desk and three mismatched chairs. He indicated two of the chairs, then took the better chair behind the desk and turned on a shaded reading lamp. He said in English, 'You are Colonel Hollis of course, and this must be Lisa Rhodes.'

'That's correct,' Hollis answered. 'And you are a colonel of the KGB. I didn't hear your name.'

'Burov.' He added, 'You understand that with the death of a foreigner, Soviet law states that the KGB must process the paperwork and so forth. You should attach no further meaning to my presence.'

'If you say so.'

Burov leaned forward and stared at Hollis. 'I say so.' Burov asked, 'And am I to attach any meaning to *your* presence, Colonel Hollis?'

'No, you are not.' But of course, Hollis knew, they were both lying. As soon as the Soviet Foreign Ministry saw that it was Hollis and not a consular officer who applied for the pass, they notified the KGB, and the KGB, wanting to see what Colonel Hollis was about, told the Foreign Ministry to issue it. The simple matter of transferring the remains had escalated into something like a counterintelligence operation. Hollis wondered what would provoke the KGB to kill him and Lisa out here. Probably the Borodino side trip, if they knew about that. That's what got Fisher into the ice chest in the next room.

Burov said, 'You are several hours later than I expected. You kept me waiting.'

'I had no idea you *were* waiting, Colonel.'

'Oh, please, you knew very well . . . anyway, what caused your delay?'

Hollis looked closely at Burov in the dim light. He placed Burov in his mid-forties. He was a tall, well-built man with those pursed boyish lips that were prevalent in the north around Leningrad and Finland. His skin was fair, his eyes were blue, and his hair was flaxen yellow, reinforcing Hollis' impression that Burov was more Nordic than Slavic. He may have had

Finnish blood, or he may have been one of the many legacies left by the German army. His age was right for that. In fact, Hollis thought, if Mosfilm were looking for a typical Nazi heavy for one of their innumerable war movies, Burov would do nicely.

'Colonel Hollis – what caused your delay?'

Hollis replied, 'Your Foreign Ministry held up the passes.' Hollis leaned toward Burov and added sharply, 'Why does everything in this country take twice as long as it does in the civilized world?'

Burov's face reddened. 'What the hell do you mean by that?'

'Your English is excellent. It means what you know it means.'

Lisa was somewhat surprised at Hollis' strong language, but she suspected that Hollis was putting Burov on the defensive regarding the question of their lateness.

Burov sat back in his chair and lit an oval-shaped Troika cigarette. The heat from the first two puffs caused the flimsy paper and loose tobacco to sag. Burov automatically straightened the cigarette with his fingers. He said in a calmer tone, 'That was not very diplomatic of you, Colonel. I thought diplomats would sooner bite their tongues off than say anything so offensive against their host country.'

Hollis glanced at his watch in a gesture of impatience, then replied, 'Diplomat-to-diplomat, that may be true. But you know who I am, and I know who you are. And if you ever cock your finger under my nose again, you'd better be prepared to lose it. Now, do you have something for us to sign?'

Burov stared down at the cigarette in his hand, and Hollis could only imagine what thoughts were running through the man's mind. Burov crushed out his cigarette on the floor and said, 'Many things to sign.'

'I'm sure.'

Burov opened a green file folder on the desk and withdrew a stack of papers.

Lisa said to Burov, 'I think the body could have been treated with more care.'

Burov looked at her with the expression of a man who is not used to dealing with women on a professional basis. 'Is that so? Why do *veryushchii* – he used the Russian word for believers in God – 'care about mortal remains? The soul is in paradise now. Correct?'

'Why do you assume I'm a believer?'

'You might well ask why I assumed you knew Russian, Ms Rhodes. Should I assume you're here to write a very nice press release on the joys of motor travel in the Soviet Union? Or will it be about the speed and efficiency of having one's body shipped back to the States in the event of a mishap?' Burov smiled for the first time, and Lisa actually felt a chill run through her.

Lisa drew a deep but discreet breath and said forcefully, 'I must request that the body be more carefully cleaned and that it be properly shrouded.'

'Did the young man's naked body offend you?'

'The way he was *thrown* in the freezer like a carcass offended me, Colonel.'

'Really? Well, the state of Mr Fisher's remains is no concern of mine. Take that up with the mortician.' Burov shuffled through some papers with a look of disdain, as if to show that this aspect of their business was beneath him.

Lisa seemed not to heed Burov's advice and asked, 'How do you propose we transport the body to the airport?'

Burov replied curtly, 'The mortician will provide an aluminum air coffin with dry ice. As in any *civilized* country. You must sign a charge for that. As you would in America.' He added, 'I see you are driving a Zhiguli. How do you intend to fit a coffin in that?'

Lisa answered, 'We have no intention of transporting the coffin ourselves. You will provide us with an appropriate vehicle and driver. As any other country would.'

Burov smiled again as if to suggest he found Lisa amusing. He eyed Lisa's *vatnik*, then commented, 'You both seemed to have dressed as though you intended to be gravediggers as well as pallbearers. Well, we'll work something out. May I examine your travel passes and credentials?'

Hollis and Lisa handed him their passes and diplomatic passports. Burov seemed interested in Hollis' visa stamps and made no secret of writing down the entry and departure dates to the dozen or so countries represented on the visa pages.

Hollis considered Colonel Burov. The man spoke unusually good English and was quick-witted in it as well as insulting and sarcastic. Russians dealing with foreigners, especially Western-ers, were usually polite, though if they weren't they were simply abrasive and blunt – not so sharp as Burov was. Hollis guessed that Burov had a lot of dealings with English-speaking people and perhaps he was a graduate of the Institute of Canadian and American Studies in Moscow, a place that turned out as many KGB men as it did scholars and diplomats. Hollis had seen some of those smooth Russians on American TV, explaining in American idiom their country's position on anything from human rights to why they obliterated a passenger plane full of people. Hollis would have liked to get a line on Burov, but he doubted that Alevy or anyone had anything on the man. Burov was not his name anyway, though the KGB uniform and the rank were real. Using an alias was one thing; stepping down in life was quite another. Hollis said, 'Are you quite through with our passports?'

Burov made a few more notations, then handed back the passports but kept the travel passes. Burov handed Hollis a sheet of paper and said, 'Firstly, the dead man's automobile has been impounded, and it will be easier if you sign that document waiving any claim on it.'

Hollis replied, 'I want to see the car.'

'Why?'

'To see if it has any salvage value.'

'I assure you it doesn't. In any case, the car has been shipped to Moscow. I will have your embassy informed of the location, if you wish. Will you sign that?'

139

Hollis glanced at the waiver, written in Russian and English. There were a lot of numbers showing that the car would cost more to ship out of the Soviet Union than it was presently worth. The real bottom line was that there was no way the Trans Am was getting back to the States to be examined by the FBI forensic unit. Hollis handed back the waiver, unsigned. 'After I inspect the car I'll decide what disposition should be made.'

Burov pushed it back to Hollis again. 'Then please note that on the waiver so we can proceed.'

Hollis felt that it could be a long night. The Russians were, if nothing else, patient and plodding. Hollis made a notation on the waiver but instead of giving it back said, 'I must have a copy of this.'

'Of course.' Burov gave him a faint carbon copy of the same document, simultaneously taking the original from Hollis.

Lisa had the impression that Hollis and Burov had both been through this before in one form or another. The protocols of diplomacy, the give and take, the one-upmanship, the bluffing and posturing. It didn't matter whether the issue was the disposition of mortal remains or nuclear disarmament. Men, she had observed, loved to talk deals.

'Item two,' Burov said, 'an inventory of the personal items on the body and in the automobile. The items are in an air container and can be shipped to the deceased's home address at your embassy's expense, if you authorize that.' He handed Hollis the inventory.

Hollis leaned toward Lisa, and they both read the list, written in Russian. The list seemed very complete and included in addition to clothes and luggage, two watches, a school ring, a camera, and even items that were meant to be small gifts, such as pens, razors, and postcards. It didn't appear to Hollis as if anyone had helped himself to anything. This either meant that the peasants, local militia, and morgue employees had all the Western consumer goods they needed, or more likely that this had been a KGB operation from start to finish.

Burov said, 'The lubricants and other things that were in the trunk are not in the air container because they are inflammable. You will see that there were fruits and vegetables in the car that cannot be shipped because of American customs regulations. We will be happy to send the lubricants and produce to the American embassy. In fact, you can take them back yourself. The pears look quite good.'

'*You* can take the pears, Colonel, put a light coat of lubricant on them, and shove them.'

'Shove them? Where?'

Hollis had the distinct impression that Burov knew the idiom well enough to know exactly where.

Burov shrugged and continued, 'All Intourist vouchers will be redeemed and a Western bank draft sent to the embassy for forwarding to Mr Fisher's next of kin. I have six hundred and eighty dollars in American Express traveler's checks, seventy-two dollars in American currency, and small assorted sums of European currency, which I will give you now. There were also thirty-two rubles and seventy-eight kopeks, which I can also give you.'

Hollis thought of Fisher's words on the tape. *I gave him maps and money*. And the French woman's statement that Fisher had borrowed two kopeks from her. Hollis concluded that Burov had thrown the Russian money in the kitty so as not to raise any questions. Hollis said, 'I don't see any maps listed on this inventory.'

Burov did not reply.

'Fisher surely had maps.' Hollis studied Burov's face. 'Perhaps someone took them.'

Burov waved his hand. 'They would be of small monetary value.'

'Nevertheless, I'll bet you'd like to know where those maps are now, Colonel Burov.'

Burov stared at Hollis.

Hollis was fairly convinced now that Dodson was not in KGB hands, dead or alive. Hollis pressed on. 'If the maps should somehow turn up at the American embassy, I'll let you know so you don't worry yourself about them.'

Burov pursed his lips thoughtfully as if he was considering that possibility and finding it somewhat distressing. He said, 'I'll bet you we find those maps before you do.'

'I'll take that bet. What are the stakes?'

'Very high, Colonel Hollis.'

Hollis nodded. If Dodson made it to the embassy or to a Western reporter in Moscow, his story would effectively end Soviet-American relations for about a decade.

Burov seemed to understand what Hollis was thinking and said bluntly and not too cryptically, 'The stakes are peace.'

'Indeed they are.'

Burov went back to the business at hand. 'We are holding the exposed film we found. We will have the film developed and will send the prints to your embassy. You understand that the KGB could not possibly let exposed film pass through its hands without a peek.'

Hollis looked up and saw that Burov was grinning at his own bad joke. Hollis replied, 'I don't see anything amusing about this. A young man is dead.'

Burov continued to grin, and Hollis had the impulse to smash his fist into those ripe cherry lips. Lisa began to say something, but Hollis laid a hand on her arm and said to Burov, 'And of course you returned the key or *propusk* to the Rossiya.'

'There was no key or *propusk*, Colonel Hollis. Gregory Fisher never got to Moscow.'

'You know he did. We know he did.'

The paperwork and unpleasantness continued for another half hour. Finally Burov leaned back and abruptly observed, 'You have been walking in the woods.'

Hollis looked up from a document and replied, 'Picking mushrooms.'

'Really? You are real Russians now. Can you tell which are the poisonous *gribi*?'

'I guess so. I'm still alive.'

Burov laughed with real mirth, then leaned forward across the desk and still smiling said, 'May I see the mushrooms? I'm a fancier of them myself.'

'I'm afraid we weren't very lucky.'

'I should think not in a pine forest.'

Hollis assumed that Burov had noticed a few pine needles or smelled the scent that clung to them, or perhaps he had more solid information. It was difficult, Hollis had learned, to know what these people knew for sure and what they were guessing at. They knew too much about each person in the embassy right down to the staffers in the USIS such as Lisa. On the other hand, Hollis knew very little about the Soviets with whom he came into contact, and he knew nothing about Colonel Burov, which was a distinct disadvantage. Hollis stood. 'Will you find us a truck and driver now? We'd like to set out for the airport.'

Burov remained seated. 'That's not possible at this hour. You'll have to spend the night.'

'Do you mean to tell me,' Hollis asked with a touch of sarcasm, 'that a colonel of the KGB can't round up a truck and driver because it's after six o'clock?'

'I mean to tell you, Colonel Hollis, that unescorted night driving in the countryside is not permitted for foreigners. Diplomats included.'

'Then get us an escort.'

'Secondly,' Burov continued, 'when your car arrived, I noticed that neither your taillights nor your brake lights were working. You must see to that in the morning. Unfortunately there is no service station in Mozhaisk, nor a hotel. However, there is a *sovkhoz* – a state farm – two kilometers from here. They will find you rooms in the commune building. There is also a mechanic there. I will write you a note, and they will be pleased to give you accommodations.'

Hollis glanced at Lisa, then said to Burov, 'I don't see that we have any choice. But I require a truck and driver at eight in the morning.'

Burov laughed. 'This is not America, and I am not an

American boss, only a colonel in State Security. Expect the driver between nine and ten.' He gathered the paperwork into his attaché case, then made a notation on their travel passes. 'This is valid now until noon tomorrow and also will give you entry to the state farm. See that you're within the Moscow city limits by noon.' Burov indicated the way out.

Hollis said, 'I want to call my embassy.'

'I don't think there's a phone here. Follow me, please.' Burov snapped off the light in the cubicle and led them through the dark morgue.

They stood outside on the front steps of the morgue, and Burov gave them directions to the farth. Burov added, 'There will be a large wooden sign over the entrance to the farm road that will read 'Forty Years of October; Grain and Livestock Enterprise'. You read Russian of course.'

Hollis supposed the name had something to do with the Great October Revolution, but there were only so many constructions you could make out of the words *Red, October, Revolution*, and *Great* before you had to start stretching it a bit. Hollis said, 'The Red Livestock . . . what?'

Lisa suppressed a laugh.

Burov said curtly, 'The October – no, the Forty Years of October –'

'What the hell does that mean?'

'How do I know?' snapped Burov. 'The farm was probably founded on the fortieth anniversary of the October Revolution.' He glared at Hollis. 'You damned people are so superior, aren't you? So smug and so glib. Well, one day we'll see who . . .' Burov seemed to realize he had let himself be baited and recovered his composure. 'Well, I'm sure you won't have trouble in finding it. An old couple sleeps in the administration building. Knock loudly.'

Lisa said, 'Where can we find a telephone?'

'On the state farm. And showers, so you can get that resin off you.' Burov touched his finger to a sticky smudge on her hand.

144

Lisa jerked her hand away.

Burov walked to the Zhiguli and looked at the license plate. 'A rental car?'

'There were no embassy cars available.'

'Even so, Colonel Hollis, it is not legal for you to drive this car.'

'Don't sweat the small stuff, Colonel. Do you know what that means?'

Burov walked around the car. 'This car has been driven roughly . . . mud, pine twigs . . .' He pulled a cluster of pine needles from the chrome and twirled it in his fingers. 'And the doors and fenders are newly dented. They will charge you for that. Where did you rent this?'

'My staff rented it for me.'

'May I see the rental papers?'

'No.'

'No?'

'No.' Hollis opened the driver's-side door. 'Good evening, Colonel Burov.'

Lisa opened her door and got in the car, but Burov put his hand on the door so she couldn't close it. He said, 'There are three main sights around Mozhaisk – Saint Nicholas' Cathedral, Luzhetsky monastery ruins, and Borodino. You may have time to drive by all three, if you are early risers. Borodino is especially interesting to Westerners because of *War and Peace*.'

Hollis replied, 'I have no interest in battlefields.'

'No? It's a passion with us, I'm afraid. Too much war in this land. We keep having to teach people lessons.'

Hollis observed undiplomatically, 'I don't think either side learned anything at Borodino.'

Burov looked at him quizzically. 'You must reread your history. It was a great Russian victory.'

Hollis studied the man across the roof of the car. Hollis believed that the one fatal flaw in the Soviet system was not economic, political, or military, but informational. Soviet facts had replaced truth and reality. Hollis said to Burov, 'If you have nothing further, please close Ms Rhodes' door.'

Burov moved away from the car without closing the door, and Lisa pulled it shut, locking it.

Burov stood on the sidewalk and called out to Hollis, 'Don't get lost. And be careful on the highway. We don't have room for two more bodies in the freezer.'

Hollis said, 'Go fuck yourself, Colonel.'

'And yourself as well, Colonel.'

Then, as they both understood the rules of the game, they saluted simultaneously and bade each other good-evening.

11

As Hollis drove away from the morgue, he saw a black Chaika in his rearview mirror. He drove slowly through the dark, quiet streets of Mozhaisk, and the Chaika stayed with him.

Lisa said, 'Colonel Burov was a nasty son of a bitch.'

'He must have had a fight with his wife this morning.'

'Did he know about our side trip to Borodino or not?'

'He made the correct deduction. Soon, however, when they find the two Border Guards, he will have no doubt.'

'Will he try to kill us for that?'

Hollis considered a moment before replying. 'No, not for that. Burov understands that.'

'But for what we saw.'

'Perhaps,' Hollis replied. 'Anyway, I told you in Moscow, these people are unpredictable. Our best defense is to be as unpredictable.'

'Meaning we shouldn't go to the state farm.'

'Precisely.'

'Can we get back to Moscow?'

'Not a chance.' Hollis glanced in his rearview mirror again. 'We have company, as we say.'

Lisa nodded. 'Then let's go someplace where we can be alone.'

Hollis smiled. He entered the center of town, a collection of two-story wood and stucco buildings around a traffic circle. There was streetlighting but not much other evidence that the town was inhabited. The main street of Mozhaisk was the old Minsk-Moscow road, and Hollis headed west on it toward the state farm. The Chaika followed. Hollis wondered if it was Boris and Igor in the car.

The road curved away from the Moskva River, and soon they

found themselves traveling a very dark stretch of bad pavement, utterly alone on the vast Russian plain. Hollis could not see a single light from a dwelling, only the headlights of the Chaika in his mirror.

'What's faster,' Lisa asked, 'a Chaika or a Zhiguli?'

'Don't ask.'

'You don't have any more guns on you, do you?'

'No.'

'They could kill us pretty easily out here.'

'Not that easily.'

'Maybe they just want to see that we get to the state farm.'

'Probably.' Hollis, in fact, couldn't determine what they were up to. He was sorry he'd thrown away the pistol, but in the Soviet Union he was a criminal, and criminals ditched the evidence. And in truth, if the people in the Chaika pulled him over and found the Tokarev pistol, the least they would do was charge him with murder, diplomatic immunity notwithstanding. More likely they'd kill him. On the other hand, if he had the Tokarev, he could eliminate the men in the Chaika.

Lisa looked through the envelope stuffed with papers and traveler's checks that Burov had given them. 'Even if they did murder that boy, they are very correct when it comes to legalities.'

'When it suits them. Did you get the impression Colonel Burov was worried about Major Jack Dodson?'

'Oh, yes. Major Dodson is still out there somewhere with Gregory Fisher's rubles and maps.'

'That's right. And if Dodson makes it to the embassy, which is where I suppose he's heading,' Hollis added, 'then tons of shit will hit the fan and splatter everything from here to Washington. We'll all be home in a week, leaving the night porter as chargé d'affaires.'

Lisa didn't respond.

Three kilometers out of town, Hollis and Lisa spotted the huge wooden sign set on two poles over the entrance road to the *sovkhoz* – the state farm. Beneath the name of the *sovkhoz* was the inspirational message: *We will strive to meet the quotas of the Central Committee.*

Lisa said, 'Well, pardner, welcome to the Lazy Red Revolution October Ranch.'

Hollis managed a smile and turned into the gravel road, then proceeded toward the state farm. They could make out a large group of stark wooden farm buildings, corrugated metal sheds, and a three-story concrete building that Hollis took to be the commune, which housed the salaried workers of the state farms and their families, the single and transient workers, and the technicians, all under one roof. There were individual sitting rooms and bedrooms in the apartments, but the kitchens, dining rooms, and bathrooms were communal. It seemed to Hollis that there was something of *Brave New World* in those prefab apartment blocks rising out of the farmland, something unnatural about people who worked the soil having no yard and garden of their own, climbing stairs to their apartment.

Lisa looked back and announced, 'I see the Chaika's headlights turning onto this road . . . he just killed his lights.'

Hollis drove on past the commune and spotted the small brick structure that Burov told them was the administration building. There was a single light in one window. Hollis shut off his headlights, drove past the building and continued on.

Lisa said, 'You think it's a setup?'

'Quite possibly.'

'What are we going to do now?'

Hollis replied, 'Our little Zhiguli didn't have much chance on the main road, but back here on the farm lanes we can give the Chaika a run.'

'Is this another itinerary violation?'

'Quite possibly.' There was not much available light, but Hollis could pick out the dirt and gravel road from the surrounding fields of the famous Russian black earth. Hollis sped up, hitting the brake whenever he saw an intersecting lane and turning onto it. Without brake lights or headlights the Zhiguli was virtually invisible, and after fifteen minutes

149

of random turnings Hollis announced, 'We've lost the Chaika. Unfortunately *we're* lost.'

'No kidding?'

'Did you notice any Holiday Inns back there?'

'Way back. Like two years and ten thousand miles back. Say, Sam, you really know how to show a girl a good time. Let me buy lunch next time. Okay?'

'I'm glad you've maintained your sense of humor, Miss Rhodes, as vapid as it may be. Well; better lost than dead, I say. I think we'll pull into a tractor shed and wait until dawn.'

Lisa shut off the car heater and rolled down her window. 'It's nearly freezing, and it's only nine o'clock.'

'It is a bit nippy. Do you have long johns?'

'We have to find shelter, Sam.' She thought a moment, then said, 'I think we're off that state farm by now. If we can find a *kolhoz* – a collective farm village – we can get a peasant to take us in for a few rubles, no questions asked.'

'No questions asked? In Russia?'

'A collective is different from a state farm. In a collective village you'll see Russian peasant hospitality. I'd trust them to keep quiet.'

'You've never even *been* in the countryside. How do you know the peasants are friendly?'

'Instinct.'

'Too many nineteenth-century Russian novels, I think.' He shrugged. 'Alright. I'll trust you on this.' He added, 'You get your wish to see a village sooner than we thought.'

The road had gone from gravel to dirt and was deeply rutted by farm vehicles. They drove on in a westward direction and within fifteen minutes saw the silhouettes of utility poles against the horizon. They followed the poles and came to the first *izba* of a small hamlet. Hollis slowed the car on the dirt track that ran between two rows of log cabins. He said, 'I don't see any lights.'

Lisa replied, 'It's past nine, Sam. They're in bed. They're peasants. This is not Moscow.'

'True. In Moscow they turn in at ten.' Hollis stopped the car and looked out the window. 'I think we turned left into the last century.' He shut off the engine, and they listened to the dead silence. Hollis got out of the car and scanned the narrow lane. Like most of rural Russia, this village boasted electricity, but Hollis saw no sign of telephone lines nor was there a vehicle in sight or a structure large enough to hold one. There was no evidence that the village even possessed a single horse. It was nicely isolated. Lisa came up beside him, and Hollis said, 'They don't show *this* place to the foreign dignitaries.'

A light went on in the front window of an *izba*, then a few more lights came on. The door of a cabin opened, and a man stepped out onto a dirt path. Hollis said to Lisa, 'You talk.'

The man approached, and Hollis could see he was somewhere between forty and sixty, wore felt boot-liners, and had probably dressed hastily.

Lisa said in Russian, 'Greetings. We are American tourists.'

The man didn't reply. A few other doors opened, and more people came out into the dirt lane.

Hollis looked around. There were about ten *izbas* on each side of the road, and behind them Hollis could see pigpens and chicken coops. Each kitchen garden was fenced in, and in the corner of each was an outhouse. Ten meters down the lane was a single well and next to it a hand pump. The whole place had a look of extreme neglect about it and made the villages outside of Moscow look prosperous by comparison.

A crowd of about fifty people – men, women, and children – were standing around Hollis, Lisa, and the Zhiguli now. Hollis said to Lisa in English, 'Tell them we come from Earth with a message of peace and to take us to their *vozhd.*'

She gave him a look of both annoyance and anxiety, then said to the man who had come out first, 'We are having car trouble. Can you put us up for the night?'

151

The peasants looked from one to another, but amazingly, Hollis thought, there was no sound from them. Finally the peasant she addressed said, 'You wish lodgings? Here?'

'Yes.'

'There is a state farm not far from here. They will have lodgings now that the harvest is done.'

Hollis replied, 'I don't think the car will make it. Do you have a telephone or vehicle?'

'No. But I can send a boy on a bicycle.'

'Don't go to that trouble,' Hollis said with a politeness that seemed to surprise the man. Hollis added, 'My wife and I would rather stay with the people.' At the word *narod* – the common people, the masses – the man smiled.

Hollis looked closely at the peasants around him. They were coarse people with leathery skin the color of the earth on which they stood. Their clothes were little more than rags, their quilted *vatniks* not so clean or tailored as Lisa's. The men were unshaven, and the women had that unusual Russian combination of fat bodies and drawn faces. Half their teeth were black or missing, and from where Hollis stood, he could smell the sour clothes mixed with various flavored vodkas. *My God*, he thought, *this can't be*.

Lisa said to Hollis in English, 'Maybe this wasn't a good idea. Want to leave?'

'Too late.' He said to the man. 'You must let us pay you for our lodgings.'

The man shook his head. 'No, no. But I will sell you some butter and lettuce, and you can make a nice profit on that in Moscow.'

'Thank you.' Hollis added, 'I'll put the car where it won't block the road.' He said to Lisa, 'Get acquainted.' Hollis got in the car and backed it down the lane until he came to a hayrick he'd seen. He pulled the Zhiguli out of sight of the road, took his briefcase, and got out. He walked back, where he found Lisa involved in a ten-way conversation. Lisa said to Hollis in English. 'Our host is named Pavel Fedorovich, and this is

152

his wife Ida Agaryova. Everyone is very impressed with our Russian.'

'Did you tell them you are Countess Putyatova and you might own them?'

'Don't be an ass, Sam.'

'Okay.'

'Also I've learned that this place is called Yablonya – apple tree – and is a hamlet of the large collective farm named Krasnya Plamenny – Red Flame. The collective's administrative center is about five kilometers further west. No one lives there, but there is a telephone in the tractor storage shed. Mechanics will be there in the morning and will let us use the telephone.'

'Very good. I'm promoting you to captain.' Hollis introduced himself as Joe Smith. 'Call me Iosif.'

Pavel introduced each of the twenty or so families in the village, including his own son Mikhail, a boy of about sixteen, and his daughter Zina, who was a year or so older. They all smiled as they were introduced, and some of the old ones even removed their hats in a low sweeping bow, the ancient Russian peasant gesture of respect. Hollis wanted to get off the road in the event a black Chaika happened by. He said to Pavel, 'My wife is tired.'

'Yes, yes. Follow me.' He led Hollis and Lisa toward his *izba*, and Hollis noted that neither Pavel nor his wife inquired about luggage. This could mean they knew he and Lisa were on the run, or perhaps they thought his briefcase was luggage.

They entered the front room of the *izba*, which was the kitchen. There was a wood stove for heating and cooking, around which were a half dozen pairs of felt boots. A pine table and chairs sat in the corner, and utensils hung on the log walls. Against the far wall leaned two muddy bicycles. Incongruously there was a refrigerator plugged into an overhead socket from which dangled a single bare light-bulb. On a second table between the stove and the refrigerator sat a washtub filled with dirty dishes. Hollis noticed an open barrel of kasha – buckwheat – on the floor and remembered a peasant rhyme:

153

Shci da kasha;
Pishcha nasha.

– Cabbage soup and gruel are our food.

Pavel pulled two chairs out. 'Sit. Sit.'

Hollis and Lisa sat.

Pavel barked at his wife, 'Vodka. Cups.'

The door opened, and a man and woman entered with a teenage girl and a younger boy. The woman set a bowl of cut cucumbers on the table and backed away with the children. The man sat very close to Hollis and smiled. Another family entered, and the scene was repeated. Soon the walls were lined with women, their heavy arms folded across their chests like Siamese servants ready to snap to if anyone called. The children sat on the floor at the women's feet. Ida gave some of the children *kisel* – a thick drink made with pear juice and potato flour. The men, about fifteen of them now, sat around or near the table on chairs that the children had carried in. Vodka was flowing, and someone produced an Armenian brandy. Everyone drank out of cracked and not-too-clean teacups. The table was now covered with *zakuski* – the Russian equivalent of cocktail food – mostly sliced vegetables, a bowl of boiled eggs, and salted fish. Hollis downed his second vodka and said to Lisa in English, 'Does this mean we have to have them for cocktails?'

Lisa looked at him and said with emotion, 'I love this. This is an incredible experience.'

Hollis thought a moment. 'Indeed, it is.' He held out his cup, and it was immediately filled with pepper vodka. There was not much talking, Hollis noted, mostly requests to pass a bowl or a bottle of this or that. The stench of the people around him had been overpowering, but with his fourth vodka he seemed not to notice or care. 'That's why they drink.'

'Why?'

'It kills the sense of smell.'

'It kills the pain too,' Lisa said. 'It numbs the mind and the

154

body, and eventually it kills *them*. Would we be any different if we were born in this village?'

Hollis looked around at the flat, brown faces, the misshapen bodies, blank eyes, and earthy hands. 'I don't know. I do know that something is terribly wrong here. I've seen Asian peasants who lived and looked better.'

Lisa nodded: 'These people, like their ancestors, have been ill-used by their masters. And you always have to remember the Russian winter. It takes its toll on the mind and body.'

Hollis nodded. 'That it does.' The Russian peasant, he thought. Subject of literature, folklore, and college professors. But no one understood their inner lives.

Lisa looked around the room and met each pair of eyes. She said spontaneously, 'I am happy to be here.'

Forty faces smiled back. The man beside her asked, 'Where did you get your Russian?'

Lisa replied, 'My grandmother.'

'Ah,' said a man across the table. 'You are Russian.'

That seemed to call for a toast, and another round was poured and drunk.

A man sitting behind Hollis slapped him on the back. 'And you? Where did you learn that bad Russian?'

Everyone laughed.

Hollis raised a liter of heather-honey vodka. 'From this bottle.'

Again everyone laughed.

The impromptu party went on. Hollis surveyed the hot, smoky room and the people in it. They seemed to blend into the brown wood walls, he thought; their smell, their color, their very being was of the wood and the black earth. He looked at Lisa, joking with a young man across from her, and thought he had not seen her so lively and animated all day. Something about her total acceptance of these people and her affinity with them appealed to him, and he knew at last that he liked her very much.

The women and older children were drinking tea, and Hollis

155

watched them, then studied the men. The Russian peasant, he thought again. They were considered second-class citizens by both the state and the city dwellers and until recently were not even issued internal passports, effectively binding them to their villages as surely as if they were still serfs on an estate. And even with the passports, Hollis knew, they were not going anywhere. And there were one hundred million of them – the Dark People, as they were called in czarist Russia, as Lisa's grandmother undoubtedly referred to them. And they carried the weight of the state and the world on their bent backs and got damned little in return. They'd been beaten by landlords and commissars, herded into collectives, and had their harvests seized, leaving them to die of starvation. And to complete the process of killing their souls, they'd been denied their church and its sacraments. But when Russia needed massive armies, these poor bastards were sent to the front by the millions and died by the millions without protest. For Mother Russia. Hollis said aloud, 'God help them.'

Lisa looked at him and seemed to understand. 'God help them,' she repeated.

Hollis and Lisa ate and drank. As they expected, the questions about America began, tentatively at first, them they came in a flood, and Hollis and Lisa found themselves answering two or three people at once. Hollis noticed that the questions were all asked by the men, and the women continued to stand silently. Hollis commented to Lisa, 'Why don't you stand over there with the women?'

'Why don't you go fuck yourself?'

Hollis laughed.

A man asked, 'Is it true that the banks can take a man's farm if he does not pay his debts?'

Hollis replied, 'Yes.'

'What does the man do then?'

'He . . . finds a job in town.'

'What if he cannot find a job?'

'He receives . . .' Hollis looked at Lisa and asked, 'Welfare?'

156

'*Blago*, I think. *Gosstrakh.*'

Everyone nodded. Another man asked, 'What is the penalty for withholding produce?'

Lisa answered, 'A farmer owns all his produce. He can sell it whenever and wherever he can get the best price.'

The men looked at one another, a touch of disbelief in their eyes. One asked, 'But what if he can't sell it?'

Someone else asked, 'I've read that they kill their livestock rather than sell it for nothing.'

'What if the crops fail? How does his family eat?'

'What if his pigs or cows all die of disease? Will he get help from the state?'

Hollis and Lisa tried to answer the questions, explaining they were not that familiar with farm problems. But even as he spoke, Hollis realized that the farm questions were partly metaphor. What the average Russian feared, above all else, was *besporyadok* – chaos, a world without order, a state without a powerful *vozhd*, without a Stalin, a czar-father to look after them. The ancestral memory of such times of disorder, famine, civil war, and social disintegration was strong. They were willing to swap freedom for security. The next step was believing what the government implied: Slavery was freedom.

Hollis commented to Lisa, 'If we were talking to Martian capitalists we'd have more points of common reference.'

'We're doing fine. Just stay honest.'

'When do we tell them to revolt?'

'After the vodka is gone or after we convince them American farmers all own two cars.'

A girl of about fifteen sitting on the floor suddenly stood and asked, 'Miss, how old are you?'

Lisa smiled at the girl. 'Almost thirty.'

'Why do you look so young?'

Lisa shrugged.

'My mother' – she pointed to a woman behind her who could have been fifty – 'is thirty-two. Why do *you* look so young?'

Lisa felt uncomfortable. She said, 'Your mother looks my age.'

One of the men shouted, 'Go home, Lidiya.'

The girl started for the door but took a deep breath and walked directly to Lisa. Lisa stood. The girl looked at Lisa closely, then touched her hand. Lisa took the girl's hand in hers, bent down, and whispered in her ear, 'There is too much we don't know about each other, Lidiya. Perhaps tomorrow, if there is time.'

Lidiya squeezed Lisa's hand, smiled, and ran out the door.

Hollis looked at his watch and noticed it was near midnight. He wouldn't have minded letting this go on until dawn, but that black Chaika prowling the dark roads was on his mind. He said to Pavel, 'My wife is pregnant and needs sleep.' Hollis stood. 'We've kept you all up long enough. Thank you for your hospitality and especially for the vodka.'

Everyone laughed. The people filed out as they had arrived, in family groups, and each man shook hands with Hollis and mumbled a good-night to Lisa. The women left without formalities.

Pavel and Ida led Lisa and Hollis through an opening in the kitchen wall curtained off with a quilt blanket. They passed directly into a bedroom, and Hollis realized there was no sitting room. The bedroom held two single cots piled high with quilts, but Pavel motioned them toward a rough pine door, and they entered the second bedroom through the first. This was the end room in the three-room log cabin, and Hollis guessed it was the master bedroom. The middle room was for the son and daughter, who would probably sleep in the kitchen tonight.

Pavel said, 'Here is your bed.'

The room was lit, as the kitchen had been, by a single bulb hanging on a cord from an exposed log rafter. Heat came from a single-bar electric heater beside the bed. The double bed and two wooden trunks nearly filled the room, and a rag rug covered the plank floor. Hollis noticed spikes driven into the log walls as clothing hooks, and a pair of muddy trousers hung from one of them. There was one window in the short wall that looked into the back garden. Hollis saw there was no furniture other than the bed, though he had noticed in the children's room a chest of drawers, night table, and a reading lamp. He saw that the partition wall dividing the bedrooms was made of rough-hewn pine boards with knotholes stuffed with newspaper. The thought occurred to Hollis that the minister of agriculture might want to spend a winter month here to fully appreciate the great strides made in the Russian peasants' standard of living since the czars.

Lisa said to Pavel and Ida, 'This is wonderful. Thank you for showing us the real Russia.' She added with a smile, 'I'm sick to death of the Muscovites.'

Pavel smiled in return and addressed Hollis, 'I don't think you are tourists, but whoever you are, you are honest people and you can sleep well here.'

Hollis replied, 'There will be no trouble if the people in Yablonya don't speak to outsiders.'

'Whom do we speak to after the harvest? We are dead to them until the spring planting.'

Ida handed Lisa a roll of toilet paper that crinkled. 'If you must go out back. My bladder was always giving me trouble when I was pregnant. *Spokoiny nochi.*'

The woman and her husband left.

Lisa felt the bed. 'A real *perina* – feather mattress.'

'I'm allergic to feathers.' Hollis put his hands in his pockets. 'I might have preferred a tractor shed.'

'Stop griping.'

He went to the bed and picked up a corner of the quilt and examined the seam, looking for bedbugs.

Lisa asked, 'What are you looking at?'

'Looking for my chocolate mint on the pillow.'

She laughed.

Hollis pulled down the triple quilt to examine the sheets, but there weren't any. There was only the stained mattress ticking with feather quills sticking out. *The things we take for granted.* He suddenly felt a sharp anger at Katherine for all her petty whining and bitching about embassy life.

Lisa seemed not to notice the dirty mattress and began looking around the room.

Hollis moved to the curtainless window and examined it. It was a swing-out type, factory-made, but was some inches shorter than the log opening and had had to be set in mortar, which was now cracking. He felt a cold draft and saw his breath. Hollis tried the latch handle and satisfied himself the window would open if it became necessary to leave that way.

Lisa came up beside him and looked out the window. 'That's their private plot. Each peasant family is allowed exactly one acre. These plots comprise less than one percent of the agricultural lands but account for nearly thirty percent of the value of Soviet farm output.'

'I suppose there's a lesson there for Moscow if Moscow cared.'

Lisa seemed lost in thought, then said, 'This is like my grandmother described. This is the rural past that the intellectuals in Moscow and Leningrad are always romanticizing. The Russian purity of the land. It's still here. Why don't they come out and see it?'

'Because there's no indoor plumbing.' Hollis moved away from the window and added sharply, 'And it's not here, Lisa. Not anymore. This is a rural slum, and the peasants don't give a damn. Can't you see that? Don't you see how ramshackle everything is? Every man, woman, and child in this village wants only one thing: a one-way ticket to a city.'

She sat on the bed and stared at her feet, then nodded slowly.

'And while this might not be a sterile state farm,' he added, 'it's still a state-owned collective. The only thing these people own are their dirty clothes and greasy cooking utensils. As for these cabins and their so-called private plots, the government doesn't care a damn about them. The plan is to wipe out the villages and put everyone on the state farms where they can be twice as inefficient and nonproductive in a true communist setting. If that shithead Burov came here with a piece of paper signed in Moscow, he could take these people to the Forty Years of October *Sovkhoz* and plow Yablonya into the ground. Once you understand that, you take the first step toward understanding this society.'

She didn't respond for some time, then said, 'You're right of course. The people are alienated from the land, and the land is an orphan. The past is dead. The peasant culture is dead. The villages are dead. The bastards in Moscow won.'

He said in a more soothing tone, 'Well, it's too late to talk politics and philosophy.'

'Yes, it is.'

'I hope you're right about these peasants, and we're not awakened by the infamous three A.M. KGB knock on the door.'

'I think I was right.'

It occurred to Hollis that Lisa shared Alevy's annoying and dangerous practice of dragging the Russians into things that it wasn't fair to involve them in. With Alevy it was the Jews, with Lisa now, the peasants. And the Jews or the peasants might stick their necks out for a Westerner, but the Westerner was rarely around when the ax fell.

He doubted that these poor wretches of Yablonya even knew that it was against the law for a *Soviet citizen* to talk to foreigners, much less feed them and put them up. Hollis glanced at Lisa. She pulled off her boots and socks and wiggled her toes.

There was an awkward silence as Hollis considered what he was supposed to do or say.

Lisa said, 'It's very cold in here.' Fully dressed, she lay on the bottom quilt and pulled the two top quilts up to her chin. 'Very cold.' She yawned.

Hollis took off his leather jacket and hung it on a nail, then stuck his knife in the log beside the bed. He sat on a trunk and pulled off his boots. He became aware that his heart was beating a bit faster than normal, and he was suddenly at a loss for words. He said finally, 'Would you be more comfortable if I slept on the floor?'

161

'No. Would you?'

Hollis hesitated a moment, then took off his pullover and jeans and threw them over the trunk. He pulled the light cord, then slid into bed beside Lisa, wearing his T-shirt and shorts. He cleared his throat and said, 'I didn't mean to burst your bubble about rural Russia, peasants, and all that. I know you have some emotional involvement in the subject, and I think it's good that you can see the bright side of things. I like that. The exuberance of youth.'

'Do you snore?'

'Sometimes. Do you?'

'Depends on who you ask. Am I on your side of the bed?'

'I don't have a side.'

'You're easy to sleep with. Why do you wear blue shorts? Air Force?'

Hollis rolled away from her and looked out the window. '*Spokoiny nochi.*'

'Are you tired?'

'I should be,' he replied.

'I'm sort of hyper. What a day.'

'You're welcome.'

'Do you want to talk?'

'I've said enough.'

'Are you angry about something? You sound angry.'

'I'm just tired. I think I angered you.'

'Are you annoyed because I have my clothes on?'

'They're your clothes. If you want to wrinkle them, that's your business.'

She said, 'Before I was stationed here, I had three long-term relationships, three short-term ones, an affair with a married man, and two one-night stands. When I got here, I became involved with a man who has since left. Then there was Seth, and –'

'Slow down,' Hollis said. 'I'm running out of fingers and toes.'

She leaned over him and put her hand on his shoulder.

He turned toward her and stared at her by the dim light of the window.

She said, 'You shot two armed KGB men and never flinched, but now you're shaking.'

'It's cold.'

'I'm nervous too. But I want you.' She added, 'There may not be any tomorrow for us.'

'Sounds like my fighter pilot line. But if there is a tomorrow?'

'We'll take it a step at a time.'

'Right. And Seth? How will he take it?'

She didn't reply.

Hollis felt her bare foot touch his, and he took her head in his hands and kissed her.

They undressed beneath the quilts and side by side wrapped themselves in each other's arms.

She ran her hands over his back, and her fingers came into contact with smooth, unresilient knots.

'Scars,' he said.

'Oh.'

Hollis rolled on top of her and felt himself slip into her easily.

'Sam . . . that's nice . . . warm.'

'Warm . . . yes.' He put his mouth over hers as he entered more deeply and felt her hips draw back into the soft feather bed, then she thrust upward with surprising force. She moaned into his mouth as her hips moved more quickly, then slowed to a rhythmic rising and falling.

Lisa pushed the covers off with her feet and entwined her legs around his back, then cupped his buttocks in her hands and pulled him deeper into her as she came.

Hollis came, and they lay closely embraced. Lisa put her head on his chest.

Hollis ran his fingers through her hair.

She said, 'I hear your heart.'

'That's good news. I feel your breath.'

She kissed his chest. 'Now I lay me down to sleep.'

'Amen.' Hollis lay awake, his eyes open, staring at the blackness and listening to the silence. He smelled a cigarette from the next room, and someone coughed. The window rattled, and dried leaves blew against the panes, then silence again until a rat or mouse scampered over the rafter above.

An hour later he heard the sound of a Chaika's engine on the lane, followed by the clanking of a tracked vehicle, probably a troop carrier.

He waited for the crunch of boots in the frozen garden, the smashing of the front door, then the footsteps across the wood floor.

He waited, but the engines droned off, and quiet returned. Hollis wondered if they were looking for him and Lisa, or for Jack Dodson, or all three. There were precious few citizens in this country whose whereabouts weren't accounted for, and three foreigners on the loose was a major malfunction in the system, an intolerable situation.

Hollis closed his eyes and let himself drift. He vaguely heard Lisa mumbling in her sleep, then heard her say distinctly, 'The car is stuck,' followed by, 'I'm duty officer,' then, 'He's your friend too, Seth.'

Hollis always thought it bad manners to listen to the sleep talk of people he slept with, but this was the first woman he'd slept with who dreamed in Russian.

Hollis fell into a light, troubled sleep and had dreams of his own.

12

Lisa was awakened by a sound in the back garden. She shook Hollis. 'There's someone outside.'

Hollis opened his eyes and heard the creak of a door. 'The bathroom is outside.'

'Oh.'

There were noises coming from the kitchen, and a rooster's crowing cut through the dawn. Lisa said, 'I can see my breath.' She exhaled. 'See?'

'Very nice.' Through the window, Hollis saw Zina, Pavel and Ida's daughter, coming from the outhouse. She passed by the curtainless window but kept her head and eyes straight ahead.

Lisa said, 'It's Sunday morning, Sam, and the church bells are silent all over Russia.'

Hollis nodded. 'I'd like to hear a church bell again.'

They sat in silence awhile, listening to the morning birds, then Lisa said softly, 'Do you like it in the morning?'

'What? Oh . . .'

'I'd hate to think I was a one-night stand, so let's do it again.'

'Alright.'

They made love again, then lay back under the quilts, watching their breath as the dawn lit up the window. Lisa said, 'This is called smoking in bed.'

She put her arm around him and rubbed her toes over his foot. After a while she said, 'Turn over.'

Hollis lay on his stomach, and she pulled the quilts, down. In the weak light she saw the white and purple scars that started at his neck and continued down to his buttocks. 'I guess you *did* get banged up. Does that hurt?'

'No.'

'Were you burned?'

'Hot shrapnel.'

'The plane exploded?'

'Well, not by itself. A surface-to-air missile went up its ass.'

'Go on.'

Hollis rolled onto his back. 'Okay. December twenty-nine, 1972. Ironically it turned out to be the last American mission over North Vietnam. The Christmas bombings. Remember that?'

'No.'

'Anyway, I was over Haiphong, released the bombs, and turned back toward South Vietnam. Then my radar officer, Ernie Simms, in the backseat says coolly, 'Missile coming up.' And he gives me some evasive-action instructions. But the SAM was onto us, and I couldn't shake it. The last thing Ernie said was, 'Oh, no.' The next thing I knew, there was an explosion, the instrument panel went black, and the aircraft was out of control. There was blood spurting all over the place, and the canopy was covered with it. I thought it was mine, but it was Ernie Simms'. The F-4 was in a tight roll, wing over wing and streaking straight into the South China Sea. I jettisoned the canopy, and Simms and I blew out of the cockpit. Our parachutes opened, and we came down into the water. I floated around awhile watching enemy gunboats converging on me and contemplating life in a POW camp.'

Hollis sat up and stared out the window. He said, 'I saw Simms in his flotation seat, about a hundred meters away. He'd gotten a compress bandage on his neck and seemed alert. I called to him and he answered. One of the gunboats was bearing down on him. He yelled out to me, 'Sam, they've got me.' I swam toward him, but he waved me away. There wasn't much I could do anyway. I saw the Viets pull him aboard. Then they came for me. But by that time the Marine air-sea rescue choppers had come in with guns and rockets blazing away at the gunboats. A chopper plucked me up. I saw the boat that Simms was on, cutting a course back toward the North Viet shore batteries, and our choppers broke off the pursuit . . . They flew me to a hospital ship.'

Lisa didn't say anything.

Hollis said, 'I found out afterwards that I was the last pilot shot down over North Vietnam. I saw my name mentioned in a history book once. Very dubious honor. Simms has the equally dubious distinction of being the last MIA.'

'My lord . . . what an experience.' She added tentatively, 'Do you think . . . Simms . . . I mean, he never turned up?'

'No. MIA.'

'And . . . did you think . . . does it bother you to talk about it?'

Hollis answered her unasked question. 'I don't know what I could have done for him. But he was my copilot and my responsibility. Maybe . . . maybe I don't have the sequence of events right, the distance between me and him, the time when our choppers came in . . . I think I was out of it. I don't know what I could have done for him. Except to swim to him and see to his wound and join him in captivity. Maybe that's what I should have done as the commander of the aircraft.'

'But you were wounded.'

'I didn't even know that.'

'Then you were in shock.'

Hollis shrugged. 'It's done. It's finished.'

She put her hand on his shoulder.

A few minutes passed in silence, then Hollis said, 'So, to come full circle, Ernie Simms was never on any North Viet list of KIAs, or POWs, so he's still officially missing. Yet I *saw* them take him aboard alive. And now with this Dodson business I'm starting to wonder again about all of that. All the guys whose chutes were seen opening and who were never heard of again. Now I'm wondering if Ernie Simms and a thousand other guys didn't wind up in Russia.'

'In Russia . . . ?' Lisa found her jacket under the quilts and got a cigarette out of the pocket. She lit it and took a long pull. 'Want one?'

'Maybe later.'

'This is a mindblower, Sam.'

Hollis looked at her. 'A mindblower . . . yes.' He said, 'Look, we should get moving.' Hollis swung his legs out of the bed, then walked to the trunk where his clothes lay.

Lisa whistled. 'Nice body.'

'Cut it out.' He looked at her standing naked by the electric heater gathering her clothes from between the quilts. 'You don't have fat thighs, but your feet *are* big.'

They dressed and went through the second bedroom into the kitchen, where Ida greeted them and gave them a washbowl of hot water, a towel, and a bar of soap. They washed at the side table that still had a tub of dirty dishes on it. Lisa excused herself and went out back. Hollis went out into the cold air and walked to the dirt road. The Chaika had not left any tread marks on the frozen mud, but the vehicle with it, a half-track, had left its tread marks. Why they hadn't stopped and searched the village was anyone's guess. 'Luck.' He added, 'Laziness.' Though maybe someone was looking out for them.

Hollis walked on the mud path beside Pavel's *izba*, entered the dead garden, and passed Lisa on her way back to the house. She said, 'Isn't this fun?'

Hollis assured her it wasn't and kept walking. When he got back to the kitchen, he found Pavel sitting at the kitchen table with Lisa. Also at the table were Pavel's children, Mikhail and Zina. They were sharing a math textbook and doing homework, though it was Sunday. Hollis sat and Ida served him a boiled egg, kasha, and tea. The Russian tea was, as always, excellent. There was a stack of brown bread and a bowl of butter on the table. Hollis spoke to the two teenagers about school, then asked, 'What is your favorite subject?'

The boy smiled and answered in English, 'English.'

Hollis smiled in return. He continued in Russian, 'I know all the students in Moscow take English, but I didn't know they taught it in the country.'

The girl replied in halting English, 'Everyone in school learn English. We speak it sometimes between we.'

Lisa said in English, 'Who is your favorite American author?'

Mikhail replied, 'We know a few now we are reading. Jack London and James Baldwin.' He asked, 'Does *The Fire Next Time* be printed in America?'

'Oh, yes. I've read it,' Lisa answered.

'They put him in jail?' Zina asked.

'No. They gave him a big royalty check. *Komissiya*.'

Mikhail said, 'Our teacher say they put him in jail.'

'No.'

Zina said to her brother in Russian, 'You see? Last year an instructor told us he was arrested after the book was published. This year another instructor told us he wasn't allowed to publish the book and fled to France.'

Hollis cracked his boiled egg. He wondered why the government made English so available to school children. A paranoid would say, 'So that they can run America someday.' But there had to be more to it than that. He'd actually heard Moscow school children speaking English to one another. Whatever the government's reasoning was, the students considered it the height of chic. *Maybe, just maybe*, he thought, *there is hope*.

Zina asked in English, 'Americans learn Russian?'

'No,' Lisa replied. 'Not many.'

'You speak Russian very good. But what region is your accent?'

'Maybe a little bit Kazan, Volga region. A little Moscow. My grandmother's Russian was old-fashioned, and maybe I still use her accent.'

'A very nice accent,' Zina said. '*Kulturny*.'

Hollis noticed that Pavel and Ida beamed every time one of their children used English. Hollis opened his briefcase to see if his staff had packed any reading material as was customary whenever anyone had to travel in the USSR. He found a *Time* magazine and put it in front of Mikhail and Zina. 'This may help you with your English.' He added, 'Don't let it come to the attention of the authorities.'

They both looked at him with an expression that he'd seen before in these situations. There was first a suppressed excitement, then a sort of affected indifference, as though the contraband literature meant nothing to them. Then there was a look almost of shame, a quiet acknowledgment that their government controlled them. It *was* humiliating, Hollis thought.

Mikhail and Zina examined the magazine right down to the staples holding it together. They opened it at random and spread out a two-page color ad for Buick. The next page had an ad for Lincoln. In fact, the magazine was packed with ads for the new car models. There were sexually suggestive ads for perfumes, lingerie, and designer jeans that seemed to hold Mikhail's interest. Pavel leaned over to get a better look, and Ida stopped what she was doing and stood behind her children.

It was general embassy policy to distribute into the population every Western periodical that came into the embassy. Even if it was mistakenly thrown in the trash, it eventually wound up in the hands of a thousand Muscovites before it fell apart. And though most Muscovites and Leningraders had seen at least one English language publication, Hollis doubted if anyone in Yablonya or the Red Flame collective had.

Hollis noticed that Mikhail and Zina were reading a story about the upcoming elections. Hollis looked at his watch and saw it was just seven. 'It's time for us to go.' He stood.

Mikhail stood also. 'It's my turn to gather the eggs. Excuse me. Thank you.' He left.

Zina helped her mother with the dishes. Lisa tried to help, but Ida told her to have another cup of tea.

Hollis followed Pavel outside. The peasant walked to the far end of his private plot where a small pen held three pigs. He said to Hollis, 'The trough leaks water, and I'm tired of carrying buckets from the well.'

'Can you fix the trough?'

170

'I need some pine pitch or tar. But I can't get the fools to give me any.'

'What fools?'

'The fools at the collective office. They say they have none. Well, maybe they don't.' He added, 'It's difficult to get anything for the private plots.'

'Sometimes a hollowed-out log works better for a trough.'

'Yes, that's true. I'll need a big log though. I have a good pickax.' He added, 'It would be easier if they gave me the tar.'

Hollis asked, 'Do you go to church today?'

'Church? There's no church here. Only in the big cities. I saw an old church once in Mozhaisk, but it's a museum. I didn't go in.'

'Did you ever want to go to church?'

Pavel scratched his head. 'I don't know. Maybe if I could talk to a priest I could answer you. I've never seen a priest, but I know what they look like from books. Do American farmers go to church?'

'Yes. I'd say most of them do.'

Pavel looked into the sky. 'Rain. But maybe snow. See those clouds? When they get soft grey like that instead of white or black, it could be snow.'

Pavel looked out across the brown fields behind his plot. He spoke in that faraway, heavy tone that Hollis had come to associate with their so-called fatalism. Pavel said, 'The snow becomes so deep that the children can't go to school and we can't leave the house. They are supposed to keep the roads plowed, but they don't. I sit in the house and drink too much. Sometimes I beat my wife and the children for no reason. I had another daughter, Katya, but she died one winter of a burst appendix. Someday they say they will move us to a *sovkhoz*. Maybe. But I don't know if I want to leave this house. What do American farmers do in winter?'

'Fix things. Clean their barns, hunt. Some take jobs. It's not so cold in the winter in America.'

'Yes, I know that.'

'How long has Yablonya been here?'

'Who can say? I came here as a child after the war with my mother. My father died in the war. The government sent my mother here from a bigger village that the Germans burned. A man once told me Yablonya was within the Romanov lands. Another man said it was on the estate of a rich count. Everyone says it was bigger once. There were barns and stables where people had their own horses, troikas, and plows. There were two more wells. But no pumps. Now we have a pump. Some say there was even a church between here and the next village. But that village is gone too. Typhoid. So they burned it. I think the church was burned too. The Germans or maybe the commissars. Who knows?' He asked Hollis, 'Do you miss your home?'

'I have no home.'

'No home?'

'I've lived in many places.' They spoke casually for a while, then Hollis said, 'We must be going.' He added, 'I'm afraid if someone here – the children, the babushkas – speak of our visit, it will not be good for Yablonya.'

'I know that. We will discuss it after you leave.'

Hollis took Pavel's hand and pressed a ten-ruble note into it.

Pavel looked at the note and shoved it into his pocket. 'Bring your car around, and I'll give you five kilos of butter. 'They'll give you twenty rubles for it in Moscow.'

'We're going to Leningrad. Anyway, the money was for your hospitality. *Da svedahnya.*' Hollis turned and walked back to the house. Lisa was ready to go and had a burlap bag in her hand. She said, 'Ida gave me some honey and a bag of pears.'

Hollis retrieved his briefcase from under the table. 'Thank you, Ida. Good-bye, Zina.' He took Lisa's arm, and they left. As they walked down the road, they heard an old man singing:

> *Govorila baba dedu*
> *Chto v Ameriku poyedu.*
> *Akh, ty staraya pizda*
> *Ne poedesh nikuda.*

> – Grandma says to Grandpa:
> I'm going to America, you hear?
> Oh, you old pussy,
> You ain't goin' nowhere.

They went behind the hayrick, and standing near the Zhiguli was the young girl named Lidiya. Lisa smiled at her and said in Russian, 'Good morning, Lidiya. I wondered if I'd see you.'

The girl did not return the smile, but said in Russian, 'There is a boy here, Anatoly, who is a member of the Komsomol. You know what that is – the Young Communist League? I think this boy will tell the authorities of your visit.'

Lisa took the girl's arm. 'Perhaps the other children can talk to Anatoly.'

The girl shook her head. 'Anatoly speaks to no one and listens to no one. No one in Yablonya.'

Hollis said to Lidiya, 'Is Pavel Fedorovich the head man here?'

'They don't let us have a head man. But yes, it is Pavel Fedorovich.'

'Then tell him what you told us. And be certain Anatoly does not leave this village today.'

She nodded.

Lisa said, 'Thank you. I'm sorry we couldn't speak longer.'

Lidiya said, 'I want to know more about America.'

Lisa hesitated, then took her card from her bag and gave it to Lidiya. 'If you should ever get to Moscow, with your school or on holiday, call that number. From a phone booth only, and only give your first name. Ask for me. Lisa Rhodes.'

Lidiya stared at the card with the Great Seal on it and pronounced, 'Lee-za Rhodes.'

Lisa gave the girl a kiss on the cheek.

Lidiya stepped back, looked from Lisa to Hollis, then turned and ran off.

Hollis said, 'I shouldn't have left that magazine here, and you shouldn't have given her that card.'

Lisa replied, 'You told me not so long ago that you can't let *them* dictate how you are going to live.They create fear and suspicion, and it comes between people.'

Hollis nodded. 'Let's go.' They got into the car, and Hollis started the engine. He let it warm up while the defroster ran.

Lisa said, 'I left ten rubles in the bedroom.'

'For me?'

She laughed. 'You get hard currency. Very hard.'

Hollis smiled. 'I gave Pavel a tenner. So, do you think we can get away with just dinner, or do we have to have them for the weekend?'

'I think they were nice.'

'He beats his wife.' Hollis tried to put the car into gear, but the linkage was stuck again. 'A nuclear power. I don't get it.' He played with the clutch and stick shift, finally forcing it into second gear. 'Okay.'

Hollis pulled out onto the dirt road and turned in the opposite direction from which they had come.

'Are we going to find that telephone?' she asked.

'I wouldn't chance that.'

'Where are we going? Mozhaisk is the other way.'

'We are not going to Mozhaisk. We're going to Gagarin.' Hollis honked his horn and waved to Pavel, Ida, Mikhail, Zina, and the others who were waving from their front gardens. 'Yablonya,' he said. 'This place will sit on my mind for some time.'

'Mine too.'

Hollis passed the last *izba* in the village and sped up. The Zhiguli bounced badly on the rutted and frozen mud. '*Chornaya gryazi*,' Hollis said. The black mud. This stuff will turn to pudding when the sun warms it. The panzers used to sink up to their turrets.'

'Why Gagarin?'

'Well, there are people between Mozhaisk and Moscow who are looking for Major Dodson and maybe for us. So we're heading west to Gagarin, where I hope there's not an all points out for stray Americans. We'll ditch the car, then take the train to Moscow. Okay?'

'What are my choices?'

'You can ride in the backseat. Left or right side.'

Lisa lit a cigarette. 'You're a pretty smart guy.'

'Foreign travel is educational. And we'll see how smart I am. Could you crack the window?'

Lisa rolled down the window. 'Can we stop for a pack of cigarettes?'

'Next Seven-Eleven you see.'

'Thanks.'

Hollis headed west along the straight dirt road. He couldn't imagine that the Soviet state did not have the wherewithal to pave or even gravel back roads. Perhaps, he thought, it was just another subtle means of keeping the peasants where they belonged and making their miserable lives more miserable. He knew he had to get the Zhiguli onto blacktop before the mud thawed.

'Do you know the way?' Lisa asked.

'It's about fifty K west of here on the old Minsk-Moscow road. And yes, I'm afraid this is –'

'Another fucking itinerary violation.'

'What happened to that sweet girl who was so obsequious toward me?'

She laughed. 'I *was* awed by you. That's how you talked me into bed.'

Hollis thought it best to leave that one alone. He said, 'I need a shower.'

'You sure do.'

Hollis pushed the Zhiguli hard. It was a few minutes past eight, and he could see water in the ruts now instead of ice. He figured they had about fifteen minutes left on this road before it swallowed the Zhiguli.

Lisa said, 'Do you think those people in Yablonya will be alright?'

'Well, if they don't report their contact with foreigners, and

175

the authorities find out on their own, or if the little Komsomol shit tells them, it will be bad. In the intelligence business we talk about the average Ivan's attitudinal loyalty to the state. Some say he's got it, others don't think so. In America, if Joe Smith had a Russian knocking on his door asking to be put up on the sly, Joe would be on the horn to the FBI in a flash. Joe does that because he thinks it's right, not because he thinks the FBI will torture him if he doesn't. Ivan, on the other hand, is about half patriotic and half terrorized. That's my professional analysis. Personally I think Yablonya is fucked.'

Lisa stayed silent for some time, then said, 'I should have realized the trouble they'd be in . . . it just seemed like a solution to our problem.'

'Don't worry about it. I just hope the KGB doesn't go snooping around there this morning. We need a few hours' head start.' Hollis could feel the road getting soft and heard mud splashing against the wheel wells. The muffler was thumping. Ahead he saw a horse-drawn potato wagon plodding along the narrow road. 'Damn it.' He knew he couldn't slow down behind the wagon without getting mired in the muck. 'Hold on.' Hollis came up behind the wagon, angled the car to the left, and cut back so that the Zhiguli's right side was inches from the horse and wagon while its left wheels were off the road into the drainage ditch. The car started to flip over, then settled down and flopped back onto the road in front of the horse, who got splattered with mud and reared up. The car fishtailed in the mud but kept its traction.

Lisa took a deep breath. 'Wow.'

Within five minutes they came to an intersecting road of gravel, and Hollis cut north on it. He nudged the Zhiguli up to fifty kph and listened to the muffler working itself loose.

Lisa asked, 'Do you want a pear?'

'Sure.'

She got a pear from the bag and wiped it on her sleeve before she handed it to him.

Hollis saw the main utility poles of the old Minsk-Moscow

road ahead. He bit into the pear. 'Good *grusha*.' He turned onto the paved road and headed west. 'About twenty minutes to Gagarin.' Hollis saw no traffic on the road in either direction. He pressed on the accelerator and got the Zhiguli up to ninety kph. The engine whined, and the transmission whined back, but the car held steady. The muffler had quieted down on the level surface.

Hollis saw a black car in his rearview mirror. The car was gaining on him fast and had to be doing over a hundred kph. As the car drew closer he recognized the grillwork of a Chaika. He looked at his dashboard and saw that his tachometer was already on the red line. 'Don't look now, but . . .'

She turned her head. 'Oh, shit! Is that them?'

'Don't know.'

'What can we do?'

'Bluff and bluster. Tell them we've already called our embassy and so on. If I think it's necessary and if I get a chance, I'll try to kill them.' He slid his knife out of his boot and slipped it inside his leather coat.

'Sam . . . I'm frightened.'

'You'll be fine. Be a bitch.'

The Chaika was fifty meters behind them now and swung out into the oncoming lane. Lisa looked straight ahead. Hollis glanced in his sideview mirror and smiled. 'Wave.'

'What?'

The Chaika drew abreast and honked its horn. Two young couples waved from the car. Hollis smiled and waved back. The woman in the front passenger side pointed to the crushed fender and pantomimed swigging from a bottle and jerking on a steering wheel. The young man in the back was blowing kisses to Lisa. His female companion punched his arm playfully. The Chaika accelerated and passed them. Hollis said, 'Crazy Muscovite kids. What's this country coming to?'

Lisa drew a long breath. She opened her bag, took out a compact, and brushed her face with blush, then carefully put on lip gloss. 'I'll do my eyes when you stop for a light.' She ran a brush through her hair. 'Want me to do your hair? It's messy.'

'Okay.'

She brushed his hair as he drove. She said, 'We need a toothbrush.' She added, 'I want us to look good for them.'

'For whom?'

'The people in Gagarin or the KGB or Burov. Whoever we meet first.'

Hollis said, 'You look good. Too good. Tone it down a bit.'

'We're not going to pass for Russians anyway, Sam.'

'We'll try to pass as something other than American embassy staff.'

She shrugged and blotted the blush and lip gloss with a handkerchief. 'At least I'm wearing a *vatnik*. You look like Indiana Jones with your boots and leather jacket.' She tousled her hair. 'Well, we didn't shower.'

Hollis said, 'Standard procedure is try to pass as a socialist comrade from one of the Baltic states. They don't dress half bad, look Western, and speak un-Russian Russian. How about Lithuanian? Or do you feel like a Latvian?'

'I want to be an Estonian.'

'You got it.'

Ten minutes later they saw squat *izbas* on either side of the road, then buildings with painted wood siding. Hollis slowed down. 'Gagarin.'

'Named after the cosmonaut?'

'Yes. He was born in a village near here. From a squalid *izba* to a space capsule – log cabin to the stars. You have to give these people credit where it's due.'

They came into the middle of Gagarin, the district center for the region, situated on both banks of the Bolshaya Gzhat River. It was a town of about ten thousand people, big enough, Hollis thought, so that neither the Zhiguli nor its occupants stood out. Like Mozhaisk, it looked as if everyone had gone to the moon for the weekend. The town boasted a restaurant and a memorial museum to their famous native son.

Hollis stopped the car in the middle of the empty street and rolled down his window. An enormous babushka, wrapped in black, was carrying a crate on her shoulder like a man. Hollis asked, '*Vokzal?*'

'Good, good.' She opened the rear door of the Zhiguli, threw the crate in, and piled in after it. The Zhiguli's rear dropped. Hollis looked at Lisa, smiled, and shrugged. He asked, '*Gde?*'

'There, there. Turn over there. Where are you from?'

Hollis turned down a narrow street and saw the train station, a covered concrete platform. 'From Estonia.'

'Yes? Do the police let you drive with dented fenders in Estonia? You must get that fixed here.'

'Yes, Mother.'

'Where are your hats and gloves? Do you want to get pneumonia?'

'No.' Hollis pulled up to a small empty parking area beside the concrete platform. He got out and helped the old woman up the platform steps. Lisa followed with his briefcase, and they made their way through the crowd to the wooden ticket shed on the platform. Hollis and Lisa consulted the posted schedule and saw that the next Moscow train would be along in twenty minutes. Hollis knocked on the ticket window, and a wooden panel slid back, revealing a middle-aged woman wearing a grey railroad coat. A fire blazed in an old potbellied stove behind her. Hollis said, 'Two one-way tickets to Moscow.'

She looked at him.

Hollis knew she was supposed to ask for an internal passport, but ticket agents rarely did. In his case, however, she might make an exception. Hollis said, 'Is it possible to be ticketed on to Leningrad, then to Tallinn?'

'No. You are Estonian?'

'Yes.'

The woman craned her neck to get a look at Lisa, then turned to Hollis. 'You must be ticketed in Moscow for Leningrad and Tallinn. Twenty-two and seventy-five.'

179

Hollis gave her twenty-five rubles and took the tickets and change. '*Spasibo.*'

As they moved away from the ticket booth, Lisa glanced back. 'I wonder if she's going to call the militia.'

Hollis moved around to the rear of the wooden ticket shed, looked around, drew his knife, and severed the telephone line. 'No. But if she leaves the ticket booth, we're back in the Zhiguli.'

Lisa took his arm. 'Somehow I feel you'll get us out of this.' She added, 'You got us into it.'

Hollis made no reply.

She asked, 'What would you have done if she asked us for passports or identity cards?'

'Are you asking out of curiosity, or are you trying to learn the business?'

'Both.'

'Well, then, I would have . . . you tell me.'

Lisa thought a moment, then said, 'I'd pretend I couldn't find my ID, leave, and pay a peasant to buy two tickets.'

Hollis nodded. 'Not bad.'

Lisa and Hollis walked down the cold, grey concrete platform, which looked like a scene out of *Doctor Zhivago*, crowded with black-coated and black-scarved humanity. Old peasants, men and women, with teenage boys to help them, lugged crates, boxes, and suitcases filled with dairy products and the last fresh produce of the year. They were all headed for one place: Moscow, the Center, where eight million mouths had to be fed and could not be fed properly through the government's distribution system. Some of the peasants would go to the free markets, the government's grudging concession to capitalism, and some of the peasants would get no farther than a side street near the railroad terminal. Hollis had heard from some of the wives in the embassy that by November broccoli and cauliflower could sell for the equivalent of two dollars a pound, tomatoes for twice that, and lettuce was sold by the gram. By December the fresh produce disappeared until May.

The peasant women sat like men, Hollis noticed, their legs spread and their hands dangling in their laps. Not a single man was shaven, and there was not one decent article of clothing among the two hundred or so people. The women wore rubber boots and galoshes, and though the men's shoes and boots were leather, they were raw and cracked from long, hard use. The few young girls wore plastic boots of garish colors: red, yellow, pale blue. Hollis said softly to Lisa, 'You might as well powder your nose again. Everyone's staring at you anyway.'

'My word, look at that. That man has dead rabbits in that sack.'

The Byelorussian Express came lumbering down the track, and everyone stood and moved their wares to the edge of the platform, forming a veritable wall of boxes and crates. The train stopped, the doors opened, and Hollis vaulted inside followed by Lisa. They took two empty seats by the attendant's tea cubicle.

Within ten minutes every nook and cranny of the car was packed with bundles, and the train pulled out. Hollis checked his watch. It was nine-thirty. With stops in Mozhaisk and Golitsyno, the train should arrive at the Byelorussian station on Gorky Square well before noon.

The grimness of the platform quickly gave way to animated conversations, jokes, and laughter. It was rough peasant talk, Hollis noted, but there was no profanity, and there seemed to be a bond between these people, though clearly many of them were getting acquainted for the first time. The bond was not only the journey, he thought, but the brotherhood of the downtrodden. How unlike the Moscow metro where you could hear a pin drop at the height of rush hour.

Food was being passed around now, and there was good-natured teasing about the qualities of each person's wares. Hollis heard a woman say, 'Not even a Muscovite would buy these apples of yours.'

Another woman answered, 'I tell them they are radishes.'

Everyone laughed.

An old man across the aisle pushed a dripping slice of tomato under Hollis' nose. Hollis took it from his brown fingers. 'Thank you, father.' He passed it to Lisa. 'Eat it.'

She hesitated, then popped it into her mouth. 'Good. See if anyone has orange juice.'

'Low profile. Feign sleep or simplemindedness.'

Lisa whispered in Russian, 'Can I smoke?'

'Not here. In the lav.'

'Do you want another pear? Honey?'

'No, honey.'

'This is nice.'

Hollis looked around the car. It *was* quite nice. Clean, lace curtains on the windows, and little bud vases attached to the windowsills, each with a real rosebud. The more he saw of Russia, he admitted, the less he understood it. The windows, however, were dirty, and this was somehow comforting.

They spoke as little as possible, and Hollis urged Lisa to remain in her seat unless she really had to use the facilities. The conductor, a middle-aged woman, came through, took their tickets, and marked them rather than punching them. She said, 'Are you Muscovites?'

Hollis replied, 'No. Estonians. From Moscow we go to Leningrad, then home to Tallinn.'

'Ah. Your Russian is good.' She looked Lisa over and observed, 'Those are very nice boots.'

'Thank you.'

'They have better things in our Baltic republics. I never understood that.' She handed Hollis the tickets. 'Have a safe journey.'

'Thank you.'

The train gathered speed on the straight, flat trackbed. There was piped-in music now. It was not the classical or folk music usually heard in public places, Hollis noted, but soft, easy-listening music, Soviet Muzak.

The train pulled into Mozhaisk, and there was the same crush of humanity on the platform carrying the same bursting cardboard suitcases and ungainly bundles. The train loaded the last two cars only. There were soldiers and militia on the platform. Hollis and Lisa slumped down into their seats and ferigned sleep. The train pulled out and continued its journey through the bleak Russian landscape.

Golitsyno was a five-minute stop, and within fifteen minutes of leaving the station they could see the tall spire of Moscow University in the Lenin Hills. 'Almost home,' Lisa commented. She added, 'No, not really home.'

The train made short stops at suburban stations, Setun, Kuncevo, Fili, then Testovskaya. Lisa said, 'Why don't we get off here? We can walk to the embassy from here.'

'We're supposed to be going on to Leningrad, so we get off at the Byelorussian terminal.'

'I want to get off *here*. I've had it.'

'Sit down.'

Lisa sat back in her seat. 'Sorry. Getting edgy. I trust you. You did a magnificent job. Even if something happens and we don't get into the embassy . . . How *are* we going to get into the embassy if the watchers are waiting for us near the gate?'

'I'll show you a spy trick.'

'You'd better.'

The Byelorussian Express from Minsk pulled into Moscow's Byelorussian Station at ten minutes to noon. Hollis and Lisa left quickly and pushed through the throngs packed into the hundred-year-old station. Hollis noticed that the people returning to the hinterlands had not appreciably lightened their loads, but were burdened now with plastic bags filled with clothing, new shoes, cooking utensils, and all manner of Moscow's bounty. The most worthless thing they had on them were the leftover rubles in their pockets. A few passing Muscovites, well-dressed by comparison, gave the country folk hard looks to show they didn't like the competition for consumer goods by peasants.

Hollis and Lisa passed pairs of KGB Border Guards, who were at every transportation hub in the Soviet Union but were nonetheless intimidating to foreigner and native alike.

Hollis and Lisa came out of the station into Gorky Square, dominated by a huge statue of the writer. The sky was the usual grey, and the air seemed filled with fumes compared to the fresh air of the countryside.

They crossed the square and walked down Gorky Street, Moscow's main street, toward the Kremlin. Hollis led Lisa into the Minsk Hotel, and he entered a phone booth off the lobby. He dialed the embassy, spoke to the Marine watchstander, then the Sunday duty officer, who turned out to be his own aide, Captain O'Shea. 'Ed, this is me. Okay?'

'Yes, sir.'

'This is a photoflash,' Hollis said, using the word for a personal emergency. 'Get a car to me at location delta. Ten minutes.'

'Yes, sir. I'll go myself.'

'No, stay there and find me Mr Nine. I want to see him.'

'Mr Nine was very worried about you. He's in his office.'

'Ten minutes.'

'Yes, sir. Welcome home.'

Hollis hung up the phone and said to Lisa, 'Seth is very worried about you.'

Lisa didn't reply. They left the Minsk Hotel and continued down Gorky Street. She said, 'That was neat. Where is location delta?'

'I forgot.'

She looked at him. 'Are you jerking me around?'

'Yeah. It's Gastronom One. You know it?'

'Sure. But we Muscovites still call it Yeliseyevsky's, its pre-Revolution name. Best gourmet store in Moscow. The *only* one actually.' She added, 'We're going to make it, aren't we?'

'Looks like it.'

They passed the Stanislavsky Drama Theater, walked through Pushkin Square, and crossed the Garden Ring, which once had been the outer wall of the city. They came to the ornate façade of Gastronom One, then doubled back. Hollis said, 'I'm assuming the KGB doesn't know location delta from Times Square. We change the locations every time we have to use one. So there should be no one here from the KGB to meet us. However, they will have a car or two close behind the embassy car. As soon as the embassy car slows down, you jump in the rear, scoot over quick, and I follow. Okay?'

'I saw this in a movie once.'

They waited. Lisa lit a cigarette. 'This is my last one. But I have a pack in my office. Or my room.'

'That's good news.'

A black Ford came at a good pace up Gorky Street, and Hollis saw two security men in the front and a man who looked like Seth Alevy in the back. Behind the Ford was a black Chaika. The Ford suddenly swerved to the curb and braked hard. The back door flew open, Lisa slipped in beside Alevy, and Hollis got in, then slammed the door as the car accelerated. Lisa said, 'Hello, Seth.'

Alevy addressed Hollis directly, 'You had better have a good explanation, Colonel.'

Hollis didn't reply.

'Where is the car?' Alevy asked.

'At the railroad station.'

'*What* railroad station?'

'Gagarin.'

'*Gagarin*? What the hell were you doing there?'

'Getting the train to Moscow.'

Lisa opened her burlap bag. 'Seth, do you want a pear?'

'No.' Alevy folded his arms and looked out the side window.

The Chaika got up close behind them, and the security driver sped up until another Chaika appeared in front of the Ford and boxed them in. The American driver pulled out, and the three cars continued their dangerous game, weaving through central Moscow and down Kalinin Prospect.

Within ten minutes the Ford reached the embassy and shot past the militia booth, crossed the sidewalk, and entered the gates. The Chaika behind them sounded its horn, and the man in the passenger side put his arm out the window and extended his middle finger. The security men in the front of the Ford returned the salute of the KGB men in the Chaika, while Hollis returned the salute of the Marine watchstanders. The Ford went around the flagpole and stopped at the entrance to the chancery. Hollis, Lisa, and Alevy piled out. Alevy said, 'No offense, but you both smell.'

Lisa said, 'I think I'll go and shower.'

'Not a half-bad idea.'

Hollis said to Alevy, 'Get a call through to the Mozhaisk morgue. Tell them not to wait for an escort and have them drive the body to Sheremetyevo airport freight terminal. Send a consular officer to the airport to take charge of the remains.' He took the manila envelope from his briefcase. 'Here's all the paperwork, including the export permit and a charge for the coffin that they want paid before they'll ship it out.'

'I thought you were in the damned coffin. I called the Soviet Foreign Ministry, the KGB –'

'That's like dialing M for murder, Seth.'

'Where did you spend the night?'

'Is that a professional question?' Hollis inquired.

Lisa interjected, 'We hid out in a village called Yablonya –'

'Hid out? From whom?'

Hollis answered, 'From a guy named Burov. KGB type. Colonel.' Hollis described him. 'Know the man?'

'Maybe. I'll ask around. Okay, please be in the sixth-floor safe room in thirty minutes. Both of you. Can you do that?'

Lisa said, 'I need an hour.' She turned and walked into the chancery.

Alevy stared at Hollis, who stared back. Alevy said, 'You know, it was my fault for letting you take her along.'

'I think I cured her of her fascination with espionage.'

'On the contrary, I think. Did you get along alright?'

'She was an asset.'

'Maybe I should recruit her,' Alevy said.

'She has what it takes. And we have no female types now.'

'I'll wire Langley. What was her strongest asset?'

'Humor in the face of danger.'

'We must discuss this soon.'

'Fine. But not out in the open where the directional microphones can eavesdrop.' Hollis turned and walked into the chancery. He went through the lobby and came out onto the rear terrace. She was there waiting for him. She said, 'What were you talking to Seth about?'

'Your assets.'

They walked on the birch-lined path beside the quadrangle toward her unit. She said, 'I wondered if I'd see this place again.'

'No more bitching about your unit.'

'No, sir. I love my bathroom. Kiss the tile.'

Hollis looked out on the quadrangle. John Uhlman from the consular section was teaching his son how to ride a two-wheeler. The scarecrow had been built in their absence, and there were three oddly shaped pumpkins at its feet. Hollis observed, 'No corn stalks.'

She followed his gaze. 'No corn stalks.'

'Well . . .' He glanced at his watch.

'Last chance for a pear.'

'I'll take one.'

She held out the bag. 'Take the honey too. I'm off sugar.'

'I'm off too, sweets.'

They both smiled. Finally Lisa asked, 'How do we stand?'

Hollis put his hands in his pockets and shrugged.

'Is that an answer?'

'How do you stand with Seth?'

'It's over.'

'Then what's he angry about?'

She threw the bag over her shoulder. 'Well, think about it.' She turned and walked down the path.

Hollis stood awhile, then made his way across the quadrangle.

13

Seth Alevy said to Charles Banks, 'John Uhlman from the consular section is headed for Sheremetyevo to take care of the business that Colonel Hollis did not complete.'

Hollis noticed that Alevy was talking mostly to Banks, ignoring him and Lisa.

Hollis saw that Banks was wearing his Sunday best, though since it was Sunday in Moscow, everyone else was dressed casually. Hollis had showered and put on jeans and a flannel shirt. Alevy wore pleated slacks and a V-necked sweater. Lisa, he thought, looked good in a white turtle-neck and tight jeans, though she was somewhat cool to him. Hollis sat at the far end of the conference table in the ambassador's safe room; Banks sat at the opposite end, and Lisa and Alevy sat in the center facing each other. Hollis noticed for the first time a framed piece of calligraphy hanging on the wall and read it:

The issues of diplomacy are of ever greater importance, since a stupid move could destroy all of us in a few minutes.

LORD HUMPHREY TREVELYAN, 1973

Hollis thought that Banks and the ambassador would probably prove that true in the next few weeks.

Alevy continued, 'Obviously we can't retrieve the rented Zhiguli, so we called the Intourist Hotel and told them it was broken down at Gagarin railroad station. We'll get a hell of a bill for that.'

Hollis knew that Alevy was not in the least interested in these petty administrative matters, but Charles Banks was. It was the nature of the diplomat to never break a local rule or offend a host country. Even if you were handing the foreign minister a note with a declaration of war on it, you were polite about it. Hollis perceived that Alevy was trying to make points with Banks at Hollis' expense, so Hollis thought he'd be helpful for a change. He said, 'The car needs a lot of body work too.'

Banks turned to him. 'Body work?'

'Just hit a tree. Damage to the tree was minimal.'

'Good.' Banks cleared his throat and said, 'So . . .' He looked at Lisa, then back to Hollis, and he put a stern tone in his voice. 'Neither of you returned to your quarters last night, and neither of you informed this embassy of your whereabouts. That is contrary to regulations as well as a dangerous breach of security, not to mention the element of personal danger to yourselves.' Banks looked from one to the other. 'Do either of you have an explanation for this? Miss Rhodes?'

Lisa replied, 'We were together obviously. We were unable to finish our business in Mozhaisk by nightfall. There was no room at the inn – actually there was no inn – so we spent the night on a *kolhoz* – that's a collective farm, Charles. There was no telephone there.'

Banks said, 'I appreciate the special conditions that exist in the countryside here. But it is your obligation to keep in contact with this embassy, not vice versa.'

Hollis spoke. 'As the senior person, I'll take responsibility for the breach.'

Banks nodded, satisfied.

Alevy said, 'I don't quite understand how you two got such a late start and failed to complete this routine assignment before dark.'

Hollis replied, 'Lot of paperwork involved, Seth. Drop it.'

But Alevy continued, 'How did you wind up on a collective? Why didn't you call from Mozhaisk?'

Hollis looked directly at Alevy. 'I don't think Mr Banks wants to be bored with those details.'

Alevy nodded. 'Right. Perhaps later you can bore me.' He looked at Lisa a moment, then turned back to Banks. 'Sir?'

Banks addressed Lisa. 'The ambassador is writing an official

189

letter of condolence to Mr Fisher's parents. I would like you to write a personal note indicating that you were involved with the disposition of the remains and the personal effects and so forth. And that the Soviet authorities assured you that Gregory Fisher died instantly and suffered no pain and so forth. There are sample letters on file.'

'Sample letters of personal notes from me?'

'No,' Banks replied coolly. 'Sample personal condolence notes . . .' Banks seemed to grasp the contradiction in that, so he said, 'Personalize the sample.'

Lisa tapped her fingers on the table, then replied, 'Shall I tell them I spoke to their son before his death? That he called this embassy from the Rossiya Hotel and asked for help?'

'Certainly not. I just told you what to write, Miss Rhodes.' Banks added, 'Perhaps Colonel Hollis will write a similar letter to the deceased's parents.'

Hollis replied, 'I'll study the samples.'

Lisa looked at Hollis, then at Alevy and Banks. She said, 'I have phone messages on my desk from Peter Stills of *The New York Times*, Faith Lowry of *The Washington Post*, Mike Salerno of the Pacific News Bureau, and four or five other news agencies. Apparently in my absence someone in my department issued a press release regarding Gregory Fisher. Apparently, too, some journalists smell a bigger story.'

Banks leaned toward her. 'There is no story beyond the fact that an American tourist died in an automobile accident.'

'If the auto accident had happened in France or England that would not be news,' Lisa said. 'But in the Soviet Union, people get curious. This is a curious country, Charles. You may have noticed.' She added, 'That's why we sit in windowless rooms like this when we talk. It's not paranoia; it's reality, though no one in the West would believe half of it.'

At length Charles Banks responded, 'Your office has indeed issued a press release. They may issue another if new facts warrant it. Kay is handling the press on this. You are not assigned to this story.'

Lisa drew a deep breath. 'Why didn't the press release give all the facts? The call from the Rossiya –'

Alevy cut in. 'We may reveal that in time. For now, we're not going to. We're as aware as you are that there is more to this. But we're trying to get the facts before we make any accusations. You appreciate the current diplomatic thaw. Trust us.'

Lisa nodded reluctantly.

Hollis took a piece of paper from his pocket, a decoded radio message. 'I sent a query to Defense yesterday asking if a Major Jack or John Dodson was on the Vietnam MIA list. They replied in the negative.' He threw the paper on the table.

Charles Banks said, 'We made the same inquiry of State and also received a negative. So right there we have to wonder about Mr Fisher's story.'

'Do you?' Hollis continued, 'We were talking about trust. In my business, as in Seth's, rule number one is trust no one, including your own people.' Hollis poured himself a glass of mineral water and added, 'So I went to our library here yesterday and found a book written by a former Navy flier who was a POW in Vietnam. In the book was an appendix listing some one thousand men who are still unaccounted for. Among them is an Air Force major, named Jack Dodson.'

No one spoke.

Hollis said, 'I know my query elicited a negative, but I don't know if yours did. I think someone is playing games.'

Alevy said, 'Sam, leave it alone.'

Charles Banks added, 'Colonel, we are conducting an official investigation through diplomatic and other channels. In the meantime, neither you nor Miss Rhodes are to concern your-selves with this unless requested to give testimony. This is obviously beyond your respective duties.' He added, 'The ambassador would like a written report of your activities and whereabouts from the time you left Moscow yesterday afternoon. Thank you for taking care of the remains.'

Hollis stood. 'Mr Banks, please tell the ambassador that

unless or until I receive orders from my superiors to the contrary, I will pursue my own line of investigation into this matter.'

Lisa stood also. 'Charles, an American citizen named Gregory Fisher died under mysterious circumstances in the Soviet Union. Furthermore, Gregory Fisher told me on the telephone of another American citizen whom he met in a pine forest north of Borodino and who was apparently on the run from Soviet authorities –'

Seth Alevy interrupted, 'I recall on the tape that Mr Fisher mentioned the woods, but I don't recall him saying anything about a pine forest.' He tilted his chair forward and looked at her, then at Hollis. '*What* pine forest?'

Hollis replied, 'We must compare notes one of these days.' Hollis left.

He waited for Lisa at the elevator. He gave it two minutes, then five, then took the elevator down alone.

14

Sam Hollis walked up Kalinin Prospect, Moscow's answer to Fifth Avenue. At the corner of Tchaikovsky Street, a line of hopeful diners waited in front of the popular Arbat restaurant, and Hollis had to make his way around them. Moscow's rush hour was in full swing, everyone lugging bags, trying to buy anything that was for sale. Muscovites, peasants, and townsmen from the hinterlands descended on central Moscow daily for what they called shopping, though Hollis thought it more resembled the sack of the city.

Hollis stopped in front of the window of *Podarki Pyatero* – Gift Shop Five – and examined his reflection. His dark blue overcoat of wool was Moscow-standard as was his narrow-brimmed black hat and his oversize briefcase, which was useful for carrying fresh produce and meat when available. He supposed he blended in superficially, but he knew that Muscovites picked him out as a Westerner. Aside from his facial features he knew he carried himself differently than the people around him, and he remembered what Lisa said about how Russian men walk and a joke someone in the embassy told him when he'd first arrived: Two Muscovite men were walking down the street. One was carrying a huge bundle on his back and was bowed and stooped by the weight, taking each step as though it were his last. The other Muscovite was carrying nothing at all and was bowed and stooped, taking each step as though it were his last.

Hollis went inside the gift shop. It was not crowded as were the shops selling necessities, and the section in the rear that accepted only Western currency was empty.

Hollis picked out a carved wooden bear balancing a ball on its foot and a small aluminum *znachok* – a lapel pin – on which was a profile of Lenin. He handed over six American dollars, and the clerk, claiming she had no American coins for change, pushed some foil-wrapped chocolates toward him. Hollis had a dresser drawer full of chocolate change. 'I'll take pence.'

'Nyet.'

'Centimes.'

'Nyet.'

'Green stamps. Anything, but no more chocolate.'

'Nyet.'

Hollis stuck his purchases in his overcoat and went back into the chilly dusk.

Kalinin Prospect was a recently widened thoroughfare of twenty-story glass and concrete flats with shops on the ground floors. It cut through the quaint Arbat district, and Hollis, though he did not share Lisa's fondness for old Moscow, didn't think much of new Moscow either. The street was as wide as an expressway and the shops too far apart, which might be just as well.

Hollis stopped again, this time at the window of a woman's clothing store named *Moskvichka*, which translated to something like 'Miss Moscow', a name that always amused him for some reason. He looked at the passing crowd reflected in the window but couldn't spot his tail. He continued north, crossing October Square.

Hollis walked over a stone footbridge that led to the gate beneath the Troitsky Tower set in the red brick wall of the Kremlin. Two green-uniformed guards looked him over but said nothing. Hollis entered the sixty-acre complex of magnificent cathedrals, monuments, and public buildings, the heart of Soviet power and the soul of old Russia. Sam Hollis, who was not easily impressed, was still impressed by the Kremlin.

He walked past the Arsenal across Ivanovsky Square, threading his way through hundreds of tourists snapping pictures in the last light of day, the time when the Kremlin photographed best. He spotted two men engaged in conversation near the Troitsky gate. Like him they wore narrow-brim hats and dark overcoats. The two men stood out because they carried no briefcases or bags. Their hands were stuffed in their pockets, much like policemen everywhere, and you never knew what was in those hands. Hollis walked toward Spassky Tower on the northeast wall of the irregularly shaped citadel. The tower gate was not meant for pedestrian traffic and in fact was closed as he approached. But soon a black Volga sedan pulled away from the Presidium building, and Hollis followed it, quickening his pace. The wooden gates were pulled open by two sentries, and Hollis followed the Volga out, noticing the sentries exchanging nervous glances, but no one challenged him.

As the gates closed behind him, Hollis walked into Red Square opposite St Basil's Cathedral. Only Kremlin vehicles were allowed in the square, and pedestrian traffic was heaviest now at rush hour, which was why he liked this place and this hour to lose people. Hollis darted through the throng, diagonally in front of the Lenin mausoleum where a long line of people waited to view the embalmed corpse. He walked quickly past the huge GUM department store at the north end of the square and glanced back but didn't see the two men in overcoats. Hollis went down a set of steps in the sidewalk, and the stairs split – metro to the right, an underground passage beneath Red Square to the left. He went right, put five kopeks in the turnstile, and jumped on the fast-descending escalator. He stepped off into the huge marble station with crystal chandeliers. A train came within a minute, and he squeezed on with the commuters, taking the train north one stop to Dzerzhinsky Station.

Hollis came up the stairs into a small park area at the southern end of Dzerzhinsky Square. He approached a group of twenty or so people standing in a tight crowd. A pretty young woman with flaming red hair was addressing the group. She said in barely accented English, 'Behind you is the State Polytechnical Museum, whose exhibits trace the development of Russian engineering. This is worth visiting when you have a free day.'

A middle-aged woman to Hollis' left said in a New England accent, 'Free day? *What* free day?'

Her male companion said, '*Sh-h-h-h!*'

The Intourist guide gave the couple a glance, then looked curiously at Hollis before continuing. 'To your left there is the Museum of the History and Reconstruction of Moscow. There you can see how Soviet socialist planning has made old Moscow into one of the most beautiful cities in the world.'

Hollis noticed that the American tourists were stealing glances at him, and he knew at least some of them were imagining he was KGB, which was what they wanted to believe. It was part of the tour package, a deliciously sinister tale to tell to the folks back home.

'To your right,' the redhead continued in a hoarse but sexy voice, 'is the Mayakovsky Museum, the flat where the famous poet spent the last eleven years of his life.'

Someone in front of Hollis asked his neighbor, 'Will there be a test?'

Hollis thought if there were a test, one question should be, 'Is it true that Vladimir Mayakovsky's suicide was a result of his disillusionment with Soviet life?'

'In the center of the square you see the handsome bronze statue of Felix Dzerzhinsky, eminent party leader, Soviet statesman, and close comrade of Lenin.'

Hollis thought she should add, 'Mass murderer and founder of the dreaded State Security apparatus.' How could anyone pass a test without these facts?

The guide motioned over her shoulder across the square. 'That handsome building with the tall, arched windows is Detsky Mir – Children's World – Moscow's largest toy store. Russians love to spoil their children,' she added, more from rote, Hollis thought, than from any personal experience.

A murmur came from the crowd, and a woman called out, 'Oh, can we go there?'

'On your free time.'

Someone laughed.

'But come,' the guide said curtly. 'We will go to the bus now, yes?'

'What is that large building there?' a man asked.

'That,' the guide said smoothly without even looking up, 'is the offices of the electric power agency.'

And it was, Hollis thought, if one's idea of electric power was fifty volts to the scrotum. He watched the procession wend its way back to the red and white Intourist bus. Passing Muscovites scrutinized the foreigners' clothes, and Hollis wished American tourists would learn to dress better. A few people in the group turned and took pictures of the electric power agency, knowing from some more reliable source that it was the headquarters of the KGB, the infamous Lubyanka prison.

The streetlights snapped on, though there was some daylight left. Hollis took the Lenin pin from his pocket and stuck it in his lapel, then sat on a bench that faced up Marx Prospect. From his briefcase he took a green apple, a hunk of goat's cheese, and a small paring knife. He laid a cloth napkin on his lap and went to work on the apple and cheese with his knife. On a bench to his right an older man was eating black bread. The park benches were Moscow's fastfood chain. Hollis threw an apple paring toward a group of sparrows, who scattered, then came back and pecked at it.

Hollis saw him coming down Marx Prospect, past the remnants of the sixteenth-century walls, his tailored overcoat belted at the waist, marking him as a military man in mufti. His stride, too, was military, and he wore a smart cap of fur. He carried his familiar pigskin attaché case, too thin for apples or cheese.

General Valentin Surikov, of the Red Air Force, walked directly in front of Hollis, scattering the sparrows. Surikov saw the lapel pin signifying it was safe and sat at the opposite end of the bench from Hollis. The general lit a cigarette, put on a pair of gold-rimmed glasses, and took a copy of *Pravda* from his attaché case. Without looking up he said in English, 'The cheese should be wrapped in cellophane not newspaper. We have cellophane. A peasant would use newspaper.'

197

Hollis crumpled the piece of newspaper and put it in his briefcase.

'Why did you pick this place?' Surikov asked.

'Why not?'

'This is no game, my friend. We don't do this so you can have something amusing to talk about with your friends.'

'No, we don't, General.'

'If they catch you, they kick you out with your diplomatic immunity. If they catch me, they take me there' – he cocked his head toward the Lubyanka – 'and shoot me.'

Sam Hollis did not particularly like General Valentin Surikov, but he wasn't sure why. Hollis said, 'Do you know what they did to Colonel Penkovsky when they caught him?'

'I don't know who Colonel Penkovsky is.'

'Was.' Hollis was newly amazed each time he discovered how little these people knew about the society in which they lived. Even generals. 'Penkovsky did what you are doing. Quite famous in the West. The fellows over there tortured him for six months, then threw him alive into a furnace. Firing squads are for lesser offenses.' Hollis cut out a section of apple, then made several crosscuts looking for worms. Finding none whole or halved, he put the small pieces of apple into his mouth and chewed.

General Surikov chain-lit another cigarette. 'You're absolutely certain you weren't followed here?'

Hollis shrugged. 'I do my best. How about you?'

'I certainly can't take overt evasive actions like you can. I have to walk normally.'

'What's your business in this quarter, Comrade General?'

'I have reservations at the Berlin Hotel restaurant in one hour. I'm meeting my granddaughter for dinner.'

'Good. I like that.'

Surikov asked, 'How do you know they threw him in a furnace?'

'What? Oh, Penkovsky. I don't know. I was told by my boss.

But my boss lies just like yours does. Sounds good. Supposed to make me hate the KGB more.'

'And do you?'

'Not personally,' Hollis replied. 'They haven't fucked up my whole life like they have yours and everyone else's from Vladivostok to East Berlin. Do *you* hate them?'

Surikov didn't reply, which Hollis found intriguing. He couldn't get a handle on Surikov's motivation.

Surikov said, 'Your note said it was urgent.'

Hollis nodded. They had worked out a simple expedient for arranging unscheduled rendezvous. Hollis would simply messenger a note to his counterpart, Colonel Andreyev, in the Soviet Defense Ministry and request an inconsequential bit of information regarding the ongoing arms limitation talks. Andreyev would naturally buck the request up the line, and it would eventually come across General Surikov's desk. Surikov would place Hollis' note over a small, detailed map of central Moscow. A pinprick in the note would pinpoint the meeting place. The time was always five-thirty of that day. If there was a pencil smudge in any corner of the note, the meeting was for the following day. The word 'response' anywhere in the note meant urgent.

Hollis said, 'Yes, urgent, but nothing for you to worry about.' Hollis thought he'd probably upset Surikov's day.

Surikov turned a page of the oversize newspaper and held it up to catch the light. 'What is it then?'

'Who won the battle of Borodino?'

Surikov glanced at Hollis. 'What?'

Hollis said, 'Tolstoy gives an accurate description of a French Pyrrhic victory, yet there are some Russians who think that it was a Russian victory. How do you reconcile these facts? Who won the battle?'

Surikov replied, 'What are you talking about?'

'Reality. Truth. I need the truth. The real truth, not the Soviet truth. I need some information on a former Red Air Force training facility.'

'Yes?'

'North of Borodino.'

Surikov did not reply.

'A former ground school. The *Komitet* uses it now for other purposes. You know the one I mean, don't you?'

Again Surikov made no reply.

Hollis said, 'If you know nothing about it, I'll leave now.'

Surikov cleared his throat. 'I know something about it.'

'But it must not be too important, General, or you'd have told me long ago.'

Surikov let a full minute pass before he replied, 'It is so important, Colonel, so potentially dangerous for the future of Soviet-American relations and world peace, that it is better left alone.'

Hollis did not look toward Surikov, but he could tell by his tone of voice that Surikov, usually cool as ice, was agitated. Hollis said, 'Well, that's very good of you to stand guard over the peace. However, something leaked, and before it gets misunderstood or before it gets into the wrong hands, I want to control it. But first I have to understand it.'

Surikov refolded his newspaper, and Hollis allowed himself a glance at the man and saw on his face a troubled expression. Hollis said, 'Tell me what you know and how you know it.'

'First tell me what *you* know.'

'I know to ask the question about the place. That's *all* you have to know.'

Surikov replied, 'I have to think this over.'

'You've been doing that since the first day you contacted me a year ago.'

'Yes? You know my mind and my soul? You're not even Russian.'

'Neither are you, General. You're a Muscovite, a Soviet man, and we're both modern military men. We understand each other.'

'Alright,' Surikov said decisively. 'I *have* thought this through. I want to get out.'

200

'Then consider yourself out.' Hollis finally found a worm and threw the apple core to the sparrows. 'Good luck and thanks.'

'I want to get out of *here. Russia.*'

Hollis knew what Surikov had meant. Sometimes, as with troublesome spouses, you had to begin negotations by packing their bags for them.

'I want to spend my last days in the West,' Surikov said.

'Me too.'

Surikov didn't respond.

'Do you think they're on to you?' Hollis asked.

'No, but they will be if I give you what you want. I want to go to London.'

'Really? My wife's in London. She didn't like it here either.'

'How long will it take you to get me to the West?'

'It's about a four-hour flight, General.' Hollis got a perverse pleasure in reminding Soviet officials of the kind of state they had created. He added, 'You apply for a travel visa, and I'll see to the Aeroflot reservation. One-way, correct?'

'You mean to tell me you can't get people out of here?'

'It's not real easy. You guys got a hell of a good police force.'

'Don't think that if you keep me here, I will continue to feed you secrets, my friend. If you can't get me out, I am retiring from your service.'

'I told you that was okay.'

'I am going to the British.'

Hollis wiped his hands on his napkin. Losing an agent who panicked and quit was one thing; losing him to another service was quite another. The new theory was to let a source leave anytime he wanted and not try to squeeze him as they'd done in the past. Squeezed agents inevitably got caught, and then the KGB found out everything they'd given away and took steps to fix things up. But if Surikov went to the Brits and got blown later, Hollis might never know that Surikov was singing in the Lubyanka.

'Or the French,' the general said. 'I speak passable French. I could live in Paris.'

'If you go to the French, you might as well go right to the KGB and save time. They're penetrated, General. Most of them hold secondary commissions in the KGB.'

'Don't try to frighten me. The Germans are my third choice. So now the choice is yours.'

'Well, I'll take it up with my people. It's not that we don't want to, it's just that it's dangerous. For you.' Actually, Hollis thought, it was more that they didn't want to. Some politicians loved a high-ranking defector, but for intelligence people, a defecting spy told the KGB the same thing as a captured spy, namely that everything that had come across his desk was now in enemy hands. Surikov had either to go on spying for him or just retire and shut up. But since he seemed inclined to do neither, Hollis thought a car accident was what Surikov needed. Hollis, however, didn't like that sort of thing and hoped he could think of something more creative. 'We'll think it over. You too. The West is not all it's cracked up to be.'

'Don't joke with me, Colonel.' Surikov chain-lit his third or fourth cigarette.

Hollis took a *Pravda* from his briefcase. He read modern Russian fairly well – bureaucratic Russian, journalese, communist Russian. But he had difficulty with Chekhov, Gogol, Tolstoy, and the like, and he thought he'd enjoy working on that someday if he lived long enough to sit in a rocking chair with Tolstoy.

He stole a glance at Surikov, who seemed actually to be reading his *Pravda*, The Organ of the Central Committee of the Communist Party of the Soviet Union. Reading it and believing it, in some monstrous display of triple-think. These people, Hollis decided, were hopeless. Hopeless while they were in country, childlike and bewildered when you got them out and gave them their first copy of *The Washington Post* or London

Times. Hollis perused a piece under the headline: *Afghanistan is Fighting and Building*. Hollis read: *Soviet-Afghan political and economic ties, which go back to V. I. Lenin, have a long history and serve as a vivid example of good-neighbor relations.*

Hollis glanced again at Surikov. The man had been fed empty calories for the brain all his life, and it was no wonder his intellect was malnourished. Hollis realized he had to be careful how he handled this man.

Surikov said as he rustled a page, 'You understand, Colonel, that if I give you what you are asking for, neither you nor I should remain in Russia.'

'Is that so?' Hollis recalled the first time he had met General Surikov. Surikov had approached him directly a year ago at a reception given by the Yugoslav ambassador on the occasion of Yugoslav Independence Day. Surikov had said in English, 'Colonel Hollis, my name is Valentin Surikov.' Surikov was wearing the uniform of a Red Air Force general, so Hollis had replied with the required military courtesy, 'Pleasure meeting you, General.'

Surikov had continued, almost matter-of-factly, 'I wish to pass sensitive documents to your government. Tell whoever it is who handles such things to meet me at the Finnish ambassador's reception next week.' Surikov had then walked away.

Hollis himself had shown up at the Finnish reception.

Now, sitting here in Dzerzhinsky Square a year later, Hollis agreed with Surikov that one way or the other he and Valentin Surikov were coming to the end of their dangerous liaison.

Surikov looked over his newspaper at a group of men leaving through the front doors of Lubyanka. Surikov said, 'You asked for the information. I gave you my price.'

Hollis too noticed the men standing in front of the KGB headquarters. There were six of them, talking and gesturing. They seemed in a good mood, Hollis thought. But why shouldn't they be? They were the police in a police state.

Surikov seemed to be getting anxious. He said quickly in a voice that Hollis could barely hear, 'If you know anything about the facility at Borodino, you will know that getting me out of here is a cheap price for what I can tell you.' Surikov added in one of his practiced American phrases, 'It will blow your mind, Colonel.'

Hollis smiled behind his newspaper. His eyes moved again to the Lubyanka across the square.

It was a rather handsome Italianate building of eight stories. The first two stories were grey granite; and the upper floors were cement stucco painted that odd mustard color the Russians seemed fond of. It was one of the few buildings in Moscow with clean windows, and he could see people at work under sickly pale fluorescent lighting.

What had always struck him about the place was its location, right in the heart of Moscow, a stone's throw from a children's department store in a square where tens of thousands of people saw it every day. Here was a place, Hollis thought, where thousands of Soviet citizens had been tortured and shot, a place referred to by Intourist guides as the electric power authority, and Muscovites, if they referred to it at all, whispered the despised name: Lubyanka.

Yet neither the KGB nor the Soviet government had the good grace to remove the facility, and it stood as a monument to brutality. But perhaps they knew what they were doing. It did remind one, did it not? Hollis couldn't help but think each time he saw the place that he ought not to be doing things that would put him in there.

Hollis looked away, but the image of the place stayed in his mind's eye. He asked, 'Do you know a KGB colonel who calls himself Burov?'

'Perhaps.'

Hollis watched as the six men in front of the building split up. Four headed toward Hollis and Surikov.

General Surikov stood. 'We have been here quite long enough. I will be at Gogol's grave next Sunday at one.'

As usual, Surikov picked a place that would send Hollis leafing through his Michelin guide. 'Tomorrow, General.'

'Sunday, Colonel. I need time.'

'Alright. Alternate rendervous?'

'None. Gogol's grave. Sunday. One P.M. And you will tell me how you are getting me to the West, and I will give you half a secret. I'll give you the second half when I'm in London.' Surikov tucked his *Pravda* under his arm and picked up his attaché case. He seemed anxious to leave but stood motionless as the four KGB approached. They looked at Hollis and Surikov with that keen eye of appraisal that Hollis had come to associate with muggers looking for an easy mark. They slowed their pace, then continued on.

Surikov, quite pale, Hollis noticed, turned without a word and crossed the square.

Hollis waited for Felix Dzerzhinsky's spiritual kin to reappear in the square and arrest him, but nothing happened. Life went on, the criminals – Hollis and Surikov – had once again foiled the organs of state security.

Hollis sometimes wondered if this game was worth his life. But this time he thought of Greg Fisher's life, which was over, and Major Jack Dodson's life, which was in the balance. And he thought of Ernie Simms and the thousand other fliers whose families and whose nation had given them up for dead. Hollis thought that maybe, if he did everything right, he might bring them home again.

Hollis watched Surikov disappear into the throng of people who were laying siege to Detsky Mir. 'I suppose,' Hollis said to himself, 'that it would be the lines that caused me to defect. I hate lines.'

No, Sam Hollis reflected, *I do not like General Valentin Surikov, though I'm not sure why*. But Hollis had just learned not to underestimate him. Hollis admitted that Surikov's motives for treason were not base – Surikov had never taken a ruble, a dollar, or a banked Swiss franc. Nor had he bothered Hollis for things from the American embassy stores. But Surikov's motives were not lofty either. He had had no ideological conversion as far as Hollis knew. And according to Surikov's own account, he had not suffered any personal harm from the system, no one in his family had spent time in a camp or internal exile. In fact, General Surikov did not have to join the crowds at Detsky Mir to buy his grandchildren toys. He had only the inconvenience of moving through the common people on his way to the Berlin Hotel, where he was headed for a decent meal. Surikov belonged to the communist aristocracy, the *nomenklatura*, who had shop-at-home service and special stores, who lived a life of gross hypocrisy and privilege unknown in even the most class-stratified societies of the West.

Then one day, Hollis thought, for reasons known only to himself, Valentin Surikov decided he didn't like it here anymore. He wanted to live in London, though he'd never been outside the Soviet Union as far as Hollis knew. And it wasn't a scam as Hollis had determined early on. The Surikov stuff was top grade – Red Air Force postings, unit designations, command assignments, and so forth. Stuff no spy satellite could tell you. Apparently Surikov was a – or *the* – personnel officer for the entire Red Air Force, though he never gave out that piece of information.

Now General Surikov had indicated he had the airfare to London and wanted Hollis to arrange the transportation. Half on booking, half on arrival. Hollis nodded to himself as he stuffed his *Pravda* in his coat pocket. There was a way out, but it couldn't be used too often. Hollis didn't know if he wanted Surikov to live in London. Surikov deserved to live in Moscow. Served him right.

Hollis wanted to go back to the embassy now, but the gentlemen of the KGB's Seventh Directorate – the embassy watchers – having lost him in Red Square, would at least note his time of return to the embassy compound. Somehow Hollis felt that the longer he was gone – like some errant spouse (like *his* errant spouse) – the more annoyed the watchers would become. So he decided to kill an hour in the State Polytechnical Museum. Maybe it *was* worth a visit. He was a sucker for redheads anyway. Hollis stood, removed his Lenin pin, and threw it to the ground. He picked up his briefcase and turned toward the museum.

He thought of his wife Katherine in London. Running Surikov was one reason he couldn't take leave to go settle things with her there. Now Surikov might get to London before him. The ironies on this job were endless. 'Endless,' he said aloud.

Lisa Rhodes popped into his mind though he'd tried to push her out of it all day. He realized he felt responsible for her safety, which might be one of the reasons he hadn't called her. He wanted the involvement, but since he always felt like a moving target, he didn't know if he wanted her near him. These dilemmas hadn't bothered Alevy, apparently, as Hollis had discovered in the Arbat antique store.

In this business, Hollis had observed, men's relationships with women often fell into two categories: professional/sexual or sexual/professional. Alevy, he knew, preferred the former. Hollis was comfortable with neither.

Hollis decided that maybe he ought to ask Lisa Rhodes what she thought.

15

Sam Hollis entered the bowling alley in the basement of the eight-story embassy chancery building. There were three games in progress. The place was stuffy, and Hollis bought a Heineken at the bar, then took a seat at an empty lane. He noticed four female FSPs – Foreign Service Personnel – on the adjoining alley laughing and drinking. He recognized three as secretaries and one as a nurse. They all wore jeans and T-shirts. The nurse, a petite blonde, looked at him. Her T-shirt read: *Gee, Toto, I don't think we're in Kansas anymore.*

Hollis smiled. The woman winked at him and turned back to her game. Hollis sipped on his beer. He watched them bowl. There was something oddly frenetic in the way they bowled, drank, and laughed, he thought, as though their mainsprings were wound too tight. He half expected them to fall to the floor in five minutes.

On the lane to his right were a married couple, Bill and Joan Horgan. He was in the FAS – Foreign Agricultural Service; she taught at the Anglo-American School. With them were their two teenaged daughters. Bill and Joan gave him a cheery wave. The girls looked bored senseless. One of them, Hollis recalled, was prone to hysteria and weeping.

Two lanes farther down, four Marines in civilian clothing were rolling balls. The Marine watchstanders, as they were called, numbered about twenty. They were handpicked for their height, bearing, intelligence, and quite possibly their looks, Hollis thought. As per Marine regulations, they were unmarried. These facts had caused some problems, most notably the sex-for-secrets scandal at the old embassy.

Russia, Hollis thought, more than any country he'd ever served in, changed you. You went in as one person and came out another. An American, whether a tourist, business person, or embassy staffer, was the center of attention and under constant scrutiny, from the locals and from the state. You woke up with tension, lived with tension, and went to bed with tension. Some people, such as Katherine, fled. Some cracked up, some became mildly idiosyncratic, some betrayed their country, and some, such as Lisa, embraced the Russian bear and danced with it, which, Hollis reflected, might be the only way to get out with most of your marbles.

The bowling lanes and the adjoining spaces doubled as a bomb shelter, and Hollis sometimes wondered if the day would ever come when he would be watching the automatic pinsetters while waiting for an American nuclear strike to obliterate central Moscow above.

Seth Alevy walked over and sat on the bench beside Hollis. Alevy swirled his scotch and ice cubes as he regarded the four women. 'Right,' Alevy said at last, 'we are not in Kansas. We are below the Emerald City.'

One of the secretaries threw a strike, did a little victory jig, and slapped palms with her teammate. Hollis said to Alevy, 'You want to roll a few sets?'

'"Frames." No.'

The ambient noise cover down here was good, Hollis knew, and any bugs planted during construction were ineffective, as were the KGB directional microphones in the surrounding buildings. Which was one reason Hollis understood, that Alevy liked to meet here. But the other reason that Alevy had not requisitioned one of the safe rooms in the chancery was that Alevy suspected those rooms were bugged by State Department Intelligence. As the CIA station chief in Moscow, responsible ultimately for all American intelligence in the Soviet Union, Seth Alevy had no intention of being bugged by a minor league bunch such as State Department Intelligence. Alevy was only slightly less disdainful of Hollis' Defense Intelligence Agency. Alevy had a better psychic relationship with the KGB, Hollis thought, because they didn't pretend to be his friends.

Alevy asked, 'Did Ace show?'

'Yes.'

'Can he help us with this?'

'I think so.'

Alevy nodded. 'Why did you think he could, Sam?'

'Just a hunch.'

'You didn't expose one of our best assets in the Soviet Union to a personal meeting with you on a hunch.'

'Ace is Red Air Force. Dodson is – or was – US Air Force. I went with that.'

'That's pretty thin. Now that we're alone, why don't you tell me everything the French couple told you, then tell me what you did and saw on the way to Mozhaisk. Then tell me what Ace told you tonight. And while you're at it, tell me things I haven't even thought to ask you about this case.'

'I'm really into interservice rivalry, Seth. I'm protecting my own petty little fiefdom. It gives me a sense of worth and importance.'

'I think we're being sarcastic.' Alevy added, 'Alright, we can pursue this along separate lines for a while. All I ask of you is to be careful what you tell the Pentagon, and I'll do the same with Langley.'

'Why?'

'You know why. This thing is so big they'll try to run it from there. Then State and the White House will get involved, and we'll be getting micromanagement from one of those bozos in the basement of the White House. We're the ones who risk our lives out here, Sam.'

Hollis didn't reply.

Alevy added, 'You risked your life once in a war that had enough bombing limitation rules to make sure you didn't hurt anyone but yourself. Are you still pissed about that? Would you like to even the score with Washington on that? Do you want to maybe bring a few fliers home? You know they're out there, Sam. I know it too.'

Hollis stared Alevy in the eye and said softly, 'I'll listen to reason and logic, Seth. But don't you ever – *ever* try to manipulate me with that argument. Stay out of my past. I'll deal with that.'

Alevy maintained eye contact, then nodded and turned away. 'Okay. Cheap shot.'

Hollis finished his beer.

Alevy stood and went to the bar, coming back with two more drinks. He handed Hollis a beer. Alevy said, 'You know, I've been thinking about Ace. I don't know if he rings. Do you?'

Hollis recognized the format: Prove to me your man is not a double. 'He's always had the goods,' Hollis reminded him.

Alevy looked at Hollis. 'Seems so. Everything he's given you has checked out with my people and yours. Yet . . .'

Hollis stared down at Alevy's brightly polished handmade broughams. Italian-tailored blue silk suit. Custom shirt and Liberty tie. Seth Alevy spent a good deal of money on good clothing. And yet someone who knew Alevy in the States said he dressed better in Moscow than in Washington. Hollis suspected that the sartorial splendor was just Alevy's way of annoying the Russians. Alevy, to the best of Hollis' knowledge, was the only man who ever showed up at the Bolshoi in a tuxedo. In fact, Hollis was convinced that Alevy owned the only tuxedo in all of Russia.

Alevy finished his second scotch. 'Ace's stuff is good, but he may be setting us up for a nasty sting. You might have handed him the means if you mentioned Borodino.'

'There's always that possibility.' Hollis regarded the four FSPs. The one with the Toto T-shirt threw a gutter ball and uttered an obscenity. She pulled the front of her T-shirt up and wiped the perspiration from her face, baring her midriff in the process. 'Hard fuzzy-belly.'

'What?' Alevy looked. 'Oh.'

'What do you do for sex now, Seth?'

'That's a rather personal question.'

'No, it's a professional question.'

'Well . . . I don't have to remind you, as our Marines have

211

to be reminded daily, that the local *devitsas* are off-limits. And so, theoretically, are the wives of our coworkers.'

'Theoretically.'

'There are,' Alevy said, ignoring this, 'at this moment exactly thirty-two single women in the embassy, and perhaps twenty or more of them have already formed liaisons.'

'Have they? How do you know?'

'I keep a dossier on everyone here. Isn't that disgusting?'

'No comment.'

'As for the women in other Western embassies, they are off-limits to intelligence types such as us. For you and I the policy is to date only single American women.' Alevy added, 'You could hang around the hard-currency bars and find an unattached American tourist.'

'Have you done that?'

'Maybe.' Alevy looked at Hollis. 'I assume your wife is not returning. However, until you get a divorce, you have to play by the rules.' Alevy smiled and patted Hollis' arm, a rare display of intimacy. 'You don't know how to be a bachelor anyway. You were married too long.'

Hollis didn't respond.

'Did you have someone special in mind?' Alevy asked.

'No, just checking the rules.'

Alevy regarded Hollis for some time, then asked, 'Did something happen between you and Lisa? That's a professional question.'

'Then look in your dossier.'

'Well,' Alevy said in a cooler tone, 'I want you to think now about Ace.'

'I have. So I had him meet me in Dzerzhinsky Square. And some K-goons came along, and Ace went pale. Hard to fake skin color.'

Alevy shrugged. 'Heard of a similar situation where a guy did fake it with some sort of nitrate substance. Turned him ashen. But Dzerzhinsky Square was an inspired idea. Not bad for a military guy. A little risky though.'

Hollis sipped his beer.

Alevy said, 'Regarding Ace, if you cut him loose, we're ahead of the game whether he's real or not. If you stay with him, you may find out what he's up to. But what he's up to may be murder, and it may be too late.'

'Actually there's been a new development.'

'What?'

'He wants to head West.'

'Does he?'

'So he says.'

Alevy thought a moment. 'Then maybe what he wants is to find out how we get people out of here.'

'Maybe. Maybe he just really wants to defect.' Hollis cradled the beer bottle in his hands and watched the condensation drip. Alevy had a weak spot in his professional makeup: He personally didn't like most Russians. Not liking the Soviet regime was a job qualification. But Alevy was unable to concede that anyone who had been shaped by the regime was capable of anything but treachery and vileness. Perhaps he was right. Certainly General Surikov was a good example of the New Soviet Man. 'I don't intend to cut him loose or to turn him over to you, if that's what you're getting at.'

'I'm not suggesting that. He apparently wants to deal with a brother Air Force officer. I couldn't run him. What's he offering for the ticket West? The scoop on Borodino?'

'Yes.'

'Maybe you planted that in his head. Maybe he'll make up a crock of shit just to get out of here.'

'We'll soon know.'

'Are you meeting with him in person again?'

'Yes.' Hollis put his beer bottle on the floor and wiped his hands on his trousers. 'But I don't want company.'

'I want to talk to this joker myself.'

Hollis said, 'I don't think it's a good idea for the CIA station chief, the most important man in Western intelligence in the

213

Soviet Union, to run around Moscow trying to rendezvous with Russian informers. Do you?'

'Let me worry about my job description.'

'Sure.' Hollis considered what little else he knew about Alevy. In Langley, he'd turned out to be a genius at political analysis, and his prophesies regarding Soviet intentions, particularly Gorbachev's *glasnost*, had been so accurate that it seemed, some said, he had a friend in the Politboro. Alevy had arrived in Moscow about three years before as third deputy to the CIA station chief. Now he *was* the station chief. He was not allowed to leave the embassy compound without at least two security men and one cyanide pill. Hollis knew he left without the former but was sure he never left without the latter.

Alevy's official job with the diplomatic mission was that of political affairs officer, but the cover was thin, as it usually was with this sort of thing. The KGB knew who he was, and so did most of the senior American staff. 'Maybe *that* is Ace's scam,' Hollis said baitingly. 'To draw you out so they can kill *you*.'

'Even *they* don't kill senior American diplomats.'

'In your case they'd make an exception. Anyway, you're not a diplomat.'

'I am. I have a diplomatic passport. I go to all the receptions and talk like a diplomatic dork.'

Hollis stood. 'What were you doing in Sadovniki Friday night?'

Alevy stood also. 'A Sukkot party. The harvest festival. Sort of like Thanksgiving.'

Hollis nodded. He had heard that Alevy once lived some months in the Russian Jewish community of Brooklyn's Brighton Beach section. Thus he spoke his Russian with a Moscow-Leningrad accent and was perhaps the only man in the embassy who could actually pass for a Soviet citizen under close scrutiny. Hollis imagined that Alevy had also heard some firsthand accounts of religious persecution from his friends in Brighton Beach, and had also been given quite a few names

214

to contact in Moscow, thus arriving in Moscow with assets no one else had.

Alevy asked, 'Do you know anything about Judaism?'

'I know the Soviets aren't too keen on it. I know that religious observances can attract the K-goons. I know the ambassador would not like you annoying our host government.'

'Fuck his excellency.' Alevy added, 'Jews are politically unreliable here, so you can fraternize with them.'

Hollis considered the irony in this. American Jews were once thought politically unreliable by the CIA. Now Alevy was the CIA Moscow station chief partly *because* he was a Jew. Times change.

As though Alevy had read Hollis' mind, Alevy said, 'Jewish dissidents are our potential fifth column here, Sam. We should build more bridges to that community.'

'Should we?' But beyond all that, Hollis thought, Alevy was playing a dangerous game, dangerous because it had become a personal game with no official backing or backup. Someday Seth Alevy would find himself alone with his cyanide pill. Hollis found himself saying something he'd thought about in Pavel's *izba*. 'Those people have enough problems, Seth. They don't need you hanging around making things worse.'

'Bullshit. Things get worse for Jews only when they try to accommodate their persecutors.'

'Maybe. Look, I don't talk politics or religion – only sex and football. I'm just telling you as a colleague, and yes, you idiot, even as your friend, that the KGB will forgive your spying, but not your Judaism. We need you here, especially now, until this new thing is settled.'

Alevy did not acknowledge Hollis' words at all, but asked, 'So, where and when are you meeting Ace?'

Hollis knew he couldn't very well refuse to answer. 'Gogol's grave. Next Sunday. Three P.M. Give or take a few hours.'

'Where is Gogol's grave these days?'

'Beats me.'

As Alevy and Hollis walked toward the exit, Hollis noticed

that the Marines, the three secretaries, and the nurse had joined forces and retired to the lounge. The Horgans must have left without his noticing. The lanes were empty and quiet. And so were the game rooms and the swimming pool and all the other activity centers in the compound except the bars. There was a sort of mass lethargy that gripped this place, especially with the onset of winter. Hollis had never seen this kind of aimlessness and listlessness in any other American embassy. He didn't know what a behavioral psychologist would make of this maze and its white rats, but Hollis' theory was that the people inside the walls had somehow absorbed the malaise of the people outside the walls.

Hollis stared at the exit sign above the elevator and a word came to mind: *bezizkhodnost*. Exitlessness; dead end; futility; hopelessness; going nowhere – all contained within that one expressive word that the Russian people used but *Pravda* never printed. '*Bezizkhodnost*.'

Alevy looked at him and seemed to understand. 'That's what's left when you subtract God from man.'

'But I see it here too. I think it's catching.'

'Maybe,' Alevy said, 'but not for us. We know what we're about, don't we, Sam?'

'Indeed we do.'

'Fuck the Reds,' Alevy said.

'Each and every day,' Hollis replied, but at the same time thinking that was no longer enough. Thinking that this time he had a chance to do something positive, to put Haiphong harbor to rest in his own mind, and to put the whole MIA question to rest for his country.

The two elevators came simultaneously. Hollis got in one, and Alevy the other.

16

Lisa Rhodes picked up the telephone in her office, dialed Hollis' office, then before it rang, hung up. 'Damn him.' She dialed Alevy's office, and his secretary put her through. Alevy said, 'Hello, Li –'

'Did you tell Sam Hollis to stay away from me?'

'No, I wouldn't –'

'Are you lying to me?'

'No. But to be honest with you, I don't think it's a good idea for you to get invol –'

'Don't fuck around with my life, Seth.'

'Just calm down.'

She took a deep breath. 'Okay. Sorry.'

'Look, if he's done a disappearing act on you . . . Anyway, *I* still love you. Why don't we talk –'

'We talked.'

'I should really be angry. What happened out there in that village?'

'It's in my report.'

'Lisa –'

'I have to go. Bye, Seth.' She hung up. 'Damn men.'

Lisa looked at her watch, saw it was five P.M., and poured herself a bourbon. She pulled a press release toward her and worked on it without knowing what she was writing.

A few minutes later Kay Hoffman walked in and took her favourite seat on the hot-air register. 'Ah. You ever try this?'

Lisa didn't reply and went back to the press release.

Kay Hoffman picked up a just-arrived copy of the previous day's *Washington Post* and scanned it, then glanced at Lisa. 'You alright?'

'Yes.'

'Monthly blues?'

'No.' Lisa struck out a line of the typed copy. She reflected on her job in the United States Information Service. She wrote news releases, but she was also the resident Russophile, responsible for cultural affairs. She arranged for Soviet cultural missions to tour the States. They sent the Bolshoi, and the US sent Van Halen.

Lisa Rhodes loved Russian poetry in its original language, and Pasternak moved her deeply. She was an expert on icons, enjoyed Russian ballet, traditional Russian cooking, and folk art. She thought she understood the mysticism in the Russian soul – the unsevered link between the Russian race, the land, and the Orthodox church. And since Yablonya, she thought she felt her own Russianness more.

She sometimes thought of herself as a thin rope bridge between two iron superstructures. But if the Americans and Soviets were determined not to understand each other, that was their problem. One day they'd blow themselves and the rest of the earth into oblivion. Then the two cultures would be similar.

She made a few more notes on her press release. She usually wrote two releases – one for America, one in Russian for the Soviet news service, Tass. Tass used what they wanted without attribution. In that respect, at least, the Soviet and American press were alike. She looked up at Kay. 'Do I have to be nice to Van Halen or to the audience?'

Kay glanced up from her newspaper. 'Oh . . . are you still working on that? That has to go out today. Just sound up.'

'Where do you get your orders from?'

'I don't get orders, Lisa. Only direction.'

'From *where*?'

'High up.'

'Someday I'm going to write what I want. What I really saw here.'

'Some day you can. But today you write what you're told.'

218

'That's what some *apparatchik* is being told at the Tass office tonight.'

'Maybe. But we won't shoot you if you don't do what we say. So don't tell me we are no different from them.'

'No, I meant . . . there's more to the story. The whole idea of the Russian youth enthralled by Western pop culture. Every kid there was dressed in blue jeans. They were shouting in English, "Super," "Beautiful, baby." It was . . .' She thought a moment. 'It was surreal is what it was. But was it revolution?'

Kay Hoffman stared at her awhile, then said, 'If it was, that is *not* what you will write about.'

Lisa went back to her press release.

Kay went back to her newspaper.

Lisa thought, *But what was it? What is going on here?* Questions such as that, however, were not within the purview of the USIS. Working for the USIS was like working for the Ministry of Truth; when the party line changed, you changed with it.

At the moment, Soviet-American relations were on the verge of a breakthrough. Thus all this cultural activity was a precursor to the diplomatic activity. Her orders – her directions – were to be positive, upbeat. Think peace.

Those had been her orders some years back, before Nicholas Daniloff, an American correspondent, had been arrested by the KGB on a trumped-up spy charge. Then new orders came down: cancel all cultural exchanges. And so it went, in an Orwellian about-face, in mid-sentence, the word processors ceased churning out puff pieces and began issuing terse sentences of canceled events. But for the moment, puff was required. Though now there was the Fisher affair. She said to Kay Hoffman, 'I don't appreciate you writing that press release about Fisher's death and you putting my name on it.'

Kay shrugged. 'Sorry. Orders.' She asked, 'What *did* happen to that Fisher boy?'

'Exactly what you said in my press release.'

'I guess I deserved that.'

'Maybe I should resign over that.'

Kay stayed silent, then said, 'I don't think you need bother.'

'Meaning what?'

'Forget it.'

Lisa finished her cigarette and lit another. Her tour of duty was four years. She had less than two to go. As a Foreign Service Officer, she was assigned overseas duty somewhat as a military officer was. In fact, her rank of FSO-6 was roughly equivalent to an Army captain. Her title was Deputy Public Affairs Officer. Kay Hoffman was the PAO. They had six FSPs – five women and one man – working for them. It was all very exciting, very boring; very easy, very trying.

She looked at the wall clock. It was ten past five. She thought she would go to her apartment and write captions for her photographic essay of Moscow. She stood. 'Enough of this place.' She threw a few papers in her attaché case.

Kay looked up from her newspaper. 'Are you alright?'

'No one is alright here,' Lisa replied. 'This is what State calls a hardship tour. Do you think the Soviet government is insulted by that?'

Kay smiled grimly. 'They don't give a damn. This whole fucking country is on a lifetime hardship tour, and the government put them there.' Kay added, 'It helps if you have a lover.'

'No, it doesn't.'

'Yes, it does. Did I ask you what happened to that political affairs guy? Seth.'

As she gathered her things and contemplated another lonely evening, Lisa thought of Seth Alevy. Embassy romances, she thought, were partly a result of enforced intimacy. There had been talk of marriage, of career conflicts, of two world-traveling spouses on different assignments. They both agreed it wouldn't work unless one of them resigned from service. And there it ended. She answered, 'That was nothing.'

'It must have been something, Lisa. You practically moved into his place.'

'Embassy life is like living in a small town, isn't it, Kay?'

'Yes. Population: two hundred seventy-six at last count. Didn't mean to be nosy. Just concerned.'

'I know.' She smiled. 'I'll take a Russian lover. That will complete my understanding of the Russian psyche.'

'They're awful lovers.'

'How do you know?'

Kay winked. She threw down her newspaper and stood. 'My ass is hot and so am I. I'm going to the bowling alley lounge. Come along. The Marines are bonkers over you.'

'No, thanks. I have a headache.'

'Okay. See you at breakfast.' Kay Hoffman went to the door, then said, 'Rumor has it that you and that air attaché, Hollis, ran off for the weekend.'

'Nonsense. We went to take care of Gregory Fisher's remains. Everyone here is so small-minded.'

Kay Hoffman laughed and left.

Lisa stood in the quiet room and stared at the telephone.

17

Sam Hollis answered the ringing telephone in his office. 'Hollis.'

She imitated a male bass voice. '*Hollis.*' She asked, 'Can you say hello?'

'Hello, Lisa.' Hollis looked at the wall clock. It was five-thirty, and he hadn't spoken to her since he'd left Alevy and Banks Sunday afternoon. 'How are you?'

'I feel used. You're supposed to call or have flowers delivered or some damned thing.'

'They don't deliver flowers –'

'What a bumpkin!'

'Look, I'm not good at this. I'm a married man. Don't get around much.'

'That's not what I heard.'

'Well, then you heard wrong. Can I buy you a drink?'

'No.'

'Oh . . . sorry –'

'I want dinner. Tonight. Out of the compound.'

Hollis smiled. 'Meet you in the lobby. Half an hour?'

'Thirty-five minutes.' She hung up.

Hollis called his aide, Captain O'Shea, on the intercom. 'Ed, get me a Moscow cab at the gate in forty-five minutes.'

'How about a car and driver instead?'

'No, it's personal.'

'Personal or not, let me get you a staff car.'

'A taxi will be fine.' Hollis hung up and went to the window. His office faced east into the heart of the city, and the Kremlin towers offered a magnificent view at night, all alight like perfect jewels in an ordinary setting. 'Moscow.' Not old by European standards, it had begun in the twelfth century as a trading post with wooden stockade walls on the slight rise where the Kremlin now stood. It was a nothing town on a nothing river in the middle of a nothing forest. And except for trees, snow, and mud, there were no natural resources. The place had been burned to the ground and put to the sword by a dozen armies, and instead of fading into oblivion like a thousand other villages, it came back, each time bigger and just a little stronger. With nothing going for it, it had become the center of an imperial empire, then a communist empire. The Third Rome, as it was sometimes called, but unlike Rome on the Tiber, Moscow was all shade and shadow, a city of somber moods whose citizens drifted in a void of moral weightlessness.

'It's the people,' Hollis decided. That was its one resource: Muscovites. Tough, stubborn, conniving, cynical bastards. And the city was a magnet, a mecca for every like-minded bastard in the Soviet Union. Hollis admired the bastards.

He went into the men's room, straightened his tie, and combed his hair. 'Burov.' Burov was no local Mozhaisk gendarme. He was a Muscovite by choice if not by birth. Further more Burov was somehow directly involved with the Charm School. Hollis didn't know how he knew that. But he knew.

Hollis got his topcoat and walked unannounced into Alevy's corner office down the hall. Hollis pulled the heavy drapes closed and turned on the tape player. Bob Dylan sang 'Mr Tambourine Man.' Hollis pulled a chair up close to Alevy and said softly, 'Burov.'

Alevy nodded. 'That's our only name and face, isn't it?'

'We want to draw Burov out, right? To get a fix on this guy and see if he's more than the phantom of the Mozhaisk morgue. Call Lefortovo restaurant. Make a dinner reservation for two in my name.'

Alevy stayed silent for a while, then said, 'Long shot.'

'Not really. The embassy listeners are keyed for my name. Even if Burov is somewhere around Mozhaisk, he can be in Moscow within two hours.'

'Who are you taking to dinner?'

'Not you.'

Alevy smiled wryly. 'Okay. But if Burov shows and he wants to do more than talk, I'd be hard-pressed to bail you out in Lefortovo.'

'I didn't need you to bail me out of Mozhaisk either.'

'I think you're pushing your luck, Colonel. Not to mention our friend's luck.'

Hollis stood. 'I'll put it to her straight, and she can decide.'

Alevy stood also. 'Sam, remember the lecture you gave me about helping Soviet Jews? Let me give you the same advice about possible American fliers. Make sure it's worth your life. Or at least make sure someone can pick up the ball after you're gone. In other words, fill me in on what you know before they kill you.'

'If I did that, Seth, you wouldn't be so worried about my safety.'

'My, aren't we thinking like a paranoid spy? Hey, did you find out where Gogol's grave is?'

'I'm not even convinced he's dead.' Hollis left Alevy's office and took the elevator down to the ground floor of the chancery. The big open lobby was filled with embassy men and women leaving work. Some of them waited for spouses, children, or friends; some walked to the rear of the building toward the quad, a short commute home. A few people reboarded the elevators for the ride down to the recreation areas. A few men and women, always in groups of two or more, walked toward the gate, into the city of Moscow and a night of sightseeing or something more interesting.

In some ways, Hollis thought, the scene before him resembled any highrise office lobby at quitting time. But on closer inspection, one knew that this was something quite different. These men and women, despite their respective jobs or rank, shared lives within the citadel walls, shared common bonds and experiences, problems, sorrows, and joys. They were three hundred Americans in a city of eight million Russians.

Hollis spotted Lisa talking to three men whom he recognized from the commercial section. She didn't see him, and he watched her smiling and laughing with them. Two of the men were good-looking and obviously on the make. Hollis found he was annoyed.

She glanced around the lobby and saw him. She excused herself and walked over to him. 'Hello, Colonel.'

'Hello, Ms Rhodes.'

'Do you know Kevin, Phil, and Hugh from FCS? I can introduce you.'

'Some other time. We have a cab waiting.' He walked toward the door, and she followed. They went out into the cold air and headed toward the gates. She shivered. 'Good Lord, that wind's from the north now. That's it until May.'

Hollis said, 'I wanted to call you the last two days . . .'

'Forget it, Sam. Step at a time. I was swamped with work anyway. Dinner was a good idea. Thanks.'

'Right.' He took her arm and turned her toward him. 'I still think I owe you an explanation. Just listen. Before we went to Mozhaisk, I told you it could be dangerous, and you saw what I meant. Every day is a danger now, every time we leave this gate. This is not just dinner tonight . . . I guess what I'm asking is, do you want to get involved with me and with what I'm doing?'

'Taxi's waiting.'

Hollis took her hand, and they walked through the gate. The US Marine guards saluted, and the Soviet militiamen eyed them. The KGB embassy watchers, sitting in the Chaikas, put down their newspapers and picked up their binoculars.

Hollis saw two taxis at the curb waiting for fares. Moscow taxis as a rule didn't wait for anyone anywhere, but Western embassies were an exception. Hollis picked a white Lada and got in. He said to the driver, 'Lefortovo.'

The driver glanced back at him.

Hollis said in Russian. 'The restaurant, not the prison. It's on Red-something street. Does that help?'

Lisa laughed.

The driver pulled out. 'I know where that place is.'

Hollis glanced back and saw one of the Chaikas make a U-turn and follow.

Lisa said to Hollis, 'Lefortovo is the name of a restaurant?'

'Yes.'

'Never heard of it. Is that the KGB hangout you promised to take me to?'

'That's it.'

'The State Bureau of Naming Things is not known for market research, but that name is *repellent*. Like Lubyanka or Dachau.'

'They're not looking for tourists.'

Lisa said, 'This is going to be an adventure. You're a lot more exciting than you look.'

'Thank you.'

The driver butted in as Moscow taxi drivers tended to do. 'You speak Russian?'

'A little.'

'Maybe you want to pick another restaurant.'

'Why?'

'That one is not nice.'

'Why not?'

'Police. Too many police go there. No one else likes it.'

'You mean KGB?'

The driver didn't respond. He lit a cigarette and filled the cab with acrid smoke. 'If you give me two dollars, we'll forget the meter.'

'I can't give you dollars.'

'Do you have any gum, lipstick, cigarettes?'

Lisa rummaged through her bag. 'Here's an Estée Lauder lip gloss for your wife.'

'For my girlfriend. My wife gets my pay. Thank you.'

Lisa said to Hollis in English, 'Men are such pigs.'

'I know.'

The driver said, 'You both speak good Russian. Are you spies?'

226

Hollis answered, 'Yes.'

The driver laughed. He turned off the ring road into the Avenue of the Enthusiasts and headed east toward the Lefortovo suburb. 'Traffic gets worse every year.'

Hollis didn't notice much traffic. He asked, 'Do you know that Washington and Moscow are talking about a summit meeting in January?'

'Yes. I read that.'

'What do you think of that?' Hollis asked.

The driver looked around as if trying to determine if there were anyone else in the cab, then said, 'They've been talking for forty fucking years. If they wanted peace, they'd have peace.'

Hollis listened as the taxi driver gave his somewhat rambling view of the world. Hollis knew what Soviet diplomats thought, so an Ivan-in-the-street interview was useful now and then.

The driver turned onto Krasno Kursantsky Street. They passed the grim Lefortovo prison compound, and the driver stopped in front of a modern building of glass and aluminum. The driver concluded, 'So we should get together before the black asses and the yellow asses take over the world. We're going to blow each other up, and they'll take over. Tell that to your president.'

'I'll pass it along.'

'Are you sure you want to go here?'

'Yes.' Hollis handed him five rubles and told him to keep the change, which he did. Hollis had been told that as few as ten years ago, the taxi drivers stuck to the rule of not accepting tips. But the Revolution was over, burned out, and no one took any of it seriously anymore. In two years he had not once heard anyone call anyone else comrade. The pride and fervor were gone, and everyone was on the make or on the take. The churches were crowded, party membership was down, suicides were up. The average life expectancy was dropping, and alcohol consumption, despite the anti-drinking campaign, had risen. Russia was a second-rate nation, but they had first-rate weapons and a world-class secret police.

He and Lisa walked to the door of the restaurant. She said, 'That man sounded like the last New York cabbie I had.'

'God bless the proletariat. They get down to basics.'

Lisa turned and looked up and down the street. 'I've never been in this part of town. It's dark and grim.'

'Part of the charm.'

She stared at the KGB prison across the road, then noticed a car parked with its engine running. 'Is that our favorite Chaika?'

'Could be. In a country with four makes of cars, most of which are black, it's hard to tell if you're being followed.'

Hollis showed her into the restaurant, and they handed their coats in at the checkroom. He took Lisa into the dining area, a medium-sized room, unremarkable in its decor but interesting in its clientele. Most of the patrons were men, and more than half were in one sort of uniform or another. Many of the civilian-attired men were in brown suits, better cut than those of the average Muscovite. The dining room was darker than most Moscow restaurants, Hollis noted, though the effect was not romantic.

Lisa said, 'Sinister. I love it.'

Hollis gave his name to a woman at the reservation counter. She looked him over, then looked Lisa up and down. She frowned, turned, and led them to a table in the center of the room. The table was laid with white linen and heavy flatware. Hollis pulled Lisa's chair out for her. She said, 'Everyone is looking at us.'

'You're so beautiful.'

'They know we're Americans.'

Hollis said, 'By way of background, the gentlemen you see are mostly employees of Lefortovo – prison, not restaurant. They are a collection of KGB interrogators, torturers, and executioners. They work up big appetites. The food is good, and the service is the fastest in all Moscow, all Russia. It is also underpriced.'

A man in uniform at the next table stared at Lisa. She stared back.

Hollis added, 'The KGB doesn't bug the tables here. Here, the KGB are *at* the tables.'

A waitress came by with a bottle of mineral water and set it down with two menus. Hollis ordered a bottle of Georgian wine. The waitress left without a word.

Lisa said, 'What's this country coming to when an American military spy can sit in the same restaurant with a hundred KGB thugs? Where is Joe Stalin when they need him?'

Hollis looked over the menu. 'Unlike the restaurants in central Moscow, if it's on the menu, they've got it.'

The waitress returned with the wine, and they ordered dinner. Lisa said, 'That one bastard is still staring at me.'

Hollis poured two glasses of red wine. 'I'll ask him to step outside.'

'No.' Lisa smiled. 'We're even on restaurants.' She stuck her tongue out at the man who was staring at her. Several diners laughed. The man rose from his table, and Hollis wondered if his crew cut was going to brush the ceiling.

A few of the other men hooted and howled. One yelled out, 'Viktor! Don't be an uncultured lout. Buy the Americans a drink.'

Someone else shouted, 'No, show them how much of a lout you are and throw them out.'

Lisa looked around but saw no restaurant employees. She said to Hollis, 'Do you want to leave?'

'No.'

Viktor and Hollis sized each other up.

The dining room became quiet as a tall, thin man in civilian clothes rose from a dark corner table and walked across the room. He snapped to Viktor, 'Out!' Viktor hurried for the door.

Colonel Burov motioned toward the table. 'Please. Sit. May I?' He sat in a chair at their table, still motioning Hollis into his seat. Burov snapped his fingers, and a waitress suddenly appeared. 'More wine.' He looked at Hollis and Lisa. 'I must apologize on behalf of my compatriot.'

Hollis replied, 'Why? Hasn't he learned human speech?'

Burov seemed puzzled, then got it and laughed. He turned and translated Hollis' words for the others. Everyone laughed.

Hollis said to Burov, 'Come here often?'

'Yes. This is a favourite of my organization. Did you know that before you came?'

Hollis ignored the question and asked, 'Can I assume this isn't a chance meeting?'

'It's a fateful meeting perhaps.'

'What's on your mind, Colonel Burov?'

'Many things, Colonel Hollis. Since our last unpleasant business at Mozhaisk, I've been thinking about you two.'

'And we about you.'

'I'm flattered. By the way, they tell me you never arrived at the state farm.'

'So what?'

Burov continued, 'We found your rented car where you left it at Gagarin station, and I had it examined by the Criminal Investigation Division of the Moscow police. Tire marks, mud, pine twigs, and so on. I conclude that you entered a restricted area. Specifically an area two kilometers north of Borodino Field.'

Hollis said, 'Will you pass that butter, Colonel?'

Burov slid a butter dish across the table. 'So?'

Hollis leaned toward Burov. 'I suggest that if you want to speak to us, you go through your foreign minister and arrange it with my embassy. Good evening.'

Burov drummed a spoon on the table. 'The hell with those people. This is intelligence business. I know who you are. I know you have scars on your neck and back from wounds received when you were shot down over Haiphong. I know your sister's name is Mary and your mother drank too much. Let's get down to business and forget the protocols of diplomacy.'

Hollis took the spoon from Burov's hand and said, 'Alright,

no more diplomacy. You murdered an American citizen. You beat my driver, and perhaps you would have murdered me and Miss Rhodes. Yet you sit here and talk to us as though you are a civilized human being. You are not.'

Burov seemed not to take offense. He rubbed his finger over his lips thoughtfully, then nodded. 'Alright. There's no use denying some of the details that you possess in this matter. But what you conclude from those details is probably erroneous. This matter is quite beyond your understanding, Colonel Hollis, and certainly yours, Miss Rhodes. It is, I admit, somewhat beyond my understanding as well. It is a matter that concerns the higher-ups.'

Lisa replied, 'Then why kill the little people, Colonel?'

Burov ignored this and continued, 'Yes, I'll satisfy your curiosity. It's like this; the Major Jack Dodson, who the late Mr Fisher referred to in his phone call to you, was a turncoat. While a prisoner of war in the People's Republic of Vietnam, Major Dodson sent a message to the Soviet embassy in Hanoi requesting an interview. It was granted, and during the discussion with a Soviet military attaché, Major Dodson said he would welcome the opportunity to come to the Soviet Union and exchange his military knowledge for his release from the prison camp. He felt bitter and betrayed by his country. He stated that America was not waging the war properly, that the limited air war had endangered his life, wasted his talent, and caused the deaths of his friends. Perhaps you yourself felt that way, Colonel. So, anyway, Dodson asked if we would get him out of the Vietnamese POW camp. We did.'

Neither Hollis nor Lisa spoke. Finally Hollis said, 'And why didn't the Soviet Union announce his defection for propaganda purposes?'

'Dodson didn't want that. That was part of the deal we struck with him.'

Lisa asked, 'And he let his family think he was dead?'

Burov shrugged. 'Major Dodson spoke of his wife's past infidelities. He was childless, I believe.'

Hollis said, 'Sounds like bullshit to me.' Hollis added, 'What was Dodson doing in the pine forest at night when Gregory Fisher came upon him? Picking mushrooms?'

'And,' Lisa added, 'why did Gregory Fisher leave the Rossiya, after Colonel Hollis told him to stay there, and go back to Borodino, where he got himself killed in an auto accident? Come now, Colonel Burov.'

Burov helped himself to some wine. He said, 'Mr Fisher's accident is not relevant to the subject of Major Dodson. However, as I did have the opportunity to listen to the tape of Mr Fisher's conversation with you and Miss Rhodes, I think we can all agree that he sounded agitated. The militia report says that he was also drunk. My theory is he panicked and got back in his car with the idea of . . . well, who knows what a drunk man thinks? As for Major Dodson, he was hiking, as was his custom. He met Mr Fisher, quite by chance, and out of nostalgia perhaps, told him something about himself. But he did *not* tell Mr Fisher he was a prisoner, because he is not.'

Burov took a sheet of folded paper from his pocket and handed it to Hollis. 'This is a letter in Major Dodson's hand, dated January of 1973, requesting asylum in the Soviet Union. Your government has now been made aware of this, and what both governments are trying to do is to avoid any embarrassment that Major Dodson's defection would cause. It was a silent defection, and that is the way we all want it to remain.'

Hollis pushed the letter back without looking at it. Hollis said, 'I want to speak to Major Dodson and hear all this from him.'

Burov nodded. 'Yes, alright. If he's agreeable.'

'I don't care if he's agreeable or not. You will make him speak to me. Tomorrow. Here in Moscow. I suggest the International Trade Center hotel as a somewhat neutral site.'

Burov lit a cigarette and exhaled. 'Well, I'll take it up with the proper authorities.'

'Lacking a prompt decision, which is not unusual here, I

want to see a photo of Major Dodson holding tomorrow's *Pravda*.'

'That's very clever.'

Hollis leaned toward Burov. 'If you can't produce the man or a picture of him. I'll conclude that you've killed him or that he is not under your control. In fact, I believe he is on the run from you and may surface soon in his own way.'

Burov looked at Lisa, then at Hollis. 'Westerners who come to the Soviet Union are often paranoid, filled with the drivel they read about us. They observe things through yellow eyes and misinterpret what they see. However, I expected more sophisticated judgment from people such as yourselves.'

'You're blowing smoke,' Hollis said. 'Call me at my office tomorrow regarding Major Dodson.'

'I'll try. But tomorrow I've got other things on my agenda, as you Americans say. Specifically, I'm involved with the investigation of the murder of two guards in that restricted area I told you about. Two young men, shot in the chest, left to die in agony. Who would do such a thing?' He stared at Hollis, then Lisa.

Hollis poked Burov in the chest and said through clenched teeth, 'Two young men' – he poked Burov again – 'left to die in agony? You bastard. 'You and your thugs have murdered a million young men, women, children –'

Lisa held his arm. 'Sam. It's alright. Easy.'

Every head in the quiet restaurant was turned toward them, and Burov's face seemed frozen. No one spoke or moved for a full minute, then Burov said softly, 'What a fool you are. To come here like this . . . accuse me of murder –'

Hollis interrupted, 'By the way, who was the man who answered the door of Mr Fisher's room at the Rossiya?'

'How do I know?'

'That man,' Hollis said, 'looked and talked like an American. He was, in fact, a Russian, a KGB man working in the First Chief Directorate, probably the Service A section. He was a

233

graduate of the Institute of Canadian and American Studies in Moscow, among other schools.'

Burov stared at Hollis.

Hollis continued, 'The guy was perfect, Burov, so don't fire him. But he was too perfect. Better than your schools usually put out. I knew he didn't belong in that room, so I concluded he was one of yours. But at first I figured he was a real American working for you. Then I got to thinking about Mrs Ivanova's Charm School and Major Jack Dodson and such. And I started coming to some mind-blowing conclusions.' Hollis poured wine in Burov's glass. 'You look like you need a drink, Colonel.'

Burov cleared his throat and said stiffly, 'I would like you both to accompany me so we can continue this talk in private.'

Hollis said, 'I think we'll finish our dinner. Good evening.'

'Come. A short walk to my office.'

'Go to hell.'

Burov said tauntingly, 'Are you frightened? There are two ways to go to Lefortovo. One is voluntary.'

Hollis glanced around the dining room and saw several men rise. Some of the seated men were smiling.

Lisa said, 'Our embassy knows where we are tonight.'

'No, Miss Rhodes. They knew where you were headed. Do they know if you arrived?' Burov stood. 'Come with me. Stand.'

Hollis put his napkin on the table, stood, and took Lisa's arm. They followed Burov to the door. Three KGB men fell in behind them. They retrieved their coats in the foyer and stepped out into the cold. Burov said, 'To the left.'

Hollis replied, 'I think we'll say good-bye here.' He took Lisa by the arm and turned away.

Burov motioned to the three men, one of whom was Viktor. Viktor shoved Hollis, sending him slamming into a parked car.

Lisa shouted, 'You bastard!' She kicked Viktor in the groin.

One of the other KGB men slapped Lisa across the face and pulled her to the ground by her hair.

Hollis spun around and caught Burov's jaw with his fist, then went for the man who still had Lisa by the hair. The man drew a pistol and barked, '*Stoi!*'

Hollis stopped.

Burov got to his feet, and Viktor, somewhat recovered from the kick to the groin, drew his pistol. Burov dabbed at his bleeding jaw with a handkerchief and said calmly, 'You are both under arrest.'

Hollis helped Lisa to her feet. 'Are you alright?'

'Yes . . .'

Burov snapped, 'Start walking. You know where you're going.'

Lisa and Hollis walked down the dark, quiet street toward Lefortovo prison, Burov and the three KGB men behind them. Burov said to the men in Russian, 'Viktor got kicked in the balls, so he gets to search her.'

They all laughed.

About a hundred meters from the prison a car turned into the street and put on its bright lights. Another car came from the opposite direction. Hollis identified the cars as medium-sized Volgas. They drew close and stopped. The doors opened, and four men in black ski jackets and ski masks got out.

Seth Alevy, not wearing a ski mask, stepped onto the sidewalk, passed by Hollis and Lisa, and went directly to Burov. 'Good evening. Colonel Burov, I presume.'

Burov looked at the black-clad men who had deployed around him.

Alevy said, 'They're all carrying silenced automatics. I wanted you to know that.'

Burov's eyes came to rest on Alevy. 'You're under arrest.'

Alevy added, 'I'd like to kill your three friends and kidnap you right here, in front of Lefortovo. However, if you want to be reasonable, we'll call this one a draw and part company until we meet again. Don't dawdle. Yes or no?'

Burov nodded.

'Tell them to put their guns away. Now.'

Burov told them.

Alevy stared at Burov's face as though committing each feature to memory. Alevy said, 'Do you know who I am?'

'Oh, yes. You're the dirty little Jew who is the CIA station chief here.'

'Well, we won't quibble about definitions. I just want you to know that you're having a serious career crisis. You understand the idiom?'

'Fuck you.'

Hollis joined Alevy and said to Burov, 'I still expect a call from you tomorrow regarding Dodson.' Hollis and Alevy ushered Lisa into the backseat of one of the Volgas. The other security men piled in the cars, and they all headed back toward the center of the city.

Lisa said, 'I *need* a cigarette.'

'Crack the window,' Alevy said.

Lisa lit her cigarette with a shaky hand. 'Jesus . . .'

'You okay?' Hollis asked.

'Yeah. Want a cigarette?'

'Not right now.'

Alevy said to Hollis, 'I don't think punching a KGB colonel in the face was a good idea.'

'It seemed like a good idea at the time.'

The two security men in the front laughed. The driver said, 'That was for Brennan, right, Colonel?'

'Half for Brennan, half for me.'

Alevy said curtly, 'It's best to avoid physical violence. This is not personal.'

Hollis thought it was and knew that Alevy was sure it was.

Alevy added, 'That's how these things start. Now he's going to break your jaw next chance he gets.'

'If he gets a chance, I deserve to have my jaw broken.'

Lisa interjected, 'They were manhandling us, Seth. We had a right to defend ourselves.'

Alevy snapped, 'Not here you don't. *You* are on their list too. I couldn't see exactly what you did –'

'I kicked fat Viktor in the balls.'

Again the two men up front laughed. The man in the passenger's seat said, 'Way to go, Miss Rhodes.'

Alevy shrugged. He said to Hollis, 'I'll bet you thought for a moment there I was going to let them take you inside.'

'I think your timing was a bit slow,' Hollis replied. 'I expected you sooner.'

Lisa said, 'This was all planned?'

No one answered.

'You two are crazy. Now I really feel used. I'm not bait.'

Again no one responded.

Lisa sat back and drew on her cigarette. She said, 'Look, I'll help. But in the future I want to be kept informed or it's no deal. Agreed?'

Alevy and Hollis both agreed. Hollis said, 'I'm convinced now that Burov is a main player.'

Alevy nodded. 'I didn't recognize him, but I'll go through our mug shots. Did you learn anything else?'

'I learned that when you say Mrs Ivanova's Charm School, you go to jail.'

'Interesting.'

'These are desperate men, Seth. I've never seen them get so agitated and take so many risks, like trying to kidnap Americans with diplomatic immunity, not to mention murder.'

Alevy nodded again. 'Very desperate men.' He added, 'They're breaking the rules, so we can do the same. Things are going to get hot in old Moscow. Unfortunately we can't match their resources. We have to resolve this soon, before we wind up expelled or dead.'

Hollis replied, 'If we go public, that will buy us a little protection.'

'Yes, but the word from Washington is for the diplomats to work it out quietly.'

'Work *what* out?' Lisa asked.

Alevy answered, 'The repatriation of Major Jack Dodson.'

'What if he doesn't want to be repatriated? Burov said he was a defector.'

Hollis replied, 'We'll want to speak to him about that.'

The car approached the embassy gates, and Hollis saw there were three Fords parked on the street near the Chaikas. He said, 'We're on full alert.'

'Oh, yes,' Alevy answered.

Lisa said, 'There's more to this, isn't there? It's not just Dodson. What is the Charm School? A place where they brainwash people? Does Burov really have Dodson, or is Dodson on the run? Is anyone going to answer me?'

No one was.

Lisa announced, 'I have ways of making men talk.'

18

Hollis, Alevy and Lisa stood in the lobby of the chancery.

'Come in for a drink,' Lisa offered. 'I need one.'

Alevy replied, 'I have to do some night sending before five, DC time. See you tomorrow.' He turned and headed for the elevator.

Lisa said to Hollis, 'How about you? Night sending?'

'No. I'll have a quick one.'

'Quick drink?' She smiled.

'Whatever.'

They walked out onto the rear terrace, then along the path to the housing units. She opened her door and put their coats in the hall closet, then showed him upstairs to the living room. 'What can I get you?'

'Scotch, neat.'

Lisa made the drinks.

Hollis looked around. The apartment was modern, a living room-dining room combination, and a galley kitchen. Upstairs would be the bedroom. The furniture, like most of the odds and ends, was from Finland, the closest and easiest Western country from which to import quality consumer goods. It was the apartment of a mid-level American government employee, but it would be the envy of any senior Soviet bureaucrat.

Lisa gave him his drink, and she toasted, 'Another good date.'

She put Rachmaninoff on the tape deck and they talked. Hollis examined an icon on the wall. 'Is that real?'

'Yes. My grandmother's. I'm going to have a tough time trying to get it back out of the country.'

'I'll put it in the diplomatic bag.'

'Would you? Thanks, Sam.'

'You planning on leaving?' he asked.

'No . . . but somehow I have the feeling my days here are near an end.'

Hollis nodded.

Lisa sat on the couch, and Hollis sat at the far end. She said, 'It's not just Dodson. There are hundreds of them, aren't there? That's what you were saying . . . when we . . . in Pavel's bedroom.'

Hollis glanced at her. He finally replied, 'I might have said too much.'

'I don't repeat what you tell me.' She asked, 'Don't you and Seth compare notes?'

'We *trade* notes. You don't get nothin' for nothin' in this business. My outfit, Defense Intelligence, is sort of junior to the CIA. So I have to protect my turf. All very petty. But competition is very American.'

'But you do get along. Personally.'

'Yes. He's my friend too.'

She nodded.

'Can we change the subject?'

She stood and went to the window that looked north over the brick wall. A huge banner had just been strung between two buildings across the street in anticipation of the celebration of the Great October Revolution, whose anniversary was actually November 7 by the Gregorian calendar. She said, 'Look at that. 'Peace-loving Soviet peoples demand an end to American aggression.' Do I have to look at that?'

'Call the zoning commission.'

She grumbled, 'They're getting all worked up for their big day – those bloody red banners all over the damned place, exhorting, cajoling, boasting – like state-subsidized graffiti, for God's sake. And you know, Sam, when I first got here, the hammers and sickles all over the place were jarring, almost scary, because we're so conditioned, like with swastikas, to react to certain symbols. A Party official once told me that the crosses on the Kremlin give him the creeps, and the Great Seal

240

on our embassy wall makes him see red.' She laughed without humor and added, 'I wish we could stop pumping adrenaline when we see red stars or Stars of David or whatever. But we're like Comrade Pavlov's mutts, Sam. They've got us drooling.'

'Who are *they*?'

'They are what we will be twenty years from now. We are in training to be them.'

'You may have something there.'

'Another?'

'Sure. Less glass this time.'

She poured him a triple scotch, then sat close to him. 'Can I tell you something? I was damned frightened at Lefortovo. That's twice you've done that to me.'

'Tomorrow night we'll see the movie. They're showing *Rambo – Part Eight*.'

She laughed. 'Hey, remember when that Russian kid scaled the wall, got into the theater, and watched a whole feature before anyone knew he was there?'

'I remember. The ambassador chopped some heads at Security.'

'The kid wanted to see that movie. What was it?'

'*Rocky Nine*.'

'When are these people going to break loose, Sam? I mean, they need two hundred million of those kids. When's that going to happen?'

'Probably never, Lisa.'

'Don't say that. The human spirit –'

'Lighter topic, please. Did you enjoy dinner?'

'We never got dinner.' She jumped up. 'I'm starved. I made *rasolnik* the other night. I have some left.'

'What's that?'

'Pickled vegetable soup.'

'I'll stick with the scotch.'

'I'm trying to learn traditional Russian cooking.'

'Let me know how you make out.'

She went to the refrigerator and took out a section of cold

241

kolbassa and began eating it. 'Do you like garlic? This is loaded with it.'

Hollis stood. 'You sleep with your clothes on, and you eat garlic before bed. I think I'll go home now.'

'No. Stay. Talk to me. I don't want to be alone tonight.'

'You're perfectly safe in the compound.'

'I know that.' She chewed thoughtfully on the sausage, then added, 'I've smiled at you a dozen times in the damned lobby, in the elevators –'

'Was that you? Was that a smile?'

'You don't remember, Sam, but I was at that little bon voyage they gave for Katherine. Did you know then that she wasn't coming back?'

'I suspected when I saw her packing everything she owned.'

'Ah, good intelligence work. Are you divorcing her?'

'I'm trying to figure out who has jurisdiction. I may fly to the States and file or something. But I can't figure out what state I live in. Probably Siberia, if I don't watch my step.'

'So you're in the process of divorce.'

'Yes. But what married couple isn't?'

'Do you want to know about Seth?'

'Not while you're gnawing on eight inches of sausage.'

She put the sausage on the breakfast bar. 'Do you want to see my photographs?'

'Sure.'

Lisa went to the cabinet beneath the bookshelves and retrieved two albums. She put one on the coffee table, sat beside Hollis, and opened the one in her lap. 'This is the first picture I took the day I got to Moscow. Those are the last of the wooden houses that used to line the road to Sheremetyevo Airport. They're gone now.' She flipped through the pages, and Hollis saw that all the photos had typed captions below them. Most of the pictures were black and white, but there were some color shots taken in the spring and summer. Hollis looked at churches and cathedrals with their dates of destruction noted, and in some cases, pictures of the actual wrecking crew

242

followed by a photograph of the new building on the site. Hollis was no architectural romantic, but the photography made the point jarringly well.

In nearly all the photos of old wooden homes, there were people about, leaning out windows, hanging laundry in the yards, or talking over picket fences. The people seemed weathered like the unpainted wood, and like their homes they seemed to fit in well, to belong to the narrow streets, the tangle of Russian olive trees, and the giant sunflowers hugging the fences. There were dogs and cats in the pictures, though Hollis couldn't recall ever seeing a single dog or cat in his two years in Moscow. Surprisingly, he didn't recognize any of the locales, and if he hadn't known it was Moscow, he would have guessed it was some small provincial town out on the steppe. It was as if there were another city lurking among the concrete behemoths that Moscow had become. 'This is very good, Lisa. Incredible shots.'

'Thank you.'

'Where are these places?'

'They're all within the Outer Ring Road, since I can't get out of the city. Some of these places were villages that are now within the city. Some are old districts in the central city that haven't been torn down yet, hidden between apartment projects.'

Hollis observed, 'Many American cities are undergoing the same sort of ugly growth.'

'Yes,' she replied, 'but that's a debate between aesthetics and profit. Here the goal is to get everyone into apartment blocks where they can be *watched*. And it's not just the cities; the countryside will one day look like that *sovkhoz* we saw.'

Hollis replied, 'It's not our problem.'

'You probably think I'm obsessed, and maybe I am. But I don't see what right these bureaucrats have to destroy other people's homes or cultural and religious monuments that in some ways belong to the world. Look at these shots. The Maly Theater next to the Bolshoi, Stanislavsky's Moscow

243

Art Theater, St Nicholas' Cathedral. They were all slated for destruction, but some Moscow artists and writers got wind of it and actually made a protest. Same with the Arbat district. The wrecking crews are on hold, but no one is really able to stop this onslaught on the past. They'd rip down the Kremlin if they thought they could get away with it.'

'Maybe they could sell it to an American businessman who would make a theme park out of it.' Hollis turned a page of the album and saw a picture of Lisa standing on the veranda of what could have been her own Victorian house in Sea Cliff, except that there was a very Russian-looking family standing around, and the adults were drinking Moskovaya beer from bottles. Also in the picture, his hand for some reason on Lisa's head, was Seth Alevy, wearing a rare smile. The typed caption read: *Seth and I, house hunting with real estate brokers in Tatarovo*.

She said, 'Silly,' and flipped the page. She went through the remaining photographs, but Hollis was no longer paying attention. She seemed to sense this and put the book on the coffee table. After a minute or so of silence, she said, 'That was a Jewish family. Dissidents.'

Hollis got up and made himself another drink.

Lisa said, 'So, do you think a New York publisher would be interested in the theme?'

'Maybe. The pictures are very good. You have a good eye.'

'Thanks. Can I take a picture of you for my book?'

'No.'

'Are you sulking?'

'Quite possibly.'

'Well . . . I'm sorry . . . I shouldn't even tell you this, but he was very interested in my work, in the project. He said he had contacts in a few publishing houses . . . so we went picture taking once in a while.'

'Good.' Hollis could well believe that Alevy had publishing contacts. In fact, the CIA had many such contacts, the purpose of which was to get anti-Soviet books published with mainstream publishers. Hollis didn't know what kind of incentives the CIA offered or if the publishers actually knew with whom they were dealing, but he'd heard it was a successful program. Lisa, he suspected, had no idea she was the subject of another one of Alevy's little side schemes. Whether or not the book had merit, Hollis knew that some-day he'd see it in a bookstore, courtesy of Seth Alevy and company. The man certainly knew how to mix business with pleasure.

Lisa broke into his uncharitable thoughts. 'You *did* say it would be dangerous.'

Hollis looked at her. 'What?'

'Whatever is going on. Dangerous.'

'Yes. Dangerous.'

'Can you give me any more facts?'

Hollis had a further uncharitable thought: that Lisa was reporting to Seth Alevy. But if that were true, then everything he thought he knew about people was wrong. He said, 'You have the outlines. I'll brief you on a need-to-know basis.'

She smiled. 'I'll play the game, Sam, but I won't talk the talk. Talk English.'

He smiled in return, then said, 'Whenever you want to quit, just say "I quit." Nothing further is required.'

'Do you really need me?'

'We're short on red-blooded Americans here. I know this violates the USIS rules, not to mention Pentagon rules. But yes, I need you.'

She nodded. 'Okay. You got me.' She smiled suggestively. 'What can I do for you now?'

Hollis ignored the suggestion and said, 'I bet *you* know where Gogol's grave is.'

'Sure.' She laughed. 'Doesn't everyone?'

'Not the cultural illiterates I work with, myself included. Where is it?'

'Why do you want to know? Is there a party there?'

'Oh, you've been asked that already?'

245

'Sure have.'

'Well?'

She hooked her finger under his belt. 'First things first. I'd feel awful if I thought I was a one-night stand.'

Hollis put his drink on the end table.

'So,' she said, 'let's do it again.'

'Well . . .' He looked at his watch.

She embraced him and kissed him, then ran her fingers over the nape of his neck and felt the scars again. 'You could have been in the Charm School.'

'I suppose.'

'But instead you're here. Your wife is in London. Gregory Fisher is dead, and Major Dodson is God knows where. How will this end?'

'No idea.'

'When do you finish your tour here?'

'Whenever the Pentagon wants. You?'

'Twenty months. Maybe less now. What will we do if one of us leaves before the other?'

Hollis didn't reply, and she said, 'Step at a time.' She motioned to the staircase. 'Let's do those steps first.'

They climbed the stairs to her bedroom. Like the main floor, Hollis noticed, it was Finnish modern, light ashwood, Finlandia crystal, things by Sotka, Furbig, and Aarikka, names that the American community in Moscow had come to appreciate. There was a long-tailed Chinese kite tacked in loops across the ceiling and down the wall over the bed. 'Very nice.'

'You're only the third man who's been up here.'

'It's certainly a rare privilege. Look, do you realize I'm nearly twenty years older than you?'

'So were the other two. So what?'

Hollis looked at her. There was something about Lisa Rhodes that appealed to him. She was tomboyish yet feminine, ingenuous but shrewd. And at times she showed great maturity, though there were other times she seemed refreshingly unsophisticated. He said, 'I like twenty-nine.'

'I've never tried that.'

'Your *age*.'

'Oh . . .' She laughed in embarrassment, then kicked off her shoes and unbuttoned her blouse. 'Stay the night. I want to wake up beside you. Like in Yablonya.'

'That would be nice.'

The alarm rang, and Hollis reached for it, but it wasn't there.

Lisa turned it off on her side of the bed. 'You *do* have a side.'

'Where am I?'

'Paris. My name is Colette.'

'Pleased to meet you.' The blinds were shut and the heavy drapes pulled tight as was the rule. Hollis turned on the lamp.

Lisa said, 'I used to enjoy the sun coming in the window in the morning.'

'Me too,' he said, 'but there's no sun anyway, only microwaves from across the street.'

She cuddled close to him and ran her hand over his groin as she kissed his cheek.

'You're very affectionate,' he said.

'You're not,' she replied.

'Give me time.'

'I understand.' She got out of bed and went into the bathroom.

Hollis heard the faucet running. The telephone on the nightstand rang. He let it ring. It kept ringing. Against his better judgment, he picked it up. 'Hello.'

Seth Alevy said, 'Good morning.'

'Morning.'

'I wanted to speak to you.'

'Then call me in my apartment.'

'You're not there.'

Hollis swung his legs out of bed. 'Try again.'

Alevy sounded annoyed. 'I'd like a meeting with you for eleven A.M.'

247

'I have a meeting with two Red Air Force colonels at ten-thirty.'

'That's been canceled.'

'By *whom*?'

'Also ask Lisa to be there. Her calendar has been cleared. I'll see you in the intelligence officer's safe room.' Alevy hung up.

Lisa called out from the bathroom, 'Where are you?'

'I'm on *my* side now.' Hollis got out of bed. *Bastard.* He thought that Alevy could well have waited to talk to him when he got to his office. He thought about life inside the red brick walls. Here you could bowl, swim in the indoor pool, play squash, or see the weekly movie in the theater. If none of that appealed to you, you could go crazy, as his wife claimed she had done, or you could indulge yourself in one sort of marginally acceptable behavior or another; extramarital sex, alcohol, and social withdrawal were the most common. More acceptable pursuits included reading long Russian novels, working sixteen-hour days, or trying to learn more about the land and the people, as Lisa had done. This latter hobby, however, often met with disappointments and frustrations, as this host country, in contrast to most, wasn't flattered and didn't want you to learn anything. Even a fluency in the language marked you as a potential spy. Xenophobia was as Russian as borscht, Hollis thought.

And if things inside the walls weren't enough to get you down, outside the walls were the men and women of the KGB's Seventh Directorate, the 'Embassy Watchers', who had the premises and each individual in it under constant surveillance. Hollis parted the drapes a few inches and looked out into the new morning.

The new embassy had to be built on the only site offered by the Soviet government, and in addition to the unhealthy river vapors, the low ground made it possible for the KGB to bombard the whole compound with listening-device microwaves whose long-range physical effects were unknown, though leukemia was one suspected by-product.

Even intracompound telephone calls such as Alevy's to Lisa's apartment were monitored, and the windows were watched, which was why room blinds were almost permanently shut.

Lisa walked out of the bathroom, wearing only a towel around her neck. 'Who was that?'

Hollis regarded her in the dim light. In clothes she looked lithe, almost slight. But naked, she was full-busted, and her hips were well-rounded. Her pubic hair had a nice reddish tint.

'My face is up here.'

'Oh . . .' Hollis said. 'That was Seth.'

'Oh . . .'

'He wants to see both of us at eleven A.M. Your calendar has been cleared.'

'What do you suppose they want now?'

'Who knows?'

She asked, 'Are we in trouble because of . . . this?'

He replied, 'Me, maybe. I'm married. You single people get away with everything.'

She thought a moment, then offered, 'This wasn't a good idea. I was being selfish. You have more to lose than I do.'

'Mandatory postcoital speech noted.'

They stood a few feet from each other, both naked. Lisa looked him up and down. 'That's some throttle you've got there; fly boy.'

Hollis smiled despite his annoyance at the phone call.

She said, 'Let's impress the KGB listener with our sexual appetites.' She took his hand and led him into the bathroom. They made love in the shower, and over his objections, she shaved him with her pink plastic razor. She gave him a toothbrush, then went downstairs to the kitchen to make coffee.

As Hollis dried himself, he surveyed the array of feminine products on the countertop. He supposed that Katherine had the same sort of things, but he'd never noticed them. This all seemed very new to him. Unconsciously he picked up a jar of cleansing cream and smelled it.

249

19

It was the intelligence officer's safe room this time, Hollis
noted, because the ambassador was using his own safe room,
meeting with four people from Washington who had just flown
in. Clearly, things were coming to a boil. The people in the
embassy, even the non-diplomatic and non-intelligence staff,
knew something was up because of all the activity: Brennan
being flown to London in bandages; Volgas, Fords, and Chaikas
tearing off in the night.

After leaving Lisa, Hollis had gone in the snack bar as usual
and discovered he had six breakfast companions at a table for
four. They had tried out several rumors on him, and Hollis
found himself saying things such as, 'I'm just an Air Force
guy. I don't know any more than you do.'

Charles Banks cleared his throat, made eye contact with
Hollis, then with Lisa, and began. 'Colonel Hollis, Ms Rhodes,
it is my unpleasant duty to inform you that the Soviet government has filed a formal complaint against both of you. the
details are unimportant. You have each been declared persona
non grata.' He looked at Hollis, then at Lisa. 'You have five
days in which to get your affairs in order and leave the country.
You will depart Monday A.M.'

Lisa glanced at Alevy, then at Hollis. No one spoke, then
Lisa said with emotion in her voice, 'That's not fair. Not fair,
Charles.'

Banks ignored this and added, 'As you may know, since you
both work here, Soviet-American relations are on the mend.
Sino-American relations are deteriorating as a result. The
Chinese are now making overtures toward the Soviets. There
is a new world alignment in the wind, and our government is
anxious not to be left standing alone.'

Lisa remarked sarcastically, 'I didn't mean to upset the world balance of power. And I don't think Sam did either. Did you, Sam?'

Hollis pretended he didn't hear. Alevy stifled a smile. Banks cleared his throat and leaned forward in his chair. 'The balance of world power, Ms Rhodes, is not a joking matter.'

Lisa retorted sharply, 'I'm not a bubble brain, Charles. Neither do I intend to alter my reality or compromise my principles to suit my government's momentary needs. Murder is murder. And there is an American POW who is in trouble out there. If I can't do anything about it, and you won't, then I will have to offer my resignation and go public with this.'

Charles Banks replied frostily, 'Thank you for your thoughts, Ms Rhodes. Please understand that State isn't kicking you out. The Soviet Foreign Ministry is. We don't require your cooperation or resignation or *anything* from you. We only require that you pack and leave as requested. And you will *not* go public.'

Lisa turned away and seemed disinterested in Banks.

Charles Banks said to Hollis, 'There will be nothing derogatory in your file or that of Ms Rhodes. We will issue a *bene decessit* – a statement that your leaving was not due to misconduct as we define it. Is that satisfactory, Colonel?'

'General.'

'Excuse me?'

'That's what I want, Mr Banks.'

'Oh . . . I see. Yes, I'll take that up with . . . the appropriate people. If you have time in service, time in grade, and other –'

'I don't, but you'll tell the commander in chief to waive that.'

Banks eyed Hollis a moment, then continued, 'You will both be given thirty days' home leave. You will also be given new assignments that will be beneficial to your respective careers.'

Lisa said, 'We want to be reassigned together.'

Banks glanced at Alevy, then back to Lisa. 'That's not possible.'

'Why not?'

'For security reasons.'

'What does that mean?'

Banks looked pointedly at his watch. 'I must go upstairs. Mr Alevy will give you your departure briefing at this time.' Banks added in a softer tone, 'Personally, I'm sorry to see you both go. Everyone here considers you very valuable assets to our mission. Your fluency in Russian is unexcelled. Sam, Lisa, good luck to you.' Banks left.

Alevy went to the sideboard and poured a vodka and chilled orange juice. There were trays of pastry as well. 'Help yourselves. Charles laid on some nice things to make you feel better.'

Lisa stood and drew hot water for tea from a silver urn. She said to Hollis, 'Sam, can I get you something?'

'Coffee, please.'

She brought him his coffee and sat in the chair beside him. Alevy placed a tray on the table, heaped with red and black caviar, sour cream, toast, and butter. Lisa commented, 'When they give you the shaft here, they at least smear it with *maslo*.'

Alevy chewed on a pastry. 'That's crude, Lisa.' Alevy wiped his fingers with a linen napkin. 'I will now read you certain provisions of the National Security Act and instruct you on your duties and obligations regarding not disclosing *anything* you have seen, heard, or read while posted here.' Alevy proceeded to do so, then asked them to sign standard statements of acknowledgment, which they did.

Alevy sat opposite them and put his drink on the table. He spread sour cream and caviar on a triangle of toast and said to them, 'It's better this way.'

Hollis replied, 'I think it's better with butter.'

Alevy chewed on his toast and regarded Hollis coolly. 'I mean it's better that they're booting you. If they weren't

252

booting you, that would mean the KGB has convinced the Politburo to give them another shot at you. Apparently the Politburo, acting as game warden, has told the KGB they had their chance and the season is closed for Lisas and Sams.'

Hollis finished his coffee. 'That about it, Seth?'

'No. I'm advising both of you to stay within the embassy grounds for the rest of your days here.'

Lisa said, 'I intend to buy some Russian folkcraft before I leave, take some photos, that sort of thing.'

Alevy shrugged. 'That's only sensible advice. What *is* an order is that you are not to go outside the gates alone and never after sundown.'

Hollis observed, 'I thought we were off-season.'

Alevy stood and made himself another drink. 'Where there are game wardens, there are poachers.' He added, 'If it makes you feel any better, our government has booted their air attaché and press officer out of DC. It's in tomorrow's papers.'

Lisa asked, 'Am I relieved of my duties?'

'Oh, yes. Both of you. Interdean, the West German movers, will pack you up. You need the time to supervise.'

Hollis asked, 'Who's going to meet Ace on Sunday?'

'You have to do that. Tell him that someone else will be handling him. Work out the details. Don't lose him.'

'Are we getting him out?'

'If he has what you asked for.'

Lisa asked Alevy. 'Why aren't they booting *you*? You're the one who pulled a gun on Burov.'

'Well,' Alevy replied, 'it's the KGB who wants me around, on the theory that it's better to deal with the devil you know. Also if the Soviets booted me, then we'd boot their top *rezident* in Washington as happened in '86. Then one boot leads to the other. Nobody wants that again. The score is tied, two-two.'

Lisa observed, 'Diplomacy has a certain immutable illogic to it that becomes a logic of its own.'

'I'll get that framed and hung in the ambassador's safe room.' Alevy smiled at Lisa and looked at her for some time, then asked with a forced lightness in his tone, 'So, Lady Lisa, where will you spend your home leave?'

'I don't know . . . this is unexpected. New York, I guess . . .'

Alevy looked at Hollis. 'You?'

'Not real sure. London, I suppose, to take care of that business. Then maybe Japan to see the old folks practice Zen. Then New York to see my brother who won't leave his time zone.' He added, 'I might pay a condolence visit on the Fishers in New Canaan.'

Lisa nodded. 'Me too.'

Alevy said sharply, 'Don't you dare. You two are going to be well taken care of if you cooperate. You can each pick any assignment in the world outside the Curtain. That's what they're offering.'

Lisa added, 'As long as we're not together. Is that *your* idea?'

Alevy replied, 'I won't dignify that question with an answer.'

Hollis stood. 'Well, I'll discuss this whole matter with my people.'

'My company has the primary responsibility for handling these matters.'

'Are we finished?'

'No. I would like you to tell me now about your side trip to Borodino.'

'There's not much to tell,' Hollis replied. 'However, I did kill two KGB Border Guards.'

Alevy stood. 'Jesus Christ! Are you serious?'

'Unfortunately, yes.'

'My God, that's got their blood boiling. Why the hell didn't you tell me that? You're damned lucky to be alive. Both of you.'

'It was unavoidable.'

'Okay, okay. What else happened at Borodino?'

'I'll give you a complete report before I leave.' He added, 'But as they say in diplomatic circles, we want quid pro quo.'

'Do you now?' Alevy replied. 'Well, as they also say, I won't

254

agree to any sine qua non. You'll tell me without preconditions and without any guarantee that you'll get something in return. If you don't tell me, I will guarantee that the roof will fall in on both of you.'

Hollis replied softly, 'Don't threaten a killer, Seth.'

Alevy and Hollis stared at each other, then Alevy smiled. 'Sorry. Just passing on orders.'

Lisa moved toward Alevy and said curtly, 'When you tell us how Gregory Fisher's murder is going to be resolved and what you're doing about Major Dodson, we'll tell you what we saw at Borodino. This is not going to be another case of an American citizen's death being written off in the interest of some diplomatic maneuverings.'

Alevy retorted, 'Don't play investigative journalist, Lisa. You're a writer for the USIS, and you do what you're told.' Alevy added, 'You just signed a statement to that effect. Remember?'

'Yes, alright. But certainly you understand that I'm personally upset over that boy's death . . . I never should have gone to Mozhaisk . . . to see the body.'

Alevy replied, 'I couldn't agree more.' He looked her in the eye and said, 'I might also remind you that *you* are one of the embassy's foremost cheerleaders for cozy Soviet-American relations. I don't subscribe to that, but I'll write off Fisher's death if my government determines that is the way to save their precious upcoming summit. So if that is your goal too, forget justice. There are more important issues. Okay?'

Lisa did not reply.

Hollis interjected, 'Maybe I'm willing to write off Fisher, Seth. But I have a personal interest in Air Force Major Jack Dodson and any other Americans who are being held here against their will. I'm just putting you and your company on notice about that. *That* we don't write off. We'll discuss it before I leave.'

'Noted and agreed.' He looked at Lisa and said in a conciliatory tone, 'Look, I can tell you're upset. This is all very new to you. But justice is done differently here, and it's not a matter of public record. The only justice here is revenge. Tit for tat.'

Lisa gave Seth Alevy a long, sad look, and Hollis had the impression they'd been through this before.

Alevy broke eye contact with her and said as if to himself, 'I'm not totally ruthless. I may seem so at times . . . I know violence begets violence . . . I was raised as a nonviolent person . . . I still don't like the wet stuff . . . but I know I commit psychological violence on my enemies every day.' He sipped on his drink thoughtfully, then said, 'A little over two years ago, before either of you were here, I was jumped on the street, beaten, and robbed by a bunch of hooligans, as the Russians call them.'

Hollis had heard about that, but no one seemed to know the details.

Alevy glanced at Lisa. 'I was on my way to meet Ina Shimanov, the wife of Reuven Shimanov, the Soviet nuclear biologist who defected to the West during a symposium in New York. Ina had been fired from her job and was destitute, hungry, and despondent. Our embassy was trying to get her out to join her husband. I spoke to Reuven on the telephone one night. He was calling from New York. He'd just gotten through to his wife in Moscow and spoke to her a few minutes before they were cut off. Ina, he said, was crying, begging him for help.' Alevy shifted into Russian. '"Husband, dear," she cried. "I am starving. They are going to banish me from Moscow. Please, dear Reuven, for the love of God, help me."' Alevy looked at Hollis and Lisa before continuing, 'So I went out by myself to comfort her and bring her money. I took the metro. It wasn't official, just Jew to Jew. Understand? Well, the boys of the Seventh Directorate, in conjunction with the electronic eavesdroppers, got onto me in a flash. Followed me, jumped me when I got off the metro at Universitet Station, beat me, and left me naked in the snow with internal injuries.'

Lisa put her hand to her mouth. 'Oh, dear God.'

Alevy set down his drink. 'My fault. I was responding to my

sense of decency – justice. Anyway, a group of passing students spotted me and took me to a hospital. My people wanted to reassign me to someplace nice. But I wanted to stay here. To even the score.'

Hollis said, 'I heard your friends in DC did that.'

Alevy replied, 'I had nothing to do with that.'

'With what?' Lisa asked.

'Nothing.' Alevy moved toward the padded, airtight door. 'Look, I can tell you this is a dirty, dehumanizing business, but it takes something like the events of the last few days for it to become real. Right? In military intelligence you deal with stats, numbers, capabilities, and talk about thermonuclear destruction. Means nothing. But then you get slammed against a car by a smelly goon, like I got my testicles kicked into my abdomen, and hey! The Soviet-American power struggle takes on new and deeper meaning.' Alevy opened the door. 'I have good motivations to take care of this. Charlie Banks can blow smoke and utter platitudes all fucking day, and I'll smile and nod all fucking day. But I have my job, and he has his. As for you two, the diplomats would say this matter is ultra vires – beyond your power or authority.'

'I'll make that decision,' Hollis said as he went through the door with Lisa. 'Not you or the diplomats.'

'I know you will, Sam.' Alevy added in a lighter tone, 'Oh, the party is Saturday at six-thirty, in the reception hall. The ambassador will put in an appearance. The persona non grata parties are more fun than the regular end-of-assignment parties. Be prepared for some kidding. Make up funny speeches about why you're being kicked out and all that.' Alevy extended his hand, and they all shook.

Lisa said, 'Don't let this place, this job, dehumanize *you*.'

Alevy thought a moment before responding, 'As long as I'm still capable of going out into the cold night to help a woman who is being persecuted, then I know I'm okay.'

'I hope so.'

'Me too.' Alevy closed the door.

As Hollis and Lisa walked toward the elevator, she asked, 'What happened in DC?'

Hollis considered a moment before replying, 'Seth's friends arranged to have a Soviet diplomat's teenage daughter mugged in Washington. They left her on the campus of American University with a broken jaw.'

Lisa stopped walking. 'But . . . Seth didn't know . . .'

'I think not.' But Hollis was sure he did.

She began walking again.

Hollis added, 'In Seth's company there are people who deal with the Soviets on an unofficial and personal level. They call themselves the Tit for Tat Gang. A broken arm in Moscow or Budapest is a guarantee of a broken something in Washington or London.'

Lisa shook her head.

'This philosophy of assured retaliation has actually reduced the number of broken limbs. In fact, things have been cool for a few years. The fact that Burov opted for the wet stuff is suggestive . . . indicative of the degree of the KGB's concern. A signal to Seth and me that things can quickly get out of hand.'

'They're not very subtle, are they?'

'No. They reacted too strongly and got everyone interested.'

They took the elevator up to the seventh floor and walked to Lisa's office door. She asked, 'Can we do something useful before Monday?'

Hollis replied, 'We shouldn't talk too much outside the safe areas.'

She nodded. 'Is it true that we bug ourselves? To see who's violating talk security?'

'Maybe. I get tired of whispering in the ears of people I don't know that well.'

'You're not unhappy about leaving, are you?'

'I don't like the circumstances. How about you?'

'I'm sad. But I'm glad it was both of us. We *can* get together on the outside, Sam.' She smiled. 'General.'

He returned the smile. 'They'll play ball. If we do.' He looked at his watch. 'I'm going to clean out my desk.'

'Me too.'

They stood there a moment, then Lisa said, 'For the record, I think I'm falling in love with you.'

'A little louder for the microphone, please.'

She smiled. 'Can I see you tonight?'

He opened the door of her office. 'Dinner?'

'Your place. I'll cook.'

'I only have beer and mustard. But I'll go to the commissary if you give me a shopping list.'

'No, I'll go to Gastronom One.' She said, 'I'll cook a Russian meal. You get the vodka.'

'You shouldn't leave the compound alone,' Hollis reminded her.

'Gastronom One doesn't deliver.'

'Be careful.'

'I'm only going to the grocery store.'

'Be careful.'

'Yes, sir.' She turned and walked into her office.

20

At six P.M. the telephone rang in Hollis' office. 'Hollis.'

'Alevy. Are you free for cocktails?'

'No. I have a dinner engagement in half an hour.'

'You'll have to postpone it for an hour.'

'Then why did you ask? How is it that you're running my social and business calendar?'

'Only your business calendar. We have business.'

Hollis surveyed the packing boxes around him. 'I'm out of business.'

'Oh, don't believe everything you hear. You're relieved of only your official air attaché duties. Did you really think you were relieved of your spy duties?'

'No.'

'My place in ten minutes. Do you know where I live?'

'I'll bet I could find it.' Hollis hung up and called Lisa's apartment, but there was no answer. He buzzed his side, Captain O'Shea. 'Ed, are you working tonight?'

'Yes, sir, until about eight.'

'Okay, if Ms Rhodes . . . do you know her?'

'Yes, sir.'

'If she calls or stops by – she's shopping in the city – tell her I'll be . . . in my apartment, about seven-thirty.'

'Yes, sir. Can you be reached between now and then?'

'Perhaps.'

'Will you be in the city?'

'No, Captain, I'll be here in the fort. Why?'

'Just looking out for your ass, Colonel.'

'At whose suggestion?'

O'Shea let a few seconds pass before replying. 'No one's. I'm your aide.'

Hollis hung up, and a few moments later O'Shea walked in with his slate board and wrote in chalk: *Gen. Brewer from DC has asked me to report on your activities*.

Hollis wrote on his own slate: *KMP*. Keep me posted.

O'Shea nodded and said as though just walking in, 'Excuse me, Colonel, I thought you'd want to know I've gotten calls from just about everyone in the resident press corps here, including the Brits, Aussies, Canadians, and some West Europeans too. They would like to know why you have been declared persona non grata. I referred them all to the press office, of course. But they all want to speak to you off the record.'

'Did any of them mention Fisher?'

'Yes, sir. They're trying to find a connection between Fisher's death, your trip to Mozhaisk, and you getting booted.'

'Very suspicious people.'

'Yes, sir.'

Hollis put on his overcoat. 'If a Colonel Burov calls for me, transfer the call to me in Mr Alevy's apartment.'

'Yes, sir.' O'Shea erased both slates.

'Hold down the fort, Ed.' Hollis left and took the elevator down to the lobby, walked outside to the rear terrace, and cut across the quad, avoiding the paths. It was cold, and a light snow was falling from a luminous sky. Some of the housing units surrounding the quad were lit, and he could see families in their living rooms, the blue glow of televisions that were hooked to VCRs, people in their third-floor bedrooms looking out at the first snow. Lisa's unit was dark.

It was all so red-brick American, he thought, like suburban town-house condos, or family housing at an airbase or college. Peacefully boring and ordinary. Thinking back on his marriage and his life, he realized he had taken extraordinary personal risks, more than any normal man would have taken. Katherine must have drawn some valid conclusions from that.

He came to Alevy's door and rang the bell.

Alevy showed him in, and Hollis hung his topcoat on a coat

tree in the foyer, then followed Alevy up the stairs. 'Snowing,' Alevy observed.

They came up into the living room. Hollis had never been in Alevy's place, and he was surprised at its size, not to mention its appointments. The apartment was done in the most opulent Russian antiques he'd ever seen outside of a museum. In addition to the furnishings, there were oil paintings on the walls, two Samarkand rugs on the floor, porcelain and lacquer pieces on every polished wood surface. A huge silver samovar sat gleaming in front of the window. Hollis commented, 'Not bad for a mid-level political affairs officer.'

Alevy hit a wall switch and background music filled the room, providing sound cover. The music was an orchestra of massed balalaikas playing folk tunes. Alevy responded, 'My company pays for this. Nothing comes out of the diplomatic budget here.'

'Good. I wouldn't want to think the rest of us are counting paper clips so you can go into competition with the Winter Palace.'

'Have a seat.' Alevy went to a carved mahogany side-board. 'Scotch, right?'

'Right.' Hollis sat in a plush, green velvet armchair. 'The Pentagon doesn't understand civilian perquisites like your company does.'

Alevy handed him a drink. 'So join my company. We'd be happy to have you.'

'No, thanks. I want to get back to flying. That's what I want out of this mess.'

'Well,' Alevy said, 'my company has jet aircraft too. But I think that would be a waste of your real talent.'

'What is my real talent?'

'Espionage,' Alevy answered. 'You're better at it then you probably think.' He raised his glass. 'To your safe return home.' They drank.

Hollis set his glass down stop a silver coaster on the end table. He said, 'I think flying is my area of expertise.'

Alevy settled into a facing chair of black lacquer. 'Flying may be your *love*, but the shrapnel in your ass makes me question your expertise.'

Hollis smiled. 'I dodged sixteen missiles, but all anyone remembers is the seventeenth.'

'Life's a bitch, Sam. Look, I didn't call you here to recruit you. But it's an offer. Consider it.'

'Sure.'

Alevy said, 'I don't invite many people here.'

Hollis looked over the room. Lisa, of course, had been one of those who were invited. He could appreciate how a Russophile could be seduced in such a setting.

Alevy said, 'I can explain this stuff to you because you're in the business.'

'Interior decorating?'

'No, intelligence. This stuff is worth about a million. There's even a Fabergé egg and czarist dinnerware and so forth. Anyway, this junk is tied into how we pay our Soviet assets. You've heard of the commission shops where Soviet citizens can bring family heirlooms and other items of unspecified origins.'

'I've recently heard about that.'

'Well, I can't go into details, but this quirk in the Soviet system gives us an opportunity to channel money here and there. Okay?'

'You don't owe me an explanation.'

'Nevertheless, you got one. But that's got a top secret classification.'

Hollis considered a moment, then said, 'Lisa has a low security clearance.'

'I never told her what I just told you. I told her this stuff was from our pre-Revolution embassy.' He looked at Hollis. 'One of my people happened to see you coming out of the antique shop on Arbat. So I thought something she said might have piqued your curiosity.' Alevy stood and made himself another drink. With his back to Hollis he said, 'This is what you call awkward.

Right? I mean, the same woman and all. You're sitting here thinking that Lisa and I probably did it on that ten-foot couch, and you're probably right.'

Hollis didn't respond.

Alevy continued, 'And you've discovered that you like her, so you decided you don't like me.'

'We've always gotten along.'

'Right. I could decide I don't like *you*. Because I still care for her, and I'd like to have her back.'

'She's leaving,' Hollis said.

'True. Anyway. I wanted to clear the air about that.'

'Then stop blowing smoke.'

'Right. The air is not clear. But we have to accomplish a few things, you and I, before you leave. So let's get professional.'

'Accomplish what?'

'Well, a report on Borodino. Now that we're alone we can drop the posturing we do in front of Banks and Lisa.'

'Speak for yourself, Seth.'

'Another drink?'

'No.'

'Follow me.' Alevy opened a narrow door in the hallway, and Hollis expected to see a closet but instead found himself shown into a dark windowless room, about twelve feet square, with padded walls. The room was lit by the glow of a five-foot video screen. 'This is my little safe room. A few electronic gadgets. Just enough to do homework. Have a seat.' He motioned toward a chair. Hollis sat.

Alevy took a seat beside him and swiveled his chair toward the video screen. He picked up a remote control device from the table and pressed a button. The screen flashed to a photo of a man in his thirties wearing the uniform of an Air Force officer. Alevy said, 'Major Jack Dodson. Missing in action since November eleventh, 1970. Last seen by his wingman, ejecting from a damaged Phantom over the Red River Valley between Hanoi and Haiphong. This witness said he appeared unhurt. However, Dodson never showed up on

264

Hanoi's lists of POWs. Now we think we know where he disappeared to.'

'My copilot, Ernie Simms, similarly disappeared.'

'Yes, I know that.'

The picture of Dodson disappeared, replaced by another man. It took Hollis a few seconds to recognize Ernie Simms.

Neither man spoke for a while, then Alevy said, 'I don't know if he's here in Russia, Sam.'

Hollis did not respond.

Alevy added, 'We can't refight the war, but sometimes we get a chance to make a little change in the present to make the past better.'

Hollis looked at Alevy in the blue light but said nothing.

Alevy shut off the video screen, and they sat in the dark room in silence. Alevy said, 'There's more to this slide show. But now it's your turn to do show-and-tell. Borodino. You're on, Sam.'

'Lisa and I will be assigned together if that's what we decide we want. That's the quid pro quo.'

Alevy kicked off his shoes and propped his feet on an electronic console. He unwrapped a stick of gum and popped it in his mouth. 'Well . . . I suppose that's easier to do than convincing her that justice will be done.'

Hollis stared into the darkness of the room, then began, 'We went north of Borodino Field. There's a ridge line covered with pine trees there.' Hollis related the story of their excursion, telling Alevy what he saw and what he deduced about the place.

Alevy listened intently, then asked, 'More like a prison than a restricted area?'

'Definitely. A local Gulag.'

'KGB Border Guards?'

'Yes.'

'Wearing the standard winter uniform? Olive drab, red piping?'

'Yes.'

'Soft caps or helmets?'

'Soft caps. Why?'

'AK-47s?'

'Yes. I also saw a guy in the half-track with a long rifle and scope. It could have been one of those SVD sniper rifles. The Dragunov. You know it?'

'Yes.'

'Why do you want to know all that? As if I didn't know.'

Alevy said nothing.

Hollis remarked, 'You're crazy.'

'Oh, I know that.' Alevy continued his questioning. 'You saw no Red Air Force people, signs, or markings?'

'None.'

'Okay, so when you got back to your office you started digging in your files, correct? What did you learn?'

Hollis tapped his fingers on the armrest. Sharing military secrets, saying them aloud, did not come easy to him, but he thought the time had come. 'I discovered that this area is off limits to civilian aircraft overflights.'

'So's ninety percent of this country.'

'Right. I also found an old survey of Red Air Force bases that my office did about fifteen years ago. The file was labeled Borodino North for want of a Russian name. Lacking an airfield, the survey termed it a ground school, perhaps a survival course, though the area is largely benign farmland. Even the forest is a piece of cake. But that's all the report said.'

Alevy nodded. 'We had no interest in the area until recently. But when I got interested, I had some people poke around there. It *had* been a Red Air Force installation about fifteen years ago according to local memory. That jibes with your old survey. But then the uniforms started to change to KGB and to civilian attire. The personnel inside the installation have virtually no contact with Borodino village, Mozhaisk, or the surrounding countryside, according to the locals. They helicopter back and forth, presumably to Moscow. Conclusion: Top secret stuff. Personnel have Moscow privileges and so forth.' Alevy looked at Hollis. 'Okay, your turn.'

Hollis replied, 'I found some old SR-71 photos. But these were taken in 1974 or '75 at eighty thousand feet with cameras that don't have the resolution that your recon satellites do now.'

'What did the photo analysts say about those shots?' Alevy asked.

'Well, Air Force Intelligence was only looking for things that interested *them*. They concluded that the installation, which seems to cover about three hundred hectares, a little more than a square mile, had no military significance in a tactical or strategic sense. That's where my file ends on Borodino North. Case closed.'

Alevy asked, 'What do *you* think the place is?'

'Mrs Ivanova's Charm School,' Hollis replied.

'And what,' Alevy asked, 'is Mrs Ivanova's Charm School?'

'You tell me. And if you have pictures, and I guess you do, let's see them.'

Alevy hit the remote switch again, and the screen brightened to show a slow-motion aerial view of farmland. Alevy said, 'The recon satellite is passing from northeast to southwest. Very nice, sunny summer day. That's wheat there. Let's move in a little.' The image on the screen zoomed in to a close-up of a man on a red tractor pulling a load of hay. 'Now there's the Moskva River coming up.'

The picture seemed to be taken at about two thousand feet, Hollis thought, though the satellite could have been a hundred miles above the earth.

Alevy continued, 'Alright, you see the beginning of the pine forest. Now you see what you saw from the ground – a cleared ring about fifty meters in depth, and if you look closely you can see the concentric rings of barbed wire. There . . . see the watchtower.' Alevy stopped the tape and focused even closer. 'The Border Guard chap in the tower is scratching his ass, and unbeknownst to him, the eye in the sky is recording it for posterity.'

Hollis asked, 'When was this taken?'

'This past June. Okay, moving toward the center of the installation – we see more pine trees and not much else. But hold on here –' He stopped the tape again. 'Now look at the top of the screen. That clearing is a helipad. See the way the grass is blown by the rotor blades, and see the chopper-skid indents on the ground?'

'No.'

'Well, neither do I. But that's what the photo analysts told me. Okay, move on a few seconds, and there we see just a piece of a structure, a log cabin, but you won't see much else because of the evergreen cover. The Soviets like to use their pine forests as cover from our satellites. One day this whole fucking country will be hidden under the evergreens. Okay, now you see the beginning of Borodino Field, then the old Minsk-Moscow road, then the new Minsk-Moscow highway. Pretty nifty, huh? The Soviets must shit when they think about our satellites.' Alevy shut off the video. 'That's it.'

Both men sat in the semidarkness awhile. Alevy said, 'We did spectrum and infrared analysis on the pine forest. There are heat sources and such down there. Vehicles, people, lots of small structures, and a few larger ones, mostly wood, we think, scattered about in that square mile. Population anywhere from four to eight hundred hot bodies, though the place could hold more. In fact, it probably did once.'

Hollis said, 'There are about three hundred American POWs there.'

Alevy looked at him quickly. 'How do you know that?'

'The French woman told me. Fisher told her, Dodson told him.'

Alevy nodded. 'We contacted her in Helsinki, but she wasn't talking.' Alevy asked, 'Anything else?'

'What you already know. Former Red Air Force school, now a KGB school.'

Alevy rubbed his chin. 'Three hundred?'

Hollis nodded.

'Jesus Christ.'

268

'That was my general reaction.'

Alevy looked at Hollis. 'Am I thoroughly briefed now?'

'You are. Am I?'

Alevy said, 'Well, you can guess the rest, Sam. These are not defectors, of course, but POWS from 'Nam. They were given to the Russians by the North Vietnamese, probably in payment for those neat surface-to-air missiles that knocked you guys down. They got the product of their missiles. Live American fliers. Quid pro quo.'

Hollis nodded.

Alevy continued, 'There are . . . what? A thousand fliers still unaccounted for? The North Viets thought of them as nothing more than POWs to be beaten, starved, and paraded in front of news cameras. 'The Russians thought of them as a valuable resource for the Red Air Force.'

Hollis stood. 'Yes, and they opened a Red Air Force training school with their potential enemy as instructors. We always suspected that.'

Alevy asked, 'Would these American pilots have been of real military value? What's your professional opinion on that?'

Hollis replied, 'I'll tell you a military secret because I like you. The Israelis in the past have given us captured, Soviet-trained Egyptian and Syrian pilots. Using drugs and hypnosis, we were able to reproduce a good deal of the Soviet Air Force jet fighter school curriculum.'

'Okay, but what good would that do as the aircraft and tactics change?'

'Not much if you haven't engaged the enemy during a particular period of time. The hardware and tactics change, as you say.'

'So,' Alevy asked, 'what are those Vietnam-era pilots doing there *now*, Sam? They were used to train MiG pilots fifteen, sixteen years ago. Now they're useless. Why not dispose of them? What good are they *now*? That is the question. Do you know the answer?'

'I'll think about it.'

The telephone rang, and Hollis said, 'That might be for me.'

Alevy waved his hand toward the phone, and Hollis picked it up. 'Hollis.'

Captain O'Shea said, 'Burov.'

'Put him through.' Hollis said to Alevy, 'The phantom of the Mozhaisk morgue.'

Alevy advised, 'Be nice.' He stuck a plug tap in his ear and listened.

Burov's voice came on the line. 'Colonel Hollis?'

'Speaking.'

Burov's tone was cordial. 'How are you this evening?'

'Real good. How are you?'

'I meant to call earlier during business hours. But I'm still involved with that messy double murder I told you about. Am I interrupting your dinner?'

'No, we dine at eight here in little America. I was just watching a spy satellite tape of the Soviet Union.'

Burov laughed. 'What a coincidence. I was just listening to some taped conversations emanating from your embassy.'

'Small electronic world. When can I see Major Dodson at the Trade Center?'

'Well, I spoke to him, and he's very reluctant to meet anyone from your embassy.'

'*His* embassy. Why is he reluctant?'

'He sees no point in it.'

'The point is to see if he's alive and well and wants to remain in the Soviet Union.'

'That's affirmative on all counts,' Burov replied.

Hollis was somewhat surprised at Burov's American military jargon. He said, 'It's not that I don't trust a colonel of the KGB, but how about the photo with the *Pravda*?'

'That I can show you.'

'Unretouched. I want the photograph and the negative.'

'I can't do that. For your eyes only.'

'Then keep it.'

'I don't know what more I can say, Colonel Hollis.'

'You can say yes.'

'I'll talk to Major Dodson again.'

'Will you? What if I told you that Major Dodson is here, in this embassy, and that he has told us a most incredible story?'

Alevy whispered to Hollis, 'Don't push it.'

Burov skipped a beat, then replied, 'That's not possible, Colonel. I just spoke to the man twenty minutes ago.'

'I don't think so.'

'Well, if he's there, put him on the phone.'

Hollis replied, 'I may put him on TV in a few days.'

Burov's tone was controlled but anxious. 'I'll get back to you on the whole question of Major Dodson.'

'Swell. Where can I contact *you*, Colonel Burov?'

'You may call Lefortovo and leave a message.'

'Do you have a home number where I can reach you on weekends?'

'I'm afraid not. Just call Lefortovo. We're open day and night.'

'Not Mozhaisk or Borodino?'

'No, I work here.'

'In what directorate?'

'That's not important for you to know.'

'Do you have a first name?'

'Petr.'

'Very Christian. I'll bet your parents were Christians.'

Burov replied stiffly, 'None of that concerns you.'

'Alright, Petr.'

'Don't try to bait me, Hollis. I already owe you one.'

'That's my old Burov. How's the jaw today?'

Alevy smiled.

'A constant reminder,' Burov replied. 'You know, Sam, from what I know of you, you've led a charmed life. But your luck may run out.'

'Is that a threat?'

'No, a prophecy. I wouldn't make a threat over the phone. You people record everything.'

'Well, let's record your answer to my next question. Where is Mr Fisher's car?'

'That's a question for the Moscow police.'

'They claim they don't have it. A team of forensic experts has arrived from America to examine the car. Where is it, Colonel Burov?'

'I'll look into it.'

'Please do. And try to be more helpful than you've been with other things I've asked you for. Well, Colonel, I have to get back to the spy satellite photos, if you have nothing further. The new solid-fuel rocket plant outside of Kaliningrad is coming along nicely, but I see a lot of loose material lying around. Tell someone to get it squared away out there.'

Burov ignored this and said, 'By the way, a friend of mine in London told me your wife spends half her days in Bond Street. I hope she doesn't have your credit cards. Or perhaps the man she's with is paying. He looks prosperous from what I'm told.'

Alevy whispered, 'Drop it, Sam. You can't win that game.'

Hollis nodded. 'Okay, Burov, I'll keep you informed about Major Dodson.'

'I'll do the same for you. Incidentally, another friend of mine, from the Foreign Ministry, called and told me the disturbing news of your unscheduled departure. I enjoyed working with you. Perhaps we can have lunch before you leave, Monday. Would you consider Lefortovo restaurant again?'

'Of course. I'll try to work it into my schedule.'

'Good. Who will I be dealing with after Monday?'

Alevy pointed to himself.

Hollis said into the phone, 'Seth Alevy. You remember him.'

'Oh, yes. We all know Mr Alevy here. I'm very much looking forward to meeting him again. Send him my regards.'

'I most certainly will.'

'If I don't see you, Colonel, or don't speak to you, have a very safe trip home.'

'I plan to.'

'Good evening.'

'Good evening to you, Colonel Burov.' Hollis hung up. 'You son of a bitch.'

Alevy said, 'Jesus, that guy has a command of English, doesn't he?'

'He's been hanging around a lot of Americans.'

Alevy nodded. 'Well, you got him exercised about Dodson. He's wondering now if we know only a little bit about the Charm School or if we know everything. Sometimes it's good to beat the bush and see what comes out. Sometimes it's rabbit, sometimes it's bear.'

'Bear's okay. I'm loaded for bear.'

Alevy smiled. 'This is bear country.'

'No sweat, Seth. You can handle it. Write me about it.'

Alevy laughed. 'You bastard. You piss him off, then leave me to face him.'

'You volunteered. I'd hand him over to my replacement.'

'No, I'll take charge of Burov. He's a good contact. I think I might even get along with him down the road after this business is resolved. I could work with him.'

'Birds of a feather.'

Alevy didn't respond.

'I have to go.' Hollis opened the safe-room door and left, Alevy followed him down the hallway.

In the living room Alevy said, 'I have some sending and receiving to do tonight. Come back here at one A.M.'

Hollis moved toward the top of the stairs. 'Why?'

'I might have more answers by then. I know I'll have more questions. Think about what goes on in the Charm School.'

Hollis went down the stairs, retrieved his coat, and let himself out. He said aloud to himself, 'What the hell do you think I've been thinking about?'

21

Sam Hollis looked for a dish towel, couldn't find one, and wiped the kitchen counter with his handkerchief, then threw the handkerchief in the trash can.

Hollis missed the Russian maids, but the number of FNs inside the embassy was down to about a dozen. While security was improved, housekeeping was hit or miss. The American couple who did the cleaning now, Mr and Mrs Kellum, were more thorough than the Russian women had been. But then, the Kellums were looking only for dirt, whereas the Russians had had other things to look for. Unfortunately, the Kellums got around to his place only about once every two weeks, and it showed. Hollis threw coffee cups and beer glasses into the dishwasher and slammed it shut. The doorbell rang. 'Damn it.'

He went into the living room and kicked magazines and newspapers under the couch, then scooped up three ties and dumped them behind the books on his bookshelf. The doorbell rang again. 'Hold on.' He placed an ashtray over a scotch spill on the coffee table and bounded down the stairs. He opened the door. 'Hello.'

She came inside wearing an ankle-length white wool coat, a Russian blue for hat, and carrying a canvas bag. She kissed him lightly on the cheek, which he thought was more intimate than on the mouth. She stomped her boots on the rug and handed him the bag. 'Snowing,' she said.

He helped her off with her things and put the hat and coat in the foyer closet. Hollis saw that under the stylish coat she'd worn into the city, she was wearing a black velour sweat suit.

She sat on the stairs, pulled off her boots and socks, and massaged her feet. 'Where were you?' she asked.

'I was in the kitchen.'

'No, I mean earlier this evening.'

'Oh, I was sending and receiving.'

'Boy, I wish I had a secret room where I could tell people I was, even if I wasn't. That could come in handy sometimes.'

He led her up the stairs.

'Captain O'Shea got all shifty when I asked him where you were. I looked for you in the lounge.'

'I was in the radio room. Sending and receiving.'

They stepped into the living room. She asked, 'Are you seeing anyone else? I never asked you that, because I'm naïve. But I'm asking you now.'

Hollis was momentarily nostalgic for a wife who didn't care where he was. 'There's no one else. What's in the bag?'

'The best that Gastronom One has to offer.' She walked into the center of the living room and looked around at the eclectic collection of Asian, South American, and European furniture. 'Is this your wife's taste?'

'We picked up pieces all over the world.'

'Really? Does she want it back?'

'I don't know.'

'Where are you having it moved?'

'My next duty station, I guess. Do you want this stuff in the kitchen?'

'Yes.' She followed Hollis into the kitchen and unpacked the canvas bag. Hollis looked at the jars and cans – pickled vegetables, horseradish, salted fish, canned sausage, a piece of smoked herring, a box of loose tea, and a carton of cookies labeled cookies. The Russians were into generics. Hollis had tried those cookies once and thought they smelled like rancid lard and pencil shavings. He said, 'Where's the beef?'

'Oh, they don't carry real food at that Gastronom. Only specialty items. I'll just make a platter of zakuski, and we'll pick. I'm not very hungry.'

'I am. I'll go to the commissary.'

'There's enough here. Make me a vodka with lemon while I put it together. Where's your can opener?'

'Right there.' Hollis got his Stolichnaya out of the freezer and filled two frozen glasses. 'I don't have lemon. No one has lemon.'

Lisa reached into her pocket and produced a lemon. 'Got this in the lounge. The bartender is in love with me.'

Hollis cut the lemon and put a wedge in each glass. They drank, opened cans and jars, and looked for bowls, plates, and serving pieces. Hollis found that he didn't know his kitchen very well.

'Go sit on the couch,' she said. 'I'll serve you there. Go on.'

Hollis went into the living room and found a magazine under the couch.

She came in with a tray of food and placed it on the coffee table, then sat beside him and tried to push the ashtray aside. 'This is stuck.'

They ate zakuski, drank vodka, and talked. Hollis asked her about her work.

'I'm a fraud. I write what I know they want, in the style they want, the word length they want –'

'Who is "they"?'

'I don't know. That's the scary thing. Do you know?'

'In the military you *know*.'

She nodded. 'Actually, I'm a good writer. I can do some good stuff. But I like the glamour of the Foreign Service. What should I do?'

'Stay with the service. Write the good stuff on the side, under a pen name.'

'Good idea. Do you think they'll reassign us together?'

'Is that what you want?'

'Have I been too subtle, or are you dense?'

He smiled. 'I'll work it out.'

'Can you?'

'I think so.'

She took out her cigarettes. 'Do you mind?'

'No.'

'Want one?'

'Later.'

She drew the ashtray toward her. 'Why does this stick?'

Hollis poured himself another vodka.

She lit her cigarette and said, 'How have the last six months gone, Sam? You miss her?'

'No, but my bachelorhood hasn't been too thrilling either. There aren't many social opportunities in merry Moscow and fewer here on the compound. I can't play bridge with the marrieds anymore, and I don't hang around with you unmarrieds in the lounge. I'm in limbo.'

'You've been horny.'

'It's been a *hard* half year.'

'So the stories I heard about your amorous adventures were not true?'

'Well, maybe three of them were.' He smiled.

'Am I the first woman who's been up here?'

'You're into counting, aren't you?'

She gave him a look of mock anger and grabbed his tie. 'You remember how I kicked Viktor in the balls? Answer me, Hollis.' She pulled his tie.

'You're making my tie hard.'

She suppressed a smile. 'Answer me.'

He laughed. 'Yes, yes. I told you. I've been alone.' He grabbed her wrists and pinned her to the couch. They kissed.

She moved away. 'Later. I have a videotape in my bag.' She stood, retrieved the tape, and put it in his VCR. '*Doctor Zhivago*. There was a month wait for this, so we have to see it.' She went back to the couch and lay down, putting her bare feet in his lap. 'Are you into feet?'

'I never gave it much thought.'

'Would you mind rubbing my feet?'

'No.' He rubbed her feet as they watched the tape and drank vodka.

'I've seen this movie four times,' she said. 'It always makes me cry.'

'Why don't you run it backwards? The czar will be on the throne at the end.'

'Don't be an idiot. Oh, look at him. He's gorgeous.'

'Looks like a used-rug salesman.'

'I love "Lara's Theme".'

'I love Lara. I could eat that woman.'

'Don't be gross. Oh, Sam, I wanted to go out to Peredelkino and put flowers on Pasternak's grave and listen to the Russians read his poetry in the churchyard.'

'It seems you won't do many of the things you wanted to do here to satisfy your Russian soul.'

'I know. It's sad. I almost got home.'

'Watch the movie. This is where Lara shoots the fat guy.'

They snuggled on the couch and watched the videotape. A cold wind rattled the windowpane, and a few flakes of snow fell.

They made love on the couch and fell asleep. At one A.M. Hollis awakened and put on his trousers. She opened her eyes. 'Where are you going?'

'To the Seven-Eleven for a pack of cigarettes.'

'Whom are you meeting?'

'The ambassador's wife. I'm going to break it off.'

'You're meeting Seth.'

'Correct. Jealous?'

She closed her eyes and rolled over.

Against his better judgement, Hollis said, 'You never told me he lived like a czar. Did he give you the icon?'

'I told you it was my grandmother's.'

'That's right. And you sounded so appreciative when I said I could get it out in the diplomatic pouch. Christ, your friend Alevy could get the Kremlin's domes out for you.'

'Don't be a postcoital beast.' She closed her eyes and rolled over.

Hollis left, slamming the door behind him.

Part 3

The Russian is a delightful person till he tucks in his shirt. As an Oriental, he is charming. It is only when he insists on being treated as the most easterly of western peoples instead of the most westerly of easterns that he becomes . . . difficult to handle.

– Rudyard Kipling

22

The background music on the tape deck in Alevy's apartment was the Red Army Choir singing patriotic songs.

Hollis asked, 'Could you change that?'

'Sure.' Alevy opened the door on the sideboard and stopped the tape. 'Sometimes I play things they like to hear too.'

Hollis looked out the window toward a ten-story apartment building across the street. The top floor was where the KGB manned its electronic gadgets aimed at the embassy compound. He wondered just how much they saw and heard.

'Tina Turner or Prince?'

'Whatever turns you on, Seth.'

Alevy put the Prince tape on and hit the play button. 'That should send them to their vodka bottles.' He turned to Hollis. 'So to pick up where we left off, what are those three hundred American fliers doing in that prison to earn their keep? To keep from being shot?'

'Let's back up a minute,' Hollis said. 'If we know that American POWs are being held at the place, why isn't our government doing something about it?'

Alevy poured brandy into his coffee. 'We didn't *know* until Friday night.'

'You people knew *something* before then.'

'What were we supposed to do about it? If the president made discreet inquiries or demands of the Soviet government, they would say, 'What are you talking about? Are you trying to wreck the peace again?' And you know what? They're right. And if the president got angry and made a *public* accusation, he would recall our ambassador, kick their ambassador out, and cancel the summit and arms talks. And we still wouldn't have a shred of evidence. And the world would be pissed off at us

281

again. This guy they've got in the Kremlin gets good press, Sam. He says he wants to be our friend.'

Hollis observed, 'Then he shouldn't let his K-goons kill and harass Americans.'

'Interesting point,' Alevy conceded. 'And that's part of the complexity of the problem we face. This new guy has inherited three hundred American POWs. But it's the *KGB* who runs that camp. How much has the KGB told him about the camp? How much have they told him about what *we* know about the Charm School? For that matter, we're not telling our government much, are we, Sam? The KGB may be looking to hand the Kremlin an embarrassing and serious problem at the last possible moment. The KGB and the Soviet military have pulled that stunt before. They don't want peace with the West.'

'Don't your people sabotage peace initiatives?'

'Not too often,' Alevy gave a sinister laugh. 'How about your folks at the Pentagon?'

Hollis replied, 'No one's hands are clean.'

'And you personally, Sam?'

'Peace with honor,' Hollis replied. 'How about you? You're no fan of the Soviets or of détente.'

Alevy shrugged. 'I'm just giving you the party line. I do what they tell me. They tell me not to embarrass the Soviet government with revelations that they might be holding American citizens as prisoners.' Alevy sprawled on the couch. 'So I don't. Then Burov moves the camp or just shoots all those airmen.'

Hollis said, 'That's why we have to move fast, Seth.'

Alevy stared up at the ceiling. 'Right. Those men would be dead right now, if it weren't for Dodson. Dodson is living evidence, and Dodson is on the loose. So Burov has the Charm School and its population on hold. If Burov gets Dodson before we do . . . I keep waiting for Dodson to show up here.'

Hollis said, 'I keep thinking about the thousand missing fliers

282

and the three hundred we know are in the Charm School. I suppose there were more, but through attrition . . . natural causes, suicide, executions . . . Three hundred. I think it's up to us, Seth, to save them. Screw the diplomats.'

Alevy regarded Hollis a moment, then spoke. 'You know, Sam, in the two years I've been working with you, I never understood where you were coming from.'

'Good.'

'But now I've got a handle on you. You're willing to break the rules on this one, risk your career, world peace, and your very life to get those fliers out. Cool Sam Hollis, Colonel Correct, is a wild jet jockey again, ready to bomb and strafe anything in his way.' Alevy smiled. 'Yet everyone still thinks you're a team player and I'm the rogue. They don't know what I know about you. That could be useful. Welcome to my world, Sam Hollis.'

Hollis made no reply.

Alevy said, 'Think of the downside of your goal. Let's say we got those men out, through negotiations or otherwise. Christ, can you imagine three hundred middle-aged American POWs landing at Dulles airport on a flight from Moscow? Do you know what kind of public outrage that would produce?'

'Yes, if my outrage is any gauge of American public opinion.'

'Right. Scrap the summit, the arms talks, trade, travel, the Bolshoi, the works. We might have our honor intact, but I wouldn't give odds on the peace.'

'What are you saying, Seth? Washington doesn't want them home?'

'You figure it out.' Alevy got up and poured more coffee and brandy from the sideboard. He shut off the tape. 'What do you want to hear?'

'In the last two years I've heard every piece of music written since 1685. I really don't care any more.'

'How about bagpipes? Listen to this. The Scots Highland Regiment. A limey in the UK embassy gave me this one. He says the Russians hate the sound of bagpipes.' Alevy put on the tape of pipes and drums, and the regiment swung into 'The Campbells Are Comin'.'

Alevy said, 'Let's return to the question of *why* these fliers are still in Soviet hands. After they were wrung dry by the Red Air Force and GRU, why did the KGB come in and co-opt the place?'

Hollis sipped on his coffee. 'Mental labor. A sort of think tank. A KGB think tank. An extension course of the Institute of Canadian and American Studies.'

'Something like that,' Alevy replied. 'But a little more sinister.'

'Meaning?'

'We think the POWs are causing us damage, God forgive them. So our concern is not purely humanitarian. If it were, then you'd be correct in your cynical assumption that we'd just as soon let them rot in order to save détente. Fact is, Sam, our concern – my company's concern – is very deep and has to do with urgent matters of national security.' Alevy walked toward Hollis and said, 'To put it bluntly, we think that fucking prison camp is a training school for Soviet agents who talk, look, think, act, and maybe even fuck like Americans. Do you understand?'

Hollis nodded. 'I know that. I've known that from the beginning. A finishing school, graduate school, charm school . . . whatever.'

'Right. If our theory is correct, a graduate of that place is indistinguishable from a man born and raised in the good old US of A. When an agent leaves there, he has a South Boston accent like Major Dodson or maybe a South Carolina accent or a Whitefish, North Dakota, accent. He can tell you the name of Ralph Kramden's wife and beat you at Trivial Pursuit. See?'

'Whitefish is in Montana, Seth.'

'Is it?'

'Who played shortstop for the 1956 Dodgers, Seth?'

Alevy smiled grimly. 'Phil Rizzuto.' He waved his arm. 'Anyway, I can't be one of them.'

'Why not?'

'My company doesn't let you in just because you talk the talk. They want to interview mothers, fathers, and high school teachers. Point is though, most private companies just want to see documentary evidence that you were born, educated, and so forth.' Alevy grinned. 'But it was a good question. You'll be asking it again.' Alevy added, 'You've met a graduate of the Charm School.'

'The man in Fisher's room. Schiller.'

'Yes. Was he perfect?'

'Chillingly so.' Hollis thought a moment. 'So you think these . . . graduates of this school have entered American life, in America?'

'We believe so. They might not work for my company, but they could work for contractors we hire, and they could live next door to me in Bethesda or empty the trash in CIA headquarters. They could install my telephone and audit my taxes. They can go to computer schools or other technical schools and could most probably join the military.' He looked at Hollis. 'Who *did* play shortstop for the 1956 Dodgers?'

'Howdy Doody.'

'Bang, you're dead.' Alevy poured brandy into his empty coffee cup. 'Want anything?'

Hollis could see that Alevy was fatigued, high on caffeine, and low on alcohol. Hollis went to the sideboard and poured the last of the coffee. He said, 'So they quack like a duck, look like a duck, and even lay eggs like a duck. But they ain't ducks.'

'No, they ain't, Sam. They're red foxes. In the chicken coop. Or if you prefer, Satan in the sanctuary.'

'How many do you think have graduated that place?'

'When the school was first started, there were probably more Americans – let's call them instructors. The Charm School, as an offshoot of the Red Air Force school, has been in existence maybe twelve to fifteen years. The Charm

School course would have to take at least a year. Probably a one-on-one situation. The little Red student assimilates the sum total of the American's knowledge, personality, accent, and so forth.'

'The invasion of the body snatchers,' Hollis said.

'Precisely. So the school may once have had the capacity to graduate several hundred agents a year. But we assume some of the Russkies flunked out, and we assume some of the American instructors flunked in the ultimate sense, and also we don't think the KGB undergraduate schools here in Moscow or in Leningrad could supply that many qualified students to the graduate school – that's what we called it. But Major Dodson called it Mrs Ivanova's Charm School, and that's from the horse's mouth. I guess the Americans there call it that as a joke. We still don't know what the Russians call it. Probably Spy School Five. Anyway, we can't be sure all of the graduates were infiltrated into the States. So to answer your question, I would guess maybe fifteen hundred to two thousand. Maybe more.'

'You mean there may be as many as two thousand Russian agents in America posing as Americans?'

'Posing is not the word,' Alevy said. 'They *are* Americans. The earlier graduates have been there nearly fifteen years. Long enough to have realized the American dream – with a little help from their friends. Long enough to have married and have kids in Little League. Long enough to be in positions to do real harm.'

'And none of them has been caught?'

Alevy shook his head. 'Not that I know of. No one was even looking until recently. And what do we look for? Someone who drinks tea from a glass and writes his *k*'s backward?'

'Someone who is caught spying.'

'They probably don't spy in the conventional sense. Their people are probably divided into several categories: sleeper agents, agents in place, agents of influence, and so forth. Their covers are perfect, and they never draw attention to themselves.

Even if we nabbed one spying, we'd be hard-pressed to prove the guy was born and raised in Volgograd, as long as he stuck to his legend.'

'If you attached electrodes to his balls and jolted him until he spoke Russian, you'd know.'

'You know something? I don't think the guy would speak Russian. And even if he exposed himself, what good would it do? He's not part of a cell or a ring. He's got to be on his own if this thing is going to work for them.'

'But he's got to have a control officer, Seth. Someone in the Soviet embassy in DC or the UN delegation in New York or the consulate in San Francisco. What good is he if he's really on his own? How does he deliver his work product? They're not going to trust clandestine radios or drop sites.'

'No. He's got to hand over his product and make oral reports. So he goes on foreign vacations like other Americans. Maybe he even takes one of these package tours to Moscow. As far as we can figure, all agent contact is made overseas.'

Hollis walked to a tall curio cabinet. The shelves contained small figurines in porcelain and bisque, eighteenth-century ladies in low-cut gowns and goldilocks curls, and gentlemen in knickers and wigs. They could be Frenchmen or Englishmen of the same period, Hollis thought, but, there was something about them that was not quite right, not quite like the real thing you'd see in a London antique shop. Hollis opened the cabinet and took out a six-inch statuette of a man in riding livery. He said, 'What is it, Seth? The Tartar influence? The Kazak influence? Why aren't they exactly like us? I know they can look Scandinavian or Germanic, like Burov, but it's something more than genetic. It's a whole different soul and psyche, an ancestral memory, it's the deep winter snow, and Mongols sweeping over the steppe, and always feeling like they're inferior to the West and getting shafted by Europe and Cyrillic letters and Slavic fatalism and an off-brand Christianity and who the hell knows what else. But whatever it is, you can spot it, spot *them*, like an art expert can spot a forgery across

287

the room.' He looked at the figure in his hand and threw it to Alevy. 'You understand?'

Alevy caught it gingerly. 'I understand. But we can't find two thousand of them that way.' Alevy put the figure down.

'No.' Hollis began to close the cabinet door and saw the Palekh box that Lisa had bought in the Arbat. He recalled his conversation with her and understood that he'd known then what Alevy was telling him now about the nature of the Charm School. He had the bizarre thought that Lisa herself could be a product of the Charm School, but of course that wasn't possible considering her verifiable background, which was double-checked by State Department Intelligence. But if he had that passing thought, he could imagine the fear and distrust that would run rampant in American society, defense industries, institutions, and government offices if it became known that there could be two thousand KGB agents among them.

Alevy said, 'Actually, I think we have found two. Right here. In the embassy, Sam. Right under our noses. Any guesses?'

Hollis thought a moment. He had to discount the men and women with high-level clearances, which left the nonworking spouses, the Marines, and the service people. Suddenly two names came immediately to him, as if he'd known all along. Bits and pieces of conversation ran through his mind, small details that had struck him as odd but had not fully alerted him because he had not known about the Charm School then. He said to Alevy, 'Our nice handyman and housekeeper. The Kellums.'

Alevy replied, 'Great minds think alike. When they were hired, they were given only low-level security investigations commensurate with the job. I wired Langley a while ago. Now it seems their backgrounds are not checking out.' Alevy rubbed his eyes wearily and continued, 'I'm having the bartender, the cooks, the chauffeurs, and the whole American service staff rechecked. We thought when we kicked out the FNs, we were getting rid of the security problem we had. But with the Russian staff, you watched them like hawks and kept them in designated areas. Now with all these low-level, low-security classification Americans, they wander around freely because they're American. But evidently some of them are Russian wolves in designer clothes.'

Hollis thought about the Kellums' going through his rooms, his desk, his letters. Burov even knew how much scotch he drank and the brand of undershorts he preferred. He pictured the Kellums, a pleasant middle-aged couple, ostensibly from Milwaukee, and recalled his brief conversations with them.

Alevy seemed to be reading his thoughts. He asked, 'So, could you tell the Kellums weren't *exactly* like us?'

'No, but then we're not exactly like each other either. America is as diverse as the Soviet Union. You and I do the Baltic bit when we're snooping around in Russia, but in the Baltic, we're Ukrainians or Byelorussians. They must do the same sort of thing. The ones who have developed, say, a Boston accent and legend, won't operate in Boston, because they couldn't pull it off there. But to answer your question, the Kellums had me fooled.'

'Me too. But now that we know, we can clean house a bit. However, a lot of damage has been done. And we have only two down and about two thousand to go. We have to come up with a hell of a lot better way to find these people who are scattered from one end of America to another. Not to mention overseas military bases and, as we are embarrassed to discover, our embassies.'

Hollis seemed lost in thought, then said, 'But something you said before . . . these Soviet agents have married, formed relationships, have American children, live the good life.'

'And may now, as you are suggesting, Sam, be having very mixed feelings. And yet, not one has defected. Why not? Partly, we think, because there's no reason to defect. In a bizarre sort of way some of them have already defected. The KGB knows that but doesn't care as long as they go on their overseas vacations a few times a year and turn in good work product. And maybe

the reward for fifteen or twenty years' service is retirement –
in America, if they wish. Irony of ironies. Of course, there are
other inducements to lead a double life: ideology, money, and
fear. The KGB is perfectly capable of wiping out a person's
family in Russia *or* in America if that person betrays them. But
realize, too, that these are handpicked agents. Many of them
need no threats or inducements. Many of them are not going
to be seduced by the American lifestyle or by democracy or
anything they see.'

'You don't think so?'

Alevy massaged his temples. 'You know, Sam, we tend to
overrate the seductiveness and quality of our system. That's
heresy, I know, but it's true. Two hundred million Ivans and
Natashas do not want to move to America just because they
know we have freedom and dishwashers. There *is* a certain
purity of the Russian soul, a fierce patriotism somewhat like
our own and a half-assed belief which still lingers, that things
will one day get better for them.' Alevy refilled his glass.
'That's not to say we won't get a defector or two one day,
but as I said, that won't roll up the operation.'

Hollis looked at Alevy in the dim light. Alevy was far more
understanding of the Russians than Hollis had been led to
believe. A lot of CIA types liked to dwell on all the signs and
portents of a Soviet society that was falling apart. They made
reports on this to succeeding administrations, who enjoyed
the good news. But this was a society that had been falling
apart for as long as anyone could remember, and it was still
around, and in the end the Russians always stood and fought
to protect their identity, their culture, their language, and their
motherland.

Hollis poured himself a scotch and fished a half-melted ice
cube out of a sterling silver bucket. 'Where's the weakness in
their operation, Seth?'

'I'm not sure. I have some thoughts. But I know what *our*
problem is. We have two major ones. The first is to identify
and roll up this network that isn't a network but is more like

toxic organisms in American society. Then we have to stop this school from pumping out more disease. I didn't make up that analogy. That's from headquarters. They like analogies.'

'You forgot the third thing, Seth. Getting the fliers out of there.'

Alevy glanced at Hollis. 'Yes. But that's part of closing up the school. The tough nut to crack is the two thousand agents already entrenched in America. I hate to say it, or even think it, but we may have to live with that for another forty or fifty years.'

'If America is around that long.' Hollis said.

Alevy didn't reply to that but said, 'So that's the story you've helped uncover, Sam.'

'What am I supposed to do with this information?'

'Well, Colonel, we had several options a few days ago. But now, with you getting booted, with Dodson on the loose and Fisher dead and then with you snooping around out there, and your goading Burov, now they know that we know, and our options are shutting down fast. They're going to shut that place up and remove every scrap of evidence. They'll transfer the operation someplace and they'll offer to take an American delegation through the suspected site. By the time we get there, it'll be a rest home for Moscow pensioners or something. So, as you said, we have to act quickly.'

'Why don't we start by arresting the Kellums and making them talk?'

'I'd like to, but we haven't absolutely proven they're Russian agents yet, and we don't want to tip off the KGB any more than they're already tipped. So we'll be careful with the Kellums. Also, they may be real Americans, complete with civil rights.'

'Are you asking me to help you or not?'

'You can help by not becoming part of the problem.'

'I never *was* part of the problem. I want those fliers out of prison, and I'll work with you to do that, or I'll pursue my own course of action.'

Alevy nodded. 'Yes, of course you would. I guess if you or any military man was jeopardizing the lives of three hundred CIA agents, I'd do the same. Loyalty is okay.'

'I don't need you to tell me that.'

Alevy replied, 'Listen, Sam, I told you everything – State secrets and diplomatic policy and an issue so hot it could blow Soviet-American relations to hell for years to come. I did that to convince you we're not sleeping on this. We're working on getting those pilots home. I'm taking it on pure faith that you will be reasonable. Don't get your people in the Pentagon all worked up. Okay?'

'Okay.' Hollis did not think for one second that Seth Alevy took anything on faith. He also didn't think that Alevy intended to follow the government's line of pursuing détente. Alevy would like nothing better than for him to get the Pentagon all worked up. And neither did Hollis think that Alevy spent an hour briefing him just to tell him to keep his mouth shut. With a few days left in the country and officially relieved of his duties. Hollis knew he hadn't heard the last of the Charm School or of Seth Alevy.

'Don't tell Lisa any of this. It's your job to neutralize her. Okay?'

'Okay.'

'And remember that your persona non grata status raises some questions about your diplomatic immunity. Tell Lisa that. Be very cautious if you decide to go outside the gate.'

'Right.'

'Oh, one last thing. I want you to do me a favor.'

'What?'

'Come up on the roof with me.'

'What for?'

'Once a month or so I go on the roof and vilify the Union of Soviet Socialist Republics. I get up there and yell, "Hello, KGB shits!" Then I go into my analysis of why Soviet society sucks.'

'Christ, no wonder they beat the shit out of you.'

'Fuck them. I'm in the mood tonight. Come up with me.'

Hollis glanced at his watch. 'Well, I –' he wondered if Lisa had stayed at his place or gone home.

'Come on. Don't be so stuffy. You'll feel good.'

'I guess the fresh air will do me good.'

'That's the spirit. What are they going to do to you? Kick you out? Kill you?'

'They can't do both,' Hollis observed.

Hollis took the brandy bottle from the sideboard, and Alevy led him up to the third-floor hallway, climbed a ladder, and opened the roof hatch.

Alevy and Hollis came up on to the flat roof above Alevy's apartment. They stood in the gently falling snow and looked out over the city as the bells of the Ivan Tower chimed two. Alevy said, 'Early snow,' The stars on the Kremlin's domes and towers were luminous red, but the crosses, which for some inexplicable reason had never all been taken down, were dark and invisible. 'There is probably not one thing open in Moscow at this hour,' Alevy said, 'except the militia and KGB offices. Even the metros are closed. In Stalin's day Lubyanka would start disgorging its predators at this hour.' He took the brandy bottle from Hollis and took a long pull, then shouted, 'Do you hear me out there? Wake up, K-goons! This is Seth Alevy, super-spook, super-Jew!' He turned to Hollis and continued in a slurred voice. 'The goons would prowl the city with lists, and all Moscow would hold its breath until morning. And each dawn would break over a city of frightened human beings, hurrying to offices and factories, pretending not to notice if someone did not show up at work. And they say you could really hear the sounds of screams and gunshots coming out of Lubyanka. What a barbaric place this was! I look out there, Sam, and I see an alien cityscape. Strange lettering on signs, fantastic-shaped buildings, and the sky above the city always tinged with that eerie red glow, and I think I'm on Mars sometimes.'

Hollis looked at Alevy a moment. 'Why don't you take the next space-ship back?'

Alevy smiled self-consciously. 'Oh, I will. Another year or so.'

Hollis wanted to tell Alevy that if he kept baiting them he wouldn't last another year. But he didn't want to say that with them listening. And Alevy knew that anyway.

Alevy shouted, '*Yeb vas!*' Fuck you.

A window on the top floor of the apartment house across the street opened, and a man called down in English, 'Fuck you, Jew.'

Alevy laughed and shouted back, '*Sosi khui, chitai Pravdu budesh komissarom,*' which Hollis translated as something like 'Suck cocks and read *Pravda*, and you'll become a commissar.' Hollis said, 'Let's go, Seth.' He took Alevy's arm.

Alevy pulled away. 'No.' He took another swallow from the bottle and handed it to Hollis. 'Here. Get drunk and think of a good one. You know the one about . . . how does it go . . . ? KGB men never go out with girls, they just live with Mary Palm.' Alevy made a jerking motion with his cupped hand.

'Seth . . .' Hollis could see that Alevy was quite drunk by now, and there was no talking to him. This was apparently Alevy's monthly catharsis, and Hollis had learned to respect people's intermittent periods of insanity here.

A second voice from the window called down in English, 'Who's the other fag with you? Is that Hollis?'

Hollis thought he recognized Igor's voice. Hollis took a pull from the bottle and shouted back in Russian, 'I saw your mother on her knees in Gorky Park trying to make the rent money!'

Alevy roared with delight. 'That's a good one.'

The insults flew through the snowy night for fifteen minutes. Hollis, who was feeling somewhat drunk himself now, had the vague thought that this East-West meeting should have been on a higher plane, but Alevy and the two Russians seemed to be happy with their ritual. Hollis said to Alevy, 'Has the ambassador spoken to you about this?'

Alevy finished the brandy and let the bottle drop in the snow.

'Fuck him.' Alevy staggered to the open roof hatch and gave a parting wave. '*Spokoiny nochi!*'

The Russians both shouted back, 'Good night!'.

Alevy climbed unsteadily down the ladder.

Hollis looked back at the apartment building and saw the two men waving. One shouted in English, 'Have a safe journey home, Sam.' They both laughed.

Hollis didn't think they sounded any more sincere than Burov.

23

Hollis stood among the packing crates, glass in hand, trying to find the one with his liquor in it. The big furniture was still in place, and the German movers, with Teutonic efficiency, had left some necessities unpacked until the last day. Thus the bathroom was largely intact, and he had three days of clothing available, plus some odds and ends in the kitchen. But they hadn't left a bottle of scotch out. He found a fiberboard crate marked *Alkoholisches Getränke* that looked promising. He tore open the lid and rummaged through the Styrofoam filler, finding a bottle of Chivas. He poured a few ounces into his glass and went into the kitchen for ice. He looked at his watch, waited for noon, then took a swallow.

Hollis heard the front door open and assumed it was Lisa, since she had asked for and gotten a key. He went to the top of the stairs and saw the Kellums coming toward him. Dick Kellum smiled. "Oh, hi, Colonel. We didn't expect you in."

Hollis returned the smile. 'Not much to do in the office.' He stepped aside as the Kellums came into the living room.

Ann Kellum, carrying a bucket of cleaning things, said apologetically, 'We can come back another time.'

'No, Mrs Kellum, you can give it a once-over.'

She looked around. 'Oh, they've got you all boxed up.'

'Pretty much. Just hit the bathrooms and kitchen, if you would.'

Dick Kellum, also carrying a utility bucket, walked over to the boxes. 'You speak German, Colonel?'

'No, I don't, Dick.'

'You know, sometimes I wonder what the Russkies think of us getting German movers, sending sick people to Finland

and England, flying in Europeans to fix things in the embassy. They've got to be a little insulted. Right?'

Hollis thought, *You tell me, Ivan*. He said, 'They don't insult easily.' He looked at the Kellums. They were in their mid or late forties, both somewhat swarthy, with black, greying hair and dark eyes. They moved like people who'd done heavy menial labor all their lives, and their accents seemed to be working class, though they were far from stupid. Hollis recalled a somewhat interesting conversation he'd had with Dick Kellum on the virtues and varieties of Milwaukee beer. Ann Kellum had once confided in him that her husband drank too much of those famous brews.

Ann Kellum asked, 'Did they pack your vacuum cleaner?'

'Probably. Don't worry about that. You can do a complete job for the next tenant after I've gone.'

'You got a replacement yet, Colonel?' Mr Kellum inquired.

'Yes, a lieutenant colonel named Fields. I know him and his wife. They're trying to get him here before I leave, and if they do, I'll introduce you to him. His wife will probably come in later.'

'I hope he speaks Russki like you so someone can talk to that crazy Russian groundkeeper for me.'

Hollis smiled at Dick Kellum. *You son of a bitch. I'd like to cut your heart out*. 'He's fluent too but likes to keep that under his hat, if you know what I mean. So don't push him on it.'

'Gotcha.' Mr Kellum winked.

Mrs Kellum asked, 'This will be their unit then?'

'Yes.'

'Will the lady be working, do you know?'

'I believe so. She's an accredited teacher and will probably try to get a position at the Anglo-American School.'

'Okay,' Mrs Kellum said. 'That makes things easier to schedule.'

'I know,' Hollis replied.

Mr Kellum hefted his bucket. 'I'll get going on the head.' He walked to the second-floor bathroom.

Mrs Kellum watched him go, then said in a low voice, 'Colonel, this is none of my business, and you can tell me to shut up, but are you joining Mrs Hollis? She still in London?'

'I'm not sure, Mrs Kellum.'

The woman seemed to be fighting some sort of inner battle, then blurted out, 'Colonel, Dick and me like you, and I talked to him about this, and he told me to keep quiet about it, but I think you got to know. Your wife . . . Mrs Hollis . . .' She glanced at Hollis, then looked away. 'Well, she was seeing a gentleman here, a gentleman from the commercial section. I can't say his name, but he'd come by whenever you were in the city or something or up to Leningrad on business.' She added quickly, 'They could've just been friends, you know, and maybe they were, but I don't think it's right for a woman to be having male friends in her place without her husband being around.' Mrs Kellum fidgeted for a moment, then picked up her bucket and went into the kitchen.

Hollis took a drink of his scotch. *Spies lie*, he thought. Maybe the KGB were just indulging themselves in a last joke before he left. Then again, it might be true. In fact, the gentleman in question could have been Ken Mercer, one of the men Lisa had been speaking to in the lobby of the chancery. Hollis said. 'Who gives a damn?'

He heard the front door open again, and this time it was Lisa who came up the stairs. 'Are you alone?' she called out. 'Did I catch you? Are you screwing someone, Hollis?'

Hollis greeted her at the top of the stairs. 'Hello, Lisa.'

'At least you have your pants on.'

'Mr and Mrs Kellum are here.'

She put her hand over her mouth, and her cheeks reddened. She whispered, 'You idiot, why didn't you tell me?'

'I just did.'

'Did they hear me?'

'I'm sure they did.'

She buried her face in his chest and muffled a laugh.

'That'll be all over the compound in an hour. Oh, my God. I'm embarrassed.'

'They're discreet.' He kissed her. 'Why don't we go to your place?'

She looked around. 'My place is a mess too. Let's go into town. It's not raining or freezing today.'

Hollis hesitated, then replied, 'All right, but . . .'

'Oh, don't let *them* run your life. Isn't that our motto?'

'Yes, it is.' He called into the kitchen, 'Mrs Kellum, I'm leaving.'

She appeared at the kitchen door. 'Oh, Ms Rhodes, I didn't know you were here.'

Lisa exchanged a smirking glance with Hollis. She said, 'Hello, Ann. Not much to do here, is there?'

'No. Have they packed you too?'

'All packed.'

'Are you sad to be leaving?'

'Yes, very.'

'I don't see why they couldn't give you another chance.'

'Well, they take minor violations very seriously here.'

'Everything's a violation here. No freedom of anything. Will your replacement be moving into your unit?'

'I don't think I'm getting a replacement. No use sending someone here if they have to start shipping people –'

'Let's go,' Hollis interrupted. 'Good-bye, Mrs Kellum. See you before I leave.'

'I hope so, Colonel.'

'I'll make a point of it.'

He took Lisa's arm, and they went down to the foyer, where Hollis got his trench coat and a black felt fedora.

'You look like a spy in that getup.'

'No, that blue topcoat and porkpie hat is my spy outfit.'

They walked outside into the thin sunshine. There was a damp chill in the air, but it was above freezing, and the snow of a few nights before lay in patches on the quad. They left through the rear pedestrian gate beside the Marine barracks, and Hollis said, 'Where do you want to go?'

'Nowhere in particular. We'll just be tourists. We'll walk up Gorky Street, hand in hand, and stop in a funny little café for cappuccino and pastry.'

'There are no cafés with cappuccino on Gorky or any other street.'

'Pretend.'

'All right.' They walked through the streets of the old Presnya district, past a sculpture of a barricade fighter and then another sculpture entitled 'The Cobblestone – Weapon of the Proletariat.' Nearby was an obelisk erected to the Heroes of the 1905 Insurrection. Hollis said, 'This is romantic. Can we kiss in Insurrection Square?'

'Oh, stop griping. Romance is in the heart, not in stone or marble, even on the Via Veneto.'

'Well said.'

'Anyway, I've developed a perverse fondness for this city and its people.'

'Some of its perverse people have been following us. You know what "embassy watchers" are, of course.'

'Yes. Are they following us?' She glanced around.

'Yes.'

'Are you sure? I don't think I've ever been followed.'

'Well, they follow everyone once in a while. But with military attachés, they stick like glue all the time. We're going to lose them. It's fairly simple to do on the metro. Just stay with me. Here's some five-kopek pieces.'

They walked up Rampart Street and entered the 1905 Street Metro, taking the first train to come along. Sitting in a half-empty car, Hollis said, 'We'll have to make a few random transfers until I'm sure we've lost them.'

'Okay. But who cares if they follow us? We're not doing anything.'

'It's the principle. Also, they may still have a room waiting for us at Lefortovo.'

'Oh.'

They rode the metro toward the city center and made several last-minute transfers at the more crowded stations, then took the Prospect Mira line to the northern reaches of the city. Hollis settled in his seat and said, 'We lost them back at Revolution Square.'

She sat beside him in the nearly empty car. 'How do you know?'

'I saw them looking upset on the platform as our train pulled away.'

'You knew what they looked like?'

'I hope so.'

'This is neat. *This* is romantic. Running from the KGB.' She looked at her watch. 'It's nearly one. I'm starving. Whose turn to buy?'

'I think you forgot to pay at Lefortovo. So it's your turn.'

'Right.' She took his hand. 'You know, Sam, my boss, Kay Hoffman, says I shouldn't get involved with a married man.'

'Really? Does she write an advice column on the side?'

'Be serious. She's an experienced woman –'

'So I've heard.'

'And she's sort of my mentor. She said that married men either go back to their wives, or they consider you a transitional woman.'

'Here's Cosmos Station. The next stop is the woods. We better get off here.'

They came out of the metro pavilion and looked around. To their left was the soaring space obelisk, a three-hundred-foot curved shaft of polished titanium that represented the blast and plume of a rocket, atop which was the huge rocket itself.

Lisa observed. 'It's so *phallic* . . . look at that curve . . . that thrusting power . . . that rocket –'

Hollis smiled. 'Calm down.'

She laughed. 'Sorry, lost my head.' She surveyed the vast open spaces around her. 'I've been up here once. It's all so *Soviet* here, almost nothing of old Russia.'

301

Hollis nodded. Beyond the space obelisk was the Cosmos Cinema and beyond that the Moscow TV tower, a rocket-shaped structure nearly 1,500 feet high, which held a revolving restaurant with the odd name of Seventh Heaven. Fifty yards from the metro pavilion was the huge entrance arch to the USSR Economic Achievements Exhibition, a two-hundred-acre park with some two dozen pavilions. A sort of theme park, Hollis thought, and the theme was Soviet power. He'd toured the place once, and it *was* impressive. The buildings, like the obscenely expensive titanium rocket, were built of the finest stone and metals. The exhibits, ranging from atomic energy and rocketry to agriculture and animal husbandry, were well-preserved and well-maintained. Yet, a few kilometers to the north were the log cabins, the mud streets, the outhouses, and the women carrying water buckets on yokes.

Lisa said, 'We can try to get into the Seventh Heaven or one of the snack bars in the exhibition, or maybe we can try the Cosmos Hotel.'

Hollis looked across the six-lane Prospect Mira at the massive concave facade of the thirty-story aluminium-and-glass hotel. It had been a joint French and Yugoslav project, completed in time for the 1980 Olympics, and though it was stunning to look at, Hollis had heard rumors that the last maintenance and cleaning people had departed with the Olympic guests. He said, 'All right, the hotel.'

They crossed the wide avenue and walked up a long concrete ramp that took them to the front doors. A doorman asked for their *propusks*, and Hollis gave him two rubles instead, which got the door open.

They entered the massive, blondwood-paneled lobby, surrounded by a mezzanine level, and consulted a wall directory. The theme here, as across the street, was rocketry and space travel. There was the Orbit Lounge, the Lunar Restaurant, and so forth. Hollis said, 'I hope they don't serve drinks in space capsule glasses.'

'With rocketship stirrers.' She looked around the crowded

lobby. The furniture was discolored and sagging, the floors were dirty, and half the lights didn't work. She said, 'What is that smell?'

'I'd rather not speculate.'

She shrugged. 'I hope it's not one of the restaurants. Let's try the Lunar.'

They walked up the closest out-of-order escalator to the sweeping mezzanine level and found the Lunar Restaurant. Hollis spoke to the hostess in English, which she partly understood. She seemed surprised to discover they weren't hotel guests and had actually come from somewhere else to eat at the Lunar. She showed them into the dining room, a fairly pleasant if plain room with clean blue tablecloths.

The Cosmos was an Intourist hotel, and as the Soviets considered it one of the best, they put Americans and West Europeans there, though Hollis thought it was inconveniently far from central Moscow. The restaurant was crowded with tourists on their lunch break, the two-hour respite between the bus jaunts of their Intourist-planned stay. The hostess pointed to the far end of the restaurant and said, 'British and Americans.'

'How about Canadians and Australians?'

'Yes, yes. There, please.'

They walked unescorted through the restaurant, which consisted entirely of tables for eight and twelve. Hollis said, 'Tables for two in Russia are only in interrogation rooms.'

'Always griping.'

'Just making observations.' Hollis determined that they were now walking through the German section of the restaurant. There were well over a hundred of them, predominantly middle-aged couples. Most of them, like a good many Germans he'd seen in Moscow, looked dour and withdrawn. He could not imagine how they felt comfortable in a country that had lost twenty million of its people to the German armies and where half the tourist sights were memorials to the dead. He wouldn't have been surprised to discover that some of the men had last seen Russia from the turret of a Panzer tank.

In the English-speaking section of the dining room, Hollis and Lisa found a table occupied by only one other couple, and Lisa introduced herself and Hollis as Sam and Lisa Randall, tourists.

The couple introduced themselves as George and Dina Turnbill of Rhode Island.

Hollis and Lisa sat. The table, Hollis noticed, was set for ten, and he knew the busboys had no intention of removing the other settings. On the table were two bottles of mineral water, four bottles of a popular pear soda that Hollis had tried once, and two bottles of Russian Pepsi-Cola. Hollis had tried the Pepsi once, and it wasn't.

There was a basket of the ubiquitous black bread near them, white butter that was more like stiff cream than butter, and a bowl of pickled beets. There was apparently no menu, and a waitress brought four *pannikins* of mushrooms floating in hot cream. A waiter set down a tureen of borscht on which floated a film of sour cream.

Hollis and Lisa fell into conversation with the Turnbills. They were a casually dressed couple, attractive and in their mid-thirties. They were both instructors at Brown; he taught anthropology and she taught psychology. Hollis told them he was a used car salesman from Hoboken, New Jersey, and Lisa was a housewife, which earned him a kick under the table.

George Turnbill said to Hollis, 'Our tour group is having lunch at the downtown Intourist so they can go to GUM department store afterward. But Dina and I came back here to see more of this Economic Exhibition across the street.'

Hollis replied, 'We're in the same situation.'

Dina said, 'Isn't it marvelous?'

'What?'

'The exhibition. They've done so much in so short a time.'

Hollis thought the old 'so short a time' tagline was wearing a little thin after seventy years.

George exclaimed, 'You can eat off the streets here! Have you seen the subways yet? My God, they're marble and brass!'

Lisa smiled. 'We've been exploring the subways quite a bit.'

Dina said, 'George and I walked around Red Square last night – eleven o'clock at night, and we never once felt afraid. Right, George?'

'There's no crime here,' George agreed. 'This is a very well-run city and country. The people seem content, prosperous, healthy, and well fed.'

Hollis poured the *pannikin* of mushrooms into the beet soup and studied the result.

Lisa responded. 'I've noted that almost no one smiles –'

'That,' Dina interrupted, 'is just a national character trait. It doesn't mean they're not happy.'

'For instance,' George explained, 'Orientals smile when they're embarrassed.'

Hollis had the feeling he was getting a combined psychology and anthropology lecture. He tried the pear soda, then washed the taste out with the mineral water, then tried the borscht and mushroom concoction. Hollis badly wanted a drink, but the anti-alcohol campaign made it impossible to buy the stuff before four P.M., not even wine or beer in a tourist restaurant. He poured Pepsi, pear soda, and mineral water into one glass and swirled it around.

George asked him, 'Did you notice how cheap everything is? Five kopeks for the metro, two kopeks for the telephone. I bought a beautiful photo book of Moscow for two rubles, and the room here is about thirty rubles, and there's no tipping.'

Hollis thought about mentioning the price of fresh food if you could get it, or that badly made shoes cost about sixty dollars, junk cars about nine thousand dollars, and freedom couldn't be bought at any price. He said to George. 'What exactly did you come here to find?'

305

George answered without hesitation. 'The truth. I came to Moscow to look for the truth.'

'That,' Hollis said, 'is sort of like going to Forty-second Street to look for virtue.'

'What is that supposed to mean?'

Lisa interjected, 'We're having a somewhat different experience here than you.'

'You have to stay open-minded,' Dina advised.

Hollis turned to Lisa and said in Russian, 'I'm not sure I want to go back to America if there are any more shitheads like these two here.'

Lisa replied, 'Just stay away from college campuses.'

George asked, 'Is that Russian?'

'Polish,' Hollis said.

They finished the mushrooms, the bread, the mineral water, and the pickled beets, but there was no sign of the main course. From where he sat, Hollis could see behind the screen that shielded the kitchen door. Six waiters and waitresses sat there at a table, drinking tea and talking. Hollis said dryly, 'I'm glad they're having a good time on their day off.'

The Turnbills were extolling the virtues of black bread, mineral water, and pear soda, though they couldn't find much good to say about the communist Pepsi.

Lisa asked the Turnbills, 'Did you hear since you've been here that the Soviets have expelled two Americans from the embassy?'

'We heard that right before we left, Tuesday,' George answered. 'In fact, we read it in *The New York Times* at Kennedy Airport.'

Dina said, '*The Times* story said they went into an unauthorized area, that the man was a military attaché, and that those people are usually intelligence people. Spies.'

George added, 'I blame a lot of this tension on our government, I'm afraid. If we show we have peaceful intentions, then the Soviets will respond. They have a very responsive government in the Kremlin right now. You can see what a big

306

thing they make of peace here. *Mira*,' George said, trying out his Russian. 'Peace. Same word as for world. *Mira*. I wonder if they say *mira mira* for world peace. That sounds Spanish. Anyway, there are peace exhibits, things named for peace, Prospect Mira, banners all over saying peace. *Peace*.'

'Peace,' Hollis said. '"They have seduced my people saying, Peace; and there was no peace." Ezekiel.'

The Turnbills decided they couldn't wait for the main course and were anxious to get to the Economic Exhibition. They stood to leave.

Hollis said to them, 'A word of advice because you are my compatriots. Avoid black marketeers because they can get you in serious trouble, don't force your friendship on ordinary Russians because that can get *them* in trouble. Also, every dark street is not safe at night. And if you can get permission – which you need – see if you can get into the countryside for a day. Also, try not to criticize your own country too much, and above all, remember that you are free and they are not.'

The Turnbills smiled tightly and departed.

Lisa commented, 'That's not like you to wave the flag.'

'I was just trying to help them see.'

'We all see what we want to see, Sam. This system here still has seductive powers as you indicated. Like an old whore on a good night.'

Hollis nodded. 'I remember when I first got here. I was impressed with what I saw, but I forgot to think about what I couldn't see – concepts and abstractions such as freedom of speech, the pursuit of happiness, and the right to assemble, to travel, and ultimately to emigrate. It takes a few months here before you realize what's missing from the picture.'

Lisa smiled. 'Maybe the Turnbills will be picked up by the KGB for taking a picture of a railroad bridge or something. A week in Lefortovo or Lubyanka will straighten them out.'

'One wonders. The old Bolsheviks who were shot by Stalin were true believers to the end.'

The main course finally came, a mystery meat covered with

307

more heavy creamed mushrooms and the standard mashed potatoes on the side. Hollis said to the waitress, 'Could you bring us asparagus tips and hearts of palm?'

The waitress shook her head, pointed to the food, and left. They ate in silence for a while, then Lisa said, 'It doesn't have to be this awful. Russian food can be quite good. I've done better myself. And there are about six good Russian restaurants in New York that serve authentic stuff. No one here cares.'

'They'd care if they had to pay New York rents and get the customers in. That's the motivation to take care with any product. Not Socialist altruism, but capitalist greed. The only demanding and discerning consumer in this country is the military.'

The waitress brought tea and ice cream. For some reason that Hollis could not fathom, Russian ice cream was quite good and quite plentiful, and the Russians ate it two or three times a day, all year long. Lisa said, 'I saw another press release my office put out this morning. The ambassador again denies any wrongdoing on our part.'

'If he keeps denying it every day, people might start to wonder.'

'I know. I wish I had been allowed to write the damn thing. I used to have to rewrite everything his bitch of a secretary gave me for release. Now without my magic typewriter, he's starting to sound like the fool he is.'

'My, my,' Hollis said, 'aren't we sounding self-important? Do you think the diplomatic mission to the Soviet Union will survive your departure?'

Lisa smiled good-naturedly. 'Sorry. Just feeling mistreated.' She asked, 'What's the first thing you're going to do when you get back to the States?'

'I'm not sure. Maybe just get acquainted with my country again.'

'Where will you stay?'

'Here and there. Maybe on a military base around D.C. Go to the Pentagon and pester them for an assignment.'

They drank tea and talked awhile, watching the other diners rise in mass groups each time an Intourist guide announced a bus tour departure. The dining room was nearly empty now. Lisa took out a cigarette. 'Want one?'

'Not right now.'

'Do you smoke, or not?'

'Oh, yes.'

She looked at him doubtfully as she lit her cigarette. 'I saw another press release on the Fisher business. It was in response to charges made by his parents that the embassy was being evasive regarding the circumstances of his death. Mr and Mrs Fisher want to know if there is any connection between their son's death and our expulsion. You remember you signed all that paperwork for Burov, Well, the Fishers have it all, and they're wondering about Colonel Samuel Hollis.'

'And well they might. That's one of the advantages of having a free citizenry and an inquiring press.'

'Yes. So my office said the two events were purely coincidental. That's so lame it might even pass as the truth.'

'It might,' Hollis agreed. 'But we don't lie very well, and the USIS Ministry of Truth should stick to covering cultural and scientific events.'

Lisa waved her hand. 'Not my problem anymore.'

'Well, what are *you* going to do when you get home?'

'Watch the six o'clock news, get my wardrobe updated, buy an avocado, see a football game, rake leaves –'

'You're staying with your parents?'

'Yes. I still have my room there. My little time capsule, my home base. You don't have that, do you?'

'No. No nest for this eagle, if you'll pardon the bad analogy.'

'Metaphor. I'll pardon anything but bad English.'

'I'd like to get you in a high-performance jet, smart-ass.'

'I'd love to get in one with you.' She leaned across the table and looked him in the eye. 'Well, are we going to be together?'

'I hope so.'

'And you think you can work it out?'

'Yes, it's called blackmail.'

She took his hand and squeezed it. 'I don't care what it's called as long as it gets us together. And I don't care if it's Paris or Borneo.'

'That's very nice, Lisa. I was thinking, maybe the States. Maybe it's time to go home.'

'Maybe it *is* time to go home, Sam.'

The waitress presented them with a bill for six rubles, which Hollis thought very reasonable for lunch in the abstract but too much for the food that was served during the lunch. Lisa paid.

They left the dining room, and Hollis found the Intourist Service Bureau. With some difficulty he booked a car and driver pre-paying in American dollars.

'Where are we going?' she asked.

'Surprise.'

A man in his thirties, scruffily dressed, introduced himself as Sasha and led them outside to a black Volga. Hollis wrote in Cyrillic on a piece of paper and handed it to him. Sasha looked at it and shook his head. '*Nelzya,*' he said, using one of the Russians' most used words. Not allowed. '*Nyet.*'

Hollis handed him a ten-dollar bill and said in Russian. 'Be a good fellow. No one will know.'

Sasha glanced back at Hollis, then took the ten and put the Volga in gear. 'Okay.'

Lisa slid next to Hollis and put her arm through his. 'An itinerary *and* a currency violation. You've outdone yourself this time.

The Volga, like every Russian cab Hollis had been in, was dirty. They headed north on Prospect Mira, hit the Outer Ring Road and followed it southwest on its great circle around Moscow. There was still snow outside the city, and the vast stretches of evergreens were dusted with white powder.

Sasha turned onto the Minsk-Moscow highway. Lisa said to Hollis, 'Not Borodino . . . ?'

Hollis smiled. 'Please.'

They left the highway, went down a two-lane paved road, and entered a good-sized village of pre-Revolution clapboard houses. Lisa asked. 'Where are we?'

Hollis pointed to the train station, and Lisa read the name, Peredelkino,' She kissed Hollis on the cheek. 'Oh, what a sweetheart you are.'

Sasha said in Russian, 'I have to ask where the cemetery is.' He stopped the car and asked a passing boy on a bicycle. The boy pointed. 'That road. You'll see his grave easily enough. There are students there.'

Sasha drove up a narrow street that passed through the village and came out into open farmland again. By the side of the road was a grove of pine trees and bare birch surrounded by a low brick wall. Sasha stopped the car. Hollis and Lisa got out and walked through the small opening in the wall.

A group of ten young men and women stood in the snow-dusted cemetery around a white tombstone into which was carved an impression of the poet's craggy features and the simple line, 'Boris Pasternak, 1890–1960.' Fresh flowers lay in the snow, and a book of Boris Pasternak's poetry was being passed around, the students reading from it in turn. They barely took notice of Lisa and Hollis, but then a young girl motioned to the book questioningly and Hollis replied in Russian, 'Yes, I'd like to read.' He picked one of the Lara poems, which made Lisa smile, then passed the book to Lisa, who read from 'Garden of Gethsemane':

And peering into these Black abysses –
Void, without end and without beginning –
His brow sweating blood. He pleaded with His father
That this cup of death might pass from Him.

Afterward, on the way back to the city, Lisa said, 'Could

you imagine that in America? People traveling to a poet's grave?'

'No, I suppose not. But the Russians do it as much out of love of poetry as out of political protest. If the government made the place a national shrine, you'd see fewer poetry lovers around here. And if church attendance were encouraged, you might see fewer people there too.'

'That's cynical. I think you're wrong.'

'Maybe I see too much of the dark side of the Russian soul because I deal with the darker elements.'

'Probably.'

They had Sasha drive them around Moscow, revisiting places that had some memories for one or the other. Lisa said. 'I want to share every place with you so we can talk about them after we leave.'

'How about Gogol's grave?'

'Later.'

At dusk they went up to the Lenin Hills and looked out over the city from the observation platform of the Moscow University campus. Lisa huddled against Hollis. 'Thank you for a beautiful day. No matter what happens, this was our day.'

Hollis looked at the city spread out beyond the Moskva. 'I guess we can tell people we fell in love in Moscow.'

'Yes, that's true, and our first lovemaking was in a peasant's cabin.'

'I don't think we should go into details.'

'Oh, Sam, I'm so happy and sad at the same time. And optimistic and frightened . . .'

'I know.'

Sasha stood ten feet or so down the stone parapet, chainsmoking. He and Hollis made eye contact and Sasha smiled. He called out in Russian, 'Many lovers come here. And over there, you see that hill? That is Farewell Hill where the old Muscovites would go to say good-bye to their family and friends when they left on a long journey westward.'

Sasha moved closer to his customers. 'There is Mosfilm

down there. See the buildings? Soviet films are good, but sometimes I like American films. We don't get many. I saw *Kramer vs. Kramer*, and I took my daughter to see *Lady and the Tramp*.' He turned back to the city. 'There is the Ukraina Hotel. Stalin knew how to build things to last. Today, everything they build is cheap and falls apart. Stalin would have shot half the building supervisors they have today. See, over there is the old Kiev Station, and there is the new circus – the round building. The best circus in all the world. And right here where we stand, every December the students gather to commemorate the death of John Lennon.'

'Not Vladimir Lenin?' Hollis asked mischievously.

Sasha roared with laughter. 'No. The party takes care of that great man each twenty-first of January. Does it surprise you that the young people come here and sing John Lennon's songs? He was a poet, like Pasternak. The Russians love poets. Did you like John Lennon?'

'Yes,' Lisa replied. 'He was a great musician and poet.'

'We need more poets and fewer generals,' Sasha declared.

Lisa pointed to a cluster of gold-domed buildings about half a kilometer away. 'Sasha, isn't that Novodevichy Convent?'

'Yes. Peter put his first wife and his bitchy sister there for all their lives.' Sasha smiled at Hollis. 'It's not so easy now to get rid of troublesome women.'

'Amen, brother,' Hollis replied in English.

Lisa poked him in the side.

Sasha continued, 'You should go there on Sunday. The believers have mass in the cathedral there. I went once. It was very . . . interesting. Then go to the cemetery there too. You like our writers? Chekhov is buried there.'

'And Gogol?' Hollis asked.

'Oh, yes. He's there too.'

Hollis glanced at Lisa, who was smiling.

Sasha went on, 'Also Khruschev is there and other party members. Why do you suppose they wanted to be buried in holy ground and not at the Kremlin wall? Who can say? Maybe they're taking no chances.' Sasha laughed again.

They all got back into the Volga. Sasha said, 'You have almost two hours left for what you paid.'

'I think we've had enough,' Hollis said.

'Good. Me too. I invite you to my flat for food. My wife always wanted to meet Americans. I told her someday I'd bring some home. You're the first I've met who speak our language. Also, I like you.'

Lisa looked at Hollis and nodded. Hollis said to Sasha, 'Thank you, but we can't.'

'I know who you are. I saw both your pictures on television last night. But we have *glasnost* now. It doesn't matter.'

Hollis wondered how Soviet TV had gotten their pictures Hollis replied, 'I'm afraid this is beyond *glasnost*, and it does matter. For you, not for us.'

Sasha pulled the car away and chuckled. 'Maybe they'll kick me out too.'

'Do you know where the American embassy is?'

'Who doesn't?'

'We'll go there now.'

The Volga came down from the Lenin Hills, crossed the Moskva, and headed toward the embassy along the embankment road.

Lisa put her head on Hollis' shoulder. 'Busy tonight?'

'Meeting until about nine.'

'With whom?'

'Spies.'

'Do you want to come over afterward?'

'I'd love to.'

'Stay the night?'

'Stay the rest of the week, if you want.'

She smiled. 'Good. Move in. Shake up the diplomats and their stuffy wives.'

'Hang my underwear from your clothesline.'

'I don't have a clothesline, but I'll put your name on my buzzer.'

The Volga slid along the misty embankment road following the loop of the Moskva. The red brick chancery building appeared all alight through the river fog. Lisa said, 'I thought you were relieved of your duties.'

'I'm just briefing and being debriefed.'

'Kay won't even let me in my office. I guess this really is serious business. Are we in more trouble than we know?'

'Not at the moment. But we will be if we don't keep our mouths shut.'

'You're still on the case, aren't you? You're still working with Seth.'

Hollis didn't reply immediately, then said, 'Discharges don't come so easily in this war.'

He leaned over the front seat and said to Sasha, 'Don't slow down until you're at the gate, then stop quickly, as close to the gate as you can.'

Sasha glanced at him. 'I can't cross the militiamen on the side walk.'

'No, but get *close*. We'll be leaving the car quickly, so I'll say good-bye now.'

'*Da svedahnya*,' Sasha replied.

'Someday we'll have that dinner.'

'Someday.'

Hollis pulled his hat down and slid back low in his seat.

Lisa slid down beside him. 'Is this necessary?'

'No, it's my idea of fun.'

Sasha maintained his speed, then suddenly pulled over to the curb and hit his brakes. Hollis opened the curbside door, and he and Lisa jumped out. He took Lisa's arm and moved her quickly past the militia guards just as they stepped out of their booth '*Stoi! Pasport!*'

Hollis called out to the Marine guard. 'Hit it, son.' The electric gates began to part as Hollis heard running boots behind him. He pushed Lisa through the opening, then followed, returning the guard's salute. Hollis looked over his shoulder at the two militiamen glaring at him through the gate. Beyond them he saw that Sasha now had two embassy watchers in his Volga and was looking rather uncomfortable.

Lisa remarked, 'I think I've had enough cloak and dagger for the day. I think what I'll do is have a drink, then I'll move your things over while you're at your meeting. Maybe I can have someone from housekeeping help me. I'll call the Kellums.'

'No, I'd rather you and I did it later. Okay?'

'Okay.'

They walked into the chancery building, and Hollis said, 'I'm going up to my office awhile, then to my meeting.'

'Will Seth be there?'

'I guess. Why?'

She hesitated, then said, 'You're jealous that we were involved . . . I'm jealous of his relationship with you.'

Hollis didn't think it was quite the same thing but didn't reply.

Lisa added, 'Be careful of him, Sam.'

Hollis glanced at his watch. 'Well, see you later.'

'Thank you for today.'

Hollis walked to the elevator as Lisa walked out the back toward the residence. As Hollis rode up to meet Alevy, it occurred to him that two of the great puzzles in life were women and espionage and that he was up to his eyeballs in both.

24

Hollis buttoned the blue tunic of his Air Force uniform and straightened his tie. 'How do I look?'

'Very sexy,' Lisa said. 'I'm going to lose you to some young secretary tonight.'

Hollis adjusted his row of ribbons.

Lisa asked, 'Do you arrange them by color, chronologically, or what?'

'By order of importance. Good conduct last. Which secretary?'

She smiled. 'Will you teach me how to put your uniform together?'

'It's not important. I can do it.'

'Did your wife do it?'

'I don't think she knew I was in the military. Do you have any scotch?'

'One bottle left in the kitchen. Help me with this zipper.'

Hollis zippered her black silk dress, then reached around and cupped her breasts in his hands. 'World-class jugs.'

'Gross. You're getting very gross. You used to be an officer and a gentleman.'

He kissed her on the neck, and they went downstairs. Lisa got the scotch and a bottle of soda. Hollis filled two glasses with ice.

She said, 'These packing boxes are getting on my nerves.'

'Where's the icon?'

'Over there on the bookshelf. I'm going to send it to my boss at the USIS in DC. I wrote and asked him to hold it. Will you get it into the diplomatic bag for me?'

'I said I would.'

'Thanks. Can you pick it up for me when you go to Washington?'

'Sure.' He took the icon from the bookshelf and looked at it. It was a square, about two feet on each side. The painting was of a male saint, but Hollis couldn't identify him. 'Who's this guy?'

She came up beside him. 'That guy is the Archangel Gabriel. See his trumpet?'

'Right.'

'This is painted on larch. Too many of them were done on pine, which warps and cracks.'

'I see.'

'A lot of people don't like icon painting. The figures have no perspective, no depth or movement. They're just flat, and the faces seem stiff and distant.'

'Like eight million Muscovites.'

'But there's a warmth to the colors they used, and there's a certain serenity in that beatific face, don't you think?'

'Oh, yes. How much?'

'Is it worth? Well, they're hard to get appraised in the West, but I found an art historian at Columbia once who said it was sixteenth century, Kazan region, which I knew. Worth maybe twenty-five thousand.'

'Jesus. What if I lose it?'

She poured scotch in his glass. 'I can't imagine a spy losing things. I trust you.'

'Okay.' He put the icon carefully back on the shelf.

She said, 'The icon has a very special importance in Russia. During the Tartar invasions, when churches were burned and priests massacred, the icon was small enough to be hidden, and each household had one. For hundreds of years these deeply religious people came to see the icon as the symbol of survival of the Russian culture and Christianity.'

Hollis nodded. 'You see parallels?'

'Of course. Everyone does. If the Orthodox church and Russian culture could survive almost three hundred years of wild horsemen, it can survive those fools in the Kremlin. That's part of the symbolic meaning in the revival of iconography. The portraits themselves may be uninspiring, but people here who keep icons are making a statement of dissent. I think they know and the Kremlin knows who are the keepers of the culture and who are the Tartars.'

'Interesting. Sometimes I think there's more to this country than meets the eye. We forget they have a history.'

'They don't forget for a minute.' Lisa sipped on her scotch. 'I'm a little anxious about this party.'

'Why?'

'Well . . . it's sort of . . . I guess I'm basically shy. I don't like being the center of attention, especially a party celebrating my getting kicked out.'

'I hadn't noticed your shyness,' Hollis ventured. 'Anyway, it's all good fun. I went to one in Sofia once. The deputy CIA station chief there had seduced the wife of a Bulgarian official or something. Long story short, he got caught and booted. Anyway, the party lasted all weekend and the poor guy . . . what's the matter?'

'Men are pigs. That's not a funny story.'

'Oh. Seemed funny at the time. Maybe you had to be there.'

'You know, this espionage business is sort of . . . anyway, it's not you. Can you get out of it? Do you *want* to get out of it?'

'I'd like to fly again.'

'Do you? Or have you been saying that too long?'

Hollis sat on a packing crate and didn't reply.

'I'm sorry, Sam. I'm pushing too much. I don't own you.' She finished her scotch. 'Yet. Want another?'

'No.'

'I do. I'm jumpy.'

'I see that.'

She poured another drink, then found her cigarettes on an empty bookshelf. 'Want one?'

'After I finish my drink.'

She lit her cigarette. The doorbell rang. 'I'll get it.' She went down the stairs and came back with Charles Banks.

Banks said, 'Hello, Sam. Lisa assures me I'm not intruding.'

'Then you're probably not. Take off your coat, Charles.'

'No, this will only take a few minutes.'

'Drink? Scotch only.'

'A short one. Soda or water.'

Lisa went into the kitchen.

Banks looked around. He said to Hollis, 'I've seen this scene so often in my career and in my life. My father was a Foreign Service man.'

Lisa came back with a glass of ice water and filled it with scotch. She handed it to Banks.

He raised his glass. 'Let me be the first, before your soirée begins, to wish you both the best of luck in your careers and personal happiness.'

They touched glasses and drank.

Banks remained standing and said to Lisa, 'I was telling Sam, I was a diplomatic brat, like he's an Air Force brat.'

'I didn't know that, Charles. No one here knows much about you, to be frank.'

'Well, some people do. I've spent my life in diplomatic posts and in fact, my father, Prescott Banks, was with the first post-Revolution diplomatic mission here in 1933. I was eight at the time, and I remember Moscow a bit. It was a grim place then.' He smiled. 'I know, I know. Anyway, I met Stalin when I was about ten, I guess.'

'How fascinating,' Lisa said. 'Do you remember him?'

'I remember he smelled of tobacco. My father told me jokingly that I was going to meet the czar of all the Russias. Then when I was introduced to him at his apartment in the Kremlin, I told him he didn't look like the czar of all the Russias. Stalin laughed, but my mother nearly fainted.'

Hollis smiled. 'You weren't always so smooth, were you?'

Banks chuckled. 'No, that was my first diplomatic faux pas.' He shook the ice in his drink, then said, 'Well, then, the first order of business . . .' He looked around the room. 'A bit of music would be nice.'

Lisa nodded and went to a tape player on the shelf. 'They've packed my stereo. Here're a few tapes. Charles, do you know Zhanna Bichevskaya, the Joan Baez of Russia?'

'I'm afraid I don't know much about contemporary Russian music. I'm sure it will be fine for our purposes.'

'Right.' Lisa put the tape in and hit the play button. A soft guitar, then a beautiful, clear Russian voice filled the room. Lisa said, 'Her songs make me melancholy. I've tried to get her on a tour of America, but the bastards won't let her out of the country. I can't even speak to her. I don't know where she lives or much about her, except I love her voice. I assume she's politically unreliable.'

Banks said, 'She does have a lovely voice. At least they let her sing.'

They all moved nearer the tape player, and Lisa adjusted the volume. Hollis said, 'I think that's about right. Go on, Charles.'

Banks cleared his throat. 'Yes, first thing. You both disappeared the other day for some time, and there was some fear here and in Washington that you'd met with foul play. Therefore, the ambassador has requested that you stay inside the compound until you are both driven to the airport by security personnel, Monday morning. That will not cause you any hardship, I trust.'

Hollis replied, 'No, it won't, since I'm not taking orders from the ambassador. Lisa and I intend to go to church in the city on Sunday.'

Banks replied in an impatient tone, 'Why do you want to provoke them and expose yourself and Lisa to danger?'

'Surely, Charles,' Hollis said in a baiting tone, 'you don't think the Soviet government or its organs of State Security would make an attempt on our lives even as our diplomats are discussing a new era of Soviet-American friendship?'

Banks replied coolly, 'Not the Soviet government, perhaps, but I can't fathom what the KGB is up to, and neither can you. We have a similar problem right here with Mr Alevy, whose organization seems to be pursuing its own foreign policy. In fact, if the KGB and the CIA have one thing in common, it's their desire to wreck any rapprochement between their respective governments.'

'That's a very strong statement,' Hollis observed.

'Nevertheless it's what the diplomatic community believes.'

'Charles, I don't like it when the diplomatic community here or anywhere tries to take the moral high ground. My work and Seth Alevy's work may not be to your liking or your superiors' liking. But it is, unfortunately, necessary work. And there is an implied understanding that the Foreign Service will provide support services to the intelligence personnel within the mission. No one in my office or Alevy's has ever asked anything of you more than room and board and an atmosphere of cooperation and understanding. We have never compromised the diplomatic personnel here. Whoever takes over from me has a tough enough job, and he deserves your respect if not your sympathy.'

Banks set his drink down on a bookshelf. 'Personally, I agree with you. The world has changed since the days when the only spies in an embassy were a few Foreign Service people known unofficially as State Department Intelligence. However, the ambassador's fear in this current problem . . . the fear of the White House itself, if you want to know the truth . . . is that one of you – you, Seth Alevy, the naval attaché, the Army attaché, or any of the people who work for you – will seize on this current Fisher and Dodson business as a tool to wreck the diplomatic initiatives. Enough said.'

Hollis poured more scotch into Banks' glass and handed it back to him. 'I'm afraid I have to have the last word on that, Charles. You're afraid of us troglodytes, but I want to remind you that many of the fruits of hard-won military and intelligence victories, paid for in blood, were lost by the State Department and the Foreign Service. I fought a war, and my father fought a war, and your father . . . well, I know the name Prescott Banks. I want to remind you of the sterling performance of the State Department at Yalta and Potsdam, when your forebears gave Stalin everything but the west lawn of the White House. That's why we're in the goddamned mess we're in now.'

Banks' ruddy face turned even redder. He took a long breath, then sipped on his drink. 'That was not our finest hour. My father regretted his role in that in his later years.'

Lisa poured more scotch for everyone and said, 'I know that the past is prologue for the future, but you old duffers are talking about things that happened before I was born.'

Banks said, 'Well, more recent news then. As you know, Gregory Fisher's parents have had an autopsy performed on their son. We've received information on the results of that autopsy.'

'And?' Lisa asked.

'The medical examiner's report states that the injuries were not the immediate cause of death.'

'What,' Lisa asked, '*was* the cause of death?'

'Heart failure.'

Hollis observed, 'Heart failure is the cause of all deaths. What caused the heart to fail?'

'Partly trauma. But mostly alcohol. Mr Fisher had a deadly amount of alcohol in his blood and brain tissue.'

'The KGB introduced the alcohol before death,' Hollis said, 'through a stomach tube. The perfect poison, because nearly everyone takes it now and then.'

Banks seemed uncomfortable with this type of talk. 'Really? Is it possible to do that?' He looked at Hollis as though he were discovering a new species of human being. 'That's terrible.'

Lisa said, 'So, we have no evidence that could be used in a court of law or in a diplomatic note of protest if anyone considered such a course of action?'

'That's correct,' Banks replied.

Lisa asked, 'Do you believe Greg Fisher was murdered?'

Banks considered a moment. 'The circumstantial evidence seems to point in that direction. I'm no idiot, Lisa, and neither is the ambassador.'

'That's reassuring.' She added, 'I do appreciate your position.'

Banks smiled tightly. 'Do you? Let me tell you that I personally admire your sense of integrity and moral courage. And *entre nous*, the ambassador is similarly impressed. However, I'm here to restate to you in the strongest possible terms that if either of you so much as breathes a word of this incident back in the States, you will both be unemployed and unemployable and perhaps subject to legal action. Is that clear?'

Hollis moved closer to Banks. 'I don't think you or anyone outside the Pentagon is in a position to tamper with my military career.'

'On the contrary, Colonel. And as for Miss Rhodes, while you have the option of a private career in journalism, you might find it more difficult than you think to ever be accredited to cover any agency of the United States government.'

She put her drink down. 'I think, Charles, that you've been in the Soviet Union too long. We don't make threats like that in *my* country.'

Banks seemed somewhat abashed. 'I apologize . . . I'm passing on information.'

There were a few moments of awkward silence, then Banks extended his hand. 'I'll see you both at your farewell party.'

Lisa took his hand. 'You probably will, if you come. We have to be there.' She smiled. 'I like you, Charlie.' She kissed his cheek.

Banks smiled awkwardly, then took Hollis' hand and said, 'The least free people in a free society are people like us who have a sworn duty to defend the constitution.'

'It's one of the ironies,' Hollis agreed.

After Banks had left, Lisa commented, 'He hit us with the carrot and tried to make us eat the stick.'

'He's having a rough time of it.'

'Who isn't these days?'

25

Sam Hollis gave his uniform a quick once-over, then strode into the large diplomatic reception hall.

The protocol of a farewell party didn't require that he or Lisa stand in a receiving line, nor was there a head table, which suited him fine. Protocol did demand however, that, as a married man whose wife was temporarily out of town, he arrive without a woman. Lisa had gone on ahead, and he saw her across the room, talking to some people from her office.

The reception hall was an elegant, modern wing off the chancery building, with tall windows, walls of Carrara marble, and three large contemporary chandeliers of stainless steel hanging from the high ceiling. The floor was parquet, which for some reason the Russians equated with elegance, hence its choice for the hall.

Of the approximately three hundred men and women living in the compound, nearly all had been invited, and Hollis guessed that most of them had shown up. He would have been flattered by such a Saturday night turnout for him in London or Paris, but in Moscow you could get five hundred Westerners to a Tupperware party if you had music and food.

Hollis assumed that the staffers whose turn it was to use the Finnish dacha for the weekend had wisely done so. Missing also was most of the thirty-man Marine contingent. Some had duty, but the rest, Hollis figured, were in a nearby foreign-residents apartment house where they had somehow secured a suite of rooms that they called *Studiya 54*. Hollis understood it was mostly disco, drinking, and *devitski*, the latter being an infraction of the rules. But since the great sex-and-spy scandal, the Marine Corps had concluded that though their men were made of iron, their libidos were not. The *Studiya 54* gatherings were actually encouraged so as to keep the Marines and Russian women in one place. Unknown to any of them, but known to Hollis, four of the Marine guards were actually Marine counterintelligence officers. It struck him that the world was full of professional snoops, and it was sad that Americans didn't even trust Americans anymore.

Hollis noticed that round tables had been placed along the walls, but most people were standing in groups, glasses in hand. There was a long buffet table against the far wall where a few people helped themselves. Early in his tour of duty, Hollis had been advised that if he went to an embassy reception where Russians were present, he should not stand near the buffet table when the food was uncovered, or he would be trampled.

Hollis glanced at his watch. The party had been in progress about an hour, and he figured everyone was three drinks ahead of him by now. He scanned the room to see where the bar had been set up and saw James Martindale, the protocol officer, making his way toward him.

'Hello, Sam.'

'Hello, Jim.' Hollis had a perverse liking for the man despite his inane job and decorous manner.

Martindale announced, 'We have a nice turnout for you, Colonel.'

'I see that. I'm very flattered. I would have thought everyone would rather have seen the changing of the guard at Lenin's tomb.'

Martindale seemed to miss the humor and continued, 'You understand, I hope, that we did not invite any Soviet air force personnel with whom you've become acquainted, nor any other Soviet officials because of the circumstances under which you are leaving.'

Hollis thought that was self-evident. 'You didn't want to feed them, did you?'

'Also I did not send invitations to certain other embassies so as not to put them in an awkward position.'

'You're a very sensitive man.'

'However, I did extend verbal and informal invitations to your friends and counterparts in the British, Canadian, Australian, and New Zealand embassies.'

'We Anglo-Saxons have to stick together against the Slavic hordes.'

'Yes. And some other NATO military attachés will drop in to say goodbye.'

'You mean my spy friends from the rest of Christiandom? I hope you invited the Irish.'

'I did. It's best to keep this sort of thing informal so as not to give the host country the impression that we are insulting them.'

'But we *are*, Jimbo. Do you think I'd have *any* party if I'd been kicked out of England or Botswana?'

'Well, from the strict standpoint of protocol –'

'Where's the bar?'

'In the far corner there. Also I've invited the thirty or so American resident press people and their spouses as a courtesy. Most of them will stop by, but they are not to talk business.'

'Good thinking.'

'I explained to Ms Rhodes all of what I've just told you, and she understands.'

'Was I supposed to wear sackcloth and ashes?'

'No, this is business dress.'

'May I go to the bar now?'

'I'd like to take this opportunity to extend to you my best wishes and my appreciation for the work you've done here.'

'Thank you. I –'

'This was the best I could do under the circumstances.' He waved his arm around the room.

'Look, I didn't get caught buggering a militiaman. I just got caught spying. No big –'

'The ambassador and his wife will put in an appearance of course, but they should not be detained as they have another engagement.'

'Are you drunk?'

Martindale smiled a lopsided grin. 'I've had a few.'

Hollis laughed.

Martindale took Hollis' arm. 'Come with me.'

Hollis was led to the front of the reception hall where there was a raised platform on which stood a podium and microphone. A four-piece combo of volunteer musicians were grouped around the big Steinway piano. Hollis recalled that the Steinway had once been in the ambassador's official residence, Spaso House, where it had been vandalized a few hours before the performance of Vladimir Feltsman, a prominent pianist and Jewish dissident. The KGB were strong suspects, and Alevy sent a copy of the repair bill to Lubyanka. Some KGB wag there sent a return note saying, 'Check is in the mail.'

Hollis stepped on to the wooden platform, and Lisa, escorted by Martindale's secretary, joined him. Hollis and Lisa exchanged brief smiles.

Martindale nodded to the combo, and they struck up a few bars of 'Ruffles and Flourishes', which got everyone's attention. Martindale tapped the microphone. 'Ladies and gentlemen, thank you for coming. May I present our guests of honor, Colonel Sam Hollis and Ms Lisa Rhodes.'

There was a round of applause, and Hollis could see a lot of silly smiles out there. Clearly, everyone was in a merry mood for the occasion.

Martindale said, 'I must issue a reminder that this is not a secure room and that everything you say is being heard across the street. So I urge you to observe talk security, not to make derogatory remarks about our host country, and to keep in mind that the expulsion of Colonel Hollis and Ms Rhodes is an occasion of great shame.'

A few people chuckled.

Martindale reached behind the podium and produced two lengths of blue satin, which he unfurled and held up. Everyone laughed. Hollis saw they were bogus ambassadorial sashes on which was written in red glitter: *Persona non grata.*

Lisa put her hand over her mouth and laughed.

329

Martindale turned to them and ceremoniously draped the sashes across their chests. Martindale said into the microphone, 'For the nondiplomats here who don't know Latin, *persona non grata* means "someone who doesn't tip".'

Lisa whispered to Hollis, 'This is embarrassing.'

'You're lucky Martindale didn't pin a scarlet A on you.'

'On *me*? On *you*.'

Martindale announced, 'Before we begin the music and dancing, and especially before the ambassador and his wife arrive, we'll have the presentations and speeches. I would like to introduce our first presenter, Comrade Vladimir Slizistyi.'

The people who understood Russian laughed at the word for 'slimy'.

One of the young consular officers, Gary Warnicke, came through the door, wearing a brown suit about six sizes too big. His hair was slicked back, he had a red tie painted on his shirt, and he was barefoot. There was a burst of loud laughter.

Warnicke stepped on to the platform, kissed Hollis perfunctorily on both cheeks, then planted a long kiss on Lisa's lips. Hollis got the feeling it was going to be a long night.

Warnicke addressed the audience. 'Comrade American swine, thank you for here me inviting. I make now presentation to Colonel Hollis.'

Martindale led Hollis to the podium as Warnicke bellowed, 'Colonel, by order of Central Committee, I present now to you, for consistently inferior work product, Order of Lemon.' Warnicke hung a red ribbon around Hollis' neck from which was suspended a pear. Warnicke explained, 'Sorry, no lemons.'

'I understand.'

Everyone applauded. Warnicke motioned Lisa to the podium. 'And for you, sexy lady, by order of Central Committee, I present Medal of Socialist Loafing, for spending whole year sleeping in supply closet. Warnicke reached into his jacket and produced another red ribbon from which hung a red plastic alarm clock. Warnicke said, 'Wakes you at quitting time.'

Lisa said, 'I'm honored to have done my part.'

Warnicke took the opportunity to give her an intense kiss on the neck.

The guests, who hadn't interrupted their drinking for the show, began to hoot and whistle.

Warnicke barked, 'Silence, comrades! Serious business here.' He took two pieces of paper from his pocket and said to Hollis and Lisa, 'Here two *putyovki* – worker vacation passes – for five-year stay in Siberian Gulag of your choice. Separate rooms.'

This brought some guffaws from the crowd.

Warnicke made a few more light remarks, then said, 'Now I have pleasure of calling to podium, great American diplomat, great statesman, peace-loving friend of Soviet peoples, good dresser, expensive shoes, Comrade Charles Banks.'

Everyone applauded as Banks stepped on to the platform. 'Thank you very much, comrade, ladies, and gentlemen. As you know, every year about this time, we present the Barlow award to one or more deserving individuals. This coveted award is named in honor of Joel Barlow, American ambassador to the court of Napoleon, who in the year 1812 acompanied the French army into Russia in order to maintain diplomatic contact with the emperor. After the burning of Moscow, Mr Barlow found himself caught up in Napoleon's retreat and, tragically, died of exposure, making him the first American diplomat to freeze to death in Russia.'

Banks' timing was good, and everyone laughed.

Banks held up his hand. 'So each autumn to commemorate that sad event and to honor Mr Barlow's memory, we pay tribute to one or more of our compatriots who made it through the previous winter without bitching and griping and without running off on thirty-days' leave to the Bahamas. This year it is my honor to present the Joel Barlow award to two people who have demonstrated a unique ability to work together in keeping warm. Ladies and gentlemen, this year's recipients of the Joel Barlow award, Colonel Sam and Miss Lisa.'

331

The guests applauded and laughed as Charles Banks retrieved a full ice bucket from behind the podium and handed it to Hollis and Lisa. 'Congratulations.'

Lisa said, 'Thank you, Charles. This is a dubious honor but a nice bucket.'

Hollis found himself holding the dripping ice bucket.

Banks said into the microphone, 'Now for the more serious business, may I present Colonel Hollis' aide, Captain Ed O'Shea.'

Captain O'Shea, carrying a small parcel, took over the podium from Banks, who stepped aside. O'Shea said, 'It has indeed been a rare opportunity to work for such a talented officer.' O'Shea made a few more salutatory remarks, then said, 'On behalf of the military attachés here and their staffs, I would like to present Colonel Hollis with a farewell gift.' O'Shea opened the box he was carrying and withdrew a small plaster bust of Napoleon. O'Shea said, 'Colonel, this is courtesy of the French embassy. As you pass from duty station to duty station and wherever your service to your country takes you, let this be a reminder of your time here in Moscow and of your last interesting weekend in the Russian countryside.'

Hollis held out the ice bucket, and O'Shea stuck the plaster bust in it.

The guests applauded, and there was some subdued laughter. Hollis assumed there were at least a dozen versions of the itinerary-violation weekend going around, and most of them somehow included Borodino, hence the Napoleon bust. Hollis said to O'Shea, 'I'm very grateful for the memento, and I'll have it on my desk when I write your last efficiency report.'

The military personnel in the crowd laughed.

O'Shea smiled weakly and introduced Kay Hoffman, who climbed on to the platform carrying a beautifully hand-painted balalaika. Kay Hoffman smiled at Lisa and said into the microphone, 'In all my years with the United States Information Service, I have rarely encountered an individual who had such a profound knowledge of the host country, its language, its culture, and its people.' Kay Hoffman delivered a short tribute to her assistant, then said, 'On behalf of everyone in the USIS here and also in our Leningrad consulate, we would like to present to Lisa this going-away present. Obviously this is not a joke gift, but a very special piece of Russian art, which, though it was difficult to come by, was worth the search because it is passing into the hands of a very fine lady who appreciates such native craftsmanship. Lisa . . .' Kay Hoffman held out the balalaika. 'May I present you with this exquisite electric samovar.'

The joke caught everyone off guard, and there was a silence followed by a burst of laughter and applause.

Kay Hoffman continued, 'You loosen these strings here and shove them into an electrical outlet. The tea goes in this big hole here. I'm not sure where you put the water.'

Lisa took the balalaika. Kay embraced and kissed her, saying in her ear, 'Don't let that stud get away, honey.'

Lisa winked and wiped a tear from her eye. She said, 'I don't play it – the samovar – but I love its music, and I promise to learn to play it in memory of the thoughtfulness of my coworkers.'

James Martindale stepped back to the podium carrying a display easel on which was mounted a blowup of a newspaper article written in Russian. Martindale said, 'For those of you who want the truth about the unfortunate incident that has brought us here, I direct your attention to the Soviet free press. For your convenience we've had the *Pravda* article blown up and mounted. *Pravda*, as you know, means 'truth', and *Izvestia* means 'news', and I've heard it said that there is no news in the *Truth* and no truth in the *News*. Nevertheless I'll read you the English translation of this incisive Soviet reporting.' Martindale read from a piece of paper. '"The Soviet Foreign Ministry has announced the expulsions of S. Hollis and L. Rhodes, a man and a woman, American embassy employees, for activities inconsistent with their diplomatic status. This is yet another example of American agents hiding behind their diplomatic immunity to engage in anti-Soviet activities. However, the organs of State Security had been watching this S. Hollis and L. Rhodes for some time and finally put an end to their abuse of Soviet hospitality."' Martindale looked up from the translation and shook his finger at Hollis and Lisa. 'Bad, bad.'

Warnicke called out, 'Let this be a lesson for all of you. Three cheers for organs of State Security.'

Martindale turned back to the microphone. 'Now, ladies and gentlemen, I'd like to introduce our first guest of honor, holder of the Order of Lemon, not to mention a chestful of real medals, our departing air attaché, Colonel Sam Hollis.' The people who were still sitting at the tables stood, and everyone clapped loudly. The four-piece combo struck up 'Off we go into the wild blue yonder' as Hollis put the bucket down and waited at the podium. Unexpectedly Lisa came up beside him and squeezed his hand momentarily.

Hollis said into the microphone, 'Thank you all for that very nice welcome. And thank you, Jim Martindale, chief of protocol, alcohol, and Geritol, for the sash and the introduction. I want to express my appreciation also to Gary Warnicke for making a fool of himself in public, and my deepest gratitude to Charles Banks for arriving here sober. And of course, warm thanks to Captain O'Shea and my staff for their personal devotion, which they will transfer to their next boss without skipping a beat.' Hollis made some serious farewell remarks, then concluded on a lighter note. 'When I get home, and as I'm tooling down the highway in my 'Vette through the glorious Virginia countryside, listening to the Air Force-Army game and eating a banana, my thoughts will be of you here, drinking your breakfast vodka as you watch the snow rise over your windowsills.'

This brought some hisses and laughter. Everyone was clearly drunk by now, Hollis thought, except him. He saluted and stepped away from the podium to the accompaniment of applause.

Martindale introduced Lisa, who also got a standing ovation, as the combo played 'Lara's Theme'. She took the microphone. 'Thank you all so much. I've never been kicked out of a country before, and I never knew it could be so much fun.' Lisa thanked the people in her office who made her tour of duty tolerable and said, 'I also want to thank Charles Banks, who tried so hard to keep me out of trouble. Charles, for those of you who are not honored to know him, is a man torn between his duty as the ambassador's personal aide and his desire to be a human being. A man whose familiarity with Russia has prompted him to declare that Borodino is the best Italian red wine produced in the Soviet Union.'

Banks called out, 'I always order it with babushka.'

Lisa concluded, 'I wish I could stay with you and continue my work here. I know that somewhere down the line we'll all cross paths again, but this will remain the incomparable assignment of a lifetime for all of us. Thank you.'

As everyone clapped, Hollis unexpectedly took the microphone again and said, 'I would be remiss if I did not thank a man who has become a friend of mine and of Lisa Rhodes, for his wise counsel and for showing me the ropes in Moscow. I'm speaking of a very industrious political affairs officer, Seth Alevy.'

Alevy was standing off to the side, his thumbs hooked in the pockets of his vest. He nodded perfunctorily in acknowledgement of the scant applause. It was obvious to Hollis that very few of the three hundred people present knew Seth Alevy, and those who did were not his fans.

Lisa glanced over at Hollis with a warm smile and a wink.

Hollis and Lisa stepped down from the platform as Martindale said, 'Dance music, maestro, please. Have fun, everyone.'

The combo played 'In the Still of the Nite,' and Lisa took Hollis on to the dance floor. As they danced, she said, 'That was very nice of you to thank Seth.'

Hollis grumbled a reply.

'My alarm is crushing your pear.'

Hollis took a bite out of the pear and passed it to her. She bit into it and laughed. She said between chews, 'This is the first time we've danced. I love this song.'

'Five Satins, 1956.'

'Who? When?'

Hollis smiled.

She held him closer, and they glided over the parquet floor. 'Did you grind to this when you were a horny little guy?'

'Sure did.'

'God, I can't believe you were getting erections before I was born.'

'I couldn't wait for you.'

The combo segued into 'Since I Don't Have You.'

Lisa said, 'I'm not being facetious, but there's obviously some degree of status attached to being kicked out of the Soviet Union. I never realized just how much contempt and disdain we have for this country. I mean, Gary Warnicke's skit was a mockery – no wonder the ambassador is coming late.'

'It's just a lot of frustration and nervous energy pouring out.'

'It's more than that, and you know it. It's scary, Sam.'

'What is?'

'How much we *hate* them.'

Hollis didn't reply.

Lisa looked around the dance floor. 'These press people won't report –'

'They damned well better not, or they'll never see the inside of this or any other American embassy again. This is strictly off-the-record, and they knew that when they were invited.'

'Yes, they're a good crew. Here in Moscow we realize we're on the same side. They're pleasant to work with.' She said, 'I'm sad. I don't want to leave.'

'Things could be worse. We could be dead.'

She didn't reply.

'Never look back on this place, Lisa. Never go back, even if they allow you to. Promise me that.'

'No, I won't promise that.'

336

Hollis stepped away from her. 'I badly need a drink.'

'Stay sober enough to do me some good tonight.'

'I won't promise. You can dance with Alevy if you want. You don't need my permission anyway.'

'No, I don't. But thanks for saying that.'

Hollis made his way across the dance floor and found the bar, where he fell into conversation with four NATO attachés.

The band suddenly stopped, and James Martindale announced the ambassador and his wife. Hollis noticed that the party calmed down a bit. Hollis excused himself and walked toward the ambassador, meeting Lisa heading the same way. She said to him, 'Is it alright if we present ourselves to the ambassador together?'

'It's alright with me. Listen, I'd like to spend part of my home leave with you.'

'I'll think about that.'

'What is there to think –'

The ambassador and his wife approached and greeted Hollis and Lisa. They exchanged pleasantries for a few minutes, and everyone smiled. Neither the ambassador nor his wife commented on the sashes or the pear and alarm clock, which struck Hollis as the height of savoir faire if not stupidity. Lisa said, 'You both missed some very funny speeches.'

'Oh,' the ambassador's wife said, 'we're so sorry we were detained.'

They chatted a moment longer, then the ambassador said, 'I'm deeply appreciative to both of you for your contributions to the diplomatic mission here. Charles tells me he's spoken to you on certain matters of national importance and that you both understand the reasoning and so forth. I'm very happy that you do. Colonel Hollis, Ms Rhodes – Sam and Lisa – have a pleasant and safe journey home.' Everyone shook hands.

The ambassador's wife said, 'Please excuse us, we have another engagement that we accepted before this was arranged.'

Lisa watched them go and commented, 'They could send programmed androids for that job, and no one would notice.'

'What is there to think about?'

'Nothing. That's the point. It would take ten minutes to program the 'droids.'

'What is there to think about spending some time with me?'

'Oh, that. I have to think about . . . well . . . my parents . . . you're a little older than I, and you're married.'

'Did you just discover that?'

She smiled wanly. 'Let me think about how to make it right.'

'Do that.'

'Are we having our first fight?'

'Quite possibly.' Hollis turned and walked toward his staff, who were standing together talking.

Hollis was intercepted by Mike Salerno, a reporter for the Pacific News Service. Salerno took Hollis aside. 'Funny speech, Colonel. Everyone is in a rare mood tonight. You guys should do that once a month. Catharsis. When one of us leaves, we get together at somebody's place, and we do the same kind of thing.'

'No wonder the KGB harasses you.'

'Yeah . . . I guess they listen in, don't they?'

'Wouldn't surprise me in the least.' Hollis had met Salerno on a few occasions and found him somewhat pushy but straightforward and down to earth.

Salerno went on, 'You know that we've kicked out your counterpart in DC and also some Soviet Tass dork in retaliation for Lisa. The Reds are probably having a similar party in Washington tonight. Doing Uncle Sam skits.' He laughed, then finished his drink and said, 'What's the actual reason behind you guys leaving?'

'Pretty much what the official version is, Mike. We took an unauthorized trip.'

'Yeah. But they usually give you a break the first time for something petty like that. Especially with the sweet smell of détente in the air.'

'It was actually the second time for both of us.' To forestall further questions, Hollis added, 'As you may have deduced, we went to see the site of the famous Russian nonvictory at Borodino. Moscow gets claustrophobic.'

'Hey, don't I know it? It takes me a month to get permission to visit some godforsaken tractor factory in the Urals.'

'Tell them you don't want to see a tractor factory in the Urals. You'll be on the next train.'

Salerno laughed. 'You got that right, Br'er Bear.' He took two glasses of champagne from a passing waiter and handed one to Hollis, saying, 'To a safe trip.'

Salerno finished the wine, seemed to consider a moment, then asked, 'Are you leveling with me, Sam?'

'Yes.'

'You went out that way to take charge of the body of Greg Fisher.'

'Right.'

'And you detoured a few K's to Borodino and were spotted.'

'Correct.'

'Hell of a fucked-up country, isn't it?'

Hollis replied, 'When in the third Rome, do as they tell you. Excuse me.'

'Hold on a second, Sam. Look, I know there's more to this Greg Fisher story than anyone is saying. One theory is that he was killed by robbers and the Soviets don't want that getting around. Makes the world's first workers' state look a little less like paradise. Right?'

'I saw the inventory of the boy's effects. Everything from money to felt-tip pens. There was no foul play.'

'No? Can I tell you something I found out?'

'If you'd like.'

'I called Greg Fisher's parents in New Canaan and found out that an autopsy has been performed. They told me a few other things. So I'm thinking about this kid who's tearassing along the Minsk-Moscow highway at night, under the influence of alcohol according to the autopsy, and I'm not buying it. I'm thinking about all the rules the kid had to sign in Brest when he crossed the border – seat belts, drinking and driving puts you in jail, and night driving can get you in trouble with the KGB. And Mr and Mrs Fisher tell me Greg was a very careful kid – okay, parents say that about dead kids. But I'm starting to wonder now.'

Hollis said, 'We're not supposed to talk business here.'

'Just hear me out, Sam. Okay? So, the other day I go on my own unauthorized trip in a car. First I poke around Mozhaisk, and for a few rubles a truck driver leads me to the accident site west of Mozhaisk. The car is gone by now of course, but I see where it went off the road heading east and plowed into the tree. I even find some glass from the windshield where the kid's head went through. Okay. But the truck driver says something about the kid's car causing a big stir in Mozhaisk. How did the kid get to Mozhaisk if he died west of the town?'

'Beats me.'

'Right. Me too. I think something stinks, Sam, and I'm wondering if you'd like to give me an off-the-record clue.'

'I don't have a clue,' Hollis replied. 'But if what you say is true, it's possible that Greg Fisher did pass through Mozhaisk, then doubled back for some reason, then later headed back for Moscow and ran off the road before he got to Mozhaisk again.'

'Why is he running up and down the Minsk-Moscow road at that hour? Was he on some kind of cloak-and-dagger assignment for the spooks here in the embassy?'

'There are no intelligence personnel in the American embassy,' Hollis said, 'but if there were, they wouldn't send people out in Pontiac Trans Ams.'

'True.' Salerno added, 'Look, I'm booked on that Pan Am flight to Frankfurt tomorrow. Let's sit together, and I'll tell you a few other things I discovered about this business.'

'Maybe.' Hollis turned to leave.

Lisa approached, and Salerno greeted her warmly. He said,

'Going to miss you, Lisa. The only straight shooter in the embassy Ministry of Propaganda.' They spoke for a moment, then Salerno moved off. Lisa said, 'What was he talking to you about?'

'What do you think? He smells a rat.'

'Eventually we may have to go to the press with this.'

Hollis said curtly, 'We are employees and representatives of the United States government. We are not press informants.'

She put her hand on his shoulder. 'True.'

He said coolly, 'If I'm more cautious than you, it's because I'm much older than you.'

She gave him a conciliatory smile and patted his arm. 'Now, now . . .'

Hollis, for the life of him, could not understand women. It seemed to him that she aggressively pursued him, then the moment he stopped being evasive, she backed off. He vaguely recalled that he'd had similar experiences with women when he was younger. There were some women and men he knew who enjoyed only the chase, and like fox hunters, had little use for the kill. He said, 'Excuse me,' turned, and headed back to the bar.

Hollis saw Alevy standing there and had the impression that Alevy had been waiting for him. Alevy said, 'It's not a good idea to draw attention to the CIA station chief.'

Hollis ordered a scotch and soda.

'It makes some people uncomfortable.'

Hollis moved away from the bar with his drink. 'I thought you were a political affairs officer. Now you tell me you're the CIA station chief.'

Alevy smiled. 'Well, I thank you for your thoughtfulness. What did Salerno want?'

'He knows a few things, Seth. Any reporter in this room with a little pluck could come up with some inconsistencies in the Fisher story. Coupled with me and Lisa getting the boot, it smells a little.'

'I suppose. You and Lisa have a spat?'

341

'No.'

'Good. I want you to stay close to her at least as far as Frankfurt.'

'Don't worry about it.'

'Okay. By the way, if you have no other plans tonight, would you do me a favor?'

'No.'

'Stop by around midnight. My place.'

'When do you sleep?'

'At the ambassador's staff briefings.' Alevy asked, 'Do you know anything about the Mi-28 chopper?'

'Only the technical stuff. Newest Soviet transport helicopter. Why?'

'I have to do a report. Can you bring me what you have?'

'I'll have O'Shea drop it off.'

'You can drop it off. Midnight, my place.' Alevy turned and walked off.

Hollis said to himself, 'I knew it.'

Hollis spent the next hour talking to the various air attachés from the NATO member nations. There was information to be exchanged, thank-you's to be said, and promises to stay in touch, professionally. The good thing to be said for military spies, Hollis thought, was that they were military first and spies second. Hollis made his farewells, then slipped out of the reception hall and went up to his office, where he intended to stay until his midnight meeting with Alevy.

His phone rang, and he answered it, 'Hollis.'

'What are you doing in your office at eleven o'clock?'

'Saying good-bye to my secretary.'

'You'd better not be, Hollis. Are you coming home tonight?'

Home. The word took him by surprise. 'I have a midnight meeting with the political affairs officer.'

'Where?'

'His place.'

'I expect you in my bed before dawn.'

'I'll think about it.'

'What's there to *think* about?'

'I have some work to do here,' he said. 'I have to go.'

'I have your underwear. And your toothbrush.'

'These are not secure phones.'

'There was that thing I wanted to try, where I bring my legs up over my head –'

'Okay, okay.' He smiled. 'I'll see you later.' He hung up.

Hollis went to the window and looked out into the darkened city. 'Meeting with Alevy. Then Novodevichy Convent tomorrow. Sheremetyevo Airport, Monday morning. Pan Am to Frankfurt.' Then London, Washington, or New York as the mood struck him. That was the plan. That was *his* plan. There were other, conflicting plans out there. He liked his plan the best.

26

The blue Ford Fairlane sat in the underground garage, deep below the trees and grass of the embassy compound's main quad. Betty Eschman, the wife of the naval attaché, was behind the wheel. 'Ready, Sam?'

'Ready.' Sam Hollis sat on the floor in the rear of the car, his back to the door. Lisa was opposite him. In the rear seat, their legs tucked under them, were two young women from the consular section, Audrey Spencer and Patty White. In the front passenger seat was Jane Ellis, a commercial officer.

The engine started, and Hollis felt the Ford move forward. He said to Betty Eschman, 'Remember, they're not allowed to stop you when you're leaving. If a mili-man steps in the driveway, hit the horn and keep going. He'll move. Okay?'

'Okay. I did this for my husband once.'

Jane Ellis said, 'Why bother with the horn? He'll move. Sideways or horizontally.'

The two women in the back laughed, a bit nervously, Hollis thought.

Lisa offered, 'Two points for a mili-man, Betty.'

The Ford went up the ramp and surfaced beside the chancery building, into the grey morning that was gloomier than the subterranean garage. Betty Eschman drove slowly through the forecourt of the embassy compound.

Hollis ran the simple plan through his mind again: There were only two places in all Moscow where Protestant services were being held this Sunday morning. One was a small Baptist church in a far suburb. The other was the chapel in the British embassy where an Anglican chaplain flew in from Helsinki on alternate Sundays. The American embassy did the honors on the alternating sabbaths and holy days. It was fortunate that today was the turn of the British and that the four women normally went over there together. There was nothing, therefore, that should arouse the curiosity of the embassy watchers, who knew the routines of the American embassy.

Betty Eschman said, 'We're passing the Marine guards now. Here goes.'

As she approached the sidewalk, one of the militiamen stepped out of his booth, walked into the driveway, and held up his hand. Betty Eschman blasted the horn and stepped on the accelerator. The militiaman jumped back and shouted, '*Pizda!*'

The Ford cut right and proceeded up the street. Mrs Eschman asked, 'What does *pizda* mean?'

Lisa replied, 'Cunt.'

'Why that son of a bitch!'

Jane Ellis added, 'I'm going to make a formal complaint. I'm tired of their harassment.'

Patty White laughed. 'I never saw a Soviet citizen move so fast.'

Hollis asked, 'Anyone behind us?'

The two women in the front looked in their side-view mirrors, and both reported that they didn't see any cars.

Betty Eschman cut on to the embankment drive and accelerated up the nearly deserted road that hugged the north bank of the Moskva. It was not the most direct route to the British embassy, which was on the Maurice Thorez embankment opposite the Kremlin, but Hollis knew it was a fast road, an easy road on which to spot tails. Also it passed directly beside Novodevichy Convent. Hollis settled back against the door and looked at Lisa. She stretched out her legs and put her shoeless foot in his groin. 'Am I crowding you?'

The two young women in the back chuckled.

Jane Ellis said, 'What's going on back there? Behave, Sam.' The women all laughed. Hollis thought his original idea of riding in the trunk might have been better. The Moskva and the road turned south in the river's great loop below the Lenin

Hills. Hollis said, 'You're all going to catch some harassment when you return. Sorry.'

'Screw them,' Jane Ellis said, who added quickly, 'Oh! We're going to church.'

Everyone laughed.

Betty Eschman announced, 'There's the convent straight ahead.'

Lisa said, 'Pull off into that little park in front of the convent, and we'll tumble out.'

Hollis said, 'Thanks for the lift, ladies.'

Jane Ellis responded, 'It was an honor to have the holders of the Joel Barlow award in the car.'

Betty Eschman cut off the embankment road into the park and stopped on a paved lane. Hollis and Lisa opened their doors and got out quickly. The car pulled away, and Hollis watched it disappear around the curving river road, then he looked around and said, 'I think we're alone.'

Lisa brushed off her black trench coat. 'Hell of a way to get to church.'

'Let's move away from the road.'

They began walking through the park toward the high crenellated walls of limestone and brick that surrounded the twenty-acre convent grounds.

Lisa asked, 'Are we still fighting?'

'No.'

'Good. Are you sorry?'

'For what?' Hollis asked impatiently.

'For being difficult. For sleeping on the couch. For –'

'Yes, yes. I'm sorry.' He looked at his watch. 'What time is the service?'

'At ten. The Soviet government has designated two times for Christian services in all of Russia: ten A.M. and six P.M.'

'Keeps it simple.' Hollis regarded the ornate battletowers of the convent walls. 'Incredible place. Nicer walls than the Kremlin. Which way in?'

'Follow me.'

They made their way around to the north wall, which held the Church of the Transfiguration. A stream of people, mostly elderly, came from the nearby metro station and passed through the massive church portals. Hollis looked up at the spires and gold onion domes rising over the wall, set against a sky of Moscow grey, and he became aware of a fine mist settling on his cheeks. 'I won't miss the weather.'

'No.' Lisa took his arm, and they joined the people going through the arched gates. Lisa asked, 'What were you talking to Seth about until four A.M.?'

'Sex, sports, and religion.'

'He doesn't know beans about any of those things, and neither do you.'

'We figured that out about four, and I left.'

'You know, every human life needs a spiritual dimension, or it isn't a complete life. Do you feel there's something missing from your life?'

'Yes. Sex, sports, and religion.'

'I thought I was part of the team. You two are not being fair. You can't use me and keep me in the dark.'

'Take it up with Seth.'

'I don't think you want me talking to him.'

'You can talk to whomever you please.'

'Remember you said that.'

They passed through the tunnellike entrance of the gate church and came out into the convent grounds. The people around them glanced curiously at Lisa's well-cut trench coat and examined her footwear. Hollis wore his baggy blue overcoat, narrow-brimmed hat, and shoes that squeaked. Hollis recalled that Captain O'Shea had stood in line two hours for the Soviet shoes. The leather was synthetic, the shoes were a size too small, and the cordovan color was a bit on the red side. O'Shea claimed that was the best he could do, but Hollis always suspected he was getting even for the two hours in line.

Hollis and Lisa walked arm in arm, following a wet cobblestone lane covered with broken branches and dead leaves. Lisa said, 'That's the Lopukhin palace. Boris Gudonov was elected czar there. Also, as Sasha said, Peter the Great put his sister in there. Peter used to hang his sister's political supporters outside her windows.'

Hollis regarded the long stucco palace. 'If the windows were as dirty then as they are now, she wouldn't have noticed.'

Lisa ignored him and continued, 'Novodevichy used to be a retreat for high-born ladies as well as a nunnery. It was also a fort, as you can see, the strongpoint on the southern approaches to Moscow. Odd sort of combination, but common in old Russia. It remained a nunnery until after the Revolution when the communists got rid of the nuns – no one seems to know exactly what became of them – and this place became a branch of the State History Museum. But they never really cared for Novodevichy.'

Hollis could see that the gardens were choked with undergrowth and the trees so badly in need of pruning that the branches touched the ground and blocked the paths.

Lisa said, 'But it's still lovely and peaceful here. People come here to meditate. It's sort of the unofficial center of the religious reawakening here in Moscow.'

'And probably crawling with KGB because of it.'

'Yes. But so far they seem content to take names and photographs. No incidents yet.' She squeezed his hand. Thanks for coming with me. You can visit Gogol's grave while you're here.'

'I might just do that.'

'I thought you might. That's why you're wearing that silly outfit.'

'Yes, it's business.'

'Can I come with you?'

'I'm afraid not.'

The lane took them into a paved square from which rose a beautiful six-tiered bell tower. On the far side of the square was a white and gold multidomed church. Lisa said, 'That's the Cathedral of the Virgin of Smolensk.'

'Is she home?'

Lisa announced, 'If I ever get married, I think I'd want an Eastern Orthodox wedding.'

Hollis wondered if she'd ever informed Seth Alevy of that.

'Did you get married in church?'

'No, we were married in a jet fighter, traveling at mach two, by an Air Force chaplain on the radio. When he pronounced us husband and wife, I hit the eject and blew us out into space. It was all downhill after that.'

'I see I can't talk to you this morning.'

Hollis regarded the throngs of people. Most of them were old women, a few old men, but there were also a number of young people – teenage boys and girls and university students. Here and there he saw intact Muscovite families.

As they passed the Cathedral of the Virgin of Smolensk, many of the people in the square stopped, bowed, and made the sign of the cross toward the cathedral. A few of the old women prostrated themselves on the wet stone, and people had to step around them. Hollis recalled the first time he'd been inside the Kremlin walls, when an old woman suddenly crossed herself in front of one of the churches, bowed and repeated the process for several minutes. A militiaman walked over to her and told her to get moving. She paid no attention to him and prostrated herself on the stone. Tourists and Muscovites began watching, and the militiaman looked uncomfortable. Finally the old woman had risen to her feet, crossed herself again, and continued her walk through the Kremlin, oblivious of time and place or soldiers and red stars where crosses had once risen. She'd seen a church – perhaps of her patron saint, if Russians still had such a thing – and she did what she had to do.

Lisa watched the people performing their ritual outside the cathedral that had been closed for worship for seventy years and was now the central museum of the convent complex. She said, 'After seventy years of persecution, their priests shot, churches torn down, Bibles burned, they still worship Him.

349

I'm telling you, these people are the hope of Russia. They're going to bring about an upheaval here.'

Hollis looked at what was left of God's people here in unholy Moscow and didn't think so. It would have been nice to think so, but there were neither the numbers nor the strength. 'Maybe . . . someday.'

They crossed the square, and Lisa steered him toward another church, a smaller single-domed building of white stucco. She said, 'That's where we're going to mass. The Church of the Assumption.'

'It needs some care.'

'I know. I was told that the churches of Moscow and this place in particular – because it's so close to Lenin Stadium – got some quick cosmetics for the 1980 Olympics. But you can see how run-down everything is.'

Hollis nodded. He surveyed the ancient trees and buildings of the fortress-convent. It was well within the city limits now, not two kilometers from Red Square, but from inside the walls there was no sign of any century but the sixteenth. He could easily imagine a grey, misty October day in the early 1500s, soldiers on the battlements watching the woods and fields, ready to ring the alarm bells of the huge tower, to signal the Kremlin of any approaching danger. And on the paths the nuns would stroll, and the priests would be sequestered in prayer. The world may have been simpler then, but no less terrifying.

Lisa stopped about ten yards from the church. Hollis saw six men outside the doors stopping some of the younger people and the families, asking for identification. The men jotted information from the ID cards into notebooks. Hollis spotted another man, posing as a tourist, taking pictures of the people going inside. One of the six men at the door got involved in an argument with a young woman who apparently refused to show her identification. Hollis said, 'I assume those men are not church ushers.'

'No, they're swine.'

Hollis watched a moment. The young woman finally managed to get away from the KGB without showing her identification, but she didn't try to enter the church and hurried away.

The old babushkas moved ponderously past the KGB men, ignoring them and being ignored by them. Those black-dressed women, Hollis had learned, were invisible. They were also free, like the animals and proles in George Orwell's nightmare world. Free because no one cared enough about them to enslave them.

Lisa said, 'They don't usually stop anyone who looks Western.'

'Well, I'll look Western. I'll smile.'

'But your shoes squeak.' She took his arm as they approached the doors of the church. The KGB man who had been arguing with the young woman intercepted them and said to Hollis, '*Kartochka!*'

Hollis replied in English, 'I don't understand a fucking word you're saying, Mac.'

The young man looked him over, waved his arm in dismissal, and began to turn to someone else when he noticed Lisa. He smiled and touched his hat, then said in Russian, 'Good morning.'

She replied in Russian, 'Good morning to you. Will you join us in celebrating Christ's message to the world?'

'I think not.' He added, 'But be sure to tell Christ that Yelena Krukova's son sends his regards.'

'I will. Perhaps you'll tell Him yourself someday.'

'Perhaps I will.'

Lisa led Hollis up the steps of the church. He said, 'I take it you come here often.'

'I take turns among the six surviving Orthodox churches in Moscow. That fellow back there must have permanent weekend duty. I've seen him nearly every Sunday I've come here for two years. We have that little ritual. I think he likes me.'

'That's probably why he volunteers for Sunday duty.'

They entered the vestibule of the Church of the Assumption.

351

To the right of the door sat a long refectory table laden with bread, cakes, and eggs. Adorning the whole spread were cut flowers, and stuck into the food were pencil-thin brown candles all alight. Hollis moved through the crowd to examine the display. 'What's this?'

Lisa came up beside him and said, 'The people bring their food here to be blessed.'

As Hollis watched, more food was laid on the table, more flowers strewn over it, and more candles lit. Off to the side he noticed an old woman standing at a countertop selling the brown candles for three kopeks apiece. Lisa went to her, put a ruble on the table, and asked for two candles, refusing the change. Lisa took Hollis' arm and led him into the nave.

The church was lit only by the weak sunlight coming through the stained-glass windows, but the raised altar was aglow in the fire of a hundred white tapers.

The nave had no pews and was packed wall-to-wall, shoulder-to-shoulder with about a thousand people. Hollis became aware of the smell of strong incense, which competed for his olfactory attention with the smell of unwashed bodies. He could see, even in the dark, that whatever exterior cosmetics had been done in 1980 had not been carried through inside. The place was in bad repair, the water-stained stucco crumbling, and the heating had either failed or was nonexistent. Yet there was still a magnificence about the place, he thought. The gold on the altar gleamed, the iconostasis – the tiered altar screen made of individual icons – was mesmerizing, and the ruined architecture was somehow more impressive and appropriate than the fussily kept cathedrals of Western Europe. Lisa took his hand, and they made their way forward, finally meeting a solid block of bodies about midway through the nave.

Long-bearded priests in gilded vestments swung censers and passed a jeweled Bible from one to the other. The litany began, repetitious and melancholy, lasting perhaps a quarter hour.

Immediately after the litany ended, from somewhere behind the iconostasis, a hidden choir began an unharmonized and unaccompanied chant that struck Hollis as more primitive than ecclesiastic but nonetheless powerful. Hollis looked around at the faces of the people, and it struck him that he had never seen such Russian faces in the two years he'd lived in Moscow. These were serene faces, faces with clear eyes and unknit brows, as if, he thought, the others really *were* soul dead and these were the last living beings in Moscow. He whispered to Lisa, 'I am . . . awed . . . thank you.'

'I'll save your spy's soul yet.'

Hollis listened to the ancient Russian coming from the altar, and though he had difficulty following it, the rhythm and cadence had a beauty and power of its own, and he felt himself, for the first time in many years, overwhelmed by a religious service. His own Protestantism was a religion of simplicity and individual conscience. This orthodox service was Byzantine Imperial pomp and Eastern mysticism, as far removed from his early memories of white clapboard churches as the Soviet 'marriage palaces' were removed from the Church of the Assumption. Yet here, in these magnificent ruins, these medieval-looking priests spoke the same message that the grey-suited ministers had spoken from the wooden pulpits of his youth: God loves you.

Hollis noticed that the worshipers crossed themselves and bowed low from the waist whenever the mood seemed to strike them, with no discernible signal from the altar. From time to time, people would manage to prostrate themselves on the crowded floor and kiss the stone. He saw, too, that the murky icons around the walls were now illuminated by the thin candles that were being stuck into the gilded casings that framed the icons. People were congregating around what he presumed to be the icons of their patron saints, kissing them, then moving back to let someone else through.

For all the ritual on the altar, Hollis thought, the worship in the nave was something of a free-for-all, quite different from the mainstream Protestant churches he'd once attended, where the opposite was sometimes true.

Suddenly the chanting stopped, and the censers ceased swinging. A priest in resplendent robes moved to the edge of the raised altar and spread his arms.

Hollis looked closely at the full-bearded man and saw by his eyes that he was young, no more than thirty perhaps.

The priest began talking without a microphone, and Hollis listened in the now-quiet church where nothing could be heard but the young priest's voice and the crackling of the tallow candles. The priest delivered a brief sermon, speaking of conscience and good deeds. Hollis found it rather unoriginal and uninspiring, though he realized that the congregation did not hear this sort of thing often.

Lisa, as if knowing what was on his mind, whispered, 'The KGB are recording every word. There are hidden messages in the sermon, words and concepts that the clergy and congregation understand, but which the KGB cannot begin to comprehend. It's a start anyway, a spark.'

Hollis nodded. It was odd that she used that word: spark – *iskra* in Russian. It was the word Lenin often used and what he named his first underground newspaper – *Iskra*. The concept then, as now, was that Russia was a tinderbox, awaiting a spark to set the nation ablaze.

Hollis heard the young priest say, 'It is not always convenient to let others know you believe in Christ. But if you live your life according to His teachings, no power on this earth, no matter what they deny you in this life, can deny you the Kingdom of God.'

The priest turned abruptly back to the altar, presumably, Hollis thought, leaving the more educated worshipers to draw their own moral or finish the sermon in their minds.

At a particular point in the mass, toward the end, a large number of people either prostrated themselves completely, or if they couldn't find the room, knelt and bowed their faces to the floor. Lisa dropped to her knees, but Hollis remained standing. He was able to look across the church now, and he saw standing to his left front, about twenty feet away, a stooped old man with disheveled hair, grey stubble on his face, dressed in a shabby dark coat that almost reached his ankles. At first sight there was nothing remarkable about the old man, and Hollis thought that what had initially caught his eye was the young woman standing beside him. She was about seventeen or eighteen, Hollis reckoned, and she too was dressed in a shabby coat, a shapeless red synthetic. But her manner and her bearing, if not her uncommon beauty, marked her as someone special. More than that, Hollis, who was trained to see such things, picked out the coat as a disguise. She was quite obviously someone who should not be seen in the Church of the Assumption. This discovery led Hollis to look more closely at the old man, who in an unusual gesture for a Russian, especially in church, was holding the girl's hand affectionately.

As Hollis stared at the man, people began to stand, and Hollis' view was becoming blocked, but in a second before he lost sight of the strange couple, he realized that the stooped old grandfather was actually somewhat younger than he appeared. In fact, it was General Valentin Surikov. Suddenly things were becoming more clear.

27

Sam Hollis and Lisa Rhodes moved with the crush of worshipers through the open doors of the church. The people carried their blessed food in bags, and many of them clutched a handful of the thin brown candles. Hollis looked out over the converging paths. These people, he realized, did not seem to know one another, did not speak, nor did they try to make acquaintances. They had come by metro and bus from all over Moscow to an inconveniently placed church, and now they scattered like lambs who smelled wolves. 'Do the K-goons usually hang around?'

'Who? Oh, those men. Sometimes. But I don't see them now.'

Hollis didn't see them either. But he worried more about the KGB when he didn't see them. He moved off the path and watched the people coming down the steps.

'Are you looking for someone?'

'Just people watching.' Hollis realized that not only were the worshipers scattering, but the priests had not come out to speak with their flock. As he watched for Surikov, he said to Lisa, 'No tea and fellowship afterwards?'

Lisa seemed to understand. 'The Orthodox Christian comes to God's house to worship Him. The priests don't come to your house and ask how you're getting along.'

'The Kremlin must find that useful.'

'True. In fact, the Russian church has always preached subservience to the state. When the czars were on the throne, it worked for the church and the czars. But when Lenin became the new czar, it backfired.'

'You mean there's something I can't blame on the Reds?'

'The communists didn't help the situation.'

Hollis watched the last of the worshipers leave the church but did not spot Surikov or the girl with him.

He and Lisa walked away from the church and sat on a stone bench occupied by a stout babushka who seemed to be sleeping in a sitting position. Lisa asked, 'Did you like the service?'

'Very much. We take so much for granted in the West.'

'I know. Thanks for coming, even if you came because you had to go to the cemetery anyway.'

'I came to be with you.'

She nodded and looked up in the sky. 'This is not like autumn at home, and it's not like winter either. It's something else. It's like a time of foreboding, grey and quiet, mist and fog obscuring the world. I can't see a sun or a horizon or even the end of a block. I want to go home now.'

Hollis took her hand. 'We'll be in the air this time tomorrow, heading west.'

She moved closer to him. 'Do you have to go to the cemetery?'

'Yes.'

'It's not dangerous, is it?'

'No. I just have to meet an old Russian friend to say good-bye.'

'A spy? A dissident?'

'Sort of.'

'The old lady stood and moved aimlessly down the path.

Lisa said, 'At Gogol's grave. Was that his idea?'

'Yes.' Hollis looked at his watch. The service had lasted about two hours, and it was nearly noon. Now he knew why Surikov had picked this hour and this place. 'I won't be more than thirty minutes. Where can I meet you?'

'At that bell tower there. See it? Don't get lost.'

Hollis stood. 'How do I get into the cemetery?'

'Just keep on this path. You'll see another gate church set in the wall like the one we entered through. Go through the gate, and you'll find yourself in the cemetery.'

'Thanks. Are you going to walk around?'

'Yes. I like to walk here.'

'Don't walk in the cemetery.'

'Okay.'

'Try to walk where there are people.'

'If they come for you, it doesn't matter how many people are around. You know that.'

'Yes, I know that.' He added, 'I don't think they know we're here. But be careful.'

'*You* be careful. They might have followed this friend of yours.' She gave him one of the thin brown candles. 'Here. To light the way.'

He kissed her on the cheek. 'See you later.' Hollis turned and walked down the path, carrying the candle. Within a few minutes he passed another large church of brick and white stone that looked forlorn among the bramble and bush, unused as either a church or a museum. The path curved around it, and he saw the towering south wall of the convent grounds, then spotted the gate church built into the center of it.

Hollis looked around. A few people straggled past him, apparently headed for the cemetery. He slid his hands in his overcoat pockets and leaned back against a thick rowan tree. His right hand let go of the candle and found the silenced 9mm Polish Radom automatic, another Colt-Browning knockoff. His left hand slid through his coat to the handle of the knife in his belt sheath. Hollis watched awhile, then fell in behind three young couples and followed them down to the gate church. He passed through the portals into a tunnellike passage and found himself in the quiet cemetery.

The convent grounds, like the Kremlin, had been built on a rare high spot on the banks of the Moskva, and Hollis could see down the slope out to the south and west over the brick cemetery wall. The Olympic complex and Lenin Stadium were five hundred meters to the south, nestled in the loop of the Moskva on reclaimed bog land. Beyond the stadium was the river, and rising from its south bank were the Lenin Hills and the towers of Moscow University. He could pick out the observation platform where he, Lisa, and Sasha had shared a brief and pleasant moment.

Hollis followed a brick path into the sloping cemetery. It was heavily treed, and most of the graves were overgrown. The tombstones were higher than a man, in the old Russian style, creating a maze of limestone and granite. The cemetery was as wide as the convent grounds but not as deep, and Hollis estimated it covered about six acres. It would take some time to find Gogol's grave here.

There weren't many people in the cemetery, which was good for privacy, but there were enough so that he and Surikov wouldn't stand out. Surikov had picked a good Sunday spot.

The visitors were mostly students apparently looking for graves of the famous. They stood in knots in front of tombstones, pointing and discussing the man or woman interred there. Hollis saw the graves of Chekhov, Stanislavsky, and the painter Isaac Levitan. Six young men and women, Bohemian types in peasant-chic *vatniks*, baggy corduroys, and high boots, sat on the path and talked in front of the grave of the filmmaker Sergey Eisenstein. Hollis walked around them.

An old lady in a dirty red coat stood facing the grave of Nikita Khrushchev. The woman crossed herself, bowed to the stone, and walked off. Hollis wondered if she was a relative.

He turned up an intersecting path and found himself in a patch of ground mist. A tall, attractive woman, smartly dressed in a long, black leather coat, came out of the mist toward him. As she drew close, Hollis asked her in Russian, 'Gogol's grave?'

She looked him over, then said in an unusually cultured accent. 'You might try over there. Near that very tall pine tree. I think I passed it.'

'Thank you.' Hollis moved past her.

She said to him or to herself, 'But you never know. Even the dead disappear here.'

Hollis kept on walking. A week ago, he thought, he'd have stopped and spoken to the woman. But his quota for Russian adventures was filling up fast, and he hadn't even spoken to Surikov yet.

Hollis saw him standing on the path under the spreading boughs of a tall pine tree, smoking a cigarette, contemplating a decaying slab of lichen-covered limestone. Hollis stood beside him and looked at the tall stone.

Surikov said, 'Do they read this fellow in the West?'

'Not so much. Colleges, I guess.'

'Can I get things to read in Russian there?'

'Yes.'

'Dead souls,' Surikov said. 'Dead souls.' He stared at the grave a while longer, then looked Hollis up and down through his cloud of cigarette smoke, and a thin smile came to his lips. 'Do we dress so badly as that?'

'I'm afraid so.'

'It looks worse on you.'

'Thank you.' Hollis added, 'Why are *you* dressed badly today?'

Surikov ran his hand over his stubble. 'It's Sunday.' He turned and walked away. Hollis waited a full minute, then followed.

Surikov stood near the base of the corner battletower where it joined the brick wall of the cemetery. There were ancient tombstones along the wall with old Cyrillic that Hollis couldn't read.

Surikov pulled a *Pravda*-wrapped parcel from the pocket of his baggy coat and said, 'Do you want to buy fresh carp?'

Hollis could actually smell the fish. 'Perhaps.'

Surikov tapped the package as if extolling the virtues of the fish. He said, 'So, my friend, *Pravda* tells me you are leaving Russia. I was quite shocked to hear that. I didn't know if you would come today. I was worried.'

Hollis could well imagine what was worrying Surikov. Hollis replied, 'My diplomatic immunity is in some doubt right now. So you don't have to ask me if I'm sure I wasn't followed, because today I'm as worried as you are.'

'Yes? I could lose my life. You would only go to prison.'

'I would envy you a bullet in the head if I was sent east for five or ten years.'

Surikov shrugged. 'So, how will this affect our deal?'

'We have no deal.'

'We will. When are you leaving?'

Hollis replied in a sarcastic tone, 'It was in your *Pravda* wasn't it?'

'They didn't say *when* you were leaving.'

'Really? Well, I'm leaving Wednesday.'

Surikov's face seemed to show some surprise. He asked, 'Who will replace you as air attaché?'

'I'm not certain.'

'Will I deal with the new air attaché or someone else?'

'We'll discuss that before we part.'

A young couple appeared on the path and moved over to the worn tombstones. At the base of the wall the man knelt and traced his fingers over the lettering. The woman held a notebook. The man said, 'This was a nun. Gulia. I don't hear that name much anymore.' The woman made some notes in her book.

Surikov waved the carp under Hollis' nose. 'I caught them this morning in the Setun. My wife cleaned them so a lazy bachelor would pay good money for them.'

The young couple moved down the row of stones.

Surikov said, 'I think you're telling me little lies. I know you are leaving tomorrow, and I know the name of your replacement is Colonel Fields.'

Hollis nodded. It may have been the embassy listeners, who heard him telling the Kellums, or it may have been the Kellums, who told the KGB directly. Whatever the route, it was a little scary to hear that from General Surikov. Hollis said, 'The KGB told you that.'

'Yes. They told me the name of the new air attaché. They told me you were leaving Monday, not Wednesday.'

'Why did they tell you any of that?'

'They like to impress people with their knowledge. I'm not a military intelligence officer, if that's what you're thinking.'

361

Hollis never thought Surikov was. He didn't have the moves or the jargon of a GRU man.

Surikov added, 'Actually, the KGB wanted to know if I or my staff or any of our overseas air attachés knew a Colonel Fields. The KGB is apparently having trouble building a dossier on him, so they came to me.' Surikov smiled. 'Perhaps you can help me impress them.'

'What exactly is your position with the Red Air Force, General?'

'I am what you would call a G-l. Chief of Air Force personnel.'

'For what command?'

'The whole Red Air Force, Colonel. I keep the files and paperwork of a half million men. Not so glamorous a job, but interesting things come across my desk. Don't you agree?'

'How did the KGB know the name of Colonel Fields?'

Surikov looked Hollis in the eye and replied, 'I think they've penetrated your embassy.' He studied Hollis' face for a reaction.

Hollis asked, 'How was this KGB inquiry directed to you? Memo? Phone call?'

'In person. I was summoned to Lefortovo. The KGB can even summon generals. They take delight in asking us to stop in to see them at Lubyanka or Lefortovo. One never knows if one will leave there alive. This happened a few days ago.'

'Were you frightened, General?'

'Very much.'

'To whom did you speak at Lefortovo?'

'A colonel named Pavlichenko.'

'Tall, blond, pouty lips, blue eyes?'

Surikov's eyebrows rose. 'Yes. You know the man?'

'By a different name.' Hollis realized that Surikov was in an answering mood for a change. It was often so when the final deal was at hand. Hollis didn't know if Valentin Surikov, a Christian, was any more trustworthy than General Surikov of the Red Air Force, but he was willing to gamble that he was.

Surikov said, 'After Lefortovo, I am more resolved than ever to leave here.'

'I know how you feel.'

'Can you get me out?'

Hollis had no authorization to say yes, but the time had come to bring this whole thing to a head. 'I can if you have the fare.'

'Half now, half in the West.'

'I understand.'

'Is it dangerous? The getting out, I mean.'

'Of course.'

'It's not for me that I'm worried.'

Hollis already knew that. 'Is she your granddaughter?'

Surikov's head snapped around, and he opened his mouth, but no words came out.

Hollis continued matter-of-factly, 'It's dangerous, but it doesn't require much from you except nerve. Does she have nerve?'

Surikov drew on his cigarette. 'She has faith.' He glanced at Hollis but did not hold the eye contact. 'You saw us?'

'Yes.'

'Then you know why I want to leave.'

'I suppose.'

Surikov stared stupidly at the wrapped carp in his hands and spoke, but not to Hollis. 'I curse the day I found God. My life has been a misery ever since.'

Hollis didn't know quite how to respond to that statement, but he understood it.

Surikov said, 'Yes, my granddaughter. Natasha. My only daughter's only daughter. The light of my life, Hollis.'

'She's a beautiful girl. Does she speak English?'

'Yes.'

'She'll do well. She'll marry a rich American or Englishman and live happily ever after. Do you believe that?'

'I would like to. Unfortunately, she wants to become a nun.'

'Does she? Well, she'll do what she wants, General. That's what it's all about over there.'

'Is it? And me?'

'We'll find something for you to do.'

'Yes.' Surikov wandered away, down the line of tombstones. The sky was more overcast now, and a few drops of rain fell, splattering the headstones and the damp leaves. A wind came up, and the rowan and birch trees swayed.

Hollis walked past Surikov, then stopped to look at the next tombstone. 'Borodino, General.'

Surikov spoke. 'Some kilometers north of Borodino was once located a Red Air Force ground school. Classroom instruction on American fighter tactics, capabilities, and weaponry.' Surikov paused for effect, then said, 'The instructors were Americans.' He looked briefly at Hollis. 'This is an incredible story, and you must listen closely.'

Hollis drew a long breath. The one prayer he'd allowed himself in church was that Surikov would confirm what he and Alevy had discussed. Hollis said abruptly, 'That's the half-secret? I know all about that.'

Surikov turned his head toward Hollis. 'What . . . ?'

'You can't get to London on that fare. I'm sorry.' Hollis walked away. He kept walking, like a man walking away from a bad deal or an unfaithful lover, hoping that the deal or the lover would get better in the next ten steps.

Surikov caught up with him. 'You can't . . . but how do you . . . ?'

'I was out to Borodino. That's why I'm being kicked out. I know there are Americans out there. I'm sorry. I thought you knew more –'

'I do!'

Hollis stopped and turned toward Surikov, who still held the carp in his hand. 'What were you going to give me in London? What is the other half of the secret?'

Surikov licked his lips. 'The school . . . you know they don't train pilots there any longer . . .'

364

'Yes. I know they train KGB men to be Americans. How do *you* know that?'

'I . . . I supply the students. They're not actually KGB. The KGB doesn't trust its own recruiting methods. They get very odd personalities who want to be KGB, and they know that. They wanted honest Russian patriots. Men who had volunteered to be Air Force pilots. Men, I suppose, who would have something in common with their American instructors.'

Hollis nodded. 'Like when it was a training school for pilots.'

'That's my understanding. From what I've heard, when it was a Red Air Force training school, our pilots seemed more interested in asking the Americans about America than in learning their fighter tactics. The political commissar was very angry and worried about this situation and reported several pilots to the KGB. It was then that the KGB had their brilliant idea. They eventually took over the school. There was no formal announcement to the American prisoners, but gradually the nature of the school changed from fighter tactics to what it is now. A spy school. This is what I heard.'

'And how are you involved with this school now, General?'

'I'm not directly involved, but Air Force Personnel has to handle the paperwork on the candidates for this school, since they are all members of the Red Air Force. So I –' Surikov stopped. 'There's more. Much more. Is it worth it to you, Colonel, to get me out of here?'

'Perhaps. But you know, General, we don't need any more information on this school. We know where it is, and we have enough information already to precipitate an international crisis.' He looked at Surikov. 'You know what I need.'

Surikov didn't reply.

'The *names*,' Hollis said. 'The names of Soviet agents already in America. I assume you have some sort of list, or you wouldn't still be trying to make a deal. The *names*. *That* is your ticket west, General.'

'But . . . if I got that for you . . . how do I know you wouldn't abandon me and my granddaughter? I have nothing to offer for my passage if I gave you the list of names here.'

'You simply must trust me.'

'I can't.'

'You *must*. Listen to me, General. You are, as we say in English, a babe in the woods. You understand? Once you took that first step you were as good as dead. And so is Natasha. I could expose you here, or shoot you in London. I can also give you back your life. I could be lying, but you don't know if I am or not. You simply have no choice but to do what I say, to understand that the game is being played on my terms now.'

General Surikov's body seemed to sag. Beneath the erect military man was a tired old grandfather trying to do one last thing right and cursing himself for it. Surikov said, 'We don't understand faith and trust here. We're not taught those things as children. Here we trust no one but family. We have faith in nothing.'

Hollis said, 'Do you understand that if you gave me that list, and I let something happen to you, I could not live with myself? Do you understand that concept? Conscience. Did you listen to the priest, or was your mind somewhere else?'

'I heard him,' Surikov snapped. 'It's all new to me. Less than two years. Do you expect me to become a saint in two years? Do you think I believe you are a saint because you go to church and use saintly words?'

Hollis smiled. 'I'm no saint, my friend.' Hollis didn't think the words *trest, vera*, and *sovest* – 'trust', 'faith', and 'conscience' – were particularly saintly words, but he supposed if one rarely heard them, they could be jarring or moving or both.

'I need time to think this over. I'll meet your replacement next Sunday –'

'No. There is nothing to think about. It would be best if you made your decision now and gave me your word on it. Then I will give you my word, and I will see to it that you get out of here. I'll meet you in the West if you wish.'

366

General Surikov seemed to rediscover his backbone and stood straight. 'Alright. You're a lot more ruthless than I thought, Colonel. But perhaps you do have a conscience. Here is what you're getting: a microfilm of the personnel records of every man who's gone to the American Citizenship School – that's what the KGB calls it. On the microfilm you will find photographs of the men, their Russian names, their fingerprints, places of birth, birthdays, blood types, identifying scars, dental records, and so forth. A complete personnel file. You will not find their new American names or addresses, and I cannot even tell you how many of them actually made it to America. Only the KGB has that information. So your people over there – the FBI – will have to do a great deal of work. That's all I can give you.'

Hollis nodded. It was a start. 'How many?'

'A little over three thousand.'

'Three thousand . . . ? All on microfilm?'

'Yes. These men, incidentally, are all officially dead. Killed in training accidents. The Red Air Force gave them military funerals. Closed coffins. We buried a lot of sand. We also paid out a lot of death benefits. The KGB finds it convenient to use our logistics, our money, our pilot candidates, and the cover of military deaths for so large an operation.'

Hollis nodded to himself. Three thousand military training deaths in the States would cause something of a national scàndal. Here, not even one such death ever made the newspapers. The three thousand families of the supposed deceaseds only knew of their own loss. Amazing, Hollis thought. Only a totalitarian society could mount an operation such as that. The world's largest Trojan horse, the biggest fifth column in history, or whatever Washington would call it. Hollis asked, 'Where is the microfilm?'

'I'll tell you where you can find it when I get to London. That was the deal. Half now, half in London.'

'I told you, I already have the first half. You'll give me the microfilm now.'

'Why now?'

'Because you may be arrested anytime between now and the time we try to get you out of here. Because I want it now. That's why.'

Surikov stared off into space, and Hollis could see he was angry, but that didn't matter.

Surikov nodded. 'Alright. My life and my granddaughter's life are in your hands. I'll bring the microfilm to my next meeting, or I'll leave it in one of our dead drops, whatever you prefer.'

Hollis considered a moment. A dead drop was preferred, but his instincts told him that this was a case for hand-to-hand transfer. 'Tomorrow at nine A.M. you will go to the antique store in the Arbat. A man will ask you where he can find czarist coins. He speaks fluent Russian. Have the microfilm with you.'

Surikov lit another cigarette. 'And that's the last I'll hear from the Americans.'

'If you believe that, then you don't want to live in the West, General. You might as well stay here.'

'Well, we will see if my cynicism is well-founded. And this man will tell me how I'm going West?'

'Yes.'

'I have a better idea. You tell me now. I want to know. Before I bring the microfilm.'

Hollis thought General Surikov needed a victory, but he remembered Alevy's words of caution. *Then maybe what he wants is to find out how we get people out of here.* But there was no time for caution. Hollis said, 'Alright, I'll tell you our secret. Can you get to Leningrad on a weekend?'

'Yes.'

'You'll go to Leningrad this Saturday. The man in the Arbat antique store will tell you how to meet someone there who will give you more details. But it's basically simple. You go to one of the Kirov Island recreational parks carrying fishing equipment. You and Natasha rent a boat and take it to the mouth of the Neva, but not so far as to attract the attention of patrol boats. You will fish in the marked channel. Whenever you see a freighter flying the flag of a NATO country coming in or going out, you will give a signal that you will be advised of by the man in Leningrad. One of these freighters will take you and Natasha aboard, and someone on board will take charge of you. When the authorities find your boat capsized, it will appear you've both drowned. If the rendezvous fails on Saturday, you'll do the same thing Sunday.'

'And if it fails Sunday?'

'Then the next weekend.'

'There's not much boating weather left up that way, Colonel.'

'General, if you are being honest with us, you will not be abandoned. There are other ways. But with luck . . . and God's help . . . by this time next week, you will be in a Western port city.'

'This thing will need all of God's help. Natasha thinks she is blessed by God. We'll see.'

'I'll see you in London.'

'And you will buy me a drink.'

'I'll buy you the whole fucking bar, General.'

Surikov tried to smile. 'Just a drink will do.' He handed Hollis the carp. 'You poach them in sour cream.'

Hollis didn't think so. He said, 'I shake your hand.'

'And I yours.' Surikov added, 'Safe journey west. I will see you in London.' He turned and walked back into the cemetery.

Hollis looked at the wrapped carp, slipped it into his pocket with the candle and the pistol, and headed toward the gate church. About ten yards from the church, someone tapped him on the shoulder and asked in Russian, 'What's in that package?'

Hollis gripped the 9mm automatic, pointed it through his coat pocket, and spun around.

Seth Alevy asked, 'What did he give you?'

'Carp.'

'Oh. I grew up on carp. Very Jewish and Russian. I hate the stuff.'

369

Hollis turned and continued toward the gate church.

Alevy fell into step beside him. 'I thought you said the meeting was for three.'

'I was going to tell you when I got back that I remembered it was earlier.'

'I thought it might have been. Where's Lisa?'

'At the bell tower.'

They walked through the arched passage into the convent grounds. The drizzle was turning to light rain. Alevy asked, 'Did we get lucky?'

'We hit the jackpot.'

'The Charm School?'

'Yes. The KGB, incidentally, calls it the American Citizen-ship School.'

'How is Surikov involved with that?'

'I'll tell you later. Are we covered?'

'Well, I'm covering you, and you're covering me. I couldn't call out the troops again like I did at Lefortovo. The KGB tripled their embassy stakeout, and they're looking for a confrontation. I snuck out in the van going to the Finnish dacha. If I had any brains, I'd have gone there and gotten laid.'

'Why didn't you? Nobody asked you to come here.'

'I wanted a look at Surikov.'

'You'll meet him soon enough.'

They kept walking quickly up the tree-lined path, toward the bell tower. Alevy said, 'The other reason I came is that we got a communication this morning from the Soviet Foreign Ministry. They've revoked your diplomatic status. And Lisa's.'

'I see.' Hollis added, 'Thanks for coming then.'

'According to international law, your immunity is now good only between the embassy and a point of departure from the country. Therefore, your ass is hanging out here. So is hers, obviously.'

'Sort of like going vampire hunting and losing your cross,' Hollis observed.

'Sort of. I assume you have your wooden stake though.'

'Yes,' Hollis said. 'You nearly got it through your heart.'

They came out into the paved square on the far side of which rose the bell tower. Hollis didn't see Lisa. They crossed the open square walking normally so as not to attract attention. The rain was heavier now, and the strollers were disappearing. They reached the base of the bell tower, then split up and circled around it.

Alevy snapped, 'God damn it!'

'Relax, Seth. She'll be along.'

Alevy turned to him, and Hollis saw he was not going to relax. Alevy pointed his finger at Hollis and said irritably, 'You shouldn't have brought her here!'

'Hey, hold on. She wanted to go to church here, and she can do –'

'Oh, don't give me that shit. This is not a fucking lark, Colonel, or an ego trip for you two. This is Moscow, buddy, and –'

'I know where the hell I am. And I'll run my operations my way.'

'I should have had both of you shipped out a week ago. You've caused more problems –'

'Go to hell.'

Alevy and Hollis stood very close, then Alevy turned and began walking across the square. He called back, 'I'll wait at the main gate for fifteen minutes. Then I'm leaving, with or without you, her, or both of you.'

Hollis followed Alevy into the square. 'Hold on.' He walked up to Alevy. 'Listen, in case I don't get back to the embassy – you have an appointment with Surikov. The antique shop on Arbat. Tomorrow at nine A.M. He has microfilmed personnel files of all the Charm School students, past and present. Three thousand, Seth.'

'Jesus . . . three thousand . . . how the hell did he get that information?'

'He's the G-1 for the entire Red Air Force.' Hollis explained briefly and concluded, 'I gave him my word that we'd get him and his granddaughter out. You understand? Don't fuck around with that, Seth. You get them out.' He stared at Alevy.

Alevy nodded. 'I'll take care of it.'

'Now get out of here.'

Alevy hesitated. 'I'll wait at the gate.'

'No. You get your ass back to the embassy and stay there until you go to meet Surikov. I don't need you here. I've passed the baton to you, Seth, and either way I won't be around to meet Surikov tomorrow. It's all yours now, buddy. Beat it.'

Alevy looked around the rain-splashed square, then nodded. 'Good luck.' He walked off through the rain toward the main gate.

Hollis moved back to the bell tower and put his back to the wall. He drew his pistol and kept it at his side. He saw Alevy disappear on to a tree-covered path.

Hollis watched the square, watched the cold falling rain, and watched his breath mist. The minutes passed. For all he knew, they had Surikov, Lisa, and Alevy and were just letting him stand alone in the rain. 'You worry more about them when you don't see them.' But if he saw them, he'd take a few with him. 'No more diplomatic immunity, no more nice guy.'

He glanced at his watch. It had been fifty minutes since he'd left her. He thought about Alevy's coming out to cover them, then about Alevy's agreeing to leave. Professionally that was right. What was wrong, he realized, was the profession.

He heard footsteps on the wet square and looked out.

She came hurrying across the square, splashing through the puddles, and threw her arms around him. 'I lost track of the time. Forgive me.'

'No problem.'

'That coat is soaked.'

Hollis took her arm, and they walked toward the main gate.

'You found your friend at Gogol's grave?'

'Yes.'

'How was your meeting?'

'Fine.' That question, Hollis thought, conjured up pleasant

372

images of conference tables and hot coffee, not heart-pounding encounters in the cold rain. He said, 'Nice cemetery.'

'It is. Did you see any famous graves?'

'A few.'

'Were you waiting here long?'

'Not too long.' He said lightly, 'I thought you'd gotten picked up.'

'I never get in trouble on holy ground. Well, once at a church dance . . .' She laughed. 'Did anything interesting happen to *you*?'

'No, not really.'

They approached the gate church.

She said, 'I smell fish.'

'Oh, I bought some carp from an old man.' He patted his pocket.

'You poach it in sour cream.'

'I know.'

'I missed you. I was worried about you.'

'Thanks.'

'Will we have any problem getting back into the embassy?'

'I'm going to find a phone and call security. Location Foxtrot is close. That's the Lenin statue on the north side of the stadium. Remember that, if we get separated.'

'How will we get separated?'

'Just in case.'

They walked into the arched passage where about a dozen people stood sheltering from the rain. Hollis stopped and let his eyes adjust to the dim light. Lisa took off his rain-soaked hat and wiped his face with her handkerchief.

Seth Alevy stepped out of the darkness. He didn't say much, just 'Follow me,' but Hollis thought it was enough under the circumstances.

373

28

Sam Hollis and Lisa Rhodes stood beneath the portico of the chancery building and said their final farewells to the people who had come to see them off. Lisa kissed her coworkers, while Hollis shook hands with his former staff and exchanged salutes.

The ambassador had sent his car, a stretch Lincoln with the Great Seal on the sides, and the driver opened the rear door.

Kay Hoffman gave Hollis a big kiss and said, 'I want an invite to the wedding.'

Hollis didn't know about the wedding but answered, 'Okay.'

Charles Banks said to Lisa, 'I once told you that your picture-taking would get you booted.'

She smiled. 'I'm glad it wasn't that, Charlie. I'm glad it was for something important.'

'Send me a copy of your book.'

'I will.'

Hollis and Lisa got into the Lincoln. The driver, Fred Santos, closed the door and got behind the wheel.

Everyone waved as the Lincoln pulled away. At the Marine guard booth, ten Marines had assembled with rifles and presented arms. Hollis returned the salutes. The two Soviet militiamen stared at the Lincoln and its occupants as the car pulled into the street. The embassy watchers peered from the windows of the surrounding buildings and from their black Chaikas. A man who Hollis recognized as Boris stood beside his Chaika and waved. Hollis waved back. '*Da svedahnya.*' He added, 'You son of a bitch.'

Fred Santos laughed.

Lisa turned and looked back through the rear window at the

chancery building and the walls of the American embassy as the iron gates with the eagles closed shut.

Hollis opened a two-day-old *New York Times* and read. '"Clear and sunny today" – that was Saturday – "seventy degrees." Nice. Mets took the second game of the Series.'

Lisa faced the front. 'I'm going to cry.'

'Are you a Detroit fan?'

The Lincoln wound through the narrow streets of Krasnopresnya. Hollis put down the paper and glanced back through the rear window. Following closely was a Ford with Seth Alevy in the front seat, accompanied by three security men. Behind the Ford was the embassy van, loaded with their luggage and personal items. To their front was another Ford with three more security men and Bert Mills, a CIA officer and Alevy's deputy station chief. Hollis observed, 'No air cover, no tanks.'

Lisa said, 'This is a little silly.'

'Seth is very protective of you.'

She retreated into a moody silence.

Fred Santos said, 'Well, this has got to be a relief. Right?'

'Right,' Hollis answered.

'Funny thing though, everybody I drive to the airport looks sad. People say things like, 'I wish I could have done more here.' Or they think about embassy friends they left here. Some people feel sorry for Russian friends who they'll never see again. I guess you get used to a place. This is one tough assignment. But maybe it's the one place where you feel needed and appreciated. You know?'

'I know,' Hollis replied. 'How long do you have to go?'

'A year and two weeks. Then it's back to DC. A year and two weeks. Not too long.'

'Goes fast,' Hollis said.

'Maybe.'

Hollis had come to Moscow at the time the State Department decided that perhaps the Foreign Nationals had to be replaced with American service personnel. The ambassador's former chauffeur, Vasily, a nice old gentleman who everyone knew was a KGB colonel, was getting about two hundred dollars a month, and State thought it was a good deal. Alevy had pointed out the inherent security risk in having a KGB colonel as one's chauffeur, and also that if money were the issue, Vasily would pay the Americans twice that to keep his job. The State Department, after having Soviet citizens snooping around the embassy for over fifty years, began to see the point. It was no wonder, Hollis thought, that the intelligence people thought the diplomats were bozos.

The American service personnel, like Santos, cost about three thousand a month with benefits, and they needed places to live. But Hollis thought it was worth it as long as they weren't graduates of the Charm School, such as the Kellums. Hollis said, 'Hey, Fred, who played centerfield for the '81 Mets?'

'I don't follow baseball, Colonel. You wanna talk NFL, I'll talk your ear off.'

'Maybe later.'

The Lincoln swung into Leningrad Prospect, a broad, six-lane road with a treed center divide. They headed north, out of Moscow. Hollis regarded the massive grey apartment blocks, the bare trees, and the dark sky. He suspected that this was how he would remember Moscow.

Leningrad Prospect became Leningrad Highway, and the four-vehicle convoy picked up speed.

Lisa said, 'I'm feeling better. This is for the best. It's good for us.' She reached forward and slid the glass partition closed. 'You know, Sam, we fell in love here, under stressful circumstances, which can cause emotions that are ambiguous and unreliable.'

Hollis opened the small bar refrigerator. 'There's a box of Belgian chocolates and a split of French champagne.'

'Are you listening to me?'

'No.'

'Well, listen!'

'I'm listening.'

'Okay. In Moscow, our love was safe from outside reality. That's ironic because Moscow is unreal. But now, being expelled so soon after we've found each other, our feelings didn't have time to take root, and I'm afraid –'

'Did you rehearse this?'

'Yes.'

'Could you put it in the form of a short memo?'

'Stop being an idiot.'

'Do you want a chocolate or not?'

'No!' She slammed the refrigerator door shut. 'Let me ask you something. Did Katherine leave *you*, or did she leave Moscow?'

Hollis worked on the champagne cork.

'Answer me.'

'She left Colonel Hollis, spy, in Moscow.' The cork popped, hit the ceiling, and Fred Santos rose off his seat. Hollis called through the glass partition, 'Sorry, Fred!'

'Jesus, Colonel . . .' Santos put his hand over his heart in a theatrical gesture.

Hollis observed to Lisa, 'This country makes people jumpy. Have you noticed that?' He poured the champagne into two fluted glasses and handed one to her. He said, 'Not the end, but the beginning.'

'Oh . . . oh, I love you!' She embraced him, spilling champagne on his trench coat. Hollis kissed her. The security driver behind them beeped his horn playfully. Hollis glanced over Lisa's shoulder and saw Alevy staring at them from the front seat of the car.

They entered the main terminal area of Sheremetyevo Airport on their way to the diplomatic wing. Alevy's deputy, Bert Mills, said, 'Please wait here a minute.'

Hollis and Lisa stood in the concourse of the large new terminal. Hollis thought that the architect's previous experience must have been designing tractor sheds. The low ceilings were a copper-toned metal, making the whole place dark and grim, harsh, and unwelcoming.

As in all Soviet transportation terminals, there was a profound lack of services or amenities. Hollis spotted a single food kiosk under attack by at least a hundred people.

Soviet citizens coming from or heading to domestic flights pushed large crates around the grey slate floor. Hollis never understood where they stowed all that stuff. He said to Lisa, 'Pan Am measures my flight bag to the last centimeter. On Aeroflot, people bring livestock. Like on that train we took. Remember?'

'I'm not likely to forget.'

'Right.' Hollis went to the currency window and dumped his rubles on the counter but held on to some loose kopeks. 'American dollars, please.'

The cashier, using an abacus, converted the amount, then gave Hollis some forms to sign. He signed, and she pushed some dollars toward him, saying. 'No coins.'

'Chocolate?'

'*Shokolad?*'

'Forget it. *Da svedahnya*, sweetheart.' He joined Lisa and said, 'That was the last Russian I'm ever using.'

From where they stood in the concourse, Hollis could see the international arrivals area where there were crowds at passport control and larger crowds at customs. Most of the arriving people looked to be from the Third World, and there were a good number of youth groups; pilgrims on Soviet-sponsored tours, coming to Moscow to talk peace, progress, disarmament, and equality. It never ceased to amaze him how a discredited philosophy and a repressive nation still attracted idealists.

Hollis scanned the rest of the terminal. Grey-clad militiamen were all over the place, and Hollis spotted a few KGB Border Guards in their green uniforms. He picked out his embassy security people strategically placed around him and Lisa. He saw one man in a brown leather car coat and tie who might have been KGB, but he couldn't spot any others. Hollis normally wouldn't expect any trouble in a crowded public place, but to the KGB, the entire country was their private hunting preserve. He realized that Alevy had disappeared, then he noticed that Lisa was looking a bit tense. He said to her, 'Did you ever fly Aeroplop?'

She laughed. 'Aero*plop*? Yes, once to Leningrad on business.'

'I used to take it once a month to Leningrad. The pilots are all military. There's not much difference between civil and military aviation in this country. Did you notice how they circled the airport at high altitudes, then dove in?'

'Yes. Scared me.'

'Me too. And I used to fly fighter-bombers. In the States, the drinking rule for pilots is twenty-four hours between bottle and throttle. Here, Aeroplop pilots aren't allowed to drink within twenty-four feet of the aircraft.'

She laughed again. 'You're terrible. What are you going to complain about in the States?'

'The quality of winter strawberries.' Hollis glanced at his watch.

Lisa noticed and asked, 'Do you think there's something wrong?'

'No. I think we're getting jumpy. Oh, I was going to tell you about my last Aeroplop flight. It was a Yakovlev 42, a tri-jet with huge wheels so it can land on grass and dirt. It's actually a military transport, but when they get old, they slap an Aeroflot logo on them and put in seats. The cabin had been painted by brush, and you could see the brush marks. Anyway, the stewardesses were Miss Piggy look-alikes, and the lav had backed up –'

'That was *my* flight. And the cabin smelled of sewage. And my barf bag had been previously used. I'm not kidding. I collect barf bags from different airlines, and I took this one out of the seat pocket, and –'

'You collect *barf* bags? Disgusting.'

379

They were both laughing now. She said, 'Only *unused* ones. So, anyway, I –'

Alevy came up behind them. 'Okay. Everything's set. Let's go.'

Hollis and Lisa picked up their flight bags and followed Alevy, accompanied by the six security men. They entered a long, narrow corridor off the concourse that took them to the diplomatic wing, where Alevy's man, Bert Mills, was waiting.

The DPL wing consisted of a front desk and a comfortable modern lounge with small conference rooms to the sides. It was not much different from a private airline club or any VIP lounge in any airport except for the presence of a smartly uniformed KGB Border Guard near the front desk and another Border Guard with a submachine gun at the rear exit door that led to the tarmac.

Their luggage, which had diplomatic seals, had already been passed through X-ray and was now piled in a coatroom near the front desk. A passport control officer arrived and stamped their passports with exit visas, then left.

Hollis, Lisa, and Alevy sat in the small lounge. An embassy security man stood near the front desk, a few feet from the KGB Border Guard. Two more security men stood near the rear entrance, keeping the Border Guard there company. Bert Mills sat on the other side of the lounge. Hollis remarked to Alevy, 'Why all the firepower? One or two would have done.'

'Show of force.'

It occurred to Hollis, not for the first time, that Seth Alevy relished the fact that his lifelong game against Moscow was being played in Moscow. Hollis wondered what would become of Seth Alevy when he had to leave here.

Three Hispanic-looking men walked into the lounge, wearing red Lenin pins on the lapels of their suit jackets. They gave Hollis, Lisa, and Alevy an unfriendly look, and one of them said something in Spanish that made the other two laugh. They sat down in the adjoining club chairs.

Alevy commented, 'There's a direct Aeroflot to Havana in half an hour.'

Lisa said, 'I think they said something insulting. I heard the word *gringo*.'

'Let it pass,' Alevy advised.

There were drink lists printed in several languages on the coffee table, and Alevy said, 'They sometimes have orange juice here. How about a little vodka with it?'

'Fine.'

He looked around for the waitress he'd seen before, then stood and went to the woman at the front desk. After a minute he came back and said, 'No orange juice. So I got Bloody Marys. Okay?'

'Fine.'

A waitress came with four glasses of green fluid. Alevy said in English, 'Everything in this fucking country is red, but the tomato juice is green. Would you call this a Bloody Grasshopper?'

The waitress set the four glasses down, then placed a plate of salmon and black bread on the table. 'For hungry. Good-bye. Good trip.'

'Thank you.' Alevy remarked to Hollis and Lisa, 'Every once in a while, somebody here is nice to you, and it makes you think.' Alevy raised his glass. 'Safe trip.' He finished his entire drink and sighed. 'Vodka. The one thing they do right, by God.'

Lisa said to Alevy, 'You're in a good mood today. Glad to see us go?'

'No, no. Just happy for you. Both of you.'

There were a few seconds of awkward silence, then Lisa said to Alevy, 'Is that extra drink for you?'

'Oh, I forgot. It's for Bert Mills.' Alevy picked up the drink and stood, seemed to lose his balance, and spilled the green tomato juice on the head of one of the Cubans. 'Oh, I'm terribly sorry. Mucho fucking clumsy –'

The three Cubans sprang to their feet.

381

Hollis stood, and Bert Mills was suddenly there too. The Cubans sized up the situation quickly. They gathered their attaché cases amid a flourish of handkerchiefs and retreated to one of the side rooms. Alevy said, 'I feel just awful.'

Mills laughed and walked back to his chair. Hollis noticed the two KGB Border Guards grinning.

Hollis always marveled at Alevy's little army of well-mannered thugs. In addition to the twenty or so CIA intelligence officers, there were about a dozen embassy security men whom Alevy had use of. Alevy had once told Hollis that if he could get the thirty-man Marine contingent under his control, he could take the Kremlin.

Alevy wiped his hand with a cocktail napkin. 'I always meet interesting people in the diplomatic lounge.'

Lisa smiled at Alevy but said nothing.

Hollis realized that Alevy was showing off one last time for Lisa. Hollis excused himself and left the lounge.

Levy and Lisa remained standing. Alevy said, 'I'm not happy to see you go. I'm sad to see you go.

Lisa didn't respond.

Alevy added, 'I thought we could give it another try.'

'I thought about it too. But other things have happened.'

'I know.' Alevy picked up her glass and drank from it. 'Well . . . maybe our paths will cross again, in some other godforsaken place. This is a strange life we've chosen.'

'The Russians say, "To live a life is not as easy as crossing a field."'

'The Russians say a lot of things that don't make any sense. Tartar haiku. You like the place. I don't.'

'But you like being the premier spy in the capital of the evil empire.'

'Oh, yes.'

'That's what bothers me. Try to see the evil side of what *you* do.'

'I don't have time for moral abstractions. My job is to try to fuck the Soviets, and they respect me for it.'

'Alright, we've been through this. I just ask you to try to understand these people. As people. It will help you professionally as well as personally if you understand them.'

'I try. We all try.'

'Do we?' She glanced at the door, but there was no sign of Hollis. She put her hand on Alevy's arm. 'Be careful, Seth. I worry about you.'

'Do you? You be careful yourself. You're not home yet.' He finished her drink. 'Piece of advice, Lady Lisa. His age is not that important. Neither is his present marital status. But if he enters that macho world of jet jockeys again, you've got a problem.'

'I'm not considering marriage. What, by the way, were you two talking about until six A.M.? You both look like hell.'

'I just needed some Red Air Force stats, and I needed Hollis' name on the report as a cosigner. They respect him in Langley. Sorry if I intruded on your plans. Won't happen again.' Alevy glanced at his watch. 'I'm going to find Sam and say good-bye. You'll be alright here.' He looked at her. 'Well . . . there's more I'd like to say, but they know too much about my personal life already.' He jerked his thumb up at the ceiling. 'The evil ones. 'They get lots of tidbits from this room.'

She shook her head. 'I still never think about it.'

'You don't have to anymore. Just watch what you say when Sam returns. When you board the Pan Am 747, you can say whatever you like all the way to Frankfurt and beyond. The free world. I like that old Cold War phrase. The free world.'

They both stood awkwardly for a moment, then Lisa said, 'Write to me.'

'Of course.'

'I'll let you know where I wind up.' She suddenly laughed. 'How stupid of me. You'll probably know before I do. I guess that was part of our problem. A woman likes to have a little privacy and a little mystery about herself. But you knew everything inside the walls of our castle. You were our Merlin.'

'I never thought of it quite that way. Maybe that's why no one asks me to bowl.' He smiled.

She gave him a kiss on the cheek. 'Good-bye, Seth. Thank you for everything –' She wiped her eyes. 'We'll meet again.'

'I know we will.'

Alevy suddenly pulled her close to him, put his mouth to her ear, and whispered, 'Listen to me. You don't have to leave on this flight . . . you have until midnight to leave Russia. There are two more flights to Frankfurt today. Tell Sam you're not feeling well, and –'

'Why?'

'I . . . I thought we could . . . spend some time . . . a proper good-bye.'

She looked at him. 'Is that a proposition?'

'No. Really, I just . . . look, what I'm trying to say is that Hollis is a target. I don't like the idea of you being near him –'

'I know that. He told me that, and I could figure that out for myself. But I'm not a wilting flower, Seth. I was willing to share any danger with you, and I will give him the same loyalty.'

Alevy looked at her, and a sad smile came across his face. He nodded. 'That's why I love you.'

They kissed, and Seth Alevy turned and walked quickly from the waiting room, the Russians and Americans in the room looking at him, then at Lisa.

She sat down again and dabbed her eyes with a handkerchief as she leafed through an old copy of *Time*. 'Damn you, Alevy. Damn men.' She looked at her watch. 'Come on, Sam.'

Alevy found Hollis in the narrow corridor that led back to the main concourse. Alevy pointed at the ceiling, and they walked back to the crowded terminal building. They stood quietly among the milling people for a minute, then Alevy said, 'Did you want to speak to me?'

Hollis replied, 'I assume the meeting went well, or you'd be in a less playful mood.'

'It went fine.'

'You got the microfilm?'

'I did.'

'Did you look at it?'

'Briefly.'

Hollis drew a deep breath of impatience. 'I can either pull teeth, or I can knock them all out, right here.'

Alevy regarded Hollis a moment, then his eyes became unfocused as though his mind just got a phone call. He refocused on Hollis and said, 'Sam, I promise you, you're still on the case. You have my word on that.'

Hollis studied Alevy's face a moment. 'Okay. Was the microfilm good stuff?'

'The jackpot. But I don't know how the FBI is going to proceed with it.'

'That's ther problem, not ours.'

'Well, it's everyone's problem. I'd like to see us just go public with the photos – TV and newspapers, movie theaters, shopping malls. That would blow every one of those Russian agents whether they're White House janitors, defense workers, or congressional sides.' Alevy added, 'However, I think the government wants the FBI to try to round them up quietly.'

'But you'd like it public. That would finish the summit and arms talks once and for all.'

'All that nonsense deserves to be dead and buried. What benefit is there to us to talk peace and trade, when the Soviets have massive economic problems and social unrest? As our mutual hero, Napoleon Bonaparte, said, "Never interrupt an enemy while he's making a mistake."'

Hollis smiled. 'You *are* a manipulative son of a bitch.'

'Thank you. Speaking of manipulators, do you know who Charlie Banks works for?'

'Probably State Department Intelligence.'

'Right. You're sharper than you look.' Alevy moved toward

a group of Japanese businessmen who were talking loudly and animatedly, providing good sound cover from directional microphones. Hollis followed him. Alevy said, 'State Department Intelligence here in Moscow spend most of their time spying on people like you and me. They think we're trying to sabotage their diplomatic initiatives.'

'Where would they get an idea like that?'

'Beats me. Anyway, SDI would be harmless except that they're an arm of the venerable and powerful Department of State. And in the matter of the Charm School, Charles Banks is watching the situation very closely and reporting, I believe, directly to the President.'

'He's watching *you* very closely. What I don't understand is how anyone is going to resolve the problem of the Charm School without all hell breaking loose.'

'There are ways to resolve it quietly. As long as Dodson doesn't show up.'

'What if he does show up?'

Alevy replied, 'I doubt if he'd make it over the wall. The militia and KGB have orders to shoot on sight. But if he did, by some miracle, get inside the embassy or get to a Western reporter in Moscow, then Banks, the Secretary of State, and the President will be singing my company song.'

Hollis said, 'I keep thinking that if Dodson did get over the wall, he might not be home free. Is that an insane thought?'

'Yes, but it's a good thought. I think old affable Charlie Banks is under orders to have Dodson killed to shut him up.' Alevy added, 'And you think I'm nuts and immoral? Our government is ready to write off three hundred American airmen for some abstraction they call détente. Hell, I can't even pronounce it, and the fucking Russians don't even have a word for it.'

'Seth, I'll try to separate the white hats from the black hats on the plane. Meet me in DC, and we'll talk to some of my people in the Pentagon. I won't get involved in conspiracies, but we can talk about ways to bring those men home and not make them pawns in everyone's power game.'

'Alright. I'll meet you in DC.'

Hollis asked, 'By the way, what did you think of General Surikov?'

'I spoke to him in the basement of the antique shop for half an hour. I don't think he liked me.'

'He doesn't have to like you. You're not going to be his control officer. He's leaving.'

'Well, that's the other thing. I agree with you that he's a legitimate defector. But I don't think he's going to make it in the West.'

'A lot of people who already live in the West aren't making it. That's not your concern. Just get him there.'

'I'm telling you, Sam, he'll die when he leaves mother Russia. I know the type.'

'He has religion.'

'I'd love to keep him here in his job. He would be the highest-ranking agent we've ever had in the Soviet military. I'd turn him over to Bert Mills and –'

'Don't give me that crap about him not surviving in the West. If you had an ounce of human compassion left in you, you'd see the man was suffering. If we ever do beat this system, it will be because we hold out an honest light to the decent people here. I never understood Surikov's motives because I wasn't thinking of the most obvious motive – the man wants to be free, whatever that means to him. He delivered, now *you* deliver.'

'Alright . . . it was a thought –'

'Take a leave, Seth. You need it.'

'Oh, I know. By the way, I scanned that microfilm and found a picture of our custodian, Mr Kellum, born Anatoli Vladimirovich Kulagin, in Kursk, USSR.'

Hollis nodded. 'So we bagged the first one. How about Mrs Kellum?'

'Didn't come across her yet. Lots of work to do on that. She may be a real American, and she may or may not know who her husband is.'

'What are you going to do with the Kellums?'

'I'll debrief them in the cellar for a few months. Dick, we know, is guilty, and as far as I'm concerned Ann is guilty by association. However, we can't get them back to stand trial. And I can't keep them locked up here forever. Also, they're no good as trading cards because the Soviets will never claim them. So . . .' Alevy scratched his head. 'I don't know. Any ideas? What should I do with Dick and Ann, Sam?'

'Why don't you shoot them in the head and drop them in the Moskva?'

'Excellent idea. Why didn't I think of that?'

Hollis said, 'I have to go.'

Alevy put his hand on Hollis' arm. 'When I was a young college liberal, I used to wonder how American airmen could drop bombs on the Vietnamese. Now I'm all grown up, contemplating cold-blooded murder for my country, and an airman is looking down his nose at me. Can't win.'

'You've made your point. I apologize. Do what you have to do.'

'Thank you. I will. Well, so much for bad business. The good news is that the microfilm was an incredible counter-intelligence coup. Three *thousand* agents. My God, Sam, that's the biggest single catch in history. And now with those Russian Americans in our hip pocket, we can tackle the problem of the Charm School itself.'

'A trade?'

Alevy nodded. 'Three thousand of theirs for three hundred of ours. It's a possibility. And we have you to thank for that. You did it, Sam. I think you got your people home.'

'But I thought there were people in Washington who didn't want them home.'

'We'll work on that. You have some clout yourself now. When you get to DC, you're going to be treated like a conquering hero. No parades, of course. Very quiet. But the top CIA people and your people in the Pentagon are going to present you with some awards. Real awards. And, you're going to have an interview with the President, and don't be surprised if he pins a general's star on you. I just got that over the wire. I'd like to be there if you don't mind.'

'Fine.'

'You outdid me this time, Sam.'

'Surikov just fell into my lap, Seth. You know that as well as I do.'

'Don't be modest. Well . . . a personal note . . . on the subject of Lisa, all I can say is that I'm glad it was you and not some Foreign Service wimp.'

Hollis didn't reply.

'Good luck. I wish you both happiness.'

'Thank you.' Hollis put out his hand. 'And thanks for showing me around.'

Alevy took his hand. 'We'll meet again, in a better place than this.'

Hollis turned and walked toward the diplomatic wing. He said to himself, 'That would be just about anyplace, Seth.'

Hollis also had the impression that Alevy liked it here, or more accurately, needed to be here. He needed to breathe Moscow air and smell Moscow river fog. He needed the KGB, and in some perversely reciprocal arrangement they needed him, or they'd have had him expelled or killed long ago.

Possibly Seth Alevy was a living legend at the Lubyanka, and his stature increased the self-worth of his adversaries. But now their macabre dance of death and destiny was drawing to an end.

The further thought occurred to him that what Seth Alevy was saying about the Charm School wasn't computing. If three thousand Russians were heading east and three hundred Americans were heading west, and that balanced the equation, then what was in it for Seth Alevy? Answer: zero. So back to the problem.

29

A man in a heavy overcoat opened the outside door to the diplomatic lounge and looked at Lisa and Hollis. 'Pan Am. Frankfurt. Follow, please.'

Hollis and Lisa put on their coats and picked up their overnight bags.

Bert Mills came up to them. 'I'll go with you.'

Hollis said, 'No need.'

'I have orders.'

Hollis, Mills, and Lisa walked past the Border Guard with the submachine gun and followed the Russian with the overcoat outside, down a set of steps where a small airport bus waited on the tarmac. A fine powdery snow sifted down from a softly overcast sky, and a wan sun peeked through, casting a sickly yellow haze over the snowy tarmac. They boarded the bus, on which they were the only passengers, and the driver headed out to a taxiway where they saw a mammoth 747 bearing the blue and white markings of Pan Am.

Mills said, 'Look at that. Look at *that*.'

Hollis said, 'Looks good, guys.'

Mills said, 'Let's switch identities, Sam.'

'Can I go back to the embassy and sleep with your wife?'

Mills laughed. 'Sure. I'll wire her from Frankfurt.'

Lisa muttered, 'Pigs.'

As they got closer to the plane, Hollis noticed four Border Guards around it with submachine guns.

They pulled up to the boarding stairs and got out of the bus. Mills said, 'I'll hang around awhile. But I think you're home free.' He shook hands with Hollis and said, 'It's been a pleasure working with a pro;' He also took Lisa's hand. 'Safe trip.'

Hollis and Lisa went up the stairs and were met by a smiling woman who said in a twangy voice, 'Hi, I'm Jo, your flight attendant in Clipper Class. How're you folks this morning?'

Hollis noticed that she was deeply tanned, something he hadn't seen in a while. He replied, 'Just fine, Jo. You?'

'Real good. You folks traveling together?'

'Yes,' Lisa replied.

Jo looked at a boarding manifest. 'You're our DPLs, right?'

'Right,' Hollis replied. 'That's why we got the private bus and the bodyguard.'

Lisa poked him in the ribs.

Jo smiled and said, 'Clipper Class is right up that little spiral staircase there. Can I help you with your bags?'

'That's alright,' Hollis replied.

'How long you folks been here?'

'About two years,' Lisa replied.

'My Lord! I'll bet you're happy to be going home.'

'Yes.'

'Well, I'm sure glad we can help get you there.'

Hollis realized it had been a while since he'd had service with a smile, and it was sort of jarring. He said, 'I'm glad too.'

'Make yourselves at home up there. Soon as the boarding buses get here, I'll be up.'

Hollis led the way up the spiral staircase into the business section located in the dome of the 747. They hung their coats and stowed their bags in a closet, then took two seats near the front. There were two backward-facing seats across from them.

The domed cabin seemed eerily quiet, and Hollis had the fleeting thought that the 747 was a sham and Jo was a graduate of the Charm School. He laughed.

'What's funny?'

Hollis took her hand. 'I think this place finally got to me.'

'Well, the timing is good.'

The cockpit door opened, and a man in a blue uniform came through it. 'Hi. I'm Ed Johnson, the captain. Colonel Hollis and Ms Rhodes?'

'Right.'

Johnson looked around the empty cabin, then leaned over with his hands on the armrest. 'I have a message from the embassy in Bonn saying you folks got into a little scrape here.'

Hollis nodded.

'They were just advising the crew to keep an eye on things. I don't have any particulars except what I read in the papers.'

'That's about all of it.'

'You Air Force, Colonel?'

'Right.'

'Flew what?'

'F-4's mostly.'

'Nice.'

Johnson and Hollis talked airplanes for a while, and Lisa flipped through that week's *Time*. Johnson went back to the cockpit, and Lisa observed, 'You sounded like you were interested in a subject for a change.'

'I'm only interested in sex, sports, and religion.'

'Have you come to any decisions about flying?'

'I don't think the decision is mine to make.'

'But would you go back if you could?'

'I don't know. I know that the last aircraft I piloted came down without me in it. Yet . . . sometimes I can feel the controls in my hands and feel the engines spooling up, and the vibrations through the airframe, full power, then the dash down the runway, rotate, climb out . . . you understand?'

'I guess if you put it that way, I do.' Lisa went back to her magazine, then looked up again. 'I always feel like a stranger in my own country when I go home on leave.'

Hollis replied, 'It takes a few weeks to get into sync with any country, including your own.'

'I know.' She added, 'You know, Sam, I almost feel like Moscow and the embassy was home and I'm heading to a strange country. I miss my apartment and my office, my friends. I miss Moscow. I think I'm going to cry again.'

'I understand.' And he did, because he felt an inexplicable twinge of nostalgia himself. Though why he should feel that for a country that had almsot killed him was a mystery. But he'd felt that for Vietnam too. He supposed there were some countries that in a perverse way alerted your senses and put you on full throttle every day. And whatever came afterward was just cruise control. 'It's a common emotion. You make good friends on hardship tours. Sort it out.'

She wiped her eyes with a tissue. 'Sorry.'

The passengers started to board, and Hollis could hear footsteps on the stairs. Mike Salerno was the first person up the stairs, and he sat in one of the seats facing them. He said, 'You guys get boarded before first class.'

'One of the lesser perks,' Hollis replied. 'How did you get up here so fast?'

'Pushed and shoved. I'm a reporter.'

Lisa asked, 'Are you going home for good?'

'No, I put in for two weeks' therapeutic leave.'

On the tarmac below, Hollis saw two men in brown overcoats standing in the snow, speaking to two armed men who wore the green overcoats of the KGB Border Guards.

Lisa looked at her watch. 'I hope this snow doesn't delay the takeoff.'

Hollis noticed that only six more people had come into the Clipper Class section, which could hold about fourteen passengers. There was a middle-aged couple sitting near the staircase whom Hollis could hear speaking with British accents and four German businessmen sitting across the aisle in the other facing seats. One of them had spoken to Jo in English.

Jo went to the front of the cabin and announced without a PA microphone, 'There'll be a few minutes' delay until we get clearance. The weather is slowing up takeoffs. Soon's we get airborne, we'll get the free drinks moving.' She turned to the four Germans. 'Okay, gentlemen?'

The one who spoke English nodded to her and translated for the other three.

393

Hollis stood, went to the back of the small dome, and looked out the window. Their bus was still there, and Bert Mills was leaning against it. One of the men in a brown coat walked over with an armed Border Guardsman and had some words with Mills. Mills pulled out his diplomatic passport and shook it at the KGB men. Hollis could see that the bus driver was getting agitated, probably never having seen anyone argue with a gentleman of the *Komitet*. Mills didn't speak much Russian, which was probably an advantage in that situation, Hollis thought. Mills was pointing to the ground at his feet, and Hollis could imagine him saying. 'I'm staying right fucking here until that plane leaves.'

Finally the KGB man in the brown coat said something to the bus driver, and the bus moved off, leaving Mills on the snowy taxiway, a half kilometer from the terminal. The KGB man smirked, turned, and went back to his car. Mills made an uncomplimentary gesture with his middle finger, then stood with his hands in his pockets. The KGB man watched him from the car. Hollis went back to his seat.

Lisa asked, 'Everything alright?'

'Yes.'

Salerno commented, 'You guys jumpy? Don't blame you.'

Hollis read that morning's *International Herald Tribune*. Salerno read a pulp detective novel featuring a character named Joe Ryker, NYPD, and Lisa had exchanged her *Time* for *Vogue*. She said to Hollis, 'If we're going to live in the States, I'll need clothes like this.'

He glanced at her magazine. 'Maybe we should live someplace else.'

She commented, 'I could have bought a black sable coat here for ten thousand and resold it in the States for forty.'

Hollis mumbled something behind his newspaper.

'What's holding us up?'

'Weather.' Hollis heard the engines spool up, then wind down.

Jo came out of the cockpit and said, 'Cleared for takeoff.

Seat belts, please. No smoking.' She rattled off the preflight safety regulations, then took an empty seat. The 747 began to move.

As the aircraft rolled down the taxiway, Hollis saw Bert Mills waving, and Hollis waved back. The aircraft lumbered to the runway and turned on to it. The engines roared, the aircraft strained against its brakes, then began its race down the snowy concrete. No one spoke. The 747 nosed up, and the wheels bumped into their wells. Salerno said, 'Airborne.'

The big aircraft began its climb over the white knobby hills northwest of Moscow. Lisa said, almost to herself, '*Da svedahnya*.'

Salerno snorted, 'Good riddance. For two weeks.'

Lisa looked out of the window at the snow-dusted landscape. She saw the Minsk-Moscow highway to the south, the tiny villages that dotted the open fields, and the dark green pine forests that covered much of the countryside. Her eyes followed the Moskva River west toward Mozhaisk and Borodino. The aircraft rose into the cloud cover, and she turned from the window. 'I'll never see this place again.'

Salerno commented, 'Lucky you.'

Hollis said to him, 'She likes Russia.'

Salerno grumbled, 'Easy to say when you lived in decent housing and shopped in the embassy commissary. Try living like a Russian. I did it for a story.'

'Alright,' Lisa said. 'We all know that. But you can like the people without liking the system.'

'The people *are* the system. The KGB is made up of Russian people.'

'You sound like *him*.' She pointed at Hollis.

Hollis turned the page of his newspaper. 'I don't even know what you two are talking about. Who are these Russians?'

Salerno laughed. 'I love it, Sam.' Salerno looked at Lisa. 'Listen, Lisa, I've been on assignment in a half dozen countries. I found good and bad in all of them. But this place is beyond hope.'

Lisa let out a breath of exasperation.

Salerno added, 'Well, maybe you can appeal your non-person status. The Soviets sometimes rehabilitate people for reasons known only to themselves.'

Hollis said, 'Who are the Soviets?'

Salerno laughed again. 'Look, Lisa, I understand you have mixed feelings. But bottom line, you're feeling a little easier already. Right? That place' – he jerked his thumb toward the window – 'is *tense*. I've seen it on other flights out of here – tourists and business people – smiling, giddy. Do you know that the pilot *announces* when we cross into West German airspace? What does *that* tell you?'

Hollis yawned.

Lisa picked up a magazine.

Salerno said, 'I'll tell you something else I learned about that Fisher business.'

Neither Hollis nor Lisa responded.

Salerno went on, 'I found out from his parents that he was booked at the Rossiya, so I went there on the hunch that he'd actually gotten to Moscow. And guess what? I found an English tourist who remembered the car parked in front of the Rossiya with Connecticut license plates.'

Lisa lowered her magazine. Hollis asked, 'What do you think that means, Mike?'

'I'm not sure. What do the people in the embassy think it means?'

Hollis replied, 'How can I tell you that, if we're hearing this for the first time?'

Salerno leaned forward. 'You know damned well that Fisher got to the Rossiya. Fact is, guys, he called the embassy from the hotel. Spoke to you, Lisa.'

Lisa asked, 'How do you know that?'

'You got a leak. So how are the people there going to handle this? What is Seth Alevy's office making of this?'

Hollis replied, 'Seth Alevy is a political affairs officer and has nothing to do with the Fisher business.'

'Come on, Sam.'

Hollis thought a moment. He couldn't conceive of how that call from Fisher to the embassy was leaked. Only he, Lisa, Alevy, Banks, and the ambassador knew of it. Although it might have been the Marine who took the call. Hollis said, 'I'll discuss this with you after we're out of the USSR.'

Salerno said, 'You're on an American aircraft at twenty thousand feet and climbing.'

'Nevertheless, it will keep until Frankfurt.'

Jo came by with champagne, and they each took a glass. Salerno held out his glass. '*Na zdorovie.*'

They drank, and Hollis commented, 'Your accent is terrible.'

'Is it? I seem to get by.'

'Where did you learn your Russian?'

'Berlitz.'

'Ask for your money back if you can't even pronounce a standard toast.'

Salerno said, 'Sam, can I talk to you in private a minute? Nothing to do with the Fisher business. Promise.' He motioned toward two empty seats.

Hollis replied, 'Lisa Rhodes is a representative of the United States government. She has a secret clearance. You can talk right here.'

Salerno nodded. 'No offense. Okay. Listen, I heard something weird. I heard that you guys were holding an American in the embassy. I don't know if this guy is supposed to be a spy, or if he was somebody who got into trouble in Moscow and made it into the embassy, or both. It was a very strange story.'

'Sounds strange,' Hollis agreed.

Lisa took a cigarette from her bag. 'Mind if I smoke? Mike, you smoke. Go ahead.'

'Yeah.' Salerno took a pack of Marlboros from his pocket and lit one. 'Come on, guys. Give me a break on this one. You holding someone in the embassy? I know you got underground cells there. Someone, one of the service people, tipped me.' He

397

drew on his cigarette. 'Says there's at least one American in an isolation cell. Maybe two.'

Hollis studied Salerno a moment. He wondered if Salerno was fishing for the Kellums or for Dodson. He wondered, too, where this man got his information. Salerno didn't know it yet, but Frankfurt was as far as he was going for a while.

Lisa said to Salerno, 'That's absurd.'

Salerno replied, 'No, it's not. And I heard too that this guy in the isolation cell is also wanted by the KGB. He's either one of theirs or a defector or something like that. But they want him.'

Hollis noticed that the fingers in which Salerno was holding his cigarette kept moving in a habitual way to straighten the cigarette to keep it from sagging. But since it was an American cigarette, it did not sag, giving Hollis the impression that Mike Salerno sometimes smoked cigarettes that did sag. Hollis said, 'You two enjoy your nicotine, don't you?' He asked Salerno, 'You smoke the local brands?'

'Hell, no.'

'Did you ever?'

Salerno glanced at him quickly. 'No, why?'

'Just wondered.'

Salerno stubbed out his cigarette and picked up his paperback.

The flight attendant, Jo, came over to them, carrying a brown-paper parcel. 'Ms Rhodes?'

'Yes?'

'I was asked to give you this after we got airborne.' She handed the package to Lisa.

Lisa asked, 'Who gave it to you to give to me?'

'A Russian guy. An airport official.' She added, 'It's usually against regulations to take anything aboard like that, but it was from an airport official, and he said it was x-rayed and all. So it's okay.' She glanced at Hollis, then said to Lisa, 'The Russian said it was a farewell gift.' She smiled and moved away.

Lisa sat looking at the package on the seat tray. She said

to Hollis, 'This is the icon, Sam, addressed to USIS in DC.' She stared at it awhile, then looked at Hollis. 'You said it was cleared for the diplomatic pouch.'

'It was,' Hollis replied. 'I told them in the mailroom. What did they say when you brought it there?'

'I . . . didn't. Mrs Kellum saw it and said she was going to the mailroom, so she took it. I told her it was cleared for the pouch.' She looked at Hollis. 'It's been opened. The tape is broken.' She touched the brown paper. 'The foam rubber I used is missing.'

Hollis didn't say anything.

'I'm going to open it.'

'Don't.'

She ripped at the paper, and Hollis held her wrist. She pulled her hand away and tore the paper off, then let out a stifled sob. 'Oh . . . oh, my God . . . Sam . . .'

Hollis looked at the icon lying on the table. Deeply gouged into the painted wood, obscuring the face of the archangel, was a hammer and sickle.

Lisa looked at him and tried to say something, but no words came out. Tears formed in her eyes.

Hollis threw a piece of paper over the icon and took her hand.

Salerno looked up from his book and said, 'What's that? What's the matter?'

The PA system crackled, and a voice came over the loud-speakers. 'Ladies and gentlemen, this is Captain Johnson speaking. We're experiencing a minor electrical problem, and we've been instructed to land in Minsk. Nothing to be concerned about. We'll be on the ground in fifteen minutes, and hopefully airborne again shortly. Please fasten your seat belts for an approach to Minsk. Thank you.'

The seat-belt lights and no-smoking lights blinked on.

Salerno said, 'It looks like our farewell to Russia was premature.' He looked at Hollis and smiled.

30

The Pan Am 747 touched down at Minsk Airport, its rollout bringing it near the end of the short runway. The sky was still overcast, but Hollis noticed it hadn't snowed here. Lisa had slid the paper off the icon and was staring at it. Hollis asked, 'How are you?'

She didn't reply.

The aircraft taxied toward the small modern terminal building, and Hollis saw four mobile stairways coming out to meet them, which was not normal for a routine deplaning. Behind the stairways were four buses. Hollis also noted that the 747 was some distance from the terminal.

Hollis looked back at Lisa. 'It can be restored. A museum restorer can do it. You'd never know.'

She looked at him blankly.

Salerno turned the icon toward him. 'Goddamned shame. Who would do something like that?'

Hollis replied, 'I can think of one outfit right away.'

'You mean the KGB?' Salerno plucked at his lip. 'You mean they got the embassy penetrated? Hey, remember the ambassador's Steinway? What a bunch of shits. But I thought you were all secure there now. Maybe it was that gardener you guys got. Vanya?'

Lisa took Hollis' hand. 'I feel so . . . violated.' She looked at him. '*Why?* Why, Sam?'

'You know.'

'Yes . . . but it's so senseless. So petty and vengeful.'

'That's them.'

'Those bastards . . . bastards!'

The four Germans looked over at them.

Salerno said, 'It probably *can* be fixed up. A little wood

filler, paint brush, good as new. Could have been worse.'

Lisa looked at the icon. The hammer and sickle had been gouged into the wood with a rough tool, the sickle's curved blade running around three edges of the painting. The hammer's handle slashed diagonally across the body, and the hammerhead was a rectangle of raw splintered wood where the angel's face had been. Lisa took a deep breath. 'I'm going to keep it just as it is.'

Hollis squeezed her hand. 'Good.'

'Just the way they gave it to me.'

Salerno shrugged and glanced out the window. 'Never been to Minsk.' He looked at Hollis. 'You?'

'No.'

Salerno's lips formed a thin smile. 'Hey, guys, is your diplomatic immunity good here?'

Lisa looked up from the icon. 'You know that it's good all over the Soviet Union. But why would we need diplomatic immunity?'

'You never know.'

Before the 747 came to a halt, Jo stood near the forward galley door. She announced, 'Ladies and gentlemen, the electrical repair might take a while, so what we're going to do is deplane. Please take all your personal things. Okay?' She opened the closet and handed out coats and bags. The aircraft came to a halt.

The pilot, Ed Johnson, appeared at the door between the galley and cockpit and motioned to Hollis. Hollis said to Lisa and Salerno, 'Go ahead.' He went over to Johnson, and they stood in the small galley. Johnson said, 'It's not an electrical problem. We got a radio message directly from Sheremetyevo tower saying they got a bomb threat.'

Hollis nodded.

'The Soviet civil aviation authorities instructed me to set it down in Minsk, which was the closest airport that could handle this craft.'

'So why aren't we sliding down the emergency chutes?'

'Well, that's the thing. As we're making the final approach, Sheremetyevo calls again and says they have information the bomb is an altitude device, so we're safe. That's pretty screwy. I mean, do they actually have the guy who made the threat? Are they believing him about what kind of bomb it is? They wouldn't answer any questions, they just said to land at Minsk and no emergency evacuation. They said they didn't want to upset the passengers or have any injuries on the chutes. I demanded four stairways and got them.' Johnson looked Hollis in the eye. 'I think it's a hoax. Somebody wants this plane down in Minsk.'

'Could be.'

'Does this have anything to do with your problem?'

'Quite possibly.'

'Anything I or the crew can do?'

'Not without jeopardizing yourselves. If I don't get to Frankfurt with you, call a General Vandermullen in the Pentagon. He's my boss.' Hollis took a paper napkin from the galley counter and wrote the telephone number on it. 'Just give him your professional opinion of this emergency landing.'

'Will do.'

'And not a word to anyone while you're in East Bloc airspace. Not even your copilot.'

'Okay. Good luck.'

They shook hands, and Hollis went down the spiral stairs to the door, where the mobile staircase had already been set up. Hollis descended the stairs. In the bus were Lisa, Salerno, the English couple, and the four Germans from the Clipper Class, plus about a dozen people from first class. The door closed behind him, and the bus pulled away. Hollis sat in an empty seat beside Lisa. She asked, 'What did that pilot want?'

'Your phone number.'

'Why do I ask you questions?'

'Beats me.'

Salerno, in the seat behind them, asked Hollis, 'Did he tell you what the hell is going on?'

'No.'

The bus took them to the terminal, where they were shown into a small waiting room not large enough to accommodate the coach passengers. Hollis had the feeling that he and Lisa had been neatly cut from the main pack, and there would be a further isolation when someone offered them diplomatic courtesies.

A short, squat man in a ludicrous mustard-colored suit walked into the room, followed by an attractive woman. The man held up his hand and said in accented English, 'Please, please.' The room became quiet, and the man said, 'I am Mr Marchenko, the Intourist representative here. I must inform you that there is no electrical problem on the aircraft. Soviet authorities have received a bomb threat –'

There was a gasp from the group.

'Please, please. Nothing to fear. However, the entire aircraft must be searched, and all luggage must be searched. This takes a long time. So, Intourist will take you all to Sputnik Hotel to have lunch, and maybe you may stay overnight.'

The woman with him repeated the announcement in German, then in French. Hollis was impressed with this uncharacteristic Soviet efficiency on such short notice. Obviously, they'd had help from another, more efficient Soviet agency.

Lisa said, 'I don't like this, Sam.'

Salerno lit a cigarette. 'I hope the damned Sputnik has a bar.'

Hollis said, 'I'll be right back.'

'Where you going?' Salerno asked.

'Men's room.' Hollis walked out the door of the waiting room and into a corridor, but a Border Guard with a holstered pistol motioned him back. Hollis said in Russian, 'I have to use the toilet.'

The Border Guard seemed surprised at his Russian. 'There's a toilet in the waiting room.'

'It's occupied.'

'Can't you wait?'

'No. I have a bad bladder.'

The Border Guard pointed down the hallway.

Hollis went into the small men's room, picked up a metal trash can, and threw it against the tile wall.

A second later the door swung open, and the Border Guard charged in as Hollis' foot shot up into the man's groin. The man made a grunting sound and doubled over. Hollis grabbed him by his high tunic collar and gunbelt and propelled him headfirst into the wall. The man moaned and sank to his knees. Hollis, still holding his collar, dragged him into a stall and sat him on the toilet, then closed the stall door, righted the trash can, and threw the man's cap into it. Hollis went back into the corridor and moved quickly to the main concourse of the terminal. He found the pay phones in a recess of a wall and put two kopeks in the slot and dialed the Minsk long-distance operator. 'Put me through to Moscow, two five two, zero zero, one seven.'

'Have sixty kopeks ready.'

Hollis heard a series of clicks as the call was routed through the Moscow operator, then through the KGB listening station on the way to the embassy. The phone rang twice before his direct office line was picked up. He barely heard a faraway voice say, 'Captain O'Shea.'

The operator cut in, 'Deposit sixty kopeks now.' Hollis shoved the first twenty-five-kopek piece in the slot, and O'Shea, knowing by the loud humming that someone was paying for a long-distance call, held the line. Hollis pushed the remainder of the kopeks in the slot, cursing the Soviet phone system. The humming stopped, and Hollis heard a clear line. 'Hel –'

A hand reached over Hollis' shoulder and pushed down the phone cradle. Hollis turned around and found himself looking down at the short, squat Mr Marchenko, now wearing an overcoat and flanked by two Border Guards whose shoulder boards were higher than the short man's head. Marchenko said, 'Colonel Hollis, everything is all arranged. No need to call.'

Hollis snapped, 'Where the hell do you get off interrupting my phone call?'

'Please?'

Hollis said in Russian, 'Move away!' He turned and put another two-kopek piece in the coin slot.

Marchenko said, 'Come, sir, Ms Rhodes is waiting for you. She seems anxious about you.'

Hollis turned back to the man. 'Where is she?'

'In the car. Please allow me to introduce myself again. I am Mr Marchenko, the senior Intourist representative in Minsk. The Soviet Foreign Ministry has wired, instructing me to extend special courtesies to you and Ms Rhodes. Will you follow me?'

'We require no special courtesies. We'll stay here at the airport.'

Marchenko shook his head. 'No, Colonel. I have strict instructions. Ms Rhodes is even now in the car awaiting you.'

Hollis' eyes went past the two uniformed Border Guards, and he spotted three men in brown leather trench coats in the center of the crowded concourse, hands in pockets, looking at him. He said to Marchenko, 'I want Ms Rhodes brought here to me. Now.' He turned and dialed the long-distance operator again and said in Russian, 'Connect me with Moscow, two five two, zero zero, one seven.'

'Colonel, there is no need to call. We will be late!'

'For *what*?' Hollis heard humming, buzzing, faraway voices, and other assorted sounds in the earpiece.

'A helicopter, sir. To take you back to Sheremetyevo. There is a Lufthansa flight leaving there at three-fifty-five for Frankfurt. This Pan Am flight in truth will not leave today. Come.'

Hollis considered several courses of action, none of which seemed promising. 'We're in no hurry. We'll stay here. I told you I want you to bring Ms Rhodes here.'

'But we have no choice. I have a cable from Moscow.'

'I'm sure you do. The question is, was the cable from the Foreign Ministry or Dzerzhinsky Square?'

'I don't comprehend you. Please, at least come out to the car and talk to Ms Rhodes and see what she wants to do. Come, she is most anxious about you.'

Hollis heard a voice come on the line. 'Moscow Central.' Hollis said, 'I want to be connected with two five two, zero zero, one seven.'

Marchenko added, 'And you perhaps are anxious about her.'

'You son of a –' The operator came on again. 'I cannot complete your call.' Hollis knew how to argue with Ma Bell, but if Moscow Central said they couldn't complete your call, that could mean anything from a busy phone to a KGB intercept on the line. Hollis would have faked a conversation with O'Shea, except that his coin was still half in the slot and wouldn't go in unless the call were completed. Hollis put the phone back on the hook.

Marchenko said, 'Intourist has already wired your embassy with your new departure. Please, sir, Miss Rhodes –'

Salerno suddenly appeared out of the corridor. 'There you are. What's all this?'

Hollis said, 'This is the answer to your question about my diplomatic status. It's still good.'

Marchenko said to Salerno, 'Do you hold a diplomatic passport?'

'Hell, no. I work for a living.' He pulled his Soviet press credentials from his pocket. '*Zhurnalista.*'

Marchenko responded, 'Then I must ask you to go back to the waiting room. Your bus will be leaving shortly.'

'Hold your horses.' He said to Hollis, 'They told Lisa you wanted her. What the hell's going on?'

'We're being offered a helicopter ride to Sheremetyevo to catch a Lufthansa to Frankfurt.'

'Well, lucky you. While I'm eating lard with mushroom gravy in the Sputnik, you guys will be landing in Frankfurt. In my next life I want to be a diplomat.'

'What were you in your last life?'

'A Russian.' Salerno laughed, then said to Marchenko, 'Hey, any chance of taking me back to Sheremetyevo?'

'Impossible.'

Salerno said to Hollis in Russian, '*Nelzya*. That's all you hear in this country. Everything is *nelzya*. Somebody ought to teach them "can do".'

Marchenko was at the end of his patience. 'Please, Colonel! Your companion is waiting.'

Salerno said to Hollis, 'I don't think you can refuse the honor, Sam.' Salerno motioned to the phones. 'I'll call the embassy right now and tell them that Intourist has rolled out the red carpet, pardon the pun. I doubt if there's anything funny about this, but the ambassador will straighten these people out if there is. So rest easy. Maybe I'll catch up with you in Frankfurt.'

Hollis said to Salerno in Russian, 'It was the cigarette, Michael. You kept straightening it with your fingers.'

Salerno smiled and winked, then replied in Russian, 'Don't tell anyone, and I'll owe you a favor. You'll need one shortly.' Salerno slapped Hollis on the shoulder, turned, and walked away.

Marchenko motioned toward the front doors of the terminal. Hollis walked through the small lobby, flanked by the two KGB Border Guards. They went out the glass doors, and Marchenko opened the rear door of a waiting Volga sedan.

Hollis saw Lisa in the rear seat. 'Lisa, get out of the car.'

Before she could respond, the driver pulled the car forward a few feet, and Marchenko slammed the door shut. Marchenko said to Hollis, 'Colonel, you're making this more difficult than it has to be.'

Hollis found himself being crowded by the two KGB Border Guards. The three men he'd seen in trench coats were standing a few feet away in front of the terminal doors. He thought he'd feel better if he made them work a bit, but the end result would be a clubbing or a chloroforming, followed by handcuffs and a bad headache. He walked to the car, and Marchenko again opened the door with a silly courtliness. Hollis got in, and Lisa threw her arms around him. 'Sam! I was worried – what's going on –?'

'It's alright.'

Marchenko got into the front, and the driver pulled away from the terminal.

Lisa took Hollis' hand in both of hers. 'They told me you were waiting for me, then –'

'I know.'

'Are we going back to Sheremetyevo?'

'Good question.' Hollis pushed on the door handle, but it moved only a fraction of an inch. A bell sounded, and a light on the dashboard came on.

Marchenko said, 'Colonel Hollis, you must be leaning on the door handle.'

Hollis didn't respond. He glanced out the rear window and saw another Volga in which were the three men in brown leather coats.

Lisa whispered into his ear, 'Are we being kidnapped?'

'In this country it's hard to tell. Sometimes you just have to ask.' Hollis leaned toward Marchenko. '*Komitet?*'

Marchenko moved around in his seat and looked back. 'No, no. Please. *Intourist.*' Marchenko smiled. 'Like you are an air attaché.' He laughed. 'So, winter is here now. How was Moscow?'

'Colder,' Hollis replied.

'It is always colder in Moscow. Do you know why?'

'No. Why?'

'Eight million cold hearts in Moscow. That is why. Me, I'm Byelorussian. The Great Russians are half Tartar, all of them. We're more Western here. Did you like Moscow?'

'Loved it.'

'Yes? You're joking. I hate Moscow. But sometimes I go there for business. Minsk is a beautiful city. The Germans destroyed ninety percent of it and killed a third of the population, including most of my family. What bastards. But we rebuilt it all. With not much help from Moscow. You see? The arrogant Germans and the cruel Muscovites. And who got caught in the middle? Us.'

'I know the feeling.'

The Volga turned on to a narrow concrete road that paralleled the airport fence.

Marchenko shifted his bulk back toward the front and continued his talk. 'But when Moscow gets a cold, we sneeze. Is that the expression?'

'The other way around,' said Hollis.

'Yes? When Moscow sneezes, we get a cold?' He shrugged and turned his head back to Lisa and Hollis. 'We are going to the helipad of course. There was no time to disengage your luggage from the others', so it will go on to Frankfurt airport tomorrow. You can have it sent to your Frankfurt hotel. But for tonight, you have your flight bags in the trunk. If there is anything I can do through Intourist, please let me know.'

Lisa replied, 'You've done enough.'

Marchenko chuckled.

The Volga turned into a wide concrete apron on which was painted a yellow X. 'Ah,' Marchenko said. 'Here we are. But no helicopter. We rushed for nothing.'

'Perhaps,' Hollis said, 'someone has misappropriated it.'

'Yes, we have that problem here. You know about that? Too much misappropriation. But I think this is the other problem we have. Lateness.'

The Volga sat at the edge of the concrete apron, its engine running. The backup car pulled alongside, and the three men got out but stayed near their car.

Marchenko looked at his watch, then leaned forward to peer through the windshield at the sky. 'Ah, there it is. You will make your Lufthansa flight,' Marchenko said, not bothering to put any sincerity in his voice any longer.

Lisa put her mouth to Hollis' ear. 'Tell me not to be frightened. Tell me everything's alright.'

'I think a little apprehension might be appropriate. Let's see what they're up to. They might just want to chat.'

Marchenko said, 'I don't like helicopters myself. In fact, there was a crash not far from here just today. The pilot and

409

copilot and two passengers, a man and a woman, were killed. All burned beyond recognition. Cremated, really. How are the families to know if they have the correct remains?'

Hollis understood now how it was being done. He could hear the sound of helicopter blades beating the dank, heavy air. A black shape appeared over the bare tree line, silhouetted against the grey sky. The helicopter hung for a second, then began its sloping descent toward them. Hollis recognized the shape as that of the Mi-28, a six-seat passenger craft with a jet turboshaft, somewhat like the Bell Jet Ranger. Aeroflot, in fact, did use these for VIP service between Moscow's airports and the city heliports. However, as the Mi-28 dropped in closer, Hollis saw it had the markings of the Red Air Force. He said, 'Mr Marchenko, this is very special treatment indeed.'

'Oh, yes,' Marchenko replied. 'You are very important people. In fact, I have been instructed to escort you. Please step out of the car.'

Hollis and Lisa got out of the Volga. The driver retrieved their bags and Lisa's icon from the trunk and set everything on the concrete near their feet. One of the men from the other Volga stood behind Hollis. Marchenko moved to Hollis' side and shouted over the noise of the approaching helicopter. 'The gentleman behind you is called Vadim. He will accompany us.'

Hollis thought he might have had a chance to try his hand at flying an Mi-28, but apparently Marchenko thought he'd remove the temptation.

The Mi-28 set down on the yellow X, and Marchenko shouted, 'Go, go!'

Hollis and Lisa moved toward the helicopter with Marchenko and Vadim behind them. A crewman slid open a small door in the side of the fuselage, and Hollis got in first, then helped Lisa up. The crewman motioned them to the two rear seats. They stowed their bags beneath the seats and sat. Vadim climbed in and sat in front of Lisa. Marchenko struggled to climb aboard, but the crewman didn't seem inclined to help, so

Vadim reached over and pulled Marchenko into the cabin. The crewman slid the door shut and settled into the copilot's seat. The helicopter rose.

Marchenko fell heavily into the last empty seat in front of Hollis and tried to catch his breath. 'Ah . . .' He turned to Hollis behind him. 'I'm getting old.'

Hollis replied in Russian, 'And fat.'

Vadim turned his head and gave Hollis a nasty look, confirming Hollis' suspicion that Marchenko was Vadim's boss and that neither Marchenko nor Vadim were Intourist guides.

The helicopter spun around and headed east, back in the direction of Moscow. Hollis noted that the pilot and the copilot were both Red Air Force officers. Hollis then looked at the profile of Vadim. He was a man of about thirty and looked muscular beneath his leather trench coat. He had one of the thickest necks Hollis had ever seen outside a zoo. Hollis doubted if he could get his hands around that neck, though perhaps he could garrote him with his tie and go for the man's pistol. But he knew not to underestimate fat Marchenko or indeed the two Red Air Force officers. He thought about how it could be done.

Marchenko, as though guessing at his thoughts, turned in his seat and said, 'Relax and enjoy the flight. We'll be in Sheremetyevo within three hours. You'll catch the Lufthansa flight in good time.'

Lisa replied, 'You're full of baloney, Marchenko.'

'Baloney?'

Hollis noticed that the helicopter was at about two thousand feet, traveling on a due east heading, the pilot land-navigating by the Minsk-Moscow highway. Snow began to appear on the ground, and a stiffening north wind caused the pilot to tack to port to compensate for the drift. The Mi-28 was capable of close to three hundred knots, and Hollis thought they'd get where they were going very fast.

Hollis put his arm around Lisa and massaged her shoulder. 'How you doing, kid?'

'Awful.' She looked down at the icon lying in her lap. 'This is what real faith is all about, isn't it? The belief that someone up there is looking after you.'

'Yes.' The key, Hollis thought, was to take out Vadim immediately, then find Vadim's pistol before Marchenko drew his. Shoot Marchenko and the two pilots, then fly the Mi-28 to the embassy quad. This was all presupposing, of course, that Marchenko was not simply a helpful Intourist man who was under strict orders from the Soviet Foreign Ministry to get the American diplomats on that Lufthansa flight to Frankfurt. But Hollis had to act on what he believed, not what Marchenko wanted him to believe. He thought about how to take out Vadim quickly.

Lisa said to Hollis, 'This icon has probably been kissed ten thousand times over the last three centuries. I've never kissed it . . .'

'Go ahead. Can't hurt.'

She brought the icon up to her face and pressed her lips to it.

Vadim sensed the movement and turned quickly in his seat. He looked at the heavy wooden icon, seeing and thinking what Hollis was simultaneously thinking. As Lisa lowered the icon, Vadim reached back with his right hand and grabbed it. Hollis brought his left knee up under Vadim's forearm and sliced the edge of his right hand down on Vadim's wrist. Above the sound of Vadim's scream, Hollis heard the wrist snap. Hollis snatched the icon from Lisa's lap and raised it, aiming the corner edge at the top center of Vadim's head where it would penetrate the coronal suture of the skull.

Marchenko had reacted faster than Hollis anticipated, sliding off his seat on to the floor, and he was now kneeling on one knee, pointing a heavy revolver at Hollis' chest. 'Stop! Stop!'

Hollis hesitated a moment, and Vadim slid down in his seat, then reappeared with his own pistol in his left hand. Hollis noticed that the color had drained out of Vadim's face and his right arm hung limply. The copilot had come back into the cabin holding a small-caliber automatic, suitable for inflight gunplay. He aimed the pistol at Lisa.

Marchenko said to Hollis, 'Put that down, slowly.'

Hollis lowered the icon, and Marchenko grabbed it away from him, then said to Vadim in Russian, 'Put your gun away.'

Vadim shook his head. 'I'm going to kill him.'

'Then I'll kill you. Put that away,' Marchenko snapped with authority.

Vadim put his pistol in the pocket of his trench coat. The Russians, Hollis recalled belatedly, like many Europeans, were not fond of holsters and preferred their pockets for their pistols, which was how Marchenko had gotten his out so quickly.

Marchenko stood and his head just touched the top of the cabin. He said to Hollis, 'It has always been my experience that people will believe any little lie that will comfort them and allow them to behave well while on the way to their execution. But I see you don't believe you're going to Sheremetyevo to board a Lufthansa flight, and you're quite correct.'

Hollis replied, 'I also know I'm not going to my execution, or you'd have taken care of it in Minsk.'

'Well, they want to talk to you first. And yes, I have orders not to kill you in transit under any circumstances. But I can and will kill Miss Rhodes the very next time you try something foolish.' He reached into his pocket and took out a pair of handcuffs. 'We don't have much need for these here, as Soviet citizens do what we tell them. However, I took these along as I know Americans have no respect for the law. Put them on.'

Hollis looked at Lisa, who was pale but composed. She said, 'I'm alright.'

Hollis snapped the cuffs on his wrists and sat back in his seat. Marchenko nodded to the copilot, who took his seat. Marchenko, too, sat down and said to Vadim in Russian, 'Is it broken?'

'Yes.'

'You can inquire what can be done about it when we land.'

Hollis suspected that Marchenko wasn't talking about a cast for Vadim's wrist, but a break for Hollis' wrist.

Marchenko examined the icon, which was now on his lap. 'This has been desecrated. Did *we* do this?'

Lisa replied, 'Who else?'

Marchenko made a clucking sound with his tongue. 'I don't like all this destruction of cultural treasures. I have my differences with the Russians, but we are all Slavs nonetheless. This is terrible.'

Hollis felt that Marchenko meant it, but if Marchenko were ordered to burn every church in Byelorussia he'd do it, with no more moral protest than the clucking of his tongue. Hollis said, 'Why don't you shut up?'

Marchenko turned his head and looked at Hollis with a hurt expression. 'There's no need to be rude.'

'On the fucking contrary, fat boy. You're more despicable than the swine in Moscow because you're a traitor to your own country and a Muscovite lackey.'

Marchenko seemed to be trying to control himself. He took a deep breath, then forced a smile. 'You see? I tell you a little about myself, and you exploit it. A typical treacherous Westerner. And you think you can abuse me because you know you are to be taken alive. Well, let me tell you something – you're going to stand trial for the murder of two Border Guards and perhaps a third one if the one you left in the toilet dies. We don't let that sort of thing go unpunished as you well know. You will probably be convicted and sentenced to death. They will tell you to write an appeal to the president of the Supreme Soviet, as that is a right under the Soviet constitution. As you are writing your appeal, someone will shoot you in the back of the head. That's how it's done. Very humane if you don't know what's coming. But I wanted you to know, Colonel Hollis, so that if they tell you you're going to draft an appeal of your death sentence, now you know you are probably going to your death. I thought I'd extend that kindness to you. Even if you are a murderer.'

'Shut up, Marchenko.'

Marchenko looked angry for the first time. He turned to Lisa. 'You seem alright, which is why I don't want to shoot you. But your friend here . . . well, I don't meet many Westerners. Perhaps I shouldn't judge by one spy. Yes?'

Lisa said, 'Will you give me my icon back? I promise not to bash it over your head.'

Marchenko laughed. 'I must have your oath to God.'

'I swear to God I won't bash it over your head.'

'Good.' Marchenko leaned back and handed it to her. 'You see? This religious relic started all of this unpleasantness. But I respect the believers. I have a female cousin my own age who believes in God. She became a Baptist for some reason. Another Western corruption, this Baptist religion. At least she could have become Orthodox if she wanted to be a martyr. Does this religion bring you comfort even now?'

'Yes.'

'Good. Perhaps someday when I'm old, right before the end, I will talk to a priest about getting into heaven. God will understand. No?'

Lisa replied, 'I think God can get pissed off by some people.'

'"Pissed off?"'

Hollis said, 'Marchenko, please, I implore you, shut the fuck up.'

'Yes? I think perhaps I talk too much. Not good in my job. Perhaps I *should* work for Intourist. I could talk all day to Westerners.' He turned to Vadim and asked in Russian, 'Do I talk too much?'

'No, sir.'

'See? Well, maybe I'll be quiet for a while.' Marchenko settled back in his seat.

Hollis looked at Lisa. 'Relax.'

She forced a smile and took his cuffed hands in hers. 'Don't feel bad.'

'Okay.'

They didn't speak much for the next two hours, and true to his word, Marchenko didn't say much either. Vadim was in worsening pain, and Hollis could see his wrist was twice its normal size. Vadim muttered an obscenity from time to time. The copilot belatedly remembered his first aid kit, and Vadim found codeine tablets in it. He took several of them.

Hollis was certain that the pilot and copilot remembered perfectly well they had the first aid kit all along. Hollis had observed that casual cruelty in Russians before, a real indifference to the suffering of strangers. Once you drank with them or ate with them or had your little *dusha dush*, they'd give you the shirt off their backs, no matter how brief the relationship. But if you weren't kith, kin, lover, or soul mate, you shouldn't expect anyone to volunteer painkillers for a smashed wrist, and Hollis had even heard of that sort of indifference in hospitals. And to add insult to cruelty, the copilot offered the painkillers not to make Vadim feel better, but to let Vadim know they were available for the last two hours. Also, Hollis thought, the flight crew being Red Air Force, and the charter passengers being KGB, the cruelty was not altogether casual. Even more bizarre, Hollis thought, was the fact that Vadim was not angry with the pilots for their lack of sympathy, but was still glaring at Hollis as the source of his pain. *Primitive*, Hollis thought. But Russians reacted to the moment, not to abstractions. That was something to keep in mind in the days ahead.

Hollis said to Lisa in a light tone, 'Well, do you want to say the words, "I quit"?'

She looked at him and said softly so no one else could hear, 'I've been thinking. You and Seth promised I would be kept informed in exchange for my help.'

'I'm keeping you informed. We've been kidnapped.'

'Not funny, Sam. I think you both *knew* this might happen.'

Hollis stayed silent a moment, then replied, 'We suspected.'

'More than suspected, I think. Do you know that Seth didn't want me to get on that flight?'

416

'No, I didn't know that.' But that was very interesting, Hollis thought. He said, 'No one ever promised to keep you informed, Lisa. Not in this business. *I'm* not fully informed, obviously.'

She nodded. 'He . . . he was trying to tell me something, but I guess I wasn't listening.'

'Nor were you telling me what he said.'

'Sorry.' She added, 'He said you were a target and I should stay away from you.'

'But you came along anyway.'

'I love you, stupid.'

Marchenko piped in, 'I hear whispers. No whispers. No secrets.'

Lisa ignored Marchenko and said to Hollis, 'If I didn't love you, I'd really be pissed at you.'

'I'll make it up to you. Dinner?'

'At Claridge's.'

'You got it.'

Marchenko said, 'Dinner? Yes, we missed our lunch. I'm hungry.'

Hollis said to him, 'You can live a month on your fat.'

Marchenko turned and looked at Hollis. 'You will be eating rats to stay alive in the Gulag.'

'Go to hell.'

'That's where we are going, my friend.'

Nearly three hours after they'd begun their flight, the helicopter began to descend. Hollis spotted the old Minsk road running along the Moskva River and noticed a dozen clusters of *izbas*, any one of which could have been Yablonya. Then, unexpectedly, he did spot Yablonya. He knew it was Yablonya because it was a stretch of black charred log cabins along a dirt road. Grey ash lay where kitchen gardens and haystacks once were. A bulldozer had dug a long slit in the black earth, and half the burned village had already been pushed into it. Hollis looked away from the window. To the list of scores to be settled – Fisher, Bill Brennan, and the three hundred American fliers – was now added the village of Yablonya.

About three minutes later, Hollis looked back out the window. They were at about five hundred feet now, and he saw the beginning of Borodino Field, the earthworks, monuments, then the museum. The pine forest came up, and the helicopter dropped more quickly. He saw the wire fence and the cleared area around it, then the helipad that Alevy had pointed out in the satellite photograph.

Lisa leaned over beside him and looked out the window. 'Are we landing?'

'Yes.'

'Where?'

'At the Charm School.'

Part 4

Wherever your travels in the Soviet Union take you, consult our Guidebook, and you will find the addresses of the camps, jails, and psychiatric prisons in your area: Slaves are building Communism . . . Visit them!

– Avraham Shifrin
The Guidebook to Prisons and Concentration Camps of the Soviet Union

'The Charm School,' Lisa said. 'Mrs Ivanova's Charm School.'

'Yes.'

She spoke as if to herself. 'The place Gregory Fisher mentioned, the place Major Dodson came from, where we went on the way to Mozhaisk . . . We're going to get a closer look at it now, aren't we?'

'Yes.' Hollis added, 'They are going to question you, so the less you know, the better.'

'Question me? Interrogate me?'

'Yes.' He could feel her hand tightening over his. He said, 'Just prepare yourself for some unpleasantness. Be brave.'

She drew a deep breath and nodded.

Marchenko turned in his seat and smiled at them. 'Not Sheremetyevo. But you knew that.'

'*Yeb vas*,' Hollis said.

'*Yeb vas*,' Lisa agreed.

'Fuck *you*,' Marchenko replied.

Vadim poked his head between the seats, looked at Hollis and Lisa, and made a cutting motion across his throat.

The helicopter continued its sloping descent toward the landing area, which Hollis noted was a natural clearing of tall yellow grass in the pine forest. On the south edge of the clearing was the log cabin he'd seen in the satellite photo. A narrow dirt track, barely visible among the pine trees, began at the cabin and ran a hundred yards south to the main camp road.

Most of the mile-square camp was not much more discernible from a few hundred feet, Hollis saw, than it had been from the satellite a few hundred miles up. Yet, because he had seen much of the world from the air, he could sense the general layout. There was a roughly circular gravel road that ran around the inside of the perimeter, probably a service road for the watchtowers. The main camp road was two lanes of winding blacktop that roughly bisected the camp from east to west. This road passed through the main gate and was actually a continuation of the one they had taken up from Borodino Field.

As they descended to about a hundred feet, Hollis saw on the main road a grim-looking concrete building in the center of the camp, probably the headquarters. Not far from that was a long wooden building with a green roof whose purpose he could not guess.

Some distance south of these two buildings was another clearing, but this one was man-made, a perfect rectangle, the size of a soccer field, which it undoubtedly was, and which could double as a parade ground or assembly area, a standard facility for any school or prison camp. In fact, as the helicopter got lower, he could see bleacher stands that would accommodate close to five hundred people.

Between the soccer field and the south perimeter of the camp, he saw the metal roofs of long barracks-like buildings that would be the separate compound within the compound for the KGB Border Guard detachment.

Hollis sketched an serial map in his mind and committed each detail to memory.

As they descended to about fifty feet, his eye caught something odd, and he looked at an area of the treetops about midway between the dachas and the headquarters. He realized that he was looking at a huge camouflage net covering about an acre, supported by living pine trees whose tops poked through the net. An axiom of both combat flying and spying was that neither aerial photographs nor overflights were a substitute for a man on the ground. He was about to be the man on the ground.

The helicopter settled on to the snow-dusted landing field. the copilot drew his pistol and slid open the door. Marchenko climbed out first, followed by Vadim. The copilot motioned with his gun at Lisa, and she took her bag and icon and jumped

422

down from the helicopter, refusing Marchenko's hand. The copilot looked at Hollis a moment and asked, 'Where did you think you were going to take this helicopter?'

'That's my business.'

'The American embassy, perhaps?' He glanced at the pilot and said, 'Neither of us would have flown you there.'

Hollis got his bag and held it in his cuffed hands. He stood, crouched over in the low cabin. 'Then I would have killed you both and flown it myself.'

'The copilot backed away from Hollis. 'You're a real murderer.'

'No, I'm an American Air Force officer who is being kidnapped.'

'The copilot's eyes widened in surprise. 'Yes?'

Marchenko called out, 'Come along!'

'Call my embassy and tell them Colonel Hollis is here. I'll see you get fifty thousand rubles for you and your friend here.'

Again, the copilot glanced over his shoulder. 'Get moving.'

Hollis edged towards the open door.

The copilot said softly, 'You shouldn't have broken that man's wrist. Do you know who those two are?'

'Intourist guides. Remember my offer.' Hollis jumped down from the helicopter to where Marchenko stood with Lisa and Vadim near a Zil-6, a Red Army vehicle somewhat like an American jeep but larger. Hollis heard the helicopter lift off and felt the rush of wind pushing him forward.

Marchenko opened the rear door of the Zil and said, 'Colonel Hollis, then Vadim, then Miss Rhodes.'

Hollis pushed his cuffed wrists under Marchenko's nose. 'Unlock these.'

Marchenko shook his head. 'Get in, please.'

Hollis said to Lisa, 'Get in first.'

She got in, and as Vadim tried to follow, Hollis shouldered him aside and got in the middle beside Lisa. Vadim sat beside

Hollis and said in Russian, 'I'm going to beat your fucking face to a pulp.'

'With which hand?'

'You shit –'

'Please!' Marchenko shouted. 'Enough!' He got into the front passenger seat and said to the driver, 'Headquarters.'

The Zil moved across the grass field toward the log cabin about a hundred yards off. Hollis looked at the cabin as they drove by and guessed it was probably once a woodsman's *izba*, a relic from a time when such a thing as a lone woodsman existed in this communal nation. But now it sprouted two antennas and was probably the radio shack for the helipad.

The Zil entered the narrow track that cut through the dark pine forest. Lisa took Hollis' hand and said into his ear. 'I'm going to be brave.'

'You *are* brave.'

The Zil came to the end of the track and turned left on to the main blacktop road. Hollis noticed that the pine trees on either side of the road were huge, rising forty to fifty feet into the air, and the spreading bough canopy was so heavy that little light reached the ground. Now and then he saw log-paved lanes, what the military called corduroy roads, leading off the main road. Down some of these lanes he saw houses that he hadn't seen from the air. He was surprised but not shocked to catch sight of an American ranch house, then a white clapboard bungalow. They were most probably residences, he thought, for the Charm School students and their American instructors, set in the Russian *bor* to enhance the illusions that made this place so unique.

Lisa spotted one and said to him. 'Look!'

'I see them.'

'This is *bizarre*. What is –?'

'No questions.'

She nodded. 'Alright.'

Marchenko, too, was staring out the window. He said to

424

Hollis, 'This is very odd indeed. Do you know what this place is?'

Hollis had assumed that Marchenko didn't know much beyond his kidnapping assignment. Hollis replied, 'It's a secret CIA base camp. You're under arrest, Marchenko.'

Marchenko turned around in his seat and looked at Hollis in a way that led Hollis to think the man almost believed him. *What a country.* Marchenko finally smiled. 'You joke. Tell me, what kind of structures are those in the wood?'

'They're called houses.'

'Yes? I saw American houses in a movie once. Those are American houses.'

'Very good.

Marchenko turned back to the front and peered out the windows. 'I don't understand this place.'

Hollis noticed that the light snow was mostly on the pine branches and little of it had reached the moss-covered ground. This was a place, he thought, of perpetual darkness, a place where even at high noon in the summer there would be little light.

Lisa said, 'I haven't seen a single person.'

Hollis nodded. Neither had he, and the unsettling thought came to him that they were all gone, moved to another location as had happened when the American rescue force had raided Son Tay POW camp in North Vietnam. But as he peered through the forest he saw lit windows in some of the houses, and smoke rose from the chimneys. *No*, he thought, *they are still here*. The KGB had not properly evaluated the situation and had not broken camp yet.

The Zil continued slowly along the road, and coming up on the right was the long green-roofed building Hollis had spotted from the air. It was a single-story building of white clapboard with a very homey-looking front porch. There were rockers on the porch and a red-and-white Coke machine against the wall near the double front doors. Through a large picture window Hollis got a glimpse of some men and women, and on a wall

425

hung a large American flag. Hollis had the impression of a small-town Veterans of Foreign Wars hall, and as the Zil passed by, he saw a black-and-white sign over the double doors that said just that: VWF, POST 000.

The Zil moved on, then came to a halt in front of the headquarters building, a grey two-story hulk of precast concrete slabs, most of which had the familiar cracks that were a trademark of the prefab industry in these parts. Steel reinforcing rods protruded here and there and bled orange rust over the deteriorating concrete. A KGB Border Guard stood in a plywood booth, and to the right of the booth was the headquarters' entrance. Standing in front, wearing the long green greatcoat with red shoulder boards of the KGB, was Colonel Petr Burov.

Marchenko got out and said, 'Come, come. You don't keep a colonel waiting.'

Vadim opened the rear door and got out, followed by Hollis and Lisa.

Burov looked at them a long time, then said, 'Well, this is what you wanted to see, wasn't it, Hollis?'

Hollis didn't reply.

Burov said to Marchenko, 'Why is he handcuffed?'

'He tried to hijack the helicopter.' Marchenko explained to Burov with great diffidence in his voice, altering somewhat the exact events at the airport and on the helicopter.

Burov looked at Vadim's swollen wrist, now the size of an orange, then looked at Hollis but said nothing. Burov stared at the icon in Lisa's hand. He said to her, 'If you were Catholic or Protestant, you'd have to carry only a small cross for comfort.' He laughed, and Marchenko and Vadim laughed also.

Lisa said in Russian, 'Go to hell.'

Burov slapped her hard across the face, knocking her to the ground.

Hollis bent down to help Lisa to her feet, and as he did, Burov swung at him, catching him on the jaw and sending him staggering back. His knees sagged, and he dropped to the ground, then stood uneasily.

Burov flexed his right hand and watched Hollis as he straightened up. Burov said, 'Well, that evens the score for Lefortovo.' Burov looked at Vadim and said in Russian, 'The stomach.'

Vadim's right foot shot out and caught Hollis in the solar plexus, causing him to double over, but he managed to stay on his feet.

Hollis straightened up and tried to catch his breath. Coming at him, as if in a bad dream, was the towering hulk of Viktor from Lefortovo. Hollis heard Burov's voice. 'The balls.'

Viktor's foot came up between Hollis' legs and caught him full in the testicles. Hollis heard himself yell, then found he was on the frozen ground rolling around in blinding pain. He heard Lisa scream, then the scream was cut off by the sound of a blow. Lisa fell beside him, holding her midsection, her eyes dull with pain.

Viktor took a step past Hollis, and Hollis got the handcuff chain under Viktor's foot and around the man's ankle. Hollis pulled and sent Viktor sprawling to the ground with a thud.

Burov came at Hollis but walked over him and planted his heavy jackboot in Lisa's side, causing her to cry out. Burov said to Hollis, 'Any more heroics?' He put his boot on Lisa's head. 'No? Get up.'

Hollis got to his feet at the same time as Viktor. Viktor grabbed Lisa by the collar of her coat and pulled her to her feet.

Burov motioned to Marchenko. 'Uncuff him.'

Lisa moved unsteadily toward Hollis, but Burov pushed her away. Burov said to Marchenko in Russian, 'That vehicle will take you and your subordinate to the Center, where you will make a full report. If you ever breathe a word about anything you saw here, you'll both be shot. Dismissed.'

Marchenko and Vadim saluted, did an about-face, and got back into the Zil.

Burov said to Hollis and Lisa. 'Get inside.'

The Border Guard opened the door, and Hollis and Lisa entered with Burov and Viktor behind them.

They found themselves in a lobby or waiting room where a duty officer sat at a desk facing the door. The man stood when he saw Burov. Burov said to Hollis and Lisa, 'Leave your bags and that religious thing with this man.'

Hollis set his bag down and noticed an open door to the left through which he could see a telephone switchboard and a radio transmitter.

Burov said to them, 'Now take off your coats and shoes.'

Hollis removed his trench coat and shoes while Lisa pulled off her boots and overcoat.

The duty officer put the coats and footwear on his desk, examining them as he did.

Viktor fingered Hollis' tie, then pulled it off him and stuffed it in his own pocket. He unbuckled Hollis' belt and ripped it off, throwing it on the desk, then took Hollis' watch and put it on his wrist.

Burov snapped, 'This way.' He led them down a long corridor toward the rear of the building. A Border Guard with an AK-47 followed. The guard threw open a steel door and shoved Lisa inside. Burov said to her, 'Take off your clothes and wait for the matron to come and search you. Or, if you have a means to end your life, do it before she comes. You have a few minutes.'

Viktor said to her in Russian, 'I'm not through with you, bitch.' He slammed the door shut and bolted it.

Burov opened the next door and pushed Hollis into a small, windowless cell, then followed him in. He said to Hollis, 'For your information, I am the camp commandant here. I never had an escape for the ten years I've been here. Then Dodson escapes and two of my men are murdered.' He glared at Hollis. 'I know you killed them, and I think you and your Jew friend Alevy know too goddamned much about this place. Don't you?'

Hollis said nothing, and Burov punched him in the stomach.

Burov waited for Hollis to straighten up, then said, 'I'll tell you something else, smart guy – from the moment I laid eyes on you and your snotty girlfriend I wanted you both here. The Center said impossible, but I showed them how we could kidnap two American diplomats. They thought it quite brilliant. Your death in a helicopter crash is now being reported to your embassy. Your incinerated remains – actually a male and female prisoner – are being gathered from the crash site. No one knows you're here, Hollis. No one is looking for you. You're all mine now, and you're dead.'

Hollis tried to clear his head. Between the lines he read that Burov was in trouble and was trying to redeem himself with Lubyanka. So far, Burov was doing fine.

Burov snapped, 'Take off your clothes and give them to Viktor.'

Hollis removed his suit, shirt, and underwear, handing each piece to Viktor while the Border Guard kept his AK-47 trained on him.

Burov said, 'If I find any of your stupid spy gadgets, I'll kill you with my own hands. Someone will be along shortly to see if you've got anything up your ass. Welcome to the Charm School, Hollis.' Burov, Viktor, and the guard left. The door slammed, and Hollis heard the bolt drive home.

Hollis stood naked in the cell and looked around. Four bare concrete walls enclosed a space about ten feet square. There was no window, and the only light came from a dim recessed bulb in the ceiling, covered by a steel grating. Somewhere up there, though he could not see it, was a fiber-optic device watching him.

There was no furniture at all in the cell, and as far as he could see, no heat source either. In the far left corner of the cell a water spigot protruded from the wall about four feet off the floor. Beneath the spigot was a waste hole. Hollis turned on the spigot and rinsed the blood out of his mouth, then splashed cold water on his face. He felt his jaw swelling, and one of his teeth was loose. His testicles were beginning to swell too, and his midsection was turning purplish. He washed his hands, then drank some water, but his stomach heaved, and he spit it into the waste hole.

The door opened, and two uniformed men came in. One of them held a pistol in one hand, and the other performed a body search, then both men left.

Hollis stood in the center of the cold, concrete room. He had once spent ten very unpleasant days in prison, an intelligence school training facility located in a building similar to this one in northwest Washington, DC, called Lubyanka West. The first few days there and probably here were the standard 'shock days', a blur of dehumanizing treatment, psychological torture, and physical abuse. This softened you up, stripped away your self-esteem, and set you up for what was to come. Then they left you alone to think about things, but the welcome solitude soon became maddening isolation. Then when you yearned to hear and see another human being, they scheduled 'interviews' with you and were conditionally pleasant, and you began to like them for letting you live. You began talking, enjoying the company, and when you were talked out, you were sent to a regular prison camp or shot.

There was some advantage in knowing what was coming, Hollis thought, but no comfort in the knowledge. He was glad Lisa didn't know anything.

He went to the wall that separated their cells and struck it with his palm, but it was solid, and he heard no answering signal.

Hollis sat in a corner with his back against the warmer interior wall, pulled his legs up to his chest, and wrapped his arms around his knees. He slept fitfully.

On what he thought was the second day, the door opened. Someone threw a ball of clothes on the floor and shut the door. Hollis found a blue warm-up suit and sweat socks but no footwear. He dressed and treated himself to some water. He felt very weak. The light overhead went off, and the cell was in darkness. He'd noticed that the light came on and off at random intervals, apparently without any pattern or any reason except to play games with his biorhythms. Hollis walked awhile in the dark, then curled up and slept in his new clothes.

On what he reckoned was the third day, the door opened again, and a sleeping bag flew in, followed by a boiled potato that steamed in the cool air. Hollis looked at the potato but did not move toward it while the guard stood at the door.

The guard asked in Russian, 'How do you feel?'

'Fine.'

The guard snorted and spoke the traditional phrases used to greet new camp prisoners in the Gulag, *'Zhit' budesh', no est ne zakhachesh'.'* *You'll live, but you won't feel much like fucking.* The guard laughed and closed the door.

As Hollis moved toward the potato, the light went off, and he had to get down on all fours to find the food. He climbed into the sleeping bag to conserve body heat and ate the warm potato.

Some hours later, the door opened again, and a guard shouted in Russian, 'Get up! Come here!'

Hollis got to his feet and followed the guard down the long corridor, then up a narrow flight of concrete stairs. He was led into a small room and immediately saw it was set up for a tribunal. There was a long table at the far end of the room at which sat five KGB officers in uniform facing him. Burov sat in the middle and seemed to be the ranking man. The other four stared at him with stolid Russian faces.

On the wall behind the table hung a picture of Felix Dzerzhinsky, founder of the secret police, and next to that a color photograph of a man whom Hollis recognized as the present chairman of the KGB. Above both pictures was a large painted sword and shield, the emblem of the Committee for State Security. Hollis noted there was no Soviet flag, nor a picture of any political or party leader. The symbolism was obvious; the KGB was a law unto itself.

Hollis saw weak sunlight coming through the window,

looking more like dusk than dawn. The KGB Border Guard snapped, 'Sit!'

Hollis sat in a wooden chair facing the five men.

Colonel Burov spoke in Russian from his seat. 'This special tribunal of the Committee for State Security has been convened for the purpose of trying Colonel Samuel Hollis of the United States Air Force for the murder of Private Nikolai Kulnev and Private Mikhail Kolotilov, members of the Border Guards Directorate of the KGB.' Burov recited dates and circumstances, then asked, 'Colonel Hollis, how do you plead to the charge of murder?'

The Border Guard behind Hollis kicked his chair, and Hollis stood. He said, 'I plead guilty.'

If Burov or the other four men were surprised, they didn't show it. Burov asked, 'Do you want to say something in extenuation or mitigation?'

'No.'

Burov cleared his throat and said, 'Very well. If the accused raises no extenuating circumstances; then there is only one penalty that this tribunal can adjudge for the murder of a KGB man, and that penalty is death by firing squad.' Burov looked at Hollis closely, and Hollis stared straight ahead.

Burov said to Hollis, 'You are required to write a full confession of the crime for which you stand convicted. If the confession is satisfactory, you will be allowed to write an appeal of your death sentence to the chairman of the Committee for State Security. If the appeal is turned down, there are no further appeals, and you will be executed. Do you understand?'

'Yes.'

'Take the prisoner to his cell. Bring in the next prisoner.'

The guards moved Hollis toward the door, and as he reached it, it opened and Lisa stepped into the room, wearing a grey prison dress. She looked, he thought, pale, shaky, and disoriented. Hollis said to her, 'Plead guilty. Be brave. I love you.'

She focused on him as if trying to place him, then the guards

432

moved them past each other, and Hollis found himself in the corridor. He was escorted back to his cell on the ground floor. The cell was dark, but then the light snapped on, and he saw a writing tablet on the floor. He knelt and picked it up, noticing also an American ballpoint pen.

Hollis sat on his sleeping bag and rested the tablet on his knees. His instructions as an intelligence officer superseded the Rules of Conduct for a POW. He was to confess to everything and anything and write whatever they asked as long as it didn't endanger another prisoner or compromise national security or ongoing operations. In short, he was to play their game because they thought so much of it.

His primary obligation was to escape, and to do that he was to preserve his mind and body. He'd been assured that if he stayed within his instructions, that whatever he signed, wrote, or said would not be held against him if he should ever make it back. Hollis thought he preferred the moral certainty and rigid guidelines of name, rank, and service number. But he was no longer a pilot, and in this new business there were no certainties, moral or otherwise. Hollis began writing his confession. He chose to write it in Russian, so if there were any problems of fact, he could plead ignorance of the finer points of the language.

He knew that if they had the time, they'd make him rewrite it again and again. The Russians took the written word very seriously, and as former Orthodox Christians they were obsessed with confessions of guilt; thus the legendary written confessions that poured out of the Lubyanka. But Hollis suspected that Burov was on tight schedule to get on with the important business, the interrogation to find out what he and Alevy knew and what the embassy knew and what Washington knew. Hollis reflected on the sequence of the criminal justice system here: trial, confession, interrogation. He supposed it didn't matter. The bullet still came at the end. Hollis continued to write.

Hollis paused to collect his thoughts, then continued his confession. In truth, there wasn't much to tell. He'd been spying on the Charm School, ran into two Border Guards, and shot them. His chance sighting of Yablonya from the helicopter removed that moral problem and gave him an opportunity to betray people who were already liquidated. He knew, too, that the KGB wanted not only details, but philosophical motivations for what he'd done, an enlightened awareness of his shortcomings as a decadent product of Western capitalism. They also wanted apologies. He'd written several sample confessions in the Washington Lubyanka, but he didn't want to make it appear that he was a pro at it.

As he started a new page, Hollis thought about Lubyanka West, the Charm School, and the many other manifestations of Washington's and Moscow's obsession with and emulation of each other. He always thought that if either side were ultimately defeated in a future war, the victor would feel a sense of loss and purposelessness. He recalled the almost disappointed expression on Burov's face upon passing the death sentence on him. There was no doubt that each side got something out of the conflict, drew some sort of unnatural psychic energy from it.

Hollis filled the writing tablet with words, then read what he'd written. It was a good confession, a mixture of hard fact and hard-to-prove fiction. The facts were things Burov probably already knew. The fiction was that Greg Fisher's phone call to the embassy was the first time they'd heard of an American POW in Russia. Burov would believe that because he wanted to believe it.

Two hours after he'd begun writing. Hollis signed the confession and lay down in his sleeping bag. He thought briefly about Lisa, then forced her out of his mind, but he fell into a restless sleep and dreamt about her anyway.

On the fifth or sixth day of his imprisonment, after the third draft of his confession, the door to his cell opened, and the lieutenant who had been the duty officer when he arrived walked in and said in Russian, 'Your confession is accepted. Now you will write an appeal of your death sentence. Come with me.'

Hollis, half starved by now, stood unsteadily and followed the lieutenant out into the corridor. The man pointed, and Hollis walked toward the rear of the building. It was at this point where they usually put the bullet into your neck. But why that odd custom of the hallway execution – begun in the 1930s in Lubyanka – persisted was beyond him. It *would* have been humane if no one knew about it, but as it was fairly well-known in the Soviet Union, Hollis thought he'd just as soon face a firing squad outdoors.

He could hear the lieutenant's boots on the concrete floor and listened intently for the snap of a holster flap, wondering if he'd misjudged Burov's need to interrogate him. He remembered his own advice to Lisa at the restaurant in the Arbat, that the KGB were not rational, and he could well believe that Burov had let his emotions get the better of his intellect.

'Stop!'

Hollis stopped and heard a door open to his right. The lieutenant said, 'In there.'

Hollis entered a small windowless room that was just another cell like his own except that there was a table and chair in it. On the table was a sheet of paper and a pen.

'Sit down.'

Hollis sat, and the lieutenant moved behind him. Hollis saw that the table was of yellow pine, and the boards of the table were stained with what could only have been blood. Against the wall in front of him were stacked bales of straw to keep a bullet from ricocheting.

'Address your appeal to the Chairman of the Committee for State Security.'

Hollis picked up the pen and asked, 'In Russian or English?'

'It doesn't matter.'

Hollis began writing, and the lieutenant remained behind him. In contrast to confessions, the appeal was obviously supposed to be short, as he had only one sheet of paper.

Hollis heard the metal snap of the holster, the pistol sliding over the leather, and the click of the hammer being cocked.

435

Hollis continued to write. He found that his mouth had gone dry and his palms were moist. He controlled his hands as he finished the last line of the appeal of his death sentence. Hollis signed his appeal, put the pen down, and waited, wondering if he'd actually hear the blast or feel anything.

He heard the hammer click again, the pistol slide into the holster, and the snap close. The lieutenant chuckled softly and said, 'Leave it there. Stand.'

Hollis stood, and the lieutenant brought him back to his cell. The Russian said, 'Your appeal will be decided within twenty-four hours. It is not humane to have you waiting much longer to learn your fate.' He closed and bolted the door.

The light was on, and Hollis knew Burov was taking some pleasure in watching him. Hollis wanted to urinate but didn't. He sat on his sleeping bag and closed his eyes. He knew that he should be playing the game for Burov, should be shaking with fear at the waste hole, drinking water to wet his dry mouth. He knew that if he didn't give Burov any pleasure, then Burov, in his pique, would consider Hollis a malfunctioning toy and get rid of him.

Hollis rose slowly, went to the waste hole, and urinated. He drank from the spigot, retched, then drank again. He took a deep breath, went to his sleeping bag, and pulled it over his head. The lights went off.

An image of Lisa walking beside him on that sunny Saturday in Arbat Street filled the darkness behind his eyes. He pictured her face with various expressions, and each expression froze for a moment, as if he were taking photographs with his mind. He found himself slipping into a sort of twilight sleep, the only sort of sleep he'd been capable of for some time. There seemed to be less and less difference between his waking periods and these periods of shadowy consciousness, and he could not distinguish dreams from waking hallucinations. What he longed for was a deep, recuperative sleep, but that no longer seemed possible.

Finally he slipped into real sleep and had a real dream, a dream he never wanted to have again – his F-4, its controls dead in his hands, the cockpit filled with blue smoke and red blood, and the sea rushing up at him, then the sky, sea, sky, as the aircraft rolled wing over wing and his hand clutched at the eject trigger.

Hollis jumped to his feet, his face covered with sweat and his heart trying to get out of his chest. He screamed, 'Simms! Simms!' then sank to the floor, covered his face, and remained motionless.

The door opened, and a guard said tonelessly, 'Come with me.'

Hollis stood and followed the man into the corridor. A second guard fell in behind them, and they began walking. The guard to his rear said to Hollis, 'Mikhail Kolotilov was a friend of mine, you fucking murderer.'

Hollis made no reply. The guard to his front turned into the narrow staircase along the wall, and they went to the second floor. The Russian knocked on a door and opened it. The man behind him poked Hollis toward the door, and Hollis entered.

Colonel Burov sat at his desk in a spartan concrete office. There was a single window in the wall, and Hollis saw it was evening. The concrete walls were painted the color and texture of crusty yellowed cream, and on the concrete floor was a brick-red rug with a central Asian design. On the wall behind Burov's desk hung the same two pictures as in the tribunal room, but in addition, there was the necessary picture of Lenin.

'Sit down, Hollis.'

Hollis sat in a wooden chair facing the desk, and the door closed behind him.

Burov held up Hollis' written confession. 'Fascinating. I'm quite impressed with your ability to avoid capture. As you know, we discovered your car at Gagarin station. What you don't know is that we found out about Yablonya as well. I'm glad to see you were truthful about that.'

Hollis rubbed the stubble on his chin and suppressed a cough.

'Your girlfriend, however, was not. In fact, her confession has fewer interesting details than yours does.'

'She doesn't know much.'

'No? She knew about Yablonya and didn't put that in her confession. She, too, has been condemned to death by the tribunal. Unless her confession is satisfactory, she will not have an opportunity to make an appeal for her life.'

Hollis said nothing.

'And she will be shot.' Burov studied Hollis a moment, then picked up a single sheet of paper and glanced at it. 'Your appeal for clemency is interesting. You say you are willing to work here if you are not shot.'

'Yes.'

'What do you think we do here?'

'Train KGB agents to pass as Americans.'

Burov studied Hollis a moment, then inquired, 'How do you know that?'

'We guessed.'

'You and Alevy?'

'Yes.'

'I see. And have you caught any of our graduates from this place?'

'Yes. The Kellums.'

Burov leaned across the desk. 'When did you discover them?'

'Only . . . I guess it was last Thursday or Friday. What day is this?'

Burov didn't answer, but asked, 'And Dodson? Where is Dodson?'

'I don't know.'

Burov stood and went to the window. He stared out at the dark pine forest, then asked, 'If you people know about this place, why aren't you doing anything about it?'

'My government is pursuing a policy of peace at the moment.'

'So they want to keep it quiet?'

'That's my understanding.'

'But if Dodson somehow got in touch with your embassy . . . ?'

'They'll shut him up.'

Burov smiled. 'Will they?'

'I believe so. I don't know everything that goes on there.'

'No. I'd rather have Alevy here. But you'll do for now.'

Hollis rubbed his eyes. He knew that what he said was being recorded, and perhaps it was being fed into a voice-stress analyzer. Later, he'd be asked the same questions when he was attached to a polygraph and perhaps again under drugs. Any inconsistencies discovered then would be resolved with electric shock interrogation.

Burov continued what was called in the trade the 'soft' interrogation, and Hollis answered the questions, tonelessly and with an economy of words. Burov was good, but he was not a professional KGB interrogator of Special Service II. Hollis thought the bogus SS II interrogators at Lubyanka West in Washington were somewhat better. On the other hand, Hollis, as an air attaché with diplomatic immunity, was not supposed to have ever gotten into such a situation, and his training was somewhat limited.

Hollis suspected, however, that Burov was enough of an egoist to think he could handle the situation himself, and that was why Burov, the camp commandant, had gone to Mozhaisk and Lefortovo restaurant on his own counterintelligence missions. Also, Hollis reminded himself, Burov and his whole Little America operation were probably in trouble with the politicians if not the Lubyanka. It was Hollis' job to assure Burov that everything was alright. He did not want this place to disappear. Yet.

Burov said, 'I can't imagine your government would let our operation continue. Even in the interests of peace. There are thousands of our agents in America already, and we're graduating over two hundred a year. What does Washington intend to do about *that* situation?'

And that, Hollis thought, was the crux of the matter. He

replied, 'It is my understanding that the State Department is looking for a negotiated settlement.'

'Are they? The diplomats are such women. What does the CIA want to do?'

'Blow the whistle. Leak it to the world press.'

'Ah, yes. And the White House?'

'They're sort of in between.'

'And your people? The Defense Intelligence Agency?'

'They have a moral interest in the fate of the captured fliers.'

'And you? You, Colonel Sam Hollis?'

Hollis allowed himself a small smile. 'I just want to kill you.'

Burov smiled in return. 'Yes? I thought you wanted to work for me.'

'That depends.'

Burov nodded to himself, then said, 'And has anyone proposed direct action against this school?'

'What do you mean?'

'Something like rescuing one or two of these men and presenting them to the world as evidence?'

'Not that I know of. From what I see here, that's not possible.'

'No, it's not. And Dodson's escape was wholly an internal conspiracy here. No outside help. Correct?'

'We had no part in that.'

'And Fisher's meeting with Dodson was totally chance?'

'Of course. You heard Fisher on the taped phone conversation. He's not ours.'

'And your snooping around here – that was not an attempt to rescue a prisoner?'

'No. There was only Lisa Rhodes and I. We did that on our own.'

'You have no contact with any prisoners inside the camp?'

'No.'

'With any staff?'

'No.'

'Do you have Soviet citizens on the outside who are your agents?'

'None that have any connection with this camp.'

'But you do employ Soviet citizens as American agents.'

Hollis thought it was time to get one point on the board. 'Not employ. They don't take a kopek. They do it because they hate the Communist Party and the KGB.'

Burov said nothing for a while, then asked, 'You'll give me their names.'

'I don't have any actual names. Just code names.'

'We'll see.'

'Why should I tell you anything if I'm going to be shot?'

'Because being shot is not as bad as what I can do to you.'

'And I could kill myself before you do *anything* to me.'

'I don't think you have any lethal means at your disposal.'

'I could have pushed that ballpoint pen through my jugular vein. You're not supposed to give trained intelligence officers things like that.'

'Ah, yes. The pen. So, you think that as an intelligence officer your brains are too valuable to be blown out?'

'Perhaps.'

'Well, then let me ask you something. What do you propose? Intelligence officer to intelligence officer.'

'My appeal makes that clear. I realize I'm officially dead. I'd rather work here, among my peers, than go to Siberia or be shot. I want Lisa Rhodes with me.'

'Yes, you are officially dead. I'll show you the American newspaper accounts. The Center wants you actually dead after your debriefing. But perhaps I can convince them that you and your girlfriend will be an asset here. Perhaps a life sentence here, helping us to destroy America, will be worse than death. I'd enjoy that, Hollis.'

'I know you would.'

Burov smiled, then said, 'I don't think you defense attachés are as tough as your CIA people. However, if I begin to think that your capitulation is a ruse of some sort, I'll torture your girlfriend to death. Right in front of you.'

Hollis didn't reply.

Burov walked over to Hollis and looked down at him. 'You thought you were quite the man, didn't you? In the Mozhaisk morgue, then in Lefortovo restaurant, then on the telephone with me. What abuse I took from you.'

'I had diplomatic immunity.'

Burov laughed. 'Yes, you did. Big shot. Now I can do whatever I please to you.' Burov grabbed Hollis' hair and yanked his head back. 'Look at me, you smug American bastard. You shits in the embassy look down your noses at us, don't you? I've heard some of the tapes of embassy conversations. You laugh at our drinking, you think we don't bathe enough, you make fun of our women, you joke about Moscow, the food, the housing, and just about everything else about us.' Burov pulled harder on Hollis' hair. 'Do you think you look or smell so good now, you son of a bitch?' Burov released Hollis' hair and slammed the heel of his hand against Hollis' forehead. 'Do you think your delicate girlfriend looks or smells so good now? Do you think you look so civilized now? What are you without your tailored clothes and your deodorants? You're nothing, that's what you are. A Russian can stand more suffering because we don't start with so much. And because we have more inner strength. You people fall apart as soon as you miss a shower or a meal.' Burov paced around the room, then came to Hollis and barked, 'Stand up!'

Hollis stood.

'Hands on your head!'

Hollis put his hands on his head.

Burov glared at him. 'Can you imagine the things I could do to you and Lisa Rhodes? Things that wouldn't leave a mark on your bodies, but would completely destroy you inside, your humanity, your souls, your minds. Answer me!'

'Yes. I know.'

Burov stood off to Hollis' side and said, 'Your girlfriend is a lover of Russian culture. Perhaps she would like a Russian boyfriend. Maybe several dozen of them.'

Hollis didn't reply.

'Did you know that she and Alevy were lovers? Answer me.'

'Yes.'

'I told you that your wife has taken up with an English gentleman.'

'I don't care.'

'She's in Washington now for your funeral. I think it's tomorrow.'

Hollis made no response.

'Who is Simms?'

'I don't know.'

'I think I know.' Burov looked at his watch and said, 'Well, Hollis, do you want to see your slut?'

Hollis nodded.

Burov opened the door to his office and said something to the guard, then turned to Hollis. 'You may take your hands down. Get out.'

Hollis walked to the door, and Burov said, 'You may have sex if you wish.'

'Thank you.'

Burov smiled and closed the door.

The guard marched Hollis down the stairs. The man opened the door of Lisa's cell and shoved Hollis in. The door closed behind him.

Lisa sat in a sleeping bag, curled up in the corner. She looked at him but said nothing.

Hollis knelt near her and examined her face. Her cheeks were drawn, and her eyes seemed sunken. He noticed her lips were dry and cracked, and there was a bruise on her neck. On her left cheek there was still a smudge of blush, and this somehow caused him more pain than the rest of her appearance. 'How are you?'

She didn't reply.

'Do you need a doctor?'

She shook her head.

Hollis felt weak and sat down beside her, putting his arm around her shoulders. She didn't move toward him or move away. She sat still, staring straight ahead.

They sat in silence for a long time, then Lisa put her face in her hands and wept.

Hollis drifted off from time to time, but the numbing cold and his empty stomach woke him every fifteen minutes or so.

The light went on and off, and there were bootsteps in the corridor that stopped outside the cell door, then continued. Now and then someone slid the bolt back, but the door never opened. A few minutes later, the bolt would slide closed again.

Lisa stared at the ceiling and spoke in a barely audible voice. 'I was sentenced to death.'

Hollis didn't reply.

She reached her arm out along the wall, then held her hand out in front of Hollis.

He didn't know at first what she was holding, then recognized a heap of ash and charred pieces of paper. Photographs. Her photographs of Moscow. He turned her hand so the ash spilled out, and wiped her palm on his knee.

She said, 'It doesn't matter.'

Hollis knew the room was wired to pick up the slightest whisper, and even in the dark, the fiber-optic device could see them. He wanted to comfort her but thought it best to say nothing that Burov could use. In fact, he knew he should not have even told Burov he wanted to see her.

She asked, 'Why did you tell them about Yablonya?'

'I'm sorry.'

She stood unsteadily and went to the waste drain in the floor, and used it. The guard picked that moment to come in, confirming Hollis' belief that they could see as well as hear. Lisa stood and pulled her sweat pants up as the guard leered at her. The Russian looked at Hollis, then threw a piece of black bread in the center of the floor. He said to Hollis, 'I

444

told you that you wouldn't feel much like fucking.' He laughed and closed the door.

Lisa washed in cold water, then put her mouth under the spigot and drank. She picked the bread up off the floor and carried it back to her sleeping bag. She slid into the bag and took a bit of bread, chewing it slowly, Hollis noticed, more like a person who is starving than merely hungry.

Hollis estimated they were getting about three hundred grams of bread a day, about four hundred calories. They'd been here about eight days, though it could have been longer. There were enough calories to stay alive, but as the guard suggested, he didn't feel much like doing anything but breathing. He suspected, too, that the food was drugged, probably with sodium pentothal or a similar truth serum, which, along with the sensory deprivation and numbing cold, would account for their extreme lethargy.

Lisa stared at the black bread awhile, then offered him the piece. He broke off about a third and handed the rest back to her.

After they'd finished the bread, Hollis said, 'Feeling better?'

She shrugged. After a few minutes she reached out and took his hand. 'You must be cold. Didn't they give you a bag?'

'I'm alright.'

'Come in here. There's room.'

He slipped into the sleeping bag beside her.

She said, 'I don't blame you for this. You warned me.'

Hollis made no reply.

They slept fitfully. Lisa cried out in her sleep several times, but he couldn't understand what she was saying.

Hollis got up to get water. The water pressure was low, and he knew from experience that this meant it was dawn. He heard footsteps, and the door opened. The guard said, 'Stand up. Follow me. No talking.'

Hollis helped Lisa to her feet. She said, 'I love you, Sam.'

'I love you.'

'No talking!'

Hollis took Lisa's hand, but the guard pushed them apart. 'Walk!'

They walked down the long corridor, and another guard opened the door to the room where Hollis had written the appeal of his death sentence, the room with the blood-stained table and the straw bales against the wall. The execution room. Lisa hesitated, but the guard shoved her inside.

32

On the bloodstained table was hot tea, boiled eggs, bread, and jam. The guard said, 'Eat all you want, but if you throw it up, you'll clean it. No talking.'

Hollis and Lisa sat. Hollis glanced at the bloodstains beneath the food. They were actually rust-colored, not bright red, and he suspected that Lisa didn't know what they were. He wondered, too, if it was animal blood, put there to frighten prisoners and amuse the guards.

They ate slowly, but they both got stomach cramps just the same. The guard let them out of the room and into what looked like a locker room, probably, Hollis thought, used by the night guard. There were wall lockers, a sink, a toilet, and in the corner an open shower. The guard motioned toward the shower. 'Go ahead. Use it.'

They both undressed and showered with hot water and soap. A matron brought in towels, a shaving kit, underwear, and clean warm-up suits. Hollis dried himself, shaved, then dressed, noticing that the clothes had Jockey labels. Lisa dressed quickly, avoiding the guard's eyes. The matron pointed to a box full of Adidas running shoes; and they each found a pair that fit.

The guard said, 'Come with me.' He led them to the east wing of the building and through a door marked *Klinika*. They were met by a female nurse, who took them into separate examining rooms. The guard stayed with Hollis. Presently, a plump middle-age woman entered the room and introduced herself as the camp doctor.

She gave Hollis a perfunctory examination, being interested mostly in his heart, Hollis thought, recalling the Russian obsession with heart disease. He said curtly in Russian, 'I am malnourished and have been sitting in a cold cell for about two weeks. I've been punched in the jaw, kicked in the testicles and the solar plexus. Also, I hear fluid in my lungs.'

She moved the stethoscope back to his lungs, told him to breathe deeply, listened, and tapped his chest. 'Yes. A little congestion. You'll be alright.'

'Alright for two more weeks of starvation?'

The guard said, 'No talking.'

Hollis looked at the man. 'I'll talk to the doctor. Why don't *you* shut up?'

The guard snapped back. 'Only medical talk!'

The doctor gave Hollis a pill and a glass tumbler that looked as if it could use a washing.

Hollis asked, 'What is this?'

'Just a vitamin.'

'Then you take it.' He handed it back to her.

She looked at him a moment, then put the pill in her mouth and washed it down with the water. She said in a low voice, 'I too am a prisoner here. A political prisoner.'

'I see. I apologize for my rudeness.'

She gave him another vitamin, and he took it. She said, 'You'll be fine. Your heart is good.'

Hollis got down from the examining table and dressed. He asked, 'What dies first here, the heart or the soul?'

'The soul dies. The heart breaks.'

Hollis looked closely at the woman. He should have seen immediately that she was not free, but in Russia it was sometimes hard to tell and very relative. Hollis said to her, 'Thank you.'

The guard took Hollis to the waiting room, and within five minutes, Lisa joined him. The guard said, 'Follow me.' He led them upstairs to Burov's office. As they entered, Burov said, 'Sit down.' They sat in chairs facing Burov.

Burov said, 'Now you are Americans again. Right, Hollis?'

'Yes.'

'Do you feel well?'

'Yes.'

'Good. You'll feel much better when I tell you that both your death sentences have been conditionally commuted to life in prison.'

'What,' Hollis asked, 'is the condition?'

'Two conditions. One is that you pass a polygraph test. The other is that you agree to work for us here.'

Neither Hollis nor Lisa replied.

Burov added, 'If you say no, you'll be executed for murder.'

Lisa said, 'What you're asking is that we become traitors. The answer is no.'

Burov didn't respond to that, but said, 'You should know, Ms Rhodes, that your friend has already indicated he would work for us here in exchange for his life.'

She looked at Hollis.

Hollis said to Burov, 'I didn't say I would subject myself to a polygraph interrogation.'

'No,' Burov replied, 'but you will be thoroughly debriefed nonetheless. There are several methods of interrogation. I prefer polygraph and sodium pentothal over electroshock and a truncheon, especially as the results of the former are more reliable than the latter. I'm sure you and Ms Rhodes would prefer that too.'

Hollis said, 'Working here for you is one thing. But I cannot give you intelligence secrets that would compromise or endanger the lives of other agents.'

Burov tapped his fingers on his desk and looked from one to the other. 'You're not in a position to make deals. You're already dead, and no one knows you are here. And the reason you are here is that you know entirely too much about this place, and we want to know what you know.'

'We're here for killing two Border Guards,' Hollis reminded him. 'That's what we are under a death sentence for.'

'Well, that too, of course.' Burov regarded Hollis a moment. 'You know, as soon as the blood sugar goes up, people revert to their former selves. In your case, Hollis, I don't like your former self. Please try to control your sarcasm.'

'Yes, sir.'

Burov turned to Lisa. 'In your case, a debriefing would most probably yield very little and would in no way endanger anyone. Correct?'

Lisa nodded hesitantly.

'So the question for you is this: Do you want to live and work here, or do you want to be shot? Answer.'

'I . . . I want to be with Colonel Hollis.'

Burov grinned. 'Here? Or in heaven?'

'Anywhere.'

Burov looked at Hollis. 'Such loyalty. So what is your decision?'

Hollis thought a moment, then replied, 'I would like for both of us to be let out of the cells, to live here awhile before we decide if we want to become willing instructors in this place.'

Burov nodded. 'Alright. I think when you see how comfortable you can be here, you'll decide you don't want to die in front of a firing squad. But we haven't resolved the question of your interrogation.'

Hollis replied, 'Let's resolve that after Ms Rhodes and I resolve the question of working here or not. We'll need ten days.'

Burov smiled. 'You're stalling.'

'For what? I'm dead. We are both dead.'

Burov stood and went to the window. He stared out into the trees for a while, then nodded. 'One week.' He turned to Hollis and stared at him. 'The very first moment I think you are up to something or lying to me' – Burov pointed to Lisa – 'she dies. And as I told you, not by firing squad.'

Neither Hollis nor Lisa spoke.

Burov walked toward them. He looked at Hollis. 'You are intelligent enough to know that I let you bargain with me because I'd rather have you alive. I want you alive so I can question you, not only now, but anytime something comes up in American intelligence matters that you can enlighten us on. I also want you alive because we went through a great deal of trouble making you dead. You are both valuable commodities here, potential assets for this school. And lastly, but not least, I want you both under my thumb. Forever. You amuse me.'

'But you're not smiling,' Hollis pointed out.

Burov stared at Hollis for a long time, his face impassive, then he turned and went to his desk. Burov took a heavy revolver from the top drawer and emptied five of the six chambers. He walked over to Hollis and Lisa. 'No, not what you call Russian roulette. Stand up.' He handed the revolver to Hollis. 'See that the loaded chamber will fire if you pull the trigger.'

Hollis checked the cylinder.

Burov stepped back a pace. 'Go ahead.'

Hollis stood with the revolver in his hand.

'I'm giving you the opportunity to be a hero to your country, albeit an unknown one, and to indulge your own fantasy. Go ahead.'

Hollis glanced at Lisa.

Burov continued, 'Well? At least make me crawl a bit. Tell me to get on my knees and beg for my life.'

Hollis said nothing.

'No? Are you learning something? How much power comes from the muzzle of a gun? That depends on who is holding the gun. Me or you. And authority never came from the muzzle of a gun.' He looked at Lisa. 'Stand.'

She stood.

'Take the revolver.'

She hesitated, then took it from Hollis.

'You see,' Burov said, 'you do what I tell you even though *you* have the gun now. Shoot me.'

'No.'

'Ah, what are we learning now? Civilized people think ahead. What happens after you kill me? Are your problems

451

over? No, they have just begun.' Burov smirked. 'But a real patriot would have sacrificed his life to take mine.'

Lisa looked at the revolver in her hand. She said, 'There is only one reason I won't shoot you. Perhaps you can comprehend it. I am a believer in God. I will not take a life, not even yours.'

Burov snatched the pistol from her. 'Yes? Christians don't kill people? Perhaps I should go back to my history books. How does that little rhyme go . . . "After two thousand years of masses, you've progressed to poison gasses?" What hypocrites you all are.'

'We're trying. You're not.'

Burov sat on the edge of his desk and stared down at her. 'Let me give you some advice, Ms Rhodes. If you can convince your friend here to submit to us, you will be safe. Without him, you are nothing. Just a woman. Do you remember at Mozhaisk morgue when you pulled your hand away from me in revulsion? Well, picture, if you will, so many more dirty Russian hands on you – no, don't swear at me. I know you both have a little backbone left. Just shut your mouths and think about everything we've discussed here. Stand.' Burov threw the pistol on the desk and spoke in an almost friendly tone. 'Well, then. Are you feeling up to a walk in the fresh air? I'm sure you're curious.' Burov motioned them toward the door and spoke to the guard. He said to Hollis and Lisa, 'I'll join you in a while.'

The guard led them downstairs and indicated a bench near the front doors where they had first entered the building, then left them alone.

Hollis looked around the lobby. Like the rest of the place, it was sparse, but there was, as always, the picture of Lenin staring down at them. The picture was hung over the front desk, and Hollis noticed that the duty officer there was the same lieutenant who had played games with his pistol when Hollis was writing his appeal. The lieutenant glanced up at him and smiled.

From where Hollis sat he could see the open door to the communications room and saw an operator sitting at the switchboard. The man connected a call manually, and Hollis realized it wasn't an automatic board. To the operator's left was the radio console he'd seen when he first entered this building. He recognized a shortwave set but couldn't see the rest of the console.

The lieutenant said in Russian, 'Curiosity is how you got here.' He stood and closed the door of the communications room. He turned to Hollis and Lisa and held out a pack of cigarettes. 'Smoke?'

They both shook their heads.

'My name is Cheltsov.'

Hollis replied in Russian, 'I really don't give a shit.'

Lieutenant Cheltsov shrugged and sat back at his desk. He stared at them. 'I've come to like Americans.'

Hollis asked, 'Do they like you?'

The lieutenant smiled. 'Everyone here gets along as best he can. This is not a prison.'

'You could have fooled me.'

'Well, you'll see. Colonel Burov is a very smart man. There is much freedom here for the Americans. That's because Americans are used to much freedom. Correct?'

'Except for American communists.'

'That's not completely true. We know what goes on in America.'

'And how does that knowledge compare with what you were taught in school? About American communists for instance?'

The young officer shrugged. 'The Party knows what's best for the people to know.'

Lisa spoke. 'You certainly don't believe that anymore.'

Cheltsov lit a cigarette. 'I certainly do. So you will be instructors here?'

'We're considering the offer,' Hollis replied. 'Tell me more about how smart Colonel Burov is.'

The man smiled. 'Well, he is smart enough to let you people

453

have the run of this place as long as you produce results. If he discovers that an American instructor has lied to a Russian student about something in America, then . . .' The man put his forefinger to his temple and cocked his thumb. 'You understand?'

Hollis asked, 'And are you the executioner, Cheltsov?'

The man didn't reply.

'Do you speak English?' Lisa asked.

'No. None of the cadre – the KGB – speaks English.'

'And the American instructors?' Hollis asked. 'Do they speak Russian?'

'They are not supposed to know Russian, but they pick up a little. You see, here the Russian students and American instructors may communicate in English only. The Border Guards may not speak to students or instructors unless absolutely necessary.'

'Then how is it,' Lisa asked, 'that you know about America?'

Cheltsov smiled. 'One picks up a bit here and there.'

'And what if Burov knew you picked things up here and there?' she inquired as she put her finger to her head.

The lieutenant went back to the paperwork on his desk. 'Your Russian is excellent. Be careful how you use it.'

They sat in silence awhile, then Hollis, said to Lisa in English, 'Did you give up smoking?'

'I guess I did.' She added, 'But there must be an easier way.'

'You'll live longer.'

'Will I?' After a few minutes she said, 'Sam . . . I know we're in a bad situation here. But . . . I'm not going to . . . submit to them.'

Hollis rubbed his thumb and forefinger together, the embassy signal to remind people of electronic eavesdropping.

She touched her chin in acknowledgment and whispered in his ear, 'It was an act, wasn't it? I mean your . . . your . . .'

'Submissiveness.'

'Yes. That.'

He said, 'We'll talk later.'

They waited for nearly half an hour, and Hollis suspected that Burov intended this to be a period of psychological adjustment, a place to reflect on the relative freedom outside the doors and the hell at the rear of the building.

Finally Burov appeared in his greatcoat, and Lieutenant Cheltsov jumped to attention. Burov said to the man, 'Get them some parkas.' He addressed Hollis and Lisa and said, 'I'd like you to do two things. First, when you walk out those doors, forget what happened to you in here. Secondly, remember what happened to you in here. Do I make myself clear?'

Hollis replied, 'We understand.'

'Good.'

The lieutenant handed them each a white parka, and they put them on. Burov said, 'Follow me.'

They went with him out of the headquarters building into the chill morning air. There was some thin sunlight, and Hollis noticed how pale Lisa looked in it. He drew a breath of pine-scented air.

Burov too seemed to be enjoying the morning. He said, 'It's a pleasant day though a bit cold. I suppose you both feel it more without that little layer of fat you had.'

Hollis replied, 'Will you be having much difficulty not making inane allusions to what happened in the past?'

Burov smiled thinly. 'Thank you for reminding me. We start with a clean slate here. Here there is no past. That is the underlying philosophy of this institution. The instructors have no personal past, only a cultural past that they transmit to the students. The students have no personal or cultural past, only a political past that they cherish but never mention.'

Hollis had the distinct impression that Burov had anticipated this moment and was looking forward to showing them his school, to see and hear their reactions. 'Fascinating,' Hollis said.

'Very,' Burov agreed. 'And please, speak your mind. You

455

have carte blanche to criticize, complain, even indulge your sarcastic wit. Come, let us walk.'

They followed Burov around the headquarters building and entered a log-paved lane that led south toward what Hollis had determined was an athletics field. They broke out of the woods behind the bleacher stands that he'd seen, and Burov took them around to the open grass field. On the field Hollis saw two teams of young men playing touch football. The quarterback was calling signals, the ball was hiked, and the passer faded back. The offensive line blocked, but the defense got through easily. The quarter-back spotted a free receiver in the right flat and threw. The ball was wide, and the receiver lunged for it but fell. Burov observed, 'It's a difficult game.'

Hollis replied dryly, 'They make it look more difficult than it is.'

'Yes?'

Hollis noticed two middle-aged men on the opposite sideline and two on the field.

Burov said, 'The coaches and two referees. I wish the students could play with their instructors as they did years ago. We used to have some good games. But in truth, the instructors are getting on in years.'

'The Americans, you mean.'

'The instructors and students are all Americans, so we don't use that term to distinguish one from the other.'

'I see.'

'Anyway, the idea is to just teach the basics. All exercise here is some sort of American or universal sport. But we're limited because of your satellites. We play a little baseball, but if we had laid out a baseball diamond, your people would wonder what that was doing in the middle of Russia.' Burov smiled. 'But now that it has been discovered that we invented baseball, we are beginning to perfect the game and I may build a court here.'

'A diamond.'

'Whatever.'

Hollis said, 'That must be particularly galling to you. The satellites.'

'Oh, yes. And it hinders so many of our activities. So we retreat to the *bor*, like we did with the Tartars, Napoleon, Hitler, and all the rest.' Burov looked up at the sky. 'We all come here to this field now and then just to see the open expanse and feel the sun. You understand?'

'Yes.'

Burov nodded and said, 'Come.' He led them across the field and spoke as he walked. 'Now they are playing much soccer in America, so my students can excel at something over there if they have an athletic inclination. Incidentally, one of the best amateur soccer teams in northern New Jersey is coached by one of our graduates.'

'Is that a fact? Do you know what becomes of all your students?'

'Alas, no. They are turned over to Directorate S for infiltration into the States. You are familiar with D-S?'

'Yes. A branch of the First Chief Directorate.'

He glanced at Hollis as they walked. 'But anyway, we get a few anecdotal stories back from Directorate S. It's good for our morale.'

Lisa asked, 'What happens to the students who flunk out?'

Burov didn't reply for a while, then said, 'Well, they're asked to sign a statement swearing never to breathe a word of anything they've seen here. The same as in any other intelligence operation.'

Lisa remarked, 'I think you probably kill them.'

'Come, come, Ms Rhodes. Really.'

They walked in silence across the field and entered the tree line by way of another path. The path ended at a small concrete structure that resembled a bunker, and they entered it. The bunker was completely bare, and Hollis wondered why they were there. Burov directed them to the middle of the steel-plate floor, then pressed a button on the wall and stood beside them. The center plate of the floor began sinking.

They rode down a shaft for a few seconds, then stopped. Two sliding doors parted, and Burov showed them out into a smartly appointed room of chrome furniture and suede-covered walls. A young man sat at a countertop desk, wearing a T-shirt and reading a *New York Times*. Burov said to Hollis and Lisa, 'Welcome to the Holiday Spa.'

Hollis in fact smelled chlorine, and he noticed that steaminess peculiar to health clubs.

The young man behind the counter put down his newspaper and said in cheery English, 'Hello, Colonel. Who you got there?'

'New members, Frank. Colonel Hollis and Ms Rhodes.'

'Great.' The young man put out his hand. 'Frank Chapman. I read your obit last week, Colonel.'

Hollis hesitated, then shook hands with him and said, 'If you're Frank Chapman, I'm Leo Tolstoy.'

Chapman did not smile.

Burov said to Chapman, 'I'll just show them around.'

'Sure thing.'

Burov led them through steamy glass doors into an anteroom. 'Men's locker there. Ladies' over there. We don't have many female students because we only have six female instructors. Maybe seven now.'

Lisa said nothing.

Burov said, 'This place is our gem. It cost over a million rubles to build underground, and there's a half million dollars' worth of Western athletic equipment here. It's boosted morale among students, instructors, and staff.'

They followed Burov down a long corridor. Burov said, 'Finnish saunas here, steam baths there, sunrooms, whirlpools. Here's the workout room. Universal gym. Those two women are new students. They're trying to get American figures like yours, Ms Rhodes.' Burov smiled and watched the two Russian women sweating on stationary bicycles. Burov said, 'We know that many important contacts are made in athletic clubs and that most successful Americans are involved in some sort of athletic pastime. Golf and tennis I know are the most important to the upper and ruling classes. But there is not a single golf course in all of Russia, so our students watch golf tournaments on video-tape, then sign up for lessons in America. We play a little tennis here, but the real game is learned there. Here we mostly stress physical conditioning for its own sake. Social sport comes later. This way, please.'

They walked to the end of the corridor, which opened into a large gymnasium. Several young men were engaged in gymnastics, working on the bars, beams, and rings. Burov said, 'This is something at which we excel. It produces very good bodies. Our students, male and female, are partly chosen for their physical attributes. Many of them, when they go West, form romantic liaisons with Americans who can be of some help. Do you understand?'

Lisa replied tersely, 'Do you have any idea how morally corrupt you are?'

'Yes, by your standards. We have different standards.'

'You have no standards. That's why this country is morally and spiritually bankrupt. Do you teach your students Judeo-Christian morality?'

'There's not an overwhelming amount of that over there as far as I can determine.'

'Have you ever been to America?'

'Unfortunately not. Do you think it would do me some good, Ms Rhodes?'

'Probably not.'

Burov smiled, He pointed to the far end of the gym where six young men in shorts were shooting baskets. 'Come.' They walked around the hardwood gym floor and approached the six students. Hollis noted that their hairstyles were very American, and he was surprised at how they carried themselves: their walk, their smiles, the facial expressions, and hand movements. They were like no Russians he had ever seen, and he thought they closely approximated the American subtleties of physical presence.

Burov said to them, 'Gentlemen, this is Sam Hollis and Lisa Rhodes. They may be joining the faculty. Introduce yourselves.'

The six young men greeted them pleasantly, pumping their hands and saying things such as, 'Nice meeting you,' 'Glad you could come,' and 'Welcome aboard.'

Their names, Hollis learned, were Jim Hull, Stan Kuchick, John Fleming, Kevin Sullivan, Fred Baur, and Vince Panzarello. Hollis thought their Anglo and ethnic names somewhat fit their appearance.

Fred Baur asked, 'Didn't I read about you two in the newspapers?'

Burov replied, 'Yes. They died in a helicopter crash.' The young men seemed to light up with recognition. They all chatted awhile, and Hollis was impressed with not only their English, but with their informal manner in front of and with Colonel Burov. This, he knew, must have been a difficult cultural breakthrough for them and for Burov.

Lisa listened to the conversation awhile, then looked at the man named Jim Hull. He was in his early twenties, blond, and rather good-looking, dressed in only shorts and sneakers. Lisa surveyed his body up and down, then caught his eye and gave him a look of unmistakable meaning. Hull seemed alternately ill at ease and interested. Finally he broke into a silly grin, dropped his eyes, and lowered his head. Burov and Hollis both noticed, and Hollis realized that Jim Hull suddenly didn't look American anymore. American men of that age could be shy and awkward with women, Hollis knew, but Hull's manner of expressing his shyness and discomfort revealed the Russian boy behind the mask.

Lisa commented to Burov, 'That man doesn't get out much, does he?'

Burov seemed annoyed and said curtly, 'I'm afraid my students aren't used to aggressive American women.' He added, 'Let's go.'

They walked through the gymnasium. Lisa spoke to Hollis

460

as though Burov weren't there. 'You know, Sam, when a young man's hormones are bubbling and his heart is racing and the color comes to his face, he is not in complete control of himself.'

'I think I remember that.'

Burov interjected, 'Well, aside from that, what did you think of them? Truthfully, now.'

'I think,' Hollis answered, 'your six basketball players smelled of kolbassa and cabbage.'

'You mean literally or figuratively?'

'Both.'

'I don't think so.'

'Then don't bother to ask me.'

Burov turned down a short corridor and opened a glass door that led to a large swimming pool. Burov motioned toward the pool in which two men and two women were swimming laps. He said, 'This is a focal point of social activity at night and, I'm afraid, for some rather uninhibited parties on Friday night. That's skinny-dipping night. The wilder bunch congregates here then. I'm not sure if that's Russian decadence or American decadence.' Burov thought a moment, then observed, 'I'll tell you something I've discovered. In America, as in Russia, there is a puritanical streak in the people, a high public morality, but privately there is a good deal of looseness. I think, as great empires we associate spiritual and moral decay with political decline and fall. We think of Rome. What do you think?'

Hollis thought that Burov had been forced into some independent thinking in his capacity here. He was not overly bright, but he was cunning, a survivor, and therefore open to outside reality.

Lisa said, 'There are better examples of the similarities between Russians and Americans.'

'Yes, but none so interesting as their attitudes toward sex. Follow me, please.'

They toured the remainder of the underground sports complex, and Hollis realized this place was at least a partial reason for Burov's not wanting to break camp and move the whole operation elsewhere. When the Charm School was in its cruder, more Russian form, it could easily be relocated. But with the introduction of good housing and this spa, Burov was bogged down in what he could call American decadence, if he thought about it.

They left the underground complex by way of the elevator, which brought them back up into the concrete bunker. Burov led them outside the bunker and pointed to the south. 'That barbed wire is the compound of the KGB Border Guard Directorate. They man the watchtowers and patrol the perimeter. There are a few of them inside the camp, mostly at headquarters. You have no reason to ever go near that compound nor to speak to any of them.' Burov added, 'They don't like you anyway, as you murdered two of their comrades. Is that clear?'

'Perfectly,' Hollis replied. Beyond the barbed wire and watchtowers of this camp and all the other camps in this country, he reflected, was the larger Gulag called the Union of Soviet Socialist Republics. And every meter of those all-encompassing prison walls was watched by the elite paramilitary arm of the KGB, called the Border Guard Directorate. Over a half million strong, they were often better trained and equipped than the Red Army, and their existence gave the KGB the means to bully not only the populace, but the military and the very party they were sworn to defend. As they walked along a path, Hollis asked, 'And you are not in the Border Guard Directorate?'

'You asked me about that once on the telephone, didn't you? Well, I can answer you now. I'm in the Executive Action Department. You know us, of course.'

'Of course. Political murderers, saboteurs, kidnappers, and blackmailers.'

'We don't define ourselves quite that way. But that's about what we do. I started my career in that department, working for some years in Scandinavia. But I've been at this camp ten years, as I said, five as deputy commandant and five as commandant. Like everyone here, I'm assigned for life. The Center does not encourage transfers out of this place. Many of the Russians who work here, including the entire medical staff, are political prisoners who have been assigned here from the Gulag.' He added, 'So, I heard on the Fisher tape that the American instructors call this place Mrs Ivanova's Charm School. Is sarcasm a trait peculiar to American pilots, or does it permeate your whole society?'

'It's endemic in American society,' Hollis replied. 'There are night classes on sarcasm.'

'Now *you're* being sarcastic.'

The three of them continued their walk through the woods, and to an outside observer, it would have looked like a companionable scene. Hollis questioned Burov on some things, and Burov answered easily, remarking several times that there were few secrets inside the perimeter of the camp. Burov pointed out, 'The real deficiency of this school is that all the male instructors are former pilots. Their premilitary backgrounds are somewhat varied, which is good, but their job experiences and adult lives are naturally too similar and limited for us to get a good cross section of American society.' Burov added, 'To have two people like you with some variables in your backgrounds would make excellent additions to the faculty.'

'Please,' Hollis said, 'spare me the college jargon.'

'But we use it here.'

'What do you call the guys with the submachine guns? Campus security personnel?'

'No, they are definitely KGB Border Guards, well-trained, with orders to shoot to kill.'

'So perhaps,' Hollis said, 'I was only acting in self-defense when I killed two of them. Were you acting in self-defense when you murdered Gregory Fisher?'

Burov thought a moment, then replied, 'In a manner of speaking I was.'

Lisa said tersely, 'I don't think so, Colonel Burov. I thought about that. I mean, how you would have had to do that. You would have had to smash that boy's head through the windshield, smash his chest against the steering wheel –'

'Please, Ms Rhodes, we don't need graphic descriptions. Also, your moral outrage is getting tiresome.'

'You said we could say what's on our minds. Don't you want to learn about Western moral outrage?'

'No, and there are limits to my patience.'

'And mine.'

Burov seemed literally to bite his lip, and Hollis thought he was having second thoughts about releasing them from the cells.

They crossed the soccer field again and came back to the main road near the headquarters building. Burov turned left, west toward the main gate. About a hundred meters down the road they saw the long wooden building with the pleasant front porch and the Coke machine. They stepped on to the porch, and Burov said, 'You both look rather tired.' Burov put a fifty-kopek piece in the machine. 'It takes our money.' He handed a can of Coke to Lisa, then the next one to Hollis, and kept the third for himself. 'It's the real thing.' He laughed.

Hollis and Lisa sipped at the cola drink and discovered that indeed it was the real thing.

At Burov's invitation they sat in rockers and looked out across the road at the pine trees. Hollis had once sat on a similar porch in a hunting lodge in North Carolina, sipping a soft drink from a can, smelling the pine, and talking to his wife.

Burov stared off into the distance and rocked slowly, giving Hollis the impression that he too was nostalgic for something, though Hollis could not imagine what. Perhaps his days in Scandinavia as an assassin.

Burov said, 'In this country there is only one master. Us. The KGB. We are known as the sword and shield of the Party, but in reality, we serve neither the Party nor the State, and certainly not the people. We serve ourselves. Even the military fears us, and they have guns too. But we've discovered that the ultimate

464

weapon is illusion. We give the illusion that we are everywhere, so people dare not even whisper our name. And what you see here' – he waved his arm – 'is illusion.' He asked Hollis, 'What did your photo analysis think this was?'

Hollis replied, 'They thought it was probably the Russians' idea of a desert training school.'

Lisa stifled a laugh.

Burov's lips puckered as he stared at Hollis. His fingers tapped rhythmically on the arm of the rocker. 'You might as well have your fun.' Burov stood. 'Let's go inside.'

Burov showed them into the building called VFW Post 000. To the right of the lobby was a large recreation room, and they stood at the door of it apart from the twenty or so people in the brightly lit room.

On the opposite wall was the large American flag that Hollis had seen through the window. Also on the walls, hung randomly, and Hollis thought without much care, were cardboard decorations of the season: pumpkins, scarecrows, a black cat, a few turkeys, and a Pilgrim couple. They all looked like good quality party goods, probably, Hollis guessed, made in the States.

Lisa scanned the autumnal display and said, 'That's depressing.'

Hollis was reminded of the Christmas tree in the rec room at Phu Bai air base. Some seasons didn't travel well.

Hollis noticed a magazine rack on the wall in which were dozens of American periodicals, from *Time* to *Road and Track, Playboy* to *Ladies' Home Journal*. In the rear corner was a reading area with shelves stocked with hundreds of books. There were game tables for cards and board games, a pool table, and even a video game. Burov said, 'The older men, of course, are your compatriots. They keep up-to-date with American life through videotapes that are sent to us in diplomatic pouches by our embassy and consulate staffs in Washington, New York, and San Francisco. Books, magazines, and newspapers come daily through normal flights to Moscow.'

A few of the middle-aged men glanced at Hollis and Lisa, but Hollis noticed none of them even looked at Burov, and no one made a move toward them.

Hollis focused on a man in his middle fifties, a handsome, well-groomed man wearing corduroy pants, a button-down shirt, and cardigan sweater. He sat with a younger man, and both were watching television. Hollis could see the screen; Tony Randall and Jack Klugman were having an argument in the kitchen of their apartment. Hollis couldn't hear the sound, but he recognized the segment from *The Odd Couple*.

The young man howled with laughter at something, then turned to the middle-aged man and spoke in New York-accented English. 'I still don't understand if these guys are supposed to be Jewish or not.'

The American instructor replied, 'It's a little vague.'

'Unger is a Jewish name, right?'

'Right.'

'So Unger is maybe a white Jew.'

'What's a white Jew?' the American asked.

'You never heard that expression? That's a Jew who acts like a gentile.'

'Never heard it,' the instructor said.

The student thought a moment. 'Bill told it to me. He said it was a compliment. But I heard from someone else it was a slur. Now you say you never even heard it.'

The American shrugged. 'I don't know everything.'

Burov turned to Hollis. 'Is it a slur? Or a compliment?'

Hollis replied, 'It's a rather nice compliment.'

Burov smiled. 'I think you're lying.' He added, 'There is some lying here. That has always been a problem. But we can usually check these things.'

Hollis looked at the Americans in the room, his brother fliers from long ago, and his heart went out to them. He took Lisa's arm and moved her out the door. Burov hurried out behind them, and they stood on the covered porch in front of the building. Burov continued his previous thought. 'You see, the lies of omission are the most difficult. Our instructors do not volunteer a great deal, so –' He looked at Hollis. 'Is something bothering you?'

'No.'

'Oh, yes, those men. How insensitive of me. They're alright, Hollis. They've adjusted.'

Lisa put her hand on his shoulder, and Hollis nodded. 'Alright.'

Burov placed his can on top of the Coke machine. He waited a minute, then said to Hollis, 'A man named Feliks Vasilevich called me from Minsk. He was upset over something you said about him, though he was somewhat vague on the details. I wonder, perhaps, if you know what and whom I am talking about.'

'You're talking about Mike Salerno.'

'Yes, that's right. How did you catch on to him?'

'He stood to attention and saluted every time a Soviet officer went past.'

'Come now, Colonel Hollis. I'll let you be sarcastic, but this is lying, and I told you about lying.'

Hollis replied, 'The way he smoked a cigarette.' Hollis explained perfunctorily.

Burov nodded. 'I see.'

Lisa looked from one to the other. She asked Hollis, 'Mike . . . ?'

Burov answered, 'Yes. Were you fooled, Ms Rhodes? Good.' He looked at Hollis. 'But you know, Colonel, if someone wasn't aware, as you were, of wolves in sheep's clothing, that minor mistake would have passed unnoticed. Oh, I don't belittle your intelligence. But smarter men than you have been completely fooled by my graduates. Ms Rhodes' good friend Seth Alevy for one has been fooled several times by some of our Americans. The Kellums, to name but two.'

'The *Kellums*?' Lisa said. 'Dick and Ann?' She looked at Hollis.

Hollis nodded.

Lisa shook her head. 'My God . . . my God . . . I don't believe this.'

Burov smiled in pure delight. 'And there are three thousand more in America, in your embassies, in your overseas military bases. Fantastic, isn't it?'

Lisa stared at Burov.

Hollis glanced from one to the other. He hoped that Burov understood and believed how little Lisa knew. He hoped too that Lisa understood why she wasn't kept as informed as she wished to be.

Burov turned to Hollis and asked, 'And how did you discover the Kellums?'

'Simple background check. They're quite good actors actually.'

Burov looked thoughtful. 'We've had no contact with them for ten days, so we assume Mr Alevy is debriefing them. That's very upsetting. Is he a good interrogator?'

'I have no idea,' Hollis replied. He asked, 'With Dodson on the loose and the Kellums in Alevy's hands, will you move the school?'

Burov shrugged. 'I'd rather not. But things are getting hot, as you say. What would you do if you were the commandant here?'

'Well, I'd say it was my country and I ran it, not the Americans. I wouldn't be pressured by Americans or the Kremlin to run and hide somewhere else.' Hollis added mockingly, 'Create an illusion.'

Burov nodded to himself. 'Perhaps it is you who is trying to create an illusion. Well, we'll see.'

Lisa stood at the porch rail watching a dozen joggers run by on the sandy shoulder of the road. The men were singing as they ran, 'Anchors Aweigh.'

Burov watched them. 'All the students seem to like that one. I prefer your Air Force song myself.' Burov looked at his watch. 'Come, we'll walk, if you feel fit.'

They followed Burov down the steps of the porch and along

the road. He turned down a log-paved path, and they came to a small wood-shingled cottage, vaguely American in design, set among the pine trees. Burov said, 'This is a four-student residence.' He knocked and opened the door. Four young men in a small sitting-room were on the floor playing Trivial Pursuit. Burov motioned to them to continue.

Hollis was struck again by their American casualness, their very un-Russian attitudes, sprawled out on the floor, shoeless, all wearing jeans and sweat shirts. And they were alone, Hollis thought, not expecting company. He noticed that one of the sweat shirts said, 'Jesus Is Lord.' Another read, 'Nuke the Whales.'

One of the men said to Burov in an accent that Hollis recognized as from the Virginia-DC Area, 'This Baby Boomer edition is a real bitch. The regular trivia shit is sort of general knowledge. But the Boomer stuff is tough. I don't think most Americans even know this crap.'

'Yes?' Burov turned to Hollis. 'You play this game?'

Hollis shook his head. 'Wouldn't be caught dead.'

Burov asked Lisa, 'You?'

'No.'

Burov shrugged, then said to Hollis, 'Do me a favor, Colonel. Ask a trivia question of my students. Please. It will be enlightening to you as well.'

Hollis thought a moment, then said to the four men on the floor, 'What is the approximate number of Soviet men, women, and children who died during the Stalin reign of terror?'

The four looked at one another, then at Burov. Burov nodded. 'Answer, if you know.'

One of the men replied, 'I've read it in books and magazines. I guess twenty million is about right.'

'Do you believe that?' Hollis asked.

Again there was a silence.

Burov spoke, 'I don't believe it, and neither do they. But when they get to America, they will say they believe it.' Burov added coolly, 'That is not the type of question I had in mind. Go on and ask them some *trivia*. You, Ms Rhodes. Go ahead.'

Lisa said, 'I don't know any trivia.'

Burov handed her a stack of Trivial Pursuit cards.

She shrugged and flipped through them. She read, '"What country built the TU-144, the first SST to fly and crash?"'

The man with the 'Nuke the Whales' sweat shirt answered, 'The Soviet Union.'

Lisa found another. '"What Russian erection started rising under floodlights shortly after midnight one fateful August thirteenth, 1961?"'

The man with the 'Jesus' sweat shirt replied, 'The Berlin Wall.'

Burov said, 'Thank you, Ms Rhodes, that will be enough.'

The young man with the Virginia accent said to Lisa, 'You know, we Americans call this trivia, but some of this stuff is heavy going for your average Russki.'

Lisa looked at Hollis, and he could see in her eyes that she couldn't quite believe these men were Russian. Burov saw this too and said to the one with the 'Jesus' sweat shirt, 'We will break the rules and you can be a Russian again for a moment.'

The man jumped to his feet and said in Russian, 'Yes, Colonel.' He looked at Hollis and Lisa and again in Russian said, 'My name was once Yevgenni Petrovich Korniyenko. Eleven months ago I entered this school that we call Chrysalis – this sheltered state of being during which I will completely metamorphose and emerge a butterfly. I will be named Erik Larson. I may have some vague memory of the caterpillar I once was, but I will have beautifully colored wings and I will fly in the sunlight. No one who sees me will think of a caterpillar.'

Burov nodded, and the man sat again. It seemed to Hollis that Yevgenni Petrovich was more believable as Erik Larson. Hollis also realized, as Burov suggested, that many of these men were picked for their physical attributes as well as intelligence.

A majority of those that he'd seen were good-looking, and many had the fair complexions of the Nordic Russians, giving them a sort of all-American look when the props and costumes were added.

Burov thanked the four men and motioned to the door, but Hollis said to the four, 'Who knows who won the Battle of Borodino?'

Larson replied, 'I'm not much on history, but I think Napoleon just squeaked by on that one. Right, guys?'

They all nodded.

Hollis said to Burov, 'You must reread *your* history, Colonel.'

Burov didn't reply, but escorted Hollis and Lisa outside. They continued their walk. Hollis saw that the buildings in the camp were spread out, and there were times when it seemed they were in an uninhabited woods, but then a building appeared, or men could be seen walking. Hollis spotted three men in overcoats walking toward them on the wood-planked path. Burov said, 'Instructors.' Hollis watched them walking and talking, almost, he thought, as if they really were three dons, at some sylvan retreat, discussing tenure or Chaucer. They met on the path, and Burov made the introductions. 'Commander Poole, Captain Schuyler, Lieutenant Colonel Mead, may I introduce Colonel Hollis, United States Air Force, former American embassy air attaché, and Miss Lisa Rhodes, United States Information Service, also late of the American embassy.'

The five Americans looked at one another. Colonel Mead broke the silence. 'How the hell did you get here?'

Hollis replied, 'Kidnapped.'

Mead said to Burov, 'Christ, you people fucked up this time.'

Burov smiled thinly. 'If you followed the newspapers more closely as you're supposed to do, gentlemen, you would have read of the deaths of Colonel Hollis and Ms Rhodes in a helicopter accident.'

Commander Poole nodded. 'That's right. You're the air attaché.'

471

'I was.'

Captain Schuyler said, 'Then you're both real? I was thinking you might be two of Colonel Burov's flying worms from a much earlier class.'

'No,' Hollis replied. 'We're real.'

Lieutenant Colonel Mead still seemed skeptical. 'I did read about you, but are you *you*?'

Burov replied, 'You'll be getting last week's news magazines tomorrow, with pictures. And last week's videotapes of network news programs also.'

Schuyler nodded gravely. 'Well, sorry to see you here.'

'We're sorry to be here,' Hollis replied. He could sense that they had a lot of questions for him, the question of Dodson being one, but this was not the time to address them. Hollis said, 'We'll talk soon.'

They nodded.

Burov made a hasty parting and led Lisa and Hollis on. He said, 'As you can see, most of the houses here are American. Also, in another underground area, we have several training environments – American kitchen, several business and professional offices, rooms filled with American gadgets and such. I'll show you that another day. But mostly we concentrate on the nuances of language and culture: facial expressions, clothing, interpersonal relationships, and that sort of thing. The day-to-day things such as supermarkets and gas stations can easily be assimilated in the States.'

Hollis remarked, 'Like how to smoke a cigarette.'

Burov walked in silence awhile, then replied, 'Little mistakes can be fatal.' He went on, 'One of our biggest problems turns out to be facial expressions. How unique faces are, and how odd that different cultures do different things with their faces for different reasons.'

Lisa commented, 'Muscovites always have an expression of quiet desperation, except when they're drunk, and then they look melancholy. They never smile except at their children.'

'Is that so?' Burov said. 'You know, I never noticed that. But that's the point. You did. And the other major difficulty is the English language. The number of words alone is overwhelming. You have close to half a million words. We have less than a hundred thousand. English is a rich language, to be sure. I'd envy you your language but for the spelling and the grammar.'

Burov continued his talk as they walked along the wooden paths through the woods. He said, 'I just remembered a story about one of our graduates who recently arrived in America and had a bad experience in a supermarket with a can crusher. It seems he put a full can of cola into the machine, though I have no idea why.' He smiled at the thought, then added, 'I suppose it's like satellite-map reading. You can see everything, but it's not like being on the ground. You have to put your feet into a country and smell its air and listen to its rhythms to really know it.'

Lisa asked, 'And what if you come to know it and love it?'

'That,' Burov replied, 'can be a problem. But we've worked that out. Again, it's illusion. Our graduates are loyal, but we create the feeling within them that they are always being watched over in America. They know too that their families here are being well taken care of. You understand?'

Hollis remarked, 'You, Colonel, certainly know the nuances of our language.'

'Thank you.'

They crossed the main road again and took a path that ran behind the VFW hall, into the woods, and down a gentle slope. Burov said, 'We are trying something new. Graduates who have spent at least six years in America are returning as instructors. This program must continue and expand; we can't rely on foreign instructors forever.' Burov added, 'Peter the Great finally realized that. He imported too many foreigners at first. That is the history of my country: trying to graft Western learning and culture on to this rough land. But eventually we have to take what we need from the West and perpetuate that learning here. This school will not die because the foreign teachers die, as happened to Peter. No, we will teach teachers to teach, and they will teach others. One day this school will put out two thousand Americans a year. By the end of the century, you will have a fifth column in your country, whose size and influence will be sufficient for the Soviet Union to consider itself a minority shareholder in America, albeit a silent one. One day we might be chairmen of the board.'

Neither Hollis nor Lisa responded.

Burov showed them toward a small clapboard cottage built in a Cape Cod style, with green shutters and a cedar shingle roof. 'This was Major Dodson's quarters. You may use it for the week you need to make up your minds. Come in.' Burov opened the door and invited them to take off their coats, then turned on several portable electric heaters. At Burov's urging. Hollis lit the kindling in the fireplace.

Hollis looked around the room. It was rustic but comfortable. He examined the books on the shelves beside the fireplace and saw that Dodson's taste ran to inspirational literature and British whodunits.

Burov said to Lisa, 'Through that door is a small kitchen. You'll find glasses and something to drink.'

'Really?'

Burov hesitated, then said, 'Would you be kind enough to make drinks?'

Lisa gave him a nasty look, then went into the kitchen.

Burov said to Hollis in a low voice, 'That woman is very . . . independent.' He added, 'American women. How do you put up with them?'

'They're interesting.' Hollis said.

'They're spoiled bitches.' Burov sat in an armchair near the fire. 'The winter is here. Have you adjusted well to Russian winters?'

'Quite well. I have the Joel Barlow award.'

Burov nodded. 'I heard that tape, you know.'

Hollis didn't reply.

'One couldn't make out everything, but I have to tell you I was enraged. It was insulting, vile, and hateful.'

'It *was* in rather bad taste,' Hollis agreed. 'Perhaps you

474

shouldn't listen to other people's conversations.

'Your friend in there likes Russia.'

'But not the people who run Russia now.'

'Now and forever.'

'I think not, Colonel Burov.'

'Be realistic, Colonel Hollis.'

'I try to be.'

Burov shrugged. He said, 'A word of advice: try to keep her mouth shut. We're very lenient here, because that's the only way we can suck your brains year after year. But a few instructors have gone too far.'

'And you shot them.'

Burov replied, 'Only as a last resort. Have a seat. You don't look your old self. *Sit.*'

Hollis sat on a love seat facing the fire.

Lisa came back with three glasses on a small metal tray and passed a glass to Hollis. 'Brandy.' She took a glass for herself and put the tray on an end table. Burov took his glass and raised it. 'To your new home.' He drank alone. 'So, do you find this preferable to torture, starvation, and death?'

Lisa replied, 'Not yet.'

Burov stared at her awhile, then said, 'Sex. You both wondered about that. You saw some women. Some were students, and there are those six American female instructors whom you haven't met. Also there are many other women here who have been provided for the American instructors. Russian women. It would be unrealistic to expect these men to function well for all these years without women. Dodson, however, was one of those who did not seem to avail himself of female companionship. Some say he was completely celibate, and I heard he was being faithful to a wife. Can you believe that?'

Burov sipped his brandy. 'Well, in the beginning most of these men were very promiscuous. But now most of them have settled down into monogamous relationships. The women are all from the Gulag, mostly politicals, but a few criminal types as well. Economic crimes mostly. Thus, the women are mainly of the educated classes, so the Americans form rather good bonds with them. And most of the women are anti-Soviet, which is how they got into the Gulag in the first place. Many of them had life sentences, and those that didn't, do now.'

Lisa inquired. 'Are these couples married in a legal way?'

'No, not under Soviet law. I know that some quasi-religious marriages have been formed. Also, as I said, we still have the wild ones, the ones who go to the spa on Friday. Everything is coed on that night. Life here is what you make it. Like in the West.' Burov added, 'I think in an ironic way you will be less homesick here than you were in the embassy.'

Hollis found that the brandy had gone to his head and found too he was sick to death of Burov. He said to Burov, 'We'd like to be alone.'

Burov stood. 'Of course. You've both had a trying few weeks.' He went to the door. 'Speak to the quartermaster at headquarters if you need anything. There's a shopping plaza at the east end of the main road. You'll find your overnight bags in the bedroom through that door. Unfortunately, your luggage has been sent to your next of kin.'

Hollis asked, 'Ms Rhodes' icon?'

'Oh, I'll have that sent over if you wish. Who cut that hammer and sickle into it?'

Hollis replied, 'The Kellums, I presume.'

'Really? I remember them from when they were here – ten years ago it was. We don't often send them over as a couple like that, but they had the idea of hiring themselves out as domestic servants to a powerful political family. Servants, I understand, are hard to come by in America and easy to place. Once they are in the house, they have unlimited access to things.' Burov added, 'We teach individual initiative here too, which is unfortunately not a Russian character trait. But in the spy business it is half the game. Don't you agree, Colonel?'

'If desecrating a holy art object is an example of the initiative you teach, you're getting it wrong.'

'That *was* rather cruel of them. But I'll send that over to you if you wish. Anything else? No? Well, I've had a pleasant morning. I hope you did too.' Burov left.

Hollis surveyed the room, then looked into the bedroom. 'Not really my taste.'

Lisa put her arms around him. 'I want you to know and to never forget that I love you.'

'I hope so. It looks like we may be here for the rest of our lives. And you thought the embassy was claustrophobic.'

'We will *not* be here for the rest of our lives. No! We are going to go home, or we're going to die trying.'

'Don't be a fool.' Hollis rubbed his fingertips together.

She nodded.

'We'll take a walk later.'

'Yes. I'm exhausted. I don't feel well. My God, that was awful, Sam . . . that cell . . . I hate that man.'

'Lie here on the couch.' He moved her to the couch and covered her with a parka, then sat in an armchair.

Lisa said, 'Was I brave?'

'Very.'

'I don't want to hate so much.'

'Go to sleep. We'll talk later.'

'Yes.'

Hollis stared at the fire awhile.

He reflected on Burov's schizoid personality: vicious and sadistic, then nearly amiable. He suspected that neither facet of that man was an act. Burov had an honest and profound hate for Hollis and the entire Western world. Yet, given a little encouragement and self-interest, he could be polite if not friendly.

Hollis tried to come to grips with his death – his staged death and his impending death. He thought of the three American officers he'd met on the path. They looked forlorn, like unhappy ghosts, lost souls, adrift in a void between the living and the dead. He tried to imagine nearly two decades in this place but could not. He tried to comprehend the sort of monstrous system that could create a place such as this but could not. He tried to think of a way out but could not.

33

Toward dusk, Hollis and Lisa left their cottage and walked south toward the soccer field. Lisa asked, 'Can we talk here?'

'Not on the paths. Later.' They found the soccer field, but it was deserted, and they moved farther south past the concrete bunker that housed the spa elevator. Lisa asked, 'Are we going to the Holiday Spa?'

'No, just walking.'

'Like the last time you took me through these woods?'

'Well, it's not quite so dangerous this time. This time we're *inside* the barbed wire.' The path ended, and Hollis climbed the ladderlike branches of a towering pine tree. He disappeared among the boughs for ten minutes, then came down and brushed himself off.

Lisa asked, 'What did you see?'

'The Border Guard compound.'

'Why did you want to see that?'

'Because it's there. That's my training.' He smiled. 'I can't help it.'

'I guess not.'

They went back along the path, and Hollis turned off the trail and led her into a small ravine. They sat side by side on the sloped ground, and Hollis said softly, 'They may have listening devices on the paths and maybe directional microphones tracking us. But we can talk here if we keep it low.'

'By now we should have been in a country where no one worries about things like that. Damn it.' Lisa picked up a twig and poked the carpet of pine needles on the ground. 'Are we here for the rest of our lives?'

'I hope not.'

'Seth knows we're here?'

'I think he knows we didn't die in that helicopter crash. He probably hopes we're here and not someplace else. We're actually lucky we *are* here and not Lubyanka.'

'So, are we going to be rescued or exchanged or what?'

'I don't know.'

'You *do* know. Why can't I have some hope?'

Hollis took her hand. 'I told you – the less you know the better. The less *I* know, the better. You understand about polygraphs and truth serums. Burov is by no means through with us.'

She nodded. 'I told Burov just about everything I knew, Sam. I couldn't help it. But I didn't betray the people in Yablonya.' She looked at him.

Hollis put his arm around her. 'It's gone. I saw the village from the air. They burned it.'

She poked at the ground awhile, then said quietly, 'Oh . . . those bastards . . .'

'It was brave of you to try to protect them.'

She shook her head. 'I wasn't brave.' After a while she said, 'I always thought I could resist . . . but within a week I was nobody. I wasn't Lisa. I feel ashamed of myself.'

Hollis replied, 'They're professionals, Lisa. They can break anyone. They've had millions of people to practice on before you came along. Don't be hard on yourself.'

She nodded slowly. 'But I had no idea what they could do to a person . . .'

'I think you did.'

She looked at him. 'Yes. I understand that now. The KGB was always an abstraction to me, a bogeyman story that you and Seth told to frighten me into being careful with my Russian friends, my church attendance . . . but now . . . my God, how evil they are. We're so naïve.'

'Don't dwell on it.'

'I'm still shaking.'

He held her closer, and she put her head on his shoulder. She said softly, 'Burov tried to make me hate you. He said

I was here because I was an accomplice to the murders you committed. But I knew that was a lie. They aren't interested in those two dead men. They're interested in what we know and who we are.'

'Yes. You know they don't subscribe to our morality, though they take every opportunity to use it against us. You're not a criminal. You're a political prisoner.'

'Yes, a political prisoner.'

'Those guards were unfortunate casualties of their own illegal operation.'

'Yes. I'll remember that.' She took a deep breath and said, 'I . . . I prayed, but I think I lost faith a few times.'

'So did Christ on the cross. He was human too.'

She took his hand. 'You've made me feel better.'

'Good. And you'll feel a lot better if we can even the score here.'

'I don't want to talk about that, Sam. I'm tired of this ongoing vendetta. All I want is to be out of here and to get our people out of here.'

He said, 'Good.' He rose to his feet. 'Then let's talk to some of our people here and see how we can help.'

Lisa rose also and put her hand on his arm.' Sam . . . I hope you'll understand . . . but I don't think we should sleep together . . . for a while at least.'

'I understand.'

'Do you? It's nothing to do with you.'

'It's alright.'

'I love you.' She kissed him, and they linked arms, walking back toward the path. She asked, 'Do you think they'll give me a Bible?'

'I think they'll give you nearly anything you want. That's the whole idea. They're not trying to brainwash us here. On the contrary. They want you to be Lisa. And they want you to turn out other Lisas.'

'I won't.'

'You most certainly will.'

'I never said I would. *You* said I would.'

'Do you want to be shot?'

'Maybe.'

Hollis glanced at her. 'Lisa, just play for time. Alright?'

'You know, I think these pilots here have been playing for time for nearly twenty years.'

'One week. Promise me.'

She nodded. 'One week.'

They got back on the path and continued their walk. The pine forest was rather nice, Hollis thought, a real Russian *bor*, alive with birds and small animals. Pinecones lay strewn on the log trail, and a carpet of needles covered the earth. Among the pines were a few scrub oaks, and red squirrels gathered acrorns from the base of them. As Hollis and Lisa rounded a bend they saw an unexpected knoll covered with yellow grass, stop which were a dozen white Russian birches, alight in the fading afternoon sun. Lisa took Hollis' hand, and they made their way to the top of the knoll and stood among the birch trees. She said, 'The circumstances notwithstanding, this is lovely.' She pointed. 'What is that?'

Hollis turned toward the setting sun and shielded his eyes. About a hundred meters off, through a thin growth of pine, he could see a tall wooden watchtower, grey and brooding in the gathering dusk. 'That is what has replaced the onion-dome church as the predominant feature of the Russian landscape. That is a guard tower.' He couldn't see the barbed wire or the cleared zone, but he knew it was there. He picked out another tower about two hundred meters beyond the first. Hollis reckoned that if the camp was about two kilometers square and the watchtowers were about two hundred meters apart, there could be as many as forty towers around the perimeter. Each one would have to be manned by at least two Border Guards in eight-hour shifts, meaning there was no fewer than two hundred forty guards for the towers alone. There would be perhaps another two hundred for the perimeter patrol and the main gate, plus the headquarters staff and helipad personnel. Based on just what he'd seen, here and from the air, Hollis thought there could be as many as six hundred KGB Border Guards in the camp. A formidable force. That was a lot of people to keep about three hundred Americans contained. But it was critically important to the KGB that not even one American should get out of here. And for nearly two decades, no one apparently had. Then Dodson had done the seemingly impossible, and the whole chain of command, from Burov right up to the Politburo, was worried. Hollis wondered how Dodson had gotten out.

Lisa looked out at the tower and said, 'This is the limit of our world now, isn't it?'

'Apparently.'

'I wish I had wings.'

'I'm sure the airmen imprisoned here remember when they did.'

They walked back down the knoll to the path and turned in the direction from which they'd come. Lisa said, 'I still feel weak.'

'Do you want to stop?'

'Later. I want to walk while the sun is shining. I'll hold your arm.'

They rounded a curve in the path and saw coming toward them a young couple dressed in jeans and ski jackets. Hollis said to Lisa, 'Be friendly and play instructor.'

'One week.'

The couple smiled as they drew closer, and the man introduced himself, 'Hi, I'm Jeff Rooney, and this is Suzie Trent. You must be Colonel Hollis and Lisa Rhodes.'

He struck out his hand.

Hollis shook hands with him and felt a firm, powerful grip.

Rooney took Lisa's hand. 'Great meeting you.'

Hollis looked at the man. He was in his mid-twenties, probably a two-or three-year veteran of the Red Air Force. He may have had some time in Air Force Intelligence school. Certainly he had spent his one year at the Institute for Canadian and American Studies in Moscow. He was dark and rather short and did not appear particularly Irish as his name suggested, but his legend would probably include a Slavic mother.

Rooney said, 'We were sort of looking for you guys. We went to your house, but someone said they saw you heading this way.'

Neither Hollis nor Lisa responded, but Jeff Rooney seemed irrepressible in his friendliness. He said, 'The colonel suggested we look you up. He wanted Suzie to meet Lisa.'

Suzie Trent smiled. She was a petite woman, in her early twenties, with dirty blond hair, a pointy nose, acne, and breasts too big for her frame. She spoke in accented English. 'It is good that you are here now, Lisa. I have been here six months and go to the women's class. It is very small. Twelve students and only six female instructors. It is time for me to go one-on-one, but there are not enough female mentors. So I hope you can become my mentor and teach me to be you.'

Lisa drew a short breath. 'Yes, if you wish.' She forced a smile. 'But you can't sleep with my boyfriend.'

Jeff and Suzie laughed very hard. Suzie said, 'Lisa, can you have tea with us this afternoon? We meet at five-thirty, after class. All the girls.'

'The women?'

'Yes. We meet in the split-level. Anyone may tell you where it is.'

'*Can* tell.'

'Yes, thank you. *Can*. I know the rule, but I still don't know always which to use.'

'When in doubt, use "can". Most Americans err in that direction. When Russians speak English, they tend to err in the other direction, using too many "may"s, and it stands out.'

'I will remember that.'

'Remember, too, that Americans don't stand as close as you're standing to me.'

'Oh, yes. Sorry.' She took a step back and asked, 'Were you

rich in your last life? Will I have to learn the manners and customs of the rich?'

Lisa glanced at Hollis and replied, 'I was born into a middle-class family.'

'Where?'

'Long Island, outside New York City.'

'Oh . . . then they will send me elsewhere. I wanted to go to New York.'

Jeff Rooney interjected. 'Suzie, I don't think Lisa cares about that. You're not real sensitive. You know?'

'Of course. I'm sorry.'

Rooney said to Hollis, 'My old man is in the Soviet Foreign Ministry, so I sort of picked up the jargon and stuff at home. I thought what we could do for my last few months here is to bat around a lot of embassy jargon. I'm up to here in American Air Force and Navy jargon. We have a few Army types too, by the way. Mostly chopper guys. So, what do you think?'

'Sounds alright.'

'Great,' Rooney said, as if Hollis could have turned him down. Rooney added, 'But I understand that you two may decide not to stay on.' He looked at Hollis closely, and the mask slipped a half centimeter as he said, 'That would be a mistake.'

Hollis didn't reply.

Rooney smiled and continued his pitch. 'Anyway, when I graduate, I was sort of thinking about a career in military intelligence, leading to an attaché posting like you had. Ultimately, I'd like to be assigned to NATO.'

'Good choice.'

'Right. Problem is, the placement people here don't think I could get a security clearance. I mean with my background. Born in Moscow, father a Party member, and all that.' Rooney laughed. 'Well, I mean, I have to come up with a whole legend, of course. But it would be a hell of a coup if I could make it into American military intelligence. I took a few Air Force placement and aptitude exams – US Air Force, I mean – and did pretty well. I think with your coaching. I could really do alright.'

Hollis cleared his throat. 'Well, that's very ambitious of you. I'd be surprised, though, if you could pass a background check. How would you do that?'

'Well, it's getting a little easier now that we have all those other guys over there. I'd start off as an orphan, you see, and list a defunct orphanage, and a few dead foster parents. Birth certificates are no problem anymore. We got a few guys in the Bureau of Vital Statistics in some cities who can take care of all that.'

'But what about personal references?'

'Well, the program here goes back fifteen years, Colonel. So I can list guys whose own bona fides are pretty well established there. It's like an old boys' network already. School ties and all that. The first wave of guys to hit the beach had it tougher. Us new guys go in there with a few beachheads already established.'

'It's my understanding that the graduates never come into contact with one another for security reasons.'

'Oh? Who told you that?'

'Can't remember.'

Jeff Rooney shook his head. 'There are small cells. Just like all over the world. That's how we made a revolution here and other places. Cells, isolated from one another for security, but all working for the same thing. It was a novel concept back before the Revolution, and it still works. Makes it impossible to round up the whole organization. That's the way I understand it is over there. Each cell works to enhance the professional life of its members.'

'That's interesting.'

'Right. So, anyway, don't worry about my security clearance, Colonel. Just give me some insights into the Air Force intelligence world and maybe some embassy Jargon and how the politics work on getting these postings. I'll do the rest. Okay?'

'Okay.'

Rooney added, 'I wish I had an old man who was an Air Force general like you do. Well, someday I'll *be* an American Air Force general, and my kids will have it easier. The great American dream – right, Colonel? Always a little harder for us immigrants.' He laughed. 'Legal or illegal. But we'll make it. We work harder.'

Hollis regarded Rooney closely. The Charm School, he thought, took the spycraft ideal of deep cover to its ultimate realization; it assaulted the very notion of identity that all human beings took for granted. Each man and woman on earth, Hollis reflected, was a complex matrix of language, habit, nuance, gesture, and shared mythology, the sum total of which identified them as members of a specific nation, culture, or society. And the thought that all of this could be replicated was a scary notion. But, Hollis thought, it was a very Russian notion. It was the old Russian nobility and upper classes speaking French, dressing English, and thinking German; it was the whole Russian obsession with trying to be something they were not. And this place, Hollis realized, was an advanced version of Stanislavsky's method acting, a bizarre and grotesque stage where all the actors exited into the night and played their stage parts in the world. It was, Hollis understood, a place where the final curtain had to be drawn.

Rooney said, 'Colonel? You there?'

Hollis focused on Rooney. 'I'm here.'

Rooney smiled. 'Well, you guys probably want to snoop around a little, so we won't keep you. But we're having a party Friday night. You'll get a chance to meet a lot of the people here. See Chuck over at supply for a mask.'

'Mask?'

'Yeah. Halloween. Friday's Halloween.'

'Right.'

Suzie looked at Lisa and said, 'Smile. It's not so bad here.'

Lisa didn't smile or reply.

Jeff added, 'No one will hassle you if you're straight with

us. Talk to the other instructors and you'll see. See you at the Grand Sabbat.'

Suzie waved. 'Nice meeting you both. Don't get lost.'

'Welcome to the campus,' Jeff added. 'Don't get too close to the perimeter.'

They moved off down the path.

Neither Hollis nor Lisa spoke for a minute, then Hollis said dryly, 'Nice kids. Lots of ambition.'

Lisa replied, 'God forgive me, but I wanted to slit their throats.'

'And they may have wanted to cut ours.' Hollis thought a moment, then said, 'Frightening.'

'Creepy,' Lisa agreed. She watched them disappear around the bend in the path and commented, 'He's a nearly finished product. She's still very rough. I guess I'm supposed to polish her. I can't believe this, Sam.'

'It is a bit surreal.' Hollis looked into the woods. Deep purple shadows lay in the ancient *bor*, and the worn wooden trail ran from nowhere to nowhere. The wind had died, and there was a stillness all around. *Here I am*, Hollis thought, *in the heart of Russia, dead to the world, surrounded by barbed wire and engulfed in a mad experiment. Fifteen years late, but here at last.*

They headed back the way they came, but took a cross path that cut east.

Lisa said, 'Did I do alright? I mean with the "may" and "can"?'

'Fine. But they didn't believe for a minute that we were willing participants.'

'Good. I'm not much of a phony.'

'No, you're not.'

They came to a ranch-style house set snugly among the pine trees. It was red brick with white trim and a green asphalt roof. A gravel driveway led to a one-car garage, but there was no sign that a car had ever driven over the gravel. On the right side of the garage was a man of about fifty, stacking a cord of firewood. A child of about five swung in a tire suspended by a rope from a tree limb. Hollis walked up the drive, followed by Lisa, and the man turned toward him. Hollis said, 'Hello, I'm new in town.'

The man looked at him and at Lisa. 'Sam Hollis! I heard you were here. And that must be Lisa Rhodes.' The man wiped his palms on his corduroy slacks and shook hands with Hollis. He spoke in a Texas twang. 'I'm Tim Landis. I think we know each other, Sam.'

Hollis was momentarily taken aback. 'Yes . . . by God, you were a flight commander in our fighter group.'

'Right. We attended some wild briefings together. I remember you used to give old General Fuller a hard time.' Landis said to Lisa, 'Sam got ticked once at all the target restrictions and told Fuller we should drop water balloons so no one would get mad at us.'

Hollis introduced Lisa, and she shook hands with Landis. She asked, 'Is this like dying and going to purgatory, or is it a living hell?'

Landis seemed to understand. 'Well, that depends on how you wake up in the morning, what you dreamed about in the night.' Landis rubbed his forehead. 'You see, I've been nearly twenty years here, and I don't feel like it's home, but I don't know what home is supposed to feel like anymore.' He added, 'Except sometimes when I wake in the night and can remember all of it and feel it again.'

No one spoke for a while, then Landis smiled at Hollis. 'Hey, Sam, I'm glad you didn't get downed.'

'Well, I did. Over Haiphong harbour. Last run of the war. But I got fished out of the drink.' Hollis hesitated a moment, then said, 'My copilot was Ernie Simms. Is he here?'

Landis replied, 'Not anymore.'

'He was here?'

'Yes.'

'And?'

'Well . . . let's see . . . it was back in '74. He'd just got here from Hanoi. In fact, now you mention it, it was you he was with. He said you blew out too, but didn't know what happened to you. So he got fished out of that same drink, I guess. Artery got opened, but the Zips fixed him up, and he was fine by the time he got here.'

'What happened to him here?'

'They shot him.'

'Why?'

'Well . . .' Landis seemed suddenly uncomfortable. 'Well, he told them to fuck off. He told the honcho here, a Red Air Force shit whose name I can't remember now, that he wasn't playing ball. So they shot him.'

Hollis nodded.

Landis said, 'They had all the pilots they needed from the Zips then, so if you got testy with them, they shot you. Then the war ended, and the KGB started taking over. You know about all that?'

'No.'

'You want to know?'

'Some other time.'

'Okay. Hey, sorry about Simms. But there are probably a few other guys here you know from our bunch. Jessie Gates?'

'"Crazy" Gates?'

'Right.' Landis rattled off a dozen other names, and Hollis recognized three or four of them. Landis said, 'Say, let me introduce you to my little guy.' He turned to the boy and called out, 'Timmy. Come here and meet an old friend of mine.'

The boy jumped down from the tire and ran over to them. Landis said, 'Timmy, this is . . . what are you now, Sam, a general?'

'Colonel.'

'Terrific. Timmy, this is Colonel Hollis and Miss Rhodes. This is Timothy Junior.'

Everyone shook hands, and the boy smiled bashfully. Landis said, 'Timmy is almost six. There are a few other kids his age

489

here but not too many. He likes the older kids anyway. Right, kiddo?'

The boy nodded. 'Joey Reeves is my best friend, and he's nine.' He looked at Hollis. 'Are you from America?'

'Yes.'

'I'm going to America someday.'

'Good. You'll like it.'

'I'm going to go there to work for peace.'

Hollis didn't reply.

'America is a good country.'

'Yes, it is.'

'But bad people run the country.'

Hollis glanced at Landis.

Lisa asked the boy, 'Do you speak Russian?'

'No. We learn things about Russia but in English.'

'What do you learn?'

'Russia is a great country that works for peace. Someday, Russia and America will be friends. Then Dad, Mom, and me can leave here and live in America if we want. Or in Russia. Russia is close to here. America is far away.'

Lisa knelt and took the boy's hands. 'America wants peace too.'

'But bad people run the government.'

Hollis put his hand on Lisa's shoulder, and she stood.

Landis said to his son, 'Go on and play.'

The boy ran off.

Landis watched him, then said, 'At first they thought that sex was enough, then they understood that some of us actually had a paternal instinct and our women had the maternal urgings. So they let us have children. They want to keep us contented here, busy with everyday things. But solutions lead to new problems. Like the kids. There are about sixty of them now. The oldest is the Brewer kid, Rick. He's ten. Ted Brewer's wife, Svetlana, was the first to conceive after they lifted the ban.'

'And what,' Hollis asked, 'is the problem?'

'Well, they didn't know how to bring up these kids. So they

490

came up with this hybrid system where they teach the kids a modified American curriculum in English, but they also teach Russian history and Soviet ideology. It's kind of screwed up. They think they can send these kids into America like they do the Russian students. But I don't know. I think all these kids are going to go bonkers as they get older and realize they're in prison.' Landis looked at his son, swinging again on the tire. 'My poor little guy.'

Lisa watched the boy awhile, then looked at Landis. 'Do you teach him the truth at home?'

'No.'

'Why not? You could in subtle ways –'

'Miss Rhodes, they told me if they discovered I was doing that, they would kill the boy. Not take him away, but *kill* him. And kill my wife too.'

'My God . . . I'm sorry . . .'

Landis shrugged. 'It's all velvet gloves over steel fists here.' He looked at Hollis. 'Say, Sam, did you ever happen to hear anything about my wife? I mean my American wife? Maggie?'

'No, I don't think so. I'll try to remember.'

'Would you? I'd appreciate that. I had two boys, Timothy . . . my other Timothy . . . and Josh. They'd be grown men now. Tim would be thirty, and Josh would be twenty-four. I sure hope they did alright. Hope Maggie remarried too.' Landis passed his hand over his face.

Hollis had a strangely empty feeling in his stomach. He said, 'Look, Tim, I think my presence is a little upsetting, so we'll –'

'No, no. Hey, I won't ask any more of those kinds of questions. You two are probably a little disoriented yourselves. Come on in and meet Jane. That's my wife. She's Russian but likes the name Jane.'

'No, thanks –'

'Come on. You'll like her. She's a political. Real anti-Red. She got thirty years, but that's like a death sentence

491

in the camps. She did two years and then got offered the job here because she had some school English. I'd like you to meet her.'

Lisa and Hollis exchanged glances, and Lisa said, 'We'd like to meet her.'

'Great.' They walked around to the front of the house, and Landis went on, 'She got here about, let's see . . . fifteen years ago. She dated around for about two years – we all did then. Wild time. Then most of us sort of paired off over the years.'

Landis opened the front door of the house and called in, 'Honey, we got company.'

A voice called out in accented English, 'Oh . . . Tim, the house is a mess.'

Hollis and Lisa looked at each other and didn't know whether to laugh or leave.

Landis indicated the way toward the kitchen. Hollis noticed that the living-room furniture was rather shabby and not particularly American-looking. It was blondewood, sort of 1950s, and may have been Scandinavian. The floor was Russian parquet, larch not oak, and the rug was an Oriental from one of the Soviet near-Eastern republics. Hollis saw a modern Sony TV with VCR and an audio system in a stack unit.

They entered the kitchen, and Hollis felt that here indeed was little America. It was a well-equipped and fairly modern kitchen, with breakfast nook. The only thing that seemed to be lacking was a dishwasher. A General Electric coffeepot was perking on the white plastic counter. Mrs Landis was scrubbing beets at the sink.

Landis said, 'Jane, these are our new neighbors, Lisa Rhodes, and an old comrade-in-arms, Captain – no, Colonel Sam Hollis.'

Jane Landis wiped her hands on her apron and looked at both of them, then took Lisa's hand. 'Hello.'

Hollis thought she was about forty. She was rather attractive and well-kept with grey-streaked black hair, cut in a pageboy style. She wore a turtleneck sweater, plaid skirt, and penny loafers. Hollis momentarily pictured a late fall day, somewhere in the Northeast. It was a Saturday afternoon, and the man of the house was stacking firewood, and his wife, still rather preppy despite her years, was brewing coffee. Through the bay window of the breakfast nook, their son could be seen playing among the pine trees. *Illusions*.

Jane Landis took his hand and said, 'So the bastards kidnapped you both?'

Hollis smiled at her. For a moment he felt like hugging her. 'Yes, the bastards kidnapped us.'

'What for? Ah, they don't need a fucking reason. Sit down. Have some coffee.' She banged four mugs on the table that extended into the bay window area and busied herself with sugar and cream. 'So, what does your presence bode for us? Are we saved, or are we doomed?'

'Neither, I think,' Hollis answered as he sat. He jerked his thumb at the ceiling in a gesture he thought she'd understand immediately.

'Oh,' Jane Landis said, 'I don't think that after fifteen years they care what we say anymore. We don't know anything they don't know. But maybe with you two here, they'll start listening again. So answer me another time.' She poured four cups of coffee. 'It's not American, it's Ethiopian. Every time they grab another country, they ship out arms to it and get some crap in return. Starting to get bananas from Nicaragua now. The only thing they get from Afghanistan is body bags.'

Landis sat across from Hollis and said to him, 'I told you she was anti-Red. She's going to get into trouble one of these days. Right, Jane?'

'Fuck them. I hope they're listening.' She said to Lisa, 'I spent two years in the Kandalaksha Camp in the Murmansk region, up near the Arctic Circle. And for what? For writing a letter to that pig Brezhnev protesting the use of Soviet troops in Poland to put down the riots there. That was December of 1970. I have a husband and two daughters. They were notified that I died in Kandalaksha. I'll never see them again.'

493

'I'm sorry.'

'Yeah. We're all sorry. I'm sorry I came here. If I'd stayed in Kandalaksha, I'd be dead now. It turns my stomach to think I'm still working for them. The Americans here, Tim included, hate them, but they hate in an American way – part-time and with idiotic gallows humor. They don't understand how a Russian can hate them.'

Lisa replied in Russian, 'My grandmother was Russian. I think I understand.'

Jane's eyes lit up. 'Ah,' she replied in English, 'we're going to be friends.'

Hollis said in English, 'Lisa has aristocratic blood.'

Jane made a face. 'Well, I'll forgive that.'

They all smiled. Hollis always marveled at how even the anti-Soviet Russians had been conditioned to hate the Romanovs and the old aristocracy. That was perhaps the one solid success the Soviets had in creating the new Soviet citizen. And without a past that they wanted to return to and with their innate fear of the future, the Russian was controllable. No one seemed to have any idea of who or what should replace the communists. It was a country of failed imagination.

Tim Landis said to Lisa, 'You shouldn't speak Russian. That's a serious offense.'

'That's rather ironic,' Lisa replied.

Jane Landis said, 'I'm not allowed to teach Tim Russian. That's one of the ways they keep the Border Guards isolated from the Americans. They fear Western contamination.'

Lisa asked, 'But do they trust the students?'

Jane replied, 'They have to, up to a point. And they must have a way of controlling them in the States.' She added, 'I understand that they polygraph the hell out of these guys before they ever leave here. If they see one glitch, the student gets washed out.'

Tim Landis tapped the table and pointed at the ceiling.

Jane Landis shrugged. 'Screw them.'

They drank coffee in silence awhile, then Lisa asked, 'This

house . . . is it just for you, or do they use it as a training . . . what would you call it?'

Jane Landis replied, 'Yes, that's it. It's for training. Not just for our comfort. We have two boarders at the moment. We're supposed to call them boarders. Two young swine who live here. We get them a few months before they ship out, so we don't have people here all the time, thank God. But when we have them, I'm a bitch to live with. Right, Tim?'

'Right.'

Hollis asked, 'And you housebreak them?'

She smiled. 'That's it. Teach them how to use a flush toilet.' She laughed.

Tim Landis added helpfully, 'Jane does their cooking and laundry. They help me with house repairs and heavy cleaning chores. It teaches them a little about domestic life, handiwork, and all.'

Jane said, 'These two are real assholes. One of them made a pass at me, then was ball-less enough to say it was only training.'

Lisa smiled and asked, 'Where are they now?'

Landis looked at his watch. 'They had a driving class today. They go up and down the main road. The Soviets buy your old embassy cars and bring them here.'

Hollis nodded. 'I always wondered what they did with them. I never saw one around Moscow.'

'Well,' Landis said, 'now you know why. Most Soviets, as you know, can't drive. Even young guys like these two, most of whom are going to become pilots, for Christ's sake. So anyway, these two – Sonny and Marty – should be here in a few minutes, if you want to meet them.'

'Alright,' Hollis replied.

Jane Landis said to Lisa, 'Sonny is the one who wants to get in my pants. Keep an eye on that pig. He has a hormone problem.'

'Okay.'

Hollis drank his coffee and stared out the bay window. He

495

tried to put himself in Tim Landis' life, tried to imagine how it would have been in a North Vietnamese POW camp, then to be transferred to a Red Air Force POW camp to train pilots, then the evolution of the POW camp to the Charm School. Then a wife, a son. Nearly two decades. Who was Tim Landis now? Even Tim Landis didn't know. *Did* they want to go home? How would Maggie Landis react? She had remarried about ten years ago. Hollis knew that because he'd known an officer who'd flown to San Diego for the wedding. And if these people got out of here, were their new wives and children supposed to go with them? With every hour that passed in this place, Hollis had more questions and fewer answers. The final answer, however, might be that they would all simply die here of old age.

Tim Landis got up from the table, found a pencil and pad, and wrote on it, then handed it to Hollis. Hollis read: *Do you know about Major Dodson? Did he make it to the embassy?*

Hollis wrote in reply: *We know about him, indirectly, through Gregory Fisher. Fisher story in American newspapers. Dodson still MIA.*

Landis read it, nodded, and turned away. Hollis thought he was crying. Hollis crumpled the paper and put in his pocket.

Jane Landis was about to say something when the back kitchen door opened and two men in their mid-twenties came in. One of them said, 'Hi. Who's this?'

Tim Landis seemed to have gotten control of himself and made the introductions. Hollis looked the two over. Marty was a bit chunky, dressed in grey sweats and a ski parks. He had a pleasant, smiley face, and Hollis thought he looked rather innocuous. Sonny was uncommonly handsome, with curly black hair, dark eyes, and a sneering mouth that Hollis thought some women would find sensuous.

Sonny smiled at Lisa. 'Glad to meet you. Everyone here is talking about you.'

'Is that so?'

Sonny's eyes held hers. 'Yes, it is. There are only six other real American women here.'

496

'Why don't you just photostat them?'

Sonny laughed. 'Say, are you and Sam involved, as they say, or just friends?'

Marty interjected, 'Lay off, Sonny.'

Lisa stared hard at Sonny. 'That's none of your damned business.'

'Sure it is. I want to date at least one real American before I cross over.' He smiled.

Hollis' swing caught Sonny in the abdomen, doubling him over. Sonny staggered around the floor, odd noises coming from his mouth, then he sank to his knees, trying to catch his breath.

Hollis said to the Landises, 'Will there be any trouble for you?'

Tim Landis shook his head. 'He had it coming. I'll square it with his Russian control officer.'

Jane Landis added, 'Good training for him. He doesn't seem to comprehend the etiquette of putting the moves on a woman.'

Marty added as he helped Sonny out of the kitchen, 'This guy's gonna get himself killed in the States by some hotheaded boyfriend.'

Hollis said to the Landises, 'Thank you for the coffee.'

Tim Landis got an electric lantern from the cupboard. 'You'll need this to find your way.'

Lisa said to Jane Landis, 'We'll speak again.'

She replied, 'I like you two already.'

Tim Landis walked out with them and handed Hollis the lantern. He said, 'Thanks for stopping by. We'll have you both for dinner one night. Jane cooks American.'

Hollis said, 'Lisa cooks Russian.'

Landis smiled. 'Good night.' He turned away, then came back. 'Oh, I remembered something, Sam. What Simms said. He didn't say that he didn't know what happened to you. That was somebody else I was thinking about.'

Hollis stood silently in the dark, holding the lantern.

497

Landis moved closer to him. 'Simms said you both hit the drink together. He said the Zips sent boats out, and they got him, but you got fished out by the Jolly Green Giant. Fate, isn't it?'

'Yes.'

Landis moved still closer and spoke in a soft voice. 'Ernie Simms said you were swimming toward him, yelling to him to come to you. He said he kept waving you off because he figured he was a goner, but you kept coming, calling to him. He said he was glad when he saw the chopper rescue you, glad for you and glad there was a witness that he'd been captured alive.' Landis added, 'He spoke highly of you, Sam.'

Hollis nodded. 'Thank you.' He turned and walked with Lisa away from the house.

Lisa squeezed his hand. 'Alright?'

He nodded again. *And so,* he thought, *I make the final entry in the pilot's log and close the book.*

They walked for a while in silence, then Lisa said, 'Do you want to be alone?'

'No, walk with me. Talk to me.'

'Okay . . . question. Did you hit Sonny because he was a Russian or because he was hitting on me?'

'Oh, I don't know. Mostly male ego, I guess. I'm actually having trouble perceiving these people as Russians. All I saw was a young punk being a boor.'

'He wasn't bad-looking.'

'Bitch.'

She smiled and grabbed his arm. They embraced and kissed. She said, 'Sam . . . Sam . . .'

'Yes?'

'Don't leave me. I'd die if you left me. If we stay here, don't take a Russian wife.'

'How about a girlfriend?'

'Don't tease.'

'Sorry.'

They walked down to the path and headed home.

Lisa said, 'How do people marry here?'

'I think they just announce it.'

'Will you marry me?'

'Yes. Does that mean you'll work here?'

'I'll live here. I'll work against them. We'll be free someday. I know we will.'

He took her arm. 'I feel free. Poor Tim Landis just gave me my freedom.'

'I know.'

They continued on the dark path toward their cottage. Hollis saw other lights moving along other paths, like aircraft, he thought, lost in the night, looking for their home base. He suddenly recalled a sign that had hung in the chapel at Phu Bai air base. It was a New Year's message from Britain's King George to his embattled people at the beginning of the Second World War, and Hollis found he could recall it clearly: *I said to the man at the gate of the year, 'Give me a light that I may go forth into the unknown.' And the man replied, 'Put your hand into the hand of God. That shall be to you better than a light, safer than a known way.'*

34

Sam Hollis knelt by the fireplace in the small living room of the cottage and lit the kindling under the logs.

Lisa said, 'I used to love a fire on a cold winter night. That's one of the things I missed in Moscow and my other assignments.'

'Well, you won't miss it on this assignment.' He blew on the fire.

She looked at the growing flames, then said, 'I suppose one can pretend. I mean, here in this room, just you and I. We can pretend we're home, instead of sixty miles from Moscow. Maybe that's how these prisoners have kept their sanity.'

Hollis wasn't sure they *had* kept their sanity. And he recalled, too, what Tim Landis had said about those sad early-morning hours. 'Could you turn on the VCR?'

She went to the bookshelves beside the fireplace and examined the videotapes. 'Anything in particular?'

'Something noisy.'

She selected *Rocky IV* and fast-forwarded it to the fight scene with the Russian, then sat down on the love seat with Hollis.

He put his arms around her and spoke in a low voice. 'How was tea with Suzie and her friends?'

'Awful. I had to get up and leave. I'm sorry.'

'That's alright.'

'Sam, there are six other American women here. Two were kidnapped in Finland on ski trips, and a woman named Samantha was kidnapped while she was hiking in the Carpathian mountains in Romania. The other three were supposedly lost in swimming accidents, two in the Black Sea, one in the Baltic off East Germany. There used to be two others, but they committed suicide.'

Hollis made no comment.

'Sam, it almost broke my heart. How can these bastards *do* that to people? Rip them away from their families . . . their lives . . . ?'

Hollis looked into the fire awhile, then said, 'They call us the Main Enemy. In caps. They believe that they are locked in a life-or-death struggle with us. They're right. They know that if the Main Enemy is defeated, most of their problems will be over. Meanwhile America gives the Soviets about ten percent of its attention.'

Lisa looked at the television. Rocky and the Russian were going at it, and the crowd was nearly hysterical. 'That movie is inane. I *know* it's inane. But why isn't it as idiotic as it was the first time I saw it?'

Hollis smiled. 'I know what you mean.'

She said, 'Do you think of *them* as the main enemy?'

Hollis put his feet on the coffee table. 'You know, sometimes I like to think that I'm doing something for *them* too. Not the Party people of course or the KGB. But the *narod*, the Russian masses, and the other nationalities imprisoned outside our prison. My mind keeps returning to Yablonya, Lisa. The way it was when we were there, the way I saw it from the helicopter, and the way it could have been if the people in Moscow were different.'

She looked at him, then put her head on his shoulder and after a while asked, 'How did Major Dodson get out of here?'

'I don't know yet.'

'What did you do while I was gone?'

'Burov stopped by.'

'What did he want?'

'He just wanted to see how we were getting on.'

'That *bastard*!'

'Don't let these people get to you, Lisa.'

'It's *him*. He . . . hit you, he slapped me . . . he . . .'

'What?'

'He . . . he was in my cell . . . when the matron . . . searched me . . .'

'Alright. Don't think about it. You have to understand that he always intended for us to work for them. That's why we're here and not in Lubyanka. That's why he hasn't done anything to us that he thinks we couldn't forgive.'

'I understand.'

Hollis said, 'He also dropped off some reading material. Are you up to reading about your death?'

She stared straight ahead for some time, then nodded.

Hollis stood and went to a cabinet beneath the bookshelf. He returned with newspapers and magazines and sat beside her. He handed her the Long Island *Newsday*, opened to the obituary page.

Lisa looked down at her picture and read the headline: *Lisa Rhodes Accident Victim*. She cleared her throat. 'My mother must have given them that old photo. She always liked that picture . . .' Hollis saw a tear splatter on the newspaper, and he took the paper from her. He stood and poured two glasses of brandy. He handed her a glass, and she drank from it.

Lisa composed herself and said, 'My family buried me . . . poor Dad . . . I can almost see him trying not to cry.' She looked at Hollis. 'And you? Your family . . . ?'

Hollis opened a *Washington Post* to the obituary page. 'I got full military honors at Arlington. My parents probably groused about having to fly in from Japan.'

She looked down at the obituary and read it silently. 'I didn't realize you were so important.'

'It was just the circumstances surrounding our deaths that generated some interest. Here . . .' He opened a later editon of *The Washington Post* to a story in the A section headlined: *US Accepts Soviets' Claim, Calls Fatal Crash 'Accident'*.

Lisa looked at him, then turned her attention back to the story and read:

502

The State Department said yesterday that it was 'substantially satisfied' with the Soviet Union's explanation of the deaths of two Americans killed last week when a Soviet military helicopter crashed near the Russian city of Minsk. In a prepared statement released here and in Moscow, the department called the crash a 'tragic accident' and said that there was no reason to suspect 'foul play'.

The US embassy in Moscow had demanded that the Soviets conduct a complete investigation of the deaths of Air Force Col. Samuel G. Hollis, 46, a military attaché, and Lisa Rhodes, 29, a deputy public affairs officer for the United States Information Service. Both were being expelled from the country when the helicopter in which they were riding crashed for unknown reasons. The fact that Hollis and Rhodes had been declared 'persona non grata' by the Soviets and were traveling in a Russian military helicopter without any other westerners present when they died had concerned the State Department.

Charles Banks, an embassy official in Moscow, was quoted in yesterday's statement as saying the embassy was 'substantially satisfied' with the Soviet explanation of the incident. Banks said there was 'no reason to believe that either Hollis or Rhodes were the targets of any foul play.'

(In Moscow, the Soviet newspaper *Pravda* carried a three-paragraph story about the helicopter crash in yesterday's editions. It said a Russian helicopter pilot and co-pilot also died in the crash. Because *Pravda* rarely prints stories about accidents inside the Soviet Union, the story was seen by US diplomats as a public apology of sorts by the Kremlin.)

The State Department released its statement yesterday a few hours after Hollis was buried at Arlington National Cemetery in a military service. Rhodes was also buried yesterday in Sea Cliff, a small New York village on Long Island. A high-level source at the State Department said yesterday's statement was issued to reassure the families of Hollis and Rhodes and also to end 'unwarranted speculation' in the press about their deaths.

The Soviet government ordered Hollis and Rhodes to leave the country about two weeks ago after it accused them of taking an unauthorized automobile trip. The State Department refused to confirm or deny the Soviets' charge, but a spokesman for the US embassy in Moscow acknowledged at the time that

Hollis had been sent by the embassy to Mozhaisk, with the Soviet government's full knowledge and permission, to claim the body of an American tourist, Gregory Fisher, 23, of New Canaan, Conn. Fisher had died in an automobile accident earlier this month outside Moscow, and Hollis was investigating the matter, the spokesman said. Rhodes had accompanied Hollis to claim Fisher's body because she and Hollis were friends, not because she was on embassy business, the spokesman said. However, both had passes issued by the Soviet government, which are necessary for embassy staff for travel outside Moscow.

In retaliation for the expulsion of Hollis and Rhodes, the State Department ordered the expulsion of two Soviet embassy employees in Washington. A State Department official denied that this round of expulsions, after years of relatively good diplomatic relations, was a signal that the diplomatic thaw was cooling. 'This was an isolated incident,' the official was quoted as saying, 'and will not affect ongoing initiatives between the two countries.'

Members of the Fisher family said yesterday that they still are not satisfied with the explanation that the Soviets and State Department have given about Gregory Fisher's death. One family member said he felt it was 'odd' that Hollis and Rhodes were expelled and later died after they began investigating Fisher's death. But the State Department said it didn't believe the matters were related.

The Kremlin's decision to expel Hollis and Rhodes was considered severe by US diplomats, who said the US and Soviets usually only file routine complaints when they discover a diplomat has violated travel restrictions. The harshness of the Soviets' action prompted some Western diplomats to speculate that Hollis and Rhodes might have used the trip to conduct surveillance on the Soviets' tightly guarded military facilities in the area. The Pentagon and USIS both categorically denied that Hollis and Rhodes were involved in any 'activities related to surveillance or espionage'. The USIS issued a strongly worded statement that said its personnel 'have never and will never' participate in espionage activities. 'The USIS is not part of that world,' a USIS spokesman said. A spokesman for the Pentagon acknowledged that some countries – including the Soviet Union – use military attachés at embassies for 'intelligence gathering', but he denied that

Hollis was involved in any such activity.

Friends of the Hollis family said Hollis' father, retired Air Force Gen. Benjamin Hollis, had asked the Pentagon for a briefing on the death of his son. A family friend said Gen. Hollis was concerned because his son's body was so badly burned that it could not be positively identified.

(A high-ranking embassy official in Moscow, who visited the helicopter crash site, told Geraldine Callahan of the *Post*'s Moscow bureau that the helicopter 'burned with surprising intensity' after it crashed. The fire was so hot that it completely consumed the four bodies aboard, this official said. 'The remains were no more than ashes and bone fragments and were impossible to identify,' he said.)

The Pentagon would not comment on the condition of the bodies or whether Gen. Hollis had requested a briefing. However, a Pentagon spokesman, Gen. Earle Vandermullen, said yesterday that the Red Air Force helicopter that crashed was a turbojet and that a 'fire of extreme intensity would not be inconsistent with that type of aircraft, especially if the jet fuel tanks were full.' The Hollis family did not issue any statements or talk with reporters at the funeral.

The State Department said the Soviets gave the following account of the accident. Hollis and Rhodes boarded Pan Am flight 415 last Monday on what was supposed to be a direct flight from Moscow to Frankfurt. The airplane was forced to make an emergency landing in Minsk after Soviet authorities radioed the pilot that a bomb had been planted on the airplane. Because of their diplomatic status, Hollis and Rhodes were told by Minsk officials that they could return to Moscow without delay by boarding a military helicopter that would take them to a Lufthansa Airlines flight to Frankfurt. The helicopter carrying Hollis and Rhodes reportedly crashed about 15 minutes after it left Minsk airport.

Mike Salerno, Moscow correspondent for Pacific News Service, said that he sat next to Hollis and Rhodes when the Pan Am flight left Moscow. He said Hollis and Rhodes both seemed grateful for the chance to return to Moscow aboard the helicopter. He said they asked him to notify the US embassy about their flight change, which he said he did. 'The Soviet authorities at Minsk offered me a ride in the helicopter back to

Moscow,' Salerno said. 'But I didn't mind staying on in Minsk. Sam and Lisa (Hollis and Rhodes) were anxious to make connections in Frankfurt.' A spokesman for Pan Am said Soviet authorities held the aircraft overnight in Minsk before allowing it to resume its flight, and the passengers were put up in a local hotel. The Soviets declined to say whether a bomb was found.

Family friends said Gen. Hollis claimed his son's body Wednesday at Andrews Air Force Base. Col. Hollis was married but had been estranged from his wife Katherine during the past six months, a friend of the Hollis family said. Katherine Hollis arrived here yesterday from her home in London for the funeral but refused to talk to reporters.

Rhodes was buried last week in Sea Cliff, NY. Her mother, Eva Rhodes, described Rhodes as an energetic woman, who was 'proud of her work' and was 'a lover of the Russian language and culture'. A USIS spokesman said Rhodes was considered a 'hard worker' by her peers with a keen interest in Russian history. She had worked at USIS for six years, the last two years in Moscow.

Hollis, a highly decorated Vietnam veteran, joined the Air Force in 1962 and was a graduate of the United States Air Force Academy. He was responsible for maintaining liaison with the Red Air Force in matters of mutual interest to both countries.

The State Department said it considered the matter closed unless there was 'substantial new information' regarding the helicopter crash.

Lisa closed the newspaper and stared at the burning logs. Hollis poured two more glasses of brandy. He saw that her cheeks were wet with wiped tears. Finally, she said, 'They don't suspect a thing.'

'Not for the record.'

'But Seth . . .'

Hollis felt himself getting somewhat annoyed but answered, 'Yes, Seth probably knows.'

She seemed to sense his irritation and added, 'We don't need him to get us out of here. We can do it ourselves. You got us away from Mozhaisk and that state farm.'

'Right. We'll work on it together.'

She looked at the newspapers spread out on the coffee table, stood, gathered them up, and threw them in the fire. The blaze lit up the room, and Hollis watched her face in the sudden light. She seemed, he thought, to be finding herself again. And he noticed too that somewhere between the Arbat and here she had gotten much older.

She sat beside him again, and they held hands on the love seat. The VCR continued to play, the fire burned, and the brandy took effect. They both slept.

Hollis was awakened by a knock on the door and sat up. The videotape had run out, and the fire was dying. The mantel clock showed 10:15 P.M. Hollis stood.

Lisa awoke and mumbled, 'Where're you going?'

There was another knock on the door. Hollis went to it and opened it. A man of about fifty, dressed in a ski parka, stood in the cold. 'Sorry to bother you, Colonel. We met earlier in the woods. I'm Lewis Poole. May I come in a moment?'

'That depends. Were you born Lewis Poole, 'or are *you* one of Burov's flying worms?'

Commander Poole smiled. 'I guess that meeting on the path could have been a setup. But I can take you to fifty guys here who were in the Hanoi Hilton with me.'

'Come in.'

Poole stepped in and greeted Lisa. He stood by the fire and warmed himself, then said, 'Can we play a little music?'

Lisa put one of Dodson's tapes in a portable player, and the voices of black gospel singers filled the room.

Poole said, 'They've about given up on house bugs because we find them and squash them. Also, we play music or just use writing and sign language. Every one of us here can communicate by signing. Someone found a book on it in the library years ago, and by the time the Russians realized it, we were all pretty adept at signing.'

Lisa nodded. 'We used a simple sign language in the embassy.'

'Right. You know what it's all about. This cottage is probably all wired for you. Soviet technology. But I don't think they've invented a simple one-family house furnace yet.'

'Brandy?' Hollis asked.

'Fine.'

Hollis poured him some brandy.

Poole took a drink and continued, 'Also, you have to be extremely aware of the directional microphones outdoors. They're in the watchtowers. You have to get low, into gullies and ravines, and swish pine branches around when you speak.'

Hollis commented, 'I suppose there are a lot of things we have to learn.'

'Yes. I can set up a briefing session for you both in the next day or two.'

'That's very good of you, Commander.'

'Lew. Let me introduce myself a bit further. I'm the aide-de-camp for General Austin. Do you know the name?'

Hollis replied, 'Of course. He was the commander of the Eighth Tactical Wing at Cu Chi. The only American Air Force general shot down. Missing, believed dead.'

'Yes. But he's very much alive. According to camp rules, there is no senior man among us and no aide-de-camp or any command structure. But we're all military, are we not? So we've set up a sub-rosa POW camp organization as we were trained to do. You understand.'

Hollis nodded.

'It may surprise you, Colonel Hollis, to discover that the spirit of resistance is still alive here after nearly two decades. But I hope it *doesn't* surprise you.'

Hollis did not respond.'

Poole continued, 'Though to be perfectly frank, we have not accomplished very much aside from sabotaging the curriculum as often as possible. In real terms – that is, bottom-line breakout – Jack Dodson is only the second man we've gotten out of here. The escape committee has tried virtually everything known in the annals of prison-camp escape, including a hot-air balloon. But there are either a few turncoats among us or perhaps it's the Russian wives, though they aren't supposed to know anything about escape plans. Maybe it's just good

508

KGB intelligence work. Whatever it is, we've been damned unsuccessful.'

Lisa asked, 'What happened to the first man who escaped?'

'That was Gene Romero, an Air Force captain. He was recaptured and shot on the athletics field along with five other men as an example. That was nine years ago.'

'And Dodson?' Hollis asked. 'How did he get out?'

'I'm not at liberty to say.'

'Alright.'

Poole glanced at Hollis and Lisa and said, 'Your presence here has sparked a lot of hope.' His eyes searched Hollis', and he asked, 'Right or wrong?'

Hollis replied, 'I'm not prepared to comment at this time.'

Poole seemed to take this as a positive statement, Hollis thought. Poole said, 'Well, the reason I'm here is to invite you to meet General Austin.'

'Now?'

'Yes. Now.'

Hollis considered a moment, then replied, 'You understand that I don't accept the authority of General Austin under these circumstances.'

'I think I understand that.'

'Well, Commander, let me be blunt so that you do understand. I hold an active and honorable commission as a full colonel in the United States Air Force. The status of you men is somewhat questionable.'

Poole stared at Hollis, then turned away and looked at the fire. 'Alright. I think General Austin knew you might say that. His invitation is not an order. In fact, if you wish, I'll ask him to come here.'

'That won't be necessary if you acknowledge my point.'

'I do.'

Hollis took the parkas from the wall hook. 'Lead on, Commander.'

Hollis, Lisa, and Poole walked out into the cold night, Poole holding a flashlight to their front.

Hollis said, 'Isn't there a curfew here?'

'No. There used to be a lot of rules. There are very few rules now.' Poole added, 'The Russians are a bit slow in the head, but they finally realized that totalitarianism doesn't suit their purposes here and takes a lot of their time. They can run the rest of this benighted country with terror and fear, but this is the most free square mile in the Soviet Union.'

'I see. That was Burov's idea?'

'Pretty much. He lived in the Scandinavian countries for a few years and learned that a well-fed and free population could be as cooperative and productive as a terrorized population. That's a big leap for a Russian.' Poole laughed without humor.

They came up to the main road near the VFW hall and turned right, east toward the headquarters, walking on the shoulder of the unlit road. Poole said, 'We follow world events closely, and we're probably better informed about Soviet-American relations than the average stateside American. Certainly we know more than any Russian below the Kremlin level.'

As they walked, headlights approached from up the road, and the vehicle slowed as it drew closer to them, then stopped, its headlights glaring in their faces.

Hollis, Lisa, and Poole moved toward the driver's side of the vehicle, out of the glare of the lights, and Hollis saw that the vehicle was a Pontiac Trans Am. Sitting behind the wheel was Colonel Burov. Burov said, 'Good evening, Ms Rhodes, Commander Poole, Colonel Hollis.'

Only Poole returned the greeting.

Hollis saw that the Trans Am's windshield was intact, and there didn't seem to be any body damage to the vehicle.

Burov said, 'Yes, Mr Fisher's car. I suppose he didn't get into an accident after all. Not in this car anyway.' Burov patted the steering wheel. 'Nice machine.'

Lisa came up beside Hollis and looked at Burov. 'You bastard.'

Burov ignored her and spoke to Hollis. 'The seats are real

leather, and there is even an air conditioner in the car. Do you all drive cars like this?'

Hollis looked at the low, sleek car, its engine humming on the lonely road in the Russian *bor* with a uniformed officer of the KGB behind the wheel.

Burov saw he wasn't going to get a reply and continued, 'I'm going for a drive. I'd ask you to come along to give me some pointers, but I'm leaving the camp. I want to get it out on the Minsk highway and see if it can really do a hundred and forty miles per hour.' Burov added, 'Unfortunately I can only take it out at night when there are no foreigners about. Someone might see it and put two and two together, as you say.'

Lisa said, 'I hope you kill yourself in it.'

Burov looked at her. 'No, you don't. I am the best thing that has happened to this camp. After me – who knows?' He looked back at Hollis. 'I assume you are on your way to pay a courtesy call on General Austin. Or are you going to pick mushrooms?'

Hollis said, 'General Austin. How about a lift?'

Burov laughed. 'I'm afraid if I let you in this car, the temptation to try something stupid would be too great for you. You and Ms Rhodes are slippery characters, as I discovered.' Burov raised his right hand and showed an automatic pistol. 'So you will have to walk. It's good for your heart. Good evening.' Burov let up on the clutch and hit the accelerator. The Pontiac chirped, lurched, then stalled. Burov restarted it and managed to leave a little rubber. Hollis watched the taillights disappear toward the main gate. Beneath the lighted license plate was a bumper sticker that read: *POWs and MIAs – not forgotten.*

Lisa said, 'I still hope he kills himself.' She turned to Hollis. 'That's ghoulish. Driving the car of the man he killed. He's sick.'

Poole asked, 'That was the car of the American boy killed in an accident? Fisher?'

'Yes.'

'We read about it in the American newspapers. And Landis

told us that you know about Jack Dodson through Fisher. They met? And Fisher contacted the embassy?'

Hollis said, 'I can't discuss this now.'

Poole nodded, then asked, 'Where *are* we exactly?'

Hollis looked at him. 'Where do you think you are?'

Poole replied, 'A few kilometers north of Borodino battle-field.'

Hollis nodded.

Poole continued, 'We know from the flight that took us from Hanoi that we were landing in European Russia. We've also done some star and sun plotting to confirm that. The climate too is probably mid-Russian and not Siberian. The biggest clue is all those aircraft we see descending to the southeast. The traffic has grown over the years. We figured that had to be Moscow.'

'And Borodino?'

'The cannon fire,' Poole replied. 'Every September seventh and October fifteenth and sixteenth, we can hear a twenty-one-gun salute a few kilometers to the south. Those are the anniversaries of the two battles of Borodino. Correct?'

Hollis nodded again. He had actually attended the September ceremony the previous year.

'Well,' Poole said, 'I guess the question is, did Jack Dodson make it to the embassy?'

'That,' Hollis replied, 'is the question.'

They continued their walk. As they passed in front of the massive grey headquarters building, Poole said, 'You spent some time in the back rooms there, did you?'

Hollis answered, 'Not long by Russian standards.'

'Almost everyone here has done time in the cooler. But Burov has more subtle means of punishment. It's counter-productive to throw instructors in the cells, so he throws the Russian wives or girlfriends in if one of us commits an offense. Most of us have wives or children now – hostages to fortune – so it makes it difficult for us to act.'

The road curved and dropped as they rounded the bend, and

Hollis realized it had become darker. He looked up at the sky and saw nothing but blackness.

Poole said, 'Camouflage net.'

Hollis thought this was the camouflaged area he'd seen from the helicopter.

Lisa said, 'Look, Sam!'

Hollis looked ahead and saw dim lights suspended from lamp poles. As they got closer Hollis saw he was looking at a paved parking lot, complete with white lines. Set back from the parking lot was a row of about ten darkened storefronts, looking very much like a suburban shopping plaza. The main store in the row was a large 7-Eleven complete with the distinctive white, green, and red sign. Hollis said to Lisa, 'See, there's the Seven-Eleven we were looking for on the road to Mozhaisk.'

Lisa stared at the stores. 'Incredible.' She moved across the dimly lit parking lot toward the row of red brick shops. Hollis and Poole followed.

To the left of the 7-Eleven was a laundromat, a Bank of North America complete with logo, a place called Sweeney's Liquors, a barbershop called Mane Event, and a beauty parlor named Tresses. To the right of the 7-Eleven was Kruger's Hardware store; a stationery and tobacco shop, Main Street Pharmacy; a bookstore that also carried audio- and videotapes; and at the end of the row, a sort of luncheonette-coffee shop called Dunkin' Donuts.

Hollis asked, 'Is that a legitimate franchize?'

Poole laughed. 'No. But we're trying to get an American Express travel agency here.'

Hollis walked past the luncheonette and peered into the bookstore.

Poole said, 'To varying degrees these stores are all functioning operations. You need camp scrip to buy things at all of them except this book and tape store. Everything there is only for loan. It's sort of the camp audiovisual department, though it's set up as a retail bookstore for training purposes. We get a wide selection of publications, videotapes, and some decent cassettes and albums.'

Lisa looked at the window display of recent American and British hard-cover fiction and nonfiction. 'I couldn't find some of this stuff in the embassy bookstore.' She saw a copy of John Barron's classic, *KGB*, and the Soviet defector Arkady Shevchenko's exposé, *Breaking with Moscow*. 'And they let you . . . and the so-called students read this stuff?'

'They don't have any choice, do they?' Poole replied. 'If they don't read it now, they'll read it stateside, where it might blow their minds. They're inoculated here with the truth.'

Hollis peered through the windows of the pharmacy and stationery store. 'You men don't lack for anything, do you?'

'Not in the material sense, Colonel. You know what we lack.'

Hollis didn't reply but moved over to the hardware store. 'Mostly American brand name goods here.'

'Yes,' Poole replied. 'Most of the hardware and housewares in the camp are American. Keeps things standard and easy to fix. That's why the plumbing works.'

'You do your own repairs?'

'Yes, with our students. Most Soviet men aren't very handy, as you know. I guess that's because they all live in government housing that's falling apart. We teach them how to be weekend handymen.' Poole smiled. 'So someday when their American wives nag them to replace a leaky washer, they don't have to call a plumber.' Poole added, 'Or as we say – How many Russians does it take to change a lightbulb. Ten. Nine to fill out the requisition forms for the bulb and one to screw it in.'

Hollis, Lisa, and Poole moved to the plate glass windows of the 7-Eleven. Poole said, 'We get most of our packaged and canned food here. Some of it is American, some Finnish, some Soviet. Supplies vary. For fresh meat and produce, we go to a warehouse near the main gate and get whatever is available on a rationed basis. *That* is the same as everywhere else in this country.'

Hollis asked, 'But you actually get paid here?'

'Yes. This scrip . . .' Poole took a five-dollar bill from his wallet and handed it to Hollis.

Hollis and Lisa examined it in the dim light of a lamp pole. The note looked like a five-dollar bill and in fact was a color photocopy of one. The only difference was the poor quality paper and the reverse side, which was blank.

Poole said, 'That's part of the psychology of keeping us from becoming complete zombies. We have to balance our personal budget and all that. The students do too. They pay to board with us for instance. Banking transactions and finance are one of the most important parts of the curriculum. It's more difficult than you might think to teach these people a sense of fiscal responsibility. They're used to blowing a month's pay on the first consumer item they see on the way home from work.' Poole added, 'It's still not a completely realistic economic model here. For instance, we don't pay taxes.' He smiled.

Lisa asked, 'Where do they get all the American-style fixtures and such for these stores? The Seven-Eleven sign for instance.'

Poole replied, 'That came from Mosfilm. Their prop shop, I guess you'd call it. Same with the Bank of North America accoutrements. The smaller items, consumer goods and so forth, came through the diplomatic pouch or through the International Center for Trade in Moscow. I saw a picture of that place in a magazine. Built by Armand Hammer. Looks like a Trump building in New York. All glass, brass, and marble. Now *that's* real Little America, isn't it? You people been there?'

'Yes,' Lisa replied. 'It's quite the place. An opening to the West.'

Poole commented, 'More so than you know. They send the students to stay in the hotel there as a graduation present. They spend a month living it up and mingling with Western businessmen and VIPs. Sort of a halfway house. Then they head West.'

515

Hollis moved down the row past the laundromat and the bank and stopped in front of Sweeney's Liquors, examining the stock and the window displays of various Western distilleries and vintners. There was a professionally done display of world-class Italian wines with posters of sunny Italy and cardboard Italian flags. A wicker basket held bottles of Principessa Gavi and the Banfi Brunello di Montalcino, both popular wines that were widely imported in America.

Lisa said, 'These are very good wines. Can you buy these?'

Poole replied, 'We can buy the wines before they turn. Sometimes we can buy the Western liquor. Depends on supply. We can buy all the Soviet stuff we want.' He added, 'Everyone here was amused when we started reading that Stolichnaya had become something of a trendy drink in America. I'll take Kentucky bourbon any day.'

Hollis commented, 'I was told there was another training environment here. Kitchens, offices, and so forth.'

'Oh, that's right here. Below our feet. A large subterranean arcade. There are staircases behind the shops. There is a sort of office suite with a reception room down there. It's mostly to familiarize the students with office etiquette and office equipment. Word processors. Photostat machines, water coolers, electric staplers. The works. There's also an auditorium where they show first-run movies that aren't on videotape yet. I don't know how they get them. Also, there are two very modern home kitchens, an extensive reference library, a hotel and motel check-in desk, airport customs, and a motor vehicle bureau desk where two nasty Russian women abuse people. They don't even have to act. They were both government bureaucrats once. The students think it's funny that a state motor vehicle bureau approximates Soviet life in general.' Poole smiled, then continued, 'They also do house closings down there, employment interviews, and so on.' He added, 'The most popular amusement down there is the brokerage firm of E. F. Hutton.'

Lisa asked, 'You play the stock market here?'

Poole smiled. 'The ultimate capitalistic parasitic endeavor. Everybody here plays – the students, the instructors, the wives. The Russians fly in a videotape of the ticket quotes, so the Charm School is two days behind Wall Street. We all got hurt in the crash of '87.' He laughed without humor. 'But I am up about six thousand dollars now.'

Hollis and Lisa glanced at each other.

Poole continued, 'It's a very wide-ranging curriculum here, but aside from language and social customs, it's impossible to go into depth, to jam the knowledge and life experiences of a twenty-five-year-old American into the head of a Russian of about the same age within thirteen or fourteen months. That's how long most of them are here. Of course they come here with good English and some knowledge of America. They're all graduates of the Red Air Force intelligence school outside Moscow and of the Institute for Canadian and American Studies.'

Hollis nodded. As an intelligence officer, he knew a good program when he saw one. Whereas the American intelligence establishment had shifted the emphasis from spies to satellites, statistical analyses, and other passive means of intelligence gathering, the Soviets still believed very much in the human factor. That, Hollis thought, was ironic, considering the relative values each society placed on the individual. Hollis always believed that the Soviets' emphasis on the human spy was the correct approach. Alevy too believed in human intelligence gathering; which, Hollis suspected, was why he and Lisa were in the Charm School.

Lisa glanced in the windows of the barbershop and the beauty parlor and asked Poole, 'Do the women in the camp actually come here to have their hair done?'

'Oh, yes. The hair stylists in both shops are barbers from the Gulag. All the employees in these places are from the Gulag, most of them women and most of them now married to or involved with American instructors. It's a strange little world we have here. The milieu is mostly suburban, as you can see. That's because most of us were suburban, I guess.'

'But no cars or PTA,' Hollis said.

'No, And no travel agency.' Poole seemed lost in thought a moment, then continued, 'The population of Anytown is a little over a thousand. There are about two hundred eighty-two former American pilots at last count and about an equal number of Russian wives, plus our children. Then there are the six kidnapped American women – seven now – and there are some Russian service people and medical staff also from the Gulag. Then of course there are the students – about three hundred at any given time. And there are about fifty Russian proctors, as they're called. Control officers, actually, one for each six students. They're KGB intelligence officers who speak and understand English. Then there is the KGB Border Guard battalion, about six hundred men, living mostly in their own compound and patrolling the perimeter. We don't really count them as part of the camp population. We never have to deal with them, and they are forbidden to try to communicate with us.'

Poole stayed silent awhile, then took a breath. 'So that's it. One thousand souls, living in this miserable square mile, spending each and every day pretending. Pretending until the pretense seems reality, and the reality we read about and see on videotape seems like reports from a doppelganger planet. I tell you, sometimes I think I'm a certifiable lunatic, and other times I think the Russians are.' He looked at Hollis, then at Lisa. 'You just got here. What do you think?'

Hollis cleared his throat. 'I'll reserve judgement, though I don't think it matters if you're all insane. My problem with this place is that it works.'

Commander Poole nodded. 'That it does. We've hatched thousands of little monsters here. God forgive us.'

They walked through the parking lot back to the main road and continued on.

Lisa said, 'Let me ask you something, Commander . . . do

you ever get the impression that these students are . . . seduced by our way of life?'

Poole motioned them both closer and replied in a low voice, 'Yes. But I think only superficially. The way an American might be seduced by Paris or Tahiti. They don't necessarily want any of this for *their* country. Or perhaps some of them do, but they want it on their terms.'

Lisa nodded. 'The Russians still equate material wealth and good living with spiritual corruption.'

Poole glanced at her as they walked. 'You do know your Russians. And yet they are schizoid about it. They have no God, but they worry about their spiritual life; they live in poverty, which is supposed to be good for their Russian souls, yet they buy or steal anything they can get their hands on and want more. And the few who obtain wealth slip quickly into hedonism and drown in it, because they have no guiding light, if you know what I mean.'

Hollis said, 'That's not peculiarly Russian.'

'No,' Poole agreed, 'but I'll tell you what is. Most of them seem to have a dark core, an impenetrable center that will not let in the light around them. It doesn't matter how many books they read or how many videotapes they watch. They will not hear, and they will not see. Of course, there are a few – more than a few, maybe twenty-five percent of them – who crack open. But when they do, they're spotted very quickly by the proctors, even though we try to cover for them. The KGB takes them away. Maybe we got a few converts out of here. But I don't think they get past the oral examination – that's what we call the marathon polygraph sessions they go through.' Poole, still speaking softly, said to Hollis and Lisa, 'We're always hoping that one of them will get to America and walk right into the nearest FBI office with the spy story of the century.' He asked, 'Has that happened yet?'

Hollis shook his head.

'Incredible.'

Hollis was glad to discover through Poole that the men here

still had a sense of themselves as American military men and that they still held the Russians in some contempt. Hollis asked, 'How many of you have been imprisoned here?'

'It's hard to say. In the early days from about 1965 to the end of the air war over North Vietnam in December 1973, hundreds of men passed through here. Most of them are dead. We've put together a list of about four hundred and fifty fliers who we know were shot, died of neglect, or killed themselves. It was a very turbulent time, and we were not in a position to keep good records.' Poole whispered, 'But we do have that list, several copies of which are hidden about the camp.'

Hollis stopped, and the three of them stood close, facing one another. 'May I have a list of the dead?'

'Yes, of course.'

'And a roster of the men who are here now?'

'Yes.'

'Did Jack Dodson have that information with him?'

'Certainly. Are you saying *you* may be able to get this information out of here?'

'I'm not saying that, but that is obviously what I have in mind.'

Poole nodded. He said, 'Something else you ought to know. After the Paris Peace Treaty and after all the POWs were supposed to have been freed, we were still receiving American fliers from North Vietnamese prisons. These men were in incredibly bad shape, as you can imagine. There were about fifty of them, back in the mid and late seventies. The last one was in 1979.' Poole looked at Hollis. 'These men said there were still American POWs in North Vietnamese camps. We have a list of those men who made the sightings and the names of the POWs they say were left behind in North Vietnam.' Poole looked from Hollis to Lisa as they stood face-to-face in the tight circle and added, 'We have signed depositions to that effect. Also, the list of the two hundred eighty-two men who are now here is in the form of signatures, all written under a statement attesting to their imprisonment in the Soviet Union and the nature of this school. It would be very good if we could get this documentary evidence to Washington.'

Hollis nodded. Not everyone thought it would be good at all.

Poole added, 'I got here in June of 1971. I'd been in North Vietnamese prisons for about six months prior to that.' He thought a moment, then said, 'As I said, I was flown from Hanoi in a Red Air Force transport on a direct flight to a Soviet air base not far from here. I had no idea where we were going. There were ten of us. We had the idea that the Russians might be acting as brokers between the Americans and the North Vietnamese – that we were going to be exchanged for North Vietnamese POWs or Russian spies or something. Even after we were transported here in sealed trucks, we couldn't comprehend that we were going to train Red Air Force pilots. But as soon as we realized that, we also knew we would never get out of here with that secret.'

Hollis nodded. The secret was out, but the men remained. He wondered if Poole and the others sensed that.

They began walking again, shoulder to shoulder on the road, speaking in whispers. Lisa asked, 'Is there a church here? Do you have services?'

'No. That's one thing they won't allow, which is very telling. We *can* hold Bible study groups now, because we demanded that. But the students are not allowed to participate even as a training exercise. In America, they can become capitalists or right wing politicians if they wish, but I've heard that they're not allowed to join a church unless it's necessary for their cover.'

Lisa remarked, 'That's not consistent with the idea that you should enjoy American freedoms here.'

Poole replied, 'I don't quite understand that either. They make such a big deal over atheism and bad-mouthing religion, you'd almost think they believed in God.'

They continued their walk along the main road, then turned left into a narrow log-stepped path that climbed a rise in the

521

heavily treed forest. This section of the camp, Hollis noted, seemed uninhabited.

At the end of the log path was a rundown *izba* with a weak light in its single window and smoke coming from its stone chimney. Poole explained, 'One of the last of the original structures. General Austin prefers it to the so-called American houses, though Colonel Burov would prefer it if the general would sell out like the rest of us.'

They approached the door of the log cabin, and Poole continued, 'The general has not taken a Russian wife, as he says he is still married to Mrs Austin. I believe he has remained faithful.' He added, 'He has more willpower than I do. Also, you should know that the general refuses to teach classes.'

Hollis asked, 'Why hasn't the KGB gotten rid of him?'

'We made it clear that we would strike or rebel if they did. We have value as a commodity here, like any slaves when the slave trade is cut off. Also, I suspect they don't mind giving us a small victory to let us think we're still men.' Poole knocked on the door.

The door opened, revealing a man close to seventy, very fit looking with a grey crew cut and steel-grey eyes. His skin was too pale, but it seemed more a result of too little sun than any unhealthiness. Hollis thought he looked like a man who had borne too much, too long, and had borne it alone.

General Austin regarded them a moment, then showed them in without speaking. He went to a stereo system strewn out on a wobbly bench and placed a record on the turntable. The strings and woodwinds of Vivaldi's 'The Four Seasons' came through the speakers and filled the small room. Austin indicated two facing wooden chairs near the crumbling stone fireplace. Hollis and Lisa sat.

Poole took a similar pine chair facing the fire. Austin lowered himself into a birch rocker.

Hollis looked around the log-walled room. It was about as large as Pavel and Ida's kitchen, but if anything, more sparse. Aside from the rocker and stereo, there was not a bit of comfort, no easy chair, no rag rug on the floor, and no kitchen facilities. There were, however, shaded reading lamps around the room, their cords all snaking toward a single electrical outlet. A half wall of rough planking separated the sleeping area, where an electric heater glowed on the floor beside an army cot. Beside the cot were stacks of books, magazines, and newspapers.

General Austin spoke in a very soft voice, barely audible above Vivaldi. 'It was good of you to come, Colonel.' He looked at Lisa, 'And you, Ms Rhodes.'

She asked, 'Would you have preferred that I wasn't here?'

'If I did, I would have said so.'

She found herself replying, 'Yes, sir.'

Commander Poole said to Austin, 'Colonel Hollis wishes you to know that he is here voluntarily.'

Austin nodded but made no comment. He addressed both Hollis and Lisa. 'You have knowledge of the Major Dodson business?'

Hollis nodded.

'And do you have any news of Major Dodson?'

Hollis replied, 'No, General,' preferring to use that form of address rather than 'sir'.

Austin asked, 'What do you think our government is prepared to do if Major Dodson makes contact with the embassy or a Western reporter?'

'General, I can't engage in any discussion of that nature with a man I've just met. A man who is not a free agent. And, excuse me, a man who has been compromised.'

Austin stared off into space awhile, rocking in his chair. Finally he said, 'I understand your reservations. However, I expected from you, at the very least, some message from the outside.'

'I am not the bearer of any message. I am an intelligence officer, and I've been trained and instructed not to speak to anyone on matters that they have no need to know, rank notwithstanding.'

'I think I'm in a better position than you to determine if I have a need to know.'

Hollis did not respond directly but said, 'General, I have been drugged and interrogated by Burov, and I have so far not divulged more than I absolutely had to in order to establish myself to Burov as a potential traitor. That's why I'm here and not in a cell. Whatever I know will do you little good anyway.'

Poole asked, 'Colonel, can't you at least tell us if our government knows we're here?'

'No, I can't.' Hollis looked at Austin. 'I want you to tell me how Dodson got out.'

Austin replied, 'Only a handful of men know that. Using your reasoning, you have no need to know.'

Poole added, 'If they catch Jack Dodson, they will torture him the way they tortured Captain Romero and make him reveal the names of the men on the escape committee. They will then torture those men to determine if there are others. Two of those men will be me and General Austin. So if we told you how Dodson got out, we might, under torture, be forced to tell the KGB that you know the secret as well. Then they might torture and execute you and Ms Rhodes. They tolerate a lot from us, but they will not tolerate an escape attempt. So if you still want to know how Jack Dodson got out of here, be advised you might get caught up in the bloodbath to follow his recapture.'

Hollis looked at Lisa, who nodded.

Austin spoke. 'Alright. A catapult.' He explained, 'We cut our own wood for our fires. We designed a catapult, cut the pieces, and scattered them about in the forest. One day a few weeks ago before the cold set in, we assembled the catapult, wrapped Major Dodson in padded blankets, and sent him over the barbed wire.' General Austin added a few more details. 'We intended to send three more men over in quick succession, then cut up the catapult and burn it in our fireplaces. But as luck would have it, a motorized patrol came along between the wire fences and shone a light on us, illuminating the catapult. We

524

abandoned the rest of the escape and made it back unseen to our houses. The alarm went up, and we didn't give Jack Dodson much of a chance.' Austin looked from Hollis to Lisa. 'So you see, they already know how we got Dodson out. I was testing your courage.'

'We don't need testing, General.'

'I don't know that. I don't even know what brought you two here.'

Hollis replied, 'Fate and destiny brought us here, General.'

Austin nodded. 'We take your presence here as a positive sign.' He leaned toward Hollis in his rocker. 'I'll tell you something, Colonel. As much as we would want to go home, I think we'd all sacrifice our lives if we thought one man could get out of here and tell the world about this place. If you are to be that man, if you have a plan from the outside, you need only give the word. We're ready for just about anything.'

Hollis nodded in acknowledgment.

Lisa said, 'That's very brave.' She looked at Hollis. 'Sam?'

Hollis made no response.

Poole spoke. 'As for the catapult, Colonel, it is now behind the headquarters building under twenty-four-hour guard. No one has told us why, but since we can read the Russian mind by now, we know why. Do you know why? You, Ms Rhodes?'

Neither replied, and Poole continued, 'If they catch Dodson, he will be the first – without the padding this time. If they don't find him and they don't learn who is on the escape committee, they will just pick ten or so names at random. So even if you find us contemptible as traitors, don't think we are the Russians' docile house pets. We did do something that we are prepared to die for.'

Hollis said to Poole, 'I am not judging you. I'm only reminding you that you've all violated the Code of Conduct for prisoners of war by collaborating with the enemy. And, yes, so did I to some extent. As long as we all understand that, then we can move on to our next obligation under Article III

525

of the Code, which is to escape. I don't think two men in two decades is a very impressive effort.'

Poole's face reddened. 'Colonel, I don't think you can say –'

'The colonel is right,' Austin interrupted. 'The Russians have long ago eliminated those of us who refused to collaborate, and others of us have committed suicide, actively or passively. What you see left here, Colonel Hollis and Ms Rhodes, are the traitors. That's why we're alive. And why Ernie Simms among others is dead. Correct, Colonel?'

'Correct, General.'

Poole stood. 'Colonel, let me quote you some rules that apply to POWs. First – "Even as a POW, you continue to be of special concern to the United States; you will not be forgotten." Two – "Every available national means will be employed to establish contact with you, to support you, and to gain your release."' Poole said to Hollis, 'Look me in the eye, Colonel, and tell me that my government has lived up to its obligations to us. Tell me we are not forgotten and forsaken. Tell me they don't know we are here.'

Hollis looked Poole in the eye. 'If they knew you were here, Commander, they would have done something to get you out.'

Poole stared at Hollis, then drew a deep breath. 'Then let me tell you what we are doing here in lieu of escape. We sabotage the curriculum at every opportunity. And we justify staying alive by saying that if we could just live long enough to get one of us out, we could warn our country about this place. And there is some truth to that, Colonel. Because, as you see, this is not just a POW camp, and other rules prevail here. We've tried to maintain our integrity and our honor as officers. I can tell you for instance that not one man here has ever been found to be a stool pigeon. We can trust one another, and we've never accepted the friendship of a single Russian. It's a very bizarre situation, and we try to deal with it as it evolves. General Austin has formed an ethics committee for that purpose.' Poole looked at Hollis and Lisa. 'I hope you're not here twenty years, but if you are, I hope you can maintain your own sense of duty and honor.'

Hollis said, 'You mean you'd like to see me eat my words.'

'That's right,' Poole replied tersely.

Hollis stood. 'Well, perhaps I will.'

Lisa stood also and addressed Poole and Austin. 'I . . . I think from what I see and hear that you've done the best you could.'

General Austin stood. 'Well, we know we haven't. And your friend knows that too.' He looked at Hollis and said, 'The fall of Vietnam, Watergate, the surrender of the Pueblo, Iran-Contra, the shameful episode of the hostages in Iran, Lebanon, and on and on. We've witnessed from afar nearly twenty years of American disasters and humiliations. But we haven't used that to justify our own shameful and weak behavior.'

Hollis replied, 'You don't have to justify yourselves to me or to anyone except a duly constituted board of inquiry should you ever get home.'

Austin's mind seemed to have wandered, and Hollis wondered if he'd heard him. Then Austin said, 'Home. You know . . . we all saw on tape the POWs coming home from Vietnam. We saw men we knew. Some of us even saw our wives and families who were there to unselfishly share the joy of other families whom they'd come to know through common grief.' Austin looked from Hollis to Lisa. 'I don't think there was a worse torture the Russians could have devised for us than to show us that.'

Lisa turned and left quickly.

Hollis walked toward the door.

Poole said, 'We also read about the continuing efforts to locate POWs, mostly by private groups and families, I should add, not our government. Do you know how frustrating that is for us? And why hasn't anyone been clever enough to make some deductions? SAM missiles for American pilots. My God, the Russians and North Vietnamese were *allies*. How smart do you have to be to figure it out? Why hasn't anyone thought we might be *here*? In *Russia*!' Poole studied Hollis' face. 'Or *have* they figured it out? And is Washington too worried about the repercussions to act? Is that it? Colonel?'

'I can't answer any of those questions,' Hollis replied, then added, 'But you have my personal word that I will do everything in my power to get you all home. Good evening, General, Commander.' Hollis took the flashlight and left.

He found Lisa on the path and saw she had been crying. He took her arm, and they picked their way down the dark log trail. They came back to the main road and turned right, back toward their cottage.

Lisa composed herself and said, 'You were cruel.'

'I know that.'

'But, why . . . how could you be so hard on men who have suffered so much?'

'I can't endorse what they've done.'

'I don't understand you. I don't understand your code or your –'

'It's not necessary that you do. That's my world, not yours.'

'Damn you. Your world got me into this.'

'No. The KGB got you into this.' He added, 'There are a lot of wrongs to be righted here, Lisa. I'm not judge and jury, but I'm damned sure a witness. I know what I see and I know I'm not one of the criminals here. You keep that in mind.'

She looked at him, and it came to her that he was very upset by the meeting. She said, 'You saw yourself in their place, didn't you? They were your people once. It's not anger and contempt you feel for them. It's pity, so deep you can't comprehend it. Is that it?'

He nodded. 'Yes, that's it.' He put his arm around her shoulder. 'I can't give them hope, Lisa. That would be crueler than anything else I could say to them. 'They understand that.'

She moved closer to him. 'Ernie Simms is dead and buried, Sam. Now you have to find peace.'

35

Halloween day dawned cold and frosty. Hollis got out of bed and went into the bathroom, a prefab unit usually used in apartment houses but now attached to their cottage off the bedroom. The tap water was barely warm, and Hollis guessed the propane water heater was having problems again.

Lisa rose and put on a quilted robe over her nightgown. She went into the living room and built a fire, then into the galley kitchen and made coffee in an electric pot.

Hollis shaved, showered, and dressed in one of the four warm-up suits he had been issued. He joined Lisa in the kitchen, and they took their coffee mugs to the living room and sat before the fire.

Lisa said, 'Tomorrow it's your turn to do coffee and fire.'

'I know.'

'Did you sleep well?'

'I suppose.'

She asked. 'Does it bother you that we sleep together without sex?'

'No. But your feet are cold.'

'Can we get a wood stove for this place?'

'I don't plan on staying.'

'That's right.'

'I was thinking,' she said, 'as primitive as this place is, it's a palace compared to a peasant's *izba*. We have an electric coffeepot, toaster, and hot plate, a refrigerator, indoor plumbing, hot water –'

'Tepid water.'

'*Again*?'

'I'll check it out later.'

'It's good to have a man around the house.'

'To fix things.'

'I'm sorry about the sex.'

'Me too. But to be pefectly frank, I'm not much in the mood either. I think this place has suppressed my libido.'

She looked at him with concern. 'Are you serious?'

'Yes. I don't feel like it anymore.'

She put her cup on the coffee table. 'Are you sure?' –

'Pretty sure.'

She thought a moment. 'Well . . . they can't do that to us.'

'It's alright.'

'No, it's not.' She put her hand on his shoulder. 'Why don't we go . . . back to bed?'

'I'm not sure I can do you much good.'

'You'll be fine, Sam.'

'Well . . . alright.' He stood and they went back into the bedroom. Hollis looked at the icon, now hanging over the double bed. He said, 'Is that an appropriate place for a religious painting?'

'Oh, yes. The Russians put them anywhere. Like Catholics put crucifixes over their beds.'

'If you say so.' He looked at the bed, and they both stood beside it awkwardly as if it were their first time. Lisa slipped off her robe, then standing beside the electric heater, pulled her nightgown over her head and laid it in front of the heater. She stood naked, the bright orange glow of the electric bars reflecting off her white skin.

Hollis got out of his warm-up suit, and they embraced. He kissed her on the lips, then the breasts, then knelt and ran his tongue over her belly, down to her public hair, and touched his tongue to her labia.

'Oooooh . . . my word . . .' She knelt in front of him, and they fondled each other beside the electric warmth. She said, 'This guy's as big as a billy club. You're alright.'

'What a relief.'

She looked at him sternly. 'You conned me out of my clothes.'

530

'Not me.'

They rose together and lay in the heavily quilted bed. Hollis got on top of her, and she guided him in, then wrapped her legs around his back. She whispered, 'Sam . . . it was silly of me . . . this is what I needed . . . your love.'

'This is all we've got here, Lisa.'

'Sam, I want to live. We need more time together . . . it's too soon to have it end.'

'Yes, it *would* be too soon. I love you, Lisa. Remember that.'

They moved slowly, unhurriedly, like people who know they have many hours to themselves but not many more days; like servicemen on leave from a war, as Hollis recalled, when time was measured in minutes, and each minute was full of self-awareness and small pleasures never before experienced or appreciated.

Lisa's hands ran smoothly and slowly along his neck and shoulders down to the small of his back, then up his spine. Hollis cupped his hands under her buttocks and brought her up as he forced his groin down deeper into her. He came, and his spasm brought her to climax.

They lay still, listening to the absolute quiet of the room, their breathing, and the blood pounding in their ears.

Lisa held him tight. 'Our victory.'

They jogged along the main road. Other joggers, mostly men, passed them in either direction. Everyone waved. Lisa said, 'Friendly group. Just like Sea Cliff on a Saturday morning. But where are the women?'

'Russian women just don't jog. I guess.'

'Right. I never saw one in Moscow.'

They turned right on the main road and walked a few hundred meters. Lisa asked, 'Where are we going?'

'To call on Burov at home.'

'You can go without me.' She turned, but he took her arm. Lisa said, 'I will *not* call on that man's home.'

531

'He's asked us to stop by.'

'I don't *care*. Don't you understand? Try to put yourself in my place, as a woman. Do you want me to be graphic? He stood there in that cell while the matron gave me a very thorough search.'

Hollis nodded. 'I understand. I'll tell him you're not feeling well.'

'Why do you want to go there?'

'I have a job to do. I have to see whatever I can see.'

'But for what *reason*?'

'I don't know exactly, but I don't want to be unprepared for whatever is going to happen.'

Lisa stayed silent a moment, then turned and walked toward Burov's house.

The main road ended at a wide turnaround on the far side of which was a guardhouse, a tall razor-wire fence, and a wire gate. Two KGB Border Guards watched them approach. One of them unslung his rifle and cradled it under his arm. '*Stoi!*'

Hollis and Lisa stopped and one of the guards walked toward them. 'Go away!' he said in English. 'Go!'

Hollis said in Russian, 'We have an appointment with Colonel Burov. I am Colonel Hollis.'

The guard looked them up and down, then said in Russian, 'Are you the new Americans?'

'That's right. Though my Russian is somewhat better than yours.'

The guard glared at him, then turned and went back to the guardhouse, where he made a telephone call. He motioned to Hollis and Lisa, and they passed through the gates on to a blacktopped path, just wide enough for a vehicle. Adjacent to the guardhouse was a kennel where six German shepherds roamed inside a wire mesh enclosure. The dogs immediately began barking and pawing at the mesh.

Hollis and Lisa continued up the path. Burov's dacha was set among towering pines that had been thinned out to let some light pass through to the house and grounds. Tree stumps dotted the carpet of brown pine needles and cones.

The dacha itself was a two-story clapboard structure with somewhat contemporary lines and oversize windows. Parked in a gravel patch beside the house and enclosed in a newly built carport was the Pontiac Trans Am. Hollis walked up to the front door and knocked.

The door opened, and a KGB Border Guard motioned them inside. They entered into a large anteroom that held the guard's desk, chair, and a coatrack.

The guard showed them through to a large pleasant living room with knotty-pine walls.

Burov stood in the center of the room wearing his uniform trousers, boots, and shirt but no tunic. 'Good morning.'

Hollis ignored him and looked around. The furniture, he saw, was all Russian but not the junk that the masses had to live with. Everything in the room looked as if it had been lifted from the lobby of the Ukraina Hotel – stolid, made-to-last-lacquered furniture of the 1930s; what might be called art deco in the West, but what the Russians officially called Socialist Realism and the people called Stalinist. Adorning the walls were oversize canvasses of uncommonly handsome peasants, happy factory workers, and Red Army men prepared to do battle. The only thing missing from this 1930s time capsule, Hollis thought, was smiling Uncle Joe himself, or at least a photograph of him.

Burov followed Hollis' gaze. 'As you say in America, they don't make it like this anymore. In recent years we've sacrificed quality for quantity. There are many who long to return to the time when shoddy goods and bad buildings were punished by firing squad.'

'There are probably less extreme methods of quality control,' Hollis said dryly. 'Are you a Stalinist then, Burov?'

'We don't use that word,' Burov replied. 'But certainly I admired the man if not all of his methods. Please, sit.' Burov motioned to the far side of the room where there was an ancient

Russian porcelain stove with a wood fire in it, the only antique piece in the room. Hollis and Lisa sat in armchairs whose frames were black lacquered wood inlaid with stainless steel.

Burov motioned to the Border Guard, who left.

Lisa said, 'If I had to guess your taste, Colonel Burov, I would have said this was it.'

He smiled doubtfully.

She focused on a large canvas of peasants harvesting wheat, well-built men and women with grinning ruddy faces and flowing red bandannas. She commented, 'I didn't see anything like that in the countryside, and I suspect the artist never did either.'

'That is what we call the ideal.' He sat on the matching sofa across from them. 'So how have you been faring?'

Hollis replied, 'We're in prison. How do you think we're faring?'

'You are not in prison,' Burov said curtly. 'Tell me, then, what do you think of our school so far?'

Hollis said, 'I'm impressed.'

Burov nodded as though he already knew that. He looked at Hollis. 'First order of business. Your physical assault on Sonny Aimes.'

'Why don't we first talk about the physical assaults on Ms Rhodes and myself by Viktor, Vadim, and you?'

'That was not assault. That was official business, and as it happened before you entered the world of the school, it cannot be discussed. Why did you hit Sonny? Because he insulted Ms Rhodes?'

'No, I was on official business.'

'*I* make the rules here, Colonel Hollis. I'm very strict about law and order. And very fair. I've given students jail time for fighting, harassing women, stealing, and so on. I shot a student for rape once. If this place is to work, there must be law and order. Unlike America.' Burov added, 'If you decide to stay on here, I will conduct a full inquiry into the matter and see who was at fault.'

Lisa said, 'The Landises were not at fault. We put them in a difficult situation. It was between me and Sonny. The man is a pig.'

Burov smiled. 'Yes? He was a fine boy before he started seeing American movies.' Burov laughed.

Lisa stood. 'Good day.'

Burov motioned her back to her seat. 'No. Please. Enough verbal jabbing. I have things to discuss with you.'

Lisa sat reluctantly.

Burov looked at Hollis and Lisa for some time, then said, 'You've probably heard a few things about me and how I run this camp. And you're probably wondering what makes me tick. That's what you people wonder about when you meet a strong personality.'

Hollis said, 'Yes, and when I meet an abnormal personality I try to guess at the type of psychosis that is affecting his brain.'

Burov smiled thinly. 'Don't delude yourself into thinking I'm crazy. I'm not. I have developed here the finest espionage school in all the world, Hollis. Every premier and each member of the Central Committee and the Politburo for the last ten years knows my name.'

'That's not always an advantage,' Hollis reminded him.

'So far, it has been. But I'll tell you what motivates me. Two things. One, my deep abiding hate for the West, which I think you know. And ironically, it is only since I've had to deal with hundreds of Americans that I've grown to hate them, hate their culture, their filthy books and magazines, their shallow movies, their selfish personalities, their total lack of any sense of history or suffering, their rampant consumption of useless goods and services, and above all, their plain dumb luck in avoiding disaster.'

Hollis smiled. 'That about covers it.' He asked, 'But certainly you didn't learn all that from your prisoners.'

'*Instructors*. No, I learned from the Western filth I've been exposed to. The irony of these fliers is that they're probably the best you've got to offer in your childish society. And your government and nation wasted them like it wastes every resource you have. As I suggested to you in Lefortovo restaurant, you might agree with that.'

'I might, but I won't. I've already worked all that out, Burov. I don't feel betrayed or used. So if this is the standard psychological pitch to get me mad at America, forget it.'

Burov leaned back in the sofa and crossed his legs. 'Alright. But *think* about it. I'll tell you something else that is ironic and that amuses me. My students, when they get to America, will make better, harder working, more knowledgeable, and more law-abiding citizens than you're able to produce yourselves over there.'

'And they'll probably pay their taxes too.'

Burov regarded Hollis for some seconds, then said, 'And my second motivation is purely intellectual. Quite simply, I am fascinated with the challenge of turning Russians into Americans. I don't believe anything quite like this has ever been done on such a scale. And it has other ramifications for the future. Do you follow?'

'I'm afraid so.'

'Yes. There are other schools in the planning.'

'And where will you get the instructors?'

'Kidnap them as we kidnapped you and the American women here. But on a larger scale. I think we will use submarines to capture entire boatloads of pleasure sailors.' He smiled. 'Perhaps in the Bermuda Triangle.'

Lisa said, 'How can that make you smile? That's so cruel.'

Burov replied, 'It's war. We know that. You don't.' He turned his attention back to Hollis. 'Within ten years we will have a school for every major Caucasian nation in the world. All of Europe, South America, Canada, South Africa, Australia, New Zealand – any place where an ethnic Russian can pass for a native – we will have Russians burrowing into the very fabric of those nations. By the end of the century we will cover the globe with men and women who look and act like Germans, Frenchmen, Englishmen, or whatever, but who work for Moscow.' Burov asked Hollis, 'What do you think of that?'

'That's very ambitious for a country that has had seventy years to create the New Soviet Man and can't.'

Burov leaned toward Hollis. 'You're entirely too glib.'

'I know. Gets me in trouble.'

Burov nodded. 'So that's what makes me tick.'

'Good. Can we leave now?'

'No. There are some other matters.'

An elderly Russian woman entered the room carrying a tray on which was a teapot and cups. She set the tray down on the stove, stared at Lisa and Hollis, then left.

Burov said, 'Help yourselves.'

Lisa replied, 'If that woman is a prisoner, I won't touch a thing that has been served by your slave.'

Burov made a clucking sound with his tongue. 'What scruples you have. That was actually my dear mother.' Burov stood and poured three cups of tea. 'Yes, I have a mother. And a wife and my little darling, Natalia.' He handed Lisa a cup, which she accepted, then he gave one to Hollis and remained standing by the stove. He stared at Lisa awhile, then asked her, 'I was wondering if you would like to work here. In this house. To teach my Natalia English. She is ten now. Perhaps you could be a sort of governess.'

'Colonel Burov, you must be joking.'

'I wasn't. Do you want to meet Natalia?'

'No.'

'Do you find us all so repulsive?'

'I have many Russian friends. You are not among them.'

Burov shrugged. 'We'll see. Time heals many hurts.'

Hollis put his cup on the floor beside his chair. 'Is that the only reason you asked us here?'

'No. Unfortunately something has come up. My superiors in Moscow did not agree with my decision to extend you a week to meditate. So I must have your decision now. I trust you'll agree that you would both rather be here than in an unmarked grave.'

Hollis stood. 'My answer is no.'

Burov looked at him incredulously. 'No, you will not work for us here?'

'That's what I said.'

'Then you will be thoroughly interrogated, then shot.'

'Then I have nothing to lose if I killed you right now.'

Burov set his cup on the stove and stepped away from Hollis.

Hollis took a step toward Burov.

Lisa rose to her feet.

Burov seemed undecided if he should call out for the guard or not. He said to Hollis, 'Are you armed?'

'I don't need a weapon to kill you.'

'No? You think you're so strong? I keep myself fit also.'

'Good. That should make it interesting.' Hollis moved closer to Burov.

Burov mapped, 'Stay where you are.'

Lisa spoke, 'Sam. Please.' She said to Burov, 'I'll work for you.' She turned to Hollis. 'Please, Sam. We discussed this. It's not worth our lives. Tell him yes. Please.' She grabbed his arm. 'What difference does it make if there are two more instructors?' She turned back to Burov. 'He'll do it. Just give me some time.'

Burov seemed to consider. He stared at Lisa awhile, then said, 'I have orders to get an answer from you today. If you don't say yes by six this evening, you'll be taken to the cells forthwith. Do you understand?'

Lisa nodded.

Burov said, 'I'm in a good mood today, and I'll tell you why. Major Dodson has been captured. He was not two hundred meters from the west wall of your embassy. So whose side is fate on?'

Hollis didn't reply, but turned to leave.

Burov said, 'Yes, you may go now. Report to me at my

office at six P.M. with your answer.' He pointed the way out.

Hollis and Lisa went out to the foyer, and the guard opened the door. They walked down the path to the guardhouse, where one of the KGB men opened the gate. As they headed back along the main road, Lisa said, 'You want to buy time, don't you?'

Hollis nodded. 'But you didn't have to do that.'

'I did it for you, Sam. I saw your ego was getting in the way of your brain. I never thought you'd lose your cool like that.'

Hollis replied, 'I was okay when I went in there. But . . . I started thinking about him.'

'About what he did to me? I shouldn't have told you that.'

Hollis didn't reply.

'And you were also angry at what he was saying about America.'

'All of the above.' Hollis said, 'Thanks for cooling the situation. I'm sure that wasn't an easy act for you.'

'You owe me one.'

'Right. And dinner.'

They continued their walk away from Burov's dacha. Lisa said, 'They captured Dodson.'

Hollis nodded. 'Damned bad break for Dodson. But maybe that takes the pressure off Burov to break camp.'

'If you're concerned that this place stay put, you obviously believe someone is coming for us.'

'That's a good deduction. You're starting to think like an intelligence officer.'

'And you talk like one. Answer the question, Hollis.'

He smiled. 'I think it's better that we're here and not someplace else if a rescue attempt is made.' He added, 'Don't press me on it, Lisa. I think out loud sometimes because I have no one to talk to about any of this. I'll think to myself now.'

Hollis thought that undoubtedly Alevy knew he and Lisa were kidnapped and, in fact, had anticipated their kidnapping,

539

which was why Alevy, in an uncharacteristic display of senti-
ment, had tried to talk Lisa out of taking that flight. And in the
two early-morning sessions he had with Alevy, Alevy hinted at
some sort of rescue operation at the Charm School – perhaps,
as Burov had guessed, an operation to get at least two or three
men out of here as evidence. Thus, all of Alevy's questioning
about the Soviet Mi-28 helicopter, which was obviously how
Alevy planned to do it.

But then Alevy, at Sheremetyevo, had indicated a swap, now
that they could lay their hands on most of the three thousand
Charm School graduates in the States. Alevy never actually
lied to his peers; he just gave ten correct answers to the same
question.

He tried to get into Alevy's mind, which was not totally
impossible because they were both in the same business and
ostensibly had to think alike to solve the same sort of problems.
He thought that Alevy not only knew he and Lisa had been
kidnapped, but guessed that they had probably been taken
to the Charm School. Alevy would not want Lisa to spend
much time in Burov's hands, because Alevy, above being an
intelligence officer, was a man in love. And Alevy would not
want Hollis to spend too much time in Burov's hands either,
because Alevy did not want Hollis' brain in Burov's possession
too long.

Lisa broke into his thoughts. 'I think we underestimated
Burov's intellect.'

'Yes, I was impressed with his little speech.' Hollis added,
'What makes him tick is a weighted chain. He's cuckoo.'

Lisa laughed. 'You *are* too glib for your own good. Let's
go back and tell him that one.'

'Later.'

'What do you want to do between now and six P.M.?'

'Explore. Discover. Are you up to a long day?'

'Sure. I like watching you work. You intrigue me.'

He put his arm around her, and they continued down the
main road.

They passed the shopping plaza, then the headquarters building and approached the VFW hall. Hollis said, 'I'm to run into Poole here by accident at ten A.M.'

They climbed the porch steps and went into the building. There were about a dozen instructors in the rec room and twice that many students. Four men played billiards at one end of the room, and a group was in front of the television watching *Platoon*.

They found Poole at a card table with three students playing poker. Poole had a stack of chips in front of him and a wad of camp scrip. One of the cardplayers was Jim Hull, the young man whom Lisa had caused some discomfort in the gym. He smiled at Lisa, but she gave him a frosty look that sent him back to his cards.

Poole looked up from his hand. 'Oh, hello, Colonel. Ms Rhodes. Do you want to sit in?'

'No, thanks. Someone told me you were on the firewood committee.'

'Oh, sure. I'll be with you in a second. Let me finish out the hand.'

Hollis and Lisa sat at a nearby table.

The men played out the hand, and one of the students took the pot with aces and sixes. Poole said to the three students, 'That's called the dead man's hand.'

'Why?' one of them asked.

Poole explained, 'It was the hand that Wild Bill Hickock was holding when he was shot in the back by someone in Deadwood. That's a town somewhere in the American West. I don't remember what state. But it's an unlucky hand, even if you win with it. Aces over sixes. When someone gets that hand in poker, you say "dead man's hand".' Poole stood. 'I'll be back late. Don't swipe my money.'

The three young men smiled.

Poole led Hollis and Lisa outside and stood at the edge of the main road some distance from the VFW hall.

Hollis remarked, 'Dead man's hand is aces over eights.'

'Really? How stupid of me,' He grinned and whispered, 'I have to pull a fast one on them at least once a day, or I'm depressed.'

Lisa asked, 'Have you ever been caught?'

'Sure. About a dozen times. Then Lena – that's my wife – does a week in the slammer.' He looked at Hollis, then Lisa. 'She doesn't care. She's proud of me when they take her away. She did four years in a logging camp before she came here. The cells here are like R and R in comparison, and she doesn't have to do laundry in the slammer or make the bed because there are no beds. I cook her a big meal when she comes home.'

Lisa said, 'But surely they can do more to her and to you if they chose to.'

'They can. But they hesitate. I explained to you, they're using more carrots and fewer sticks now. They'll go through the stick phase again one day. In fact, I kind of sense it coming.'

'And will you still sabotage the curriculum?' Lisa asked in a quiet voice.

'Absolutely. You know, it may not seem much to you – these little lies, like the aces and sixes. But I remember a true story I read once about a British flier imprisoned with other pilots in a German castle during World War Two. He was there a few years, not fifteen or twenty years, but his sense of frustration at not being able to do damage to his enemies became obsessive. So he would cut slivers of dry rot from the castle timbers and implant them in sound timbers, knowing that fifty or a hundred years later, the whole castle would be eaten by rot. Can you understand the psychology of that?'

'Yes,' Hollis replied. 'I've heard of similar stories.'

Poole put his arms around them and drew them closer. He spoke softly. 'Well, that's sort of what we feel here and what we do here. Only we have our modern version of the castle timbers. I sometimes think of these little courses we teach as silicon chips. We're supposed to implant the right microcircuitry on those chips so they can go into the big computer of the Russian student's brain. But we put little scratches on those chips as we're making them. Small imperfections that escape quality control. Then the Russian heads West with these little glitches, and maybe his computer works fine most of the time, and maybe he gets a malfunction at a noncritical moment. But one day, in the right situation, like when he's sailing along at Mach two and sixty thousand feet and the engines are at full power, he'll try a maneuver, and the imperfect microchip will fail him at a crucial moment. And the small malfunction at that time and place will be fatal. Like maybe one of those bozos in there will be playing cards someday with a CIA man and pulling aces and sixes and make a stupid comment. You understand?'

'Perfectly.'

'We try.'

'I know.'

'So, do you smoke Cuban cigars?'

'No.'

'You do now.' Poole took two aluminum cigar tubes from the pocket of his warm-up jacket and handed them to Hollis, who slipped them in his pocket. Poole said, 'All the names of the Americans past and present who've been in this place. Signatures where possible, dates of first incarceration here, and dates of death where appropriate. That's dynamite there, Colonel, if you can get that out of here and to the embassy.'

'I know that.'

'But maybe they don't want dynamite in the embassy.'

'They may not. But they'll do what they have to do.'

'Will they? Do you have any hope of – well, I won't ask you again.' Poole inquired, 'How was your morning?'

'I assume you know we went up to see Burov. Is it common to be asked to his house?'

'It used to be. Like being asked to take sherry with the headmaster. But the ethics committee ruled it out years ago. We only go if given a direct order by him to report. Never take a drink or even a glass of water. I think he's insulted, so he never asks anymore.'

'Alright.'

'Can you tell me what he wanted?'

'Well, basically he wanted to shoot us. But he'll settle for our working here.'

Poole nodded. 'If you could be sure he'd only *shoot* you, I'd advise you to tell him to shove his job. But he'll put you through an interrogation that won't be very pleasant.'

Hollis replied, 'I know that. But we have the choice of a more unpleasant interrogation by drugs and polygraph if we take his job offer. Either way, he's going to get things from us that I'd rather he didn't know.'

Poole looked at Hollis, then at Lisa, and asked her, 'Are you in intelligence?'

'Yes. But only very recently. I used to write press releases.'

Hollis continued, 'I have to give him an answer by six. We'll tell him yes, but I'm trying to buy time between then and the polygraph.'

Poole stared at Hollis. 'What you buying time *for*?'

Which, Hollis thought, was a very good question. If he were to answer Poole, he would say, 'Time to get the people in Washington moving.' He knew that Seth Alevy would be presenting to the President a very convincing case to prove that Lisa Rhodes and Sam Hollis had been kidnapped, not incinerated in that helicopter crash; and that they were being held in the Charm School. Alevy would also tell the National Security Council that Hollis had more information in his head than they would ever want the Russians to know. Alevy would hint at dark things, would cajole, plead, and threaten. And Alevy might even have General Surikov in the White House at this very moment, presenting a very chilling microfilm show of three thousand Soviet agents to a stunned President and his security advisers. Eventually, even Washington would realize that something had to be done and the hell with détente.

'Buy time for what?' Poole repeated.

Hollis did not respond to the question, but informed Poole, 'Burov says they've captured Dodson.'

'Jack . . . captured?'

'That's what Burov said.'

Poole seemed stunned, then pulled himself together. 'Now comes the bloodbath.'

'I'll speak to Burov tonight. I'll see what I can do.'

'You can't do a thing.'

'But I'll give it all I've got.'

'Alright . . . that idiotic Halloween party is tonight. Begins at seven. We all have to show up with our women.'

'I'll talk to you then.' Hollis added, 'Commander, is it too early for you to have a drink?'

'Normally, yes. But I'll make an exception this morning.'

'Good day.'

Poole walked off as if in a trance.

36

Sam Hollis and Lisa Rhodes sat in Colonel Burov's office. Also in the office were two KGB Border Guards standing at parade rest directly behind them.

Burov said, 'What have you decided?'

Lisa replied, 'We've decided to work here.'

Burov nodded and looked at Hollis. 'I want to hear it from *you*, Colonel.'

Hollis said, 'I will work here.'

'Good. And you will both submit to interrogations with truth drugs and polygraph machines. Correct?'

'Yes.'

'And you understand that you will not attempt to dissemble and confuse the machines. You will tell the truth the first time you are asked a question. If you lie even once, you go to the electroshock table. If you lie twice, you may go to the firing squad. Understand?'

'Yes.'

'Now let me ask you some questions, without drugs or polygraph. And your answers had better prove true when you get on the machine. First question – Does American intelligence know of the general nature of this facility? Colonel?'

Hollis replied, 'Yes.'

Burov stared at him a moment, then asked, 'They know there are American fliers held here?'

'Yes.'

'Do they know how many?'

'No.'

'What do they plan to do about the Americans held here?'

'I don't know.'

'You don't? That answer had better not send the needle off

the polygraph paper, or you'll find out how painful an electric shock to the genitals can be.' Burov looked from Hollis to Lisa, then asked Hollis, 'Is your presence here a result of my cleverness or Seth Alevy's cleverness?'

'I'm not following you.'

'But you are. Did you and Alevy know you might be kidnapped?'

'No.'

Burov's eyes fixed on Hollis, and he stayed silent for a long time, then asked, 'Is there an American intelligence operation of any sort planned against this facility?'

'I don't know of any.'

Burov said, 'You know, Hollis, if I see that you've lied to me twice so far, you go right to the wall, sparing yourself the electric shock. But perhaps I didn't impress that upon you. So I'm going to ask you the same questions again.' Burov proceeded to ask the questions in the same words and got the same responses from Hollis. He rephrased the final question, 'Has Seth Alevy even hinted to you of an armed or clandestine American mission directed toward this camp?'

'No, he has not.'

Burov smiled thinly. 'I hope for both our sakes that you are telling the truth.' He looked at Lisa. 'And you. Are you in any way involved in intelligence work?'

'No.'

'No? You are simply involved with intelligence men?'

Lisa nodded. 'Yes.'

'How unfortunate for you. If there were a next time for you, I would advise you to sleep with less dangerous men.'

Lisa started to reply but then simply nodded.

Burov went on, 'Your two spy friends have gotten you into this. I can't get you out of it now. But I can see to it that you live comfortably if you do what I say.'

Again she nodded.

Burov said, 'You heard Colonel Hollis' response to my question. Were his responses true, to the best of your knowledge?'

'Yes.'

'Do you know what an electroshock table is?'

'I think so.'

'Good. Next question, Ms Rhodes. Did you and Colonel Hollis speak with General Austin at his cottage two nights ago?'

'Yes.'

'Did you speak to Commander Poole at that time, and also again near the recreation building this morning?'

'Yes.'

'Was an escape plan or a rescue mission discussed on either of those occasions?'

'No.'

'No? Well, we'll see how many strikes you have when we attach you to the polygraph.'

Burov looked at Hollis. 'In baseball you get three strikes. Yes? Here we play softball. The game is easier, but you only get two strikes in softball, and you're out.' Burov smiled.

Hollis said to Burov, 'That's a bad analogy.'

'Metaphor,' Lisa corrected.

'I can't keep them straight,' Hollis admitted.

Burov's eyes narrowed and his lips pursed. 'I love your language. I really do. The spoken language. But the English-speaking peoples think that anyone who doesn't speak their language is a moron. That's a source of great amusement for you. But do you know something? When a person is strapped to the electroshock table, only one language comes out of his or her mouth, and it doesn't resemble any human language you have ever heard.'

Burov looked at them both, then said, 'Tomorrow morning two interrogators will arrive here from Moscow. The first is a polygraph and drug expert. Your sessions with this man may last several weeks, and aside from some drug hangovers, you will not be uncomfortable in any way. The second interrogator is a man they call the *elektromonter* – the electrician. He dwells in the basement of the Lubyanka, and he has seen things there

548

that would make the three of us sick.' He added, 'Luckily for you the choice is yours, not mine.'

Lisa said, 'We've chosen.'

Burov looked into Lisa's eyes a long time. 'What, I wonder, has happened to your spirit.' He shrugged. 'Well, anyway, I congratulate you on your wise decision.'

Hollis asked, 'What's going to happen to Major Dodson?'

'Oh, you know I have no control over that.'

'Why not? Who runs this place?'

Burov seemed annoyed. 'You *must* understand, Colonel Hollis, that Dodson, aside from committing a capital offense, has seen too much of the country between here and Moscow. I don't want him briefing the others about the terrain and such: The man will be executed.'

'When?'

'Tomorrow morning.'

Hollis stood. 'You –'

One of the guards put his hands on Hollis' shoulders and slammed him back into his chair.

Burov shrugged. 'We simply cannot have people trying to get out of here. It would ruin everything. For all of us. For world peace. For the Americans here as well. They'd be sent somewhere else and probably shot. You understand how important this all is.'

'I understand,' Hollis replied, 'that if Dodson had made good his escape, *you* would have been shot. I understand a system that finds merit in cruelty and uses terror as a management tool.'

Burov shrugged. 'And so do I. But that's the way we've *always* done it here, Hollis, since even before the czars. I terrorize the people below me, and Lubyanka terrorizes me. So terror breeds terror. So what? It works.' He nodded directly at Hollis. 'I value my head, and Major Dodson's head is not so valuable to me. I have a family to support.'

Lisa asked, 'Can't you just *imprison* Major Dodson?'

'No. We must make a public example of him.'

549

Hollis said, 'If you kill him, you may have trouble here.'

'Yes?' Burov looked at him. 'You've heard that? Well, you can tell your compatriots that I'm prepared to shoot as many of their wives and girlfriends as I have to if they even think of trouble. Will you tell them that for me, Colonel Hollis?'

'Yes, I will, Colonel Burov. But I was thinking too of *your* compatriots. These young students. How will their new American sensibilities be affected by this execution?'

'Don't try to balt me or cow me, Hollis. My students are not going to be affected in any way by Major Dodson's execution. Even those who knew him will not shed a single tear.'

'I ask you to consider all the possible consequences of your action, Colonel Burov.'

'It was up to Dodson and his friends to consider the consequences.'

Hollis drew a deep breath. 'May we go?'

'In a moment. I want you to report to this headquarters immediately after the execution tomorrow. Yes, it will be a public execution. On the soccer field at eight A.M. You may pass the word around. Any man who does not attend will have his woman shot. Any woman who does not attend will be shot herself. Children are exempt from attending. There will be two hundred Border Guards there, heavily armed. Tell that to General Austin. Let's try to avoid a bloodbath tomorrow. Alright?'

'Will anyone else be executed?'

'Yes. Ten others. Major Dodson is now being interrogated regarding his accomplices. If he doesn't divulge any names, I'll pick ten people at random, including women.' Burov added, 'Don't feel sorry for them. They knew the rule. I'm sure there won't be another escape attempt for at least another ten years. Good evening.'

Hollis and Lisa stood.

Burov said, 'You *will* attend the Halloween festivities tonight. The camp will turn out at the soccer field at eight A.M. hangovers notwithstanding. You may leave.'

Hollis walked quickly to the door, followed by Lisa and the two guards.

They made their way out of the headquarters building and on to the dark road, leaving the guards behind. The night was very cold, and through the pine bough canopy Hollis could see stars but no moonlight. They both walked in silence toward the VFW building. Hollis suddenly stopped and kicked savagely at a fallen branch. 'Damn him!'

Lisa put her hand on his shoulder.

'That son of a bitch! He *knows*. He knows the difference between right and wrong, between good and evil, and he chooses wrong and evil. Evil is an industry here. He has a *family* to support. Do you believe what you just heard? I thought I'd heard it all. Jesus Christ.'

Lisa said, 'Let's walk. Come on, Sam. Walk it off.'

They continued along the road. Lisa said, 'Tomorrow . . . will there be trouble? A revolt?'

'I don't know. I do know that six hundred unarmed men and women have no chance against two hundred armed Border Guards.'

'But could you use this to spark a revolt?'

'Maybe . . . as far as the people here are concerned, we just dropped in from heaven with God's last commandment. But . . . is it right to incite a revolt that will end in a massacre?'

They walked slowly up the road toward the VFW hall, which was all alight for the party. Lisa asked, 'What are we going to do about the interrogation, Sam? We both have two strikes before we even walk in there.'

'We seem to be running out of time and space, don't we?'

Hollis thought of the secrets he had to protect. He had to protect Surikov in the event. Surikov had not gotten out of the country yet. He had to protect the fact that the three thousand graduates of the Charm School were about to be blown and swapped for Burov's three hundred Americans. He had to keep Burov thinking that Alevy had no plans to grab a few Americans out of here to show the world. But he could no longer stall Burov, and Burov would get what he needed from Hollis through drugs, clubs, electric shock, or just the polygraph paper. Then Burov would evacuate the camp, and the KGB would alert its three thousand agents in America. Then that would be the end of the operation and the last of America's MIAs would finally and forever be lost.

Lisa stayed silent as they walked. Finally, she said, 'Nina Sturges and Mary Auerbach.'

'Who?'

'The two American women who killed themselves here.'

Hollis didn't reply.

'Sam . . . tomorrow we are going to watch eleven good men and women die in a horrible way. Then we are going to be interrogated for weeks. We may not ever leave that building back there. You know that.'

Again Hollis said nothing.

Lisa said softly, 'I've been thinking . . . if we went to bed tonight . . . and just kept on sleeping . . . together . . . you and I . . . forever. Wouldn't it be better? In each other's arms?' She added, 'They used the propane heater . . .'

He looked at her. For the first time since he'd met her he felt totally responsible for her fate. But now she was trying to take her destiny and his destiny into her own hands. He said to her, 'There have been a lot of sunrises I haven't looked forward to. But we'll see this one. Together. I don't want to hear any more of that.'

'I'm sorry . . . I don't want to do it without you . . . but it's going to be such a long night.'

'Maybe we'll find the answers in the long night.'

Part 5

It doesn't do to leave a live Dragon out of your calculations, if you live near him.

– J.R.R. Tolkien

37

Seth Alevy put on his trench coat, took his attaché case, and left his room on the twelfth floor of the hotel located within the complex of new buildings called the Center for International Trade.

He stepped out into the large marble lobby, which he noted was crowded, mostly with Western and Japanese business people.

As he crossed the lobby, he heard a loud shout and turned quickly toward it. At the far end of the lobby, two men in expensive-looking suits rushed toward a burly-looking man and grabbed him, pushing him against a stone pillar. One of the two men shouted in Russian, 'We are CIA! Yuri Sergunov, you are under arrest!'

The burly man, Sergunov, delivered a vicious judo chop to the neck of one of the men, who crumpled to the floor. The second CIA man drew his gun, but Sergunov got to his first and fired twice into the CIA man, who dropped to the mauve carpet, blood spreading across his white shirt.

A few people at that end of the lobby screamed and ran as Sergunov sprinted toward the glass doors, brandishing his pistol. He knocked over a doorman, and Alevy saw him disappear into the night.

Someone yelled, '*Stoi!*'

The action in the roped-off section of the lobby stopped. The CIA man who had been judo-chopped stood and shouted, 'Can't you explain to that cretin how to fake a chop? He nearly broke my neck.'

A man standing next to Alevy inquired, 'Do you speak English?'

'Yes.'

The man said in a British accent, 'They ought to announce these things, don't you think?'

'Actually, there's a sign over there.'

'It's in Russian.'

'It's a Russian movie,' Alevy pointed out.

'Can you read that?'

'A bit. Something about asking our indulgence while a film scene is being shot.'

'What sort of film? Looked like a cops and robbers.'

'It's a spy movie,' Alevy replied. 'The fellow who escaped was probably the hero. A KGB man, I'd guess.'

'You don't say. That's a different slant on things.'

'This is Russia,' Alevy reminded him.

'Who were the other two chaps, then? Not MI-6, I hope.'

'No. CIA.'

'Ah.' The Englishman thought a moment. 'It seemed the CIA men were trying to arrest the KGB fellow. They can't do that in Russia.'

'It would be good if they could. But this is supposed to be America. Mosfilm uses this place as their American locale. I've seen this hotel in ten movies already.'

The Englishman laughed. 'Don't the Russians get tired of seeing the same place?'

'The Russians, my friend, don't get tired of anything but work.'

'Right you are. Well, this is something to tell everyone back home. You know, I just stepped off the lift, and I was a bit taken aback for a moment. A man can get paranoid in this country.'

'Why is that?' Alevy asked.

The man didn't respond.

The director was setting the scene again as the CIA man changed into a clean shirt for a retake.

The Englishman said, 'This sort of thing is not in the best of taste, if you think about it. I mean, almost everyone here is Western. It's somewhat offensive.'

'It's their country.'

'Yes, but really, this is an expensive hotel. We don't need this sort of thing here. Americans being shot and all that. Though I don't suppose anyone would know that if they didn't speak a bit of Russian.'

'Art imitates life,' Alevy said.

'I always thought it was the other way around. Well, I must be going. Good evening.'

Alevy watched the scene begin to unfold again, but decided he didn't want to see the CIA man take two more shots in the gut, so he turned and left.

He made his way to the shopping arcade, a thickly carpeted concourse with six specialized Beriozkas fronting on it. In the windows of the Beriozkas were decals of American Express, Eurocard, and five other major world credit cards, and the glass was clean.

Alevy walked into the store called Jewelry Store and examined a string of amber beads. Four well-dressed Japanese businessmen browsed together through the elegant shop. An American man next to Alevy said to the woman with him, 'If the masses could see this place, they'd revolt again.'

Alevy took the beads, brought them to the counter, and presented a Eurocard issued under the name of Thornton Burns. The salesgirl placed the necklace in a satin box and slid the box into a colorful paper bag. She smiled and said in English, 'Have a good evening,' but Alevy had the impression she was reading from a sign over his left shoulder.

He went out into the concourse past the window of a store called For Men and Women that sold an odd combination of Russian furs, embroideries, china, and cut glass. He glanced at his watch and saw it was nine-thirty. The Beriozkas would be closing soon. He passed by the shops marked 'Radio Goods' and 'Bookstore' and turned into a downward-sloping passage to the food store.

Even at this hour, he noted, the small supermarket was crowded with guests of the hotel, plus diplomats and their

557

spouses from every embassy in Moscow, ranking Party officials with access to hard currency, and black marketeers who were using Western currency at the risk of doing two to five in Siberia.

The market was well-stocked with European canned goods, meat and fish, Soviet hothouse vegetables, and tropical fruits, most of which Muscovites had never seen outside of a book or movie. Alevy noticed that a new shipment of pineapples, still in crates marked 'Nicaragua', was disappearing fast into a dozen carts.

Alevy purchased some Swiss candy bars, American bubble gum, and Finnish hard candies. He paid for the items in American dollars and went back to the concourse, where he found the Intourist service desk located behind a glass wall. He placed his passport, visa, and airline tickets on the desk and said in English, 'I would like to confirm my helicopter connection to Sheremetyevo and my flight to Helsinki.'

The attractive blond woman glanced at the papers on her desk and replied snippily in excellent English, 'Yes, everything is alright. What is there to confirm?'

'I know how well everything runs in this country, but I want to be certain about my arrangements.'

She looked at him a moment, then replied a bit more civilly, 'I know that your helicopter is already here, Mr Burns. It leaves in fifteen minutes. Go to the lobby and see the bell captain. I haven't heard of any problem with your Finnair flight.'

'Thank you.' Alevy gathered his passport, visa, and tickets, slipping them into his trench coat. He walked back to the lobby and spotted his luggage, which had been taken from his room. The film crew was wrapping up the shoot, and a porter was trying to get the blood off the carpet.

Alevy approached the bell captain. 'Helicopter?' He made a whirling motion with his finger. '*Helicopter?*' he said more loudly, remembering that Americans had a reputation of shouting English to foreigners in the belief that if it was loud enough the natives would understand it. 'Hel-i-cop-ter!'

'Ah, *vertolet*.' The bell captain pointed through the glass doors to a small white Aeroflot bus.

'Swell.' Alevy pointed to his bags and showed the man his hotel bill with his room number on it.

The bell captain nodded and called a bellboy over, saying to the boy in Russian, 'You didn't think the American was going to carry his bags twenty meters, did you? Be nice to him, and he may take you to America in his suitcase.'

Alevy smiled vacuously at the bell captain and gave him a ruble.

The man touched his cap and said, '*Da svedahnya*.'

'Good-bye,' Alevy said, and followed the bellboy toward the doors where the doorman wished him a pleasant journey, making Alevy think that indeed some of them were getting it right.

Alevy boarded the Aeroflot minibus and nodded to three other men who were seated. The bellboy stowed Alevy's overnight bag and suitcase in the rear of the bus. Alevy held on to his attaché case. The driver started the bus.

The man across the aisle from Alevy said to him, 'American?'

'Yes.'

The man smiled. 'Hey, can you believe helicopter service in Moscow? They didn't have this when I was here five years ago.'

The man behind Alevy added, 'I can't believe this hotel. It was nearly up to standards.'

They all laughed.

The fourth man, in front of Alevy, looked back at the other three. 'Did you men see that cops and robbers movie they were shooting there in the lobby?'

They all nodded. Alevy said, 'It was actually a CIA-KGB caper. Silly Hollywood kind of stuff. Never hear about that in real life.'

The bus pulled away from the circular driveway, and the four men, all Americans, exchanged small talk about their stay in Moscow. It turned out that they were all taking the

10:45 Finnair flight to Helsinki, the last flight to the West until morning.

The man in front of Alevy said he was a frequent traveler to Moscow and added, 'I always feel good when I get clear of this place. I've kissed that tarmac at Helsinki so many times my lips are getting black.'

They all smiled in recognition.

The bus took them around the west side of the hotel to a concrete helipad near the International Exhibition Hall, close by the Moskva embankment road. An Mi-28 helicopter sat on the floodlit pad, its turbojet engine warming. Alevy regarded the white helicopter a moment. Rather than landing skids, it sat on wheels like most Soviet helicopters. It had four main rotor blades, sitting atop two four-hundred-horsepower Izotov turbine engines. The Mi-28 saw service in the Soviet military, as it did with Aeroflot as a transporter of VIPs. It was fast, comfortable, and reliable. Or so he'd been told. Like all Soviet aircraft, this one had a NATO code name, and as with all helicopters, the code name began with *H*. The code names were supposed to be meaningless. He hoped so. The Mi-28 was called The Headstone.

The bus stopped ten meters from the helicopter, and the four Americans carried their own luggage off, the bus driver helping them with their bags of Beriozka items.

The pilot opened the cabin door and took the luggage, stowing it in the narrow space behind the last two seats. The four Americans tipped the bus driver in rubles and climbed aboard the helicopter.

Alevy sat directly behind the pilot and noted that the copilot's seat was empty as was usually the case on these short hops to the airport.

The other three men settled into the remaining seats. One of them, the frequent Moscow traveler, commented, 'At this hour we could make Sheremetyevo by taxi in thirty minutes. The Russkies probably think we're nuts to spend this kind of money to make it by chopper in ten.'

Another man replied, 'They're learning how to part us from our greenbacks. Ten more years and you'll see hard currency strip joints on Gorky Street.'

Everyone laughed.

The helicopter lifted vertically over the Trade Center complex, and Alevy looked down at the handsome buildings below: the fifteen-story hotel, the taller office buildings, and the trade exhibition halls. 'A true window to the West,' he said. 'To the world. Even the Soviet paranoia about everything Western seems to be missing from the place.'

No one replied.

Alevy leaned forward and examined the helicopter instrument panel, its gauges and radios alight in a faint red glow. He said to the pilot, 'Do you speak English?'

The pilot glanced back as he swung the helicopter north toward Sheremetyevo. '*Chto?*'

'*Angliiski?*'

'*Nyet.*'

Alevy nodded and sat back in his seat. He said to the other men, 'Fuel gauge reads full.'

The man sitting beside Alevy, Captain Ed O'Shea, nodded. 'As I said, Seth, it's a regulation so that all aircraft, even civilian craft, are always ready for instant mobilization if the balloon goes up.'

'Good rule,' Alevy remarked. *So far, so good*, he thought. *One pilot, full tanks*. He and two of the other Americans with him, Hollis' aide, O'Shea, and Alevy's deputy station chief, Bert Mills, had flown out to Helsinki during the past week, then come back to Moscow individually, with new passports and forged Soviet visas, checking into the Trade Center. They were officially out of the country, and there would be few problems for the embassy if things went bad.

The man behind Alevy, Bill Brennan, who had come directly from his convalescent leave in London, said, 'I want to thank you for giving me a chance to even the score.'

Alevy replied, 'I thought you'd be getting bored in London.'

He added, 'They did a lousy job on your nose.' Alevy looked out the window and saw Sheremetyevo coming up on the port front. 'Well, gentlemen, are we ready?'

They all answered in the affirmative. Bert Mills, in the rear seat beside Brennan, leaned forward and said to Captain O'Shea, 'Now that you've seen it, can you fly it from the copilot's chair?'

O'Shea replied, 'Tricky, but we'll give it a shot.'

'Okay,' Alevy said, 'here goes.' Alevy took a chloroform pad from his pocket, ripped open the foil envelope, and reached around the pilot's face, clamping the pad over his mouth as O'Shea jumped forward into the copilot's seat and grabbed the controls of the wobbling craft.

The pilot thrashed around kicking the control pedals and yanking on the collective pitch stick. The helicopter began tilting dangerously as O'Shea fought for control. He shouted, 'Get him out of there!'

Alevy stood and ripped the pilot's headphones off, then with Brennan's help pulled the pilot up and over the seat, dropping him on the floor of the cabin. The pilot groaned, then lay still.

Alevy took a deep breath and leaned forward. 'Okay, Captain. The seat is yours.'

'Right.' O'Shea rose carefully from the copilot's seat. 'Hold on.' He cut the throttle, and the helicopter began to drop. O'Shea vaulted sideways into the pilot's seat, grabbing at the controls as his feet found the antitorque pedals. The dropping craft yawed and rolled, then steadied as O'Shea got control. He opened the throttle, and the helicopter began to rise. 'Okay, okay.'

Alevy crossed over to the copilot's seat as Bert Mills and Bill Brennan moved forward into the middle seats. Alevy asked O'Shea, 'Well, is it as easy to fly as it looks?'

O'Shea smiled grimly. 'This is a bitch. I haven't flown rotary-wing in ten years.' He added, 'The main rotor in Soviet choppers turns the opposite of Western rotary-wing. So the rudder pedals are opposite.'

'Is that why we're zigzagging all over the place, Captain?'

'Yeah. Takes a while to get used to.' O'Shea pointed to a switch. 'What does that say?'

Alevy leaned forward and read the Russian switch plate. '*Svet* . . . light . . . moving . . . landing.'

'Controllable landing light,' O'Shea said. He switched it off. 'I saw the pilot hit it a few minutes ago. We don't need that.' O'Shea pushed the cyclic control stick to port and worked the antitorque pedals to keep the craft in longitudinal trim, swinging the helicopter west, away from Sheremetyevo, away from Moscow. O'Shea said, 'I'll need about fifteen minutes of maneuvers before I feel confident with these controls.'

Alevy replied, 'Try ten. We need every drop of fuel. Did that training manual help?'

'Yes, but it's no substitute for hands-on.' O'Shea added, 'It's okay, men. Just relax. I'm getting it.'

Alevy put on the headphones and listened to the radio traffic from Sheremetyevo tower. He said to O'Shea, 'Don't get too far west. I have to call the tower.'

'Right.' O'Shea practiced some simple maneuvers.

Alevy looked toward the east and saw the bright lights of Moscow on the distant horizon. The sky was unusually clear, very starry, but there was only a sliver of a white, waning moon tonight, he noted, which was fine. Below, the farmland and forests were in almost complete darkness.

Seth Alevy stared out the windshield. Spread before him was Russia in all its endless mystery, the land of his grandparents, a black limitless space so dark, deep, and cold that whole armies and entire nationalities – Don Cossacks, Volga Germans, Jews, and Tartars – could disappear without a trace and without a decibel of their screams being heard beyond the vast frontiers.

Alevy looked west out to where the dark sky touched the black horizon. Soon they would be plunging into that void, and though he could smell the fear around him, nothing frightened him so much as the thought that they might be too late.

Bill Brennan, sitting now behind O'Shea's seat, with his feet on the unconscious Aeroflot pilot, asked Alevy, 'Do you want me to dump him?'

'There's no need for that.'

'Okay. Can I break his nose?'

'No. Just tie him up.'

Brennan tied the pilot's wrists and ankles with a length of metal flex.

Bert Mills looked at his watch. 'We're about five minutes overdue at Sheremetyevo.'

'Right.' Alevy said to O'Shea, 'Let's kill all the lights.'

O'Shea scanned the instrument panel and referred to an Mi-28 cockpit diagram that he and Hollis had made up with English subtitles some weeks ago.

'Here,' Alevy said. 'This says "navigation lights."'

'That's the one.'

Alevy hit the switch and the outside lights went out. 'You just fly, Captain.' He took the diagram from O'Shea and found the interior light switch and flipped it, throwing the cabin and cockpit into darkness. The instrument lights cast a pale red glow over Alevy and O'Shea's face and hands.

The effect of the nearly total darkness inside and outside was somewhat eerie, Alevy thought, and he could hear the other three men's disembodied breathing above the sound of the rotor blades. Alevy held the diagram on his lap and scanned it. He found the radio transmit button on the cyclic grip. 'Okay.' He depressed the transmit button and suddenly shouted in Russian into the mouth mike of his headset, *'Kontroler! Kontroler!'*

A few seconds later the control tower at Sheremetyevo replied, *'Kontroler.'*

Alevy said excitedly in Russian, 'This is Aeroflot P one one three – lost engine power –' He stopped talking, but continued depressing the button the way a pilot would do as he contemplated the ground rushing up at him. Alevy screamed in Russian, 'God –!' then lifted his finger from the button and heard Sheremetyevo tower in his headphones,

'– one one three, come in, come –' Alevy shut off the radio power and removed his headphones. 'That should keep them busy searching for wreckage, as well as making them reflect on man's need for divine comfort in the last second of life. Okay, Captain O'Shea, let's head west.'

O'Shea swung the tail boom around and pointed the Mi-28 west, then opened up the throttle and changed the pitch angle of the rotor blades. 'This thing moves.'

Alevy looked out over the dark landscape. 'Let's get down there, Captain, and find a place to park it awhile.'

O'Shea began his descent from twelve hundred meters. As the ground came up, Alevy, Brennan, and Mills scanned the terrain. Brennan said, 'Forest there. Open farmland over there. Too open. There's something – what's that?'

They all looked out to starboard at a light-colored area about five hundred meters away.

Alevy said, 'Get in closer, Captain.'

O'Shea slid the helicopter to the right and dropped in closer. He said, 'It looks like an excavation. A quarry or gravel pit.'

'That'll do,' Alevy said.

O'Shea banked around toward the large shallow excavation that appeared to encompass about an acre dug out of the open plains northwest of Moscow. 'Okay,' O'Shea said, 'let's see if this helicopter knows how to land.'

O'Shea looked below to see if there were any smoke-stacks or anything that would give him an indication of the wind direction, but he saw nothing. He guessed that the wind would be coming from the northwest as it usually did this time of year, and he banked around so he could make his landing heading into what he hoped was the prevailing wind.

He maintained a constant rpm so there would be no variations in torque forces that could make the craft yaw around its vertical axis. The pedals, which were reversed because the rotor direction was reversed, were his major problem; what should have been second nature was becoming a thought process, like driving a British car on the left side of the road.

Alevy said, 'You're doing fine.'

'You talking to me?' O'Shea's instinct was to glide in at a shallow angle, as with a fixed-wing, but he knew he had to maintain sufficient altitude until the last few seconds in the event he did something to stall the engine, which would necessitate an autorotative landing; a free fall that could only be made successfully if there was time to throw the transmission into neutral, adjust the pitch of the blades, allowing the uprushing air to turn the rotors to produce enough lift to cushion the crash.

He was coming in at about forty-five degrees, and the altimeter showed five hundred meters.

He began decreasing airspeed with the collective pitch stick and throttle. As the collective pitch was adjusted, he increased his pressure on the right rudder to maintain the heading and increased the throttle to hold the rpm steady. Simultaneously he coordinated the cyclic stick with the other controls to maintain the proper forward airspeed. He wished he had another hand.

The helicopter passed over the edge of the excavation at one hundred meters' altitude, and O'Shea realized the pit was deeper than he'd thought. The opposite wall of the pit was less than a hundred meters away now, and he was still about one hundred meters above the bottom of the excavation at an angle of approach that would put the craft into the fast-approaching wall. He felt sweat forming under his arms.

O'Shea immediately decreased the collective, simultaneously increasing rearward pressure on the cyclic, like reining in a horse. The craft's nose rose higher, and it began to slow. He resisted the temptation to cut the throttle, which seemed the natural thing to do to bleed off airspeed, but which would have led to a stall. 'Damn . . . stupid helicopter.'

The helicopter continued to slow, but O'Shea knew he was in a tail-low attitude, and the rear boom might hit the ground before the wheels did.

The rotors' downwash raised huge billows of dust and gravel, obscuring O'Shea's visibility, and he had to look at the artificial horizon indicator to see if he was horizontal to the ground. The downwash was creating a turbulence that was interfering with his ability to hold the craft steady. He could see neither the ground nor the excavation wall to his front and was hoping to touch the ground with his wheels before he touched the wall with his nose. 'I can't see . . . can anybody see?'

Alevy replied, 'Relax. You're fine.'

O'Shea knew that he was too nose-up and tail-down and that the helicopter was now tilted to the left and was still moving forward faster than it was descending. He also realized he had lost control. He made a decision and twisted the throttle shut, hoping that gravity would do what he could no longer do. 'Hold on!' The nose dropped, and the whole craft fell the last few feet but not straight down, the left landing-wheels hitting first. 'Damn it!' O'Shea shut off the engine as the entire craft rocked from side to side, the rotor blades barely clearing the ground.

Finally the craft settled into the gravel, and the rotors wound down. They all sat silently as the dust settled, clearing their view. Alevy looked around the excavation. It was indeed some sort of open quarry. He saw a few wooden sheds to the right and earth-moving equipment but no sign of workers or watchmen. Alevy commented to O'Shea, 'Are you on the upsweep of a learning curve, Ed?'

O'Shea drew a breath and nodded. He wiped his sweaty hands on his trousers. 'I got this thing figured out now.'

Brennan opened the sliding door, and he and Mills carried the unconscious Aeroflot pilot out of the helicopter. They dragged him through the gravel away from the helicopter and removed his Aeroflot flight suit, leaving him tied hand and foot in his underwear.

Alevy and O'Shea carried their luggage out and piled it some distance from the helicopter. Alevy opened one of the suitcases with a key and removed three KGB Border Guard uniforms, along with black boots, caps, four Soviet watches, pistols, and three KGB greatcoats. Alevy, Mills, and Brennan changed into the KGB uniforms, while O'Shea put on the Aeroflot pilot's flight suit.

As Alevy buttoned his greatcoat, he scanned the rim of the pit but couldn't see much in the darkness. 'I think we can wait it out here.'

Mills surveyed the pit. 'I didn't see any lights or signs of life coming in.' He looked at his Soviet watch. 'If this thing works, it's ten thirty-two. We're going to miss our Finnair flight.'

Brennan chuckled as he strapped on a leather belt with a holster that held a silenced 9mm Makarov automatic. Alevy and Mills strapped on their holsters also, and O'Shea slipped his automatic into the pocket of his flight suit. They synchronized their watches, then heaped their civilian clothes, passports, visas, watches, and wallets onto the stack of luggage then threw the Beriozka bags and attaché cases on top of that. Alevy took the satin box of amber beads from his trench coat and transferred it into his KGB greatcoat.

Brennan reached into the open suitcase and retrieved the last items: two cylindrical phosphorus incendiary grenades with timers. Brennan set the grenades' timer for three hours and shoved them into the pile of luggage and clothes.

Alevy said, 'Let's go.' They all returned to the helicopter.

O'Shea climbed back into the pilot's seat, and Alevy again sat in the copilot's seat. Brennan and Mills sat behind them. Alevy asked O'Shea, 'What is your estimate of our maximum available flight time?'

O'Shea thought a moment, then replied, 'As I said when we first discussed this, helicopter flying time is very hard to estimate. Fixed-wing craft have more defined parameters. You take off, fly, and land. With a chopper, you do other things. Like hover, which burns a lot of fuel.'

Alevy let O'Shea talk, because he knew O'Shea had to talk it out. Also, because they had three hours to kill.

O'Shea went on, 'A lot has to do with winds, air temperature, load, altitude, and the type of maneuvers we get involved with. It has to do with me not wasting fuel, but I'm not familiar enough with this craft to squeeze the most flight time and distance out of the least amount of fuel.' O'Shea said nothing for a while, then answered Alevy's question. 'Worst case would be two hours' flight time. Best, about four hours.'

'Straight line distance?'

'Figure . . . at about a hundred mph, two to four hundred miles.'

Bert Mills remarked, 'Even best case is going to be a damned close thing.'

Brennan, who didn't seem interested in the subject of fuel, was checking his Makarov automatic. He slid the magazine in and out, then worked the slide mechanism like a man who's had some bad experiences using other people's guns. He said, 'Everybody check their weapons.'

Everyone did as Brennan said, as he was the mission armorer.

Brennan then rummaged through Alevy's large overnight bag that had been left aboard and took out the broken-down pieces of a Dragunov sniper rifle and quickly assembled it in the dark. He mounted a four-power night scope on the rifle and loaded it, then pointed the rifle through the windshield and turned on the electronic scope. 'Not bad for made in the USSR.'

'They make some nice weapons,' Mills remarked.

Brennan shut off the scope and laid the rifle at his feet.

Alevy said to Brennan, 'There are two aerial survey maps in the bag.'

Brennan found the maps and handed them forward. Alevy gave one to O'Shea, who laid it out on his lap. Alevy handed him a red penlight, and O'Shea studied the map.

Brennan was still rummaging through the bag. 'Phosphorus grenades, extra ammunition, a little of this, and a little of that. Inventory complete.' He said to Alevy, 'It's none of my business, but where did you get these uniforms and hardware? And how did you keep the room maid from seeing everything?'

Alevy replied, 'That little antique store in the Arbat has a

569

costume shop in the basement. The hardware came in the diplomatic pouch. As for the nosy maids, I had that bag and the suitcase delivered to the lobby from the outside just before we boarded the bus.'

Brennan said, 'I want you to know something. Mr Alevy. I have a lot of confidence in you, and I don't think for a minute this is a suicide mission. Also, I like Colonel Hollis. He's a straight shooter. And I liked his lady. That's why I'm here and not in London.'

No one added anything to that for a few minutes. Then O'Shea said, 'I don't want anyone to get anxious about the flying. Think about what you have to do. I'll take care of the flying.' He added, 'The principles of flight remain the same even here and even if the rotors do go the wrong way.' He tried a laugh, but it came out wrong.

Bert Mills said, 'This damned uniform is pinching my crotch.'

Brennan remarked. 'That's because KGB tailors don't have to allow room for balls.'

Alevy said to Brennan, 'Bill, there's a blue Beriozka bag I left back there. I got Bazooka bubble gum and some other things. Pass it around.'

'Bazooka? Hey, thanks.' Brennan found the gum and passed the bag to Mills, who took a candy bar. He passed it up to O'Shea, who declined. Alevy sucked on a hard candy. Brennan blew a big bubble, and it popped. Brennan said, 'Hey, it's Halloween. Happy Halloween.'

No one answered.

Brennan added, 'I've seen some scary costumes for Halloween, but these outfits are the scariest fucking things I've ever seen.'

Mills forced a laugh. 'Where we're going you'll see about five hundred more of those scary outfits.'

'Thanks,' Brennan said.

The minutes passed in silence except for the ticking of the cooling engine and the sound of popping bubble gum. Alevy said to everyone, 'Relax.'

38

The VFW hall held close to a thousand people, but it was the quietest thousand people Hollis had ever been among.

The building was surrounded by armed KGB Border Guards, and no one was permitted to leave until midnight. The main recreation room was darkened, lit only by black candles and the grinning faces of jack-o'-lanterns. In the barroom and all the side rooms, men and women congregated, speaking in hushed, angry tones. Occasionally someone would weep. For the amount of food and liquor available, Hollis noticed that no one was drunk, and the food remained untouched, even by the students, whom Hollis thought seemed very uncomfortable. The masks, Hollis reflected, were off, literally and figuratively; no one was wearing the party masks, and no one was acting his part.

In the center of the recreation room sat a black-draped coffin on a bier, a party decoration that had taken on another significance. No one stood around the coffin.

Burov had not put in an appearance, and Hollis pictured him in his dacha, sitting with his wife near the porcelain stove, reading Pushkin or perhaps watching an American movie on videotape.

Hollis, who knew he would not be among the ten randomly picked for execution, felt somewhat guilty at being one of only two Americans in the hall who wasn't contemplating his imminent death. Lisa, he knew, felt the same.

When he had told Lewis Poole of Burov's plans to execute Dodson and ten others, they had discussed the possibility of not putting out the news. But Poole, Lisa, and he had concluded that everyone had a right to know.

There had been some incidents during the so-called party:

Jane Landis had spit in the face of a student, and the stereo that had been playing funereal music to set the mood of the theme party had been kicked to pieces by one of the kidnapped American women, Samantha Wells. Two American fliers, Ted Brewer and another man, had gone outside and tried to push their way past the cordon of Border Guards but were forcibly carried back inside. Captain Schuyler, whom Hollis had met on the path with Poole and Lieutenant Colonel Mead, had punched one of the students, but the fight had been quickly broken up.

To the students' credit, Hollis thought, they took the verbal abuse and looked rather sheepish. Certainly, Hollis reflected, the school would be closed for weeks if not months after this mad night.

General Austin sat in a small study, speaking briefly with groups of men and women, twenty and thirty at a time until most of the two hundred eighty-two Americans under his command and their wives and girlfriends had been addressed by him. Hollis made his way into the study and heard Austin say, 'To attempt to escape is our only pure and uncompromised act here. So we shall try again and again and again. There won't be ten years between attempts. There won't even be twelve months until the next one. And if they want to shoot us ten at a time for each attempt, so be it. This school is closed.'

Hollis listened awhile, then went into the barroom and got a glass of beer. Lisa found him and held his arm. 'Sam, I can't take much more of this.'

Hollis glanced at his watch. 'Another few minutes. At midnight it's over.'

He looked around the long barroom and spotted Sonny and Marty talking in a corner. At a small table sat the four students he'd met in their cottage. One of them, Erik Larson, was looking more like Yevgenni Petrovich Korniyenko, Hollis thought. In fact, all the students seemed not to know how to act anymore, and Hollis wondered why Burov had subjected them to this. Perhaps there was a lesson here for them too. And the lesson had to be that the state was all powerful and that disloyalty equaled death. But they already knew that.

Commander Poole came up to Lisa and Hollis. He said, 'The men – and the women – are prepared to stick together. We can start a revolt, right here and now. We can refuse to leave here and hold the students hostage. We can march on Burov's house. We can all rush the main gate, and perhaps some of us will get through and make it to the embassy.'

Hollis looked at Poole, and they both knew that Poole was not stating viable options, but was enumerating different forms of suicide. Hollis said, 'They have the guns, Commander. That's what the twentieth-century is all about. Whoever has the rapid-fire automatic weapons is in charge.'

Poole nodded with his head down. 'So we take the eleven losses and let it go at that?'

'Yes. We have to live to try again and again. Someone has to get out of here. That's what General Austin is saying, and he's the boss. And you know, I don't think things will be the same around here after tonight.'

'No.' Poole thought a moment. 'And you know what else? That's for the better. We've all gotten too cozy with these people. We have our comforts, our women, our children, our intellectual freedom . . . it was hard for us to get angry and stay angry. That's all changed now.' He looked at Hollis and Lisa. 'I think your presence here was the slap in the face that we needed to bring us out of it.'

Hollis cleared his throat. 'I may have sounded hard at General Austin's house, and I assure you my views haven't changed. But I didn't mean to leave the impression that I am not concerned for your welfare.'

'I understand.'

Midnight came, and people began streaming silently out of the hall.

Poole said to Lisa, 'We'll pray tonight.' He said to Hollis, 'Burov has imposed a curfew for twelve-thirty A.M., so we are all effectively under house arrest until dawn. We can't meet or

573

discuss this any further. The penalty for breaking curfew is to be shot on sight. So I wish you both goodnight and see you on the soccer field in the morning.' He turned and left.

Hollis asked Lisa to wait around until all the Americans and their wives were gone. Oddly, Hollis thought, most of the students stayed on. He noticed they began drinking, and as he suspected, one of them approached him and Lisa.

Jeff Rooney greeted them with less ebullience than the first time they'd met. Neither Hollis nor Lisa returned the greeting.

Rooney said, 'I just want you guys to know I feel awful about this.'

Hollis looked Rooney in the eye and replied, 'You're going to feel even worse when you get to the States and get picked up by the FBI. You can think about how sorry you are for the rest of your life in a federal penitentiary.' Hollis added baitingly, 'You can study for your Air Force tests in the big house, General.'

Rooney seemed at a loss for words. Several students began to gather around.

Hollis continued, 'They didn't tell you that the rate of capture for you people is about two hundred a year, did they?'

'No . . . they . . . I didn't read about any . . .'

'Even Western newspapers don't know everything, you idiot.' Hollis snapped, 'Get out of my sight.'

'I'm sorry –'

Lisa said, 'You *know* better, Rooney. You *know* what a monstrous system this is. You all know, and there is no excuse for you. You are contemptible. Go away!'

Rooney didn't seem inclined to move, and neither did the growing crowd of young men and women. Rooney said, 'I'm *sorry*. I really am. I . . . can't understand why Colonel Burov –'

'Then,' Hollis said, 'why don't you organize the students and make a protest to Burov?'

'We can't –'

'No, you can't because you are no more an American than

Genghis Khan or Colonel Burov. You have no idea what it means to be a free man with rights and responsibilities.'

'I do! I learned that here.'

Lisa stepped closer to him. 'You can't *learn* that.' She poked him in the chest. 'You have to live it every day. Go on, Rooney, go and exercise your right to freedom of speech, guaranteed in both our constitutions. Exercise your right to petition for redress of grievances. That would be good training for you.' She looked around. 'For all of you.'

No one spoke, and Hollis had the impression that some of the one hundred or so students in the barroom now were thinking about things, but a good number of them had that neutral vacuous expression that people wear when they hear a call to arms and pretend the speaker is addressing someone else. About half the students, however, seemed ready for some sort of action. Hollis said to them, 'Do you understand that you have no more rights to life, liberty, and the pursuit of happiness than any prisoner here? Did you ever wonder what happened to the students who wash out of this school?'

John Fleming, one of the men they had met on the basketball court, shouted, 'You're trying to seduce us in your typical Western way. We don't listen to Western treachery.'

Marty, the Landises' boarder, called back, 'If you're going to argue with them, argue like an American, not a stupid Russian.'

This brought some shouts pro and con. Suzie Trent stepped out of the crowd and walked directly to Lisa. '*What* happens to the students who wash out?'

Before Lisa could answer, Jeff Rooney snapped at her, 'Shut up! Do you want to get into trouble?'

'I want to *know*.'

The Landises' other boarder, Sonny, stepped out of the crowd surrounding Hollis and Lisa and addressed the students. '*I'll* speak like an American. These two are abusing their rights to free assembly and freedom of speech. They are inciting to riot and pose a clear and present danger to the peace. I propose we make a citizen's arrest and take them to headquarters.'

Hollis was impressed with Sonny's grasp of the law and how it could be perverted. Hollis said to him, 'Your master, Petr Burov, is going to illegally execute –'

Sonny shouted, 'There is nothing illegal about it! There are duly constituted laws in this place, Hollis, and Dodson broke one of them. He knew it was a capital offense.'

Hollis stood face-to-face with Sonny. 'What about the ten people to be executed at random? That is called reprisals and is unlawful in any civilized society.'

Sonny put his face closer to Hollis'. 'Are you saying we're uncivilized?'

Lisa pushed Sonny's chest. 'What do *you* call executing a POW who was doing his duty and exercising his right under the Geneva Convention to escape?'

Sonny glared at Lisa, keeping a watch on Hollis out of the corner of his eye.

The room was very quiet, and someone said softly, 'She's right. The execution is illegal under international law.'

A few people murmured assent.

Erik Larson cleared his throat. 'Most of us are Red Air Force. We know that's no way to execute a brother officer. Maybe we can draft a note to Burov –'

'You needn't bother,' Burov said as he strode into the room. There were six armed KGB Border Guards behind him. He looked at the students then at Hollis and Lisa. 'Well, are you trying to replay the American Revolution here? We've already had our revolution, thank you.'

Hollis walked toward Burov and said, 'I think this class will never be the same again, Colonel.'

'I think you're right.'

'Call off these executions.'

'No, I'm more convinced than ever that we need this tomorrow. All of us.' Burov looked at Marty, then at Jeff Rooney, Suzie Trent, and a few of the others. He said, 'I commend all of you on your fine acting. An outsider would have actually thought you believed what you were saying.' He smiled unpleasantly.

Suzie Trent said in a soft voice, 'I believed what I heard about this terrible killing tomorrow.'

Burov glanced at her, then looked at the others. 'Does anyone else wish to add anything to this young lady's comment?'

No one spoke immediately, then John Fleming said, 'Yes, Colonel, I think she has always harbored unorthodox and improper thoughts about our socialist motherland.'

Hollis noted that this time no one told Fleming he sounded like a stupid Russian, so Hollis said, 'You're full of shit.'

Burov looked at his watch. 'It is twelve twenty-five, Colonel. If you and Ms Rhodes leave now, you can probably get into your home before the curfew. If you don't, you may very well be shot by a patrol. Good evening.'

Hollis took Lisa's arm and led her toward the door. Lisa said to Burov, 'For everyone's sake, please reconsider.'

'You'd better hurry. I'd like to see you in my office tomorrow, not in the morgue.' He turned from Hollis and Lisa and said to the students, 'Continue your Halloween festivities.'

Hollis led Lisa into the rec room, where another two hundred or so students had been pressed close to the door of the bar. They parted quickly, letting Hollis and Lisa through.

They went out into the cold, damp air and took the trail back to their cottage. Neither of them spoke for a while, then Lisa said, 'My God, I'm proud of you, Sam Hollis.'

'You did alright yourself.'

They reached their house and went inside. Lisa bolted the door, sank into the armchair, and stared at the dead fire. 'A spark. Is that what they need? Or do they need a blowtorch?' She drew a deep breath and stared up at the ceiling. 'I simply do *not* understand these people. No one does.'

Hollis replied, 'That's because they don't understand themselves. But if the day comes when they do, when they stop worrying about how the West perceives them and start to

577

become aware of who *they* are, then the first Russian Revolution will become nothing more than a prologue to the second revolution.'

'But *when*?'

'When they're ready. When they can't deny outside reality any longer.'

'I hope I live to see it.' She smiled grimly. 'I hope I live to see *tomorrow*.' Lisa stood. 'Let's go to bed.'

'Go ahead. I need to be alone awhile.'

'Alright.' She kissed him and went into the bedroom, closing the door behind her.

Hollis shut off the lamp and sat in the darkness alone with his thoughts. It occurred to him, not for the first time, that after all was said and done, Alevy had simply betrayed and abandoned them. And Hollis could think of professional reasons why Alevy would do that – Alevy-type reasons. Yet, the feeling, if not the fact, remained with Hollis that Alevy for all his deviousness was not capable of this ultimate betrayal. Unless of course he felt he had been personally betrayed. And perhaps Lisa had betrayed Seth Alevy, her lover. Hollis didn't know. And perhaps Alevy felt that Hollis had betrayed him as well. Sexual jealousy was as potent a force in the affairs of men and women as anything else and had brought nations and kings to ruin.

Hollis stared into the darkness. The time passed, and though he was tired, he felt no need for sleep. A strange confidence took hold of him, and he knew that one way or the other this was going to be the last day for the Charm School.

39

It had become cold in the cabin of the Mi-28. Alevy, Mills, Brennan, and O'Shea each took turns outside the helicopter, scanning the rim of the gravel pit with the night scope mounted on the Dragunov sniper rifle. With a roll of black tape, Mills had changed the helicopter's identification number from P-113 to P-413, on the chance that other aircraft, or even the Charm School, had picked up radio traffic concerning the crash of 113.

The Aeroflot pilot began moaning in the darkness, and Brennan, who was outside the helicopter with the rifle, poked his head through the door and said to Alevy, 'We should have brought a blanket for him.'

Alevy wondered at Brennan's compassion for a man he had been prepared to throw out of the helicopter at a thousand meters. Alevy said, 'It's above freezing. He'll live until someone finds him in the morning.' Alevy took another chloroform pad from his pocket and gave it to Brennan. 'Put him back to sleep.'

Brennan went off into the darkness and came back a few minutes later. The pilot stopped moaning.

The next hour passed without incident. Captain O'Shea had the sentry duty and was scanning the narrow ramp road that led down into the pit. He suddenly lowered the rifle and jumped onto the rung step at the door. 'Something coming down the road.'

Brennan leaped out of the helicopter and snatched the rifle from O'Shea. He knelt, pointed the rifle toward the road, and adjusted the focus toward the dirt ramp about a hundred meters away. O'Shea scrambled back into the pilot's seat and prepared to take off.

Brennan tracked the movement, took aim, and fired. The

silenced rifle coughed, and the flash-suppressed muzzle glowed briefly. Brennan stood and went back to the open door of the helicopter. 'Big buck. Dropped him.' He added, 'Very good rifle.'

At 1:30 A.M., Alevy said, 'Let's go.'

Bert Mills, who was standing sentry, jumped back into the helicopter and gave Brennan the rifle.

O'Shea started the two turbine engines and let them warm for a few minutes, scanning the gauges.

Alevy, sitting in the copilot's seat, asked O'Shea, 'Do you remember how to fly it?'

O'Shea forced a smile. 'I do. But I don't know how to take off.' He placed the cyclic stick in a neutral position and moved the collective pitch stick in the full down position. He twisted the throttle on the collective stick, at the same time pushing the stick forward. The helicopter began to become light on its wheels, and the torque effect caused the nose to swing to the left. He put pressure on the right foot pedal to bring the nose back to a constant heading. The helicopter rose vertically in a cloud of sand and gravel.

O'Shea let it rise, checking the torque gauge and the rpm as he held it steady in its vertical climb. The helicopter rose out of the pit and into the north wind.

Below, there was a flash of brilliant light as the phosphorus grenades exploded, consuming the pile of baggage and clothing.

O'Shea eased the cyclic forward, and the Mi-28 began a diagonal climb on a northerly heading. At eight hundred meters, O'Shea swung the nose west and adjusted the controls for a straight and level flight.

Alevy commented, 'You've taken the excitement out of helicopter flying.'

O'Shea settled back in his seat. 'I've got this thing tamed.'

'Glad to hear it.'

O'Shea said, 'Bill and Bert, you spot for aircraft. They

can't see us without lights. Seth, find me the Minsk-Moscow highway or the Moskva River.'

Alevy looked out the windshield. The night had remained clear, and the starlight gave some illumination to the ground, though the moon was nearly set. Alevy scanned the terrain below, finally picking out the Moskva River, looking like a thin ribbon of tarnished pewter, winding through dark fields and forests. He said to O'Shea, 'Slip south of the river.'

O'Shea turned to a southwest heading.

Alevy stared at the ground below, and within a few minutes he said, 'There. The highway. See it?'

O'Shea craned forward. 'Okay.' He swung the helicopter on a due west heading and followed the highway.

Mills called out, 'Eleven o'clock, level.' To their front, coming toward them, they could see blinking navigation lights. The closing speed of the two craft was fast, and the lights were suddenly very near and coming toward them on a collision course. O'Shea banked the Mi-28 to the right, and the other craft, a mammoth Mi-8 cargo helicopter, shot past on their port side. O'Shea exclaimed, 'Jesus . . .' He took a deep breath and said to Alevy, 'If he spotted us without our lights, he'll make a report. We'd be less likely to arouse suspicion if we were running with our lights on.' He added, 'If they're looking for us, Seth, they'll be using airborne radar anyway.'

Alevy replied, 'I hope that where they're looking for this helicopter is in the woods outside of Sheremetyevo. No lights.'

They continued west, land navigating between the Moskva and the highway, which ran roughly parallel to the river. Alevy looked at the airspeed indicator, which showed 120 kph. He said, 'We should be seeing the lights of Mozhaisk soon.'

Brennan commented, 'I don't see *any* lights. Nobody lives down there.'

Mills leaned forward and pointed to left. 'There. Is that Mozhaisk?'

Alevy looked at the lights about five kilometers ahead. There weren't many of them at this hour, but he could definitely pick out a string of lights that appeared to cross the Moskva River. That would be the Mozhaisk Bridge. Alevy replied, 'There's not much else around here, so that must be the town. Guide on that, Captain.'

'Right.' O'Shea corrected his heading and pointed the nose of the Mi-28 directly toward Mozhaisk.

Within a few minutes they could see the illuminated center of the small town where the two main streets crossed; the north-south street leading to the bridge and the east-west street, which was the old Minsk-Moscow road.

Alevy said, 'Drop to about five hundred and follow the river.'

O'Shea descended toward the Moskva and passed over the bridge. At this altitude the river seemed more luminescent, reflecting the cold starlight and the last available moonlight. O'Shea commented, 'I used to love river flying. Went up the Hudson in a Piper Cherokee once. Did the entire Colorado in a Cessna . . . now I'm doing the Moskva . . . in a borrowed Mi-28 . . . a Headstone.'

No one spoke for some minutes, then Alevy said, 'Reduce airspeed.'

O'Shea brought the helicopter's speed down to ninety kph.

Alevy looked at his watch, then at his aerial map and said, 'Gentlemen, we'll be landing very soon.'

No one responded. They were all professionals, Alevy reflected, and each of them had at one time or another pushed his luck to the limit in the performance of his respective profession. They were, each in their own way, cool, distant, and businesslike. They had calculated the odds and found them slightly better than Russian roulette with a five-chambered revolver. They were all damned scared but damned excited too. Alevy could almost feel the energy, the anticipation of actually seeing if a chalkboard play would work on the ground.

Alevy scanned the south bank of the Moskva River. 'It's somewhere in that pine forest there.' He said to O'Shea, 'Lower and slower, Ed. Turn in over the forest.'

'Right.' O'Shea turned away from the river and cut his airspeed, dropping two hundred meters of altitude.

Alevy glanced into the rear and looked at Brennan and Mills sitting in the murky cabin, scanning the terrain from the side windows. He had never asked their motives for coming or given them any sort of recruiting pitch. He'd only outlined the plan and asked if they thought it was feasible and if they wanted to come along, and they said yes on both counts. And that was that.

Alevy looked out the windshield at the expanse of dark pine forest passing below. The forest ended, and he could see a broad rolling field dotted with what he knew were stone monuments. Borodino Field. He said to O'Shea, 'We've overshot it. Swing around.'

O'Shea brought the helicopter to a hover, then swung it around 180 degrees and made the transition back to forward flight. They passed again over the edge of the forest, and without Alevy's saying anything. O'Shea cut the airspeed further and dropped to two hundred meters.

Mills saw it first. 'There. Ten o'clock, one klick.'

They all looked to port and saw a cleared swatch of ground running through the thick, dark trees. Alevy caught a glimpse of a watchtower and noted there were no floodlights on the perimeter of the camp. This was the age of electronic motion sensors and sound detectors, personnel radar and night-seeing devices. Prison walls had gone high-tech, especially in the Soviet Union.

Alevy said to Brennan, 'Let's get the wind direction.'

'Right.' Brennan reached into the leather bag and found a smoke marker. He slid a section of the Plexiglas side window open, pulled the pin on the marker, and dropped it out the window.

O'Shea put the helicopter into a hover at two hundred meters' altitude and watched the white smoke billowing through the trees below. O'Shea said, 'Wind out of the north at about five knots. About eight kph.' O'Shea added, 'The watchtowers may be able to hear the rotor blades now. If we're going in, we have to be lit.'

'Right,' Alevy replied. He threw the switch for the navigation lights and the blinking boom light, then said to O'Shea, 'You know what you have to do.'

'Right.' O'Shea went from hover to forward flight again, keeping the engine rpm up and the blades pitched at a high angle to obtain maximum lift at slow airspeed without stalling. He banked around to starboard approaching the northern edge of the camp perimeter on a parallel run from west to east. They could all see the watchtowers now, spaced about two hundred meters apart along the edge of the cleared zone.

Alevy said to Brennan, 'Hand me the canisters.'

'That's alright. I can do it.'

'Hand them to me.'

Brennan took four unmarked metal canisters from Alevy's overnight bag and passed them to Alevy. Alevy examined them a moment, then ripped a protective yellow plastic wrap off their top lids and turned a timing dial on each one. He slid open his vent window and dropped the first canister out, about five hundred meters outside the northern perimeter of the camp. He waited a few seconds, then dropped the second canister, followed by the third, then the last canister roughly opposite the northeast-corner watchtower. He was sure no one in the towers could see anything falling from the helicopter. He said, 'Okay, Captain O'Shea. Into the camp.'

O'Shea swung to starboard, and they came around, passing over the watchtowers and barbed wire at 150 meters' altitude.

Alevy said, 'The helipad is at the western end of the camp. Keep on this heading.' He hit the controllable landing light switch, and a bright beam projected from the underside of the fuselage. Alevy moved the lever that controlled the shaft of light, and the beam moved across the treetops. By now, Alevy thought, the Russians were trying to contact them by radio, but Alevy didn't have their frequency. The Russians were very jumpy and deadly earnest about protecting restricted airspace, but here in the heart of Russia, Alevy hoped they would ask questions first and shoot you later. He hoped too, if they had seen the smoke marker, they took it for what it was supposed to look like, a landing aid to determine wind direction, and not for what it actually was – a means to determine where to drop the four gas canisters so that the gas, when it was released, would blow over the camp. This was one case, Alevy thought, where their paranoia about being attacked by treacherous imperialist forces was not paranoia. He said to O'Shea, 'We shouldn't draw any groundfire. But if someone down there gets trigger happy, be prepared to floor it.'

'I know.'

Suddenly a beam of light rose into the air about a hundred meters to their front, then passed slowly over the fuselage, illuminating the cabin and, Alevy hoped, the familiar Aeroflot logo. Aeroflot and the Red Air Force being about one and the same, Alevy thought, that should cause no suspicion. The beam held them as they dropped altitude. O'Shea said, 'That's probably the helipad light.'

'Okay.' Alevy moved his landing light beam toward the spotlight, and he could see now, not three hundred meters to their front, the large natural clearing in the forest. Alevy worked the landing light switch and flashed the international codes for 'Radio malfunction, permission to land.' He said to O'Shea, 'Okay, Ed, let's take it in.'

O'Shea began a sloping descent toward the helipad. 'This is it.'

The ground light moved away from them, and the beam dropped, sweeping back and forth over the grass clearing, showing them the way.

Brennan was scanning with the night scope on his rifle, and Bert Mills said to him, 'Is there a welcoming committee waiting for us?'

Brennan replied, 'There's nobody on the field. I see a log cabin at the edge of the field. Guy there on a flatbed moving that spotlight. He's got an AK-47 beside him. But I don't see much else.'

O'Shea banked to the right so he could make his final approach into the wind.

Mills asked O'Shea dryly, 'Is this going to be as exciting as the last one?'

'No.'

O'Shea reduced power and passed over the log cabin at fifty meters, heading for the center of the large clearing.

No one spoke.

Alevy felt his heart speeding up, and his mouth went dry. He cleared his throat and said, 'There will be no money in this for you, gentlemen, no medals, no glory, no official recognition, no photo opportunities at the White House. There will just be a hell of a bad time down there and maybe an unmarked grave in this Russian forest. So I thank you again for volunteering.'

None of them responded.

Alevy looked at his watch. It was 2:03 A.M. The camp would be sleeping, unaware that release from their long captivity was close at hand.

O'Shea pulled back on the cyclic stick, and the helicopter flared out, hung a moment, then settled softly onto the grass helipad of the Charm School. O'Shea said aloud but to himself, 'Nice landing, Ed.'

40

The helicopter sat in the center of the field, its engines still turning. Brennan and Mills dropped down below the window.

Seth Alevy looked at his watch. It was just 2:05 A.M. He said to O'Shea, 'Captain, you will lift off not later than three forty-five, with or without passengers, and that includes any or all of the three of us. Understand?'

'Understood.'

'Shut it down.'

O'Shea shut off the engines, and the blades wound down.

The beam of light coming from the vicinity of the radio cabin about a hundred meters off played over the helicopter, picking out the cockpit, the cabin windows, the Aeroflot emblem, and finally the registration number, P-413, on the tail boom.

Alevy climbed back into the cabin and slid open the portside door, Brennan said, 'Good luck.'

Mills added, 'You look Russian.'

Alevy jumped down, put on his officer's cap, and strode purposefully toward the searchlight and the log cabin. He said to himself, 'I hope so.'

The man behind the light shut it off, came down from the flatbed, and walked toward Alevy. As he drew within ten meters, Alevy saw he was a young KGB Border Guard carrying an AK-47 at port arms. The KGB man stopped and issued a challenge. 'Halt! Identify yourself.'

Alevy stopped and replied in brusque Russian, 'I am Major Voronin.' Alevy strode up to the man, who had come to a position of attention, the AK-47 still at the ready across his chest, his finger on the trigger. Alevy stopped a few feet from him. 'I'm here to see your colonel,' Alevy said, not knowing if Burov used that nom de guerre here or used Pavlichenko, which

587

General Surikov had indicated was Burov's real name. Alevy snapped, 'Are you deaf, man? I'm here to see your colonel!'

'Yes, sir!'

'Has he sent a vehicle for me?'

'No, sir. And I have no instructions regarding your arrival, Major.'

'How unfortunate for you,' Alevy said, using a sarcasm favored by KGB officers. 'What is your name, Private?'

'Frolev.'

'Well, Frolev, call and get me a vehicle.'

'Yes, sir.' Frolev did an about face and marched back to the radio cabin.

Alevy followed.

Frolev walked past the spotlight's flatbed, which Alevy noted had no vehicle attached to it. The *izba* was a simple structure of hewn logs and the ubiquitous sheet metal roof. There were some windows cut into the cabin, and from the roof protruded a stovepipe and two aerials. Two wires, electric and telephone, ran from the cabin to a nearby pine tree.

Frolev opened the door of the one-room *izba* and moved aside as Alevy entered. A bare lightbulb hung from the center rafter. Inside were two other men – one more than Alevy had figured on.

One man lay sleeping on a cot along the far wall, a hardcover copy of Rybakov's *The Children of the Arbat* on his rising and falling chest. The other man, a sergeant, sat at a field desk studying a game of chess that had neared its end. As Frolev pulled the door shut, he yelled, 'Attention!'

The sergeant jumped to his feet, and the sleeping man stumbled out of the cot and stood to attention.

Alevy looked around the room. In the far corner was a ceramic tile stove atop which sat a steaming teakettle. Along the right wall was a long table on which were a VHF radio, a shortwave radio, and two telephones.

Alevy moved to the chessboard and examined the pieces.

He said to Frolev, 'Are you white? How did you get yourself into such a mess?'

The man laughed politely.

The middle-aged sergeant, standing at the desk, cleared his throat, 'Excuse me, Major.'

Alevy looked at the man. 'Yes, Sergeant?'

'Unfortunately I know nothing of your arrival.'

Frolev said quickly, 'Sergeant, this is Major Voronin to see Colonel Burov. He requires a vehicle.'

The sergeant nodded and said to Alevy, 'Sir, we were not able to raise you on the radio.'

'Nor was my pilot able to raise you. You'll do a communications check with him. Have you called the duty officer regarding our landing?'

'No, sir, but I'll do that now.' He said to the man near the cot, 'Kanavsky, call Lieutenant Cheltsov.' Kanavsky moved quickly toward the field phones.

Alevy drew a short, discreet breath. Things were going well. Or perhaps his years in this country had given him some insight into how these people reacted to given situations. The sergeant hadn't called the duty officer because he didn't want to annoy an officer, who would only have snapped something like, 'What the hell do you want me do to about it? Flap my wings and intercept the helicopter? Find out who he is and call me back.'

Alevy stepped casually off to the side so that he had the three men in his view. Kanavsky picked up the field phone and reached for the hand crank.

Without making an abrupt movement, Alevy drew his silenced automatic and put the first round through the chest of Frolev, still standing with the AK-47 at the door. Frolev gave a start but didn't seem to know that he'd been shot. Alevy spun and put the second round into the side of Kanavsky. The man shouted in surprise, dropped the phone, and his hand went to his rib cage.

The sergeant reacted quickly, drawing his revolver from his

holster. Alevy fired first, hitting the man in the midsection, causing him to double over and stagger back into the field desk, scattering the chess game. Alevy fired again into the crown of the sergeant's head, and the man dropped to the floor.

Alevy walked to Kanavsky, who was still standing, and put a bullet into his head, then went to Frolev, who was still trying to get to his feet. Alevy stood off a short distance so as to not get splattered and fired once into the side of Frolev's head.

Alevy hung up the telephone and took the kettle off the wood stove. He found a wool glove warming by the stove and wiped the wetness from his gun hand, then cleaned the blood from his jackboots. He loaded a fresh magazine into the automatic, drew a deep breath, and reminded himself that several hundred Americans had lived and died in this place for nearly two decades. He composed himself and stepped outside.

Brennan and Mills were already there, Brennan with the Dragunov sniper rifle and Mills with the black overnight bag. Alevy said in a low voice, 'Bill, you tidy up in there and stay put.'

Brennan asked, 'Are you sure I can't come along?'

Alevy liked Brennan, and Brennan was very brave and enthusiastic but had a short attention span. 'As I told you, Captain O'Shea needs some advance warning if things start to come apart. Also we don't know if these guys phone in scheduled sit reps to anyone or if anyone calls them periodically. So if somebody calls looking for a situation report, just say *nechevo* – there is nothing. That's standard radio lingo for negative sit rep. *Nechevo*.'

'*Nechevo*.'

'Sound bored and tired. Yawn.'

Brennan yawned and said through his yawn, '*Nechevo*.'

'Good. If anyone gets chatty on the phone say it again with emphasis. Be rude and hang up.' Alevy added, 'I'm assuming that calls originate from headquarters, so I'll relieve the commo man there of his duties. I'll call you from there – you answer the phone with *Da*. Not *Allo*. *Da*.'

'*Da. Nechevo.*'

'Fine. And if anyone comes around to check this post, let them in, but don't let them out.'

Brennan smiled. 'I'll let the Dragunov talk Russian.'

Mills added, 'Don't hesitate to jump on that chopper if you hear all hell breaking loose.'

Brennan didn't reply.

Alevy slapped him on the shoulder. 'Good luck, Bill.'

'You too.'

Brennan took the leather bag inside the cabin. Alevy and Mills moved quickly up the narrow pine-covered lane that led away from the *izba* and the helicopter clearing. Alevy said, 'You were supposed to wait for my signal before getting out of the chopper.'

'You were a long time in there. Did they call headquarters?'

'They said they didn't.'

'Do you think Brennan will be alright on the telephone?'

'About as good as O'Shea was with the helicopter.'

Mills commented, 'Sometimes you can overplan an operation. We don't have that problem here.'

Alevy smiled grimly. They had a pilot who couldn't fly his craft, a man on the telephone who couldn't speak Russian, and Bert Mills, who didn't look, act, or speak Russian. But it was the best Alevy could do, considering the problems inherent in mounting an operation in the heart of the Soviet Union. The word of the night was improvise. 'Improvise.'

'And bluff,' Mills added.

They intersected the blacktopped main road of the camp, and Alevy took a compass from his greatcoat. To the right, he knew, should be the main gate, beyond which was Borodino Field. To the left should be the center of the camp. The satellite photographs had shown a large concrete building that Alevy hoped was the headquarters. They turned left and moved quickly along the edge of the treelined road.

Within a few minutes they saw the lights of a long wooden building that hadn't appeared in the satellite photographs. They approached it cautiously. Alevy saw it had a porch out front, and as he got closer he heard music coming from the building. Alevy pointed to the sign above the door that read VFW POST 000. Mills nodded and motioned to the Coke machine.

Alevy stepped up to the porch, followed by Mills. Through the window they could see a large recreation room in which were about twenty men and a few women, all in their mid-twenties. Alevy said, 'Students.'

A group of men and women were watching Bela Lugosi's *Dracula* on a seven-foot video screen. The rest of the students were sitting in a group of chairs, drinking and talking. There were Halloween decorations on the walls and a large coffin in the center of the floor.

Mills said, 'Party. Halloween.'

Alevy nodded. He hadn't thought of that, though it looked as if it were about over. He focused on the huge American flag on the opposite wall. 'Bizarre.'

As they turned to leave, the front door opened, and a middle-aged man in a white ski jacket came out onto the porch and stopped short. He stared at Alevy and Mills.

Alevy and Mills looked back at him. No one spoke for a few seconds, then the man said in English, 'You speak English?'

Alevy nodded.

The man cleared his throat and said in a drunken slur, 'Well, go ahead and shoot.'

'Shoot?'

The door opened again, and a young man came out and said quickly in Russian, 'I'll take responsibility for this American, Major.'

Alevy tried to figure out what was going on and what language to reply in. Both men were clearly very drunk.

The young man spoke in Russian. 'My name is Marty Bambach. This is Tim Landis. I board with him. I'll take him home.'

Landis said in English, 'I just lost track of time. No big fucking deal.'

Alevy began to understand. Landis was the American, probably violating a curfew, and Bambach was a Russian American. Alevy said to Marty in Russian, 'I can overlook this man's curfew violation if you take responsibility for him.'

Marty replied in Russian, 'Thank you, Major.' He looked at Alevy in the dim light. 'Are you new here?'

'Yes. Why don't you go inside? I want to speak to this man a moment.'

Marty hesitated, then said, 'He doesn't speak Russian.'

'Go inside.'

'Yes, sir.' Marty turned to Landis and said in perfect English, which surprised Alevy and Mills, 'It's okay, Tim. He just wants to talk to you. I'll take you home. Marty turned and wove his way back into the building.

Landis staggered to the edge of the porch and leaned on the rail. He unzipped his fly and urinated. 'Fuck this place.' He zipped himself up and wobbled back toward the door.

Alevy took his arm and said in accented English, 'Have a seat there.'

'Let go of my arm.'

'Listen to me. Is Colonel Sam Hollis here?'

Landis looked at Alevy but said nothing.

'Hollis and Lisa Rhodes. Are they *here*?'

'Hollis . . . I felt sorry for him . . . he made it home.' Landis shook his head.

'Go on.'

'Plucked out of the drink . . . but here he is with us poor bastards . . . twenty years late . . . but here he is.' Landis suddenly attempted a salute. 'Captain Timothy Landis, United States Air Force, at your service, Major. Hey, when is this fucking tour up?'

'Very soon.'

'Yeah? Best news.'

'Where is Hollis?'

'My wife Jane thinks he's a hunk.'

'Wife?'

Landis went on, 'But he's got this woman with him. Fucking women. They're going to shoot her. She talks too much.'

'Who? Who are they going to shoot?'

'Huh?'

'Lisa Rhodes? Are they going to shoot Lisa Rhodes?'

'Probably. She talks too much too. Her and my wife. Dynamic duo.' Landis fell into a rocking chair and stared at the porch ceiling.

'Where is Hollis?'

'Oh . . .' Landis looked around as though familiarizing himself with his surroundings. 'Oh . . . they gave him Dodson's place. Behind this building. Couple hundred yards.'

'And the woman with him? Lisa Rhodes?'

Landis looked at Alevy and Mills. 'What do you want to know for? Hey, those two been through enough of your shit.'

'What shit?'

'The fucking cooler. You're all the fucking same. You and Burov and all the KGB shits.'

'Is Burov here?'

'Where the fuck else would he be?'

Mills put his hand on Alevy's shoulder and whispered, 'We have to get moving.'

'Hold on.' He said to Landis, 'The woman. Lisa. Is she with Hollis? In Dodson's place?'

Landis rose unsteadily to his feet. 'Leave them alone.' Landis suddenly took a swing at Alevy, and Alevy stepped back. Landis shouted, 'Go ahead, you bastard, shoot me! Shoot me! I want to die!' Landis staggered across the porch and fell against a post, covering his face with his hands. Alevy and Mills could hear him sobbing, and as they walked away, they heard him cry out, 'My God, get me out of here!'

Mills said softly, 'Jesus . . . Seth, this is bad.'

'I didn't think it would be good, Bert. You understand now, don't you?'

'I'm beginning to. I'm not sorry I came.' He added, 'Wives?'

Alevy shrugged. 'Camp whores, I guess.'

594

They found a path that ran behind the VFW hall and followed it down a slope into a thickly treed hollow. Mills whispered, 'That other guy. Marty Bambach. That was a *Russian*. His English was perfect.'

Alevy nodded.

'And he was protecting Landis.'

Alevy replied, 'I can't even begin to imagine what sort of surreal world has developed here. But we know they have jails and curfews and that the KGB is in charge.'

Alevy reached into the pocket of his greatcoat and took out a small radio receiver, turned it on, and extended the aerial. He put the jack to his ear and listened. 'Well, we have a signal. It's somewhere in this area.' As he walked he said, 'Getting louder.' He looked around and noticed for the first time a shingled cottage, set back in the trees with its lights off.

Mills whispered, 'It looks like an American Cape Cod. This is eerie.'

Alevy moved through the trees, and the signal got stronger. He tossed the receiver in the bushes and approached the front door. The door had no lock cylinder, only a knob, and it turned, but the door didn't move. Alevy put his shoulder to the door and pressed slowly. He felt something give, then heavy metal hitting the floor. He whispered, 'Stay here.'

Alevy opened the door and slipped inside the dark house, closing the door behind him. He turned on a red-filtered flashlight and played the beam off the walls and furniture, then noticed an open doorway in the right-hand wall, through which he could see the glow of an electric heater. He went through the doorway and found himself in the bedroom. His light picked out the icon on the wall over the double bed. Alevy walked softly over the floorboards to the bed and looked down at Lisa Rhodes, bundled under a stack of quilts. Involuntarily he reached out to touch her cheek.

The crook of an arm locked around his throat, and he saw a long serrated bread knife poised in front of his heart. Alevy managed to turn his head slightly and said softly, 'Hello, Sam.'

Hollis released his grip. 'Hello, Seth.' He motioned toward the door, and they went into the living room. Hollis turned on a table lamp, and Alevy saw he was wearing a warm-up suit similar to what Landis and Bambach had on. Hollis rubbed his thumb and forefinger together, and Alevy nodded. Hollis put a black gospel tape in the player. Alevy said softly, 'Hell of a way to greet a friend.'

'You're not dressed like any friends that I have.'

Alevy smiled. 'You're a cool customer, Colonel.'

Hollis hesitated, then said, 'It's actually good to see you for a change.' He put out his hand, and Alevy took it. Hollis said, 'I was beginning to wonder.'

'I came as fast as I could, Sam. I spent five days in Washington selling this operation.'

'What's the plan?'

'I'll brief you as we go along. Why don't you go wake Lisa?'

Hollis went back into the bedroom and closed the door. Alevy went to the front door, opened it, and spoke to Mills, who was crouched behind an evergreen with his pistol drawn. Alevy said, 'They're here. Few minutes.' He closed the door and walked around the room examining it. He picked up a stack of magazines, then looked at the videotapes on the bookshelves. 'Incredible.'

Hollis came back into the room. 'She's coming.'

Alevy nodded and motioned around the room. 'Not bad.'

'Not good, Seth.'

'I heard they gave you a rough time.'

'Where'd you hear that?'

'From a Captain Landis. Know him?'

'Yes.'

'Looks like a burnout,' Alevy said.

'They're all burnouts. How did you see Landis?'

'At VFW Post zero zero zero.' Alevy explained briefly.

Hollis nodded. 'I could spend a week telling you about this madhouse, but I suspect time is short. How did you get here?'

'I misappropriated an Aeroflot chopper from the Trade Center. Mi-28.'

'Right. The one I briefed you on. Who flew?'

'Your aide. He's rather fond of you and would also like you to reconsider some of the ratings you gave him on his efficiency report.'

'I'll think about it. Who else is with you?'

'My man, Bert Mills. He's outside. And Bill Brennan.'

'Brennan? He's back?'

'Just for the day.'

'Explain the plan to me.'

'Well, I dropped four canisters of something called THX, a new sleeping gas –'

'Sandman.'

'Yes, that's the code name. Very potent. The canisters are on timers. We have about an hour and a quarter left.'

'For what?'

'For this and that.'

'Who are you taking out of here?'

'You and Lisa and two others. That's all I can take on an Mi-28, and that's all the evidence I need to effect the release of everyone else.'

Hollis nodded. 'I'd be willing to stay here.'

'I know you would, Sam. But you know too much, and I can't leave you in their hands.' Alevy hesitated, then asked, 'They grilled you?'

Hollis nodded. 'Burov did. Minimum damage. The heavy guns come in tomorrow from Lubyanka with polygraphs and electric shock.'

'I was just in time.'

'Right. Are Surikov and his granddaughter out?'

'Yes. Last Saturday. Lenigrad route.'

Hollis stared at him in the dim light. 'You're sure?'

'Yes.'

Hollis said, 'You have to negotiate for the wives and everyone else here too, Seth.'

'Landis mentioned his wife. Who are these wives?'

'Russian women. Mostly politicals. And sixty some children –'

'Good God . . .' Alevy shook his head. 'I figured there would be women for them. But *wives . . . children* . . . ? Are they attached to . . . ? Well, I guess they must be. My mind is trying to process this –'

'Plus there are six kidnapped American women, and there are other Russians from the Gulag, such as the camp doctor and nurses. They go into the deal for the three thousand moles that we're going to swap.'

Alevy looked at Hollis. 'You know something, Sam, you're a real American. I mean that. You really want to save the world, or at least as many of its inhabitants as you meet and like. Well, okay, we'll be in good shape to bargain after tonight.'

Hollis asked, 'How far do you intend to fly in an Mi-28 with eight people aboard?'

'Depends on how the winds are blowing.'

Hollis said, 'I don't think the ambassador or Charlie Banks would appreciate seeing a hijacked Soviet helicopter landing in the embassy quad.'

'We can discuss this after we're airborne.'

'Seth, you can't get an Mi-28 with eight people to any part of the free world from here. Do you have a refueling station, a relay chopper –?'

Lisa came into the room, wearing a blue warm-up suit and running shoes, and Alevy guessed that this must be the camp uniform. She stood back a moment, taking in Alevy in his KGB uniform, then moved quickly to him and put her arms around him. 'Seth. Oh, my God . . .'

Alevy disengaged himself. 'We have to move quickly.'

She nodded and took her ski parka from the coat hook. 'I have to get my icon –'

Alevy held her arm. 'It's not your icon.'

'What do you mean?'

'It's a reproduction, Lisa. It's got a transmitter in it. That's how we found you.'

Lisa stared at him, then at Hollis.

Alevy said, 'It was a contingency plan. In case something like this happened. I checked out Lubyanka and Lefortovo with a radio receiver and got a negative signal.' He added, 'I hoped with the hammer and sickle carved in the icon, they'd let you keep it. They probably think the Kellums did that. The real icon is safe.'

Lisa stood quietly a moment and looked from one to the other, then moved close to Alevy. 'Do you know what they *did* to me here?'

'I'm afraid I probably do. That's the point: what they do to people.' He said to Lisa, 'Bert Mills is outside. He, I, and Sam have a few things to take care of here. You will have to make your way to the helipad by yourself. Brennan is in the radio shack there. He could use some help with his Russian if anyone telephones him. Captain O'Shea is on the pad with a helicopter. We'll be along shortly.'

Lisa replied, 'Forget it, Seth. Sam and I have come this far together, and we're not separating.'

Hollis said to Alevy, 'Don't even bother to argue with her.'

Alevy nodded. 'I know.' He drew two 6.35mm Tokarev automatics with silencers from the inside pockets of his greatcoat and handed them to Lisa and Hollis.

Hollis got his parka and reached for the door.

Alevy held his arm. 'One last thing, and I guess we can spare sixty seconds for it.' Alevy drew a small leather box from his pocket and handed it to Hollis.

Hollis opened it and saw inside the silver star of a brigadier general.

Alevy said, 'There are orders signed by the President, but I couldn't bring those along, for security reasons of course. Congratulations, General.'

Hollis closed the box, wondering briefly if this promotion could be considered posthumous, or perhaps preposthumous. He wondered too how the government was going to get his death benefit back from his wife if he actually made it home

599

or if they'd increase it if he didn't. The last thing he allowed himself to wonder was if the general's star was a reward or a bribe. He said, 'Thank you for delivering it.'

Lisa kissed him on the cheek. 'Congratulations, Sam. General Hollis.'

'Thank you.'

Lisa turned off the tape player and the lamp, and they left the cottage quietly.

Bert Mills stood with his hands in the pockets of his green KGB coat. 'Hi, folks. Ready to go home? For real this time.'

'Hello, Bert.'

Alevy said, 'Lisa is coming with us.'

They moved quickly to the lane and headed back toward the main road. Hollis whispered, 'Directional microphones. Talk low and talk Russian.'

Alevy nodded. He whispered in Russian, 'Are there patrols out?'

Hollis replied, 'Tonight there are.' He explained briefly about the curfew, the reason for it, and the morning executions.

Alevy shook his head. 'That bastard. Eleven people . . . ? We did get here just in time.'

Hollis said, 'But tonight you have to watch for curfew patrols.'

They came to the main road near the VFW hall, which was now dark and quiet. Hollis whispered, 'Where do you want to go?'

Alevy replied, 'Headquarters.'

Hollis pointed to the right.

They hurried at a jog along the road and within a few minutes saw the lighted façade of the grey concrete structure. They stopped and knelt in the drainage ditch by the side of the road. Alevy remarked, 'There's no Soviet flag or marking.'

Lisa said, 'This is America. Inside the building, however, is another story.'

Hollis asked, 'What do you have in mind, Seth?'

600

'We have to knock out the headquarters and all their communications and listening devices if this thing is going to work. Then we need two more passengers for the helicopter.'

Hollis thought of the Landises and knew their son wouldn't make much difference in an already overloaded helicopter. He also thought of General Austin and Commander Poole. He said, 'That's a tough call, Seth. But I have a few candidates.'

'I'll make it a little easier for you. Is Burov in the camp?'

Hollis looked at Alevy and nodded. 'I guess that's the professional thing to do.'

'Sure as hell is. Not to mention my personal annoyance over the "dirty Jew" remark. I'll bet you guys have a few things to settle too.'

Lisa replied, 'This is not a vendetta, Seth, but if you need him, we know where he is.'

Alevy nodded. 'The second person I want is the ranking man here.'

'That would be General Austin,' Hollis replied.

'And you know where to find him?'

'Yes.'

'Good.' Alevy poked his head over the drainage ditch and looked at the headquarters building. He said, 'Tell me about HQ.'

Hollis answered, 'There'll probably be a guard in that booth. There will be a duty officer at the desk as soon as you walk in. Commo room to the left.' Hollis gave Alevy and Mills a description of the layout, concluding with, 'The cells are on the first floor in the center rear.' He added, 'Jack Dodson is in one of those cells, and he's the American I want with us.'

'No,' Alevy replied, 'we are taking General Austin.'

'Wrong.'

Lisa said, 'You can't find Austin *or* Burov without our help, Seth. If Sam wants Dodson, you'll take Dodson.'

Alevy replied angrily, 'I won't take him if he's not ambulatory.'

Hollis said, 'You'll take him if he has a breath left in him.

I don't know the man, Seth, and neither do you, but he's the one who's earned the right to leave with us. Subject closed.'

Alevy said tersely, 'Alright. How many men do you think are in the headquarters building at this hour?'

Hollis replied, 'According to the briefing I got from Austin's aide, Commander Poole, there will be the duty officer, commo man, sergeant of the guard in the guard room near the cells, one or two KGB Border Guards, and one or two drivers who may or may not be in the building at any given time.' He added, 'There are also six or seven men in the listening room where all the camp's sound sensors and listening devices are monitored. That's the room we have to shut down, if we're going to move freely around this place.'

Alevy replied, 'We're going to shut down the whole building.' He said to Hollis and Lisa, 'You two obviously can't pass as KGB officers, so you stay –'

Lisa interrupted, 'We'll pass fine as prisoners. Let's go, Seth.'

Alevy glanced at Mills, who nodded. They quickly went over the plan, then stood and walked toward the building, Lisa and Hollis in front, their hands behind their backs, followed by Alevy and Mills.

The guard peered at them from the booth, and as they drew closer into the light, he stepped out, his rifle across his chest.

Alevy motioned him to the front door. 'Two for the cells. Open.'

The guard hesitated, then went to the front door and opened it. He peered at Alevy and Mills in the light, and it was obvious he did not recognize them as any of his battalion officers. Alevy motioned him into the building. Mills brought up the rear and closed the door.

The duty officer was Lieutenant Cheltsov, the man Hollis and Lisa had spoken to when they were released from the cells. Cheltsov stood to attention behind his desk. He glanced at Hollis and Lisa and said, 'Again?' then looked quizzically at the Border Guard, who shrugged. Cheltsov addressed Alevy, 'Yes, Major?'

Mills drew his silenced automatic and put a single shot through the Border Guard's head. Lieutenant Cheltsov watched the man fall, but nothing seemed to register with him. He stared at the dead man on the floor, then turned to Alevy, who shot him once in the forehead. Cheltsov fell back into his chair, his arms outstretched, and stared wideeyed at the ceiling, the bullet hòle in the center of his forehead spouting blood.

Lisa put her hand to her mouth, turned away, and faced the front door.

Alevy said to Hollis, Lisa and Mills, 'Bolt the front door, wait five seconds, then bring those bodies into the commo room.' He crossed the lobby and opened the door to the communications room. The commo man sat at the telephone switchboard, reading a magazine. He turned and looked at Alevy, then stood. 'Yes, sir?' He saw the automatic in Alevy's hand.

Alevy motioned him away from the switchboard, then shot him twice in the chest, sending the man crashing into the radio console. Alevy walked to the telephone switchboard. It was a manual board, he noticed, and with the operator dead, no calls could be connected.

Hollis and Mills came in, dragging the bodies of Lieutenant Cheltsov and the guard. They pushed the two dead men under the radio table.

Alevy looked at the switchboard connections and found the contraction *Verto* – 'helicopter'. He plugged the wire in, pushed the ringer button, and held the headset to his ear. A voice, sounding bored and tired – and nervous, he thought – said, '*Da. Nechevo.*'

'Bill, it's me.'

'That's good.'

'Anyone else call?'

'No, thank God –'

'Anything to report there?'

'No. Quiet. *Nechevo.*'

'Okay, you won't be getting any calls on the telephone except from us.'

'Both radios are squawking away.'

'Hold on.' Alevy moved to the radios and turned the volume up on the speakers. He listened a few seconds, then said to Brennan. 'Normal traffic. Don't worry about it.'

'Right. You in charge there now?'

'Getting there.'

'You find them?' Brennan asked.

'Yes, they're both with us now.'

'Great. Say hello.'

'Alright. Listen, Bill, if your end of the operation starts to come apart, you and O'Shea beat it. And if you're still around at three forty-five, and we don't show up, you leave before that gas gets to you. Okay?'

'Okay.'

'Lisa will be at this switchboard until further notice.'

'Good.'

'See you later.' Alevy said to Lisa, 'Hold Brennan's hand awhile. Connect any calls going through this switchboard and listen in. With your other ear, monitor the traffic on these two radios. Okay?'

She nodded.

Alevy said to her, 'We shouldn't be more than fifteen minutes. If you hear trouble, call Brennan, then get out of here and make it to the helipad. I'd like one witness to this place to make it out. Okay?'

She glanced at Hollis, who nodded.

'Okay,' Alevy said. 'Sam, let's go to the room where they monitor the listening devices.'

Hollis squeezed Lisa's hand and went to the door, opening it slowly. 'Clear.' Alevy and Mills followed him into the lobby.

Hollis led them to a short corridor off the lobby that ended in a black metal door marked MONITORING STATION. The three men held their pistols at the ready, and Hollis twisted the doorknob slowly. He took his hand off the knob and shook

604

his head to Alevy. 'Locked.' He raised his hand to knock, then noticed a button on the doorjamb and pressed it.

A few seconds later a voice called out. 'Who is it?'

Hollis replied, 'Cheltsov.'

'Yes, sir.'

Hollis moved to the blind side of the door as Alevy and Mills holstered their pistols. Alevy whispered to Hollis, 'Stay here and keep watch.'

The door swung out, revealing a young man in his shirt-sleeves. The man looked at Alevy and Mills, jumped back quickly, and saluted, his eyes scanning left and right for Lieutenant Cheltsov.

Alevy and Mills strode into the monitoring station, a small windowless room of precast concrete, lit by fluorescent bulbs. Six men sat at individual consoles with earphones, listening, Alevy assumed, to the input from various electronic security devices around the camp, switching channels from time to time.

Along the far wall was a bank of reel-to-reel tape recorders. On the left-hand wall, Alevy saw a large map of the camp, marked with numbers showing, Alevy guessed, the locations of the listening devices.

The young man in his shirtsleeves, still holding his salute, asked, 'Can I help you, Major?'

Alevy replied tersely, 'Carry on.'

The young man hurried back to his console and put on his earphones.

Alevy and Mills stood in the center of the room and looked around. Alevy noticed a red light over the door, which he guessed must flash when the door button was pushed so as to alert the men with headphones that someone was there. Alevy spoke to Mills in a soft voice. 'How do you want to take them?'

Mills cleared his throat. 'They're unarmed, Seth. Can we take them without blood?'

'I would, Bert, if we had a bit more time.' Alevy noticed a

few of the men glancing at him and Mills, and he gave them a stern look, sending them back to their monitoring. Alevy said to Mills, 'You do those three, I'll do these three here, and we'll meet at the middle. On three . . . one, two, three –' Alevy and Mills drew their silenced automatics and began firing.

Hollis, outside the door, heard bodies hitting the floor and thrashing around. Someone screamed. He reached for the door, but it opened, and Mills came out, looking, Hollis thought, as though it was he who had lost blood. Alevy followed, closing the door behind him. Alevy said to Hollis, 'The cells.'

Hollis led them back to the lobby, then turned into the long corridor that ran to the rear of the headquarters building. They came to the cell doors and quickly checked the bolts until they found one that was shut. Hollis opened it and looked inside. A man lay on the floor and even in the dim light Hollis could see his clothes were torn and he was badly battered.

Alevy said, 'I guess that's Dodson.'

Hollis knelt beside the man and checked his pulse. 'Alive.'

Alevy said to Hollis, 'Take him to the commo room. Wait there with Lisa.'

Hollis stood. 'Where are you two going?'

'Where can we get a vehicle?'

'Should be one or two Zils out back.' He moved to the door of the cell. 'Down that corridor.'

'Okay,' Alevy said, 'we'll bring it around front.' He added, 'Sam, if you don't see us in ten minutes, you and Lisa take off for the helipad. Okay? Don't try to carry Dodson.' Alevy asked, 'If I don't catch up with you later, where can I find Burov?'

'East end of the main road,' Hollis answered. 'Big dacha. Guards and dogs. Think about that.' Hollis added, 'Don't forget about the men in the guard room down the corridor.'

Hollis went back to Dodson and lifted him onto his shoulders.

Alevy and Mills walked rapidly into the corridor that Hollis had indicated and came to a door marked GUARD ROOM. Alevy opened the door, and he and Mills walked into a small barracks room in which was a field desk and telephone and six double bunk beds, all unoccupied except for one bottom bunk in which was a naked man and woman. A sergeant's KGB uniform and the woman's clothes were strewn on the floor. The sergeant sat up quickly and hit his head on the top bunk, then scrambled out of the bed and stood naked at attention. The women pulled the sheets over her head.

Alevy asked 'Sergeant, where are the other guards and drivers?'

The sergeant seemed to have trouble finding his voice, then replied, 'One guard and driver are making the rounds of the posts with the corporal of the guard. The other guard and driver are at their fixed post at the rear door of this building.'

'Is anyone else in the building?'

'The duty officer, the communications specialist, and the men in the monitoring room. Major, I can explain about –'

'About-face, Sergeant.'

The sergeant did an about-face, and Alevy drew his pistol and shot him in the back of the head, sending him sprawling over the strewn clothes. Mills put three rounds into the huddled figure beneath the blanket. The woman thrashed around, then lay still. Mills and Alevy caught each other's eye for a moment, then turned away and went out into the corridor.

They found their way to a rear foyer and opened a metal door that led down a ramp to a concrete slab on which sat a Zil-6. A harsh mercury-vapor light on the building illuminated the rear courtyard, and beyond the Zil, Alevy saw what looked like a medieval catapult. A KGB man sat on the running board of the Zil, smoking a cigarette. Standing near him was a bulky Border Guard with an AK-47 slung over his shoulder. The two men saw the door open, and the driver stood. The other man turned and faced Alevy and Mills.

Alevy walked up to them, and when they saw he was an officer, they came to rigid attention. Alevy said to the driver, who was wearing a holster and revolver, 'I am Major Voronin, from Moscow, and this is Captain Molev. We are making a security check of this installation.'

'Yes, Major.'

'Is this your fixed post?'

'Yes, Major.'

'What is your name?'

'Strakhov, sir.'

'What are your duties?'

'I and Private Filenko here secure the rear door of the headquarters. I provide transportation to the sergeant of the guard if he requests it.'

Alevy glanced at Filenko, whose AK-47 was still slung over his shoulder. He turned back to Strakhov. 'When do you expect the other driver to return?'

'There is no set time, Major. It depends on how long the corporal of the guard spends at each post.'

'Does he check the three men at the helipad during his rounds?'

Strakhov looked at Alevy a moment, and Alevy could see he was thinking about something. Alevy knew his Russian was good as long as he kept it short and if he didn't have to make extensive use of specific occupational jargon. Obviously he was sounding less like a KGB major from Moscow on a snap inspection.

Alevy noticed too that Filenko no longer had his head and eyes straight ahead, but was looking at Mills. Mills, Alevy suspected, was probably looking less like a KGB captain by the second. Alevy recalled the question that he and Hollis had batted around – the question of Americans passing for Russians and vice versa. Alevy turned to Filenko. 'Let me see your weapon.'

Filenko unslung his automatic rifle and as per regulations, stood with it extended at the position of present arms. Alevy grabbed the forestock with his right hand, but Filenko did not release his grip. The two men stared at each other a moment, and Filenko said, 'Major, may I have the password for the night?'

Mills didn't understand what was being said, but he didn't

like what he saw. His hand moved slowly toward his holster.

Suddenly the door through which they'd come burst open, casting a shaft of light over the concrete.

The four men looked toward the door and saw a naked woman standing there, her body red with blood. She staggered out onto the ramp and stumbled toward them, pointing at Alevy and Mills and crying out in Russian, 'Murderers! Murderers!'

Before Alevy could react, he felt the AK-47 yanked from his hand and felt the muzzle press into his stomach. Filenko shouted, 'Hands on your head.'

Alevy placed his hands over his service cap, and Mills followed as Strakhov drew his revolver.

The woman staggered a few feet closer toward them, then fell to her knees, grasping the folds of Mills' greatcoat. Alevy noted the location of the three wounds: one in the buttocks, one in the lower back around the right kidney, and a grazing wound along the woman's right temple. He noticed too that Mills was quite pale and looked as if he might become sick. The woman collapsed at Mills's feet.

Strakhov asked, 'Who are you?'

Mills didn't understand a word and stared at the man.

'Answer me, or I'll shoot you on the spot.' He pointed his pistol at Mills' face.

Alevy said, 'He cannot speak. Throat operation.'

Strakhov shouted, 'On your knees!'

Alevy knelt, and Mills did the same. Strakhov said to Filenko, 'Keep a watch on them. I'll get Lieutenant Cheltsov.' He ran, pistol in hand, toward the rear door of the building and disappeared inside.

Hollis moved quickly through the front lobby with Dodson over his shoulders. He approached the door of the commo room and said, 'Lisa, coming in.'

The door opened, and Lisa, pistol in hand, stepped aside.

Hollis laid Dodson on the floor.

'Sam . . . is that Jack Dodson?'

'I'm sure it is.'

'He's been . . . tortured.' She asked, 'Is be going to live?'

'I'm certain Burov left enough life in him to make the execution worthwhile. His vital signs are good. He's probably heavily drugged so he can't try to kill himself. He'll come out of it. We'll take him home.'

She nodded, then fell into his arms. 'Sam, let's get out of here.'

'Soon. How's Brennan?'

'I just spoke to him.' She smiled. 'He says he's bored.'

'Good. What's on the radio?'

She glanced at the two radios on the table. 'Not much. Normal talk so far. Towers calling one another, motorized patrols talking to one another.'

'Has anyone tried to radio here?'

'I haven't heard any calls for headquarters.'

Hollis nodded. The standard military procedure was that headquarters called the posts, asking for situation reports. The posts called only if there was a problem. He wondered when the dead commo man was scheduled to call the towers, gate, and other posts again. He asked, 'Has anyone tried to place a telephone call?'

'No. The switchboard is quiet.'

'Good.' Hollis thought that this operation had all the 'S' elements of a successful covert operation – surprise, speed, security, and secrecy. But if the secrecy was blown, they'd have to contend with six hundred Border Guards. Hollis glanced at the two bodies on the floor. *Very angry Border Guards*. He said to Lisa, 'You're doing fine.'

She forced a smile. 'Thanks.' She asked, 'Where are Seth and Bert?'

'Getting a vehicle.' He looked out the long slit window that faced the main road out front. 'They should be around in a minute or two. I'm going back in the lobby to unbolt the front door and keep watch. You stay here. I can see this door from the front door. Just take a deep breath and think about . . . autumn in New York.'

'With you.'

Hollis squeezed her hand and went out into the lobby and unbolted the front door. Suddenly the sound of running footsteps echoed from the corridor at the rear of the lobby, and Hollis spun around. A man in a KGB topcoat burst into the lobby at full speed, a pistol in his hand. Before he saw Hollis, he shouted, 'Lieutenant Cheltsov!' He stopped short at Cheltsov's desk, then his eyes took in the blood-soaked chair and the smear of blood trails where Cheltsov and the Border Guard had been dragged into the commo room. His eyes followed the blood, then he turned his head and found himself looking at Hollis.

Hollis pointed his TD automatic, knowing the distance was too long to ensure a hit, and the 6.35mm round too small to ensure a kill. Hollis said in Russian, 'Drop your gun.'

The man suddenly spun around and ran for the corridor. Hollis fired his silenced automatic twice, both rounds hitting the concrete wall above the man's head before he disappeared into the corridor.

Hollis followed at a run into the corridor. The man was a good thirty feet ahead of him, heading toward the cells, then suddenly drew up short, skidded over the painted concrete floor, and turned his body toward the intersecting corridor as his legs pumped. Hollis fired twice, and the man fired back once before he disappeared into the next corridor.

Hollis took off at full speed, came to the intersecting corridor and without slowing, cut like a broken-field runner into the narrower corridor, his running shoes holding to the floor. He saw the man duck into the guard room and heard him shout, 'Sergeant! Sergeant!'

Hollis hit the half-open door with his shoulder and rolled into a prone firing position as the man spun around and fired at the swinging door.

Hollis emptied his last three rounds into the man's chest and watched him backpedal as though he'd been pushed. The man pointed his pistol at Hollis's face, then suddenly seemed to lose his balance and toppled backward.

Hollis sprung up and rushed at the man, then stopped short as he saw what he had tripped over; lying on the floor was the naked body of another man, blood pooled around his head.

Hollis bent down and pulled the pistol out of the hand of the man he'd shot, then looked around the dimly lit guard room. He saw clothes strewn about the floor, a KGB uniform and women's clothing. He noticed the bottom bunk of one of the beds soaked with blood and knew that Alevy and Mills had already been there.

The man he'd shot moaned, and Hollis knelt beside him. The man wore a topcoat that was still cold to the touch, so he had just come from outside, which meant he had to come through the back door where Alevy and Mills were supposed to be getting a vehicle. Hollis stood with the man's pistol in his hand.

The man looked up at him and tears formed in his eyes. Hollis recognized the man as one of his guards during his time in the cells; the man who had told him he wouldn't feel much like fucking. The man said in Russian, 'I am sorry . . . I am sorry . . .'

'That makes two of us.' Hollis unloaded the magazine from the man's pistol and transferred it into his own silenced automatic. He pointed the pistol at the man's head, hesitated, then turned and moved quickly into the corridor.

Filenko knelt and rolled the naked woman on her back. 'This is the sergeant's woman. Why did you shoot her? You!' He shouted at Alevy, 'Answer me!'

Alevy answered, 'Filenko, I'll have you shot –'

'Shut up! You are not a Russian. Who are you?'

'Estonian.'

'Then speak Estonian. I know a few words.'

'Alright.' Still looking at Filenko, Alevy said in English, 'Bert, count of three . . . One, two –'

The door opened again, but Filenko kept his eyes on Alevy and Mills as he called out, 'Ivan, did you –?'

Suddenly Filenko's body lurched twice, then he dropped his rifle and sank to the ground, his hands clamped to his side.

Hollis ran down the ramp as Alevy and Mills stood. Mills grabbed Filenko's rifle, and Alevy said to Hollis, 'One of them went inside –'

'He's out.'

'Good. Let's get these two inside.'

Hollis saw that Filenko was still alive, lying on his back now, his eyes following the three of them as they spoke. Hollis went to the semiconscious woman who was moaning on the cold pavement and knelt beside her. 'Jane Landis . . .'

Alevy asked, 'You know her?'

'Yes. This is the wife of the man you met – Tim Landis. Did you shoot her?' He stared at Alevy.

Alevy said, 'She was in the sack with the sergeant of the guard.'

'No . . .'

'Yes.'

'She was very anti-Soviet.'

'Not when I saw her.'

'She may have been spying on them.'

'Or *for* them,' Alevy observed.

'Maybe she was doing it to help her husband – I don't know.'

'Neither do I, Sam.'

Hollis looked at Jane Landis, who stared back at him. She moved her mouth to speak. 'Sam . . . help me.'

Mills cleared his throat and said, 'My God, I'm sorry.'

Alevy said, 'It doesn't matter. Move her inside.'

As Hollis took her in his arms, Alevy asked him, 'What's that thing over there, Sam?'

Hollis replied, 'That is how Dodson got out. I think that's how Burov was going to execute Dodson and ten others tomorrow morning.'

Mills exclaimed, 'Jesus Christ!'

Alevy nodded. 'I want this guy.'

Hollis put Jane Landis over his shoulder and carried her up the ramp. Mills and Alevy followed, dragging Filenko by his arms into the headquarters building.

They turned into the narrow corridor of cells and pulled Filenko into one and bolted it.

Alevy said to Hollis, 'You have to lock her up, Sam. I don't know who she is, and I don't care.'

'She's dying, Seth.'

'I don't *care*.' Alevy opened a cell door. 'In there.'

Reluctantly Hollis placed Jane Landis on the cold floor and knelt beside her.

'Don't leave me, Sam.'

Hollis wanted to ask her for an explanation, but thought that Jane Landis, or whatever her name had once been, was as multilayered as a *matrushka* stacking doll, a shell within a shell, within a shell – each real, each hollow, each neatly embodied within the next.

Alevy put his hand on Hollis's shoulder, and Hollis stood and looked around the cell. 'This was where they had me. Lisa was next door.'

Alevy made no comment.

Hollis left the cell, and Alevy shut and bolted the door. He said to Hollis, 'If she lives, she'll be included in the swap.'

Hollis doubted that on both counts.

Mills said to Hollis, 'Thanks for coming to look for us.'

Alevy, who didn't seem as appreciative, said, 'We should try to stick to our prearranged plans when we agree to them.'

Hollis asked, 'Did you plan to have those guys get the drop on you?'

Alevy said to Mills, 'Go back to the commo room. Call Brennan one more time, then jam the radios and destroy the switchboard. Sam, you come with me, and we'll get the Zil and bring it around front. Let's move.'

Hollis and Alevy moved quickly toward the rear of the

building, guns drawn. They opened the back door and saw the Zil parked on the concrete under the glare of the light. Alevy said, 'I'll go first. Cover.' He ran to the Zil and jumped into the driver's seat. Like most military vehicles, the Zil had a keyless ignition, and Alevy pushed the starter button. The engine caught on the first try. Hollis jumped in beside him, and Hollis threw the floor shift into gear, then drove around the building. Alevy said, 'I don't want you or Lisa to question my handling of this operation.'

'I think it's your sanity we're questioning.'

Alevy glanced at Hollis. 'I know what I'm doing. Sam.'

'I know what you're doing too. Do it without me.'

'Then go. I don't need either of you.'

'I'll go if you let me take Mills. He doesn't deserve to die for your immortality.'

'What the hell are you talking about?'

'About you getting a chapter in the secret histories of Langley and Lubyanka.'

Alevy replied, 'You think you have me figured out, don't you?'

'I'm getting close.'

'Well, I'm not suicidal. I'd like to be in London tomorrow.'

Hollis didn't reply.

Mills moved quickly through the lobby, unbolted the front doors, then approached the commo room. He stood to the side of the door and said softly. 'Lisa, it's Bert Mills.'

'Okay, Bert.'

Mills entered the commo room and closed the door.

'Where's Sam?' she asked. 'He was out in the lobby –'

'With Seth. They're bringing a vehicle around front.'

Lisa nodded.

Mills noticed Dodson laid out on the floor near the two dead Border Guards. He knelt beside Dodson and looked at his battered face. 'My God . . .' He checked his pulse. 'He's alive.' He looked at Lisa. 'I understand why Sam wants to take him, Lisa, but this guy is a burden that we don't need.'

Lisa replied, 'Nevertheless, if Sam wants him out, that's what we will do.'

Mills glanced at her, then shrugged and stood.

'What took you so long back there?'

'We ran into a few things,' he answered without mentioning Jane Landis. 'Everything is alright.'

She looked at him and said, 'Bert . . . all this killing . . . it's making me sick to my stomach.'

'We'll talk about it when we're out of reach of the KGB. They make me sick to my stomach.'

She nodded.

Mills went to the switchboard and put the headset on, then pushed the ringer.

A voice came through the earpiece. '*Da. Nechevo.*'

'Bill, it's Bert Mills.'

'Oh . . . everything okay?'

'So far. How about there?'

'I don't know . . .'

'What's the problem?'

'Well, one of the watchtowers turned its spotlight on our chopper for a few seconds. Probably got O'Shea a little nervous. But nothing came of it. I still have radio traffic, but it's still Greek to me.'

'Give me the frequencies on the radios.'

'Hold on.' Brennan came back a few seconds later and gave Mills the frequencies. 'They're quiet now.'

Mills checked the corresponding radios on the counter and found the frequencies were the same. 'Okay, Bill, I'm going to jam both radios, and you do the same. Then I'm going to destroy the switchboard, so this is a final sign-off. We'll see you later. Stay awake.'

Brennan chuckled. '*Da.*'

Mills aimed his automatic at the switchboard and fired into the connectors. Sparks flew, and the smell of burning insulation filled the room. He went to the two radios, which were crackling, and turned up the volume on both of them. He asked Lisa, 'What's he saying?'

Lisa listened at the speaker of the shortwave radio as a voice spoke in Russian. Lisa said, 'Someone identifying themselves as "Tower One." calling the helipad.'

'That's what I was afraid of.'

Mills reached in his pocket and took the roll of tape he'd used to change the helicopter's identification number. He taped the transmit keys down on both handsets.

Lisa asked, 'The radios are jammed now?'

'Only on those frequencies.' He studied both radios, then pointed to a metal nameplate. 'What's that say?'

She read the plate. 'Auto search . . . something like that.'

'That's it.' He turned on the toggle switch above the nameplate, and the frequency dial began scanning the band. Mills said, 'That's used to pick up the strongest transmissions in the area, like a car radio scanner. But when the mike is continuously keyed, the radio becomes a broadband jamming device.' Mills did the same to the shortwave radio. 'This will play havoc with their radio traffic.'

'But it might also alert them that something is wrong,' Lisa said.

Mills had the uneasy feeling that the KGB Border Guard detachment already suspected that. 'We're nearly done here.'

'Are we?'

'Well, almost nearly.' Mills glanced at his watch, then at Lisa. Neither spoke.

Hollis and Alevy parked the Zil in front of the headquarters building and entered the lobby. Alevy called into the commo room, 'Coming in.' Alevy and Hollis entered the commo room, and Lisa ran into Hollis' arms.

Alevy knelt beside Dodson and looked him over. His warm-up suit was ripped and stained with blood. His body was filthy, and his hair was matted. Dodson's unshaven face was bruised

617

and puffy, and his nose looked broken. Alevy pushed back Dodson's eyelids. 'Really bad shape.'

'Obviously,' Hollis replied. 'He's been in the open country a couple of weeks, and he's been beaten for a few days. But mostly he's drugged up. He'll be fine. He comes with us.'

Alevy stood. 'Alright. Let's go.'

Lisa asked, 'Are we going to the helicopter?'

'No,' Alevy replied. 'We're going to get Burov.'

'*Why*, Seth?'

'Because that's what I came here for.'

She grabbed his arm. 'Is *that* why you came here?'

'Well . . . I came here for you and Sam. But –'

'Seth, this place is full of *Russians*.' She looked at Hollis. 'Sam, how many? Six or seven hundred?'

Alevy said tersely, 'What difference does that make? I don't plan to get into a firefight with them. I just want to be out of here before they wake up. I have no time to argue.' He looked at Lisa. 'Why don't you and Sam take Dodson in the vehicle and go to the helipad?'

Hollis said to Alevy, 'We'll stay with you.' He looked at Lisa. 'Are you alright?'

'I'm scared out of my mind.'

'Well,' Alevy said in an uncharacteristic display of candor, 'so am I. So let's get it over with and get home.'

Mills helped get Dodson on Hollis' back, and they moved quickly through the lobby. Alevy opened the front door and looked out. 'Clear.' They rushed down the steps of the headquarters, and Mills dropped the tailgate of the Zil and helped Hollis place Dodson in the space behind the rear seats. Mills got in the vehicle beside Alevy, and Hollis and Lisa jumped into the rear seats. Alevy said, 'You two stay low.'

Hollis and Lisa dropped to the floor as Alevy moved the Zil to the road and turned right toward Burov's dacha.

41

The Zil-6 moved over the dark road.

Lisa said from the rear, 'Seth, we don't need Burov. Just take another American. General Austin's house is right off this road. You wanted him.'

'But you wanted Dodson. Only room for one more, and that will be Colonel Petr Burov. Right, Sam?'

Hollis didn't reply.

Mills said, 'Seth, we got some problems at the helipad.' Mills explained about the spotlight and about the tower trying to raise the helipad radio.

Alevy stayed silent a moment, then said, 'Let's not get jumpy. We're very close to pulling off the snatch operation of the decade. What do you think, Sam?'

Hollis thought that a reasonable man would have accepted the evidence and concluded that the operation was starting to unravel. Alevy, however, was a driven man, and Hollis did not trust driven men.

'Sam?'

'I think we're all living on borrowed time.' Hollis said to Mills, 'Bert? What do you say?'

Mills seemed torn between reason and loyalty to Alevy, which they both knew were mutually exclusive. Mills looked sideways at Alevy. 'Seth . . . we got Sam and Lisa, we got an American . . . chopper's crowded. Maybe it's time to shuffle off.'

Alevy turned and looked back at Hollis. 'Sam, it's your call. Do *you* want to get Burov yourself, or would you be content to let him live? Maybe tomorrow when he wakes up from the Sandman, he'll murder *twenty* Americans.'

Hollis replied curtly, 'This isn't a balls contest.'

'I'm not questioning your nerve. I want to know if you have any personal scores to settle. In our business, you can't let personal considerations help you make an operational decision. Well?'

Hollis glanced at Lisa, then said to Alevy, 'Drive on.'

Alevy remarked, 'I think we have each other figured out.'

Lisa slumped against the door and stared at Hollis. He stared back. Hollis recalled the trip to Novodevichy Convent, sitting on the floor, with Jane Ellis and Betty Eschman in front. That had been a lark, Hollis thought, compared to this. But this was the inevitable result of what they had begun in Moscow. Lisa kicked his foot and forced a smile. 'Novodevichy?'

He nodded. They had a short but memorable history.

Hollis said to Alevy, 'Keep it at about fifteen K, or you'll attract attention.'

They continued on, and Alevy navigated a bend in the road, then said, 'What the hell is that?'

Hollis raised himself up and looked out of the window. 'That's Pine Corners Shopping Plaza. You never saw a shopping plaza before?'

Mills laughed. 'Jesus Christ . . .'

Alevy looked up at the camouflage net that blocked the night sky, then cut into the parking lot and drove slowly past the stores and shops. 'Seven Eleven?'

'Mosfilm does the props.'

'Really?' He looked at each shop window as they drove by, nodding his head several times. 'Not bad . . . do they –?'

'I'll brief you,' Hollis said curtly, 'in London. Let's move it.'

Suddenly a pair of headlights appeared on the road, and they saw a huge Zil-131 troop carrier pass the parking lot, heading toward the headquarters building.

Mills said, 'If he stops at headquarters, he's not going to like what he sees there.'

Alevy hit the accelerator and swung back onto the road, falling in behind the troop carrier. In the canvas-covered rear compartment, Alevy honked his horn and flashed his lights. The carrier's driver put his arm out of the window, then stopped the vehicle. The driver got out and walked back toward them. He called out, 'Stakhov?'

Alevy said to Hollis and Lisa, 'Stay low.' He opened his door and said to Mills, 'Get behind the wheel.' Alevy jumped out and walked toward the driver of the troop carrier, who was shielding his eyes against the glare of the headlights. The driver asked, 'Who is that?'

'Major Voronin.'

The man snapped to attention and saluted.

Alevy asked, 'Where are you taking those men?'

The driver replied, 'To relieve the guard posts.'

'Which guard posts?'

'Towers one and two, the main gate, the headquarters, and the helipad, sir. I've just relieved the guards at the dacha.'

'Colonel's Burov's dacha?'

'Yes, sir.'

'How many guards do you mount there?'

'Three.'

Alevy glanced at the twenty armed men in the rear of the truck whose heads were turned toward him. Alevy addressed the driver. 'The personnel in the headquarters and the helipad have two more hours' punishment duty for sloppy attitudes.'

'Yes, sir. By whose authority, Major?'

'Mine, Corporal. Go directly to the towers and the main gate, then bring the rest of your men back to the guard house.'

'The barracks, sir.'

'Yes, the barracks.' Alevy felt a bead of sweat form under his cap and roll down his forehead. 'Dismissed.'

The driver hesitated, then saluted and turned on his heel.

Alevy walked back to the Zil and got into the passenger side. 'Turn it around, Bert.'

Mills had trouble finding reverse, then got it into gear, and the Zil stalled. 'Damn it!' The big troop carrier sat on the road in front of them. Mills restarted his vehicle and made a choppy three-point turn on the narrow road as the troop carrier moved off slowly. No one spoke. Mills got the Zil moving back down the road toward Burov's dacha. He said softly, 'I don't drive Russian.'

Hollis said to Alevy, 'I heard most of that, and I don't think he completely bought it.'

'You don't understand the Russian mind.'

'I understand the military mind. Men will take orders from their own officers, but not necessarily from an officer they don't recognize.'

'I seem to be doing alright.' Alevy asked, 'Do you want to turn back or go on?'

Hollis replied, 'Go on.'

Lisa made a sound of exasperation. She said to Mills, 'Please, Bert, can't you reason with these two?'

Mills thought a moment, then replied, 'No.'

A minute later, Alevy asked, 'Is that the dacha's guard booth ahead?'

Hollis peered out the windshield. 'That's it. The dacha is surrounded by barbed wire. Dogs run loose between the wire and the house. There should be two KGB at the guard booth and one inside the dacha itself. But you never know.'

'That driver confirmed three.' Alevy said to Mills, 'You take the guard that approaches, I've got the other one.'

'Right.'

'Down in back.'

Mills slowed the vehicle and drew closer to the guard booth. Alevy looked past the gate at the rather plain-looking dacha sitting in darkness about a hundred meters away. Mills brought the Zil to a bucking halt, and it stalled. He started it again. 'I never got the hang of a stick shift.' He drew his pistol and held it in his lap.

One of the guards walked up to the driver's side and looked in the open window. 'Yes, Captain?'

Mills pumped a single shot between the man's eyes as Alevy opened his door and stood on the running board. The second guard was still in the small booth, and Alevy could see him furiously cranking the field phone as he reached for his rifle. Alevy steadied his aim over the roof of the Zil and fired all eight rounds from his pistol into the booth. The glass and wood splintered, and the man dropped to the floor.

Mills shut off his headlights.

Hollis got out of the Zil as Alevy moved to the gate. Hollis grabbed Alevy's shoulder. 'He's mine.'

Alevy nodded. 'Okay. But don't kill him.'

'I know.'

Alevy looked at his watch. 'We have thirty-four minutes to get to the helipad.'

Lisa said to Hollis, 'Let me go with you. I can help you get past the guard inside.'

Hollis nodded. He opened the wire gate, then turned to Alevy. 'On the left side of the house is Greg Fisher's Trans Am. We'll take that out of here.'

Hollis seemed not to understand. 'Fisher's Trans Am? Here . . . ?'

'Burov drives it. Keys are most probably in the ignition.'

Alevy nodded. 'Good idea, Sam. They might be on the lookout for a Zil-6 by now. And if the Trans Am is Burov's car, we might not be challenged.'

Mills added, 'And we may need the speed and handling. The Zil's a pig.'

Hollis replied, 'All that may be true. But I want the Trans Am, because . . . I want the Trans Am.' He took Lisa by the arm and began running up the long blacktop path toward the dacha.

Two German shepherds suddenly appeared out of the dark, tearing toward them from opposite directions. Hollis dove into a prone firing position, steadied his aim, and fired at the closer dog to his left. The automatic coughed softly, but the dog yelped loudly. Hollis rolled to his right just as the second shepherd reached him and Lisa. Hollis could actually smell the big dog in the split second before he put a bullet into its open mouth.

Hollis stood and helped Lisa to her feet. 'Okay?'

'Okay.'

They got to the front door, and Hollis nodded to her. She turned the doorknob and found it open. Lisa put her pistol in her parka and slipped inside.

The guard was sitting in a chair in the large foyer by the light of a dim lamp, aiming his automatic rifle at her. Lisa partly closed the door behind her and stood motionless. The guard said, 'Who are you?'

She put her finger to her lips and whispered in Russian, 'I am Lisa Rhodes, the new American woman. The colonel wishes to see me.'

The guard said, 'He never told me.'

'He told the men outside.'

The guard grinned. 'And what do you suppose the colonel wants to see you about at this hour?'

'He wants to have sex with me.'

The guard smirked and put his rifle on the desk. He said, 'I'll have to sneak upstairs and nudge him.' He pulled off his boots. 'Get into the living room and get out of your clothes. That's where he has to do it with his old lady upstairs.' The guard stood in his stocking feet.

Lisa pulled the door open and jumped aside.

Hollis ran through the door and fired as the man reached for his rifle, then rushed forward and grabbed him before he fell. Hollis sat the man back in his chair and saw the frothy blood forming at his lips and could hear the sucking chest wound as the guard tried to breathe.

Hollis took Lisa by the arm and propelled her toward the front door. He whispered, 'Go. No arguing.'

'Please . . . Sam, be careful –'

Hollis opened the door and pushed her out, then turned back to the guard, who was staring at him. Hollis walked past him, then turned, clamped his hand on the man's shoulder, and fired a bullet into the back of his head, holding him in his seat.

Hollis left the foyer and went toward the staircase.

The stairs creaked, but he continued on up. A woman's voice said, 'Natalia, is that you, darling?'

Hollis stopped. He heard footsteps, then the woman's voice called out, 'Petr, Natalia is in her room.'

Burov's voice came back. 'It is the guard. Come back to bed.'

Hollis heard footsteps again and the sound of a door closing. He climbed the remaining steps and came to a large upper hallway. To the left were two half-open doors that would be the bedrooms of Burov's daughter, Natalia, and probably his mother. To the right was the closed door that would be the master bedroom. Hollis went to the closed door, listened, then turned the knob, threw the door open, and shoulder-rolled into the room, coming up into a firing position, his pistol aimed at the bed. 'Don't move!' The room was dark except for a small red bulb, and as Hollis's eyes adjusted to the light, he saw it was actually a red star glowing stop a wood model of the Kremlin's Spassky Tower. That seemed odd, but odder still was the single empty bed on which lay a rag doll. Hollis understood, but it was too late.

He heard the revolver's hammer click behind him, and Burov's voice said, 'Drop the gun.'

Hollis dropped the gun.

Burov said, 'Don't stand. Turn around on your knees.'

Hollis turned his body slowly toward Burov. Burov flipped on an overhead light, and Hollis saw Burov standing in the doorway, barefoot, wearing flannel pajamas and pointing a big revolver at him.

Burov said, 'Some families practice fire drills. We have other sorts of drills here. And you think Russians are stupid.'

Hollis didn't reply.

'The stupid one,' Burov said, 'is the one who is on his knees looking into the barrel of a gun.' Burov regarded Hollis curiously. 'What is your purpose here?'

'To kill you, you idiot.'

'No, you would have simply shot bullets into that bed. You

said, "Don't move." You wanted to capture me. Where did you get that gun?'

'None of your business.'

'Are you alone?'

'What do you think?'

'I think not. Did you kill the guards?'

'Yes.'

'And my dogs?'

'Yes.'

Burov nodded thoughtfully, then said, 'My phone doesn't work, and I think you have people downstairs. So we are both in a bad position.'

Hollis said nothing.

'Is this a rebellion? That would be lunacy. There are six hundred armed Border Guards here. Do you want to negotiate for Dodson's life?'

'I want to give you a lecture about how much power comes from the muzzle of a gun. It depends on other factors. And authority never came from the muzzle of a gun. Are we learning something?'

Burov snapped, 'Get on all fours and crawl out here.'

Hollis dropped to all fours and moved out into the hallway as Burov stepped back.

Burov said, 'To the right.'

Hollis crawled down the hallway, and Burov came up beside him close enough to kick Hollis in the head with the heel of his bare foot. 'I'll show you who has the power and the authority here.'

Burov led Hollis into the master bedroom. 'On your back.'

Hollis rolled over on his back, and Burov walked out of his line of vision, then stomped his foot down on Hollis' face.

'Take off your jacket and sweat shirt, and pull your pants down around your ankles.'

Hollis sat up slowly, Burov still behind him, and removed his parka and shirt, then slid his pants down.

Burov snatched the jacket away, then said, 'Lie down, hands under your ass.'

Hollis lay down and put his hands under him.

Burov went through Hollis' parka. He tossed a spare ammunition clip aside, then said, 'What is this?' He threw the silver general's star on Hollis' bare chest.

Hollis made no reply, and Burov kicked the top of his head. 'And what is this in these aluminum cigar tubes, Hollis? Names . . . ah, a class roster, living and dead. Where are you bringing this?'

'One copy to Washington, one to Moscow.'

'Yes? You think so? I don't think so.'

Hollis thought Burov's voice sounded strained. He heard Burov move to the far side of the room and glanced over at him. In an alcove near a window was a radio transmitter, and as Hollis watched, the radio glowed to life. Burov said, 'I'm going to call out the entire Border Guard detachment from their barracks, Hollis.' He picked up the handset.

'Where is your wife, daughter, and your mother?'

Burov turned toward him. 'Why do you ask?'

'This place is surrounded, and there will be shooting. I'll guarantee them safe passage out of this house.'

'You can't guarantee anything, you shit.'

'They can leave now. Before you call.'

Burov, still holding the handset, came toward Hollis. 'There is no one surrounding this house.' He kicked Hollis in the side of the face.

'You know there is. The guards are dead, and your phone is cut.'

'But not my radio.'

Hollis said in Russian, 'Then make the call, you stupid shit, and fuck you, your wife, your daughter, and your ugly old mother.'

Burov again kicked Hollis in the face. He held the handset to his ear and listened to the intermittent jamming as the radio in the headquarters and the one in the helipad cabin transmitted their open microphones across the band. He swore softly, went back to the radio, and switched to the alternate frequency. He heard snatches of conversation cut off as the jamming swept the frequencies. He glanced at Hollis, then said into the mouthpiece in Russian, 'All stations, all stations, this is Colonel Burov. Full alert, full alert. Send a detachment of guards to my quarters at once. Be on the lookout for armed prisoners —'

'Students!' Hollis called out. 'Students!'

'Shut your fucking mouth!'

'Why don't you shut yours? No one can hear you anyway. Can't you tell the radio is jammed, you stupid shit?' Hollis added in Russian, 'Don't the Russians understand electronics?'

Burov dropped the handset and took a long running stride toward Hollis, his foot shooting out toward Hollis' head. Hollis sat up quickly, causing Burov to lose his balance as his foot sailed through the air. Hollis lifted himself on his hands and pivoted his legs around, knocking Burov off his feet. Hollis' right hand wrapped around Burov's revolver, and he held the cylinder in place as Burov tried to squeeze off a round. Hollis jabbed the fingers of his left hand in Burov's eyes, then jabbed into his larynx. Burov let out a gasp but did not loosen his grip on the pistol. Burov's left hand chopped down on Hollis' neck twice before Hollis could grab Burov's wrist. Hollis kicked his shoes and pants off and brought his knee up into Burov's testicles.

The two men rolled and thrashed around on the floor, Hollis holding his grip on Burov's revolver and Burov's wrist, each trying to position their knees for another blow to the groin, and each aware that the other was trained in the same deadly arts. Hollis smashed his forehead down on Burov's nose and heard it crack. Burov got his teeth into the maxillary nerves of Hollis' cheek and drew blood before Hollis could pull his face away. Hollis stuck his thumbnail into the fleshy part of Burov's wrist, digging at the veins until he opened one of them and felt the blood squirting. Neither man uttered a word or a sound of pain.

628

Hollis realized that Burov had not been lying about his physical condition, but Hollis' condition was not as good as it had been some weeks before, and he was tiring, unable to roll Burov over on his back again. Hollis found himself under Burov's heavy weight and felt Burov's gun hand working free. Both men looked at each other in the dim light, and Hollis saw that Burov was bleeding from the nose and the right eye. Burov said softly, 'I'm going to shoot you in the balls.'

Hollis suddenly released his grip on Burov's wrist and with his freed hand delivered a judo chop to the back of Burov's neck, then reached around Burov's head and grasped his chin in his hand and pulled, turning the man's head and neck until he could hear the cartilage cracking. Burov reached for Hollis' hand to break the grip before his neck broke.

Hollis kept up the pressure, and he could see Burov's tongue protruding from his mouth and his left eye beginning to bulge. Burov's free hand was pulling at Hollis' arm. Hollis brought his knee up into Burov's groin twice, realizing the man's defenses were failing. He tried to pull the pistol from Burov's hand, but Burov held tight.

Then, to keep his neck from breaking, Burov suddenly released his grip on his pistol and let his body roll over on his back, rolling out of Hollis' twisting jaw hold. Burov got to his feet.

Hollis stood also, and the two men faced each other, hunched over and panting. Hollis let Burov's pistol fall to the floor. 'Come on.'

But Burov didn't move, and Hollis could see he was finished. Both eyes were filled with blood, and his breathing came in short raspy gasps. Blood poured from Burov's nose and spurted from his wrist. Hollis moved closer to him, caught his breath, and said, 'For Dodson, Fisher, the airmen, their women, and the children.' Hollis drove his fist into Burov's face and heard the cracking of teeth.

Burov toppled backward and lay still on the floor. Hollis sank to his knees and turned Burov over on his face so he wouldn't drown in his own blood. He ripped off the collar of Burov's pajamas and tied it around the open vein of Burov's wrist.

Hollis sank to the floor, trying to clear his head and catch his breath. His hand went to his right cheek where Burov's teeth had ripped into the flesh and nerves, and he felt a searing pain flash through his brain.

A figure appeared in the doorway, and Hollis could make out a pair of jackboots coming toward him. He looked up into the face of Seth Alevy. Behind Alevy was Lisa. Hollis tried to stand, but Alevy's hand pressed down on his shoulder. 'Sit awhile.' Alevy took the revolver from the floor and went over to Burov.

Lisa hurried to Hollis' side. 'Sam, are you alright?'

He nodded, then turned toward Alevy. 'Radio.' He pointed.

Alevy moved from Burov to the radio and ripped the handset out of its cord, then smashed the plastic handset against the steel radio casing. 'Was he able to get a call through?'

'I don't think so.' Hollis pulled on his sweat pants, and Lisa helped him on with his shirt and parka. He got on his running shoes but found he couldn't tie the laces, and Lisa did it for him. Hollis stood unsteadily, stuffing the loose papers from the cigar tubes into his pocket. Lisa handed him his star.

Alevy turned Burov over and looked at his face, then looked at Hollis and said, 'You guys don't like each other.'

Hollis didn't reply.

A voice said in Russian, 'Why did you hurt my father?'

They all turned toward the door. A frightened-looking girl of about ten stood in her nightgown at the open door. Behind her was a rather plain, middle-aged woman in a heavy quilt robe, and barely visible behind her was the old woman whom Burov had introduced as his mother.

The middle-aged woman looked at Hollis, then at Lisa, then at Alevy in his KGB uniform. 'Is my husband dead?'

Alevy replied in Russian, 'No, madam, he is only unconscious.'

She sobbed. 'But I don't understand what is happening.'

Alevy and Hollis glanced at each other. Lisa said to them in English, 'You will not kill them.'

The girl, Natalia, said, 'Will my father be alright?'

Lisa replied in Russian, 'Yes.'

Suddenly the old woman pushed past her daughter-in-law and granddaughter and hurried into the room, kneeling beside her son, tears falling on his face, her fingers caressing him. 'Oh, God, my poor boy. Petr, Petr, God love you, my little one.' Hollis recalled those World War II newsclips of the old babushkas keening over the bodies of their sons and husbands. He thought, *My God, how many Burovs have been carried in the big bellies of these saintly old ladies?*

Alevy said in English, 'We can't take them, and we can't leave them . . .'

Lisa snapped, 'No, Seth!'

Hollis said to Alevy, 'I want Burov to know they're alive. That could be useful to us later.'

Alevy nodded. 'Alright.' He said to Burov's wife in Russian, 'All of you will remain in the house, or the dogs will get you. Some soldiers will be along in a while.' Alevy knelt to pick up Burov, but Hollis pushed him aside and with some difficulty got Burov in a fireman's carry and took him toward the door, the old woman still caressing him.

Lisa put her hand on Natalia's head. 'We're taking him to the hospital. He will be home soon.'

Burov's wife and mother tried to follow Hollis down the staircase, but Alevy stopped them. 'Don't worry. Everything will be alright.'

Lisa and Alevy made their way down the stairs after Hollis. Lisa said to Alevy, 'You were kind to them.'

Alevy didn't reply.

The Trans Am was now outside the front door, its hatchback open. Mills got out of the car, and with Hollis, they put Burov in the rear compartment with Dodson. Mills tied Burov's wrists with a piece of steel flex. Hollis looked down at both battered men: Dodson in his torn warm-up suit, Burov in his blood-splattered pajamas, neither face recognizable. The circle was closing on itself, Hollis reflected, the events set in motion by Dodson's catapult over the wire were nearing resolution. Hollis said to Alevy, 'I'll drive. Bert, give me your topcoat and hat and get in the back with Lisa.' Hollis put on the KGB topcoat and cap, and then slid into the driver's seat and started the car. Mills and Lisa climbed into the rear, and Alevy got in beside Hollis. Hollis threw the Trans Am into gear and accelerated quickly up the path, through the gate, and on to the dark, curving road.

They passed the shopping plaza, and Alevy said, 'We have twenty-two minutes before Sandman. Lots of time.'

Lisa said, 'Is that it, Seth? We can go now?'

'Yes. Helicopter's full.'

'Damned full,' Hollis added. He stepped on the accelerator and brought the speed up to sixty mph.

As they approached the headquarters building, a piercing siren cut the air. Alevy said, 'I assume that has something to do with us.'

Ahead they could see the lighted headquarters building with several Zil-6's in front of it and about a dozen KGB Border Guards milling around. One of them stepped to the side of the road and began waving to Hollis to pull into the parking area in front of the headquarters.

Hollis put the pedal to the floor, and the headquarters shot by in a blur.

Alevy said, 'What do you suppose that fellow wanted?'

'I don't know.' Hollis saw the speedometer climb to ninety mph. They shot past the dark VFW building, and Hollis said, 'Watch for the helipad turnoff.'

Mills commented, 'They're not real sure who's who or what's what yet.'

Alevy said, 'Well, I hope they figure it all out after we're gone.'

Hollis glanced in his rearview mirror. 'Two vehicles coming up.'

Alevy looked over his shoulder, and his eyes made contact with Lisa's. He said, 'You're unusually quiet.'

She smiled nervously. 'Thinking about the helicopter.'

'We'll be airborne in a few minutes.'

Hollis said, 'They're still back there.'

Alevy said to Mills, 'Burn them.' He handed his hat to Mills. 'Use this.'

'Right.' Mills took a phosphorus grenade from its Velcro holder on his ankle, set the timer dial at zero, and laid the grenade in the hat. He asked Alevy, 'What's the delay for zero?'

'Seven seconds.'

'Right. Could you open your door a crack?' Mills pulled the timer dial out to arm the grenade and counted to four, then pushed the hat out the door onto the road. 'Five, six.'

The lead vehicle, a Zil-6, was about two hundred meters behind them, flashing its lights now and sounding its horn.

'Seven.'

The phosphorus exploded under the first Zil, which veered off the road and crashed into the trees, its fuel tank exploding. Balls of burning phosphorus lofted into the air and ignited the pine trees. The second Zil, a big troop carrier, kept coming, but they drew no fire from it. Mills said, 'He's thinking about where that came from. He doesn't really want to open fire on the colonel's car.'

Lisa called out, 'Sam! There's the road to the helipad.'

Hollis hit the brakes and cut the wheel to the right, the Trans Am fishtailing but holding the road. He downshifted, then accelerated up the narrow gravel track. The Pontiac bounced as Hollis floored it, and the speedometer climbed to sixty mph, then seventy.

About two hundred meters ahead Hollis saw the outline of the radio cabin and a dim light in one of its windows. He also saw part of the clearing but couldn't see the helicopter.

The siren was still wailing, and now the searchlights in the towers were probing into the woods beyond the perimeter. The camp was alive, the six hundred Border Guards were on the move. Hollis said, 'We can pick up Brennan on the run.'

Alevy looked out the rear. 'That damned troop carrier is coming up. Stop it here and block the road, or they'll follow us right up to the helicopter.'

'Right.' Hollis hit the brakes, and the Trans Am skidded to a halt diagonally across the gravel path. He pulled the keys out of the ignition, then shut off the lights as everyone scrambled out.

The Zil behind them slowed to a stop about a hundred meters away, its headlights illuminating them. Alevy carried Dodson, and Hollis took Burov on his back. Alevy said, 'Lisa, run on ahead and tell Brennan we're coming in.'

Lisa pulled her pistol, then ran down the path.

Hollis could see the shadows of at least ten men leaving the troop carrier and coming toward them. Someone shouted in Russian, 'Identify yourselves.'

Alevy said to Mills, 'Hold them for a few minutes, Bert.'

'Right.' Mills drew his automatic, rolled under the Trans Am, and waited for the men to draw closer.

Hollis and Alevy began running toward the cabin, carrying Burov and Dodson on their backs.

Mills steadied his aim and fired a full eight-round magazine from his silenced pistol. Someone screamed and immediately the air was cut with the hollow popping noise of AK-47s on full automatic, sounding like a string of tightly packed firecrackers. The windows of the Trans Am began shattering, and the streaks of green tracer rounds sliced through the black night. Mills reloaded and fired off another eight rounds.

Hollis and Alevy ran hunched over, their feet trying to find traction in the gravel as their burdens became heavier. Hollis still could not see the helicopter in the field.

Lisa, ahead of them, came within twenty meters of the log cabin and called out, 'Bill! Bill Brennan!'

A voice called back, 'Lisa Rhodes? Come on! Run!'

Lisa sprinted the last twenty meters and ran into the arms

of Brennan. He said, 'Okay, okay. Take a breath. What's happening?'

She motioned back down the lane. 'Seth and Sam . . . carrying Dodson and Burov.'

'Who? Oh, yeah. Good. And Mills?'

'Back there. They're coming. We were chased.'

'I guess so. Okay, get to the chopper, out there in the field –'

'No. I'm waiting –'

'Well, then get into the cabin and stay low. Be right back.' Brennan ran up the lane and met Alevy and Hollis coming toward him. A burst of automatic fire ripped into the boughs above their heads, and they all dove for the ground. Brennan looked at Burov and Dodson and asked, They hit?'

'No,' Alevy replied. 'Resting. Did Lisa –?'

'Yeah, she's in the cabin.'

'Okay, you take Dodson here and get back to the cabin.'

Brennan got to one knee, and Alevy put Dodson on Brennan's back. Brennan said, 'Couldn't you find people who could walk?'

The fire from the AK-47s was pruning the branches above their heads, and the lane was becoming covered with boughs and cones. Hollis saw a mangled squirrel drop beside him. Hollis couldn't tell if Mills was firing back because of his silencer, but the Border Guards seemed to be moving closer, and he could actually see muzzle flashes through the trees.

Brennan got into a crouch and began running back toward the cabin with Dodson.

Alevy said to Hollis, 'Go on, Sam. Mills is my responsibility. Beat it.'

Hollis hefted Burov over his shoulder. 'Try to stay alive long enough for me to kick the shit out of you.' Hollis followed Brennan in a low crouch.

Alevy knelt behind a large pine tree to the side of the lane, drew his pistol, and fired randomly into the trees on both sides. Suddenly there was an explosion, and Alevy saw a ball of orange fire erupt up the lane, and he knew the Trans Am had blown. He called out for Mills, but got no answer. Alevy slapped his last magazine into his pistol and began making his way toward the cabin, firing as he went.

Hollis covered the last few feet between the lane and the cabin and sank to his knees in the doorway. Brennan took Burov off his shoulder and laid the unconscious man beside Dodson just inside the door. Hollis stood and noticed that the cabin was dark now, but he could pick out Lisa crouched below a window and nearby three corpses in uniform stacked neatly against a wall. Lisa said, 'Sam . . . are you alright?'

'Fine. Stay low.' Hollis took off the KGB topcoat and threw it over Dodson.

Brennan picked up his Dragunov sniper rifle and went to the window, focusing the night scope on the nearby tree line. He said, 'I don't see Alevy or Mills on the path, but I see figures moving through the trees.' He took aim and fired, the operating rod of the silenced rifle making a metallic noise louder than the muzzle blast. He reaimed and fired again. 'It's a nice rifle, but the scope is not as sharp as ours.'

Hollis saw three AK-47s stacked against the other window, and near them was a metal ammunition box filled with thirty-round banana clips. He knelt at the window, took a rifle, and knocked out the glass.

Brennan said, 'Don't fire yet, Colonel. They don't have a fix on this place yet.'

'Right.' Hollis looked at Lisa kneeling beside him. 'I'm going back for Seth and Bert.'

She grabbed his arm. 'Don't you owe me something?'

Brennan glanced over at them. 'Hey, why don't one or both of you guys get out there and see if O'Shea's still hanging around? Tell him what's happening.'

Hollis took Lisa's hand and led her to the door. 'Keep low.' He pulled her away from the cabin and toward the clearing where they knelt in the knee-high grass. About a hundred meters out, Hollis could see the white helicopter against the black tree line beyond it. Above the sound of the gunfire, Hollis could hear the turbines running. 'Do you see it?'

'Yes.'

'Tell O'Shea we're alright and we're coming.'

She looked at him. 'You're coming with me.'

'Later.'

'Now!'

Hollis grabbed her shoulders and looked into her eyes. 'I need you to go out there and tell him we're coming or he might take off. I have to go back for the others, Lisa.'

'I'll jump off, Sam. I swear I will. If you're not there, I'll come back for you –' Tears filled her eyes and her body began to shake.

Hollis turned her toward the helicopter. 'Run. Low. Go on!'

She glanced back at him, then began running through the grass toward the helicopter, turning her head back to him every few strides.

Hollis watched her silhouette getting smaller against the distant helicopter, then turned toward the cabin and found himself face-to-face with Alevy.

Alevy watched Lisa disappear into the night, then looked at Hollis. 'Go ahead, Sam.'

'I'll get Burov.' Hollis moved past Alevy and headed back toward the cabin, Alevy beside him. Alevy said, 'At least she listens to you. She never listened to me.'

Hollis didn't reply. The sound of gunfire was closer now, and Hollis could see green tracer rounds streaking through the woods, though most of them were impacting in the trees.

Hollis and Alevy sprinted the short distance to the open door of the cabin and dove onto the floor. Brennan said, 'There are a lot more of them now. They've fanned out into the woods and are moving tree to tree. They're playing it cautious, but they'll be here in about ten minutes.' Brennan added, 'If they break out of the tree line over there by the clearing and see the chopper, we have a problem.'

Alevy nodded. 'We have to slow them up a little.' He grabbed an AK-47, poked the muzzle through the window, and fired long bursts into the nearby trees until the thirty rounds were expended.

The firing from the woods slackened for a few seconds as the Border Guards took cover. When the firing picked up again, Hollis noticed that most of it now seemed to be directed toward the cabin. He could hear the thud of impacting rounds on the far side of the logs, and an occasional green tracer sailed through the shattered windows, hit the opposite wall, and glowed briefly before it burned out. Overhead, tracers ripped through the sheet metal roofing, and the rafters began to splinter. Brennan said to Alevy, 'Maybe you want to hold off on that until you see the whites of their eyes.'

Alevy reloaded another magazine. 'Okay, Bill, you take Burov and get to the chopper.'

Hollis said, 'No, Dodson goes first. I'll take Burov.'

Alevy nodded to Brennan.

Brennan gave his sniper rifle to Alevy. 'You can track them through the night scope, and the muzzle makes no noise or flash. Use this until they get closer. Then use the AKs and the stuff in the bag.' Brennan added, 'Better yet, let's all get the hell out of here.'

Alevy raised the sniper rifle above the windowsill, aimed at a muzzle flash, and fired off a round. He said, 'I have to wait a bit longer for Bert. See you later.'

Brennan was kneeling beside Dodson now. 'He's got an okay pulse, but he's really out.' He put Dodson over his shoulder and moved toward the door, which was not in the direct line of fire from the woods. 'Okay, see you on board,' Brennan said with no conviction. He charged out the door, and Hollis watched him as he moved rapidly away from the cabin toward the clearing and disappeared in the darkness.

Hollis dropped down on one knee beside Burov and checked his pulse and breathing. 'He's okay. Worth taking.'

Burov stirred and tried to raise his head, but Hollis pushed

638

him back. Burov mumbled through his swollen lips and broken teeth. He spit up blood and gum tissue, then said in Russian, 'You . . .' he opened his eyes. 'You . . . Hollis . . . I'll kill you . . . I'll fuck your woman.'

Hollis said in Russian, 'You'll live, but you won't feel much like fucking.'

'*Yeb vas.*'

Alevy moved beside Burov and said to him, 'Do you know where you're going. Colonel? To America. Lucky you.'

'No . . . no . . .' Burov raised his tied hands and swung weakly at Alevy.

Alevy removed a spring-loaded Syrette from his pocket and jabbed it into Burov's neck, releasing a dose of sodium pentothal. He said to Burov, 'You can send postcards to Natalia.'

'You bastard.'

'Look who's talking.'

Burov seemed to notice the sound of gunfire. 'See . . . they are coming for you.'

Alevy said to Hollis, 'Well, Sam, it's your turn. Take your prize home.'

Hollis replied, 'Why don't you come along? Mills is dead.'

'Doesn't matter.'

'Come on home, Seth. You deserve it. Lunch at the White House.'

'I'll give the orders, General Hollis. Get moving.'

Hollis and Alevy looked at each other a moment, then Alevy said, 'The sleeping gas will pop in a few minutes. I'll be alright. You'd better go.'

They heard the sound of running footsteps outside, and they both grabbed rifles as a voice called out, 'I'm coming in!'

Mills dove headfirst through the open door and rolled into Burov, who gave a grunt. Mills sat up on the floor and caught his breath. 'They're close. Less than a hundred meters.' He looked at his watch. 'Jesus . . . time to go.'

Hollis noticed blood on Mills' hand and on his neck. He

smelled of burnt gasoline, and his clothes were singed. 'You hit?'

'I'm alright. I got away from the car before it blew. Well, are we waiting for anything?'

'Just you,' Alevy replied. 'You take Burov. We'll cover you with smoke.'

'Right.'

Hollis lifted the unconscious Burov onto Mills' shoulders as Alevy tore open the black leather bag and removed a smoke canister. he stood to the side of the door and peered around the jamb. 'They're damned close.' He pulled the pin on the canister and flung it out the door. The black smoke billowed and began drifting southward with the wind toward the advancing Border Guards. Alevy took a CS gas canister from the bag and flung that out also. The CS riot gas hissed into the air and wafted along with the smokescreen. He said, 'Okay, Bert, see you in a minute or so.'

Mills stood in a crouch near the door with Burov on his back and watched the ground-clinging smoke roll away from the cabin into the tree line. The sound of a man gagging could be heard above the sporadic weapons' fire. Mills said, 'Good luck.' He held on to Burov and ran from the cabin, the smokescreen behind him. Hollis lay in the doorway with an AK-47 and fired a full thirty-round magazine in a sweeping motion across the tree line, getting little fire in return. He glanced back toward Mills and saw he had disappeared.

Hollis rolled back into the *izba* and sat with his back against the log wall. As he reloaded, Alevy knelt by the window and fired long bursts into the black smoke. Spent shell casings clattered to the floor, and the smell of burnt cordite filled the cabin.

Hollis said, 'Okay, Mills and Burov are on board by now. You want to go first? I'll cover.'

Alevy glanced at his watch. 'No, you go first. We have a few minutes.'

Hollis moved toward the door, then looked back at Alevy.

640

Alevy smiled. 'Go ahead.'

Hollis could hear the sound of the helicopter turbines coming from the clearing. 'He's going to leave. Come with me.'

Alevy sat with his back to the wall beside the door but didn't respond. Hollis thought he looked very relaxed, very at peace with himself for the first time since Hollis had known him. 'It wasn't sleeping gas that you dropped from the helicopter, was it?'

Alevy replied, 'No, it wasn't.'

'Nerve gas?'

'Yes. I used Sarin. Tabun is good too, but –'

'Why? Why, Seth?'

'Oh, you know fucking well why.'

'But . . . Jesus Christ, man . . . nearly three hundred Americans . . . the women, children –'

'They can't go home, Sam. They can never go home. They have no home. *This* is their home. You *know* that.'

Hollis glanced out the window and saw the smokescreen beginning to dissipate. He rummaged through the leather bag and found the last smoke grenade and the last of the CS riot gas. He pulled both pins and flung the grenades out the door. There was still some firing directed toward them, but the predominant sound now was of vomiting and swearing. He said to Alevy, 'So, the State Department and the White House got their way. This place never existed. And you went along with it?'

Alevy glanced at his watch. 'Go on, Sam. I'm not asking you to die here.'

'Are you going to die here?'

Alevy did not reply directly, but said, 'I'm about to murder a thousand people.' He looked at Hollis. 'It was my idea. The poison gas. It's good for the country.'

'*How* is it good for the country?'

'It's a compromise. In exchange for the CIA and the Pentagon not wrecking the peace initiatives and all that crap, we can keep as many as we want of the three thousand or so gradutates of the Charm School that we'll eventually round up in America.

641

The rest we can dispose of without benefit of trial. That was made possible by you and General Surikov's files. That's what broke the deadlock. We're starting our own Charm School in America. Get it?'

'I'm afraid so.'

'Don't be a goddamned Boy Scout. We're turning their intelligence offensive against them on this one. We'll have a class A school for our agents, and Burov and Dodson will be sort of deans of students. Pretty neat, don't you think?'

'Your idea?'

'Of course.' Alevy added, 'But I'll tell you something else that wasn't my idea. Neither you nor Lisa were supposed to leave here alive. Your own people in Defense Intelligence, including your boss, General Vandermullen, agreed to that, though somewhat reluctantly, I'll admit.'

'Then why –?'

'Oh, I'm not *that* inhuman, Sam. Could I really leave *her* here to die?'

'Nothing you do would surprise me anymore, Seth.'

'Thank you. But *that* I couldn't do. As for you . . . well, I like you, so I'm giving you a chance to get out.'

Hollis listened to the sounds of the helicopter's turbines running up. He said to Alevy, 'How about Surikov and his granddaughter, Seth? Did you lie to me?'

'I'm afraid so. They'll stay in Moscow awhile longer. They have to or the KGB will know that Surikov blew the Charm School graduates. We can't have that until the FBI is ready to round them all up. You know that.'

'You're a bastard.'

'I'm a patriot.'

Bullets began slapping into the log walls again, and Hollis could now hear the deep chatter of a heavy machine gun. The walls began to splinter, and Hollis lay prone on the floor. 'Get down.'

Several rounds hit the radios, and they disintegrated. The porcelain stove shattered, and smoke and ash billowed out of it. The three corpses on the far wall took some hits, and Hollis could hear the sound of popping body gases and smelled death. Hollis reached out and pulled an AK-47 toward him, then rolled to the door and fired at some nearby muzzle flashes. 'They're here, at the front of the cabin now.'

Alevy didn't seem interested. He remained sitting with his back to the wall. He remarked, 'And to add insult to injury, Sam, my people are going to smuggle the Kellums out. They'll get teaching positions in our American Charm School. They're quite bright as it turns out and willing to cooperate in exchange for not being thrown in the Moskva.'

Hollis reloaded another magazine. 'What a fucking mess. The people you were supposed to rescue here are going to die –'

'Right. Quite painless though. Sarin is quick.'

'And Lisa and I were supposed to die. And Burov the sadist lives, and the fucking Kellums live, and Surikov and his granddaughter who risked their lives for us are stuck here, and Dodson whom you all wanted to kill to shut him up is going from a living death here to another living death in your goddamned new Charm School –'

'That's about it. Except taking Dodson was your idea. I wanted the general. Anyway, Charlie Banks and his crowd are quite pleased. Your people are sort of pleased because the honor of the missing airmen remains unblighted. It would be hard to explain all those traitors –'

'They weren't –'

'They *were*. And needless to say, the CIA got what it wanted.'

'And you? Did you get what *you* wanted, Seth?'

'I guess. Maybe I just got what I had coming.'

Hollis looked at Alevy in the dim light. 'Do you understand how monstrous this is?'

'Absolutely. But do you realize how brilliant it is? This is a classic turnaround of a massive espionage offensive against us into an unmitigated disaster for them. We've bought a little more time for the fat, decadent West to consume more designer jeans, play at democracy, talk about peace and understanding, write diet books –'

Hollis sprang across the room and knocked Alevy over. He pinned his shoulders against the floor and put his face near Alevy's. 'Do you know what you've *done*? Has everyone in Washington gone stark fucking crazy?'

Alevy shouted, 'They're scared shitless is what they are! Get off your high horse, General Hollis. This is bottom-line survival.' He pushed Hollis away and sat up.

'Then you're all missing the goddamned point!' Hollis shouted. 'We can't survive by becoming like them. People like Surikov and his granddaughter . . . we're their light in this darkness . . . don't you understand, Seth? I've just gone through two fucking weeks of totalitarianism. You and I lived here for two years, Seth. Jesus Christ, man, haven't you learned anything –?'

Alevy pulled his pistol and pointed it at Hollis' face. 'I don't want a goddamned lecture. I know what the hell I did. At least admit that it had to be done. Or just shut up.'

Hollis lay prone on the floor and listened to the gunfire getting closer. He could hear men shouting orders and guessed they were getting their nerve up for the final assault across the open space between the road and the cabin. He took a deep breath and said to Alevy, 'Alright . . . I understand.' He thought of Jane Landis, then of Tim Landis and their little boy. He recalled the quiet suffering of General Austin, the understated bravery of Lewis Poole, and the tragedy of all the Americans he'd met here and their Russian wives and their children. He remembered the female doctor who had checked him over and remembered the other political prisoners who were victims of this madness. He even had a passing thought about the students, especially those who had raised their voices at the VFW hall. And there were the five or six hundred Border Guards, who to some extent were blameless, and there was Burov's wife, his mother, and his daughter. 'Damn it!'

Alevy threw away his pistol and grabbed one of the AK-47s from the floor. He stood at the window and fired a continuous stream of bullets until the rifle overheated and jammed. He threw it down and stooped for another rifle as a burst of bullets tore at the shards of glass and window frame.

Hollis picked up the remaining AK-47 and moved to the window that faced away from the gunfire. He raised the butt of the rifle and smashed away the glass and wood.

Alevy looked up at him. 'Where are you going?'

'Home.'

'No, you're not.' Alevy swung his rifle around and aimed it at Hollis. 'You know too much now.'

'That's why I'm going home.' Hollis lifted himself into the window. 'Let's go.'

Alevy fired a burst of rounds into the wall above Hollis' head. 'Stop!'

'No. I'm doing it my way, Seth. Not yours.'

'You *owe* me, Sam. For saving Lisa's life. Cover me.'

'I don't owe you a thing. Hey, Seth.'

'What?'

'You cover *me*. Okay?'

Alevy looked at him across the dark cabin. 'Sure. I always have.'

Hollis nodded. 'Thanks, Seth.'

'Yeah. You too. I'll be right behind you, Sam. See you on board.'

Hollis rolled out the window and lay still on the ground. Suddenly, he heard a shout from a chorus of voices. 'OOORAH!' The air was split by the deafening sound of AK-47s on full automatic, coming closer as the Border Guards began their final charge across the open space toward the cabin.

Hollis ran toward the clearing, keeping the solid cabin at his back. Stray rounds streaked by to his right and left, but he ignored them, focusing only on the field ahead. He reached the grass and dove into a prone position.

Behind him he could hear footsteps beating on the soft earth.

He watched Alevy coming toward him, then Alevy seemed to stumble and fall, disappearing in the tall grass. Suddenly, the undulating grass became the swells of Haiphong harbor, and the figure trying to rise up out of it was not Alevy, but Ernie Simms. A voice called out, 'Sam! Sam!' And Hollis could not in truth tell if it were Alevy's voice or Simms' voice echoing down through the years. Hollis stood and ran toward the voice.

He reached Alevy crawling through the yellow grass, and Alevy clutched at Hollis' leg, then rolled to his side as Hollis dropped low beside him. 'Sam . . .'

Hollis tore open Alevy's tunic and saw the dark stain spreading over his snow-white shirt. 'Damn it, Seth.'

Alevy rolled over on his back, and Hollis pressed the heel of his hand against the sucking chest wound. 'Lay still, Seth. Shallow breathing.' But already Hollis saw the frothy blood bubbling from Alevy's lips. 'Easy. It's alright.'

Alevy's eyes seemed clouded, and his breathing was coming in gasps, but he spoke distinctly, 'Go . . . go . . . they're waiting . . . don't let them wait . . .'

Hollis hesitated just a split second, then said, 'Not this time. We sink or swim together, buddy.' He grabbed Alevy under the arms and began to pull him up but felt Alevy's body stiffen, then go limp. He looked into Seth Alevy's dead open eyes and let him slip easily back on to the damp Russian earth. Hollis drew a deep breath, then said softly, 'I think I'm going to miss you, my friend.' And when the KGB found his body, Hollis thought, they would know that it was Seth Alevy who had beaten them, and that there would be no tit for tat this time.

Hollis rose slowly to one knee and peered out into the dark clearing. The helicopter was gone, and he looked up and saw it rising vertically into the air. He looked at his watch and saw it was 3:48. They had waited, but not long enough. He supposed that O'Shea, Brennan, and Mills had seen to it that Lisa did not leave the helicopter. Still, he thought, she might be out there in the dark field. He stood, cradled his rifle, and began moving toward the center of the field where the helicopter had been.

He heard a noise behind him and glanced back at the radio cabin. It was burning now, and by the light of the fire he saw the figures of KGB Border Guards moving into the clearing, coming toward him.

Hollis turned back toward the field and continued walking, though with each step he was more certain that she wasn't out there. He was glad she wasn't, but he would have liked to see her once more just the same.

He reached the place where the helicopter had been and stood in the flattened grass. He looked up but could no longer see the aircraft in the dark sky.

Hollis heard a noise, and he looked out toward the opposite tree line. He could make out another line of men moving in his direction. The searchlights on the closest watchtowers were turned inward now, and two of them were sweeping the field. One of them caught him in its beam.

From the direction of the cabin, a voice called out in Russian, 'Surrender. You are surrounded. Put your hands up.'

Hollis dropped to one knee and fired back toward the cabin, then turned and fired at the advancing line approaching from the other direction. Both lines of men hit the ground, but he drew no return fire as they couldn't shoot toward each other. He watched them coming in short rushes through the knee-high grass, then taking cover, both skirmish lines of KGB Border Guards converging on him. The spotlight remained fixed on him, and he fired along its beam until it went black.

'Surrender! Stand up!'

Hollis fired off the remaining rounds from his rifle, then drew his pistol and waited. Both groups of men were within fifty meters of him, and they were calling to one another. Someone gave an order, and the group from the direction of the cabin dropped low into prone firing positions. The other line knelt with rifles raised towards him, like a firing squad. He fired his pistol at them and waited for the fusillade of bullets to rip into him.

He waited, but nothing happened. He looked toward the men

who had been kneeling, but he couldn't see them any longer, and he realized they must have also dropped into prone firing positions in the grass. He called out in Russian, 'I do not surrender! Come and get me!'

He waited, but no one replied. He heard someone retching, then a moan, and he understood. The nerve gas, coming from the north, had reached the first group of men before it had reached him. He noticed, too, that the spotlights from the towers were no longer moving but were pointed motionless into the air.

He looked back at the guards who had come from the cabin, downwind of him, and he saw they were still moving through the grass. Hollis stood with his pistol drawn, waiting for the nerve gas or the last of the Border Guards, and knowing it made no difference which reached him first.

The sky was clear, and the gentle wind still blew from the north. He felt no particular fear of dying, knowing in his heart that but for a matter of minutes in Haiphong harbor, he might have spent the last fifteen years of his life here. Fate had given him some extra time, but it was borrowed time, and now the debt had to be paid, as he always knew it would.

There was already an occupied grave for him at Arlington, and he didn't suppose it mattered that the ashes in it were not his, but were those of some unfortunate Russian. Everyone had paid their respects and were getting on with their lives. This death then was somewhat redundant, just as the deaths of the airmen here were redundant. In truth, he knew that by playing Alevy's game he had contributed to this outcome, and he thought it fitting that he should be here with the men who would never go home.

And in truth, too, he knew he could have left that cabin two minutes sooner. But for reasons better known to Alevy than to himself, he had stayed, had found himself too drawn to Alevy and too involved with the man's seductive madness.

But Alevy he could forgive, because Alevy was willing to die for his convictions. Someone such as Charles Banks

648

and the people who played global chess in Washington and Moscow were another matter. They were the ones, he thought, who needed a whiff of cordite, dead bodies, and gas to bring them back to reality.

Hollis closed his eyes and conjured up a picture of Lisa the first time he'd ever really noticed her, in the duty office the night of Fisher's disappearance. Looking back, he realized that something had passed between them that night and that he knew where it was going to lead; just as he'd also known that the business of Fisher and Dodson would eventually lead him to this moment. But as these were conflicting premonitions, he had tried to distance himself from her. If he had any regrets, it was that he should have loved her more, should have given her what she gave with such enthusiasm to him.

The wind picked up, and he took a deep breath. The pine and the damp earth still smelled good, its essence, at least, untainted by the deadly manmade miasma. He felt a slight nausea and an odd tingling sensation on his skin. He heard a man cry out briefly in the distance, then another one moaned. He wondered how the gas was killing the Russians downwind of him before it had killed him.

Somewhere in the back of his mind – he heard a steady flapping sound, like the wings of dark angels, he thought, coming to lift his soul away. The wind picked up and he opened his eyes. The sky was pitch black above him, and he saw the darkness descending on him like some palpable thing. Then he saw the wings of the angel whirling in the night sky and understood that it was no gas-induced apparition but a helicopter, clearing the air around him, creating a small pocket of life in the dead zone.

Hollis shook his head. 'No! Go away!' Haiphong harbor was his second chance. He deserved that one, but he didn't deserve this one. 'Go away!'

The helicopter slipped to the side, and he saw her kneeling in the open door, ten feet above him, her hand extended toward him. Beside her was Brennan, and in the window was Mills. In the pilot's seat O'Shea was flying with far more skill than he was capable of.

Hollis shook his head and waved them off.

'Sam! Please!' She leaned farther out the door, and Brennan pulled her back, then threw a looped line down to him.

The helicopter hovered a moment, and Hollis saw it was being buffeted by its own downdraft. He realized that O'Shea would sit there until he either crashed or was killed by the gas. Hollis drew the looped line under his arms and felt his body leave the ground, swinging through the air, then he felt nothing.

42

Sam Hollis felt his body swinging through the black void. The sensations of weightlessness and motion were soothing and pleasant, and he wanted it to last, but by stages he realized he was not floating but sitting still.

He opened his eyes to blackness and stared at distant lights until they came closer and took the familiar form of a cockpit instrument panel. He focused on a clock in front of him and saw it was nearly six. He assumed it was A.M. He turned his head and looked at O'Shea, sitting in the pilot's seat beside him. 'Where the hell are you going?'

O'Shea glanced at him. 'Hello. Feeling alright?'

'I feel fine. Answer my question, Captain.'

Lisa leaned between the seats and kissed him on the cheek. She took his hand. 'Hello, Sam.'

'Hello to you. Hello to everyone back there. Where the hell are we going? The embassy is only twenty minutes –'

Bert Mills, sitting behind him, said, 'We can't go to the embassy with this load, General. Captain O'Shea, Bill, and I are officially in Helsinki. You and Lisa are officially dead. Dodson died almost twenty years ago, and Burov is a major complication.'

Hollis nodded. He knew all that. 'We're going to the gulf.'

O'Shea replied, 'Yes, sir. Gulf of Finland. To rendezvous with a ship.' O'Shea added, 'Congratulations on your promotion.'

Typical military, Hollis thought. No congratulations on being alive, but promotions were important. He grunted. 'Thanks.'

Mills asked, 'How do you feel physically?'

Hollis moved his legs, then his arms, but didn't feel any lack of coordination. His vision was good, and his other senses seemed alright. He smelled a faint odor of vomit and realized it was coming from his sweat shirt. He hadn't voided his bladder or bowels, which was good. He realized the right side of his face was numb and put his fingers to his cheek, feeling a gauze pad over the area where Burov's teeth had ripped his flesh. The numbness, he assumed, was caused by a local anesthetic and not the effects of nerve gas. 'I'm alright.' He turned in his seat and stared at Mills. 'You administered pralidoxime?'

Mills nodded, acknowledging that what they were discussing was the antidote for nerve gas, not sleeping gas.

'Did I convulse?'

'Slight. But if you feel alright, then you're alright. That's how that stuff is.'

Lisa said, 'I didn't think sleeping gas could make you so sick.'

No one replied.

Hollis turned and looked around the dark cabin. Lisa was kneeling on the floor between the seats, Mills was directly behind Hollis, and Brennan was sleeping peacefully in the seat behind O'Shea. In the two rear seats were Dodson and Burov, odd seating companions, he thought. They both were held upright by shoulder harnesses.

Mills said, 'Dodson will be okay. He just needs a few square meals. Burov . . . well, he needs his face rebuilt. I hope there's no brain damage.'

'He started with brain damage,' Hollis replied. Hollis felt Lisa squeeze his hand, and remembering his one regret, squeezed it in return. He said, 'Good to see you.'

She said, 'We waited for you, but . . .'

'You weren't supposed to wait, and you weren't supposed to come back and risk everything.'

Mills said, 'We took a vote, and I lost. Nothing personal, General. Just for the record.' Mills added, 'Also for the record, you and Seth shouldn't have waited for me. But thanks.'

Hollis turned back to the front and scanned the instrument

panel, his eyes resting on the fuel gauge. 'How far are we from the gulf?'

O'Shea replied, 'Based on average airspeed and elapsed traveling time, I estimate about a hundred and fifty klicks. I have a land navigational chart, but I can't see any landmarks below. We're on a heading for Leningrad. When we see the lights of the city, we'll take a new heading.'

Hollis looked at the airspeed indicator and the altimeter. They were travelling at 150kph at 1,600 meters. He read the torque gauge and tachometer gauges, then checked the oil pressure and oil temperature, battery temperature, and the turbine outlet temperature. Considering the load weight and the distance already traveled, the helicopter was performing well. The only problem he could see was with the fuel: there didn't seem to be enough of it. He tapped the fuel gauge to see if the needle moved.

O'Shea thought Hollis was drawing attention to the problem and said softly, 'I don't know.' He forced a smile and using an old pilot's joke said, 'We might have to swim the last hundred yards.'

Hollis replied, 'You burned some fuel coming back for me.'

O'Shea didn't reply.

No one spoke for some time, and Hollis noted that for all the euphoria they must have felt over a narrow escape, the mood in the cabin was anything but jubilant. He suspected that everyone's thoughts were flashing back to the Charm School and forward to the Gulf of Finland. The here and now, as Brennan was demonstrating, was irrelevant. He said to Mills, 'If I understand you correctly, you, Brennan, and my former aide here are still in Helsinki and most probably will not be returning to Moscow to resume your duties, diplomatic or otherwise.'

Mills replied, 'That's a safe assumption.'

'And Burov and Major Dodson will disappear into the American Charm School.'

Mills nodded tentatively.

'And Lisa and I will get a ticker tape parade in New York.'

Mills stayed silent for a moment, then said, 'Well . . . did Seth speak to you?'

'Yes. I know that Lisa and I were not supposed to be on this helicopter. But now that we are . . .'

'Well . . . I suppose we can say your helicopter accident was a case of mistaken identity. I guess we can work out your resurrection.'

'Thank you. You worked out our death real well.'

Mills smiled with embarrassment.

Lisa looked from one to the other. 'I'm not completely following this, as usual.'

Hollis looked at her. 'It wasn't sleeping gas. It was nerve gas. Poison.'

'What . . . ?'

'There will be no negotiating or swap for the others. Everyone back there, including Seth, is dead.'

'No!'

'Yes. You and I were supposed to be dead too.'

'Why . . . ?' She looked at Mills. 'Seth . . . dead? No, he can't be *dead*. Bert said he would be taken prisoner and exchanged for Burov. Bert?'

Mills stood. 'Sit here.' He took her arm and moved her into his seat. Mills squatted on the floor and drew a deep breath. 'It's very complicated to explain, Lisa.'

Hollis said, 'No, it's not, Bert. It's very simple. You just don't want to say it out loud.' Hollis said to Lisa, 'The State Department, White House, Defense Intelligence, and the CIA cut a deal. Mrs Ivanova's Charm School is closed forever, and Mrs Johnson's Charm School is about to open.'

Mills said, 'I don't think you should say anything else, General. I don't think Seth would have wanted her to know any of this.'

Hollis ignored him and continued, 'The two seemingly

insolvable problems were, one, how to identify the Russians in America, and two, how to deal with the Americans held prisoner in Russia. A man named General Surikov provided the solution to the first problem, which allowed Seth to provide his solution to the second.' Hollis related to Lisa what Alevy had told him.

Lisa stared at Hollis' reflection in the Plexiglass window as she listened. When Hollis finished, she said in a surprisingly strong voice, 'And that was all Seth's idea?'

Hollis nodded. 'To his credit, he felt remorse over the consequences of his finest moment. And he couldn't bring himself to let you die. He was ambivalent about me right to the end. I shouldn't even tell you that, but you have a right to know everything.' He added, 'That's what you always wanted.'

'I don't think that changes how I feel about him right now.' She thought a moment. 'I can't picture all those people dead – All those men, their wives, the children . . . Jane, the kidnapped American women . . .' She shook her head. 'I can't believe he made up that lie about sleeping gas and prisoner exchanges.' She looked at Hollis. 'You knew it was a lie, didn't you?'

'It seemed a bit too good and didn't fit the facts.'

She nodded but said nothing.

Hollis said to Mills. 'I consider that my life and Lisa's life are still in danger.'

Mills seemed uncomfortable. 'I'm not the source of the danger. We'll work something out.'

'Like what? Life tenure in the new Charm School?'

'I think that all Seth ever wanted from you two is a promise never to reveal a word of this to anyone.'

Hollis noted that Mills' voice had that tone in it that one uses in speaking of recently deceased heroes. *The legend begins.* Hollis looked at Lisa and saw she had her hand over her face and tears were streaming down her cheeks.

Hollis turned back toward the front and concentrated on the problem at hand. His eyes swept the gauges again, and he noted an increase in oil temperature and a drop in pressure. The fuel needle was in the red, but the warning light was not on yet. He said to O'Shea, 'You've done an admirable job of burning fuel. Reduce airspeed.'

'I can't.'

'Why not?'

'Well, according to my instructions, which I opened only after I was airborne, our rendezvous with the ship must occur before dawn. The ship won't identify itself after daylight. There may be Soviet naval and merchant vessels in the area.'

'I see.'

O'Shea added, 'First light in that part of the world isn't until zero seven twenty-two hours. We're cutting it close even at this speed.'

Hollis nodded. He'd thought the problem was only fuel. Now it was the sunrise. Hollis looked at the airspeed indicator, then the more accurate ground-speed indicator. Airspeed was still 150 kph, but actual ground speed was only 130. They were obviously bucking into a strong headwind.

Hollis looked out the windshield. Thin, scudding clouds flew at them, and occasionally he could feel the turbulence of the gusting north wind.

The sky above was layered with clouds, and there was no starlight. Below, Hollis could not see a single light. He'd flown this route to Leningrad with Aeroflot, and he knew this part of Russia. Much of it was an underpopulated expanse of forest, small lakes, and marshes. Last autumn he'd taken the Red Arrow Express from Leningrad back to Moscow, and the train had passed through the same country he'd seen from the air. The villages had been dilapidated, and the farms badly kept. It was a cold, unforgiving stretch of country below, not the sort of place where one would want to force-land a helicopter.

Hollis said to O'Shea, 'Did you try a higher altitude?'

'No, sir. I didn't want to burn any more fuel on the climb.'

Hollis took the controls on his side. 'Take a break. Stretch.'

O'Shea released the controls and stretched his arms and legs. 'Do you want to fly it from the right-hand seat?'

'No, but I don't want to try a crossover either. I'll let you sit in the pilot's seat as long as you don't take it seriously.'

'Yes, sir.'

Hollis knew that helicopter flying, which needed continuous concentration and constant hands-on, could fatigue a solo pilot within an hour. O'Shea had been behind the stick for close to two hours, alone with the falling fuel needle.

Hollis said, 'Let's go upstairs.' He increased the collective pitch for a slow rate of climb, increased the throttle, and held the craft level with the cyclic stick. The increased torque caused the nose to yaw to the left, and O'Shea reminded him, 'It's backwards.'

'Thank you, Captain. Does that mean our fuel level is rising?'

'No, sir.'

Hollis pressed down on the right rudder pedal and put the helicopter in longitudinal trim. 'It seems to handle alright. But I wouldn't want to have to try something tricky like landing on a pitching ship in the dark with a strong wind.'

O'Shea glanced at Hollis to see if he was making a joke. O'Shea said, 'Well, I've logged enough time on this to give it a try. But if you want to take it in, you're the skipper.'

'We'll arm-wrestle for the honor as we make our final approach.'

Mills looked from Hollis to O'Shea. Pilots, he thought, like CIA operatives, resorted to black humor when things were least funny.

Hollis watched the altimeter needles moving. At three thousand meters he arrested the ascent, and the airspeed climbed back to 150 kph. The ground-speed indicator read nearly the same. 'That's better.'

O'Shea said, 'Maybe I should have climbed earlier.'

'Maybe. Maybe the headwinds were stronger up here earlier.'

'It's hard to know without being able to call for weather conditions.'

'Right.' Hollis familiarized himself with the controls and with the instruments. He played around with the data available: speed, altitude, load, fuel, elapsed flight time, estimated distance to landing – but he couldn't say with any certainty whether or not they'd see the Gulf of Finland before dawn or for that matter even see the Gulf of Finland or the dawn.

O'Shea seemed to be thinking along the same lines. 'If we spot a landmark, we can figure our distance to landing. But I don't have a feeling for that fuel gauge.'

Hollis replied, 'We have the speed we need to arrive on time at the only landing site we have. Those are close parameters, and there's nothing more we can do at the moment.'

O'Shea said, 'Maybe we'll pick up a tailwind.'

'Maybe.'

Mills, who had been listening intently, asked, 'What if we pick up another headwind?'

O'Shea glanced back at him. 'No use worrying about something we can't do anything about.'

Mills said to Hollis, 'Basic question, General – what are the odds?'

Hollis replied, 'I just got here. I'm not giving odds on *your* game plan.'

Mills asked, 'Look, would it help if we dumped some weight?'

'I assume you've already done that.'

O'Shea replied, 'Yes. Coats, baggage, drinking water, some hardware, and all that. Lightened us maybe a hundred pounds.'

Mills said, 'I had something else in mind.'

Hollis inquired, '*Whom* did you have in mind, Bert?'

'Well . . . Dodson or Burov, I guess.'

'You need them,' Hollis said. 'Would you like *me* to jump?'

'No. I don't want Captain O'Shea flying again. He makes me nervous.' Mills smiled, then added, 'Look, we *can* get rid of Burov if it would make a difference.'

Neither Hollis nor O'Shea replied.

Mills said, 'Well, forget it. I'm not playing that lifeboat game. That's your decision if you want to make it.'

Hollis rather liked Mills when Mills was being Mills. But when Mills was trying to be Alevy, the result was an affected cynicism without his boss's style or moral certainty.

Lisa, who hadn't spoken in some time, said, 'I don't want to hear about any more murders, please.'

No one said anything, and the only sound was from the turbines and rotor blades.

Hollis asked O'Shea, 'Have you sighted any aircraft?'

'No, sir.'

Hollis nodded. He didn't think anyone at the Charm School had had the opportunity or ability to radio out any information. But by now, the Soviets might have discovered that their facility had been wiped out, and they might have made the connection between the missing Aeroflot Mi-28 helicopter and the disaster at the Charm School. And if they had put it all together, they were probably thinking of the only safe place other than the American embassy that an Mi-28 could reach: the Gulf of Finland.

Hollis turned to Mills and asked, 'Did you people consult any Air Force types when you put this scheme together?'

'Of course,' Mills said in a slightly offended tone.

'How did you expect to escape Soviet radar detection?'

'Well,' Mills replied, 'the Air Force guys we spoke to figured we'd be out of reach of Moscow's radar by the time they drew any conclusions. We knew we couldn't be spotted visually with our navigation lights off.' Mills said to O'Shea, 'You have some technical written orders, don't you?'

O'Shea replied, 'I was supposed to get down low to avoid airborne radar – to blend in with the ground clutter – and take an evasive course toward the gulf. But I sort of figured that the available fuel wouldn't allow for that.'

'You were sort of right,' Hollis said. 'Even if they're not looking for us, we're going to show up on someone's screen as we approach Leningrad's air traffic control area.'

O'Shea said, 'At that point we're going to have to get in low, below the radar. We can risk a visual sighting over a populated area at that time because we'll be in the home stretch. We should be landed before they can scramble a flight to intercept us.' He looked at Hollis. 'What do you think?'

'I think someone forgot to consider Red Navy radar that watches everything in the gulf. I think if they're specifically looking for us, they'll find us. I'm going on the assumption they haven't connected an Mi-28 Aeroflot helicopter bearing a certain ID number with the nerve gas attack on their training facility outside of Borodino.'

Mills said, 'We're gambling that no one even knows that the Charm School is dead until someone comes by in the morning with a delivery or someone calls from Moscow or something. As for the helicopter, I changed the ID number, and they're probably still looking for the crash site of P-113. This is a very compartmentalized country, and information does not travel freely. Therefore connections aren't easily made. That's working in our favor.'

Hollis replied, 'You may be right.' He asked O'Shea, 'How are we supposed to rendezvous with the ship in the gulf?'

O'Shea glanced at a piece of paper clipped to the instrument panel. 'Well, first we look for Pulkovo Airport, which you and I would recognize from the air. Then we drop below two hundred meters to get under the radar. About a klick due south of the control tower, we take a three-hundred-ten-degree heading. We'll pass over the coast west of Leningrad and continue out until we see the lighthouse on the long jetty. From a point directly over the lighthouse we take a three-hundred-forty-degree heading and maintain a ground speed of eighty kph for ten minutes. According to what it says here, somewhere down in the main shipping lane we'll see three yellow fog lights that form a triangle. Those lights are on the fantail of a freighter heading out of Leningrad. The lights won't blink or project a beam that might attract unwanted attention. But they should glow bright enough for us to see them at two hundred meters' altitude and about half a klick radial distance around the ship – even in one of those gulf fogs. We land in the center of that triangle, deep-six the chopper, and the ship takes us to Liverpool. O'Shea added, 'I'll buy dinner when we get to London.'

Hollis glanced at O'Shea but said nothing.

They continued north for another fifteen minutes, and Hollis saw that the ground speed was dropping, indicating they were picking up headwinds again. The needle on the fuel gauge was buried in the red zone. One of the things Hollis recalled from the Mi-28 manual – which he'd purchased indirectly from an Aeroflot mechanic for blue jeans and American cigarettes – was that the fuel gauge shouldn't be trusted. In fact, he noticed that though the needle was deeper in the red, the fuel warning light still wasn't on.

O'Shea said, 'Want me to take it?'

'No. I need the practice.'

A few minutes later O'Shea said, 'We should have seen the lights of Leningrad by now.'

Hollis nodded.

Mills asked, 'Will we have any warning before the fuel runs out?'

Hollis replied, 'Do you want a warning?'

'What do you mean?'

'Do you want to land in Russia?'

'I guess not. I guess we just keep flying until we go down.'

'I guess so,' Hollis replied.

Five minutes later the fuel warning light flickered. A few seconds after that a reedy voice said in Russian, 'Your fuel reserves are nearly gone.'

O'Shea replied to the recording, 'Screw you.'

The voice said, 'Make preparations to terminate your flight.'

Hollis and O'Shea exchanged glances.

Mills asked, 'What did he say?'

Hollis replied, 'There're only forty-two shopping days left until Christmas.'

Lisa said to Mills, 'Fuel is low.'

Mills nodded. 'I figured that's what he said.'

They continued on north through the black night. No one spoke, as if, Hollis thought, everyone were waiting for the sound of the turbines to cut out. Finally, Lisa leaned forward and put her hand on his shoulder. 'How are you?'

'Fine. How're things back in business class?'

'You tell me. How much fuel is left after that announcement?'

'It's more a matter of how much flight time you can get out of the available fuel. That depends on load, temperature, humidity, winds, altitude, speed, engine performance, maneuvers, and the good Lord.'

'Should I pray?'

'Can't hurt.'

'I'll let you fly.'

'Okay. You pray. I'll fly. Later we'll switch.'

Lisa looked at Hollis' hands on the controls. This was a different Sam Hollis from the one she'd known in Moscow or in the Charm School. It struck her that he belonged in this aircraft, and she recalled what Seth Alevy had said to her at Sheremetyevo Airport about the world of pilots: They were a different breed, but she thought she could love him just the same.

The voice said again, 'Your fuel reserves are nearly gone,' then, 'Make preparations to terminate your flight.'

No one spoke for some minutes, then O'Shea said, 'Hey, did you hear about the Aeroflot pilot who ran low on fuel crossing the ocean and dumped fuel to save weight?'

No one laughed, and O'Shea said, 'It's funnier on the ground.'

Hollis looked at the instrument panel clock. It was 6:59. Sunrise was in twenty-three minutes, after which time the freighter was to turn off its landing lights, making it indistinguishable from any other freighter in the area. At their present speed they could cover about sixty kilometers before sunrise. But for the last ten minutes of the flight they would have to reduce their speed to eighty kph, according to the instructions. Hollis said to O'Shea, 'Our options are two: We can decrease speed, conserve fuel, and we'll probably make it to our rendezvous, but it will be well after dawn. Or we can increase speed and our rate of fuel consumption, which is the only way we could possibly make our rendezvous before dawn. Of course, if we increase fuel consumption, we may not get that far. What's your professional opinion, Captain?'

O'Shea replied as though he'd given it some thought. 'I'm betting that there's more fuel left than we think. That's just my gut feeling. I say full speed ahead.'

Mills said, 'I vote to cut speed and conserve fuel. Our primary obligation is not to get to that freighter before dawn – it's to get out of the Soviet Union, and out of the reach of the KGB. I want to make sure we reach the gulf. I'd rather go into the drink than have them get their hands on us. We know too much.'

Hollis replied, 'You have no vote, Bert. This is a technical matter. But your opinion is noted. Lisa?'

'I'm with Bert. I'd rather drown than run out of gas over land.'

Hollis nodded. 'Should we wake Brennan for his opinion?' Hollis heard the sound of popping bubble gum, followed by Brennan's voice saying, 'We dead yet?'

Mills replied, 'We're working on it.'

Brennan stretched and cleared his throat. 'Hey, Colonel, glad to see you up and around. How you doing?'

'Fine. I'm a general.'

'Oh, right. Sorry. Hey, did we do a tit for tat on them, or what? I mean to tell you, we kicked some ass. Right?'

'Right. Did you hear our problem?'

'Yeah. That's a tough one. Whatever you guys decide is okay with me.'

Hollis wished everyone was as unopinionated.

Brennan added, 'I hate flying. Glad we'll be down soon.'

O'Shea said, 'Your call, General.'

The disembodied voice said again, 'Your fuel reserves are nearly gone. Make preparations to terminate your flight.'

'Full speed ahead.' Hollis pushed forward on the cyclic stick, dropping the craft into a nose-down attitude, and simultaneously increased the throttle and adjusted the collective stick. The airspeed indicator rose to 180 kph with a corresponding rise in ground speed. Hollis said, 'Never believe a Russian.'

They continued north. The fuel warning light glowed steady red, and the recorded voice gave its warning in the same indifferent tone. Hollis had always thought that these cockpit recordings should get shriller each time they came on. But tape players did not fear death.

O'Shea called out, 'Look!'

Hollis, Mills, O'Shea, and Brennan looked to where O'Shea was pointing. Slightly to starboard of their flight path, on the black distant horizon, they could see a faint glow. Hollis announced, 'Leningrad.'

O'Shea said, 'About twenty klicks. Maybe seven minutes' flight time.'

Hollis looked at the clock. It was 7:04. Eighteen minutes to sunrise. If they got to Pulkovo in seven minutes and changed heading, they would get to the lighthouse in about another five minutes. Then a ten-minute flight to the rendezvous point with the freighter. That sounded like twenty-two minutes.

O'Shea said, 'We're racing the sun now, General.'

Hollis replied, 'I thought it was the fuel gauge. You're confusing me.'

O'Shea smiled grimly.

Hollis increased the craft's speed to two hundred kph.

O'Shea observed, 'We're operating at full power at the end of a long flight. Do you trust these turbines?'

Hollis glanced at his instruments. The turbine outlet temperature was redlined, and so was the oil temperature. 'Never trust the reds.' Hollis called back to Brennan. 'So what made you come back for this, Bill?'

'Oh, I don't know. Seth Alevy said you were in trouble. That's why Captain O'Shea volunteered too. Right, Captain?'

'Right.' O'Shea said to Hollis, 'I want you to reconsider my evaluation report.'

'I'll think about it.' Hollis began a long sloping descent.

O'Shea said to him, 'How many hours of rotary wing do you have, General?'

Hollis glanced at the clock. 'Counting the last thirty minutes, one hour.'

O'Shea said, 'Seriously.'

'I don't know . . . ten or twelve. Is this a test?'

'No. I'm just wondering who should put it down.'

'If it's a power-off landing in the freezing gulf, you can do it. If it's power on, on the deck of the freighter, I'll do it.'

'Okay.'

The Mi-28 continued descending, and Hollis noticed its ground speed bleeding off, indicating increasing headwinds. At five hundred meters its airspeed was still 200 kph, but its actual speed relative to the ground, which was the speed that mattered, was not quite 130 kph. Hollis knew they were encountering those infamous winter winds from the Gulf of Finland, winds so strong and steady that they sometimes caused the gulf to rise as much as five feet, flooding Leningrad. He thought about heavy seas and their freighter rising, falling, rolling, and pitching in them.

Hollis could now see the main arteries leading into the city and saw some predawn traffic below.

Leningrad. The most un-Russian city in Russia. A city of culture, style, and liberal pretensions. But a city where the KGB was reputed to be particularly nasty, a counterweight to the westward-looking populace. Hollis had sometimes liked Leningrad and felt some sense of loss as he flew over it for the last time.

O'Shea said, 'I think that's the Moscow highway down there. So Pulkovo should be to port.'

Mills said, 'I haven't heard the recording for a while.'

665

Hollis replied, 'I think he gave up on us.'

O'Shea said, 'Is that it?' He pointed out the left side window.

Hollis looked and saw the familiar blue-white aircraft lights. 'Yes.' He added, 'That was a remarkable piece of land navigation, Captain.'

'Thank you, sir. I tried to allow for wind drift, but I wasn't sure how much we were being blown off our heading.'

'Apparently not enough to miss a whole city.' Hollis banked left as he increased the rate of descent. The altimeter read two hundred meters, and he leveled off. He estimated he was a kilometer south of Pulkovo's tower, and he took a heading of 310 degrees. They were so low now that Hollis could make out passengers in a bus below. He saw a few factories slide by and saw a train speeding away from the city. To the north, the great city of Leningrad seemed to grow brighter minute by minute as it wakened from its long autumn night.

O'Shea said, 'I think I see the gulf.'

Hollis looked out and could see where the scattered shore lights ended and a great expanse of black began. 'Another few minutes. Look for the lighthouse at the end of the jetty.'

The minutes passed in silence. The coast slipped below them, and they were suddenly out to sea. Hollis looked at the clock: 7:14.

Mills said, 'That's it. No going back.'

Hollis nodded. If they went down and survived the crash, survival time in the near-freezing gulf would be about fifteen minutes.

O'Shea pointed directly ahead. 'Lighthouse.'

'See it.' Hollis continued on and within a half kilometer of the lighthouse began to throttle back and pick up the nose. The ground speed hit eighty kph as he passed over the lighthouse on the end of the two-kilometer-long concrete jetty. He swung the nose around to the new heading of 340 degrees and noted the time on the clock: 7:17. 'Captain, keep the time.'

'Yes, sir.'

Hollis watched the compass and maintained the north-westerly heading but had no doubt that the north wind was blowing them off course. He tried to calculate how much drift there might be in a ten-minute flight if the wind was as strong as thirty to forty knots. He had a sudden desire to meet Mills' flight advisers. He said to Mills, 'What air force was that?'

'Excuse me?'

'The guys with whom you consulted.'

'Oh . . . what's the problem? Besides fuel, I mean?'

'Navigation. Two moving objects. He has to contend with the seas: we have to contend with the air.'

O'Shea observed, 'Sort of like threading a moving needle.'

'In the dark,' Hollis added.

Mills didn't reply.

Brennan said, 'I guess we only have one shot at this rendezvous.'

'O'Shea said, 'If that many.'

A voice said in Russian, 'Fuck you . . . I'll kill you all.'

Hollis enquired, 'Is that a prerecorded announcement?'

Brennan chuckled. 'I think that's our passenger in coach. What did he say?'

'He said he needs another shot of sodium pentothal,' Hollis replied. 'Bert, shut him up.'

Mills made his way to the rear and looked at Burov. He called out to Hollis, 'He's in bad shape already, General. I don't want to kill him.'

Burov said indistinctly through swollen lips, 'I'll have you all back in the cells.'

The recorded warning came on again, and Burov said, 'You see? Land this helicopter immediately.'

Hollis called back in Russian, 'Shut your mouth, Burov, or I'll throw you out.'

Burov fell silent.

Mills looked Dodson over and announced, 'Our other passenger seems okay.'

O'Shea said, 'Time, seven-nineteen, two minutes elapsed.'

Mills looked out the rear window toward the southeast. 'The sun is coming up.' He added, 'They won't take us aboard if it's light.'

Lisa asked, 'What choice do they have?'

Mills replied, 'Well, they have the choice of shutting off their landing lights. Then we wouldn't know what ship it is down there. All I know is that it's a freighter. I don't know anything else about the ship, not even its nationality. We're not supposed to know anything for security reasons, and I guess also so that we can't make a landing in the daylight and endanger the ship. All we know is to look for three yellow lights on a freighter.'

Hollis said, 'Maybe your friends in Washington picked a Soviet ship for us.'

Mills smiled weakly. 'That's not funny.'

Burov spoke in English through his broken teeth. 'Listen to me. Listen. Land this helicopter and let me out. You can make good your escape. I will guarantee you that no harm will come to the men and women at the school. You have my word on that.'

There was a silence in the cabin, then Hollis said to O'Shea, 'Take the controls.' He made his way to the rear of the cabin and stood over Burov, whose wrists were bound to the chair with steel flex. Hollis stared at Burov, and Burov stared back. Finally Hollis said, 'Would you like something for the pain?'

Burov didn't respond for a second, then shook his head.

'Are you thirsty?'

'Yes. Very.'

Hollis turned around. 'Anything left to drink?'

'Just this,' Mills said, handing him a flask. 'Cognac. Real stuff.'

Hollis took the flask and held it to Burov's blood-encrusted lips. Burov's eyes stayed on Hollis, then his mouth opened, and Hollis poured half the flask between Burov's lips. Burov coughed up dried blood, but got most of the cognac down. Hollis saw tears forming in the man's eyes and assumed it was because of the burning alcohol on his split lips and gums. Hollis said, 'We have no water.'

Burov didn't reply.

Hollis put the cap back on the flask and said to Burov, 'It's over, you know.'

Burov said nothing.

'Within a few minutes you will be either a prisoner on a ship or will be dead in the water. There's no other fate for you.'

Burov nodded.

'Do you pray?'

'No. Never.'

'But your mother taught you how.'

Burov didn't reply.

'You might consider it.'

Burov seemed to slump further into his seat, and his head dropped. 'I congratulate you. All of you. Please leave me alone.'

Hollis looked at Dodson's battered face, then looked back at Burov. Hollis said to Burov, 'You've got a lot to answer for. I'm going to see to it that you answer directly to Major Dodson on behalf of the other airmen.' Hollis moved to the port-side windows and looked out to the southeast. He saw a small red rim poking above the flat horizon, casting a pink twilight over the city of Leningrad. But out here, in the gulf, the waters were black. He went back to the copilot's chair and sat. 'I'll take it.'

Hollis looked at the clock: 7:21. About six minutes' flight time to their rendezvous site, but only one or two minutes to first light. They weren't going to reach the freighter before dawn.

O'Shea was looking intently out the front windshield. Mills and Brennan were looking out the port side, Lisa was looking out to starboard. They all searched the dark sea below. There were lights down there, Hollis saw, boats and channel markers, but no triangle of yellow lights.

As Hollis watched, the water became lighter, and he could

669

see its texture now, the rising swells picking up the new sunlight. At least, he thought, he'd seen the dawn, and regardless of what happened, it was a better dawn than it would have been in the Charm School.

O'Shea announced, 'It's seven twenty-seven. Elapsed flight time since the lighthouse is now ten minutes.'

Lisa said, 'I don't see it.'

Brennan said, 'I guess they've shut off their landing lights. Maybe we should just put it down on any ship. You see that big tanker out there? About ten o'clock, half a klick.'

Hollis could see the massive flat deck in the grey morning light. It was inviting, but like a woman beckoning from a dark doorway, it was not necessarily a safe bet. Hollis said, 'It may be a Soviet or East Bloc ship. We can't tell.'

Mills concurred. 'We agreed that we wouldn't fall into their hands. We owe that to our country as well as to ourselves.'

Brennan nodded. 'You're right. It could be a commie ship. I guess you find a lot of those here. I'd rather drown.'

Burov spoke. 'You can't be serious. Wouldn't you all rather live than die horribly in the cold water?'

Lisa replied, 'No.'

Brennan turned and said to Burov, 'I don't want to hear your voice again.'

Another few minutes passed, and the sky went from grey dawn to morning nautical light. Hollis could see the heavy cloud bank overhead now and the gulf mist below. Sea gulls and terns circled over the water, and in the distance he saw a rain squall. A typical dreary day in the Gulf of Finland.

Mills said, 'Well, he's killed the lights by now. He won't risk a Soviet ship seeing an Aeroflot helicopter land on his deck. I can't say I blame him.'

Lisa said, 'But I don't see anything that even looks like a freighter. I see a few tankers and a few fishing ships. I saw one warship with guns back there. We've missed him.'

O'Shea said, 'Maybe he's off course or we're off course. An air-sea rendezvous with radio silence is hit or miss.'

Hollis looked at his flight instruments. The Mi-28 had been pushed beyond its limits, and he found it ironic that the last Soviet product he would ever use was the best. Every component had performed admirably except the fuel gauge. He said to O'Shea, 'You were right about the fuel.'

'I figured that the gauge was an extension of Soviet life. They don't trust people to make rational choices, so they lie to them for their own good.' O'Shea smiled, then added without humor, 'But I think by now that empty means empty.'

Mills stopped looking out the window and sat back on the floor between the seats. 'Well, good try though.' He produced the flask, took a swig, and handed it to Brennan. Brennan drank and gave it to Lisa. She offered it to Hollis and O'Shea, who declined, O'Shea saying, 'I'm flying.' Lisa, Brennan, and Mills finished the flask.

Hollis looked out at the water below. The seas were high, and he could see white curling breakers rolling from north to south. At two hundred meters' altitude, his range of vision encompassed an area large enough to insure that he wouldn't miss the freighter even if he was two or three kilometers off course. Something was very wrong, and the thought crossed his mind that this was yet another Alevy double cross, a joke from the grave. But even if Alevy had wanted O'Shea, Brennan and Mills silenced, he had apparently promised to deliver Burov and one American, so it couldn't be that. Hollis realized just how much Alevy's thinking had affected *his* thinking for him to even consider such a thing. Yet, he would wager that the same thought had passed through everyone's mind.

O'Shea said, 'See those buoys? We've crossed out of the shipping lane.'

Hollis nodded. He suddenly put the craft into a steep right bank and headed southeast, into the rising sun, back toward Leningrad.

Mills asked, 'What are you doing?'

Hollis began a steep descent. Ahead, he could make out the lights of Leningrad about fifteen kilometers away.

Mills repeated, 'What are you doing?'

Hollis replied, 'I'm going on two assumptions. One is that the freighter did not reach the rendezvous point in time and is still steaming out of the harbor. Two, if that holds true, then the skipper of that boat feels some sense of failed duty, and if he sees us, he will come to our aid.' Hollis leveled the helicopter at less than one hundred meters above the churning sea and cut the speed to a slow forty kph.

O'Shea said, apropos of nothing. 'I feel fine. We did good.'

Mills concurred. 'We beat most of the odds, didn't we? We're here.'

Brennan said, 'We stole this chopper, got into the Charm School, rescued Dodson, kidnapped Burov, shot our way out, flew cross-country over Russia, and got to where we were supposed to be. Shit, as far as I'm concerned, we made it.'

Hollis said, 'I find it hard to refute that logic, Bill. If we had a bottle of champagne, I'd say pop it.'

Mills said, 'Damn, Seth was supposed to buy champagne at the Trade Center.'

At the mention of Alevy's name, there was a silence during which, Hollis thought, everyone was probably cursing him and blessing him at the same time. Such was the fate of men and women who move others toward great heights and dark abysses.

Lisa said to Mills, 'Change places with me.' She got out of her seat and knelt on the floor to the side of Hollis. She said to him, 'I know you can't hold my hand now. But if you don't have to hold the controls in a minute or two, can you hold my hand then?'

'Of course.'

O'Shea took the controls. 'I've got it, General. Take a stretch.'

Hollis released the controls and took Lisa's hand.

The helicopter continued inbound, toward Leningrad, and no one spoke. The steady sound of the turbines filled the cabin, and they listened to that and only to that, waiting for the sound to stop.

O'Shea cleared his throat and said in a controlled voice, 'Twelve o'clock, one kilometer.'

Brennan, Mills and Lisa stood and looked out the front windshield. Steaming toward them was a medium-sized freighter, and on its fantail were three yellow lights.

Hollis released Lisa's hand and took the controls. He figured they needed about thirty seconds' flying time if he brought it in straight over the bow. But if they flamed out, they could smash into the freighter, and neither the freighter nor its crew deserved that.

He banked right, away from the oncoming ship, then swung north, approaching the freighter at right angles, flying into the strong wind for added lift. He noticed that the three yellow lights were off now, which probably meant they'd seen him making his approach.

Hollis knew that a shallow approach from a hundred meters was not the preferred way to land a helicopter on a moving deck. But a flame-out during an ascent was no treat either. All his instincts and what was called pilot's intuition told him that his remaining flight time could be measured in seconds. 'Relax.'

'Your show.' O'Shea scanned the instrument panel as Hollis concentrated on the visual approach. O'Shea called out airspeed, tachometer readings, torque, and altitude. He said, 'Ground speed, about thirty.'

Hollis saw that the freighter's stern was going to pass by before he reached it, so he put the helicopter into a sliding flight toward port as he continued his shallow powerglide approach.

He adjusted the rudder pedals to compensate for the decreased torque, keeping the nose of the helicopter lined up with the moving ship, while continuing a sideways flight.

He tried to maintain constant ground speed by use of the cyclic pitch, coordinating that with the collective pitch and the throttle.

673

O'Shea called out, 'Ground speed, forty.'

Hollis pulled up on the nose to bring down the speed.

O'Shea said, 'Altitude, fifty meters.'

Hollis kept the nose lined up amidships. The distance to the freighter was about one hundred meters, and he estimated his glide angle would take him over the stern for a hovering descent.

'Ground speed, thirty; altitude, thirty.'

A horn sounded, and O'Shea said, 'Oil pressure dropping. We must have popped a line or gasket.'

The recorded voice, which had stayed inexplicably silent about the fuel, said, 'Imminent engine failure. Prepare for autorotative landing.'

They were within ten meters of the ship's upper decks now, and Hollis picked up the nose of the helicopter, reducing ground speed to near zero. The ship slid past, and the aft deck was suddenly in front of him. The deck was pitching and rolling, but never had a landing zone looked to so good to him. He felt his way toward the retreating deck, and as he passed over it, the helicopter picked up ground cushion and ballooned upward. 'Damn it.' The stern was gone now, and he was over the water again. Without the ground cushion, the helicopter fell toward the water.

Hollis quickly increased the throttle and the collective pitch of the blades, causing the helicopter to lift, seconds before the tail boom would have hit the churning wake. Hollis turned the nose back toward the stern and followed the ship, focusing on its stern light, trying to hold it steady in the strong crosswind. He felt like a man trying to grab the caboose rail of a moving train.

Written in white letters across the stern of the ship was its name, and Hollis noted it irrelevantly: *Lucinda*.

The recorded voice said, 'Imminent engine failure. Prepare for an autorotative landing.'

Hollis pushed forward on the collective stick, increased the throttle, and literally dove in, clearing the stern rail by a few feet. He pulled back on the collective pitch, and the helicopter flared out a few meters from the rising quarterdeck.

O'Shea shut the engines down as the rear wheels struck the deck and the Mi-28 bounced into the air. The pitching and rolling deck fell beneath them, then rose and slammed the two starboard wheels, nearly capsizing the aircraft. Hollis yanked up on the brake handle, locking the wheels.

Finally the helicopter settled uneasily onto the moving deck. Hollis looked up at the ship's mainmast and saw it was flying the Union Jack.

No one spoke, and the sound of the turbines and rotor blades died slowly in their ears, replaced by the sound of lapping waves. A salty sea scent filled the cabin, and the relatively smooth flight was replaced by the rocking of a wind-tossed ship. Hollis saw that there were no crew in sight and assumed that all hands had been ordered below.

O'Shea cleared his throat and said quietly, 'I don't like ships. I get seasick.'

Brennan said, 'I fucking *love* ships.'

Mills said to Hollis and O'Shea, 'You both did a splendid job. We owe you one.'

Hollis replied tersely, 'If "we" means your company, Bert, then we all owe you one too.'

Lisa suddenly threw her arms around Hollis' neck. 'I love *you*! You did it! Both of you.' She grabbed O'Shea's shoulders and kissed him on the cheek. 'I love you both.'

O'Shea's face reddened. 'I didn't do . . . well, talk to him about my efficiency report.'

Hollis smiled. 'I'll reconsider it.'

O'Shea said to Hollis, 'Right before I shut the engines down –'

'I heard it.'

'What?' Mills asked.

'One of them,' O'Shea replied, 'went out. There isn't enough fuel in the tanks to fill a cigarette lighter.'

'Well, we don't need any more fuel. See, it worked out fine.'

675

Mills reached under his seat and pulled out a plastic bag filled with black ski masks and handed it to Brennan. 'Here, everyone put on one of these. No talking to the crew, no names.'

Mills went to the back of the cabin and slid a mask over Dodson's face. He looked at Burov and said, 'Well, Colonel, the good guys won.'

Unexpectedly, Burov laughed. 'Yes? The CIA are the good guys? Your own countrymen don't think so, no more than my countrymen think the KGB are the good guys. You and I are pariahs, Mr Mills. That's what sets us apart from humanity.'

'Could be. Glad to see you learned something in your own school.' Mills took a Syrette from his pocket and jabbed the spring-loaded device into Burov's neck. 'You talk too much.' He slid a ski mask over Burov's head. 'That's much better.'

Brennan slid open the door, and a rush of cold air filled the heated cabin. Brennan jumped down onto the rolling deck, followed by Lisa, O'Shea, and Hollis. Mills got out last and said, 'I'll have Dodson and Burov taken to the infirmary.' He looked up at the Union Jack. 'I sort of figured it would be British. There aren't many of our intrepid NATO allies we can count on anymore.'

Hollis observed, 'For this operation, I don't even trust our allies in Washington, Bert.'

'Good point.'

Lisa asked, 'Are we home free, or not?'

Hollis didn't think they would ever be home free as long as they lived. He replied, 'We're in the right neighborhood.'

The door of the quarterdeck opened and six seamen dressed in dark sweaters appeared. They approached the helicopter and looked at their five passengers curiously: four men, one woman, all wearing black masks. Three men were in Russian uniforms, one in a sweat suit. The woman wore a sweat suit and parka. And on board the helicopter, Hollis thought, were two unconscious and battered men in black masks, one in pajamas and one in a shredded sweat suit. If the seamen had been asked to pick out the good guys from

676

the bad guys, Hollis realized, they would probably guess wrong.

One of the seamen made a pushing motion toward the helicopter as if he didn't think anyone spoke English. Mills shook his head, held up two fingers, and pointed. The six men went to the helicopter and removed Dodson and Burov, laying them on the cold, wet deck.

Hollis jumped back into the cockpit and released the brakes, then joined O'Shea, Brennan, and the six sailors in rolling the helicopter to the portside rail. One of the men swung open the gangplank section of the railing. They all pushed from the rear of the fuselage, sending the Mi-28 over the side, nose first, its long tail boom rising into the air as the front plunged down toward the churning sea. Instinctively, they all went to the rail and watched as the helicopter bobbed a moment until the sea rushed into its open door and it slid, cockpit first, into the dark water. Its tail section seemed to wave a farewell, and Hollis found himself touching his hand to his forehead and noticed that O'Shea did the same.

The crewmen moved quickly to the three fog lights, which were portable and connected by cords running to electrical outlets. They disconnected the lights and threw them overboard. Hollis thought there was something disturbing about that. Getting rid of the helicopter was an obvious thing to do. But getting rid of three small lights indicated that the captain was taking precautions in the event of a possible boarding and search by Soviet authorities or at the very least a flyover. Hollis wondered what other evidence the captain was prepared to throw overboard.

Hollis looked over the port rail to the south and saw two ships on the distant horizon. They may have seen the helicopter landing, and through binoculars they could have seen it pushed overboard. If they were Soviet ships or even East Bloc craft, they might radio a report. More to the point, Red Navy radar had probably picked up the unidentified flight and had recognized its flight characteristics as that of a helicopter. They could have seen the blip descend to sea level, and perhaps had even concluded that it had landed on the ship that also appeared on their screens. Three-mile limit notwithstanding, the Soviets claimed this whole part of the gulf as their private pond.

Mills seemed to guess what Hollis was thinking. Mills nodded toward the two ships on the horizon. 'That's why we wanted a night landing.'

'Yes, but radar works at night.'

Mills replied, 'I was told it would look like a crash at sea on radar.'

'It might. Depends on the Ivan who was staring at the screen.'

'Well, then this is a test to see whose side God is really on.'

Hollis smiled grimly. 'After what we did at the Charm School, I think we're on our own.' Hollis turned and walked away from the rail. Four of the seamen had stretchers now and were carrying Dodson and Burov toward the quarterdeck. One of them said to Mills, 'Infirmary.'

One of the other two sailors motioned to them, and they followed him into a door on the quarterdeck, then went up a narrow companionway to the upper deck and walked along a passageway without meeting another person. The seaman took them up one more deck and showed them into a white-painted chart room with large portholes that was located behind the bridge. The seaman left wordlessly, and Hollis pulled off his ski mask. Lisa, O'Shea, Mills, and Brennan did the same.

They all looked at one another, not knowing what their mood was supposed to be. In truth, Hollis thought, they were all so numbed by fatigue, tension, and sadness that he wouldn't be surprised if they all stretched out on the chart tables and fell asleep.

Finally Mills broke into a grin and said in a buoyant voice. 'Well, my friends, next stop is Liverpool.'

Brennan gave a long hoot and yelled, 'We did it!'

There was some backslapping and handshaking, and Lisa got a kiss from Mills, Brennan, and O'Shea.

O'Shea, in an expansive mood, said to Hollis, 'You're a hell of a chopper pilot, General. Where'd you learn to fly rotary wing?'

Hollis replied, 'Somewhere between Novgorod and Leningrad.'

Mills laughed. 'You fooled me. Hey, look, there's coffee and brandy.' Mills went to a chart table along the starboard side bulkhead on which sat an electric urn. He drew five mugs of coffee, then poured brandy into each one and passed them around. He raised his mug and said, 'To . . .'

'To Seth Alevy,' Hollis said, 'and the men and women we left behind.'

Everyone drank, but the toast had its effect of subduing the celebration. They all had more coffee and more brandy. There were chairs at the chart tables, and everyone sat but Hollis, who stood at one of the four starboard portholes and stared out to sea. The Gulf of Finland, the few times he'd seen it, reminded him of molten lead, as it did now, seeming to roll in slow motion, heavy, turgid water, all shades of greyness, its surface strangely unreflective. He saw a thin fog rolling in from the north, and through the fog, a squall suddenly burst forth like a gauze veil passing through smoke. The grey sky, the grey water, and the adjoining land masses, an unchanging landscape of grey-green pine forests, continually dripping a wetness onto the soggy earth. It was a dank and bleak corner of the world, making the Moscow region look sunny and picturesque by comparison.

Hollis rubbed his eyes and rubbed the stubble on his chin. The anesthetic was wearing off, and he could feel his cheek beginning to throb. It occurred to him that the rendezvous with this ship should be listed under minor miracles, right after their escape from the Charm School.

The door to the chart room opened, and a tall, red-bearded man of about fifty strode in. He was wearing a heavy white cable-knit sweater and blue jeans. He said nothing, but helped himself to a mug of coffee, then sat casually at the edge of a chart table. 'Welcome aboard the *Lucinda*,' he said in a British accent. 'I am Captain Hughes. Your names, I am told, are no concern of mine.'

Hollis said, 'I want to thank you for leaving the lights on beyond the sunrise.'

Captain Hughes looked at Hollis. 'I'll tell you, they were off, but I left the watch on, and he spotted you. So I argued with myself a bit and turned them on again.'

Mills said, 'That was good of you.'

Hughes shrugged. 'We were a bit off schedule ourselves. The bloody Russians don't move very quickly with the paperwork, and our pilot boat was late.'

Captain Hughes looked at O'Shea, Mills, and Brennan in their KGB uniforms, then at Lisa and Hollis. 'I'll wager you've got quite a story to tell. By the way, that landing was either the best air-to-ship landing I've ever seen or the worst. I expect you know which it was.' Hughes added, 'We're carrying timber, if you're interested. Pine, birch, and aspen. They grow good wood because God manages the forests, not them.' Hughes smiled and added, 'We dropped off a load of fresh vegetables. They like to lay on some nice things for the anniversary of the glorious Revolution. Can't say I approve of trading with them, but a job's a job. Which brings me to my next point. I was given ten thousand pounds to say yes to this, and I'll get another fifty thousand when I hand you over. You're quite valuable.'

Hollis replied, 'I hope we haven't cost you more than we're worth. Do you have any radar indications of ships approaching?'

'No, but you can be assured we're watching Kronstadt naval base very closely. Once we sail past there and get into the wider gulf waters, I'll breathe a sigh.'

'So will we all.'

Hughes said, 'There isn't enough money around to entice me to do this. They told me it was important to both our countries.'

'Indeed it is.'

680

Hughes said, 'Before I left Leningrad this morning, a stevedore pressed a piece of paper into my hand.' He gave it to Hollis.

Hollis unfolded it and saw it was a page from a one-time cipher pad. It had that day's date on it and a frequency. A handwritten note said: *Sit rep, attention C.B.*

Mills looked over Hollis' shoulder and whispered, 'That's our diplomatic code.'

Hollis nodded and gave it back to Hughes. 'Captain, will you be good enough to have your radio man encrypt a message from this pad as follows: "Attention Banks. Landed this location. Situation report to follow." Leave it unsigned. Send it out on that frequency.'

Hughes nodded. He said, 'Your two friends in the infirmary are resting comfortably. The medic would like to be briefed on their history.'

Mills replied, 'They've both suffered obvious physical trauma. Both have had sodium pentothal recently. The one in the sweat suit is the friend. The one in pajamas is not. He must be restrained for the duration of this voyage.'

Hughes walked to the door. 'I'll have a steward bring you some breakfast. I'll arrange for sleeping quarters. In the meantime, feel free to use this room as long as you wish.'

'Thank you.'

Hughes left the chart room.

Hollis went back to the porthole but saw nothing out there except the thickening fog. He said, 'We've all done a good job. I don't like what we did, but we did it well.'

Mills poured himself more brandy. 'Yes, and for whatever it's worth to you all, I wanted to see those men come home . . . with their new families.' He added, 'I'm not a religious man, but perhaps they're better off where they are now. I don't think even they really wanted to go home anymore.'

No one responded.

Hollis' mind returned to the Landis house, and he thought of Landis' little boy, Timmy, and of Landis' saying about him,

'My poor little guy.' Maybe, Hollis thought, just maybe they were all at peace now.

Hollis sat at the chart table and found a pencil and paper. He said to Mills, 'I'll write Charlie a note.'

Mills smiled. 'Be nice. He probably sat up all night worrying about us.'

Hollis drew the paper toward him and began writing in standard, non-radio English:

Dear Charles,

This is Sam Hollis sending you this message, not from the grave, but from the *Lucinda*. With me are Lisa Rhodes, Bill Brennan, Bert Mills, and Captain O'Shea. Also with us are Major Jack Dodson, USAF, and Colonel Petr Burov, KGB, our prisoner. Seth Alevy is dead. Before he died, he told me about your arrangement with CIA, White House, Defense Intelligence, et al. Charm School is permanently closed, as per this arrangement. I must tell you, Charles, I think you and your crowd are far more treacherous and cold-blooded than me or Alevy, or any combat general or spy I've ever met. I would like someday to take you out with me on a field operation to expand your horizons a bit. But lacking that opportunity, I demand you meet as personally in London four days from today. The people with me are surviving witnesses to the murder of nearly three hundred Americans by their own government. We must discuss that to reconcile it with our personal sense of morality and the legitimate needs of national security. Come prepared for a long session.

(*Signed*) Hollis.

Hollis handed it to Mills, who read it, nodded, and passed it on to the others.

Hollis said to O'Shea, 'Captain, go to the radio room and encrypt this. Stay with the operator as he sends, then wait for a reply.'

682

'Yes, sir.'

O'Shea took the message and left the chart room.

Lisa put her arm around Hollis. 'Can British sea captains marry people?'

Hollis smiled for the first time. 'Yes, but the marriage is only good for the length of the voyage.'

'Good enough.'

Mills sat in a chair, yawned, and said as if to himself, 'In the last twenty-four hours, I've been in a Moscow taxi, an Aeroflot bus, an Aeroflot helicopter, a Zil-6, a Pontiac Trans Am, and now, thank God, a British merchant ship.'

Brennan took a pack of bubble gum from his pocket, started to unwrap a piece, then looked at it. He said, 'Seth Alevy bought this for me in the Trade Center. He was a funny sort of guy. You always thought he was kind of cool and someplace else. But if you ran into him in the embassy, he'd call you by name and remember something about you to say. I always noticed that the senior people never said much to him, but the security men, Marine guards, secretaries, and all thought a lot of him.' Brennan rewrapped the gum and put it in his pocket.

No one spoke for a while, and some minutes later O'Shea came back into the chart room and handed Hollis a piece of paper.

Hollis looked at it and read it aloud: 'From Charles Banks. "Delighted to hear from you. Congratulations on a fine job. Very sorry to hear about Seth. We'll miss him. You'll be met in Liverpool. Very much looking forward to seeing you all in London. Drinks are on me. Special regards to Lisa." Signed, "Charles."'

Hollis looked at O'Shea, Mills, Brennan, and Lisa. The radio reply was so typically Charles Banks that everyone seemed on the verge of laughter.

Mills finally said, 'What a lovable son of a bitch. I'd like to beat the hell out of him, but I can't bring myself to do it. So we'll have a drink with him instead.'

683

Lisa added, 'I always liked him. I still like him. But I don't trust him anymore.'

Hollis reflected that he had never trusted Banks. He wouldn't trust him in London either.

An elderly steward entered with a galley pitcher of orange juice and a tray of hot biscuits. He set them down on the chart table and said in an accent that reminded Hollis of a Horatio Hornblower movie, 'Compliments of Captain Hughes.' He added, 'The first officer extends to the lady the use of his quarters. For you gentlemen, bunks have been set up in the officers' wardroom. The captain wishes you to know that there are no radar sightings of any note. If there's anything further you'll be needing send a message to the bridge, and someone will see to it.'

Mills thanked the steward, who left. Mills said, 'Sometimes when we're in Russia, we lose sight of what and who we're fighting for. Then you come West on leave or business, and you run into a London cabbie or someone like that steward, and you remember the word "civility", and you realise you never once experienced it in the workers' paradise.'

They all sat at the chart table, and O'Shea observed, 'Real orange juice.'

They ate in silence awhile, then Brennan said, apropos of nothing. 'I liked London. I like the way the women talk.'

O'Shea smiled and said, 'I didn't think helicopters could be so much fun to fly. I might try rotary-wing school one of these days.'

Hollis observed, 'School would be a good idea.'

Mills chewed thoughtfully on a buttered biscuit, then said, 'I'm anxious to debrief Burov and Dodson. That will be one hell of an interesting assignment. I wonder how they'll relate to one another in a different environment.'

Lisa looked around the table. 'Don't anyone laugh, but I'm going back to Russia someday. I swear I will.'

No one laughed. Hollis said, 'Me too.'

O'Shea stood and looked at Mills and Brennan. 'Why don't we go find that wardroom and catch some sleep?'

Mills and Brennan stood. Mills said to Hollis, 'I'll look in on the infirmary, and I'll keep in contact with the bridge regarding radio messages or unfriendly radar sightings. But somehow, I think we've made it. We beat them.'

Hollis replied, 'We were due.'

Mills took his ski mask and moved to the door. He said to Hollis, 'When you were passed out in the helicopter, I noticed that you snored, so why don't you find other sleeping accommodations?' He left the chart room.

Lisa and Hollis looked at each other across the table. Lisa said finally, 'You look sad.'

Hollis didn't reply.

Lisa said, 'We're all sad, Sam. We're happy that we've saved our own necks, but sad about all the others.'

Hollis nodded. 'This was the ultimate betrayal. The government betrayed those men once and now again. We've swept the last wreckage of that war under the rug for all time.'

'Will you try to put it behind you now?'

'I'll try. Once you've come full circle, any further movement along that route is just going around in circles. I'll try to move on now.'

Lisa removed a satin box from her pocket and laid it on the chart table and opened it. She stared at its contents awhile, then lifted out a string of amber beads and held them draped over her fingers. 'Seth gave me these while we were waiting for you outside Burov's house. May I keep them?'

'Of course.' He added, 'Just don't wear them.'

She looked at him and couldn't tell if he was serious. She dropped the beads back in the box and closed it.

Hollis took some crumpled sheets of paper from his pocket and spread them on the chart table, holding them down with lead map weights. 'These are the names of the men, living and dead . . . all dead now, who were in the Charm School from the beginning.'

'That was what Lew Poole gave you?'

'Yes.' He stared at the curled papers. 'Simms . . . here's Simms . . .' He looked off into the distance and spoke. 'On the Vietnam memorial they have crosses beside the names of the missing.'

'Yes, I've seen that.'

'And if a missing man is confirmed dead, they carve a circle around the cross.' He looked at Lisa. 'I want these men to be officially recognized as dead and their families notified. I want this list put to some good use.'

She nodded, then asked, 'Is that list . . . dangerous to have . . . I mean, the Charm School never existed.'

Hollis replied, 'I think it would be dangerous for us *not* to have it. This is the only real evidence that you and I have that the Charm School did exist. It is our insurance policy.'

She nodded in understanding.

Hollis said, 'I'll send this along with a letter to my father in Japan. I'll have a seaman post it in Liverpool before we get off the ship. Then when we get to London, we'll talk about things with our friend, Mr Banks.' He looked at her. 'So what do *you* want from all this?'

She smiled. 'I've got it. *You*.'

He smiled in return.

She added, 'And we have Gregory Fisher's murderer, don't we? I mean, I know that Burov is not the sole murderer. The system is a killer. But a little justice was done.'

Hollis sipped on his coffee. Lisa yawned. Through occasional breaks in the clouds, shafts of sunlight came in through the portholes and lay on the table for a time. A seaman appeared at the door and said, 'Captain Hughes wishes you to know that we've passed Kronstadt. We are in undisputed international waters.'

'Thank you.'

Lisa looked at Hollis. 'Another step home.'

'We'll get there.' Hollis stood and went to the starboard porthole. He stared out to sea awhile, then turned and found

Lisa standing in front of him. They looked at each other, then spontaneously she threw her arms around him.

The steward opened the door of the chart room, mumbled something, and backed out.

She buried her face in his chest. 'My God, Sam, I'm so tired . . . Can we make love this morning . . . ? My parents buried their daughter . . . They'll be delirious to see me . . . Come home with me . . . I want to meet your odd family . . . Sam, can I cry for Seth? Is that alright?'

'Of course. You're shaking. Let me take you to your room.'

'No, hold me.' She said softly, 'Can we pretend that after our lunch in the Arbat we flew to New York and nothing happened in between?'

'No, we can't do that. But we can try to make some sense of it. Try to understand this whole mess between us and them. Maybe I'll teach you about Soviet air power, and you explain Gogol to me. We'll both learn something that no one else cares about.'

She laughed. 'I'd like that.' She hugged him tighter. 'Later I'll tell you a Russian bedtime story.'

They stood silently for a long time, listening to the sounds of the ship and the sea, feeling the roll and forward momentum of the freighter as it moved westward, away from Russia.